This book belongs to

_____

Child Care Books from
the American Academy of Pediatrics

Caring for Your Baby and Young Child
Birth to Age 5

Caring for Your School-Age Child
Ages 5 to 12

Caring for Your Adolescent
Ages 12 to 21

CARING FOR YOUR BABY AND YOUNG CHILD

Birth to Age 5

Steven P. Shelov, M.D., FAAP,
Editor-in-Chief
Professor and Vice Chairman of
   Pediatrics
Albert Einstein College of Medicine and
   Montefiore Medical Center

Robert E. Hannemann, M.D., FAAP,
Associate Medical Editor
Visiting Professor, Child Psychology
Purdue University

Leonard P. Rome, M.D., FAAP,
Executive Board Reviewer
Clinical Professor of Pediatrics
Case Western Reserve University

Joe M. Sanders, Jr., M.D., FAAP,
Medical Reviewer
Associate Executive Director
American Academy of Pediatrics

Lisa Rae Reisberg, Technical Reviewer
Director, Division of Public Education
American Academy of Pediatrics

Mark T. Grimes, Project Manager
Division of Public Education
American Academy of Pediatrics

Editorial Board:

Catherine DeAngelis, M.D., FAAP
Associate Dean for Academic Affairs,
Professor of Pediatrics,
Johns Hopkins Hospital

Morris Green, M.D., FAAP
Perry W. Lesh Professor of Pediatrics
Indiana University School of Medicine

Robert J. Haggerty, M.D., FAAP
Former President, William T. Grant
   Foundation

Andrew P. Mezey, M.D., FAAP
Medical Director, Bronx Municipal
   Hospital Center
Associate Dean, Albert Einstein
   College of Medicine

Jack P. Shonkoff, M.D., FAAP
Chief, Division of Developmental &
   Behavioral Pediatrics
University of Massachusetts
   Medical School

BANTAM BOOKS
NEW YORK · TORONTO · LONDON · SYDNEY · AUCKLAND

Bantam hardcover edition published May 1991
Ten additional printings through May 1993
Revised edition May 1993
Additional printings:
October 1993
September 1994

Revised trade paperback edition / May 1993
Additional printings:
March 1993
July 1993
February 1994
April 1994
September 1994
December 1994

A note about revisions:
Every effort is made to keep CARING FOR YOUR BABY AND YOUNG
CHILD *consistent with the most recent advice and information available*
from the American Academy of Pediatrics. In addition to major revisions
identified as "Revised Editions," the text has been updated as necessary for
each additional reprinting listed above.

Drawings on pages 396–99
by Nancy Beaumont.
Used by permission.

ISBN 0-553-07186-6 (hc)
ISBN 0-553-37184-3 (pbk)

Published simultaneously in the United States and Canada

Bantam Books are published by Bantam Books, a division of Bantam
Doubleday Dell Publishing Group, Inc. Its trademark, consisting of the words
"Bantam Books" and the portrayal of a rooster, is Registered in U.S. Patent
and Trademak Office and in other countries. Marca Registrada. Bantam
Books, 1540 Broadway, New York, New York 10036.

PRINTED IN THE UNITED STATES OF AMERICA
27 26 25 24 23 22   (hc)
RRH   20 19 18 17 16   (pbk)

Reviewers and Contributors

Judy Hopkinson, Ph.D.
Nancy Hutton, M.D.
Barbara J. Ivens, M.S.R.D.
Michael Steven Jellinek, M.D.
John Kattwinkel, M.D.
Connie Keefer, M.D.
Avanelle Kirksey, Ph.D.
Ronald Ellis Kleinman, M.D.
Barry Allan Kogan, M.D.
John Kraft, M.D.
Richard Krugman, M.D.
Ruth A. Lawrence, M.D.
Nathan Litman, M.D.
Martin I. Lorin, M.D.
Stephen Ludwig, M.D.
Ronald B. Mack, M.D.
M. Jeffrey Maisels, M.D.
S. Michael Marcy, M.D.
Robert W. Marion, M.D.
Morri Ezekiel Markowitz, M.D.
Anna McCullough, M.S.R.D.
Lottie Mendelson, R.N., P.N.P.
Robert A. Mendelson, M.D.
Claes Moeller, M.D., Ph.D.
Howard C. Mofenson, M.D.,
   F.A.A.C.T.
James H. Moller, M.D.
Corinne Montandon, Dr. P.H.
George Nankervis, M.D.
Kathleen G. Nelson, M.D.
Buford L. Nichols, Jr., M.D.
Lucy Osborn, M.D.

Mark Papania, M.D.
Jack L. Paradise, M.D.
James Perrin, M.D.
Stanley Alan Plotkin, M.D.
Shirley Press, M.D.
Gary S. Rachelefsky, M.D.
Isabelle Rapin, M.D.
Arnold Rothner, M.D.
Lawrence Schachner, M.D.
James E. Simmons, M.D.
Frank R. Sinatra, M.D.
Lynn T. Staheli, M.D.
Martin Stein, M.D.
Ruth E. K. Stein, M.D.
Russell Steele, M.D.
George Sterne, M.D.
James Anthony Stockman, III, M.D.
Robert R. Strome, M.D., F.A.C.S.
Janice Stuff, R.D.
Ciro Valent Sumaya, M.D.
Lawrence T. Taft, M.D.
Edward Tank, M.D.
Daniel M. Thomas, M.D.
George R. Thompson, M.D.
Vernon Tolo, M.D.
Ellen R. Wald, M.D.
Esther H. Wender, M.D.
Claire Wenner, R.D.
Mark Widome, M.D.
Modena Hoover Wilson, M.D.
Peter F. Wright, M.D.
Michael W. Yogman, M.D.

Acknowledgments

Illustrations:
Wendy Wray (Part I)
Alex Grey (Part II)

Writer:
Aimée Liu

Designer:
Richard Oriolo

Secretarial Support:
Patti Coffin
Debbie Cruz
Christine Esposito-Torres
Helen Fischman
Nancy Ingraffia
Donita Kennedy
Jamie McDowell
Jane Nosek
Giselle Reynolds
Nancy Wagner

Additional Assistance:
Susan A. Casey
Sarah Hale
Eleanor Hannemann
Marlene Lawson, R.N.
Nancy Macagno
Leslie Nadell
Marsha L. Shelov, Ph.D.
Richard Trubo
Kathy Whitaker, R.N.

This book is dedicated to
all the people who recognize that children
are our greatest inspiration in the present
and our greatest hope for the future.

Contents

PLEASE NOTE

The American Academy of Pediatrics constantly monitors new scientific evidence and makes appropriate adjustments in its recommendations. For example, throughout this book is the recommendation that babies can be changed from breast milk or infant formula to cow's milk at 6 months of age. New research, however, may indicate that this change should not occur before 12 months of age. If and when this is confirmed, the Academy will modify its recommendation. Another example is that future research and the development of new childhood vaccines may alter the regimen for the administration of existing vaccines. Therefore, the schedule for immunizations outlined in this book is subject to change. These and other potential situations serve to emphasize the importance of always checking with your pediatrician for the latest information concerning the health of your child.

Foreword

Caring for Your Baby and Young Child: Birth to Age 5, is the first in a three volume series of child-care books developed by the American Academy of Pediatrics and Feeling Fine Programs. The other books in this series will include *Caring for Your Adolescent: Ages 12 to 21,* due for publication in Fall 1991, and *Caring for Your School-Age Child: Ages 5 to 12,* due for publication in Spring 1992.

The American Academy of Pediatrics is an organization of 40,000 pediatricians dedicated to the health, safety, and well-being of infants, children, adolescents, and young adults. This book is part of the Academy's ongoing education efforts to provide parents with quality information on a broad spectrum of children's health issues.

What distinguishes this child-care book from the many others in bookstores and on library shelves is that it has been developed and extensively reviewed by members of the American Academy of Pediatrics. A seven-member editorial board developed the initial material with the assistance of over 75 contributors and reviewers. The final draft was then reviewed by countless numbers of pediatricians. Because medical information on children's health is constantly changing, every effort has been made to ensure that this book contains the most up-to-date information available.

It is the Academy's hope that this book will become an invaluable resource and reference guide for parents. We believe it is the best source of information on matters of children's health and well-being. We are confident readers will find the book extremely valuable, and we encourage readers to use this book in concert with the advice and counsel of their own pediatrician who will provide individual guidance and help on issues related to the health of their children.

JAMES E. STRAIN, M.D.
Executive Director

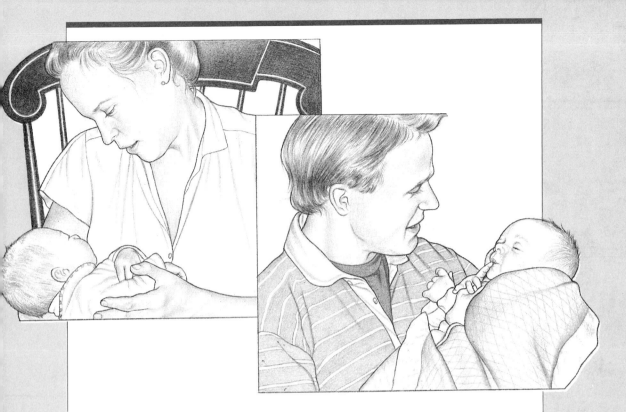

Introduction:
The Gifts of Parenthood

Your child is the greatest gift you will ever receive. From the moment you first hold this miracle of life in your arms, your world will be broader and richer. You will experience a flood of feelings, some of wonder and joy and others of confusion and of being overwhelmed and wondering whether you can ever measure up to the needs of your new baby. These are feelings you could barely imagine before—feelings that no one can truly experience without having a child.

Even describing them is difficult because the bond between parent and child is so intensely personal. Why do tears come to your eyes the first time your baby smiles or reaches for you? Why are you so proud of his first words? Why does your heart suddenly start to pound the first time you watch him stumble and fall? The answer lies in the unique two-way giving relationship between you and your child.

Your Child's Gifts to You

Although simple, your child's gifts to you are powerful enough to change your life.

Unqualified Love. From birth, you are the center of your child's universe. He gives you his love without question and without demand. As he gets older, he will show this love in countless ways, from showering you with his first smiles to giving you his handmade valentines. His love is filled with admiration, affection, loyalty, and an intense desire to please you.

Absolute Trust. Your child believes in you. In his eyes, you are strong, capable, powerful, and wise. Over time, he will demonstrate this trust by relaxing when you are near, coming to you with problems, and proudly pointing you out to others. Sometimes, he will also lean on you for protection from things that frighten him, including his own weaknesses. For example, in your presence he may try out new skills that he would never dare alone or with a stranger. He trusts you to keep him safe.

The Thrill of Discovery. Having a child gives you a unique chance to rediscover the pleasure and excitement of childhood. Although you cannot relive your life through your child, you can share in his delight as he explores the world around him. In the process, you probably will discover in yourself abilities and talents you never dreamed you possessed. You will find your abilities to communicate at different levels enormously satisfying. Feelings of empathy mixed with growing self-awareness will help shape your ability to play and interact with your growing child. Discovering things together, whether they be new skills or words or abilities to overcome obstacles, will add to your experience and confidence as a parent and will better prepare you for new and interesting challenges that you never even envisioned.

The Heights of Emotion. Through your child, you will experience new heights of joy, love, pride, and excitement. You probably also will experience extremes of anxiety, anger, and frustration. For all those delicious moments when you hold your baby close and feel his loving arms around your neck, there are bound to be times when you're convinced he's in danger and you cannot reach him. The extremes sometimes become sharper as your child gets older and struggles to establish his independence. The same child who at three gaily dances across the room with you may at four have a rebellious and active period that catches you unaware. Such periods are no less a demonstration of your child's unqualified love. The extremes are not contradictions, but simply a reality of growing up. For you as a parent, the challenge is to accept and appreciate all the feelings your child expresses himself and arouses in you, and to use them in giving him the best guidance possible.

The Gifts You Give Your Child

As his parent, you have many vital gifts to offer your child in return. Some are subtle, but all are very powerful. Giving them will make you a good parent. Receiving them will help your child become a healthy, happy, capable individual.

Unconditional Love. Love lies at the core of your relationship with your child. It needs to flow freely in both directions. Just as he loves you without question, you must give him your love absolutely. Your love shouldn't depend on the way he looks or behaves. It shouldn't be used as a reward or withheld as a threat. Your love for your child is constant and indisputable, and it's up to you to let him know that, especially when he misbehaves and needs to have limits set or behavior corrected. Love must be held separate and above any fleeting feelings of anger or frustration over his conduct. Never confuse the actions with the child, and never let him think that you do. The more secure he feels in your love, the more secure he will feel with himself as he grows up.

Self-Esteem. One of your most important gifts as a parent is to help your child develop self-esteem. It's not an easy or quick process. Self-respect, confidence, and belief in oneself, which are the building blocks of self-esteem, take years to become firmly established. Your child needs your steady support and encouragement to discover his strengths. He needs you to believe in him as he learns to believe in himself. Loving him, spending time with him, listening to him, and praising his accomplishments are all part of this process. If he is confident of your love and respect, it will be easier for him to develop the self-esteem he needs to grow up happy and emotionally healthy.

Values and Traditions. Regardless of whether you actively try to pass on your values and beliefs to your child, he is bound to absorb some of them just by living with you. He'll notice how disciplined you are in your work, how deeply you hold your beliefs, and whether you practice what you preach. He'll participate in family rituals and traditions and think about their significance. You can't expect or demand that your child subscribe to all your opinions, but you can present your beliefs honestly, clearly, and thoughtfully from the very start. Give him guidance and encouragement, not commands. Encourage questions and discussions, when age and language permit, instead of trying to force your values on your child. If your beliefs are well reasoned and if you are true to them, he will probably adopt many of them. If there are inconsistencies in your beliefs, something we all live with, often your children are the ones who will make that clear to you, either subtly by their actions or, when they are older, more directly by simply disagreeing with you. The road to developing values is not straight and true. It demands flexibility built on firm foundations. Self-awareness, a willingness to listen to your children and change when appropriate, and above all, a demonstration of your commitment to traditions will best serve your relationship with your child. While the choice of values and principles will ultimately be his to make, he depends on you to give him the foundation through your thoughts, shared ideas, and most of all, your actions and deeds.

Joy in Life. Your baby doesn't need to be taught to be joyful, but he does need your permission and occasional encouragement to let his natural enthusiasm fly free. The more joyful you are, particularly when you are with him, the more delightful life will seem to him and the more eagerly he will embrace it. When he hears music, he'll dance. When the sun shines, he'll turn his face skyward. When he feels happy, he'll laugh. This exuberance is often expressed through his being attentive and curious, willing to explore new places and things, and eager to take in the world around him and incorporate the new images, objects, and people into his own growing experience. Remember, different babies have different levels of temperament, some more apparently exuberant than others, some more noisily rambunctious, some more playful. But all babies demonstrate their joy in life in their own ways, and you as the parent will discover what those ways are and nurture your child's joy. This is a gift every child deserves.

Good Health. Your child's health now and in the future depends significantly on the care and guidance you offer him during these early years. You begin giving this gift during pregnancy, by taking good care of yourself and by arranging for quality obstetric and pediatric care. By taking your child to the doctor regularly for checkups, keeping him safe from accidents, feeding him a nutritious diet, and encouraging him to exercise throughout childhood, you help protect and strengthen his body. You'll also need to maintain good health habits yourself, while avoiding bad ones, such as smoking, excessive drinking, and drug use. In this way, you'll give your child a healthy example to follow as he grows up.

Secure Surroundings. As a loving parent you naturally want to give your child a safe, comfortable home. This means more than a warm place to sleep and a collection of toys. As important as it is to provide shelter that is physically safe and secure, it is even more important to create a home that is emotionally secure with a minimum of stress and a maximum of consistency and love. Your child can sense problems between other family members and may be very troubled by them, so it's important that *all* family problems, even minor conflicts, be dealt with directly and resolved as quickly as possible through cooperation. This may entail seeking outside help, but remember, your family's well-being maintains an environment that promotes your child's development and will allow him to become all that he has the potential of becoming. The family's dealing effectively with conflicts or differences will ultimately help him feel secure in his ability to manage conflicts and disagreements and will provide him a positive example for resolving his own difficulties.

Skills and Abilities. As your child grows up, he'll spend most of his time developing and polishing a variety of skills and abilities in all areas of his life. You should help him as much as possible by encouraging him and providing the equipment and instruction he needs. Books, magazines, play groups, and nursery schools will fast take on a central role as your toddler becomes a preschooler. But it's important not to forget some of the most important learning tools: Your child will learn best when he feels secure, confident, and loved; he will learn best when information is presented in a way that he will respond to positively. Some information is best presented through play. Young children learn a tremendous amount through play, especially when with parents or playmates. Other information is best learned or incorporated through actual experience. This may mean learning through exposure to diverse places, people, activities, and experiences. Other things are learned through stories, picture books, magazines, and activity books. Still other things are learned by watching—sometimes just watching you, sometimes watching other children or adults.

If you enjoy learning and enjoy making discovery fun for your child, he will soon recognize that achievement can be a source of personal satisfaction as well as a way to please you. The secret is to give him the opportunities and let him learn on his own terms and at his own rate.

How to Make Giving a
Part of Your Daily Family Life

Giving your child the guidance and support he needs to grow up healthy involves all the skills of parenthood: nurturing, guiding, protecting, and sharing. Like other skills, these must be learned and perfected through practice. Some will be easier for you than others. Some will seem easier on certain days than on others. These variations are a normal part of raising a child, but they do make the job challenging. The following suggestions will help you make the most of your natural parenting skills so you can give your child the best possible start in life.

Enjoy Your Child as an Individual. Recognize that your child is unique—different from everyone else—and appreciate his special qualities. Discover his special needs and strengths, his moods and vulnerabilities, and especially his sense of humor, which starts to show itself early in infancy. Let him show you how to play again. The more you enjoy your child and appreciate his individuality, the more successful you'll be in helping him develop a sense of trust, security, and self-esteem. You'll also have a lot more fun being a parent!

Educate Yourself. You probably know much more than you think you do about being a parent. You spent years studying your own parents and other families. Perhaps you've taken care of other people's children. And you have many instinctive responses that will help make you a giving parent. In other times, this probably would have been all the preparation you needed to raise a child. However, our society is extremely complex and is constantly changing. In order to guide your child in this new world, you probably will need some extra education. Talk to your pediatrician and other parents, and ask questions. Read about issues and problems that affect your family. Contact your local religious organizations, school systems and PTAs, child-care centers, and other groups that specialize in child-related concerns. Often these groups serve as networks for concerned and interested parents. These networks will help you feel more comfortable and secure when issues seem puzzling or frustrating, a not uncommon state in this complicated and controversy-ridden world of ours.

As you gather advice, sift through it for information that is right for you and your child. Much of what you receive will be very valuable, but not all of it. Because child rearing is such a personal process, there is bound to be disagreement. You are not obligated to believe everything you hear or read. In fact, one of the purposes of educating yourself is to protect your child from wrong advice. The more you know, the better equipped you'll be to decide what works best for your family.

Be a Good Example. One of the ways your child shows his love for you is by imitating you. This is also one of the ways he learns how to behave, develop new skills, and take care of himself. From his earliest moments he watches you closely and patterns his own behavior and beliefs after yours. Your examples become permanent images, which will shape his attitudes and actions for the rest of his life.

Setting a good example for your child means being responsible, loving, and consistent not only with him but with all members of the family. The way you conduct your marriage, for example, teaches your child about male and female roles and how he's "supposed" to behave as he gets older. Don't be afraid to show your affection or to take time for yourselves as a couple. If your child sees his parents communicating openly, cooperating, and sharing household responsibilities, he'll bring these skills to his own relationship.

Setting good examples also means taking care of yourself. As an eager, well-meaning parent, it's easy to concentrate so hard on your family that you lose sight of your own needs. That's a big mistake. Your child depends on you to be physically and emotionally healthy, and he looks to you to show him how to keep himself healthy. By taking care of yourself, you express your self-esteem, which is important for both you and your child. Getting a sitter and resting when you're overtired or ill teaches your child that you respect yourself and your needs. Setting aside time and energy for your own work or hobbies teaches your child that you value certain skills and interests and are willing to pursue them. Ultimately, he will pattern some of his own habits after yours, so the healthier and happier you keep yourself, the better it will be for both of you.

Show Your Love. Giving love means more than just saying "I love you." Your child can't understand what the words mean unless you also treat him with love. Be spontaneous, relaxed, and affectionate with him. Give him plenty of physical contact through hugging, kissing, rocking, and playing. Take the time to talk, sing, and read with him every day. Listen and watch as he responds to you. By paying attention and freely showing your affection, you make him feel special and secure, and lay a firm foundation for his self-esteem.

Communicate Honestly and Openly. One of the most important skills you teach your child is communication. The lessons begin when he is a tiny baby gazing into your eyes and listening to your soothing voice. They continue as he watches and listens to you talking with other members of the family and, later, as you help him sort out his concerns, problems, and confusions. He needs you to be understanding, patient, honest, and clear with him.

Good communication within a family is not always easy. It can be especially difficult when both parents are working, overextended, or under a great deal of stress, or when one person is depressed or angry. Preventing a communications breakdown requires commitment, cooperation among family members, and a willingness to recognize problems as they arise. Express your own feelings, and encourage your child to be equally open with you. Look for changes in his behavior that may signal sadness, fear, frustration, or worry, and show that you understand these emotions. Ask questions, listen to the responses, and offer constructive suggestions.

Listen to yourself as well, and consider what you say to your child *before* the words leave your mouth. In anger or frustration it's sometimes easy to make harsh, even cruel, statements, which you don't really mean but which your child may never forget. Thoughtless comments or jokes that seem incidental to you may be hurtful to your child. Phrases like "You stupid idiot," "That's a dumb question," or "Don't bother me" make your child feel worthless and unwanted and may seriously damage his self-esteem. If you constantly criticize or put him off, he may also back away from you. Instead of looking to you for guidance, he may hesitate to ask questions and may mistrust your advice. Like everyone else, children need encouragement to ask questions and speak their minds. The more sensitive, attentive, and honest you are, the more comfortable he'll feel being honest with you.

Spend Time Together. You cannot give your child all that he needs if you only spend a few minutes a day with him. In order to know you and feel confident of your love, he has to spend a great deal of time with you, both physically and emotionally. Spending this time together is possible even if you have outside commitments. You can work full time and still spend some intimate time with your child every day. The important thing is that it be time devoted *just* to him, meeting his needs and your needs together. Is there any fixed amount? No one can really say. One hour of quality time is worth more than a day of being in the same house but in different rooms. You can be at home full time and never give him the undivided attention he requires. It's up to you to shape your schedule and direct your attention so that you meet his needs.

It may help to set aside a specific block of time for your child each day and devote it to activities he enjoys. Also make an effort to include him in all family activities—meal preparation, mealtimes, and so forth. Use these times to talk about each other's problems, personal concerns, and the day's events.

Nurture Growth and Change. When your child is a newborn, it may be difficult for you to imagine him ever growing up, and yet your main purpose as a parent is to encourage, guide, and support his growth. He depends on you to provide the food, protection, and health care his body needs to grow properly, as well as the guidance his mind and spirit need to make him a healthy, mature individual. Instead of resisting change in your child, your job is to welcome and nurture it.

Guiding your child's growth involves a significant amount of discipline, both for you and for your child. As he becomes increasingly independent, he needs rules and guidelines to help him find his limits and move beyond them. You need to provide this framework for him, establishing rules that are appropriate for each stage of development and adjusting them as your child changes so they encourage growth instead of stifling it.

Confusion and conflict do not help your child to mature. Consistency does. Make sure that everyone who cares for him understands and agrees on the way he is being raised and the rules he's expected to follow. Establish policies for all his care-givers to observe when he misbehaves, and adjust these policies along with the rules as he becomes more responsible.

Another way you nurture your child's growth is by teaching him to adapt to changes around him. You can help him with this lesson by coping smoothly with change yourself and by preparing him for major changes within the family. A new baby, death or illness of a family member, a new job for a parent, unemployment, and chronic illness all deeply affect your child as well as you. If the family faces these challenges as a mutually supportive unit, your child will feel secure in accepting change and adjusting to it. By being open and honest with him, you can help him meet these challenges and grow through them.

Minimize Frustrations and Maximize Success. One of the ways your child develops self-esteem is by succeeding. The process starts in the crib with his very first attempts to communicate and use his body. If he achieves his goals and receives approval, he soon begins to feel good about himself and eager to take on greater challenges. If, instead, he's prevented from succeeding and his efforts are ignored, he may eventually become so frustrated that he quits trying and either withdraws or becomes angry and even more frustrated.

As a parent, you must try to expose your child to challenges that will help him discover his abilities and achieve successes while simultaneously preventing him from encountering obstacles or tasks likely to lead to too great a series of frustrations and defeats. This does not mean doing his work for him or keeping him from tasks you know will challenge him. Success is meaningless unless it involves a certain amount of struggle. However, too much frustration in the face of challenges that really are beyond your child's current abilities can be self-defeating and perpetuate a negative self-image, often with disastrous implications for future happiness. The key is to moderate the challenges so they're within your child's reach while asking him to stretch a bit. For example, try to have toys that are appropriate for his age level, neither too young nor too difficult for him to handle. See if you can find a variety of playmates, some older and some younger. Invite your child to help you around the house and have him do chores as he gets older, but don't expect more of him than he realistically can manage.

As you raise your child, it's easy to get carried away by your hopes and dreams for him. You naturally want him to have the best education, all possible opportunities, and eventually a successful career and life-style. But be careful not to confuse your own wishes with his choices. In our highly competitive society, a great deal of pressure is placed on children to perform. Some nursery schools have entrance requirements. Some colleges accept applications (and tuition) for babies still in diapers. In some professions and sports, youngsters are considered out of the running if they haven't begun training by age ten. In this atmosphere, the popularity of programs that promise to turn "ordinary babies" into "super babies" is understandable. Many well-meaning parents want desperately to give their children a head start on lifetime success. Unfortunately, this is rarely in the children's best interests.

Children who are pressured to perform early in life do not learn better or achieve higher skills over the long run than do other children. On the contrary, the psychological and emotional pressures may be so negative that the child develops learning or behavioral problems. If a child is truly gifted, he might be able to handle the early learning barrage and develop normally, but most gifted children require less pressure, not more. If their parents push them, they may feel overloaded and become anxious. If they don't live up to their parents' expectations, they may feel like failures and worry that they'll lose their parents' love.

Your child needs understanding, security, and opportunity geared to his own special gifts, needs, and developmental timetable. These things cannot be packaged in a program and they don't guarantee he will graduate three years ahead of his class, but they will make him a success on his own terms.

Offer Coping Strategies. Some disappointment and failure are inevitable, so your child needs to learn constructive ways to handle anger, conflict, and frustration. Much of what he sees in movies and on television teaches him that violence is the way to solve disputes. His personal inclination may be either to erupt or withdraw when he's upset. He may not be able to distinguish the important issues from the insignificant ones. He needs your help to sort out these confusing and potentially dangerous messages and find healthy, constructive ways to express his negative feelings.

Begin by handling your own anger and unhappiness in a mature fashion so that he learns from your example. Encourage him to come to you with problems he can't solve himself, and help him work through them and understand them. Set clear limits for him so that he understands that violence is not permissible, but at the same time let him know it's normal and okay to feel sad, angry, hurt, or frustrated.

Recognize Problems and Get Help When Necessary. An enormous challenge, parenthood can be more rewarding and fun than any other part of your life. Sometimes, though, problems are bound to arise, and occasionally you may not be able to handle them alone. There is no reason to feel guilty or embarrassed about this. Healthy families accept the fact and confront difficulties directly. They also respect the danger signals and get help promptly when it's needed.

Sometimes, all you need is a friend. If you're fortunate enough to have parents and relatives living nearby, your family may provide a source of support. If not, you could feel isolated unless you create your own network of neighbors, friends, and other parents. One way to build such a network is by joining organized groups, such as "Mommy and Me" and baby gym classes at your local YMCA or community center. The other parents in these groups can be a valuable source of advice and support. Allow yourself to use this support when you need it.

Occasionally, you may need expert help in dealing with a specific crisis or ongoing problem. Your personal physician and pediatrician are sources of support and referral to other health professionals, including family and marriage counselors. Don't be afraid to discuss family problems with your pediatrician. Many of these problems can eventually affect the family's health if not resolved. Your pediatrician should know about them and is interested in helping you resolve them.

Your journey with your child is about to begin. It will be a wondrous time filled with many ups and downs, times of unbridled joy and times of sadness or frustration. The chapters that follow provide a measure of knowledge intended to make fulfilling the responsibilities of parenthood a little easier and, hopefully, a lot more fun.

PART I

PREPARING FOR A NEW BABY

*P*regnancy is a time of anticipation, excitement, preparation, and, for many new parents, uncertainty. You dream of a baby who will be strong, healthy, and bright—and you make plans to provide him with everything he needs to grow and thrive. You probably also have fears and questions, especially if this is your first child. What if something goes wrong during the course of your pregnancy, or what if labor and delivery are difficult? What if being a parent isn't everything you've always dreamed it would be? Fortunately, most of these worries are needless. The nine months of pregnancy will give you time to have your questions answered, calm your fears, and prepare yourself for the realities of parenthood.

Some of these preparations should begin when you first learn you're pregnant. The best way to help your fetus develop is to take good care of yourself, since proper medical attention and good nutrition will directly benefit your baby's health. Getting plenty of rest and exercising moderately will help you feel better and ease the physical stresses of pregnancy.

As pregnancy progresses you're confronted with a long list of related decisions, from planning for the delivery to decorating the nursery. You probably have made many of these decisions already. Perhaps you've postponed some others because your baby doesn't yet seem "real" to you. However, the more actively you prepare for your baby's arrival, the more real that child will seem, and the faster your pregnancy will appear to pass.

Eventually it may seem as though your entire life revolves around this baby-to-be. This increasing preoccupation is perfectly normal and healthy and may actually help prepare you emotionally for the challenge of parenthood. After all, you'll be making decisions about your child for the next two decades—at least! Now is a perfect time to start.

Here are some guidelines to help you with the most important of these preparations:

GIVING YOUR BABY A HEALTHY START

Virtually everything you consume or inhale while pregnant will be passed through to the fetus. This process begins as soon as you conceive. In fact, the embryo is most vulnerable during the first two months, when the major body parts (arms, legs, hands, feet, liver, heart, genitalia, eyes, and brain) are just starting to form. Chemical substances such as those in cigarettes, alcohol, illegal drugs, and certain medications can interfere with the developmental process, as well as with later development, and some can even cause serious birth defects.

Take smoking, for instance. If you smoke cigarettes during pregnancy, your baby's birthweight may be significantly decreased. Even inhaling smoke from the cigarettes of others (passive smoking) can affect your baby. Stay away from smoking areas and ask smokers not to light up around you. If you smoked before you got pregnant, and still do, this is the time to stop—not just until you give birth, but forever. Children who grow up in a home where a parent smokes have more ear infections, more respiratory problems, and are more likely to smoke themselves when they grow up.

There's just as much concern about alcohol consumption. Excessive alcohol intake during pregnancy increases the risk of miscarriage. It also can cause a condition called the fetal alcohol syndrome, which causes birth defects and below-average intelligence. To date, no one has determined exactly how much alcohol is too much for a pregnant woman, but there is evidence that the more you drink, the greater the risk to the fetus. Until there is more data, it is safest not to drink alcoholic beverages during pregnancy.

You should also eliminate all medications and supplements except those your physician has specifically recommended for use during pregnancy. This includes not only prescription drugs that you may have already been taking, but also nonprescription or over-the-counter products such as aspirin, cold medications, and antihistamines. Even vitamins can be dangerous if taken in quantities larger than the recommended doses. (For example, excessive amounts of vitamin A have been known to cause birth defects.) Consult with your physician before taking drugs or supplements of any kind during pregnancy.

Your caffeine intake also should be limited while you are pregnant. While no adverse effects from normal caffeine intake have yet been proven, caffeine does tend to keep adults awake and make them irritable, which can only make things less comfortable and restful for you.

Another cause of birth defects is illness during pregnancy. Some of the most dangerous diseases you should take precautions against include:

German measles (rubella), which can cause mental retardation, heart abnormalities, cataracts, and deafness. Fortunately, this illness can now be prevented by immunization, though *you must not be immunized against rubella while pregnant.*

The majority of adult women are immune to German measles because they had the disease during childhood or have already been immunized against it. If you're not sure whether you're immune, ask your obstetrician to order a blood test for you. In the unlikely event that the test shows you're not immune, you must do your best to avoid young sick children, especially during the first three months of your pregnancy. It is then recommended that you receive this immunization after giving birth to prevent this same concern in the future.

Chicken pox is particularly dangerous if contracted shortly before delivery. If you have not already had chicken pox, you should avoid anyone who might have or be coming down with this disease, particularly young children who have been around others with chicken pox.

Toxoplasmosis is primarily a danger for cat owners. This illness is caused by a parasitic infection common in cats. The infected animal excretes a form of the parasite in its stools, and anyone who comes in contact with infected stools could themselves become infected.

If you own a cat, have it checked for toxoplasmosis before you become pregnant or as early as possible in your pregnancy. You can reduce the chances that your cat will contract toxoplasmosis by feeding it only commercially prepared cat food, which is processed in a way that destroys the organisms. Also, to decrease your own chances of being infected, have someone who is not pregnant clean the litter box daily. (The toxoplasmosis organisms cannot infect humans until forty-eight hours after the cat excretes them.)

CHOOSING A PEDIATRICIAN

Every pediatrician is committed to helping parents raise healthy children with the greatest possible ease, comfort, pleasure, and success. However, different pediatricians have different approaches, so you may want to interview several candidates before selecting the pediatrician who best suits your family's particular preferences and needs. Conduct this search *before* the baby arrives, so the pediatrician you choose can give your newborn his very first exam.

Here are some considerations to help you make your choice:

The Training of Pediatricians

Pediatricians are graduates of four-year medical schools with three additional years of residency training solely in pediatrics. Under supervised conditions, the pediatrician-in-training acquires the skills necessary to treat a broad range of conditions, from the mildest childhood illnesses to the most serious diseases.

With the completion of residency training, the pediatrician is eligible to take a written examination given by the American Board of Pediatrics. If he passes this exam, a certificate is issued which you will probably see on the pediatrician's office wall. If you see the initials FAAP after a pediatrician's name, it means he is a Fellow (member) of the American Academy of Pediatrics. Only Board-certified pediatricians can become members of this professional organization.

Following their residency, some pediatricians receive an additional one to three years of training in a subspecialty, such as neonatology (the care of sick and premature newborns) or pediatric cardiology (the diagnosis and treatment of heart problems in children). These pediatric subspecialists are generally called upon to consult with general pediatricians when a patient develops uncommon or acute problems. If a subspecialist is ever needed to treat your child, your regular pediatrician will help you find the right one for your child's problem.

How to Find a Pediatrician for Your Baby

A good place to start looking for a pediatrician is by asking your obstetrician for referrals. He should know local pediatricians who are competent and respected within the medical community. Other parents also can recommend pediatricians who have successfully treated their children.

Once you have the names of several pediatricians you wish to consider, arrange a personal interview with each of them during the final months of your pregnancy. Most pediatricians routinely grant such preliminary interviews. Both parents should attend these meetings if possible, to be sure you both agree with the pediatrician's policies and philosophy about child rearing. Don't be afraid or embarrassed to ask any questions. Questions that seem insignificant actually may be the most important. Here are a few suggestions to get you started:

■ *How soon after birth will the pediatrician see your baby?*
Most hospitals ask for the name of your pediatrician when you're admitted to deliver your baby. The delivery nurse will then call that pediatrician as soon as your baby is born. If you had any complications during either pregnancy or the delivery, your baby should be examined at birth. Otherwise, the exam can take place anytime during the first twenty-four hours of life. Ask the pediatrician if you can be present during that initial exam. This will give you an opportunity to learn more about your baby and get answers to any questions you may have.

■ *When will your baby's next exams take place?*
Pediatricians routinely examine newborns and talk with parents before the babies are discharged from the hospital. This lets the doctor identify any problems that may have arisen and also gives you a chance to ask questions that have occurred to you during your hospital stay, before you take the baby home. Your pediatrician will also let you know when to schedule the first office visit for your baby (usually at 2-3 weeks of age), and how he or she may be reached if a medical problem develops before then.

■ *When is the doctor available by phone?*
Many pediatricians have a specific call-in period each day when you can phone with questions. If members of the office staff other than the doctor routinely answer these calls, you should find out what their training is. Also ask your pediatrician for guidelines to help you determine which questions can be resolved with a phone call and which require an office visit.

■ *What hospital does the doctor prefer to use?*
Ask the pediatrician where to go if your child becomes seriously ill or is injured. If the hospital is a teaching hospital with interns and residents, find out who would actually care for your child if he was admitted.

■ *What happens if there is an emergency?*
Find out if the pediatrician takes his own emergency calls at night. If not, how are such calls handled? Also, ask if the pediatrician sees patients in the office after regular hours or if you must instead take your child to an emergency room. When possible, it's often easier and more efficient to see the doctor in his office, because hospitals frequently require lengthy paperwork and extended waits before your child receives attention. On the other hand, serious medical problems are usually better handled at the hospital, where staff and medical equipment are always available.

- *Who "covers" the practice when your pediatrician is unavailable?*

If your physician is in a group practice, it's wise to meet the other doctors, since they may treat your child in your pediatrician's absence. If your pediatrician practices alone, he probably will have an arrangement for coverage with other doctors in the community. Usually your pediatrician's answering service will automatically refer you to the doctor on call, but it's still a good idea to ask for the names and phone numbers of all the doctors who take these calls—just in case you have trouble getting through to your own physician.

If your child is seen by another doctor at night or on the weekend, you should check in by phone with your own pediatrician the next morning (or on Monday). Your doctor will probably already know what has taken place, but this phone call will give you a chance to bring him up to date and reassure yourself that everything is being handled as he would recommend.

- *How often will the pediatrician see your baby for checkups and immunizations?*

The American Academy of Pediatrics recommends checkups by one month, and at two, four, six, nine, twelve, fifteen, eighteen, and twenty-four months, and annually after that. If the doctor routinely schedules examinations more or less frequently than this, find out why.

- *What are the costs of care?*

Your pediatrician should have a standard fee structure for hospital and office visits as well as after-hours visits and home visits (if he makes them). Find out if the charges for routine visits include immunizations. If not, ask how much they will cost.

After these interviews, you need to ask yourself if you are comfortable with the pediatrician's philosophy, policies, and practice. You must feel that you can trust him and that your questions will be answered and your concerns handled compassionately. You should also feel comfortable with the staff and the general atmosphere of the office.

Once your baby arrives, the most important "test" of the pediatrician you have selected is how he cares for your child and responds to your concerns. If you are unhappy with any aspect of the treatment you and your child are receiving, you should talk to the pediatrician directly about the problem. If the response does not address your concerns properly, or the problem simply cannot be resolved, don't hesitate to change physicians.

Circumcision

At birth, most boys have skin that completely covers, or almost covers, the end of the penis. Circumcision removes some of this foreskin so that the tip of the penis (glans) and the opening of the urethra, through which the baby urinates, are exposed to air. Routine circumcisions are performed in the hospital within a few days of birth. When done by an experienced physician, circumcision takes only a few minutes and is rarely complicated. A few doctors provide local anesthesia in an effort to reduce the stress for the baby, but most circumcisions are done without medication. The option of using local anesthesia to minimize discomfort is one that should be carefully considered, since there are potential complications associated with its use.

ISSUES TO DISCUSS WITH YOUR PEDIATRICIAN

Once you have found a pediatrician with whom you feel comfortable, let him help you plan for your child's basic care and feeding. Certain decisions and preparations should be made before the baby arrives. Your pediatrician can advise you on such issues as:

Should the Baby Be Circumcised?

If you have a boy, you'll need to decide whether or not to have him circumcised. Unless you are sure you're having a girl, it's a good idea to make a decision about circumcision ahead of time, so you don't have to struggle with it amid the fatigue and excitement following delivery.

Circumcision has been practiced as a religious rite for thousands of years. In the United States most boys are circumcised, but usually for social rather than religious reasons. It is done because "all the other men in the family were circumcised," or because parents don't want their sons to feel "different."

At present, there is controversy over whether or not circumcision is advisable from a medical standpoint. New information suggests there are potential medical benefits to circumcision. Recent studies have concluded that male infants who are not circumcised may be more likely to develop urinary tract infections than those who are. Further studies are needed to confirm this observation, however, and the significance of these urinary tract infections needs to be better understood.

Cancer of the penis, a very rare condition, has long been known to occur almost exclusively in uncircumcised men. New reports find that cervical cancer may be more common among females whose partners are uncircumcised. Thus far, these reports are inconclusive. Also inconclusive is new evidence regarding the relationship of circumcision to sexually transmitted diseases.

Circumcision does, however, pose certain risks such as infection and bleeding. If the baby is born prematurely, has an illness at birth, or has congenital birth defects or blood problems, he definitely should not be immediately circumcised. The procedure should be performed only on stable, healthy infants.

The Academy does not recommend that circumcision be routinely performed; rather, the decision of whether to circumcise a male infant (other than for religious reasons) is one that should be made by parents in consultation with their pediatrician. Your pediatrician will discuss with you the benefits and risks of circumcision.

Should I Breast-Feed or Bottle-Feed?

Before your baby arrives, you'll want to decide whether you're going to breast-feed or feed formula. While not identical to breast milk, most formulas are ap-

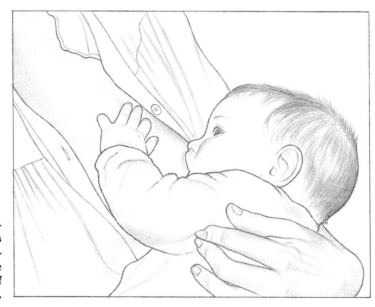

The American Academy of Pediatrics advocates breast-feeding as the optimal form of infant feeding.

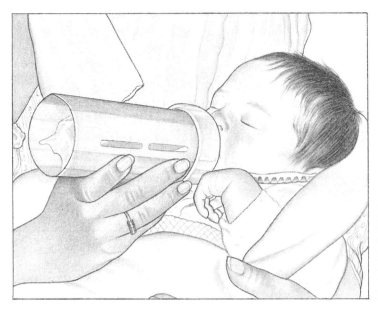

If you cannot breast-feed or you choose not to do so, you can still achieve similar feelings of closeness during bottle-feedings.

proximately as nutritious and digestible as human milk. Both approaches are safe and healthy for your baby and each has its own unique advantages. The American Academy of Pediatrics advocates breast-feeding as the optimal form of infant feeding.

The most obvious benefits of breast-feeding are convenience and cost, but there are some real medical benefits too. Breast milk provides your baby with natural antibodies that help him resist certain kinds of infection. Breast-fed babies also are less likely to suffer from allergies that occasionally occur in babies fed cow's milk formulas.

Mothers who nurse their babies also say that there are many emotional rewards. Once the milk supply is established and the baby is nursing well, both mother and child experience a tremendous sense of closeness and comfort, a bond that continues throughout infancy.

If you cannot breast-feed or you choose not to do so, you can still achieve similar feelings of closeness during bottle-feedings. Rocking, cuddling, stroking, and gazing into your baby's eyes will enhance the experience for both of you, regardless of the milk source.

Before making your decision on this issue, read Chapter 4, so that you thoroughly understand the advantages and disadvantages of breast- and bottle-feeding, and you are aware of all the options available to you.

PREPARING YOUR HOME AND FAMILY FOR THE BABY'S ARRIVAL

Choosing a Layette

As your due date nears, you'll need to acquire a layette, the basic collection of baby clothes and accessories that will get your newborn through his first few weeks. A suggested starting list includes:

3 or 4 pajama sets (with feet)

6 to 8 T-shirts

3 newborn sacques

2 sweaters

1 sleeping bag or bunting

2 bonnets

4 pairs of socks or booties

4 to 6 receiving blankets

1 set of baby washcloths and towels
(look for towels with hoods)

3 to 4 dozen newborn-size diapers
(plus diaper pins and 4 plastic pants
if you use cloth diapers)

If you have other children, most of this layette probably will consist of hand-me-downs. If this is your first child, you may receive many of the items from friends and relatives. Here are some guidelines to help you make your selections for the rest of the items you need.

- Buy big. Unless your baby is born prematurely or is very small, he will probably outgrow "newborn" sizes in a matter of days—if he ever fits into them at all! Even 3-month sizes may be outgrown within the first month. You'll want a couple of garments that your child can wear in the very beginning, but concentrate on larger sizes for the rest of the wardrobe. Your baby won't mind if his clothes are slightly large for a while.

- To avoid injury from burning garments, all children should wear flame-retardant sleepwear and clothing. Make sure the label indicates this. These garments should be washed in laundry detergents, not soap, because soap will wash out the flame retardant. Check the garment labels and product information to determine which detergents to use.

- Make sure the crotch opens easily for diaper changes.

- Avoid any clothing that pulls tightly around the neck, arms, or legs. These clothes are not only safety hazards but are also uncomfortable.

- Check washing instructions. Clothing for children of all ages should be washable and require little or no ironing.

- Do *not* put shoes on a newborn's feet. Shoes are not necessary until after he starts to walk. Worn earlier, they can interfere with the growth of his feet. The same is true of socks and footed pajamas if they're too small and worn for a prolonged period of time.

Buying Furniture and Baby Equipment

Walk into any baby store and you probably will be overwhelmed by the selection of equipment available. A few items are essential, but most things, while enticing, are not necessary. In fact, some are not even useful. To help you sort through the options, here is a list of the basic necessities you should have on hand when your baby arrives.

- A crib that meets all safety specifications (see *Cribs,* page 16). New cribs sold today must meet these standards, but if you're looking at used cribs, check them carefully to make sure they meet the same standards. Unless you have money to spare, don't bother with a bassinet. Your baby will outgrow it in just a few weeks.

Safety Alert: Bassinets and Cradles

Many parents prefer to use a bassinet or cradle for the first few weeks, because it's portable and allows the newborn to sleep in the parents' room. But remember that infants grow very fast, so the cradle that is sturdy enough one month may be outgrown the next. To get the longest and safest possible use from your baby's first bed, check the following before buying:

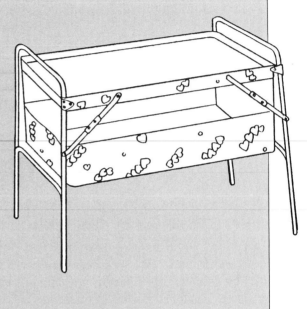

1. The bottom of the cradle or bassinet should be well supported so it cannot possibly collapse.

2. The bassinet or cradle should have a wide base so it can't tip over even if someone bumps against it.

If the bassinet or cradle has folding legs, they should be locked straight whenever the bed is in use. Your baby should graduate to a crib around the end of the first month or by the time he weighs ten pounds.

- A crib mattress that is firm and covered with material that can be easily cleaned. If this covering is made of plastic or other nonabsorbent material, place a thick fabric pad on top of it so your baby won't lie in moisture caused by perspiration, drooling, or spit-up.

- Crib bumpers to keep your baby from hitting his head on the crib bars. Make sure these bumpers are tied to the crib railings using all the strings. The bumpers should be removed when your child starts to stand; otherwise he may climb up on them and out of his crib. It is unnecessary and potentially dangerous to use pillows in a newborn's crib.

- Bedding for the crib, including a flannel-backed, waterproof mattress cover (which is cooler and more comfortable for your baby than plain plastic or rubber covers), two fitted sheets, and a quilt or soft full-size blanket. Never use infant cushions that have soft fabric coverings and are loosely filled with plastic foam beads or pellets. These cushions have been banned by the U.S. Consumer Product Safety Commission because they have been involved in thirty-six infant suffocations.

- A changing table that meets all safety specifications (see *Changing Tables,* page 383). It should be placed on a carpet or padded mat and against a wall, not a window, so there is no danger of your child falling. Put shelves or tables to hold diapers, pins, and other changing equipment within immediate reach (but away from the baby's reach), so you will not have to step away from the table—even for a second—to get anything.

- A three-gallon diaper pail with deodorizer. If you are going to wash your own diapers, you'll need a second pail so you can separate wet diapers from "soiled" ones. If you use a diaper service, they usually will provide the pail.

- A large plastic washtub for bathing the baby. As an alternative to the washtub, you can use the kitchen sink to bathe your newborn, provided the faucet swings out of the way. After the first month, however, it's safer to switch to a separate tub, because the baby will be able to reach and turn on the faucet from the sink. Always make sure the bathing area is very clean prior to bathing your baby.

Everything in the nursery should be kept clean and dust-free. (See Chapter 13 for safety specifications.) All surfaces, including window and floor coverings, should be washable. So should all toys that are left out. Although stuffed animals look cute around newborns (they seem to be a favorite shower gift), they tend to collect dust and may contribute to stuffy noses. Since your baby won't actively play with them for many months, you might consider storing them until he's ready for them.

If the air in the nursery is extremely dry, your pediatrician may recommend using a cool mist humidifier. This also may help clear your child's stuffy nose when he has a cold. If you do use a humidifier, clean it frequently as directed in the package instructions and empty it when not in use. Otherwise, bacteria and molds may grow in the still water. Steam vaporizers are not recommended because of the danger of scalding.

One object that your baby is sure to enjoy is a mobile. Look for one with bright colors and varied shapes. Some also play pleasant music. When shopping for a mobile, look at it from below so that you'll know how it appears from your baby's point of view. Avoid the models that look good only from the side or above—they were designed more for your enjoyment than for the infant's. Make sure you remove the mobile at five months of age, or as soon as your baby can sit up, because that's when he'll be able to pull it down and risk injury.

A rocking chair, music box, and record or tape player are also wise additions

Safety Alert: Cribs

Your baby usually will be unattended when in his crib, so this should be a totally safe environment. Falls are the most common injury associated with cribs, even though they are the easiest to prevent. Children are most likely to fall out of the crib when the mattress is raised too high for their height, or when the side rail is left down.

If you use a new crib or one manufactured since 1985, it will meet current safety standards. If you plan to use an older crib, inspect it carefully for the following features:

- Slats should be no more than 2⅜ inches apart so a child's head cannot become trapped between them.

- There should be no cutouts in the headboard or footboard, as your child's head could become trapped in them.

- If the crib has corner posts (sometimes called finials), unscrew them or cut them off. Loose clothing can become snagged on these and choke your baby.

Many older cribs were painted with lead-based paint, which can poison children if they gnaw on the crib rails (it does happen). As a precaution, strip the old paint and then repaint the crib using high quality, new enamel. Let it dry thoroughly in a well-ventilated room. Then place plastic strips (available at most children's furniture stores) over the top of the side rails.

You can prevent other crib hazards by observing the following guidelines:

1. If you purchase a new mattress, remove and destroy all plastic wrapping material that comes with it, because it can suffocate a child. If you cover the mattress with heavy plastic, be sure the cover fits tightly; zippered covers are best.

2. As soon as your baby can sit, lower the mattress of the crib to the level where he cannot fall out either by leaning against the side or by pulling himself over it. Set the mattress at its lowest position by the time your child learns to stand. The most common falls occur

when a baby tries to climb out, so move your child to another bed when he is thirty-five inches tall, or the height of the side rail is less than three quarters of his height.

3. When fully lowered, the top of the side rail of the crib should be at least four inches above the mattress, even when the mattress is set at its highest position. Be sure the locking latch that holds the side up is sturdy and can't accidentally be released by your child. Always leave the side up when your child is in the crib.

4. The mattress should fit snugly so your child cannot slip into the crack between it and the crib side. If you can insert more than two fingers between the mattress and the sides or ends of the crib, replace the mattress with one that fits snugly.

5. Periodically check the crib to be sure there are no rough edges or sharp points on the metal parts, and no splinters or cracks in the wood. If you notice tooth marks on the railing, cover the wood with a plastic strip (available at most children's furniture stores).

6. Use a crib bumper when your child is an infant. Be sure the pad goes all the way around the crib and is secured with at least six straps or ties, to keep the bumper from falling away from the sides. To prevent strangulation, the ties should be no more than six inches long.

7. As soon as your child can pull to a standing position, remove crib bumpers as well as any toys, pillows, or stuffed animals that are large enough to be used as a step for climbing out.

8. If you hang a mobile over your child's crib, be sure it is securely attached to the side rails. Hang it high enough so your baby cannot reach it to pull it down, and remove it when he starts to sit, or when he reaches five months, whichever comes first.

9. Crib gyms should be removed as soon as your child can get up on all fours. Even though these gyms are designed to withstand a child's grabbing and tugging, he could fall forward onto the gym and become entangled.

10. To prevent the most serious of falls, don't place a crib—or any other child's bed—beside a window.

to the nursery. The rocking motion of the chair will increase the soothing effect your baby feels when you hold him. Playing soft music for your baby will comfort him when you're not nearby and will help him fall asleep.

You will want to keep the lights in the nursery soft once your newborn has arrived, and leave a night-light on after dark. The night-light will allow you to check on the baby more easily, and as he gets older, it will reassure him when he awakens at night. Make sure all lights and cords are kept safely out of the baby's reach.

Preparing Your Other Children for the Baby's Arrival

If you have other children, you'll need to plan carefully how and when to tell them about the new baby. A child who is four or older should be told as soon as you start telling friends and relatives. He should also be apprised of the basic facts about conception and pregnancy so he understands how he is related to his new brother or sister. Fables about storks and such may seem cute, but they won't help your youngster understand and accept the situation. Using one of the picture books published on the subject may help you to explain "where babies come from."

If your child is younger than four when you become pregnant, you can wait awhile before telling him. When he's this young, he's still very self-centered and may have difficulty understanding an abstract concept like an unborn baby. But once you start furnishing the nursery, bringing his old crib back into the house, and making or buying baby clothes, he should be told what's going on. Also take advantage of any questions he may ask about Mom's growing "stomach" to explain what's happening. Picture books can be helpful with very young children too. Even if he doesn't ask any questions, start talking to your older child about the baby by the last few months of pregnancy. If your hospital offers a sibling preparation class, take him so that he can see where the baby will be born and where he may visit you. Point out other newborns and their older siblings, and tell him how he's going to be a big brother (or sister) soon.

Don't promise that things will be the same after the baby comes, because they won't be, no matter how hard you try. But reassure your child that you will love him just as much, and help him understand the positive side of having a baby sibling.

Breaking the news is most difficult if your child is between two and three. At this age, he's still extremely attached to you and doesn't yet understand the concept of sharing time, possessions, or your affection with anyone else. He's also very sensitive to changes going on around him, and may feel threatened by the idea of a new family member. The best way to minimize his jealousy is to include him as much as possible in the preparations for the new baby. Let him shop with you for the layette and the nursery equipment. Show him pictures of

Take advantage of any questions your child may ask about Mom's growing "stomach" to explain what's happening.

Picture books can be helpful with very young children.

himself as a newborn, and if you're recycling some of his old baby equipment, let him play with it a bit before you get it in order for the newcomer.

Any major changes in your preschooler's routine, such as toilet training, switching from a crib to a bed, changing bedrooms, or starting nursery school, should be completed before the baby arrives. If that's not possible, put them off until after the baby is settled in at home. Otherwise, your youngster may feel over-

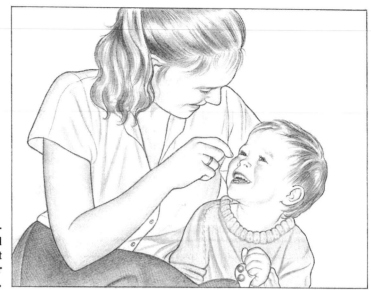

Make sure you reserve some special time each day just for you and your older child.

whelmed when the upheaval caused by the baby's arrival is added to the stress of his own adjustments.

Don't be alarmed if news that a baby is coming—or, later, the baby's arrival—prompts your older child's behavior to regress a little. He may demand a bottle, ask to wear diapers again, or refuse to leave your side. This is his way of demanding your love and attention and reassuring himself that he still has it. Instead of protesting or telling him to act his age, simply grant his requests, within reason. A three-year-old toilet-trained child who demands a diaper for a few days, or the five-year-old who wants his outgrown (you thought long-forgotten) security blanket for a week, will soon return to his normal routine when he realizes that he now has just as important a place in the family as his new sibling.

However busy or preoccupied you may be with your new arrival, make sure you reserve some special time each day just for you and your older child. Read, play games, listen to music, or simply talk together. Show him that you're interested in what he's doing, thinking, and feeling—not only in relation to the baby but about everything else in his life.

Preparing Yourself for Delivery

Toward the end of pregnancy, you may start feeling a little frantic. You'll be eager for the baby to arrive, but at the same time worried that your baby will be born before you have everything in perfect order. As your due date approaches (and in some cases, passes), you'll have to fend off countless callers who are almost as excited as you are, and also concerned about your welfare. This social pressure, added to the physical discomfort of late pregnancy, can make the ninth month seem endless. But the story does have a nice ending, so try to enjoy your leisure time as much as you can.

If you use this time wisely, you can get some chores out of the way that would otherwise have to be done after delivery. For example:

- Make a list of people who will receive birth announcements, select the announcement style, and address the envelopes in advance.

- Cook a number of meals and freeze them. You may not feel up to cooking for a while after the baby arrives.

- Look for child-care and/or housekeeping help if you can afford it, and interview candidates in advance. (See *Finding Temporary Child-Care Help,* page 152.) Even if you don't think you'll need extra help, you should have a list of names to call in case the situation changes.

Before entering your ninth month, make your last-minute preparations for delivery. Your checklist should include the following:

- Name, address, and phone number of the hospital

- Name, address, and phone number of the doctor or nurse-midwife who will deliver your baby, and of the person who covers the practice when your doctor is not available

- The quickest and easiest route to the hospital or birthing center

- The location of the hospital entrance you should use when labor begins

- The phone number of an ambulance service, in case you need such assistance in an emergency

- The phone number of the person who will take you to the hospital (if that individual does not live with you)

- A bag packed with essentials for labor and for the rest of your hospital stay, including toiletries, clothing, addresses and phone numbers of friends and relatives, reading material, and a receiving blanket and suit of clothes for the baby to wear home

- An infant seat for the car so you can bring the baby home safely. Make sure the seat meets all safety specifications. Install it facing the rear. (It should stay in this position for the first four to six months, or until the baby weighs 20 pounds or can sit up himself. Then position it facing forward. (See *Car Seats,* page 395 for complete details.)

- If you have other children, arrangements for their care during the time you will be at the hospital

Once your baby finally arrives, all the waiting and discomforts of pregnancy will seem like minor inconveniences. Suddenly you'll get to meet this new person who's been so close and yet so mysterious all these months. The rest of this book is about the child he will become and the job that awaits you as a parent.

BIRTH AND THE FIRST MOMENTS AFTER

*G*iving birth is one of the most extraordinary experiences of a woman's life. Yet after all the months of careful preparation and anticipation, the moment of birth is almost never what you had expected. Labor may be easier or more physically demanding than you had imagined. You may end up in a delivery room instead of the birthing room you'd wanted, or you could have a Caesarean section instead of a vaginal delivery. Your health, the condition of the fetus, and the policies of the hospital will all help determine what actually happens. But fortunately, despite what you may have thought when you were pregnant, these are not the issues that will make your child's birth a "success." What counts is the baby, here at last and healthy.

ROUTINE VAGINAL DELIVERY

In a routine vaginal delivery, your first view of your child may be the top—or crown—of his head seen with the help of a mirror. After the head is delivered, the obstetrician will suction the nose and mouth, and your baby will take his first breath. He doesn't need to be slapped or spanked to begin breathing, nor will he necessarily cry; many newborns take their first breath quietly.

With the most difficult part of the birth now over, there is usually one last pause before the push that sends the rest of your child's body, which is smaller than his head, gliding smoothly into the doctor's waiting arms. After another, more thorough suctioning of his nose and mouth, your child may be handed to you to hold—and behold.

Even if you've seen pictures of newborns, you're bound to be amazed by the first sight of your own infant. When he opens his eyes, they will meet yours with curiosity. All the activity of birth may make him very alert and responsive to your touch, voice, and warmth. Take advantage of this attentiveness, which may last for the first few hours. Stroke him, talk to him, and look closely at this child you've created.

Fresh from birth, your child may be covered with a white cheesy substance called vernix. This protective coating is produced toward the end of pregnancy by the sebaceous (fat-producing) glands in his skin. He'll also be wet with amniotic fluid from the uterus. If there was an episiotomy (surgical cutting) or tearing of tissue in the vaginal area, he may have some of your own blood on him. His skin, especially on the face, may be quite wrinkled from the wetness and pressure of birth.

Your baby's shape and size also may surprise you, especially if this is your first child. On the one hand, it's hard to believe that a human being can be so tiny; on the other, it's incredible that this "enormous" creature could possibly have fit inside your body. The size of his head in particular may alarm you. How could it possibly have made it through the birth canal? The answer lies in its slightly elongated shape. The head was able to adapt to the contour of the passageway as it was pushed through, squeezing to fit. Now free, it will take several weeks to revert to its normal oval shape.

Your baby's skin color may be a little blue at first, but will gradually turn more pink as his breathing becomes regular. His hands and feet will be cold, and may remain so, on and off, for several weeks until his body is better able to adjust to the temperature around him.

You also may notice that your newborn's breathing is irregular and very rapid. While you normally take twelve to fourteen breaths per minute, your newborn may take as many as sixty. An occasional deep breath may alternate with bursts of short, shallow breaths followed by pauses. Don't let this make you anxious. It's normal for the initial days after birth.

DELIVERY BY CAESAREAN SECTION

More than twenty out of every hundred babies born in the United States are delivered by Caesarean section (also called C-section or, simply, section). In a C-section, surgery is performed so the baby can be taken directly from the uterus instead of traveling through the birth canal. Caesarean sections are most often done when the mother has had a previous baby by Caesarean delivery, or when the obstetrician feels that the baby's health might suffer if born vaginally. Usually, if the fetus's heartbeat slows abnormally or becomes irregular, the obstetrician will perform an emergency C-section instead of taking the chance of allowing labor to progress.

The birth experience with a C-section is very different from that of a vaginal delivery. For one thing, the whole operation ordinarily takes no more than an hour, and—depending on the circumstances—you may not experience any labor at all. An important difference is the need to use medication that affects both mother and baby. If given a choice of anesthetic, most women prefer to have a regional anesthesia, an injection in the back that blocks pain by numbing the spinal nerves, such as an epidural or a spinal. Administration of a regional anesthesia numbs the body from the waist down, has relatively few side effects, and allows you to witness the delivery. But sometimes, especially for an emergency C-section, a general anesthetic must be used, in which case you are not conscious at all. Your obstetrician and the anesthesiologist in attendance will advise you which approach they think is best, based on the medical circumstances at the time.

Because of the effects of the anesthesia, babies born by C-section sometimes have difficulty breathing in the beginning and need extra help. A pediatrician or other person skilled in newborn problems is usually present during a Caesarean section so that he can examine and assist the baby, if necessary, immediately after birth.

If you were awake during the operation, you may be able to see your baby as soon as he's been examined and proclaimed healthy. He then will be taken to the nursery to spend several hours in a temperature-controlled crib. This allows the hospital staff to observe him while the anesthesia wears off and he adjusts to his new surroundings.

If a general anesthesia was used during the delivery, you may not wake up for a few hours. When you do, you may feel groggy and confused. You'll probably also experience some pain where the incision was made. But you'll soon be able to hold your baby, and you'll quickly make up for the lost time.

Your C-section baby may look "prettier" than newborns delivered vaginally, because he didn't have to squeeze through the birth canal. As a result, instead of being elongated, his head retains its roundish shape.

Don't be surprised if your baby is still being affected by the anesthesia for six

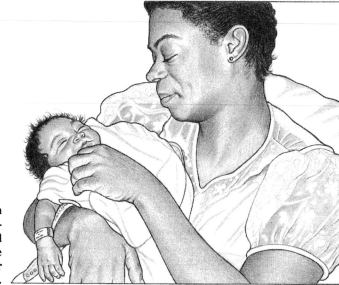

Even if you've seen pictures of newborns, you're bound to be amazed by the first sight of your own infant.

to twelve hours after delivery and appears a little sleepy. If you're going to breast-feed, try to nurse him as soon as you feel well enough. Even if he's drowsy, his first feeding will provide a reason for him to wake up and meet his new world—and you!

DELIVERY ROOM PROCEDURES FOLLOWING A NORMAL VAGINAL BIRTH

As your baby lies with you following a routine delivery, his umbilical cord will still be attached to the placenta. For several minutes the cord may continue to pulsate, supplying the baby with oxygen while he establishes his own breathing. Once the pulsing stops, the cord will be clamped and cut. (Because there are no nerves in the cord, the baby feels no pain during this procedure.) The clamp will remain in place for twenty-four to forty-eight hours, or until the cord is dry and no longer bleeds. The stump that remains after the clamp is removed will fall off sometime between ten days and three weeks after birth.

Once you've had a few moments to get acquainted with your baby, he will be dried to keep him from getting too cold, and a doctor or nurse will examine him briefly to make sure there are no obvious problems or abnormalities. One minute after birth, and again at five minutes, he will be given Apgar scores (see page 30), which measures his overall responsiveness. Then he will be wrapped in a blanket and given back to you.

Depending on the hospital's routine, your baby may also be weighed, measured, and receive medication before leaving the delivery room. All newborns are slightly low in vitamin K, which is necessary for normal blood-clotting, so they are given an injection of this vitamin to prevent excessive bleeding.

Newborns are also vulnerable to eye infections contracted while passing through the birth canal. To prevent them, your baby will be given antibiotic eyedrops or silver nitrate ointment, either immediately after delivery or later, in the nursery.

There's at least one other important procedure to be done before either you or your newborn leaves the delivery room: Both of you will receive matching labels bearing your name and other identifying details. After you verify the accuracy of these labels, one will be attached to your wrist and the other to your baby's. Each time the child is taken from or returned to you while in the hospital, the nurse will check the bracelets to make sure they match. Many hospitals also footprint newborns as an added precaution.

PROCEDURES FOLLOWING PREMATURE BIRTH

About five or six out of every one hundred births in this country are premature. Because these babies are born before they are physically ready to leave the womb, they often have problems. For this reason, premature babies are given extra medical attention and assistance immediately after delivery. Depending upon how

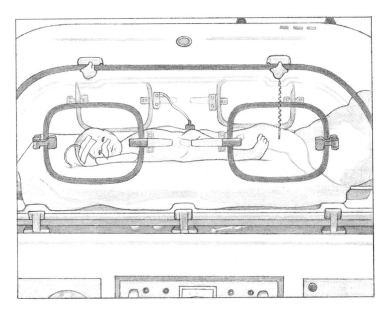

Your premature baby will be placed immediately after birth in an enclosed bed (an Isolette®) to keep him warm.

Bonding

If you have a delivery without complications, you'll be able to spend the first hour or so after birth holding, stroking, and looking at your baby. Because babies are usually alert and very responsive during this time, researchers have labeled this the "sensitive period."

The first exchanges of eye contact, sounds, and touches between the two of you are all part of a process called bonding, which helps lay the foundation for your relationship as parent and child. While it will take months to learn your child's basic temperament and personality, many of the core emotions you feel for him may begin to develop during this brief period immediately after birth. As you gaze at him and he looks back, following your movements and perhaps even mirroring some of your expressions, you may feel a surge of protectiveness and awe. This is part of the attachment process.

It's also quite normal if you do *not* immediately have tremendously warm feelings for your baby. Labor is a demanding experience, and your first reaction to the birth may well be a sense of relief that at last it's over. If you're exhausted and emotionally drained, you may simply want to rest. That's perfectly normal. Give yourself a half hour or so until the strain of labor fades, and then request your baby. Bonding has no time limit.

Also, if your baby must be taken to the nursery right away for medical attention, or if you are sedated during the delivery, don't despair. You needn't worry that your relationship will be harmed because you didn't "bond" during this first hour. You can and will love your baby just as much, even if you weren't able to watch his birth or hold him immediately afterward. Your baby also will be fine, just as loving of you, and connected to you.

early the baby is, your pediatrician may call in another pediatrician (called a neonatologist), who specializes in premature intensive care, to help determine what, if any, special treatment the infant needs.

If your baby is born prematurely, he may neither look nor behave like a full-term infant. While the average full-term baby weighs around 7 pounds at birth, a premature newborn might weigh 5 pounds or even less. The earlier he arrives, the smaller he will be, the longer his head will seem in relation to the rest of his body, and the less fat he will have. With so little fat, his skin will seem thinner and more transparent, allowing you actually to see the blood vessels beneath it. His features will appear sharper and less rounded than they would at term, and he probably won't have any of the white, cheesy vernix protecting him at birth, because it isn't produced until late in pregnancy.

Because he has no protective fat, your premature baby will get cold in normal room temperatures. For that reason he'll be placed immediately after birth in an enclosed bed (an Isolette®) in which the temperature can be adjusted to keep him warm. After a quick examination in the delivery room, he'll probably be moved in the Isolette® to a special-care nursery.

You may also notice that your premature baby will cry only softly, if at all, and may have trouble breathing. This is because his respiratory system is still immature. If he's more than two months early, his breathing difficulties can cause serious health problems, because the other organs in his body may not get enough oxygen. To make sure this doesn't happen, your doctors will keep him under close observation. If he needs help breathing, he may be given extra oxygen, or special equipment may be used temporarily to do some of his breathing for him.

As important as this special care is for your baby's survival, his move to the nursery will probably be wrenching for you. On top of all the worry about his health, you may miss the experience of holding, breast-feeding, and bonding with him right after delivery. You won't be able to hold or touch him whenever you want, and you can't have him with you in your room.

What's your best defense against the stress of an experience like this? Ask to see your baby as soon as possible after delivery, and become as active as you can in caring for him. Spend as much time with him in the nursery as your condition—and his—permit. Even if you can't hold him, touch him through the portholes of the Isolette®. Breast-feed him if possible, or ask the nurses to help you express milk to feed him; this will stimulate your own milk production so you can nurse him when he's able.

The more you participate in his process of recovery and the more contact you have with him during this time, the better you'll feel about the situation and the easier it will be for you to care for him when he leaves the nursery. If you have questions, be sure to ask them of the doctors and nurses. Also, don't forget that your own pediatrician will be participating in, or at least will be informed about, your infant's immediate care. Because of this, he will be able to answer most of your questions.

LEAVING THE DELIVERY AREA

If you've given birth in a birthing room or alternative birth center, you probably won't be moved right away. But if you delivered in a conventional delivery room, you'll be taken to a recovery area where you can be watched for problems such

Apgar Scores

As soon as your baby is born, a delivery nurse will set one timer for one minute and another for five minutes. When each of these time periods is up, a nurse or physician will give your baby his first "tests," called Apgars.

This scoring system (named after its creator, Virginia Apgar) helps the physician estimate your baby's general condition at birth. The test measures your baby's heart rate, breathing, muscle tone, reflex response, and color. It cannot predict how healthy he will be as he grows up or how he will develop; nor does it indicate how bright he is or what his personality is like. But it does alert the hospital staff if he is sleepier or slower to respond than normal and may be in need of assistance as he adapts to his new world outside the womb.

Each characteristic is given an individual score; then all scores are totaled. For example, let's say your baby has a heart rate of more than 100, cries lustily, moves actively, grimaces and coughs in response to the syringe, but is blue; his one-minute Apgar score would be 8. About nine out of ten newborns in this country score in the 8 to 10 range. Because their hands and feet remain blue until they are quite warm, few score a perfect 10.

If your baby's Apgar scores are between 5 and 7 at one minute, he may have experienced some problems during birth which lowered the oxygen in his blood. In this case, the staff will probably dry him vigorously with a towel while oxygen is held under his nose. This should start him breathing deeply and improve his oxygen supply so that his five-minute Apgar scores total between 8 and 10.

A small percentage of newborns have Apgar scores of less than 5. For example, babies born prematurely or delivered by emergency C-section are more likely to have low scores than infants with normal births. These scores may reflect difficulties the baby experienced during labor, or problems with his heart or respiratory system.

as excessive bleeding. Your baby may be taken to the nursery at that time, or he may receive his first physical examination by your side.

This exam will measure his vital signs: temperature, respiration, and pulse rate. The pediatrician or nurse will check his color, activity level, and breathing pattern. If he didn't receive his vitamin K and eyedrops earlier, they will be administered

APGAR SCORING SYSTEM

SCORE	0	1	2
Heart Rate	Absent	Less than 100 beats per minute	More than 100 beats per minute
Respiration	Absent	Slow, irregular; weak cry	Good; strong cry
Muscle Tone	Limp	Some flexing of arms and legs	Active motion
Reflex*	Absent	Grimace	Grimace and cough or sneeze
Color	Blue or pale	Body pink; hands and feet blue	Completely pink

*Reflex judged by placing a catheter or bulb syringe in the infant's nose and watching his response.

If your baby's Apgar scores are very low, a mask may be placed over his face to pump oxygen directly into his lungs. If he's not breathing on his own within a few minutes, a tube can be placed into his windpipe, and fluids and medications may be administered through one of the blood vessels in his umbilical cord to strengthen his heartbeat. If his Apgar scores are still low after these treatments, he will be taken to the special-care nursery for more intensive medical attention.

now. And once he's warm, he'll be given his first bath and the stump of his cord may be painted with a blue antibacterial dye or other medication to prevent infection. Then he'll be wrapped in a blanket and, if you wish, returned to you.

After all this activity during his first couple of hours, your baby will probably fall into a deep sleep, giving you time to rest and think back over the exciting

Nursing After Delivery

Do you plan to breast-feed your baby? If so, ask ahead of time about the hospital's policies on nursing in the delivery area. Most hospitals today encourage immediate breast-feeding following routine delivery unless the baby's Apgar scores are low or he's breathing very rapidly, in which case nursing would be delayed temporarily.

Breast-feeding right away benefits the mother by causing the uterus to contract, thus reducing the amount of uterine bleeding. (The same hormone that stimulates milk production triggers the uterine contractions.)

The first hour or so after birth is a good time to begin breast-feeding, because your baby is very alert and eager. When put to the breast he will first lick it. Then, with a little help, he'll grasp the nipple and suck vigorously for several minutes. If you wait until later, he may be sleepier and have more difficulty holding the nipple effectively.

Breast milk does not begin flowing for three to five days after delivery, but your baby does receive colostrum, a thin, yellowish fluid that contains protein and antibodies to protect him from infection. Colostrum doesn't provide as many calories or as much fluid as breast milk, but it is still an important source of nutrition and immunity. (See page 71.)

things that have happened since labor began. If you have your baby with you, you may stare at him in wonder that you could possibly have produced such a miracle. Such emotions may wipe away your physical exhaustion temporarily, but don't fool yourself. You need to relax, sleep, and gather your strength. You have a very big job ahead of you—you're a parent now!

BASIC INFANT CARE

*W*hen your baby first arrives, you may feel a bit overwhelmed by the job of caring for him. Even such routine tasks as diapering and dressing him can fill you with anxiety—especially if you've never spent much time around babies before. But it doesn't take long to develop the confidence and calm of an experienced parent, and you'll have help. While you are in the hospital, the nursery staff and your pediatrician will give you instructions and support your needs. Later, family and friends can be helpful; don't be bashful about asking for their assistance. But your baby will give you the most important information—how he likes to be treated, talked to, held, and comforted. He'll bring out parental instincts that will guide you quite automatically to many of the right responses, almost as soon as he's born.

The following sections address the most common questions and concerns that arise during the first months of life.

DAY TO DAY

Responding to Your Baby's Cries

Crying serves several useful purposes for your baby. It gives him a way to call for help when he's hungry or uncomfortable. It helps him shut out sights, sounds, and other sensations that are too intense to suit him. And it helps him release tension.

You may notice that your baby has fussy periods throughout the day, even though he's not hungry, uncomfortable, or tired. Nothing you do at these times will console him, but right after these spells, he may seem more alert than before, and shortly thereafter may sleep more deeply than usual. This kind of fussy crying seems to help babies get rid of excess energy so they can return to a more contented state.

Pay close attention to your baby's different cries and you'll soon be able to tell when he needs to be picked up, consoled or tended to, and when he is better off left alone. You may even be able to identify his specific needs by the way he cries. For instance, a hungry cry is usually short and low-pitched, and it rises and falls. An angry cry tends to be more turbulent. A cry of pain or distress generally comes on suddenly and loudly with a long, high-pitched shriek followed by a long pause

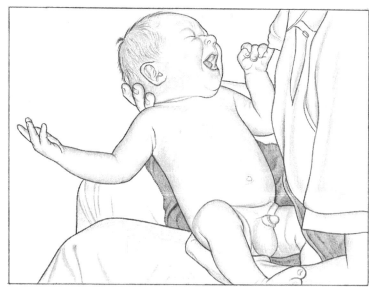

It won't take long before you have a pretty good idea of what your baby's cries are trying to tell you.

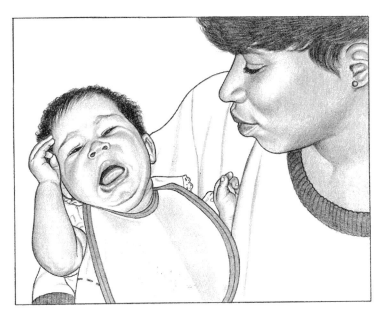

Respond promptly to your infant whenever he cries during his first few months. You cannot spoil a young baby by giving him attention.

and then a flat wail. The "leave-me-alone" cry is usually similar to a hunger cry. It won't take long before you have a pretty good idea of what your baby's cries are trying to tell you.

Sometimes different types of cries overlap. For example, newborns generally wake up hungry and crying for food. If you're not quick to respond, your baby's hunger cry may give way to a wail of rage. You'll hear the difference. As your baby matures his cries will become stronger, louder, more insistent. They'll also begin to vary more, as if to convey different needs and desires.

The best way to handle crying is to respond promptly to your infant whenever he cries during his first few months. You cannot spoil a young baby by giving him attention; and if you answer his calls for help, he'll cry less overall.

When responding to your child's cries, try to meet his most pressing need first. If he's cold and hungry and his diaper is wet, warm him up, change his diaper, and then feed him. If there's a shrieking or panicked quality to the cry, you should consider the possibility that a diaper pin is open or a strand of hair is caught around a finger or toe. If he's warm, dry, and well fed but nothing is working to stop the crying, try the following consoling techniques to find the ones that work best for your baby:

- Rocking, either in a rocking chair or in your arms as you sway from side to side

- Gently stroking his head or patting his back or chest

- Swaddling (wrapping the baby snugly in a receiving blanket)

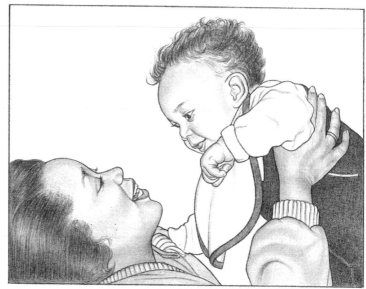

Enjoy all those wondrous moments with your child.

- Singing or talking

- Playing soft music

- Walking him in your arms, a stroller, or a carriage

- Riding in the car

- Rhythmic noise and vibration

- Burping him to relieve any trapped gas bubbles

- Warm baths (*Most* babies like this, but not all.)

Sometimes, if all else fails, the best approach is simply to leave the baby alone. Many babies cannot fall asleep without crying, and will go to sleep more quickly if left to cry for a while. The crying shouldn't last long if the child is truly tired.

If your baby is inconsolable no matter what you do, he may be sick. Check his temperature (see *Taking a Rectal Temperature,* page 58). If it is over 100 degrees Fahrenheit (rectally), he could have an infection. Contact your pediatrician.

The more relaxed you remain, the easier it will be to console your child. Even very young babies are sensitive to tension around them and react to it by crying. Listening to a wailing newborn can be agonizing, but letting your frustration turn to anger or panic will only intensify your infant's screams. If you start to feel that you can't handle the situation, get help from another family member or a friend. Not only will this give you needed relief, but a new face can sometimes calm your baby when all your own tricks are spent. No matter how impatient or angry you feel, do not shake the baby. Shaking an infant hard can cause blindness, brain damage, or even death.

Above all, don't take your newborn's crying personally. He's not crying because you're a bad parent or because he doesn't like you. All babies cry, often without any apparent cause. Newborns routinely cry a total of one to four hours a day. It's part of adjusting to this strange new life outside the womb.

No mother can console her child *every* time he cries, so don't expect to be a miracle worker with your baby. Instead, take a realistic approach to the situation, line up some help, get plenty of rest, and enjoy all those wondrous moments with your child.

Helping Your Baby Sleep

Initially, your infant doesn't know the difference between day and night. His stomach holds only enough to satisfy him for three or four hours, regardless of the time, so there's no escaping 'round-the-clock waking and feeding for the first few weeks. But even at this age you can begin to teach him that nighttime is for sleeping and daytime for play. Do this by keeping nighttime feedings as subdued as possible. Don't turn up the lights or prolong late-night diaper changes. Instead of playing, put him right back down after feeding and changing him. If he's napping longer than three or four hours, particularly in the late afternoon, wake him up and play with him. This will train him to save his extra sleeping for nighttime.

Positioning for Sleep

For many years it has been recommended that infants, particularly in the age range from birth to four months, be placed on their stomachs for sleep. This was thought to be the best way to avoid aspiration (sucking food into the trachea or windpipe) in case of vomiting or spitting up. *Recent information, however, indicates that the back or side might be a safer position, particularly as it relates to the Sudden Infant Death Syndrome (SIDS). Therefore, the American Academy of Pediatrics now recommends that healthy infants be placed on their backs or sides for sleep.* The exact reason for this finding is not certain, but it may be related to the stomach-positioned infant getting less oxygen or eliminating less carbon dioxide because he or she is "rebreathing" air from a small pocket of bedding pulled up around the nose. Although sleep position is probably not the only reason for SIDS, it seemed to be so strongly related that the Academy felt obligated to make this recommendation.

There are some exceptions to this new recommendation. They are the following infants:

1. Those prematurely born.

How Your Baby Sleeps

Even before birth your baby's days were divided between periods of sleep and wakefulness. By the eighth month of pregnancy or earlier, his sleep periods consisted of the same two distinct phases that we all experience:

1. **Rapid eye movement (or REM) sleep,** the times during which he does his active dreaming. During these periods his eyes will move beneath his closed lids, almost as if he were watching a dream take place. He may also seem to startle, twitch his face, and make jerking motions with his hands and feet. All are normal signs of REM sleep.

2. **Non-REM sleep,** which consists of four phases: drowsiness, light sleep, deep sleep, and very deep sleep. During the progression from drowsiness to deepest sleep, your baby becomes less and less active, and his breathing slows and becomes very quiet, so that in deepest sleep he is virtually motionless. Very little, if any, dreaming occurs during non-REM sleep.

At first your newborn will probably sleep about sixteen hours a day, divided into three- or four-hour naps evenly spaced between feedings.

Each of these sleep periods will include relatively equal amounts of REM and non-REM sleep, organized in the following order: 1. drowsiness; 2. REM sleep; 3. light sleep; 4. deep sleep; 5. very deep sleep.

After about two to three months the order will change, so that as he grows older he cycles through all the non-REM phases before entering REM sleep. This pattern will last into and through adulthood. As he grows older the amount of REM sleep decreases, and his sleep will become generally calmer. By the age of three, only one-third or less of total sleep time is spent in REM sleep.

2. Those with excessive spitting up or vomiting.

3. Those with certain facial deformities that make them susceptible to developing airway blockage when lying on the back.

4. Others as defined by a pediatric specialist.

If you have any questions concerning the advisability of this position for your baby, consult your pediatrician.

Also remember that this recommendation applies to infants from birth until the time that they roll over on their own. This is usually between four and seven months. Once they reach that stage, they usually are beyond the high incidence time for SIDS and will roll into the position most comfortable for them, which, in some cases, might be the stomach.

As he gets older and his stomach grows, your baby will be able to go longer between feedings. In fact, you'll be encouraged to know that more than 90 percent of babies sleep through the night (six to eight hours without waking) by three months. Most infants are able to last this long between feedings when they reach 12 or 13 pounds, so if yours is a very large baby, he may begin sleeping through the night even earlier than three months. As encouraging as this sounds, don't expect the sleep struggle to end all at once. Most children swing back and forth, sleeping beautifully for a few weeks, or even months, then returning abruptly to a late-night wake-up schedule. This may have to do with growth spurts increasing the need for food, or, later, it may be related to teething or developmental changes.

From time to time you will need to help your baby fall asleep or go back to sleep. Especially as a newborn, he probably will doze off most easily if given gentle continuous stimulation. Some infants are helped by rocking, walking, patting on the back, or by a pacifier in the mouth. For others, music from a radio or a record or tape player can be very soothing if played at moderate volume. Even the sound of the television, played quietly, can provide comforting background noise. Certain stimulation, however, is irritating to any baby—for example, ringing telephones, barking dogs, and roaring vacuum cleaners.

There is no reason to restrict your baby's sleeping to his crib. If, for any reason, you want him closer to you while he sleeps, use his infant seat or bassinet as a temporary crib and move it around the house with you. (He'll be perfectly happy in a padded basket if you don't have an "official" bassinet.)

Diapers

Ideally, you should choose between cloth and disposable diapers before the baby arrives, so you can stock up or make delivery arrangements ahead of time. There are advantages and disadvantages to each, but from your baby's point of view there is relatively little difference between cloth and disposable diapers.

Cloth Diapers. The strongest arguments in favor of cloth diapers are that they are "natural," less expensive than disposables, softer to your baby's skin, and "ecologically sound" (that is, they are recycled and do not harm the environment). If you use a diaper service, cloth diapers are almost as easy to use as disposables. You can fold them to fit an infant or a toddler and they come in a variety of absorbencies and textures.

Whether you use a diaper service or wash cloth diapers yourself, the cost is substantially less than using disposables. If you want to use a diaper service, shop around before you make your choice. Check not only prices but frequency of

How to Diaper Your Baby

Before you start to change your baby, make sure you have all the necessary supplies within easy reach. *Never* leave your baby alone on the changing table—not even for a second. It won't be long before he will be able to turn over, and if he does it when your eyes or attention are diverted, a serious injury could result.

When changing a newborn, you will need:

- a clean diaper (plus fasteners if a cloth diaper is used)

- ointment or petroleum jelly (for use only if the baby has a rash)

- cotton balls and a small basin with lukewarm water and a washcloth (commercial diaper wipes can also be used, although some babies are sensitive to them; if any irritation occurs, discontinue use)

- baby powder (advisable only during very hot weather or if the baby has a moist rash)

This is how you proceed:

1. Remove the dirty diaper and use the lukewarm water and cotton to gently wipe your baby clean.

2. Use the damp washcloth to wipe the diaper area.

3. During very hot weather, or if the baby has a moist rash, you may want to apply a light dusting of cornstarch or baby powder, especially if your baby wears disposables or plastic pants over his diapers. Do not shake out the powder near your baby's face, and make sure you never leave it within your baby's reach, as severe reactions can occur if he inhales it. Use the powder sparingly, because it may irritate your baby's skin.

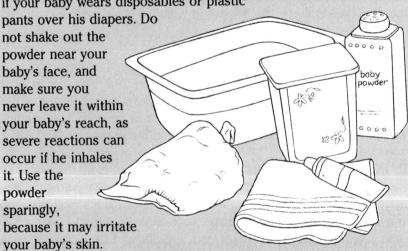

4. Put on the new diaper as shown on succeeding pages.

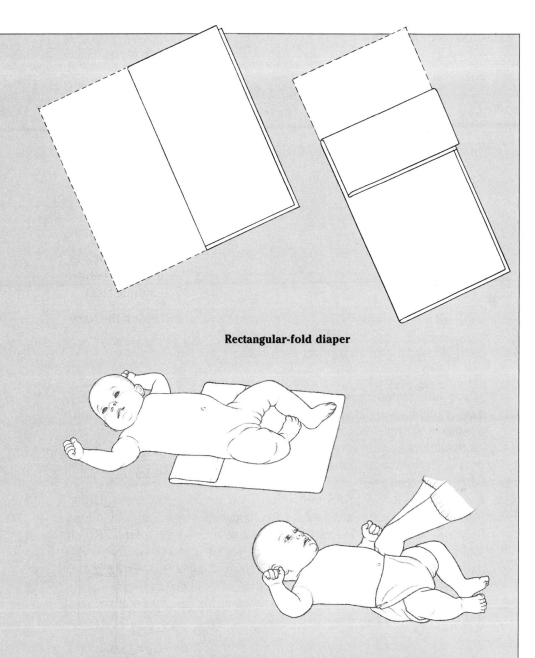

Rectangular-fold diaper

Cloth diapers are available either prefolded (14 × 20 inches) or in a 27-inch square which you can fold to fit your child precisely. Initially, you will need to fold about a third of the diaper down from the end so it's not too long. This also increases the absorbency. If the diapers have extra padding and your baby is a boy, place the padding in front. For girls, the padding goes in back.

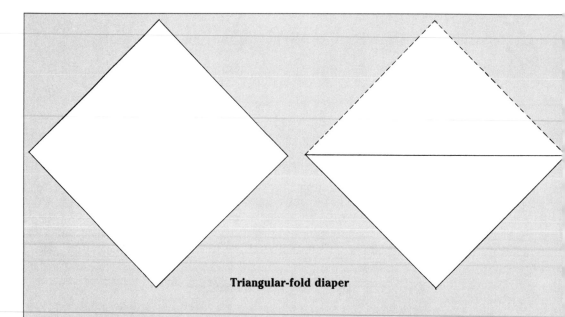

Triangular-fold diaper

The tape fasteners on disposables make the job of diapering very easy (except when petroleum jelly or lotion from your fingers gets onto the tape and prevents it from sticking), but there are also ways to fasten cloth diapers that many parents find just as convenient. Most use diaper pins (oversized safety pins with plastic heads). To prevent pricking the baby when using pins, you need to keep your hand between the pin and his skin. If this procedure makes you nervous, try using diaper tape, which comes in a dispenser like household tape and adheres to the cloth. A third alternative is the diaper wrap, which requires neither pins nor tape. Available from diaper services and most stores that carry baby supplies, diaper wraps literally wrap around the baby's body, fastening with Velcro around the waist to hold the diaper in place. You can also use these wraps when you're away from home to cover wet diapers until you can dispose of them properly.

pickups and general procedures. Ideally, a diaper service should pick up dirty diapers and drop off clean ones twice a week. Some services ask you to rinse the diapers yourself, while others prefer that you leave them intact, waste and all, in the diaper pail. (They say this makes it easier to determine the right chemical balance of the wash for your baby's diapers.) A few services even guarantee that your baby gets the same diapers from week to week, which means that any objects dropped into the pail by mistake will also be returned to you.

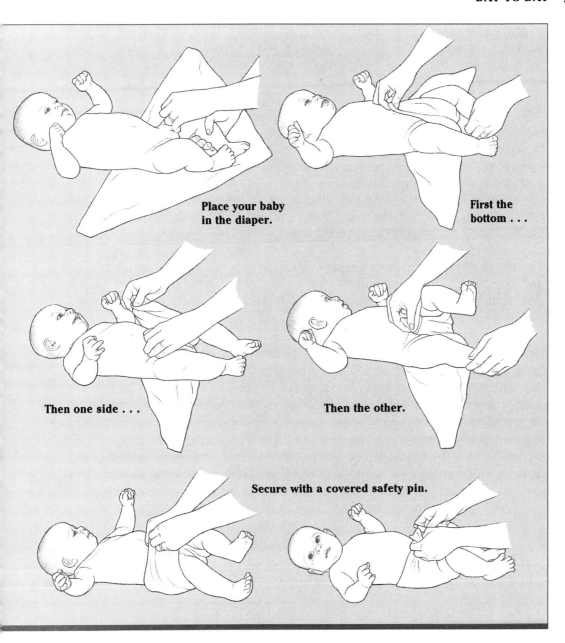

Place your baby
in the diaper.

First the
bottom . . .

Then one side . . .

Then the other.

Secure with a covered safety pin.

If a diaper service is not available or you choose to wash the diapers yourself, keep them separate from other clothes. Wash them in soap, not detergent, because soap leaves the diapers somewhat softer. Do *not* use fabric softeners or antistatic products on diapers (or any other infant clothing), since they may cause rashes in young, sensitive skin. Use hot water, and double-rinse each wash.

Most newborns go through about ten diapers a day. This means you'll need to buy seventy diapers a week if you're using disposables, or order seventy cloth diapers to be recycled through your diaper service. When using cloth diapers without a service, start with four dozen and see how you fare. This should give you extras for mopping up spills, protecting your shoulders against spit-up, and wiping your baby at changing time.

Even if you do use cloth diapers, you probably will want to keep a small supply of disposables on hand for trips and outings. Disposables come in a range of sizes, textures, and absorbencies. Buy a size larger than your baby if you're not planning to use them every day or in the immediate future. Otherwise, your baby may outgrow the supply before it's used up.

Disposable Diapers. Disposable diapers are obviously more convenient than cloth in some ways, but there are some drawbacks to them. Because of their plastic liners, disposables may protect bedding and clothing well, but they don't breathe as efficiently as cloth diapers and they trap moisture inside, increasing the risk of diaper rash. Even the new "superabsorbent" disposables can cause problems. They absorb moisture so well that many parents leave them on too long, thus actually increasing the risk of diaper rash. Superabsorbent diapers should be changed just as frequently as the less absorbent varieties.

Plastic pants over cloth diapers can create the same problem. You can help prevent diaper rash by changing diapers frequently, fastening them loosely, not using plastic pants all the time, and giving your baby some time each day to "air out" without anything on. (This last step is a little easier to do after the first few months when his bladder patterns become more regular.) Reserve the use of superabsorbent diapers and waterproof covers for the times when you can't afford to have his outfit get wet.

Disposable diapers can pose a health hazard when they are disposed of improperly. They should be rinsed and emptied of any solid waste before being

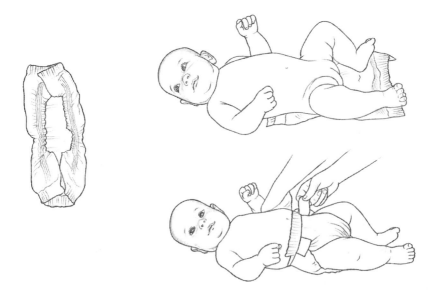

discarded—*not* into the toilet, because they can block your plumbing, but into the garbage. Because the plastic liners do not decompose, they create an environmental problem that is increasing rapidly (*each baby* averages about 2,200 diapers a year).

Urination

Your baby may urinate as often as every one to three hours, or as infrequently as four to six times a day. If he's ill or feverish, or when the weather is extremely hot, his usual output of urine may drop by half and still be normal.

Urination should never be painful. If you notice any signs of distress while your infant is urinating, notify your pediatrician, as this could be a sign of infection or some other problem in the urinary tract.

In a healthy child, urine is light- to dark-yellow in color (the darker the color, the more concentrated the urine; the urine will be more concentrated when your child is not drinking a lot of liquid). Sometimes you'll see a pink stain on the diaper which may be mistaken for blood. But in fact, this stain is usually a sign of highly concentrated urine, which has a pinkish color. As long as the baby is wetting at least four diapers a day, there probably is no cause for concern, but if the pinkish staining persists, consult your pediatrician.

The presence of actual blood in the urine or a bloody spot on the diaper is never normal, and your pediatrician should be notified. It may be due to nothing more serious than a small sore caused by diaper rash, but it could also be a sign of a larger problem. If this bleeding is accompanied by other symptoms, such as abdominal pain or bleeding in other areas, seek medical attention for your baby immediately.

Bowel Movements

In the first few days of life your baby will have his first bowel movement, which is often referred to as passing meconium. This thick, dark-green or black substance filled his intestines before birth, and it must be eliminated before normal digestion can take place. Once the meconium is passed, the stools will turn yellow-green.

If your baby is breast-fed, his stools should soon resemble light mustard with seedlike particles. Until he starts to eat solid foods, the consistency of the stools should be soft, even slightly runny. If he's formula-fed, his stools usually will be tan or yellow in color. They will be firmer than in a baby who is breast-fed, but no firmer than peanut butter.

Whether breast- or bottle-fed, if your baby has hard or very dry stools, it may be a sign that he is not getting enough fluid, or that he is losing too much fluid due to illness, fever, or heat. Once he has started solids, hard stools might indicate that he's eating too many constipating foods, such as cereal or cow's milk, before

Diaper Rash

Diaper rash is the term used to describe a rash or irritation in the area covered by the diaper. The first sign of diaper rash is usually redness or small bumps on the lower abdomen, buttocks, genitals, and thigh folds—surfaces that have been in direct contact with the wet or soiled diaper. This type of diaper rash is rarely serious, and usually clears in three or four days with appropriate care.

The most common causes of diaper rash include:

1. Leaving a wet diaper on too long. The moisture makes the skin more susceptible to chafing. Over time, the urine in the diaper decomposes, forming chemicals that can further irritate the skin.

2. Leaving a stool-soiled diaper on too long. Digestive agents in the stool then attack the skin, making it more susceptible to a rash.

Regardless of how the rash begins, once the surface of the skin is damaged, it becomes even more vulnerable to further irritation by contact with urine and stool.

Another cause of rash in this area is yeast infection. This rash is common on the thighs, genitals, and lower abdomen but almost never appears on the buttock.

While most babies develop diaper rash at some point during infancy, it happens less often in babies who are breast-fed (for reasons we still do not know). Diaper rash occurs more often at particular ages and under certain conditions:

his system can handle them. (Whole cow's milk is not recommended for babies under twelve months.)

Keep in mind that occasional variations in color and consistency of the stools are normal. For example, if the digestive process slows down because the baby has had a particularly large amount of cereal that day or foods requiring more effort to digest, the stools may become green; or if the baby is given supplemental iron, the stools may turn dark-brown. If there is a minor irritation of the anus, streaks of blood may appear on the outside of the stools. However, if there are large amounts of blood, mucus, or water in the stool, call your pediatrician

- among babies eight to ten months old

- if babies are not kept clean and dry

- when babies have frequent stools (especially when the stools are left in their diapers overnight)

- when a baby starts to eat solid food (probably due to the introduction of more acidic foods and changes in the digestive process caused by the new variety of foods)

- when a baby is taking antibiotics (because these drugs encourage the growth of yeast organisms that can infect the skin)

To reduce your baby's risk of diaper rash, make these steps part of your diapering routine:

1. Change the diaper as soon as possible after a bowel movement. Cleanse the diaper area with a soft cloth and water after each bowel movement.

2. Change wet diapers frequently to reduce skin exposure to moisture.

3. Expose the baby's bottom to air whenever feasible. When using plastic pants or disposable diapers with tight gathers around the abdomen and legs, make sure air can circulate inside the diaper.

If a diaper rash develops in spite of your efforts and the skin is dried out, you may need to use a lotion or ointment; if it is a moist rash, use a drying lotion. The rash should improve noticeably within forty-eight to seventy-two hours. If it doesn't, consult your pediatrician.

immediately. These symptoms may indicate severe diarrhea or an intestinal abnormality.

Because an infant's stools are normally soft and a little runny, it's not always easy to tell when a young baby has mild diarrhea. The telltale signs are a sudden increase in frequency (to more than one bowel movement per feeding), and unusually high liquid content in the stool. Diarrhea may be a sign of intestinal infection, or it may be caused by a change in the baby's diet. If the baby is breastfeeding, he can even develop diarrhea because of a change in the mother's diet.

The main concern with diarrhea is the possibility that dehydration can develop.

If fever is also present and your infant is less than two months old, call your pediatrician immediately. If your baby is over two months and the fever lasts more than a day, check his urine output and rectal temperature; then report your findings to your doctor so he can determine what needs to be done.

The frequency of bowel movements varies widely from one baby to another. Many pass a stool soon after each feeding. This is a result of the gastrocolic reflex, which causes the digestive system to become active whenever the stomach is filled with food.

By three to six weeks of age, some breast-fed babies have only one bowel movement a week and still are normal. This happens because breast milk leaves very little solid waste to be eliminated from the child's digestive system. Thus, infrequent stools are not a sign of constipation and should not be considered a problem as long as the stools are soft (no firmer than peanut butter), and your infant is otherwise normal, gaining weight steadily, and nursing regularly.

If your baby is formula-fed, he should have at least one bowel movement a day. If he has fewer than this and appears to be straining because of hard stools, he may be constipated. Check with your pediatrician for advice on how to handle this problem. (See *Constipation*, page 474.)

Bathing

Your infant doesn't need much bathing if you wash the diaper area thoroughly during diaper changes. Two or three times a week during his first year is plenty. If he is bathed more frequently, it may dry out his skin.

During his first week or two, until the stump of the umbilical cord falls off, your newborn should have only sponge baths. In a warm room, lay the baby anywhere that's flat and comfortable for both of you—a changing table, bed, floor, or counter next to the sink will do. Pad hard surfaces with a blanket or fluffy towel. If the baby is on a surface above the floor, use a safety strap or keep one hand on him *at all times* to make sure he doesn't fall.

Have a basin of water, a damp, double-rinsed (so there is no soap residue in it) washcloth, and a supply of mild baby soap within reach before you begin. Keep your baby wrapped in a towel, and expose only the parts of his body you are actively washing. Use the dampened cloth first without soap to wash his face, so you don't get soap into his eyes or mouth. Then dip it in the basin of soapy water before washing the remainder of his body and, finally, the diaper area. Pay special attention to creases under the arms, behind the ears, around the neck, and, especially with a girl, in the genital area.

Once the umbilical area is healed, you can try placing your baby directly in the water. His first baths should be as gentle and brief as possible. He will probably protest a little; if he seems miserable, you should go back to sponge baths for a week or two, then try the bath again. He will make it clear when he's ready.

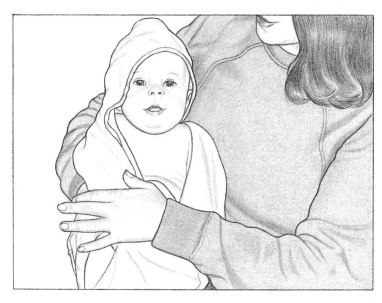

Baby towels with built-in hoods are the most effective way to keep your baby's head warm when he's wet.

Most parents find it easiest to bathe a newborn in a bathinette, sink, or plastic tub lined with a clean towel. Fill the basin with two inches of water that feels warm—not hot—to the inside of your wrist or elbow. If you're filling the basin from the tap, turn the cold water on first (and off last) to avoid scalding yourself or your child. In addition, make sure your hot water heater is set no higher than 120 degrees Fahrenheit.

Make sure that supplies are at hand and the room is warm before undressing the baby. You'll need the same supplies that you used for sponge bathing, but also a cup for rinsing with clear water. When your child has hair, you'll need baby shampoo too.

If you've forgotten something or need to answer the phone or door during the bath, *you must take the baby with you,* so keep a dry towel within reach. *Never leave a baby alone in the bath, even for an instant.*

If your baby enjoys his bath, give him some extra time to splash and explore the water. The more fun your child has in the bath, the less he'll be afraid of the water. As he gets older, the length of the bath will extend until most of it is taken up with play. Bathing should be a very relaxing and soothing experience, so don't rush unless he's unhappy.

Bath toys are not really needed for very young babies, as the stimulation of the water and washing is exciting enough. Once a baby is old enough for the bathtub, however, toys become invaluable. Containers, floating toys, even waterproof books make wonderful distractions as you cleanse your baby.

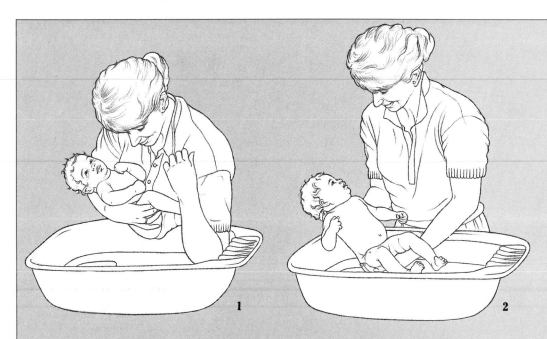

Fill the basin with two inches of water that feels warm—not hot—to the inside of your wrist or elbow. Once you've undressed your baby, place him in the water immediately so he doesn't get chilled. Use one of your hands to support his head and the other to guide him in, feet first. Speak to him encouragingly, and gently lower the rest of his body until he's in the tub. Most of his body and face should be well above the water level for safety, so you'll need to pour warm water over his body frequently to keep him warm.

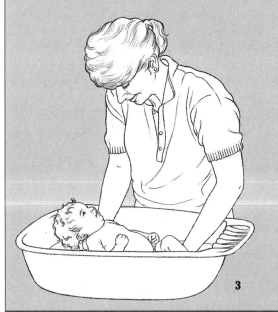

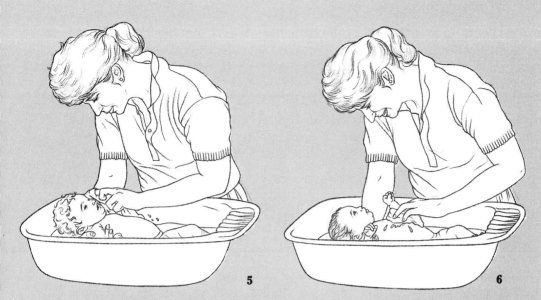

5

6

Use a soft cloth to wash his face and hair, shampooing once or twice a week. Massage his entire scalp gently, including the area over his fontanels (soft spots). When you rinse the soap or shampoo from his head, cup your hand across his forehead so the suds run toward the sides, not into his eyes. Should you get some soap in his eyes, and he cries out in protest, simply take the wet washcloth and liberally wipe his eyes with plain, lukewarm water until any remains of the soap are gone, and he will open his eyes again. Wash the rest of his body from the top down.

7

When your infant comes out of the bath, baby towels with built-in hoods are the most effective way to keep his head warm when he's wet. Bathing a baby of any age is wet work, so you may want to wear a terry-cloth apron or hang a towel over your shoulder to keep you dry.

In the early months you may find it easiest to bathe your infant in the morning, when he's alert and the house is quiet and warm. By the time he graduates to the bathtub (usually when he's sitting up or outgrows the basin) you may want to shift to an evening schedule on the days he's bathed. The bath is a relaxing way to prepare him for sleep.

Skin and Nail Care

Your newborn's skin may be susceptible to irritation from chemicals in new clothing, and from soap or detergent residue on clothes that have been washed. To avoid problems, double-rinse all baby clothes, bedding, blankets, and other washable items before exposing the child to them. (Wash his new layette, too, before he uses it.) For the first few months, do your infant's wash separately from the family's.

Contrary to what you may read in ads for baby products, your infant does not ordinarily need any lotions, oils, or powders. If his skin is very dry, you can apply a small amount of nonperfumed baby lotion sparingly to the dry areas. Never use any skin-care products that are not specifically made for babies, because they generally contain perfumes and other chemicals that can irritate an infant's skin.

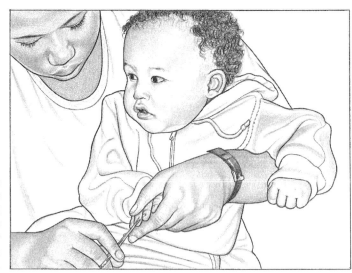

In the early weeks your baby's fingers are so small and his nails grow so quickly you may have to trim them twice a week.

Also avoid baby oil, which does not penetrate or lubricate as well as baby lotion. If the dryness persists, you may be bathing your child too often. Give him a bath just once a week for a while and see if the dryness stops. If not, consult your pediatrician.

The only care your child's nails require is trimming. You can use a soft emery board, baby nail clippers or blunt-nosed toenail scissors. A good time to trim nails is after a bath if your baby will lie quietly, but you may find it easiest to do when he's asleep. Keep his fingernails as short and smoothly trimmed as possible so he can't scratch himself (or you). In the early weeks his fingers are so small and his nails grow so quickly you may have to trim them twice a week.

By contrast, his toenails grow much more slowly and are usually very soft and pliable. They needn't be kept as short as the fingernails, so you may have to trim them only once or twice a month. Because they are so soft, they sometimes look as if they're ingrown, but there's no cause for concern unless the skin alongside the nail gets red, inflamed, or hard. As your baby gets older, his toenails will become harder and better defined.

Clothing

Unless the temperature is hot (over 75 degrees), your newborn will need several layers of clothing to keep him warm. It's generally best to dress him in an undershirt and diapers, covered by pajamas or a dressing gown, and then wrapped in a receiving blanket. (If your baby is premature, he may need still another layer of clothing until his weight reaches that of a full-term baby and his body is better able to adjust to changes in temperature.) In hot weather you can reduce his clothing to a single layer, but be sure to cover him when in air-conditioned surroundings or near drafts. A good rule of thumb is to dress the baby in one more layer of clothing than you are wearing to be comfortable in the same environment.

If you've never taken care of a newborn baby before, the first few times you change his clothes can be quite frustrating. Not only is it a struggle to get that tiny little arm through the sleeve, but your infant may shriek in protest through the whole process. He doesn't like the rush of air against his skin, nor does he enjoy being pushed and pulled through garments. It may make things easier for both of you if you hold him on your lap while changing the upper half of his body, then lay him on a bed or changing table while doing the lower half. When you're dressing him in one-piece pajamas, pull them over his legs before putting on the sleeves. Pull T-shirts over his head first, then put one arm at a time through the sleeves. Use this opportunity to ask, "Where's the baby's hand?" As he gets older this will turn into a game, with him pushing his arm through just to hear you say, *"There's* the baby's hand!"

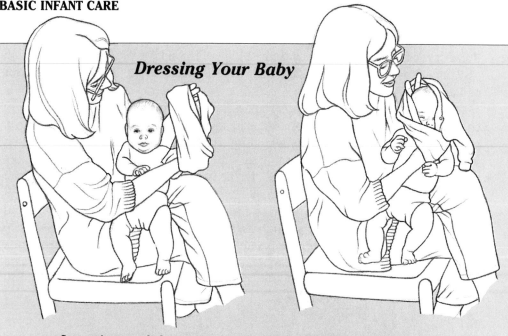

Dressing Your Baby

Supporting your baby on your lap, stretch the garment neckline and pull it over your baby's head, using your fingers to keep it from catching on his face or ears.

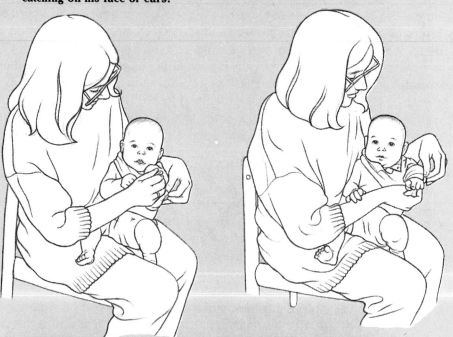

Don't try to push your baby's arm through the sleeve. Instead, put your hand into the sleeve from the outside, grasp your baby's hand, and pull it through.

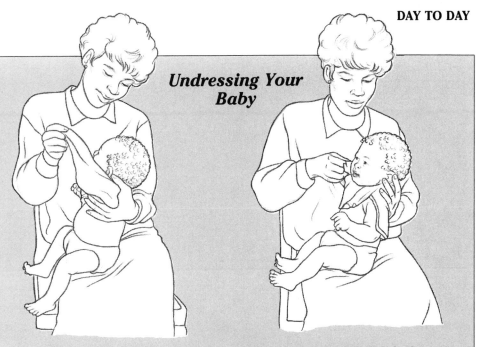

Undressing Your Baby

Take off the sleeves one at a time while you support your baby's back and head.

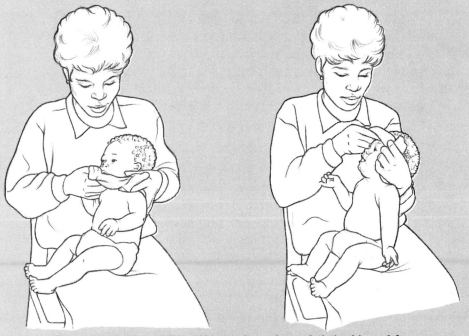

Then stretch the neckline, lifting it free of your baby's chin and face as you gently slip it off.

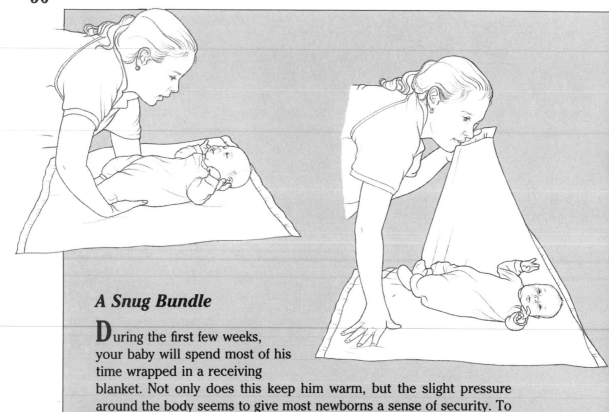

A Snug Bundle

During the first few weeks, your baby will spend most of his time wrapped in a receiving blanket. Not only does this keep him warm, but the slight pressure around the body seems to give most newborns a sense of security. To make a snug bundle, spread the blanket out flat, with one corner folded over. Lay the baby face-up on the blanket, with his head at the folded corner. Wrap the left corner over his body and tuck it beneath him. Bring the bottom corner up over his feet, and then wrap the right corner around him, leaving only his head and neck exposed.

Certain clothing features can make dressing much easier. Look for garments that

- snap or zip all the way down the front, instead of the back

- snap or zip down both legs to make diaper changes easier

- have loose-fitting sleeves so your hand fits underneath to push the baby's arm through

- have no ribbons or strings to knot up, unravel, or wrap around the neck (which could cause choking)

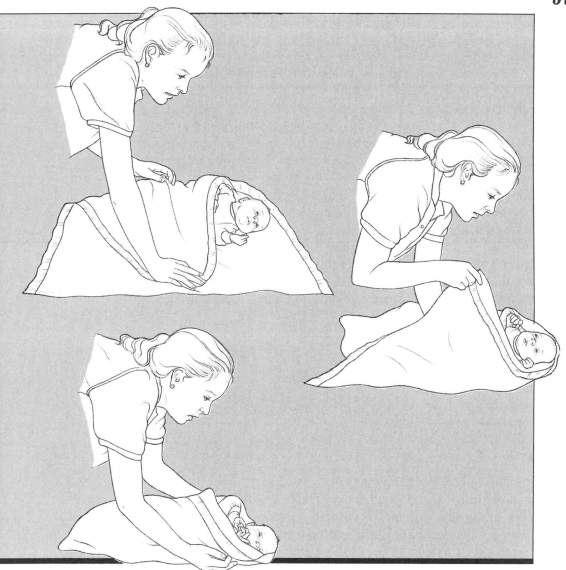

■ are made of stretchy fabric. (Avoid tight bindings around arms, legs, or neck.)

Your baby will also need a blanket or quilt to cover him when sleeping. Place it over him loosely, without tucking it in. As he gets older and becomes more active, he's bound to kick off the covers occasionally. At that time you'll need either to dress him in warmer pajamas (with feet) or keep his room warm while he's sleeping. Try not to place your baby near air-conditioning or heating vents, open windows, or other sources of drafts.

YOUR BABY'S BASIC HEALTH CARE

Taking a Rectal Temperature

Very few babies get through infancy without having a fever, which is usually a sign of infection somewhere in the body. A fever indicates that the immune system is actively fighting viruses or bacteria, so—in this respect—it is a positive sign that the body is protecting itself. But if the body temperature gets too high too rapidly (over 104 degrees Fahrenheit, 40 degrees centigrade, rising more than several degrees an hour), there may be a possibility of a convulsion occurring.

An infant or toddler cannot hold a thermometer steady in his mouth for you to take an oral temperature, and "fever strips" that are placed on the child's forehead are not accurate. The best way to measure fever in a young child is by taking a rectal temperature. Once you know how to take a rectal temperature, it is really quite simple; but it's best to learn the procedures in advance so you're not nervous about them the first time your child is actually sick.

Rectal thermometer (with short, round bulb)

Oral thermometer (with longer bulb)

Among your basic baby equipment, you should have at least one rectal thermometer with a short, round mercury bulb. Two are even better, since thermometers are breakable. Beware—it's very easy to smash the thermometer against the sink while shaking it down or drop it while juggling your baby in your arms.

Reading a thermometer takes some practice, and you should learn how before a crisis arises. The trick is to hold the thermometer between your thumb and index finger (at the end opposite the bulb) and roll it slowly back and forth until you see the mercury column. The temperature reading corresponds to the end of the column. Digital thermometers are easier to read, but are also more expensive.

The procedure for taking a rectal temperature is as follows:

1. Shake the mercury column down until it reads below 96 degrees (35 degrees centigrade). To do this, hold the end opposite from the bulb tightly between your fingers and snap your wrist (*away* from any counter tops or nearby objects).

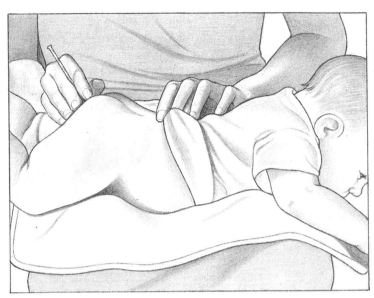

Taking a rectal temperature

2. Rub the bulb end with rubbing alcohol or soap and water, and rinse it with cool clear water.

3. Place a small amount of lubricant such as petroleum jelly on the bulb end.

4. Place your baby belly-down on a firm surface. If he's a tiny infant you can lay him across your lap, but if he's larger or squirming, you'll find a changing table or even the floor much safer.

5. Firmly press the palm of one hand against the baby's lower back just above the buttocks. If he tries to roll over, increase the pressure to hold him still.

6. With your other hand, insert the lubricated thermometer ½ inch to 1 inch into the anal opening. Hold the thermometer between your second and third fingers with the hand cupped over the baby's bottom. Hold in place for two minutes before removing and reading it.

7. A rectal reading over 100 degrees Fahrenheit (38 degrees centigrade) may indicate fever. If you think the temperature may be unusually high because your child has been physically active or too warmly clothed, retake the temperature in thirty minutes.

Rectal temperatures can be taken with children of all ages, but by age four or five your child will probably be cooperative enough to let you take his temperature orally, which requires holding the thermometer under his tongue for two minutes.

Visiting the Pediatrician

You probably will see more of your pediatrician in your baby's first year than at any other time. The baby's first examination will take place immediately after birth. The schedule below lists the minimum routine checkups for the rest of your baby's first two years. Your pediatrician may want to see your baby more often.

Ideally, both parents should attend these early visits to the doctor. These appointments give you and your pediatrician a chance to get to know each other and exchange questions and answers. Don't restrict yourself to medical questions; your pediatrician is also an expert on general child-care issues and a valuable resource if you're looking for child-care help, parent support groups, or other outside assistance. Many pediatricians hand out information sheets that cover the most common concerns, but it's a good idea to make a list of the questions you have before each visit so you don't forget any important ones.

If only one parent can attend, try to get a friend or a relative to join the parent who does. It's much easier to concentrate on your discussions with the doctor if you have a little help dressing and undressing the baby and gathering all of his things. While you're getting used to outings with your newborn, an extra adult can also help carry the diaper bag and hold doors.

The purpose of these early checkups is to make sure your child is growing and developing properly and has no serious abnormalities. Specifically, the doctor will check the following:

Growth. You will be asked to undress your baby, and then he'll be weighed on an infant scale. His length may be measured lying on a flat table with his legs stretched straight. A special tape is used to measure the size of his head. All of these measurements may be plotted on a graph in order to determine his growth curve from one visit to the next. (You can plot your baby's growth curve in the same way using the charts on pages 118–121.) This is the most reliable way to judge whether he's growing normally, and will show you his position on the growth curve in relation to other children his age.

Head. The soft spots should be open and flat for the first few months. By four months of age, the spot at the back should be closed. The front soft spot should close before your child's second birthday.

Ears. The doctor will look inside both ears with an otoscope, an instrument that provides a view of the ear canal and eardrum. This tells him whether there is any evidence of fluid or infection in the ear. You'll also be asked if the child responds normally to sounds. Formal hearing tests are rarely given to an infant unless there is suspicion that a problem exists.

RECOMMENDATIONS FOR PREVENTIVE PEDIATRIC HEALTH CARE

Committee on Practice and Ambulatory Medicine

Each child and family is unique: therefore, these **Recommendations for Preventive Health Care** are designed for the care of children who are receiving competent parenting, have no manifestations of any important health problems, and are growing and developing in satisfactory fashion. **Additional visits may become necessary** if circumstances suggest variations from normal. These guidelines represent a consensus by the Committee on Practice and Ambulatory Medicine in consultation with national committees and sections of the American Academy of Pediatrics. The Committee emphasizes the great importance of **continuity of care** in comprehensive health supervision and the need to avoid **fragmentation of care**.

A **prenatal visit** is recommended for parents who are at high risk, for first-time parents, and for those who request a conference. The prenatal visit should include anticipatory guidance and pertinent medical history. Every infant should have a newborn evaluation after birth.

AGE[4]	INFANCY[2]							EARLY CHILDHOOD[3]					MIDDLE CHILDHOOD[3]					ADOLESCENCE[3]											
	NEWBORN[1]	2-4d[2]	By 1mo	2mo	4mo	6mo	9mo	12mo	15mo	18mo	24mo	3y	4y	5y	6y	8y	10y	11y	12y	13y	14y	15y	16y	17y	18y	19y	20y	21y
HISTORY Initial/Interval	•	•	•	•	•	•	•	•	•	•	•	•	•	•	•	•	•	•	•	•	•	•	•	•	•	•	•	•
MEASUREMENTS Height and Weight	•	•	•	•	•	•	•	•	•	•	•	•	•	•	•	•	•	•	•	•	•	•	•	•	•	•	•	•
Head Circumference	•	•	•	•	•	•	•	•	•	•	•																	
Blood Pressure												•	•	•	•	•	•	•	•	•	•	•	•	•	•	•	•	•
SENSORY SCREENING Vision	S	S	S	S	S	S	S	S	S	S	S	O	O	O	O	O	O	S	O	S	S	O	S	S	O	S	S	S
Hearing	S/O	S	S	S	S	S	S	S	S	S	S	O	O	O	O	O	O	S	O	S	S	O	S	S	O	S	S	S
DEVELOPMENTAL/ BEHAVIORAL ASSESSMENT[7]	•	•	•	•	•	•	•	•	•	•	•	•	•	•	•	•	•	•	•	•	•	•	•	•	•	•	•	•
PHYSICAL EXAMINATION[8]	•	•	•	•	•	•	•	•	•	•	•	•	•	•	•	•	•	•	•	•	•	•	•	•	•	•	•	•
PROCEDURES-GENERAL Hereditary/Metabolic Screening[10]	←→																											
Immunization[11]	•←—————————————————————————————→•																											
Hematocrit or Hemoglobin						•				*								*										
Urinalysis											•											*						
PROCEDURES-PATIENTS AT RISK Lead Screening[12]						*		•				*←————————————————————→*																
Tuberculin Test[15]								*				*	*	*	*	*	*	*	*	*	*	*	*	*	*	*	*	*
Cholesterol Screening[16]																		←—————————————————————————→									
STD Screening[17]																		*←————————————————————————→*									
Pelvic Exam[18]																		*←————————————————————————→*									
ANTICIPATORY GUIDANCE[19]	•	•	•	•	•	•	•	•	•	•	•	•	•	•	•	•	•	•	•	•	•	•	•	•	•	•	•	•
INJURY PREVENTION[20]	•←————————————————————————————————————→																											
INITIAL DENTAL REFERRAL[21]												•																

1. Breastfeeding encouraged and instruction and support offered.
2. For newborns discharged in less than 48 hours after delivery.
3. Developmental, psychological, and chronic disease issues for children and adolescents may require frequent counseling and treatment visits separate from preventive care visits.
4. If a child comes under care for the first time at any point on the schedule, or if any items are not accomplished at the suggested age, the schedule should be brought up to date at the earliest possible time.
5. If the patient is uncooperative, rescreen within six months.
6. Some experts recommend objective appraisal of hearing in the newborn period. The Joint Committee on Infant Hearing has identified patients at significant risk for hearing loss. All children meeting these criteria should be objectively screened. See the Joint Committee on Infant Hearing 1994 Position Statement.
7. By history and appropriate physical examination; if suspicious, by specific objective developmental testing.
8. At each visit, a complete physical examination is essential, with infant totally unclothed, older child undressed and suitably draped.
9. These may be modified, depending upon entry point into schedule and individual need.
10. Metabolic screening (eg, thyroid, hemoglobinopathies, PKU, galactosemia) should be done according to state law.
11. Schedule(s) per the Committee on Infectious Diseases, published periodically in *Pediatrics*. Every visit should be an opportunity to update and complete a child's immunizations.
12. Blood lead screen per AAP statement "Lead Poisoning: From Screening to Primary Prevention" (1993).
13. All menstruating adolescents should be screened.
14. Conduct dipstick urinalysis for leukocytes for male and female adolescents.
15. TB testing per AAP statement "Screening for Tuberculosis in Infants and Children" (1994). Testing should be done upon recognition of high risk factors. If results are negative but high risk situation continues, testing should be repeated on an annual basis.
16. Cholesterol screening for high risk patients per AAP "Statement on Cholesterol" (1992). If family history cannot be ascertained and other risk factors are present, screening should be at the discretion of the physician.
17. All sexually active patients should be screened for sexually transmitted diseases (STDs).
18. All sexually active females should have a pelvic examination. A pelvic examination and routine pap smear should be offered as part of preventive health maintenance between the ages of 18 and 21 years.
19. Appropriate discussion and counseling should be an integral part of each visit for care.
20. From birth to age 12, refer to AAP's injury prevention program (TIPP)® as described in "A Guide to Safety Counseling in Office Practice" (1994).
21. Earlier initial dental evaluations may be appropriate for some children. Subsequent examinations as prescribed by dentist.

Key: • = to be performed   * = to be performed for patients at risk   S = subjective, by history   O = objective, by standard testing method   ←●—→ = the range during which a service may be provided, with the dot indicating the preferred age.

NB: Special chemical, immunologic, and endocrine testing is usually carried out upon specific indications. Testing other than newborn (eg, inborn errors of metabolism, sickle disease, etc.) is discretionary with the physician.

The recommendations in this publication do not indicate an exclusive course of treatment or serve as a standard of medical care. Variations, taking into account individual circumstances, may be appropriate.

Eyes. The doctor will use a bright object or flashlight to catch your baby's attention and track his eye movements. He may also look inside the baby's eyes with a lighted instrument called an ophthalmoscope—repeating the internal eye examination that was first done in the hospital nursery. This is particularly helpful in detecting cataracts (clouding of the lens of the eye). (See *Cataracts,* page 561.)

Mouth. The mouth is checked for signs of infection and, later, for teething progress.

Heart and Lungs. The pediatrician will use a stethoscope on the front and back of the chest to listen to your child's heart and lungs. This examination determines whether there are any abnormal heart rhythms, sounds, or breathing difficulties.

Abdomen. By placing his hand on the child's abdomen and gently pressing, the doctor makes sure that none of the organs is enlarged and there are no unusual masses or tenderness.

Genitalia. The genitalia are examined at each visit for any unusual lumps, tenderness, or signs of infection. In the first exam or two, the doctor pays special attention to a circumcised boy's penis to make sure it's healing properly. He checks all baby boys to make certain both testes are down in the scrotum.

Hips and Legs. The pediatrician will move your baby's legs to check for dislocations or other problems with the hip joints. Later, after the baby starts to walk, the doctor will watch him take a few steps to make sure the legs and feet are properly aligned and move normally.

Developmental Milestones. The pediatrician will also ask about the baby's general development. Among other things, he'll observe and discuss when the baby starts to smile, roll over, sit up, and walk, and how he uses his hands and arms. During the exam he will test reflexes and general muscle tone. (See Chapters 5 through 12 for details of normal development.)

Immunizations

Your child should receive most of his childhood immunizations before his second birthday. These will protect him against ten major diseases: polio, measles, mumps, chicken pox, rubella (German measles), pertussis (whooping cough), diphtheria, tetanus, Haemophilus (Hib) infections and Hepatitis B. See page 63 for the schedule of immunizations recommended by the American Academy of Pediatrics.

DTP Vaccine. At his two-month checkup your child should receive his first DTP vaccine immunizing him against diphtheria (D), tetanus (T), and pertussis (P).

Recommended Ages for Administration of Childhood Vaccines

Vaccines are listed under the routinely recommended ages. Solid bars indicate range of acceptable ages for vaccination. Hepatitis B vaccine is recommended at 11–12 years of age for children not previously vaccinated. Varicella Zoster Virus vaccine is recommended at 11–12 years of age for children not previously vaccinated, and who lack a reliable history of chicken pox.

	Birth	2 mos	4 mos	6 mos	12[1] mos	15 mos	18 mos	4-6 yrs	11-12 yrs	14-16 yrs
Hepatitis[2,3]	Hep B-1	Hep B-2		Hep B-3					Hep B[3]	
Diphtheria, Tetanus, Pertussis[4]		DTP	DTP	DTP	DTP[1,4] DTaP at 15+m			DTP or DTaP	Td	
H. influenzae type b[5]		Hib	Hib	Hib[5]	Hib[1,5]					
Polio		OPV	OPV	OPV				OPV		
Measles, Mumps, Rubella[6]					MMR[1,6]			MMR or [6] MMR		
Varicella Zoster[7]					VZV				VZV[7]	

[1] Vaccines recommended in the second year of life (12-15 months of age) may be given at either one or two visits.

[2] **Infants born to HBsAg-negative mothers** should receive 2.5 μg of Merck Sharp & Dohme (MSD) vaccine (Recombivax HB) or 10 μg of SmithKline Beecham (SKB) vaccine (Engerix-B). The second dose should be given between 1 and 4 months of age, if at least 1 month has elapsed since receipt of the first dose. The third dose is recommended between 6 and 18 months of age.

Infants born to HBsAg-positive mothers should receive immunoprophylaxis for hepatitis B with 0.5 ml Hepatitis B Immune Globulin (HBIG) within 12 hours of birth, and either 5 μg of MSD vaccine (Recombivax HB) or 10 μg of SKB vaccine (Engerix-B) at a separate site. In these infants, the second dose of vaccine is recommended at 1 month of age and the third dose at 6 months of age. All pregnant women should be screened for HBsAg in an early prenatal visit.

[3] Hepatitis B vaccine is recommended for adolescents who have not previously received 3 doses of vaccine. The 3-dose series should be initiated or completed at the 11-12 year-old visit for persons not previously fully vaccinated. The 2nd dose should be administered at least 1 month after the first dose, and the 3rd dose should be administered at least 4 months after the first dose.

[4] The fourth dose of DTP may be administered as early as 12 months of age, provided at least 6 months have elapsed since DTP3. Combined DTP-Hib products may be used when these two vaccines are to be administered simultaneously. DTaP (diphtheria and tetanus toxoids and acellular pertussis vaccine) is licensed for use for the 4th and/or 5th dose of DTP vaccine in children 15 months of age or older and may be preferred for these doses in children in this age group. Td (tetanus and diphtheria toxoids, absorbed, for adult use) is recommended at 11-12 years of age if at least 5 years have elapsed since the last dose of DTP, DTP-Hib, or DT.

[5] Three _H. influenzae_ type b conjugate vaccines are available for use in infants: HbOC [HibTITER] (Lederle Praxis); PRP-T [ActHIB; OmniHIB] (Pasteur Mérieux, distributed by SmithKline Beecham; Connaught); and PRP-OMP [PedvaxHIB] (Merck Sharp & Dohme). Children who have received PRP-OMP at 2 and 4 months of age do not require a dose at 6 months of age. After the primary infant Hib conjugate vaccine series is completed, any licensed Hib conjugate vaccine may be used as a booster dose at 12-15 months.

[6] The second dose of MMR vaccine should be administered EITHER at 4-6 years of age OR at 11-12 years of age, consistent with state school immunization requirements.

[7] Varicella zoster virus (VZV) is routinely recommended at 12-18 months of age. Children who have not been vaccinated previously and who lack a reliable history of chicken pox should be vaccinated by 13 years of age. VZV can be administered to susceptible children any time after 12 months of age. Children under 13 years of age should receive a single 0.5 mL dose; persons 13 years of age and older should receive two 0.5 doses 4-8 weeks apart.

This vaccine is given in five injections, the first three at two, four, and six months. A fourth dose is given six to twelve months after the third dose, usually around eighteen months of age. Then your child will receive another shot before he enters school, between four and six years. This "booster" shot raises your child's immunity against these diseases to higher levels.

Within the first twenty-four hours after the shot, your baby may be irritable and less energetic than usual. The area where the vaccine was injected may be red and sensitive, and he may have a low-grade fever (less than 102 degrees Fahrenheit [38.9 degrees centigrade]). These normal reactions should last no more than twenty-four hours. They can be treated with acetaminophen given every four hours. (See the chart on page 585, for appropriate doses.) Do not use aspirin.

Notify your pediatrician if your child displays any of the following less common reactions:

- Constant, inconsolable crying for more than three hours
- Unusual, high-pitched crying
- Excessive sleepiness or difficulty in waking up
- Limpness or paleness
- Temperature of 105 degrees Fahrenheit (40.6 degrees centigrade) or higher
- Convulsion (usually resulting from a high fever)

While these more serious side effects may sound alarming, there is less than a 1 percent chance that your child will have *any* of them. This risk must be balanced against the fact that if your baby is not immunized, his risk of getting one of these diseases increases greatly. Diphtheria, tetanus, and pertussis are dangerous diseases. (See Chapter 27, *Immunizations.*)

The dangers include:

- Four out of ten people who get tetanus die from it.
- Before this vaccine was available, one out of fifteen people who got diphtheria died from it.
- One out of one hundred babies under six months who get pertussis die from it. (The overall death rate is one in one thousand, including older infants.)
- Nearly three out of every four children who get pertussis require hospitalization, and one out of five develops pneumonia.

There has been controversy concerning the reactions to the DTP vaccine, but because the benefits so far outweigh the risks, *the American Academy of Pediatrics strongly recommends continuing the routine use of this vaccine, beginning at age two months.*

There are, however, some children who should have these vaccinations postponed, and a few who should not receive them at all. These include children who have one or more of the following problems:

- A serious reaction to the initial immunization
- A previous convulsion, or the suspicion of having a disease of the nervous system

If your child has any of these difficulties, make sure that your pediatrician is aware of them *before* DTP immunization is given.

Polio Vaccine. Polio is a viral disease that can paralyze some muscles of the body. The illness may be mild to very serious, depending on the muscles involved and the severity of the involvement. Fortunately, polio is not seen much in the United States anymore because there are vaccines to prevent it.

The most commonly used immunization against polio is the Sabin (oral, live-virus) vaccine, which is usually given at two, four, and eighteen months, and again between age four and six years, with an optional dose at six months for the occasional child who might travel to another country where polio is more often seen. It is preferred over the Salk (injected, killed-virus) vaccine because it is painless to administer and gives a more permanent immunity. The Salk vaccine is preferable for a child who might have an underlying immune mechanism problem or in the rare event that he is being given chemotherapy for a disease such as leukemia.

The Sabin vaccine does have some disadvantages, the main one being that the virus is passed into the baby's stools for several days after the vaccine is given. This can infect a nonimmunized individual who comes in contact with the stool. Wash your hands after each diaper change. In addition, if you or other caretakers have not been immunized, you should discuss this with your physician.

MMR Vaccine. At fifteen months your child will receive a single shot immunizing him against mumps, measles, and rubella. Though these diseases are best known for the rashes (measles and rubella) and glandular swelling (mumps) they produce, each may also cause serious medical complications. (See *Measles,* page 640; *Mumps,* page 600; *German Measles,* page 633.) Immunizations against these diseases rarely cause any serious side effects, but your child may experience the following reactions, beginning seven to ten days following the injection:

- A mild rash
- Slight swelling of the lymph nodes in the neck or diaper area
- Low-grade fever
- Sleepiness

If your toddler is allergic to eggs, he may have a reaction to the vaccine (because eggs are used in the process of manufacturing it), so you should alert your pediatrician to the fact. Also, if your child is taking any medication that interferes with the immune system, or his immune system is weakened for any reason, he should not be given the MMR. Recently, there has been an increase in the number of cases of measles. In order to give additional protection, a second MMR is now recommended at around the twelfth birthday. Some states even recommend this second dose being given earlier, so you must check with your pediatrician.

Chicken Pox Vaccine. A vaccine to protect against chicken pox is recommended for all healthy children between 12 and 18 months of age who have never had the disease. Children under 13 who have not had chicken pox and were never vaccinated also should receive a single dose of the vaccine. Although chicken pox will not cause complications in most healthy children, certain groups are at a higher risk of developing more severe problems. These include children who are under one year of age, have weak immune systems, have eczema and other skin conditions, or are adolescents.

Haemophilus B Conjugate Vaccine (Hib). A new vaccine against bacterial infections caused by the bacteria *Haemophilus influenzae B* is now recommended for children beginning at two months of age. (See also *Epiglottitis,* page 540; *Meningitis,* page 597.)

Hepatitis B Vaccine. A vaccine to prevent Hepatitis B has been added to the list of those recommended to be given to children. Hepatitis B (sometimes called serum hepatitis) is a viral illness that affects the liver. It can occur at any age, including the newborn period. It can be passed from mother to infant at the time of birth or from one household member to another. It also can be spread through sexual intercourse or contact with infected blood from needles or contaminated surgical instruments.

Infants and young children can contract the disease and not be very ill until sometime later when they may develop chronic liver problems including cancer.

Since the disease seems to be increasing and contact cannot always be predicted or avoided, health authorities, including the American Academy of Pediatrics, have recommended immunization in early infancy.

The vaccine is given in three doses beginning shortly after birth with a second dose one or two months later and a booster dose at six to eighteen months of age.

Older children, adolescents, and adults who happen to be at increased risk of contact should also be immunized. Three doses of vaccine are also needed for these individuals with a time interval of one and six months between the first and second and third doses, respectively.

There have been no serious reactions to the vaccine. However, minor side effects such as fussiness and soreness, redness, or swelling at the site of the injection may be noted.

This chapter has dealt in a general way with the topic of infant care. Your baby is a unique individual, however, so you will have some questions specific to him and him alone. These are best answered by your own pediatrician.

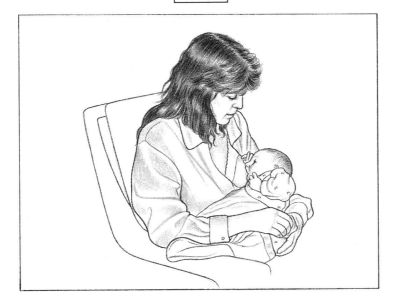

4

FEEDING YOUR BABY:
BREAST AND BOTTLE

*Y*our baby's nutritional needs during the rapid-growth period of infancy are greater than at any other time in his life. He will approximately triple his birthweight during his first year.

Feeding your infant provides more than just good nutrition. It gives you a chance to hold your newborn close, cuddle him, and make eye contact. These are relaxing and enjoyable moments for you both, and they bring you closer together emotionally.

Before your baby arrives you should decide whether to nurse or feed him infant formula. This is an important decision which requires serious consideration, so you should carefully evaluate both options before making your final decision. This chapter will provide the basic information you need to select the best option for you and your baby.

Because of its nutritional composition, human milk is the ideal food for human infants. It also contains factors that provide additional immunity against infection, and it is least likely to cause allergic reactions. As a result, most pediatricians urge expectant mothers to try breast-feeding.

But it's important not to feel guilty if you decide to bottle-feed your baby. Infant formula is an acceptable and nutritious alternative to human milk. Whatever your reason for not breast-feeding (and it could simply be that you don't want to), this is your choice. However, it's important that you give it serious consideration before your baby arrives, because starting with formula and then switching to breast milk can be difficult, or even impossible if you wait too long. The production of milk by the breast (the process is called lactation) is most successful if breast-feeding begins right after delivery. If you begin breast-feeding and then, for any reason, decide that it's not right for you, you can always switch to formula.

Approximately 44 percent of newborns in the United States are breast-fed at birth. By six months, only about 11 percent are being breast-fed, while only about 2 percent are still being breast-fed at one year. You may well use both methods with your infant before his first year is over—all the more reason to familiarize yourself in advance with the basic information about each one.

ADVANTAGES AND DISADVANTAGES OF BREAST-FEEDING

As we've already mentioned, human milk is the best possible food for any infant. Its major ingredients are sugar (lactose), easily digestible protein (whey and casein), and fat (digestible fatty acids)—all properly balanced to suit your baby. In addition, there are numerous minerals, vitamins, and enzymes that may aid the digestive process. Formulas can only approximate this combination of nutrients, and they cannot provide the enzymes, antibodies, and other valuable ingredients of breast milk.

There are many practical reasons to breast-feed, or nurse, your baby. Human milk is relatively low in cost. You should increase your own caloric intake, but that costs only about one third of what you'd have to spend for formula. Also, human milk needs no preparation and is instantly available at any time, wherever you may be. As an added advantage to the nursing mother, breast-feeding makes it much easier to get back into shape physically after giving birth, by using up about 500 calories a day and by helping the uterus tighten up and return more quickly to its normal size.

Although the psychological and emotional advantages of breast-feeding are less specific, they are just as compelling for both mother and child. Nursing provides direct skin-to-skin contact, which is soothing for your baby and pleasant for you. The same hormones that stimulate milk production may also promote feelings that enhance mothering. Almost all nursing mothers find that the experience makes them feel more attached and protective toward their babies, and more confident about their own abilities to nurture and care for their children. This advantage of breast-feeding can't be emphasized enough.

When breast-feeding is going well, it has no known disadvantages for the baby. The main drawback is for the rest of the family, especially Mom. Since no one but Mom can nurse the baby, she will have to be awake and available whenever the baby is hungry. And, because human milk takes less time to digest than formula, the breast-fed baby will have to be fed more often than one that is bottle-fed.

Breast-feeding can also make other members of the family feel a little left out. They can't enjoy the fun of holding the baby and watching him eat, and some fathers feel that breast-feeding distances them from both mother and child. They may even feel jealous of the closeness between mother and child.

A good way to keep Dad (or anyone else in the family) from feeling this way is to keep him involved in every other aspect of the baby's care. A father is invaluable when comforting is necessary and not feeding. He can hold, diaper, comfort, and carry the baby whenever he's on hand, and he can handle the feeding whenever an occasional bottle is required. But the best protection against jealousy and misunderstanding is openly discussing the issue of feeding and making sure both parents support the choice before the baby arrives. Most fathers want their children to receive the best possible nutrition from the start, and without question, that is mother's milk.

Are there medical circumstances that make breast-feeding inadvisable? Yes, but they are rare. If a mother is extremely ill, she may not have the energy or stamina to breast-feed without interfering with her own recovery. She may also be taking certain medications that would pass into her milk and be dangerous to her infant.

If you are taking medications for any reason (prescription drugs or over-the-counter medications), let your pediatrician know *before* you start breast-feeding. Your pediatrician can advise you whether any of these drugs can pass through breast milk and cause problems for your baby.

ADVANTAGES AND DISADVANTAGES OF BOTTLE-FEEDING

The main advantage of formula-feeding is that it frees Mom from being her baby's sole source of food. Dad, grandparents, sitters, even older siblings can feed an infant formula or breast milk which has been expressed into a bottle. Not only does this give the mother more flexibility, but it helps everyone else in the family to bond with the baby.

There are other reasons why some parents feel more comfortable with bottle-feeding: They know exactly how much food the baby is getting, and there's no need to worry about the mother's diet or medications that might affect the milk.

Also, because formula takes longer to digest than human milk, bottle-fed babies don't need to be fed as frequently as breast-fed ones.

But formula manufacturers have not yet found a way to reproduce all of the components that make human milk so unique. Though formula does provide all of the nutrients an infant needs, it lacks the antibodies that only mother's milk contains.

Formula-feeding is also costly and may be inconvenient for some families. The formula must be bought and prepared (unless you use the more expensive, ready-to-use types). This means trips to the kitchen in the middle of the night, as well as extra bottles, nipples, and other equipment.

BREAST-FEEDING YOUR BABY
Developing the Right Attitude

You can do it! This should be your attitude about breast-feeding from the beginning. If you feel at all hesitant, there's plenty of help available. For example, you can

- Talk to your prenatal instructors or attend a breast-feeding class.

- Talk to your obstetrician and pediatrician. They can provide not only medical information but also encouragement and support when you need it most.

- Talk to women who are breast-feeding successfully and ask their advice.

- Talk to members of La Leche League in your community. This is a worldwide organization dedicated to helping families learn about and enjoy the experience of breast-feeding. Ask your pediatrician for information about how to contact La Leche League.

- Read about breast-feeding. Recommended books include: *Breastfeeding and the Working Mother,* by D. Mason and D. Ingersoll (St. Martin's Press); *Nursing Your Baby,* by K. Pryor (Harper & Row); *The Complete Book of Breastfeeding* by M. Eiger and S. Olds (Workman Publishing). Also available, *Breastfeeding: The Art of Mothering* video and book. To order ($29.95 video, $4.95 book, plus $6.25 shipping and handling) contact American Academy of Pediatrics, P.O. Box 927, Elk Grove Village, IL, 60009-0927, (800) 433-9016.

Getting Started: Preparing the Breasts for Lactation

Whether or not you intend to nurse your infant, your body starts preparing to breast-feed as soon as you become pregnant. The area surrounding the nipples—the areola—becomes darker. The breasts themselves enlarge as the cells that

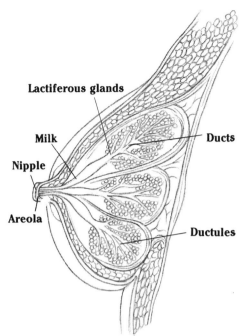

Lactiferous glands

Milk

Ducts

Nipple

Areola

Ductules

Milk is produced by the lactiferous glands. The milk then passes through the ductules into the ducts and out the nipple.

will manufacture the milk multiply, and the ducts that will carry the milk to the nipple develop. Meanwhile, your body starts storing excess fat in other areas to provide the extra energy needed for lactation.

As early as the sixteenth week of pregnancy, some women can begin expressing fluid from their breasts by squeezing the areola. This fluid—a rich, though thin-appearing, orange-yellow solution that is produced for several days after delivery until replaced by mature milk—is called colostrum. Colostrum contains more protein, salt, antibodies, and other protective properties than breast milk itself, but less fat and calories.

As your body naturally prepares for breast-feeding, there is very little that you need to do. Unless your nipples are flat or inverted, you don't have to stretch, pull, roll, or buff the nipples toward the end of pregnancy. The nipples do not need to be "toughened up" to withstand your baby's sucking. In fact, some of these tactics may actually interfere with normal lactation by harming the tiny glands in the areola which secrete a milky fluid that lubricates the nipples in preparation for breast-feeding.

There's another risk: As you approach the end of your pregnancy, excessive nipple stimulation may also cause the release of hormones that make the uterus contract, and could possibly trigger early labor. So although occasional gentle stimulation—for example, during lovemaking—is harmless, you should avoid rigorous manipulation of the nipples. Normal bathing and gentle drying is the best way to care for your breasts during pregnancy.

Although many women rub lotions and ointments on their breasts to soften them, these are not necessary and may clog the skin pores. Lanolin, the most commonly used ointment, is derived from the oil of sheep and may cause an allergic reaction in anyone sensitive to wool. Other salves, particularly those containing vitamins or normones, could cause problems for your baby if used while breast-feeding, as the substances in them can be absorbed into your system through the skin and transmitted to the baby during pregnancy or through breast milk.

Proper support of the breasts is important during pregnancy (whether one plans to breast-feed or not) and lactation, because the breasts are heavier than usual. Without a good brassiere, the additional size and weight will stretch the ligaments

Preparing Inverted Nipples for Breast-Feeding

Normally, when you press the areola between two fingers, the nipple should protrude and become erect. If the nipple seems to pull inward and disappear instead, it is said to be "inverted" or "tied." This can interfere with successful breast-feeding because the baby may have difficulty grasping the areola and getting milk from the ducts. Fortunately, if the problem is diagnosed during pregnancy, it can easily be treated before the baby arrives.

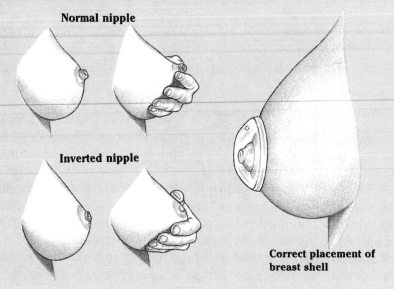

Normal nipple

Inverted nipple

Correct placement of breast shell

The simplest treatment for an inverted nipple is a special breast shell worn inside the bra during waking hours for several weeks or months prior to delivery. This plastic device, available at most baby and drug stores, is shaped like a hollow dome. The underside, worn against the skin, has a hole for the nipple. The circular area around this hole creates a gentle, uniform pressure on the areola, causing the nipple to pop through the hole. Eventually, the nipple takes on this shape even without the shell.

Rarely, in severe cases of inversion, the shell devices are not effective. In these cases a lactation consultant recommended by your pediatrician may be able to suggest techniques that make you more successful at breast-feeding. Even more rarely, surgery may be necessary.

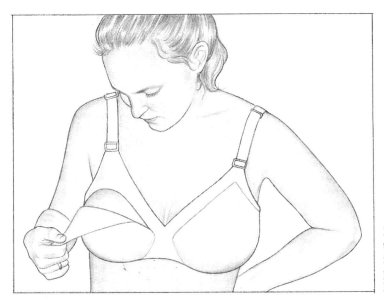

Proper support of the breasts is important during pregnancy and lactation.

of the breasts and contribute to future sagging. Some women start wearing nursing bras during pregnancy. They are more adjustable and roomier than normal bras, and are more comfortable as the breast size increases.

Letting Down and Latching On

After your baby is born and lactation begins, the breasts are ready to produce milk. As he nurses, your baby's actions will let your body know when to start and stop production. The process begins with the baby getting a good grip on the areola and starting to suck. This is called "latching on." He should do this instinctively as soon as he feels the breast against his mouth or cheek. You can help him get started by holding him so that he squarely faces the breast, and then stroking his lips with the nipple. This stimulates the reflex that causes him to search for the nipple with his mouth (the rooting reflex).

As the baby takes the breast into his mouth, his jaws should close around the areola, not the nipple. His gums will form a circular seal, creating a vacuum effect, and his tongue will press the nipple against his palate and empty the milk ducts with an undulating motion. Right after delivery, many babies prefer to lick and play with the nipple; this is normal as long as the baby begins latching on properly within the first few days.

In some cases an infant will have trouble latching on. This occurs most often in newborns who have been given bottles or pacifiers. They may simply lick,

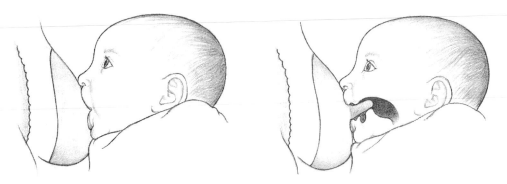

**This baby has latched on
to the breast correctly.**

**The entire areola and nipple
are in his mouth.**

nibble, or chew with their jaws instead of using the tongue. These motions, however, won't stimulate the breast to make more milk, so it will be necessary to "teach" your baby how to latch on properly. Your delivery nurse or pediatrician can help you do this.

Once your baby is sucking efficiently, his movements will stimulate the nerve fibers in the nipple. In turn, through a complex hormonal mechanism (see box on next page), these fibers will prompt the breasts to make more milk and increase its flow. This process that starts milk flowing through the milk ducts is called the "let-down reflex."

Incidentally, one of the hormones that stimulates milk flow also causes the muscles of the uterus to contract. So, in the first days or weeks after delivery, you may feel "after pains," or cramping of the uterus, each time you nurse. While this may be annoying and occasionally painful, it helps the uterus return quickly to its normal size and condition.

Once lactation has begun, it usually takes just a few seconds of sucking before the milk lets down (begins to flow), and sometimes even that isn't necessary. Just hearing your baby cry may actually be enough to trigger the milk flow.

The signs that let-down is occurring vary from woman to woman, and change with the volume of milk the baby demands. Some women feel a subtle tingling sensation, while others experience a buildup of pressure that feels as if their breasts are swelling and overfull—sensations that are quickly relieved as the milk starts to flow. Some women *never* feel these sensations, even though nursing six or seven times a day.

The way the milk flows also varies widely. It may spray, gush, trickle, or flow. It may also be quite different in each breast—perhaps gushing on one side and trickling on the other. This is due to slight differences in the ducts on either side, and is no cause for concern.

The Let-Down Process

As your baby sucks, several different hormones work together to produce milk and release it for feeding. From the moment he starts to nurse, here is what happens within his mother's body:

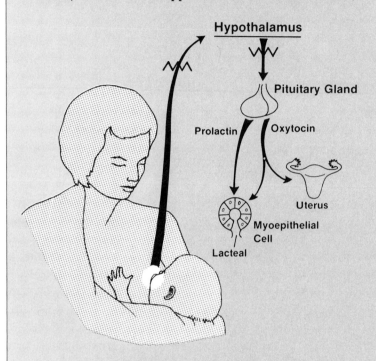

1. His sucking movements stimulate nerve fibers in the nipple.

2. These nerve fibers carry the request for milk up the spinal column to the pituitary gland in your brain.

3. The pituitary gland responds to this message by releasing the hormones prolactin and oxytocin.

4. Prolactin stimulates the breasts to produce more milk.

5. Oxytocin stimulates contractions of the tiny muscles surrounding the ducts in the breasts. These contractions squeeze the ducts and eject the milk into the reservoir under the areola.

Whichever position you choose, make sure his entire body, not just his head, is facing your body.

The First Feeding

If you had a normal delivery, and you and your baby are alert and awake, you can nurse him as soon as he's born. If there were complications with the delivery, or your newborn needs immediate medical attention, you may have to wait a few hours. But as long as the first feeding takes place within the first day or two, you should have no physical difficulty nursing.

If you do nurse immediately after delivery, you may find it most comfortable to lie on your side, with the baby lying facing you, opposite the breast. If you'd rather sit up, use pillows to help support your arms and cradle the baby at breast

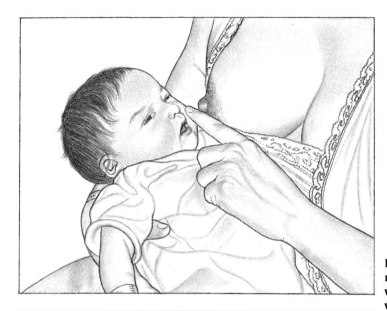

If you stroke your newborn's cheek with your finger or with the nipple, he'll instinctively turn, latch on, and begin to suck.

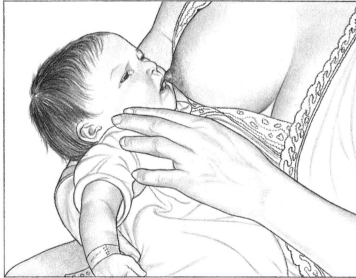

level, making sure his entire body, not just his head, is facing your body. Following a Caesarean section, the most comfortable position is what's called a "football hold," in which you sit up and the baby lies facing you at your side. Curl your arm underneath him, and support and hold his head at your breast. This position keeps the baby's weight off your abdomen.

If you stroke your newborn's cheek with the nipple, he'll instinctively turn, latch on, and begin to suck. He's been practicing this for some time by sucking

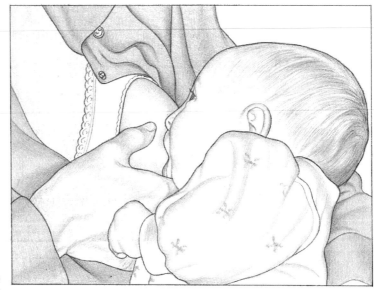

You may need to help him properly grasp the areola.

his hand, fingers, and possibly even his feet in utero. (Some babies actually are born with blisters on their fingers caused by this prenatal sucking.) It takes little encouragement to get him to nurse, but you may need to help him properly grasp the areola. You may hold the breast with your thumb above the areola, fingers and palm underneath it. Then gently compress the breast and direct it into the baby's mouth. You may use the so-called scissor grasp, compressing the areola between two fingers; however, this doesn't work well if you have a very small

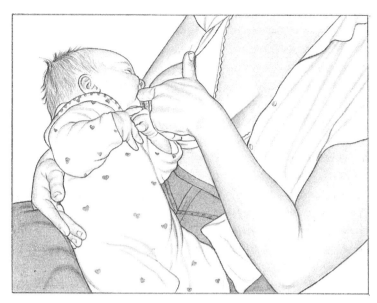

You can slide your finger into the corner of your baby's mouth, breaking his suction to see if there is a flow from the breast.

hand or a large breast. No matter which technique you try, you need to keep your fingers clear of the areola so the baby can grasp it. Be sure your fingers are no closer than two inches from the base of the nipple.

If you can persuade your baby to nurse at both breasts, this will help get lactation under way. It probably will take two or three minutes for let-down to occur in the first few feedings, after which he should receive all the available colostrum in a few minutes. Within a week or so, let-down will take place much more rapidly and your milk supply will increase dramatically.

If you are not sure you are letting down, just watch your baby. He should be swallowing after every few sucks at the start of the feeding. After five or ten minutes, he may switch to what's called nonnutritive sucking—a more relaxed sucking that provides emotional comfort rather than food. Another way to check your let-down is to expose the opposite breast while nursing and see if colostrum or, later, milk flows from it as the baby sucks. You can also slide your finger into the corner of your baby's mouth, breaking his suction to see if there is a flow from that breast.

The more relaxed and confident you feel, the quicker your milk will let down. The first feedings in the hospital may be difficult because of excitement or, perhaps, your uncertainty about what to do. If so, ask the hospital staff for help; they are very experienced at assisting nursing mothers and babies.

Once you are back home, try the following suggestions to help the let-down reflex:

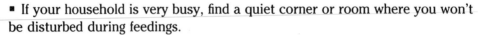

- Sit in a comfortable chair, with good support for your back and arms. (Many nursing mothers recommend rocking chairs.)

- Make sure the baby is positioned so he squarely faces the breast and is sucking properly, not biting.

- Listen to soothing music and sip a nutritious drink during feedings.

- Do not smoke, consume alcohol, or use illegal drugs, as all contain substances that can interfere with let-down and affect the content of breast milk. Check with your obstetrician or pediatrician about any prescription drugs you may be taking.

- If your household is very busy, find a quiet corner or room where you won't be disturbed during feedings.

If you still are not letting down after trying these suggestions, contact your pediatrician for additional help. Most pediatric offices have an experienced nurse or nurse-practitioner who can watch your baby as he feeds and offer constructive suggestions. If you continue to have difficulties, ask to be referred to a lactation expert (usually a registered nurse with training in the art of lactation).

When Your Milk Comes In

For the first day or so after delivery, your breasts will be soft to the touch; but as the blood supply increases and milk-producing cells start to function efficiently, the breasts will become more firm. By the third or fourth day after delivery, your breasts will be producing both colostrum and milk and may feel very full. At the end of the baby's first week, you will see only the watery white breast milk (it looks like skimmed milk), and you probably will feel engorged.

Engorgement can be very uncomfortable and at times painful. The best solution to this problem is to nurse your baby whenever he is hungry, emptying both breasts every two to four hours. But sometimes the breasts are so engorged that the baby has trouble latching on. If that happens, you can manually express some milk before you start to nurse. This may help him get a better grasp and nurse more efficiently. This is done by placing your thumb at the top of the areola, fingers underneath, and then squeezing the edges of the areola as you press back

Breast-Feeding Twins

Twins present a unique challenge to the nursing mother. At first it's best to feed them one at a time, but after lactation is established, it's often more convenient to feed them simultaneously in order to save time. You can do this using the "football hold" to position one at each side, or cradle them both in front of you with their bodies crossing each other.

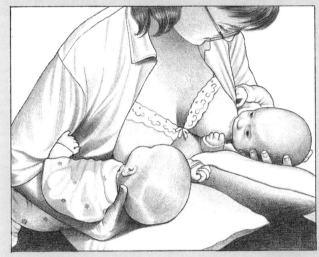

Football hold

Bodies-crossed position

Getting to Know Your Baby's Feeding Patterns

Each baby has a particular style of eating. Years ago researchers at Yale University attached names to five common eating patterns. See if you recognize your baby's dining behavior among them:

Barracudas get right down to business. As soon as they're put to the breast, they grasp the nipple and suck energetically for ten to twenty minutes. In their enthusiasm they sometimes bite down too hard, which can be painful for you, but they usually become less eager as time goes on.

Excited Ineffectives become frantic at the sight of the breast. In a frenzied cycle they grasp it, lose it, and start screaming in frustration. They must be calmed down several times during each feeding. The key to nourishing this type of baby is to feed him as soon as he wakes up, before he gets desperately hungry. Also, if the milk tends to spray from the breast as the baby struggles, it may help to manually express it first to slow the stream.

Procrastinators can't be bothered with nursing until the milk comes in. They're not interested, and it's no use trying to force them. An occasional feeding of glucose water will provide the necessary fluids in this interim period, but these babies shouldn't be given bottles of

toward the chest wall in a milking motion. If your baby is a lazy eater you can also express milk *after* he's latched on, which will encourage him to nurse more energetically. Fortunately, engorgement lasts only a few days while lactation is getting established.

The volume of milk produced by the breasts increases dramatically over this first week. You may produce as little as ½ ounce (15 cc) at each feeding in the first couple of days. But by the fourth or fifth day the volume may be up to 1 ounce (30 cc), and by the end of the week—depending on the size and appetite of the baby and the length of feedings—you may be producing 2 to 6 ounces (60 to 180 cc) at each feeding. At the end of your baby's first month he should be receiving an average of 24 to 32 ounces (750 to 1,000 cc) of milk a day. See page 85 for information on how to tell if your baby is getting enough.

formula. The best solution is to wait them out; they do well once they finally get started. For a baby who resists nursing for the first few days, you can use an electric or manual pump between feedings to stimulate milk production (see page 88). Just don't give up! Try to get some personal advice from mothers who have had similar problems.

Gourmets or *Mouthers* insist on playing with the nipple, tasting the milk first and smacking their lips before digging in. If hurried or prodded they become furious and scream in protest. The best solution is tolerance. After a few minutes of playing, they do settle down and nurse well.

Resters prefer to nurse for a few minutes, rest a few minutes, and resume nursing. Some fall asleep on the breast, nap for half an hour or so, and then awake ready for dessert. This pattern can be agonizing for a busy mother with other things to do, but these babies cannot be hurried. The solution? It's best just to schedule extra time for feedings and remain as flexible as possible.

Learning your own baby's eating patterns is one of your biggest challenges in the first few weeks after delivery. Once this is established, it will be much easier to determine when he's hungry, when he's had enough, how often he needs to eat, and how much time is required for feedings.

How Often and How Long?

Because human milk is more easily and completely digested than formula, breast-fed babies need to eat more frequently than bottle-fed infants. Some newborns need to nurse every two hours; others, every three. As they get older, they are able to go longer between feedings, because their stomach capacity enlarges and their mothers' milk production increases.

What's the best feeding schedule for a breast-fed baby? It's the one he designs himself. Your baby lets you know when he's hungry by crying, nuzzling against your breast (he can smell its location even through your clothing), and making sucking motions and fussing. Whenever possible, use these signals rather than the clock to decide when to nurse him. This way, you'll assure that he's hungry

Each feeding should start with about ten minutes on one breast, followed by burping and a shift to the other breast.

when he eats. In the process he'll stimulate the breast more efficiently to produce milk.

If you go home shortly after delivery or have your newborn "room in" with you at the hospital, it's easy to feed on demand right from the start. But if you remain in the hospital for several days and he sleeps in the nursery, his feeding schedule may be determined more by the needs of the staff than his own hunger pangs. Once you're finally home, it may take several days for him to reset his internal clock, so in the meantime try feeding him every two to three hours even if he doesn't cry for nourishment.

Each feeding should start with about ten minutes on one breast, followed by burping and a shift to the other breast. If your baby seems sleepy after the first breast, you may want to wake him up a bit by changing his diaper or playing with him a little before switching him to the second side. It's best to divide each feeding relatively evenly between both breasts so that each receives equal stimulation over the course of a day. Since your infant sucks more efficiently on the first breast he uses, you should alternate from feeding to feeding the one he uses first. Some women place a safety pin or an extra nursing pad on the side where the baby last nursed as a reminder to start first on the other side at the next feeding.

Initially, your newborn probably will nurse every couple of hours, regardless of whether it's day or night. By the end of his first month he may start sleeping longer at night, perhaps going from 10:00 P.M. to 2:00 A.M. without a feeding, and then sleeping until 6:00 A.M. You can encourage this pattern by keeping him awake during the early part of the evening, giving him a long feeding at 10:00 P.M., and keeping his room dark, warm, and quiet at night. Don't turn on the light for the 2:00 A.M. feeding. Change his diaper quickly and without fanfare before this feeding and put him right back to sleep afterward. By four months he should be sleeping six hours or more at a stretch without awakening during the night. (See *Helping Your Baby Sleep,* page 37.)

You'll also find that your infant may require long feedings at certain times of the day and be quickly satisfied at others. He'll let you know when he's finished by letting go or drifting off to sleep between spurts of nonnutritive sucking. A few babies, if allowed to do so, would nurse around the clock to satisfy their sucking needs. If your baby falls into this category, you may have to set some limits. About ten minutes on each breast provides 90 percent of the available milk; beyond this time frame, he'll receive less and less milk per suck. On rare occasions, if he seems desperate to keep sucking for a prolonged period, you might try using a pacifier as a compromise—but don't count on its working. A baby who wants to keep nursing on and on (say, for twenty to thirty minutes per side) at every feeding may be having difficulty obtaining enough milk. If you are not sure why your baby wants to nurse so long, check with your pediatrician.

How Do You Know If He's Getting Enough?

Your baby's diapers will provide clues about whether he is getting enough to eat. During the first month, if his diet is adequate, he should wet six to eight times a day and have several small bowel movements daily (usually one little one after each feeding). Later, he may have less frequent bowel movements, and there may even be a day or more between them. If your baby is otherwise thriving, this is quite normal.

Nursing Trainers

The amount of milk your breasts produce depends on the amount of milk that is removed from them. So if you miss too many feedings, your body will automatically decrease production. This can occur even if you express milk during missed feedings, because pumps do not stimulate or empty the breasts nearly as efficiently as your baby's sucking.

If you miss a number of feedings because of illness or because your baby is unable to nurse for some reason, you may be able to keep your baby well fed while reestablishing your milk supply with the help of a device called a nursing trainer. Unlike a bottle, which trains the baby away from the breast, this device provides supplemental formula while the infant is at the breast.

It consists of a small plastic bag that contains formula and hangs from a ribbon around your neck. The top of the container has a thin flexible tube that is held or taped along the breast to the nipple and placed in the corner of the baby's mouth as he sucks. His suction draws the formula from the container into his mouth, so that even if *you* aren't producing much milk, he will still be getting a full meal. This reinforces his desire to nurse at the breast. At the same time, his sucking stimulates your body to step up milk production.

The nursing trainer is also used to train babies with feeding problems. It can even stimulate lactation in adoptive mothers, or mothers who have stopped breast-feeding for a prolonged period and wish to start again. For women who would otherwise have to give up on breast-

Another way to judge your baby's intake over time is by weighing him once every week or two. During the first week of life, he may lose up to 10 percent of his birthweight (that's 10 to 12 ounces in a full-term baby), but after that he should gain steadily. By the end of his second week he ought to be back to his birthweight. If you've breast-fed other children, lactation probably will get established more quickly this time around, so the new baby may lose very little weight and return to his birthweight in just a day or two. With each successive child, your milk will come in sooner and the volume will increase more rapidly.

Once your milk supply is established, your baby should gain about ⅔ ounce a day during his first three months. Between three and six months, his growth rate will taper off to about ½ ounce a day, and after six months, it will drop even

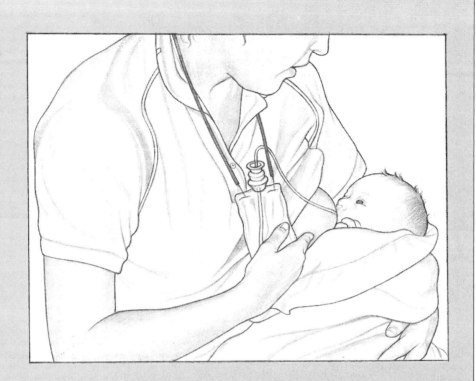

feeding, they are worth a try. Nursing trainers are available at medical supply stores and some pharmacies.

further. If your baby is gaining less than this, you should discuss the situation with your pediatrician. Depend upon the scale at your pediatrician's office for the most accurate measurements.

The Supplemental Bottle

In the hospital after delivery, some women choose to skip a nighttime feeding in order to get some extra sleep. When that happens, most hospital nurseries use a solution of 5 percent dextrose or glucose (sugar) and water to replace the missed feeding. This satisfies the infant without suppressing his appetite at the next breast-feeding.

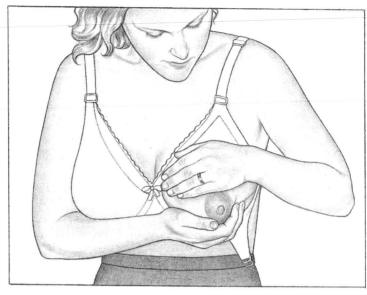

Expressing milk is easier if you stimulate the breast first by massaging it gently.

But if you must miss several feedings in a row, the baby will need to be given either expressed milk or formula. In either case, you will need to express milk, manually or mechanically, in order to stimulate continued milk production. Formula should be substituted for breast-feedings only when absolutely necessary during the first three weeks, and certainly no more than once every twenty-four hours. More frequent formula-feedings may simply get in the way of successful breast-feeding. In general, formula should be given to a breast-feeding newborn only if the mother is sick or must take medications that could pass into her milk and harm the baby.

Once breast-feeding is going well and the milk supply is established (usually three or four weeks after delivery), you may decide to use an occasional bottle of formula or expressed milk so you can be away during some feedings. This probably won't interfere with your baby's nursing habits, but it may cause another problem: Your breasts may become engorged, and they can leak milk. You can relieve the engorgement by expressing milk to empty the breasts. Wearing nursing pads will help you manage the problem of leakage. (Some women need to wear nursing pads constantly during the first month or two of lactation). Also, if you express milk in advance and store it, it can be used instead of formula for the bottle-feeding.

Milk can be expressed either by hand or by pump. If you choose to express manually, make sure your hands and the nipple area are clean, and use a sterile container to collect the milk. Hold the breast in one hand with fingers along the top and bottom of the areola, then press toward the chest wall with a rhythmic

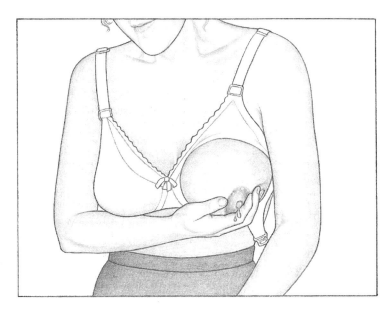

To express manually, hold the breast in one hand with fingers along the top and bottom of the areola, then press toward the chest wall with a rhythmic motion.

motion until the milk flows or squirts out. Transfer the milk into a sterile bottle for storage in the refrigerator. (See page 99.)

Most nursing mothers find using a pump easier than expressing milk manually. Hand pumps are available at most drug and baby stores. Avoid pumps that resemble a bicycle horn—this is an inefficient design that allows pumped milk to flow back into the rubber bulb, which is virtually impossible to clean properly. As a result the milk can become contaminated.

What's a better choice? The most popular pumps consist of two cylinders, one inside the other, attached to a rigid device that fits over the breast. As you slide the outer cylinder up and down, negative pressure is created over the nipple area and milk collects in the bottom of the cylinder. This collecting cylinder can be used with a special nipple to feed your baby without transferring the milk, and the entire pump can be cleaned in the dishwasher. Several different companies manufacture variations on this basic design.

Some pumps use a squeeze bulb to create negative pressure and draw the milk into a bottle, and they work well for some women. They have a soft, pliable flange that fits around the nipple and produces a milking action on the areola while pumping.

Electric pumps stimulate the breast more effectively than manual expression or hand pumps. They are used primarily to induce or maintain lactation when a mother is unable to feed her infant directly for several days or more. These pumps are easier and more efficient than hand pumps—but they're vastly more expensive. The more elaborate ones cost over $1,000 apiece, so if you will need the pump for

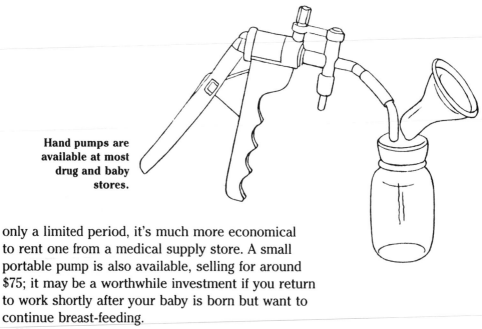

Hand pumps are available at most drug and baby stores.

only a limited period, it's much more economical to rent one from a medical supply store. A small portable pump is also available, selling for around $75; it may be a worthwhile investment if you return to work shortly after your baby is born but want to continue breast-feeding.

When shopping for an electric pump to buy or rent, make sure it creates a steady milking action with variable pressure and is not simply a suction device. You may also want to consider a pump that expresses both breasts at the same time; such a pump will increase your milk volume as well as save time. No matter which type of pump you choose, make sure all parts that come in contact with skin or milk can be removed and sterilized (see page 99). Otherwise, the pump will become a breeding ground for bacteria and the milk will not be safe for your baby. Whenever using a pump, be sure your hands are clean.

Breast milk should be stored only in sterile containers, preferably bottles or plastic nurser bags that can be used to feed the baby without transferring the milk. (Do not use ordinary plastic storage bags.) If the milk is to be given to the baby within twenty-four hours, it should immediately be sealed and chilled. If this refrigerated milk goes unused for more than forty-eight hours, it should be discarded.

If you know in advance that the milk won't be used for at least a full day, freeze it immediately. Breast milk will safely keep in your freezer for at least two weeks, and probably for up to two months. If you have a separate deep freeze, it can be kept for six months. It's a good idea to place a label with the date on each container so you know which to use first. It's useful to freeze milk in quantities of about 3 to 4 ounces—the amount of a single feeding. You can also freeze some 1-to-2-ounce portions; these will come in handy if the baby wants a little extra at any feeding.

When it's time to use this stored milk, keep in mind that your baby is accustomed to breast milk at body temperature, so the milk should be heated to at least room temperature (68 to 72 degrees Fahrenheit) for feeding. The easiest way to warm refrigerated or frozen milk is to place the container in warm water and rotate it frequently. To speed up this process, place the container in a pan of water at low heat on the stove. You can also thaw milk by leaving it at room temperature, but this takes much longer.

Microwave ovens should not be used for heating bottles. Microwaving overheats the milk in the center of the container. Even if the bottle feels comfortably warm to your touch, the superheated milk in the center can scald your baby's mouth. Also, the bottle itself can explode if left in the microwave too long.

Incidentally, once milk is thawed, its fat may separate, but it is still safe to drink. Just shake the container gently until the milk returns to a uniform consistency. Thawed milk should be used within four hours. Never refrigerate it a second time.

Not all breast-fed babies react to the bottle the same way. Some accept it easily, regardless of when it is first introduced. Others are willing to take an occasional bottle during the first few weeks, but then reject it later. And there are those who refuse the bottle no matter when it is offered if their mothers (and a potential breast-feeding) are anywhere nearby.

You can increase the likelihood that your baby will accept a bottle the first few times if someone other than Mom offers it, and she is out of sight at the time. Once familiar with the bottle, he may be willing to take it in his mother's presence, possibly even from mother herself, but don't count on it. If you want to decrease resistance to the ultimate switch from breast to bottle, offer your baby a bottle at least once a week after the first three or four weeks of breast-feeding.

Possible Problems

For some babies and mothers, nursing goes well from the start and there are never any problems. But breast-feeding can have its ups and downs, especially in the beginning. Fortunately, many of the most common difficulties can be resolved quickly if you know what to expect and how to respond. Here are some suggestions for dealing with them:

Food Sensitivities. At one time or another, almost everyone has eaten something that doesn't agree with him. In much the same way, food you eat may cause a reaction in your baby as part of it is transferred to him through breast milk. He may respond by crying, fussing, nursing more frequently, and generally being inconsolable. It's easy to confuse this problem with colic, but there's a difference: While true colic occurs on a daily basis during the first three months (see *Colic,* page 139), colicky behavior caused by food sensitivity takes place only after the nursing mother eats the offending food.

Your baby may have a colicky reaction whenever you eat a certain food, or he may react only after you eat a large quantity of a particular food that causes no trouble in smaller amounts. "Gassy" foods, such as cabbage, onions, garlic, broccoli, and turnips, cause problems for many breast-fed infants. Usually these types of food sensitivities produce what's called "twenty-four-hour colic," which persists for twenty-four hours and then disappears until the next time you eat the offending food.

In rare cases, babies may have a *true* allergy to cow's milk, and will have a colicky period several hours after their mothers eat any dairy product. In addition to the general fussiness typical of twenty-four-hour colic, a milk allergy may produce strong gastrointestinal discomfort, causing the baby to draw up his legs in pain. The only way to identify this problem is to eliminate all dairy products from your diet for at least two weeks. (This includes milk, cheese, yogurt, ice cream, and cottage cheese.) If the pattern of colic continues through these two weeks, then the baby's problem is more likely to be true colic rather than an allergy to milk products that his mother is eating. If the baby's trouble disappears during this period, the latter problem must be seriously considered.

Usually, the allergy is mild enough that some dairy products such as yogurt, ice cream, and cheese can be eaten, as long as milk itself is avoided. You can test to see if this is possible by returning these foods to your diet one at a time, with several days between each one to see if your baby has a negative reaction to any of them. Some children have such strong allergies that they cannot tolerate cow's milk in any form; their mothers have to give up all dairy products while lactating, and the babies must be given non-cow's-milk protein formula when they are weaned from the breast. Fortunately, this extreme allergy is very rare.

If a breast-feeding mother is forced to give up eating dairy products because of her infant's allergy, it is essential that she find other sources of dietary calcium, or use calcium supplements. This should be done even during the two-week period when dairy foods are eliminated as a test. Your doctor can advise you what dietary changes are important, and will recommend a dietician to help you if necessary.

Caffeine is another food substance that sometimes creates problems for breast-feeding babies. Some of the caffeine that Mom ingests shows up in the breast milk and can cause the baby to be irritable and feed more frequently than usual. Because infants don't eliminate caffeine from their bodies very efficiently, it tends to build up in their systems. Consequently, you may not notice any reaction in your baby until two or three weeks after he's born.

Even if you don't drink coffee, you may be getting more caffeine than you realize from soft drinks, chocolate, cocoa, and herb teas. These herb teas can be particularly troublesome because their manufacturers are not required to list the ingredients on the packaging. Don't forget, too, that many over-the-counter medications contain caffeine; you shouldn't use any drug without discussing its safety with your doctor.

Cracked Nipples. If your baby is not positioned properly or does not latch on well when you start breast-feeding, you may end up with cracked or sore nipples. There is no guaranteed way to prevent this. Wash the breasts only with water, not soap. Creams, lotions, and more vigorous rubbing will not help, and may actually aggravate the problem. Also, try varying the baby's position at each feeding, and limiting the length of feedings to five or ten minutes (while adding more feedings to the schedule).

The best treatments for cracked nipples are dryness, sunlight, and heat. Don't wear plastic breast shields or plastic-lined nursing pads which hold in moisture; instead, expose your breasts to the air as much as possible, even using a hair dryer on low heat (and not too close) if it seems to help. Some women prefer to use a lamp with a 60-watt bulb positioned about eighteen inches from the breasts for about twenty to thirty minutes several times a day. Also, after nursing, express a little milk from your breasts, letting it dry on the nipples. This dried milk will leave a protective coating that may help the healing process. If these measures do not solve the problem, consult your doctor for further advice.

Engorgement. As we've already mentioned, your breasts can become severely engorged if your baby doesn't nurse often or efficiently during the first few days after your milk comes in. While some engorgement is to be expected when you start lactation, extreme engorgement causes swelling of the milk ducts in the breasts and of blood vessels across the entire chest area. The best treatment is to express milk between feedings, either manually or with a pump, and make sure the baby nurses at both breasts at every feeding. Since warmth encourages milk flow, it may also help to stand in a warm shower as you manually express the milk, or use warm compresses.

If you have very severe engorgement, however, warmth may aggravate the situation (it increases blood flow to the area). If this is the case, try using cold compresses or cool water instead as you express the milk. Some women even alternate cold and warm water between feedings. Whatever approach you use, the engorgement should subside on its own in a few days.

Mastitis. Mastitis is an infection of the breast caused by bacteria within the duct system. Mastitis causes swelling, heat, and pain, usually in just one breast, and may also cause a nursing mother to feel feverish and ill. If you experience any of these symptoms, notify your doctor at once so that he can begin treating the infection with antibiotics. Make sure he knows that you will be continuing to breast-feed so he will prescribe a medication that's safe for your baby.

Mastitis is often a sign that your body's immune defenses are down. Bed rest, sleep, and decreased activity will help you recover your stamina. Also, keeping the breasts drained will help prevent the infection from spreading. Take comfort in the fact that mastitis does not cause the milk itself to be infected, so there's no reason to stop nursing your baby. Even so, some women find that it's too painful to have their baby nurse on the infected breast; in that case, open up both sides of your bra and let the milk flow from that breast onto a towel or absorbent cloth such as a clean diaper, relieving the pressure as you feed the baby on the opposite side. Then he can finish the feeding on the infected side.

The Cancer Question. Some studies indicate that breast-feeding may offer some protection against breast cancer. However, if a woman already has been diagnosed with cancer and has had a malignant tumor removed, the doctor may advise against breast-feeding. Many doctors feel that breast-feeding is safe if the mother has been clear of cancer for at least five years following treatment for a malignancy. If a woman has had a benign (noncancerous) lump or cyst removed, it is perfectly safe to breast-feed afterward.

Breast-Feeding After Plastic Surgery on the Breasts. Plastic surgery to enlarge the breasts should not interfere with breast-feeding—provided the nipples have not been moved and no ducts have been cut. However, plastic surgery to *reduce* the size of the breasts is another matter; it often makes breast-feeding impossible, especially if the nipples are transplanted. A woman who has had this procedure should consult her surgeon to find out if she is able to breast-feed.

BOTTLE-FEEDING YOUR BABY

If you have decided to bottle-feed your baby, you'll have to start by selecting a formula. Your pediatrician will help you pick one based on your baby's needs. Twenty or thirty years ago, the majority of mothers made their own formula—a mixture of evaporated cow's milk, water, and sugar. Today, there are several prepackaged varieties and brands from which to choose.

Why Formula Instead of Cow's Milk?

Many parents ask why they can't just feed their baby regular cow's milk. The answer is simple: Young infants cannot fully digest this product as completely or easily as they digest formula. Also, cow's milk contains high concentrations of protein and minerals, which can stress a newborn's immature kidneys and cause dehydration. In addition, this feeding lacks the proper amounts of iron and vitamin C that infants need. It may even cause iron-deficiency anemia in some babies, since protein can irritate the lining of the stomach and intestine, leading to loss of blood into the stools. For these reasons your baby should not receive any regular cow's milk or other dairy products for the first 12 months of life.

A few families still prepare their own infant formula, but most pediatricians discourage this. When it is done, evaporated milk is mixed with a special sugar product in precise amounts which should be prescribed and adjusted by your pediatrician. The box below describes the process most often used, but it is unwise to give your baby homemade formula without your own pediatrician's advice.

Once your baby is past one year old, you may give him whole cow's milk— provided he has a balanced diet of solid foods (cereals, vegetables, fruits, meats). But limit his intake of milk to one quart per day. More than one quart can provide too many calories, and may decrease his appetite for the other foods he needs. If he is not yet eating a broad range of solid foods, give him iron-fortified formula instead of cow's milk.

Do not give your baby any reduced-fat milk (2 percent or skimmed) before his second birthday. He needs the higher fat content of whole milk to maintain normal weight gain and his body absorbs vitamins A and D better from whole milk. Also, nonfat, or skimmed, milk provides too high a concentration of protein and minerals, and should not be given to infants or toddlers under age two. After one year of age, you should discuss your child's nutritional needs (including choice of milk products) with your pediatrician.

Choosing a Formula

When shopping for manufactured infant formula, you'll find three basic types:

Cow's milk–based formulas account for about 80 percent of the formula sold today. Though cow's milk is at its foundation, the milk has been changed dramatically to make it safe for infants. It is treated by heating and other methods to make the protein more digestible and less potentially allergenic. More milk sugar (lactose) is added to make the concentration equal to that of breast milk, and the fat (butterfat) is removed and replaced with vegetable oils and animal fats that are more easily digested by infants.

Cow's milk formulas are available with or without added iron. Some infants do not have enough natural reserves of iron to meet their needs. So, the current recommendation is that iron-fortified formula be used for all bottle-fed infants from birth to one year of age. Additional iron is available in many baby foods, especially iron-fortified cereals.

Making Your Own Formula

About 5 to 10 percent of all new mothers make their own formula. While this is certainly less expensive (costing approximately one-third the price of manufactured formulas), there are disadvantages—not only the extra labor required but, more important, the nutritional deficiencies of homemade formula. If you feed your baby homemade formula, you must also give him supplements of vitamin C and iron, which are necessary for normal growth and development, especially of the brain and nervous system. It's very important to have your pediatrician check your child regularly and prescribe the necessary supplements.

Evaporated milk is the key ingredient in homemade formula. But bear in mind that *evaporated milk is not the same as condensed milk. Don't confuse the two. And for the sake of your baby's health, follow the recipe on the facing page precisely, each and every time you make his formula.*

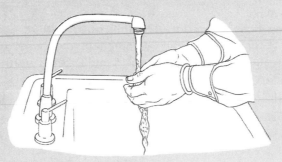

Wash hands.

Pour in one can of evaporated milk and add corn syrup or sugar.

Fill with sterile or boiled water that has been allowed to cool.

For one quart of homemade infant formula, you will need:

13 ounces evaporated milk (one can)

2 tablespoons light corn syrup or sugar (sucrose)

18–19 ounces sterile water (bottled or boiled)

Wash the top of the can with warm, soapy water. Open it with a can opener that has been scalded. Empty the can of evaporated milk into a sterile quart jar with a screw top or airtight lid. Add the corn syrup or sugar. Then fill the jar with the sterile water, which should be at room temperature (lukewarm if you're going to feed your baby right away). Close the top on the jar and shake until the ingredients are thoroughly mixed. Refrigerate any of the formula you do not use immediately, but use the refrigerated portion within twenty-four hours.

Close jar and shake thoroughly.

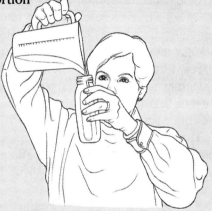

Pour into bottles.

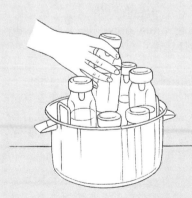

Sterilize for 25 minutes.

Refrigerate bottles not used right away.

Soy formulas contain a different protein (soy) and different carbohydrate (glucose polymers or sucrose) from milk-based formulas. They are recommended most commonly for babies unable to digest lactose, the main carbohydrate in cow's milk formula. Many infants have brief periods when they cannot digest lactose, particularly following bouts of diarrhea, which can damage the digestive enzymes in the lining of the intestines. When these babies are placed on a lactose-free formula, the enzymes have a chance to return to normal. Depending on the severity and type of diarrhea, your infant may need to stay on the soy formula for as little as a week or, rarely, as long as several months. Your pediatrician will tell you when it's safe to return to milk-based formula.

Another (and far less common) reason for placing an infant on soy formula is milk allergy, which can cause bloody diarrhea. This reaction can be so dangerous to a newborn that some doctors prescribe soy formula from birth as a preventive measure when there is a strong family history of allergies to cow's milk. Unfortunately, as many as half the infants who have milk allergy are also sensitive to soy protein, and they must be given a specialized formula or breast milk.

Soy formula is also recommended for children with a rare disorder called galactosemia. These children have an intolerance to galactose, one of the two sugars that make up lactose. Some states include the galactosemia test in the newborn screening.

The carbohydrates used to replace lactose in most soy formulas are sucrose and corn syrup (or a combination of the two). Both are easily digested and absorbed by infants. Most of these formulas cost about the same as milk-based formulas and are supplemented with iron.

A problem with these formulas is that soy is not quite as good a source of dietary protein as cow's milk (which, in turn, is inferior to human milk). Also, your baby will absorb calcium and some other minerals less efficiently from soy formulas than from milk-based formulas. Because premature infants have higher requirements for these minerals, they usually are not given soy formula at all.

Healthy full-term infants should be given soy formula only when medically necessary. Some strict vegetarian parents choose to use soy formula because it contains no animal products.

Specialized formulas are manufactured for infants with particular disorders or diseases. There are also formulas made specifically for premature babies. If your newborn has special needs, ask your pediatrician which formula is best. Also be sure to check the package for details about feeding requirements (amounts, scheduling, special preparations), since these may be quite different from regular formulas.

Preparing, Sterilizing, and Storing Formula

Most infant formulas are available in ready-to-feed liquid forms, concentrates, and powders. Though ready-to-feed formulas are very convenient, they are also the most expensive. Formula made from concentrate is prepared by mixing equal amounts of concentrate and sterile water (i.e., one can of concentrate and one can of drinking water or one bottle at a time leaving can of concentrate covered in refrigerator for no more than forty-eight hours). Powder, the least expensive form, comes either in premeasured packets or in a can with a measuring scoop. To prepare it, you'll add one level scoop of powder for every two ounces of water, and then mix thoroughly to make sure there are no clumps of undissolved powder in the bottle. The solution will mix more easily and the lumps will dissolve faster if you use slightly warmed water.

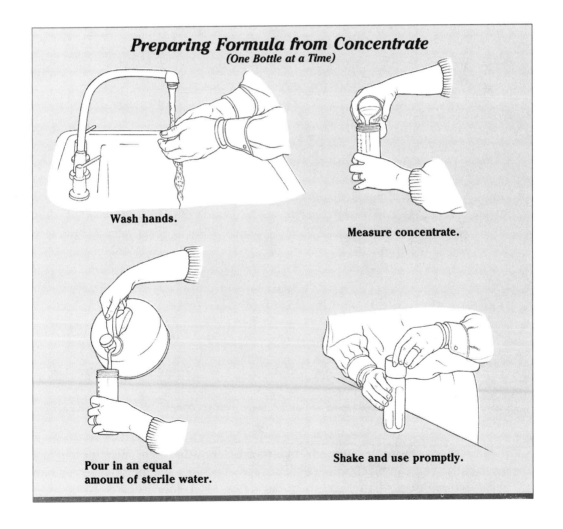

Preparing Formula from Concentrate
(One Bottle at a Time)

Wash hands.

Measure concentrate.

Pour in an equal amount of sterile water.

Shake and use promptly.

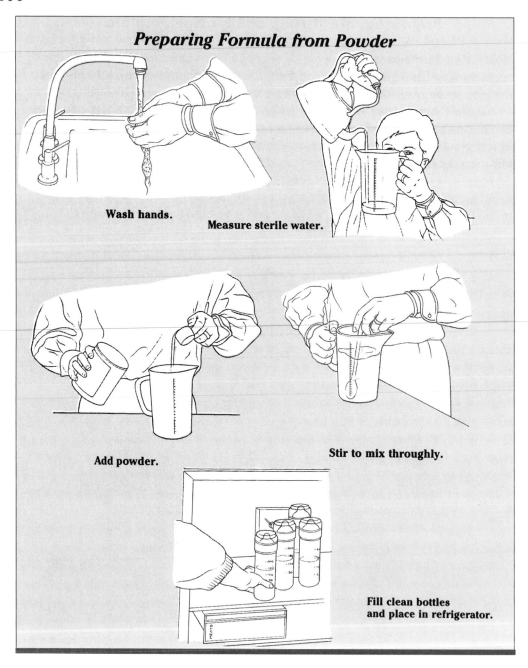

Preparing Formula from Powder

Wash hands.

Measure sterile water.

Add powder.

Stir to mix throughly.

Fill clean bottles
and place in refrigerator.

Aside from the price, one advantage of the powder is its light weight and portability. You can place a couple of scoops of powder in a bottle when you are going out with your baby, and then add water just before feeding. The powder will not spoil, even if it stays in the bottle several days before you add water.

If you choose a formula that requires preparation, be sure to follow the manufacturer's directions exactly. If you add too much water, your baby won't get the calories and nutrients he needs for proper growth; and if you add too little water, the high concentration of formula could cause diarrhea or dehydration and will give your infant more calories than he needs.

Boil the water you use in the formula for five minutes. Also make sure all bottles, nipples, and other utensils you use to prepare formula—or in feeding your baby—are clean. If the water in your home is chlorinated, you can simply use your dishwasher or wash the utensils in hot tap water with dishwashing detergent and then rinse them in hot tap water. If you have well water or nonchlorinated water, either place the utensils in boiling water for five to ten minutes or use a process called terminal heating.

In terminal heating, you clean, but do not sterilize, the bottles in advance. You then fill them with the prepared formula and cap them loosely. Next, the filled bottles are placed in a pan with water reaching about halfway up the bottles, and the water is brought to a gentle boil for about twenty-five minutes.

Any formula you prepare in advance should be stored in the refrigerator to discourage bacterial growth. If you don't use refrigerated formula within twenty-four hours, discard it. Refrigerated formula doesn't necessarily have to be warmed up for your baby, but most infants prefer it at least at room temperature. You can either leave the bottle out for an hour so it can reach room temperature, or warm it up in a pan of hot water. (Again, do not use a microwave.) If you warm it or use it immediately after terminal heating, test it in advance to make sure it's not too hot for your child. The easiest way to test the temperature is to shake a few drops on the inside of your forearm.

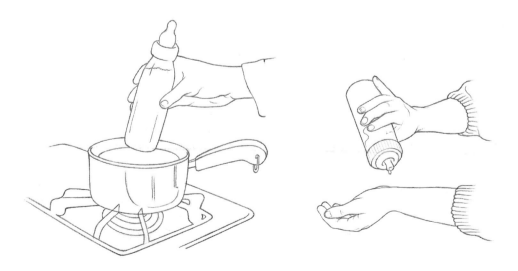

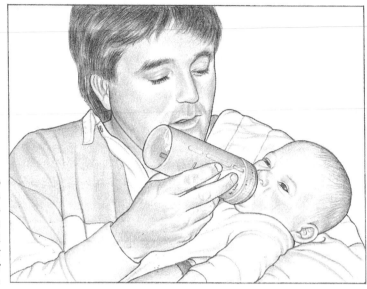

Hold the bottle so that formula fills the neck of the bottle and covers the nipple. This will prevent your baby from swallowing air as he sucks.

The bottles you use may be glass, plastic, or plastic with a soft plastic liner. These inner liners are convenient to use, and may help prevent your baby from swallowing too much air as he sucks, but they are also the most expensive. As your baby gets older and begins holding the bottle himself, you should avoid the use of breakable glass bottles. Also, bottles that are designed to promote self-feeding are not recommended as they may contribute to nursing bottle decay, since when milk is permitted to collect behind the teeth bacterial growth occurs, and to otitis media (see *Ear Infection,* page 537).

Ask your pediatrician which type of nipple he recommends. He'll choose from among the standard rubber nipples, orthodontic ones and special designs for premature infants and babies with cleft palates. Whichever type you use, always check the size of the hole. If it's too small, your baby may suck so hard that he swallows too much air; if it's too big, the formula may flow so fast that he chokes. Ideally, formula should flow at a rate of one drop per second when you first turn the bottle upside down. (It should stop dripping after a few seconds.) Many parents find that a nipple with a single small hole is adequate for feeding water but they need one with a larger hole or with several holes when feeding formula.

The Feeding Process

Feeding times should be relaxing, comforting, and enjoyable for both you and your baby. They provide opportunities to show your love and to get to know each other. If you are calm and content, your infant will respond in kind. If you are

To get him to open his mouth and grasp the nipple, stimulate his "rooting reflex" by stroking the nipple against the cheek near his mouth.

nervous or uninterested, he may pick up these negative feelings and a feeding problem can result.

You probably will be most comfortable in a chair with arms, or in one with pillows that let you prop up your own arms as you feed your infant. Cradle him in a semi-upright position and support his head. Don't feed him when he's lying down because this will increase the risk of choking; it also can cause formula to flow into the middle ear, where it can produce an infection.

Hold the bottle so that formula fills the neck of the bottle and covers the nipple. This will prevent your baby from swallowing air as he sucks. To get him to open his mouth and grasp the nipple, stimulate his "rooting reflex" by stroking the nipple against the cheek near his mouth. Once the nipple is in his mouth, he will naturally begin to suck and swallow.

Never prop a bottle in your baby's mouth and leave it there. It's an impersonal way to feed a baby and could turn him against feedings in general. It also contributes to tooth decay by allowing the sugar in the formula to pool around his teeth and gums for long periods of time. For these reasons, you should never put your baby to bed with a bottle, even after he can hold it himself.

Amount and Schedule of Feedings

Your newborn will take from 2 to 3 ounces of formula per feeding, and will eat every three to four hours during his first few weeks. During the first month, if your baby sleeps longer than four to five hours and starts missing feedings wake him up and offer a bottle. By the end of his first month, he'll be up to at least 4 ounces per feeding, with a fairly predictable schedule of feedings about every four hours. By six months, the amount consumed at each feeding should increase to 6 to 8 ounces and the feedings will number four or five in twenty-four hours.

On average, your baby should take in about 2½ ounces of formula a day for every pound of body weight. But he probably will regulate his intake from day to day to meet his own specific needs. So instead of going by fixed amounts, let him tell you when he's had enough. If he becomes fidgety or easily distracted during a feeding, he's probably finished. If he drains the bottle and still continues smacking his lips, he's probably still hungry. There are high and low limits, however. Most babies are satisfied with 3 to 4 ounces per feeding during the first month, and increase that amount by 1 ounce per month until they reach 8 ounces. If your baby *consistently* seems to want more or less than this, discuss it with your pediatrician. Your baby should drink no more than 32 ounces of formula in 24 hours.

As we mentioned in the section on breast-feeding, it's initially best to feed your newborn on demand, or whenever he cries because he's hungry. As time passes he'll begin to develop a fairly regular timetable of his own. As you become familiar with his signals and needs, you'll be able to schedule his feedings around his routine.

By two months (or 12 pounds) most babies no longer need a middle-of-the-night feeding, because they're consuming more during the day and their sleeping patterns have become more regular. Their stomach capacity has increased, too, which means they can also go longer between daytime feedings—up to four or five hours at a time. If your baby still seems to want more frequent feedings at this age, try distracting him with play and an occasional bottle of water between scheduled feedings. This should make him hungrier for the next feeding, so he'll eat more at that time and be satisfied for a longer period.

The most important thing to remember, whether you breast-feed or bottle-feed, is that your baby's feeding needs are unique. No book can tell you precisely how much or how often he needs to be fed, or exactly how you should handle him during feedings. You will discover these things for yourself as you and your baby get to know each other.

SUPPLEMENTATION FOR BREAST-FED AND BOTTLE-FED INFANTS

Vitamin Supplements

Human milk contains a natural balance of vitamins, especially C, E, and the B vitamins, so if you and your baby are both healthy, and you are well nourished, your child may not require any supplements of these vitamins.

Breast milk does *not* contain vitamin D in the concentrations your baby needs. This vitamin is naturally manufactured by the skin when it is exposed to sunlight, so if you live in a warm climate and take your baby out in the sunshine several times a week, his skin should produce all the vitamin D he needs. A total of just fifteen minutes of sunlight a week is sufficient for light-skinned children. If he is dark-skinned and you live in a relatively cold climate—or if you cannot take him out in the sun on a regular basis—you may need to give him supplemental vitamin D drops beginning at birth and continuing as long as he is nursing. (Prepared formula has vitamin D added to it.) Your baby also will need vitamin D supplements if he was born prematurely or has certain medical problems. Discuss this issue with your doctor after your baby is born.

Some pediatricians recommend that nursing mothers continue taking a daily prenatal vitamin supplement just to ensure the proper balance, but there is no definitive evidence that this is necessary. A regular well-balanced diet should provide all the vitamins necessary for both you and the baby. If you are on a strict vegetarian diet, however, you may need to take an extra B-complex supplement, since certain B vitamins are available only from meat, poultry, or fish products. If your baby is on infant formula, he generally will receive adequate vitamins.

Iron Supplements

Your baby may not be born with sufficient reserves of iron that will protect him from anemia. If he is breast-fed, there is sufficient, well-absorbed iron to give him an adequate supply so that no additional supplement is necessary. Between four and six months, you should be starting your breast-fed infant on iron-containing baby foods (cereals, meats, green vegetables), which should further guarantee sufficient iron for proper growth.

If you are bottle-feeding your baby, it is now recommended that you use iron-fortified formula from birth through the entire first year of life. Supplemental vitamins or drops containing iron can be used as a last resort, but only with your pediatrician's advice and supervision. These medications are not as well tolerated, and have been known to stain the teeth.

Water

Until your baby starts eating solid foods, he'll get all the water he needs from breast milk or formula. During very hot weather, offer a bottle-fed infant water between feedings but don't force it on him or worry if he rejects it. He may prefer to get the extra liquid from more frequent feedings. Breast-fed infants generally do not need extra water.

Once your baby is eating solid foods, his need for liquid will increase. If you offer him extra milk, formula, or juice at mealtimes, you may curb his appetite for solid foods, so instead try giving him water with his meals. Breast milk or formula-feedings should be saved for between meals.

Your bottle-fed baby may also need extra water when he's ill, especially when he has a fever. Ask your pediatrician to help you determine how much water your baby needs at these times. The best fluid for a breast-fed infant who is ill is breast milk.

Fluoride Supplements

Do breast-fed babies need fluoride supplementation? There is some controversy on this subject, so you may get different answers from different doctors. Some physicians question the need for babies under six months to get fluoride at all, since their permanent teeth have not yet started to harden with calcium. Others believe that giving fluoride supplements during these early months when the teeth are actually forming could provide added protection against cavities.

Formula-fed infants receive some fluoride from their formula and some from their drinking water (if it is fluoridated in their community). *The Academy recommends that you check with your pediatrician to find out if any additional fluoride supplements are necessary.*

BURPING, HICCUPS, AND SPITTING UP

Burping

Young babies naturally fuss and get cranky when they swallow air during feedings. Although this occurs in both breast- and bottle-fed infants, it's seen more often with the bottle. When it happens, you're better off stopping the feeding than letting your infant fuss and nurse at the same time. This continued fussing will cause him to swallow even more air, which will only increase his discomfort and may make him spit up.

A much better strategy is to burp him frequently, even if he shows no discomfort. The pause and the change of position alone will slow his gulping and reduce the amount of air he takes in. If he's bottle-feeding, burp him after every 2 to 3 ounces. If he's nursing, burp him each time he switches breasts.

Hiccups

Most babies hiccup from time to time. This usually will bother you more than your infant, but if hiccups occur during a feeding, they may distress him. So change his position and try to get him to burp or relax. Wait until the hiccups are gone to resume feeding. If they don't disappear on their own in five to ten minutes, a few sucks of some sugar water (¼ teaspoon of sugar in 4 ounces of water) should stop them. If your baby gets hiccups often, try to feed him when he's calm and before he's extremely hungry. This will reduce the likelihood of hiccups during the feeding.

Spitting Up

Spitting up is another common occurrence during infancy. Sometimes spitting up means the baby has eaten more than his stomach can hold; sometimes he spits up while burping or drooling. Though it may be a bit messy, it's no cause for concern. It almost never involves choking, coughing, discomfort, or danger to your child, even if it occurs while he's sleeping.

Some babies spit up more than others, but most are out of this phase by the time they are sitting. A few "heavy spitters" will continue until they start to walk or are weaned to a cup. Some may continue throughout their first year.

You should be able to tell the difference easily between normal spitting up and true vomiting. Unlike spitting up, which most babies don't even seem to notice, vomiting is forceful and usually causes great distress and discomfort for your child. It generally occurs soon after a meal and produces a much greater volume than spitting up. If your baby vomits on a regular basis (one or more times a day), consult your pediatrician. (See *Vomiting,* page 491.)

While it is practically impossible to prevent all spitting up, the following steps will help you decrease the frequency of these episodes and the amount spit up:

1. Make each feeding calm, quiet, and leisurely.

2. Avoid interruptions, sudden noises, bright lights, and other distractions during feedings.

3. Burp your baby at least every three to five minutes during feedings.

4. Avoid feeding while your infant is lying down.

5. Place the baby in an upright position in an infant seat or stroller immediately after feeding.

6. Do not jostle or play vigorously with the baby immediately after feeding.

7. Try to feed him before he gets frantically hungry.

8. If bottle-feeding, make sure the hole in the nipple is neither too big (which lets the formula flow too fast) nor too small (which frustrates your baby and causes him to gulp air). If the hole is the proper size, a few drops should come out when you invert the bottle, and then stop.

9. Elevate the head of the entire crib with blocks (don't use a pillow) and put him to sleep on his side (see page 37). This keeps his head higher than his stomach and prevents him from choking in case he spits up while sleeping.

How Do You Burp a Baby?

Here are a few tried and true techniques. After a little experimentation you'll find which ones work best for your child.

1. Hold the baby upright with his head on your shoulder, supporting his head and back while you gently pat his back with your other hand. You might want to put a towel or diaper on your shoulder in case he spits up.

If he still hasn't burped after several minutes, continue feeding him and don't worry; no baby burps every time. When he's finished, burp him again and keep him in an upright position for ten to fifteen minutes so he doesn't spit up.

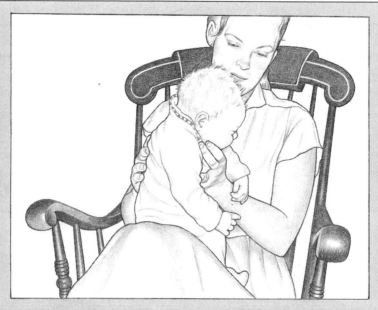

2. Sit the baby on your lap, supporting his chest and head with one hand while patting his back with your other hand.

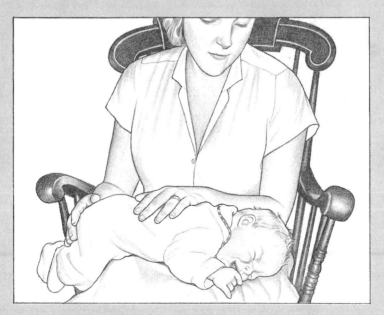

3. Lay the baby on your lap with his back up. Support his head so it is higher than his chest, and gently pat or rotate your hand on his back.

As you can tell from the length and detail of this chapter, feeding your baby is one of the most important and, at times, confusing challenges you'll face as a parent. The recommendations in this section apply to infants in general. Please remember that your child is unique, and may have special needs. If you have questions that are not answered in these pages to your satisfaction, ask your pediatrician to help you find the answers that apply specifically to you and your infant.

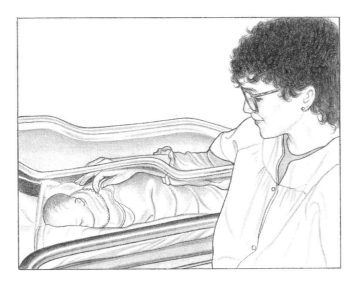

5

YOUR BABY'S FIRST DAYS

*A*fter all the months of pregnancy, you may believe that you already know your baby. You've felt his kicks, monitored his quiet and active periods during the day, and run your hands over your abdomen as he nestled in the womb. Though all of this does bring you closer to him, nothing can prepare you for the sight of his face and the grip of his fingers around yours.

For the first few days after his birth, you probably won't be able to take your eyes off him. Watching him, you may see hints of yourself or other members of the family reflected in his features. But for the most part, he is unlike anyone else. And he'll have a definite temperament of his own that will start making itself known immediately. As he turns and stretches, only he knows what he wants and feels. He may, for example, protest wet or messy diapers from the first day after birth, complaining loudly until he is changed and fed and rocked back to sleep. Infants who behave like this not only tend to spend more time awake than other babies, but they may also cry and eat more. On the other hand, some newborns may not seem to notice when their diapers are dirty, and may object to having their bottoms exposed to the cold air during changes. These babies probably sleep a lot and eat less frequently than the more sensitive infants. Such individual differences are early hints of your child's future personality.

Some mothers say that after so many months of literally "possessing" him in the womb, it becomes difficult to view the baby as a separate human being, with thoughts, emotions, and desires of his own. Making this adjustment and respecting his individuality, however, are important parts of being a parent. If you can welcome his uniqueness now at birth, you'll have a much easier time accepting the person he becomes in the years ahead.

YOUR NEWBORN'S FIRST DAYS

How Your Newborn Looks

As you relax with your baby in your own room, unwrap his blankets and examine him from head to toe. You'll notice many details that escaped you in the first moments after birth. For instance, when he opens his eyes you'll see their color. Many caucasian newborns have blue eyes, but they may change over the next year. Generally, infants with dark-skinned heritage have brown eyes at birth and they remain that color throughout life. If his eyes are going to turn brown, they'll probably become "muddy" during the first six months; if they're still blue at that time they'll probably remain so.

You may notice a blood spot in the white area of one or both eyes. This, and the general puffiness of his face, are caused by pressures exerted during labor, but both will fade in a few days. If he was born by C-section, he won't have this puffiness and his eyes should be clear.

Bathed and dry, your baby's skin will seem very delicate. If he was born after his due date he probably would have already lost his protective covering of vernix, and his skin would have been wrinkled and peeling at birth. If he was born on time or early, he may peel a little now because of the sudden exposure to air after the vernix is washed away. This is a normal process and requires no treatment.

As you examine your baby's shoulders and back you may notice some fine hair, called lanugo. Like the vernix, this hair is produced toward the end of pregnancy; however, it's usually shed before birth or soon thereafter. If your baby was born before his due date, he is more likely to have this hair still, and it may take a couple of weeks to disappear.

You may also notice a lot of pink spots and marks on your baby's skin. Some, like those that appear around the edges of his diaper, are simply due to pressure. Mottled or blotchy-looking patches are caused by exposure to cool air, and will quickly disappear if you cover him again. If you find scratches, particularly on his face, trim his fingernails. (Keep his hands covered until you have a chance to do so.) Otherwise, he'll continue to scratch himself as he randomly moves his hands and arms.

Your baby may also have rashes and birthmarks. Most will fade quickly without treatment, but some may be permanent. These are the most common newborn rashes and birthmarks:

Salmon Patches or "Stork Bites." Patches of deep pink, usually located on the bridge of the nose, lower forehead, upper eyelids, back of the head, or neck. The most common birthmark, especially in light-skinned babies, they disappear over the first few months.

Mongolian Spots. Large, flat areas containing extra pigment, which appear green or blue (like a bruise) on the back or buttocks. Very common, especially in dark-skinned babies. They usually disappear by school age and are of no significance.

Pustular Melanosis. Small blisters that quickly dry and peel away, leaving dark spots like freckles. Some babies have only the spots, indicating that they had the rash before birth. The spots disappear in several weeks.

Milia. Tiny white bumps or yellow spots across the tip of the nose or chin, caused by skin gland secretion. They appear raised but are nearly flat and smooth to the touch. They disappear in the first two to three weeks of life.

Miliaria. A raised rash consisting of small fluid-filled blisters. The fluid is normal skin secretion and may be clear or milky-white. Miliaria usually disappears with normal skin cleansing.

Erythema Toxicum. A rash of red splotches with yellowish-white bumps in the centers. They generally appear only during the first day after birth, and disappear without treatment within the first week or so.

Capillary or Strawberry Hemangiomas. Raised red spots with a rough texture. For the first week or so, they may appear white or pale, then turn red later. Caused by dilated blood vessels in the top layers of the skin, they enlarge during the first few months, then gradually shrink and disappear without treatment.

Port Wine Stain. Large, flat, irregularly shaped red or purple areas, they're caused by a surplus of blood vessels under the skin. They won't disappear without treatment, which can be performed by either a plastic surgeon or a pediatric dermatologist when the child is older.

(See also *Birthmarks,* page 627.)

If your baby was born vaginally, in addition to the elongated shape of his head, there also may be some scalp swelling in the area that was pushed out first during birth. If you press on this area, your finger may even leave a small indentation. This swelling is not serious and should disappear in a few days.

Swelling under the scalp also sometimes is visible several hours after birth, probably due to bleeding. (The bleeding occurs outside the skull bones, not inside the brain.) This swelling is often present on only one side of the head, and will seem to spring right back after you press on it. This, too, is caused by the intense pressure on the head during labor. It is not serious, though it usually takes six to ten weeks to disappear.

All babies have two soft spots, or fontanelles, on the top of the head. These are the areas where the immature bones of the skull are still growing together. The larger opening is on the top of the head toward the front; a smaller one is at the back. You needn't be afraid to touch these areas gently. They are covered by a thick, durable membrane that protects the skull's important contents.

Babies are affected by the large amount of hormones that were manufactured by their mothers during pregnancy. As a result, your baby's breasts may be enlarged temporarily and might even secrete a few drops of milk. This is equally likely in boy and girl babies, and normally lasts less than a week. Don't try to

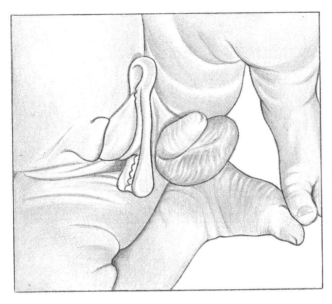

The stub of the umbilical cord is white, translucent, and shiny right after birth. The genitals of newborn babies often seem quite large for bodies so small.

compress or manipulate the breasts, since this won't reduce the swelling and could cause infection.

As you examine your baby's abdomen, it will seem prominent, and you may notice spaces between the abdominal muscles where the skin protrudes during crying spells. The spaces may be in a line down the center of the abdomen or in a circle at the base of the umbilical cord. This is normal and disappears within about one year.

The stub of the umbilical cord is white, translucent, and shiny right after birth. If it was painted with antibacterial dye, it may look blue, and quickly will begin to dry up and shrink. It should fall off within three weeks.

The genitals of newborn babies are often reddish and seem quite large for bodies so small. Girls may have clear, white, or slightly bloody vaginal discharge, caused by exposure to their mother's hormones during pregnancy. The scrotum of a baby boy may be smooth and barely big enough to hold the testicles; or it might be large and wrinkled. The testicles can move in and out of the scrotum. Sometimes they will retract as far as the base of the penis or even to the crease at the top of the thigh. As long as they are located in the scrotum most of the time, this is normal.

Some boys have a buildup of fluid in a sac called a hydrocele (see page 484) inside the scrotum. This will shrink gradually without treatment over several months as the fluid is reabsorbed by the body. If the scrotum swells up suddenly or gets larger when the baby cries, notify your pediatrician; this could be a sign of an inguinal hernia, which requires treatment.

Care of the Penis

Caring for the Circumcised Penis. If you choose to have your son circumcised, the procedure probably will be performed on the second or third day after birth, unless it is delayed for religious reasons. Afterward, a light dressing such as gauze with petroleum jelly will be placed over the head of the penis. The next time the baby urinates, this dressing will usually come off. Some pediatricians recommend keeping a clean dressing on until the penis is fully healed, while others advise leaving it off. The important thing is to keep the area as clean as possible. If particles of stool get on the penis, wipe it gently with soap and water during diaper changes.

The tip of the penis may look quite red for the first few days, and you may notice a yellow secretion. Both indicate that the area is healing normally. Within a week the redness and secretion should gradually disappear. If the redness persists or there is swelling or crusted yellow sores that contain cloudy fluid, there may be an infection. This does not happen very often, but if you suspect that it is present, consult your pediatrician.

Usually, after the circumcision has healed, the penis requires no additional care. Occasionally a small piece of the foreskin remains. This should be pulled back gently each time the child is bathed. Examine the groove around the head of the penis and make sure it's clean.

At birth the foreskin is attached to the head, or glans, of the penis, and cannot be pushed back as it can in older boys and men. There is a small opening at the tip through which urine flows. If you have your son circumcised, the connections between the foreskin and the glans are artificially separated and the foreskin is removed, leaving the glans visible. Without a circumcision, the foreskin will naturally separate from the glans during the first few years.

While you're still in the hospital, the staff will watch carefully for your baby's first urination and bowel movement to make sure he has no problem with elimination. These may occur right after birth or up to a day later. The first bowel movement or two will be dark black-green and very slimy. They contain meconium,

Occasionally circumcision must be postponed because of prematurity or other medical problems. If it is not performed within the baby's first week, it is usually put off for several weeks or months. Your pediatrician will determine the best time for the circumcision. The follow-up care is the same, whenever it is performed.

Caring for the Uncircumcised Penis. In the first few months, your baby's uncircumcised penis should simply be cleaned and bathed with soap and water, like the rest of the diaper area. Initially, the foreskin is connected by tissue to the glans, or head, of the penis, so you shouldn't try to retract it. No cleansing of the penis with Q-tips or antiseptics is necessary, but you should watch your baby urinate occasionally to make sure that the hole in the foreskin is large enough to permit a normal stream. If the stream consistently is no more than a trickle, or if your baby seems to have some discomfort while urinating, consult your pediatrician.

The doctor will tell you when the foreskin has separated and can be retracted safely. This will not be for several months to years. After this separation occurs, you should retract the foreskin occasionally to cleanse the end of the penis underneath. Once your son is out of diapers, you'll need to teach him how to do this himself so he can urinate and wash his penis.

a substance that fills the infant's intestines during pregnancy, and which must be eliminated before normal digestion and passage of new stool can take place. If meconium is not passed within the baby's first forty-eight hours, it could mean that a problem exists in the lower bowel.

If you notice a little blood in the bowel movements during these first few days, it probably means that the infant swallowed some of his mother's blood during birth or while nursing if he is breast-fed. Although the baby won't be harmed by this in any way, it's best to let your pediatrician know about it so he can make sure this is really the reason behind it; if internal bleeding is the actual cause, immediate treatment will be necessary.

National Center for Health Statistics
Girls' Weight by Age Percentiles
Ages Birth–36 Months

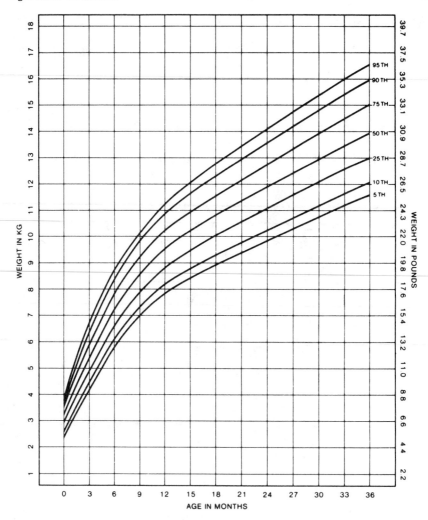

Your Baby's Birthweight and Measurements

Did your baby weigh more or less than you had anticipated? His birthweight may actually be affected by a number of factors, including:

■ Length of pregnancy before delivery: The later in the nine-month cycle he was born, the larger he may be.

■ Parents' size: If both Mom and Dad are unusually large or small, the baby may follow suit.

National Center for Health Statistics
Girls' Length by Age Percentiles
Ages Birth–36 Months

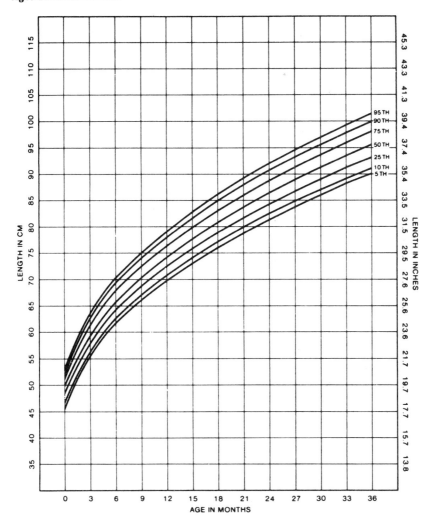

- Complications during pregnancy: If the mother's blood pressure was high or she had certain other illnesses during pregnancy, the baby might be small. If she had diabetes during pregnancy, however, the baby might be larger than expected.

- Nutrition during pregnancy: If the baby was not getting enough nourishment while inside the uterus, either because the mother's diet was very poor or because of a medical problem with pregnancy, the baby might be smaller than expected.

National Center for Health Statistics
Boys' Weight by Age Percentiles
Ages Birth–36 Months

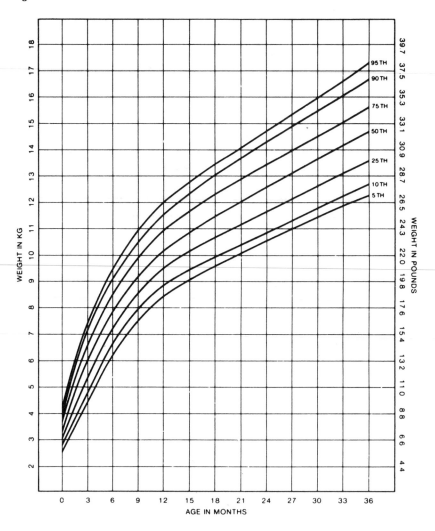

- Mother's smoking or alcohol or drug usage during pregnancy.

If your baby is either much larger or much smaller than average, he's more likely to have problems adjusting to life outside the womb. To determine how his measurements compare with those of other babies born after the same length of pregnancy, your pediatrician will use this growth chart.

As you can see in this chart, eighty out of every one hundred babies born at forty weeks of pregnancy, or full term, weigh between 5 pounds 11½ ounces and 8 pounds 5¾ ounces. This is a healthy average. Those above the ninetieth per-

National Center for Health Statistics
Boys' Length by Age Percentiles
Ages Birth–36 Months

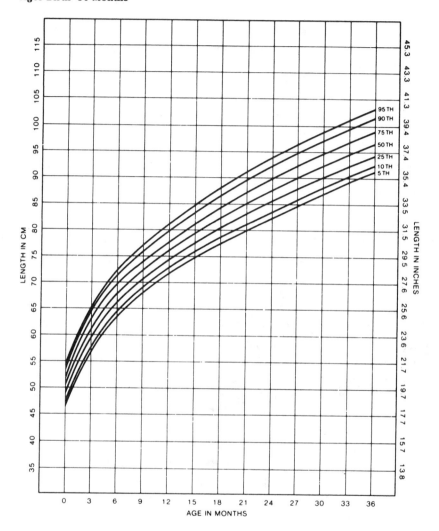

centile on the chart are considered large, and those below the tenth percentile are regarded as small. Some large babies may initially have difficulty regulating their blood-sugar levels, and require extra feedings to prevent hypoglycemia (low blood sugar). Small babies may have problems feeding or regulating their body temperature. Incidentally, these early weight designations (large or small) do not predict whether your child will be above or below average when he grows up; but they do help the hospital staff determine whether he needs extra attention during the first few days after birth.

At every physical exam, beginning with the first one after birth, your pediatrician will take certain measurements. He'll routinely measure your baby's length, weight, and head circumference (the distance around his head). In a healthy, well-nourished infant, these three measurements should increase at a predictable rate. Any interruption in this rate can help the doctor detect feeding, developmental, or medical problems.

How Your Newborn Behaves

Lying in your arms or in the crib beside you, your newborn makes a tight little bundle. Just as he did in the womb, he'll keep his arms and legs bent up close to his body and his fingers tightly clenched, though you should be able to straighten them gently with your hands. His feet will naturally curve inward, and while asleep, he'll curl his legs under him to turn face-down with his buttocks in the air. It may take several weeks for his body to unfold from this preferred fetal position.

You'll have to wait even longer for him to make the cooing or babbling sounds we generally think of as "baby talk." However, from the beginning he'll be very noisy. Besides crying when something is wrong, he'll have a wide variety of grunts, squeaks, sighs, sneezes, and hiccups. (You may even remember the hiccups from pregnancy!) Most of these sounds, just like his sudden movements, are reactions to disturbances around him; a shrill sound or a strong odor may be all it takes for him to jump or cry.

These reactions, as well as more subtle ones, are signs of how well your baby's senses are functioning at birth. After all those months in the womb, he'll quickly recognize his mother's voice (and possibly his father's as well). If you play soothing music he may become quiet as he listens, or move gently in time with it.

By using his senses of smell and taste, he can distinguish breast milk from any other liquid. Born with a sweet tooth, he'll prefer sugar water to plain water, and will wrinkle his nose at sour or bitter scents and tastes.

Your baby's vision will be good within an 8- to 12-inch range, which means he can see your face perfectly as you hold and feed him. But when you are farther away, his eyes may wander, giving him a cross-eyed or wall-eyed appearance. Don't worry about this. As his eye muscles  mature and his vision improves, both eyes will remain focused on the same thing at the same time. This usually occurs between two and three months of age.

While your infant will be able to distinguish light from dark at birth, he will not yet see the full range of colors. So if you show him a pattern of black and white, or sharply contrasting dark-red and pale-yellow, he will probably study it with interest; but if you show him a picture with lots of closely related colors, he may not respond at all.

Perhaps the newborn's most important sense is touch. After months of being bathed in warm fluid, his skin will now be exposed to all sorts of new sensations—some harsh, some wonderfully comforting. While he may cringe at a sudden gust of cold air, he'll love the feel of a soft blanket and the warmth of your arms around him. Holding your baby will give him as much pleasure as it does you. It will give him a sense of security and comfort, and it will tell him he is loved. Research shows it will actually promote his growth and development.

Going Home

If your baby was born in an alternative birthing center, you probably will go home within twenty-four hours. By contrast, you might spend up to three days in a hospital if yours was a routine delivery, and up to a week if you had a C-section or an especially difficult delivery.

From an emotional and physical standpoint, there are arguments for both the short and the long stay. Many women simply dislike being in the hospital; these women tend to feel more comfortable and relaxed at home. As soon as mother and baby are proclaimed healthy and able to travel, they're eager to leave. By keeping the hospital stay short, they'll certainly save themselves—or their insurance company—money. However, new mothers often cannot get as much rest at home as in the hospital—especially if there are older children clamoring for attention. Nor is there the support of the hospital nurses during the first days of breast-feeding and baby care. You should weigh these advantages and disadvantages carefully prior to making your decision about when to go home.

Before you do leave the hospital, your home and car should be equipped with at least the bare essentials. At home you'll need a safe place for the baby to sleep, some diapers, and enough clothing and blankets to keep him warm and protected. If you're bottle-feeding, you'll also need a supply of formula. Finally, make sure you have a federally approved car seat in which your baby can ride on his trip home.

PARENTING ISSUES

Mother's Feelings

If you're like most new mothers, your first few days with your baby will be a mixture of delight, pain, utter exhaustion, and—especially if this is your first child—some apprehension about your capabilities as a parent. When the anxiety levels peak, it will be difficult to believe that you'll ever be an expert on baby care. But rest assured. As soon as you're home, things will start to fall into place. So instead of worrying while in the hospital, take advantage of the time to rest and let your body recover.

Quite often, women are so excited about their new arrival that they don't even notice how tired and sore they are. In spite of the fatigue, it may still be difficult to relax enough to fall asleep. If you're not careful, your rooming-in arrangements can add to the problem. However, having your baby sleep in the nursery may not give you the peace you thought if you then imagine that every crying baby you hear is your own. You can solve these problems by letting him sleep in his hospital-supplied bassinet next to you, so you can sleep when he does and hold him when he awakens.

On the other hand, particularly if you had a long, hard labor or a Caesarean section, you simply may not have the strength to keep the baby with you full time. After having a C-section, you may find it uncomfortable to lift your baby for a few weeks; you may have to try different positions for holding and nursing him that put less strain on your stitches. These obstacles may make you feel that you're not bonding with your baby as you imagined you would; and you may feel especially disappointed if you had planned for a problem-free, natural delivery. Fortunately, your child's major preoccupation during these first few days also will be sleeping and recuperating, and he won't much care where he does it as long as he's warm, dry, and fed when he's hungry. So for the moment, the hospital nursery will suit him fine. You both will have plenty of time to form a secure bond with each other after your physical recoveries are complete.

If this is not your first child, there may be some questions on your mind, such as:

■ *Will this new baby come between you and an older child?*
This needn't happen if you make a point of spending time separately with each child. When developing a routine during your first weeks home with the new baby, make sure to include special times with your older child.

■ *Will you be able to give the same intensity of love to the new child?*
In fact, each child is special and will draw out different responses and feelings from you. The way you relate to your newest child will have little to do with whether he's first, second, or third.

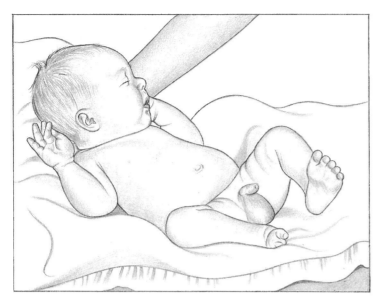

You have just given birth to a wonderful new being, but also to a new and awesome responsibility.

■ *How can you avoid comparing one to another?*

You may find yourself thinking that the new baby is not as beautiful or alert as another child was right after birth, or you may worry because he's *more* attractive and attentive. In the beginning, these comparisons are inevitable, but as the new baby's own unique qualities begin to emerge, you'll become as proud of your children's differences as you are of their similarities.

On a more practical note, the prospect of taking care of two or more young children may worry you—and with good reason. Now, greater time demands and sibling rivalry loom before you, presenting a new, awesome challenge. Don't let yourself get overwhelmed by it. Given time and patience, all of you will adjust and learn to be a family.

If the newness, fatigue, and seemingly unanswerable questions push you to tears, don't feel bad. You won't be the first new mother to cry—or the last. If it makes you feel any better, your hormones are at least partly responsible for your fragile state.

The hormonal changes you went through as an adolescent, or experience during your menstrual cycle, are minor compared to the hormonal overhaul you're undergoing after giving birth. Blame it on the hormones, and rest assured that this, too, shall pass.

In addition to the hormonal effects, significant emotional changes are taking place. You have just given birth to a wonderful new being, but also to a new and awesome responsibility. There are significant changes taking place in your family life and your relationship with your husband. It is normal to think about these things, and easy to attach too much importance to them.

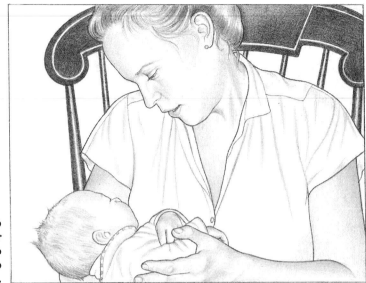

Do not be afraid to
ask for help if your
concerns seem too
great for you to
handle.

It is not wise to dwell on them, or take them *too* seriously, however. If you think you are doing that, you should discuss your concerns with your husband, obstetrician, pediatrician, and other people whose judgment you respect and value. Do not be afraid to ask for help if your concerns seem too great for you to handle, or if you feel increasingly depressed. Although a certain amount of postdelivery depression may be normal, it should not be overwhelming or last more than a few days.

Father's Feelings

As a new dad, your role is no less complicated than your wife's. No, you didn't have to carry the baby for nine months, but you did have to make adjustments physically and emotionally as the due date approached and preparations for the baby became all important. On the one hand, you may have felt as if you had nothing to do with this birth; but on the other, this is very much your baby too.

When the baby finally arrived, you may have been tremendously relieved as well as excited and somewhat awed. In witnessing your baby's birth, feelings of commitment and love may have surfaced that you had worried you might never feel for this child. You may also experience a greater admiration and love for your wife than you ever felt before. At the same time, contemplating the responsibility of caring for this child for the next twenty years can be more than a little unnerving.

So how should you deal with all these conflicting emotions? The best approach is to become as actively involved in fathering as possible. For example, depending on the hospital and your own schedule, you may be able to "room in" with mother and/or child until it's time to bring the baby home. This will help you feel less like a bystander and more like a key participant. You'll get to know your baby right from the start. It also will allow you to share an intense emotional experience with your wife.

Once the entire family is home, you can—and should—help diaper, bathe, and comfort your baby. Contrary to old-fashioned stereotypes, these jobs are not exclusively "woman's work." They are wonderful opportunities for all of you— mother, father, and even older siblings—to get to know and love this new family member.

Sibling's Feelings

Older children may greet a new baby with either open arms or closed minds. Their reaction will depend largely on their age and developmental level. Consider a toddler, for instance. There's little you can do to prepare him in advance for the changes that will come with a new sibling. To begin with, he'll be confused by the sudden disappearance of his parents when the baby is born. Upon visiting the hospital, he may be frightened by the sight of his mother in bed, perhaps attached to intravenous tubing.

He also may be jealous that his parents are holding someone else instead of him, and he may misbehave or begin acting younger—for example, by insisting

Let the older sibling know frequently that there's enough room and love in your heart for both children.

on wearing diapers or suddenly having accidents several months after being toilet-trained. These are normal responses to stress and change, and don't deserve discipline. Instead of punishing him or insisting that he share your love for the new baby, give him extra love and reassurance. His attachment to the baby will build gradually and naturally over time.

If your older child is a preschooler, he'll be better able to understand what's happening. By preparing him during the pregnancy, you can help ease his confusion, if not his jealousy. He can understand the basic facts of the situation ("The baby is in Mommy's tummy"; "The baby will sleep in my old crib") and he probably will be very curious about this mysterious person.

Once the baby is born, the older sibling still will miss his parents and resent the infant for being the new center of attention. But praising him for helping out and acting "grown-up" will let him know that he, too, has an important new role to play. Make sure he still gets some time to be the "important one" and is allowed to "be the baby" when he needs to. And let him know frequently that there's enough room and love in your heart for both children.

If your older child is of school age, he shouldn't feel threatened by the newcomer in the family. He'll probably be fascinated by the process of pregnancy and childbirth, and be eager to meet the new baby. Once the infant arrives, you can expect the older child to be very proud and protective. Let him help take care of the little one, but don't forget that he still needs time and attention himself. Even if he doesn't demand it, set aside some time each day to spend with him alone.

HEALTH WATCH

Some physical conditions are especially common during the first couple of weeks after birth. If you notice any of the following in your baby, contact your pediatrician.

Abdominal Distention. Most babies' abdomens normally stick out, especially after a large feeding. Between feedings, however, the belly should feel quite soft. If your child's abdomen feels swollen and hard, and if he has not had a bowel movement for more than one or two days or is vomiting, call your pediatrician. Most likely the problem is due to gas or constipation, but it could also signal a more serious intestinal problem.

Birth Injuries. The baby can be injured during birth if labor is particularly long or difficult, or if he is very large. Quite often the injury is a broken collarbone, which will heal quickly if the arm on that side is kept relatively motionless; your pediatrician will advise you how to do this. Incidentally, after a few weeks a small lump may form at the site of the fracture, but don't be alarmed; this is a positive sign that new bone is forming to mend the injury.

Muscle weakness is another common birth injury, caused during labor by pressure or stretching of the nerves attached to the muscles. These muscles, usually weakened on one side of the face or one shoulder or arm, generally return to normal after several weeks. In the meantime, ask your pediatrician to show you how to nurse and hold the baby to promote healing.

Blue Baby. Blue hands and feet are nothing to worry about in a newborn. His face, tongue, and lips may turn a little blue occasionally when crying hard, but once he becomes calm, his color in these areas should quickly return to normal. Likewise, if his hands and feet turn a bit blue from cold, they should return to pink as soon as they are warm. Persistently blue skin coloring is a sign that the heart or lungs are not operating properly, and the baby is not getting enough oxygen in the blood. Immediate medical attention is essential.

Coughing. If your baby eats very fast or is trying to drink water for the first time, he may choke, cough, and sputter a bit; but the coughing should stop as soon as he adjusts to a familiar feeding routine. If he coughs persistently or routinely chokes during feedings, consult your pediatrician. These symptoms could indicate an underlying problem in the lungs or digestive tract.

Excessive Crying. All newborns cry, often for no apparent reason. If you've made sure that your baby is fed, burped, warm, and dressed in a clean diaper, the best tactic is probably to hold him and talk or sing to him until he stops. You cannot "spoil" a baby this age by giving him too much attention. If this doesn't work, wrap him snugly in a blanket or try some of the tactics listed on page 35.

You'll become accustomed to your baby's normal pattern of crying. If it ever sounds peculiar—for example, like shrieks of pain—or if it persists for an unusual length of time, it could mean a medical problem. Call the pediatrician and ask for advice.

Forceps Marks. When forceps are used to help during a delivery, the baby may have red marks or even superficial scrapes on his face and head where the metal pressed against his skin. These should disappear within a few days. Sometimes a firm, flat lump develops in one of these areas because of minor damage to the tissue under the skin, but this, too, usually will go away within two months.

Jaundice. Many normal, healthy infants develop a yellowish tinge to their skin in the first few days of life. This condition, called "physiologic jaundice," is a sign that the blood contains an excess of bilirubin, a chemical formed during the normal breakdown of old red blood cells. Everyone's blood contains small amounts of bilirubin, but newborns tend to have higher levels because they have

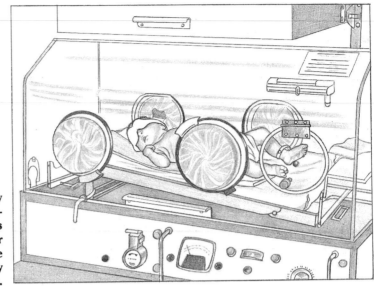

In phototherapy treatment for jaundice, the baby is placed under fluorescent-type lights for a day or two.

extra red blood cells at birth and their immature livers may have trouble processing the additional bilirubin that exists.

As bilirubin levels rise above normal, the jaundice will appear first on the face, then on the chest and abdomen, and finally on the legs. Typically, after worsening for a few days the jaundice will subside without treatment. If the bilirubin level is extremely high and does not decline, there's a risk of damage to the nervous system. Your doctor will order blood tests to determine the cause and may recommend treatment with phototherapy. In this procedure the baby is placed under fluorescent-type lights for a day or two until the liver matures enough to handle the bilirubin load. Normal daylight has a similar effect, but is not intense enough to help. Direct sunlight is *not* more effective, and should be avoided because of the danger of sunburn.

Breast milk, incidentally, sometimes interferes with the liver's ability to process bilirubin, so breast-feeding may prolong jaundice in some newborns. When that happens, your pediatrician may recommend that you consider halting breast-feeding briefly (no more than forty-eight hours) to help decrease the bilirubin levels. This approach will be taken only when absolutely necessary, since the baby's frequent sucking at the breast during these first few days is crucial to stimulate the mother's milk supply.

Lethargy and Sleepiness. Every newborn spends most of his time sleeping. As long as he wakes up every few hours, eats well, seems content, and is alert part of the day, it's perfectly normal for him to sleep the rest of the time. But if he's rarely alert, does not wake up on his own for feedings or seems too tired or uninterested to eat, you should consult your pediatrician. This lethargy—especially if it's a sudden change in his usual pattern—may be a symptom of a serious illness.

Respiratory Distress. It may take your baby a few hours after birth to form a normal pattern of breathing, but then he should have no further difficulties. If he does show any of the following warning signs, however, notify your pediatrician immediately.

- Fast breathing (more than sixty breaths in one minute)
- Retractions (sucking in the muscles between the ribs with each breath, so that his ribs stick out)
- Flaring of his nose
- Grunting while breathing
- Persistent blue skin coloring

Umbilical Cord. You'll need to keep the stump of the umbilical cord clean and dry as it shrivels and, within a few weeks, eventually falls off. At each diaper change, use a cotton swab (soaked in rubbing alcohol and then squeezed) to clean away the wet, sticky material that sometimes collects where the base of the stump meets the skin. This will help dry the cord, as will exposing it to air. Also keep the diaper folded below the cord to keep urine from soaking it. You may notice a few drops of blood on the diaper around the time the stump falls off; this is normal. If the stump becomes infected, however, it will require medical treatment, so alert your pediatrician if you notice any of these signs of infection.

- Pus at the base of the cord
- Red skin around the base of cord
- Crying when you touch the cord or the skin next to it. (If your baby cries when the alcohol is applied, that is normal, because it's cold, but crying at the touch of your finger is not.)

Umbilical Granuloma. Occasionally, after the umbilical cord has fallen off, the remaining area will continue to be moist and may swell slightly. This is called an umbilical granuloma. If it is small, your pediatrician will treat it by applying a drying medication called silver nitrate. If this is not successful, or if the area continues to enlarge or ooze, it may have to be tied off and surgically removed. This is a minor procedure that does not require anesthetic or a hospital stay.

Umbilical Hernia. If your baby's umbilical cord seems to push outward when he cries, he may have an umbilical hernia. This is a small hole in the muscular part of the abdominal wall that allows tissue to bulge out when there's pressure inside the abdomen (for example, when the baby cries). This is not a serious condition, and it usually heals by itself in the first twelve to eighteen months. In the unlikely event that it doesn't, the hole may need to be surgically closed.

YOUR NEWBORN'S FIRST PHYSICAL EXAMS

Your baby should have one thorough physical examination within his first twenty-four hours and a follow-up at some point before you and he leave the hospital. If you take your baby home early (less than twenty-four hours after delivery), your pediatrician should see the baby again at two to three days of age for follow-up. This visit will allow him to check for problems such as those listed earlier.

These early visits to the pediatrician are also opportunities to ask questions about baby care and relieve any worries you may have. Don't hesitate to ask questions that sound unimportant; the answers may provide valuable information and be reassuring to you.

Blood Tests

In all states, newborns are required to be checked for certain serious diseases. One of these is called phenylketonuria (PKU). It causes mental retardation, which can be prevented if the condition is detected early and treated with a special diet. Tests also are done for hypothyroidism (a problem that can lead to mental retardation) and, in some states, for sickle-cell anemia (a blood disease found chiefly among blacks) and other disorders. These tests involve pricking the baby's heel to obtain a small blood sample on which the laboratory work can be performed. The PKU test is best done as close as possible to the time of discharge from the nursery. If the test is done before twenty-four hours of age, you will have to visit your pediatrician to have this blood test done a second time. The repeat test should be completed no later than the third week of life.

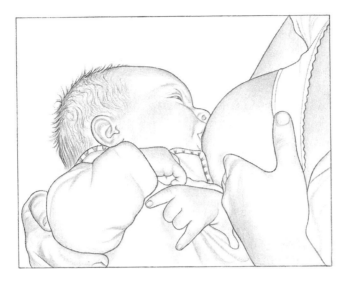

6

THE FIRST MONTH

GROWTH AND DEVELOPMENT

*I*n the very beginning, it may seem that your baby does nothing but eat, sleep, cry, and fill his diapers. By the end of the first month he'll be much more alert and responsive. Gradually he'll begin moving his body more smoothly and with much greater coordination—especially in getting his hand to his mouth. You'll realize that he listens when you speak, watches you as you hold him, and occasionally moves his own body to respond to you or attract your attention. But before we explore his expanding capabilities, let's look at the changes that will occur in his physical appearance during the first month.

Physical Appearance and Growth

When your baby was born, his birthweight included excess body fluid that was lost during his first few days. Most babies lose about one tenth of their birthweight during the first five days, then regain it over the next five, so that by about day ten they usually are back to their original birthweight. You can plot your own infant's growth on the charts on pages 118–121.

Most babies grow very rapidly after regaining their birthweight, especially during growth spurts which occur around seven to ten days, and again between three and six weeks. The average newborn gains weight at a rate of ⅔ of an ounce (20 to 30 grams) per day, and by one month weighs about 9 pounds (4 kilograms). He grows between 1 and 1½ inches (2.5 to 4 centimeters) during this month. Boys tend to weigh slightly more than girls (less than 1 pound, or 400 grams). They also tend to be slightly longer than girls at this age (about ½ inch, or 1.25 centimeters).

Your pediatrician will pay particular attention to your child's head growth, because it reflects the growth of his brain. The skull should grow faster during the first four months than at any other time in his life. The measurement around the average newborn's head is about 13¾ inches (35 centimeters), and grows to about 14¾ inches (37.75 centimeters) by one month. Because boys tend to be slightly larger than girls, their heads are larger, though the average difference is less than ⅓ inch (1 centimeter) on average.

During these first weeks your baby's body gradually will straighten from the tightly curled position he held inside the uterus during the final months of pregnancy. He'll begin to stretch his arms and legs, and may arch his back from time to time. His legs and feet may continue to rotate inward, giving him a bowlegged look. This condition usually will correct itself gradually over the next five to six months. If the bowlegged appearance is particularly severe or associated with pronounced curving-in of the front part of the foot, your pediatrician may suggest a splint or a cast to correct it, but these circumstances are extremely unusual. (See *Bowlegs and Knock-Knees,* page 620; *Pigeon Toes [Intoeing],* page 623.)

If your baby was born vaginally and his skull appeared misshapen at birth, it soon will resume its normal shape. Any bruising of the scalp or swelling of the eyelids that occurred during birth will be gone by the end of the first week or two. Any red spots in the eyes will disappear in about three weeks.

To your dismay, you may discover that the fine hair that covered your child's head when he was born will soon begin falling out. If he rubs the back of his head on his bedding, he may develop a temporary bald spot there, even if the rest of his hair remains. This loss is insignificant. The bare spots will be covered with new hair in a few months.

Another normal development is "baby acne." These are pimples that break out on the face, usually during the fourth or fifth week of life. They are thought to be due to stimulation of oil glands in the skin by hormones passed across the placenta during pregnancy. This condition may be made worse if the baby lies in sheets laundered in harsh detergents or soiled by milk that he's spit up. If your baby does have baby acne, place a soft, clean receiving blanket under his head and wash his face gently once a day with a mild baby soap to remove milk or detergent residue.

Your newborn's skin may also look blotchy, ranging in color from pink to blue. His hands and feet in particular may be colder and bluer than the rest of his body. The blood vessels leading to these areas are more sensitive to temperature changes and tend to shrink in response to cold. As a result, less blood gets to the exposed skin, causing it to look pale or bluish. If you move his arms and legs, however, you'll notice that they quickly turn pink again.

Your baby's internal "thermostat," which causes him to perspire when he's too hot or shiver when he's too cold, won't be working properly for some time. Also, in these early weeks, he'll lack the insulating layer of fat that will protect him from sudden temperature shifts later on. For these reasons, it's important for you to dress him properly—warmly in cool weather and lightly when it's hot. Don't automatically bundle him up just because he's a baby.

By the third week, the stump from the umbilical cord should have dried and fallen off, leaving behind a clean, well-healed area. Occasionally a raw spot is left after the stump is gone. It may even ooze a little blood-tinged fluid. Just keep it clean and dry and it will heal by itself. If it is not completely closed and dry in two weeks, consult your doctor.

Reflexes

Much of your baby's activity in his first weeks of life is reflexive. For instance, when you put your finger in his mouth he doesn't *think* about what to do, but sucks by reflex. When confronted by a bright light he will tightly shut his eyes, because that's what his reflexes make him do. He's born with many of these automatic responses, some of which remain with him for months, while others vanish in weeks.

In some cases, reflexes change into voluntary behavior. For example, your baby is born with a "rooting" reflex that prompts him to turn his head toward your hand if you stroke his cheek or mouth. This helps him find the nipple at feeding time. At first he'll root from side to side, turning his head toward the nipple and then away in decreasing arcs. But by about three weeks he'll simply turn his head and move his mouth into position to suck.

Sucking is another survival reflex present even before birth. If you had an ultrasound test done during pregnancy, you may have seen your baby sucking his thumb. After birth, when a nipple (either breast or bottle) is placed in your

Newborn Reflexes

The following are some of the reflexes you will see your baby perform during his first weeks. Not all infants acquire and lose these reflexes at exactly the same time, but this table will give you a general idea of what to expect.

REFLEX	AGE WHEN REFLEX APPEARS	AGE WHEN REFLEX DISAPPEARS
Moro reflex	Birth	2 months
Walking/Stepping	Birth	2 months
Rooting	Birth	4 months
Tonic neck reflex	Birth	4–5 months
Palmar grasp	Birth	5–6 months
Plantar grasp	Birth	9–12 months

baby's mouth and touches the roof of his mouth, he automatically begins to suck. This motion actually takes place in two stages: First, he places his lips around the areola and squeezes the nipple between his tongue and palate. (Called *expression,* this action forces out the milk.) Then comes the second phase, or the milking action, in which the tongue moves from the areola to the nipple. This whole process is helped by the negative pressure, or suction, that secures the breast in the baby's mouth.

Coordinating these rhythmic sucking movements with breathing and swallowing is a relatively complicated task for a new infant. So, even though this is a reflexive action, not all babies suck efficiently at first. With practice, however, the reflex becomes a skill that they all manage well.

As rooting, sucking, and bringing his hand to his mouth become less reflexive and more directed, your infant will start to use these movements to console himself. Have you already seen him nestling into his blanket or gnawing on his hand when he's tired? You may want to encourage these consoling techniques by giving him a pacifier or helping him find his thumb.

Another, more dramatic reflex present during these first few weeks is called the Moro reflex. If your baby's head shifts positions abruptly or falls backward, or he is startled by something loud or abrupt, he will react by throwing out his arms

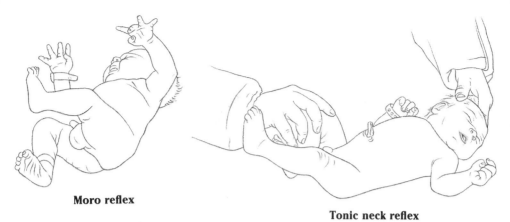

Moro reflex

Tonic neck reflex

and legs and extending his neck, then rapidly bringing his arms together as he cries loudly. The Moro reflex peaks during the first month and then disappears after two months.

One of the more interesting automatic responses is the tonic neck reflex, otherwise known as the fencing posture. You may notice that when your baby's head turns to one side, his arm on that side will straighten, with the opposite arm bent as if he's fencing. Do not be surprised if you don't see this response, however. It is subtle, and if your baby is disturbed or crying, he may not perform it. It disappears at five to seven months of age.

You'll see still another reflex when you stroke the palm of your baby's hand and watch him immediately grip your finger. Or stroke the sole of his foot, and watch it flex as the toes curl tightly. In the first few days after birth your baby's grasp will be so strong that it may seem he can hold his own weight—but don't try it. He has no control over this response, and may let go suddenly.

Aside from his "herculean" strength, your baby's other special talent is stepping! He can't support his own weight, of course, but if you hold him under the arms (being careful to support his head as well) and let his soles touch a flat surface, he'll place one foot in front of the other and "walk." This reflex will disappear after two months, then recur as the learned voluntary behavior of walking toward the end of the first year.

Although you may think of your baby as utterly defenseless, he actually has several protective reflexes. For instance, if a blanket or a pillow falls over his eyes, nose, or mouth, he'll shake his head from side to side and flail his arms to push it away so he can breathe and see. Or if an object comes straight toward him, he'll turn his head and try to squirm out of its way. (Amazingly, if the object is on a path that would make it a near miss instead of a collision, he will calmly watch it approach without flinching.) Yes, he's dependent on you, but he's not totally defenseless.

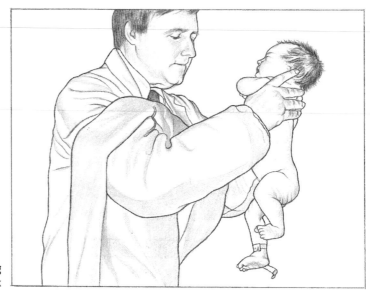

Walking/stepping reflex

States of Consciousness

As you get to know your baby, you'll soon realize that there are times when he's very alert and active, times when he's watchful but rather passive, and times when he's tired and irritable. You may even try to schedule your daily activities to capitalize on his "up" times and avoid overextending him during the "down" periods. Don't count on this schedule, however. These so-called "states of consciousness" will change dramatically in this first month.

There are actually six states of consciousness through which your baby cycles several times a day. Two are sleep states; the others are waking states.

State 1 is deep sleep, when the baby lies quietly without moving and is relatively unresponsive. If you shake a rattle loudly in his ear he may stir a little, but not much. During lighter, more active sleep (State 2) the same noise will startle him and may awaken him. During this light sleep you can also see the rapid movements of his eyes beneath his closed eyelids. He will alternate between these two sleep states, cycling through both of them within a given hour. Sometimes he'll "retreat" into these sleep states when he's overstimulated, as well as when he's physically tired.

As your baby wakes up or starts to fall asleep, he'll go through State 3. His eyes will roll back under drooping eyelids and he may stretch, yawn, or jerk his arms and legs. Once awake, he'll move into one of the three remaining states. He may be wide awake, happy, and alert but relatively motionless (State 4). Or he may be alert, happy, and very active (State 5). Or he may cry and flail himself about (State 6).

YOUR BABY'S STATES OF CONSCIOUSNESS

STATE	DESCRIPTION	WHAT YOUR BABY DOES
State 1	Deep sleep	Lies quietly without moving
State 2	Light sleep	Moves while sleeping; startles at noises
State 3	Drowsiness	Eyes start to close; may doze
State 4	Quiet alert	Eyes open wide, face is bright; body is quiet
State 5	Active alert	Face and body move actively
State 6	Crying	Cries, perhaps screams; body moves in very disorganized ways

If you shake a rattle by your baby's ear when he's happy and alert (States 4 and 5), he'll probably become quiet and turn his face to look for the source of this strange sound. This is the time when he'll appear most responsive to you and the activity around him, and be most attentive and involved in play.

In general, it's a mistake to expect much attention from a baby who is crying. At these times he's not receptive to new information or sensations; what he wants instead is comforting. The same rattle that enchanted him when he was happy five minutes earlier will only irritate him and make him more upset when he's crying. As he gets older you may sometimes be able to distract him with an attractive object or sound so that he stops crying, but at this early age the best way to comfort him usually is to pick him up and hold him. (See *Responding to Your Baby's Cries,* page 34).

As your baby's nervous system becomes more developed, he'll begin to settle into a pattern of crying, sleeping, eating, and playing that matches your own daily schedule. He may still need to eat every three to four hours, but by the end of the month he'll be awake for longer periods during the day and be more alert and responsive at those times.

Colic

Does your infant have a regular fussy period each day when it seems you can do nothing to comfort him? This is quite common, particularly between 6:00 P.M. and midnight—just when you, too, are feeling tired from the day's trials and tribulations. These periods of crankiness may feel like torture, especially if you have other demanding children or work to do, but fortunately they don't last long. The length of this fussing usually peaks at about three hours a day by six weeks, and then declines to one or two hours a day by three months. As long as the baby calms within a few hours and is relatively peaceful the rest of the day, there's no reason for alarm.

If the crying does not stop, but intensifies and persists throughout the day or night, it may be caused by colic. About one fifth of all babies develop colic, usually between the second and fourth weeks. They cry inconsolably, often screaming, extending or pulling up their legs, and passing gas. Their stomachs may be enlarged or distended with gas. The crying spells can occur around the clock, though they often become worse in the early evening.

Unfortunately, there is no definite explanation for why this happens. Most often, colic means simply that the child is unusually sensitive to stimulation. As he matures, it will decrease, and generally it stops by three months. Sometimes, in breast-feeding babies, colic is a sign of sensitivity to a food in the mother's diet. The discomfort is only rarely caused by sensitivity to milk protein in formula. Colicky behavior may also signal a medical problem, such as a hernia or some type of illness.

Perhaps you'll find it reassuring that there's a time limit to this problem, but that doesn't stop the crying now. It may be that you simply will have to wait it out, but there are also several things that might be worth trying. First, of course, consult your pediatrician to rule out any medical reason for the crying. Then ask him which of the following would be most helpful:

- If nursing, eliminate milk products, caffeine, onions, cabbage, and any other potentially irritating foods from your diet. If bottle-feeding, try a formula that has no cow's milk. If food sensitivity is causing the discomfort, the colic should decrease within a day or two of these changes.

- Walk your baby in a body carrier to soothe him. The motion and body contact will reassure him, even if his discomfort persists.

- Rock him, run the vacuum in the next room, or place him where he can hear the clothes dryer. Steady rhythmic motion and sound may help him fall asleep.

- Introduce a pacifier. While some breast-fed babies will actively refuse it, it will provide instant relief for others. (See page 150.)

- Lay your baby tummy-down across your knees and gently rub his back. The pressure against his abdomen may help relieve his pain.

- Swaddle him in a blanket so that he feels secure and warm.

- When you're feeling tense and anxious, have someone else look after the baby—and get out of the house. Even an hour or two away will help you maintain a positive attitude. No matter how impatient or angry you feel, do not shake the baby. Shaking an infant hard can cause blindness, brain damage, or even death.

The First Smile

One of the most important developments during this month is the appearance of your baby's first smiles and giggles. These start during sleep, for reasons that are not understood. They may be a signal that the baby feels aroused in some way or is responding to some internal impulse. While it's great fun to watch a newborn smile his way through a nap, the real joy comes near the end of this month when he begins to grin back at you during his alert periods.

Those first loving smiles will help you tune in even more closely to each other, and you'll soon discover that you can predict when your baby will smile, look at you, make sounds, and equally important, pause for timeout from play. Gradually you'll recognize each other's patterns of responsiveness so that your play together becomes a kind of dance in which you take turns leading and following. By identifying and responding to your child's subtle signals, even at this young age, you are telling him that his thoughts and feelings are important and that he can affect the world around him. These messages are vital to his developing self-esteem.

Movement

For the first week or two your baby's movements will be very jerky. His chin may quiver and his hands may tremble. He'll startle easily when moved suddenly or when he hears a loud sound, and the startling may lead to crying. If these movements are very pronounced or disturbing, you can contain them by holding the baby tightly against your body or swaddling him in a blanket. But by the end of the first month, as his nervous system matures and his muscle control improves, these shakes and quivers will give way to much smoother arm and leg movements that look almost as if he's riding a bicycle. Lay him on his stomach now and he will make crawling motions with his legs and may even push up on his arms.

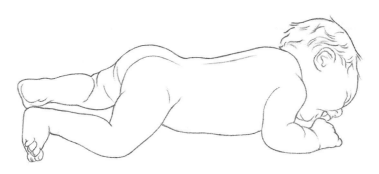

Movement Milestones
By the End of This Period

- **Makes jerky, quivering arm thrusts**

- **Brings hands within range of eyes and mouth**

- **Moves head from side to side while lying on stomach**

- **Head flops backward if unsupported**

- **Keeps hands in tight fists**

- **Strong reflex movements**

The baby's neck muscles also will develop rapidly, giving him much more control over his head movements by the end of this month. Lying on his stomach, he may lift his head and turn it from one side to the other. However, he won't be able to hold his head securely until about three months, so make sure you support it whenever you're holding him.

Your baby's hands, a source of endless fascination throughout much of this first year, will catch his eyes during these weeks. His finger movements are limited, since his hands are clenched in tight fists most of the time. But he can flex his arms and bring his hands to his mouth and into his line of vision. While he can't control his hands precisely, he'll watch them closely as long as they're in view.

Vision

Your baby's vision will go through many changes this first month. He was born with peripheral vision (the ability to see to the sides), and he'll gradually acquire the ability to focus closely on a single point in the center of his visual field. He likes to look at objects held about 8 to 15 inches in front of him, but by one month he'll focus briefly on things as far away as three feet.

At the same time, he'll learn to follow, or track, moving objects. To help him practice this skill you can play tracking games with him. For example, move your head slowly from side to side as you hold him facing you; or pass a patterned object up and down or side to side in front of him (making sure it's within his

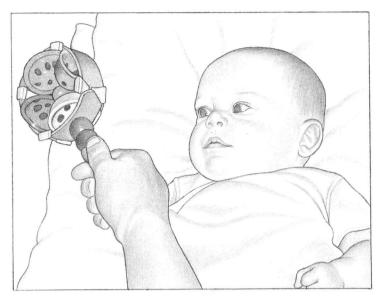

Your baby likes to look at objects held about 8 to 15 inches in front of him.

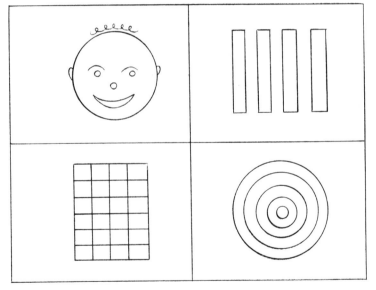

He is most attentive to black-and-white pictures or high-contrast patterns, such as sharply contrasting stripes, bull's-eyes, checks, and very simple faces.

range of focus). At first he may only be able to follow large objects moving slowly through an extremely limited range, but soon he'll be tracking even small, speedy movements.

At birth your baby was extremely sensitive to bright light, and his pupils were constricted (small) to limit the amount of light that entered his eyes. Around two weeks his pupils will begin to enlarge, allowing him to experience a broader range of shades of light and dark. As his retina (the light-sensitive tissue inside the eyeball) develops, his ability to see and recognize patterns also will improve.

The more contrast there is in a pattern, the more it will attract his attention, which is why he is most attentive to black-and-white pictures or high-contrast patterns, such as sharply contrasting stripes, bull's-eyes, checks, and very simple faces.

If you show your infant three identical toys—one blue, one yellow, one red— he probably will look longest at the red one, although no one yet understands why. Is it the color red itself? Or is it the brightness of this color that attracts newborn babies? We do know that color vision doesn't fully mature before about four months, so if you show your baby two related colors, like green and turquoise, he probably can't tell the difference at this age.

Visual Milestones
By the End of This Period

- **Focuses 8 to 12 inches away**

- **Eyes wander and occasionally cross**

- **Prefers black-and-white or high-contrast patterns**

- **Prefers the human face to all other patterns**

Hearing

During the first month, your baby will pay close attention to human voices, especially high-pitched ones speaking "baby talk." When you talk to him, he'll turn his head to search for you and listen closely as you sound out different syllables and words. Watch carefully and you may even see him make subtle movements of his arms and legs in time with your speech.

Your infant also will be sensitive to noise levels. If you make a loud clicking sound in his ear or bring him into a noisy, crowded room, he may "shut down," becoming as unresponsive as if he had heard nothing. Or he may be so sensitive that he startles, erupts into crying, and turns his entire body away from the noise. (Extremely sensitive babies also will cry when exposed to a very bright light.)

Substitute the sound of a soft rattle or quiet music and he'll become alert and turn his head and eyes to locate the source of this interesting sound.

Not only does your baby hear well, but even at this age he'll remember some of the sounds he hears. Some mothers who repeatedly read a story aloud during late pregnancy have found that their babies seemed to recognize the story when it was read to them again after birth—the babies became quiet and looked more attentive. Try reading your favorite children's story aloud for several days in a row at times when your baby is alert and attentive. Then wait a day or two and read it again. Does he seem to recognize it?

Hearing Milestones By the End of This Period

- **Hearing is fully mature**
- **Recognizes some sounds**
- **May turn toward familiar sounds and voices**

Smell and Touch

Just as he prefers certain patterns and sounds, your baby is very particular about tastes and smells. He will breathe deeply to catch a whiff of milk, vanilla, banana, or sugar, but will turn up his nose at the smell of alcohol or vinegar. By the end of his first week, if he's nursing, he'll turn toward his own mother's breast pad but will ignore the pads of other nursing mothers. This radarlike system helps direct him at feeding times, and warns him away from substances that could harm him.

Your baby is equally sensitive to touch and the way you handle him. He'll nestle into a soft piece of flannel or satin, but pull away from scratchy burlap or coarse sandpaper. Stroke him gently with your palm and he'll relax and become quiet. If you pick him up roughly, he'll probably take offense and start to cry. If you pick him up gently and rock him slowly, he'll become quiet and attentive. Holding, stroking, rocking, and cuddling will calm him down when he's upset and make him more alert when he's drowsy. It also sends a clear message of your love and affection for him. Long before he understands a word you say, he'll understand your moods and feelings from the way you touch him.

Smell and Touch Milestones By the End of This Period

- **Prefers sweet smells**

- **Avoids bitter or acidic smells**

- **Recognizes the scent of his own mother's breast milk**

- **Prefers soft to coarse sensations**

- **Dislikes rough or abrupt handling**

Temperament

Consider these two babies, both from the same family, both boys:

The first infant is calm and quiet, happy to play by himself. He watches everything that happens around him, but rarely demands attention himself. Left on his own, he sleeps for long periods and eats infrequently.

The second baby is fussy and startles easily. He thrashes his arms and legs, moving almost constantly whether awake or asleep. While most newborns sleep fourteen hours a day, he sleeps only ten, and wakens whenever there's the slightest activity nearby. He seems in a hurry to do everything at once, and even eats in a rush, gulping his feedings and swallowing so much air that he needs frequent burping.

Both these babies are absolutely normal and healthy. One is no "better" than the other, but because their personalities are so far apart, the two will be treated very differently, right from birth.

Like these babies, your infant will demonstrate many unique personality traits from the earliest weeks of life. Discovering these traits is one of the most exciting parts of having a new baby. Is he very active and intense, or relatively slow-going? Is he timid when faced with a new situation, like the first bath, or does he enjoy it? You'll find clues to his personality in everything he does, from falling asleep to crying. The more you pay attention to these signals, and learn to respond appropriately to his unique personality, the calmer and more predictable your life will be in the months to come.

While most of these early character traits are built into the newborn's hereditary makeup, their appearance may be delayed if your baby is born quite prematurely.

Developmental Health Watch

If, during the second, third, or fourth weeks of your baby's life, he shows any of the following signs of developmental delay, notify your pediatrician.

- Sucks poorly and feeds slowly
- Doesn't blink when shown a bright light
- Doesn't focus and follow a nearby object moving side to side
- Rarely moves arms and legs; seems stiff
- Seems excessively loose in the limbs, or floppy
- Lower jaw trembles constantly, even when not crying or excited
- Doesn't respond to loud sounds

Premature babies don't express their needs—like hunger, fatigue, or discomfort—as clearly as other newborns. They may be extrasensitive to light, sound, and touch for several months. Even playful conversation may be too intense for them, and cause them to become fussy and look away. When this happens, it's up to the parent to stop and wait until the baby is alert and ready for more attention. Eventually most of these early reactions will fade away, and the baby's own natural character traits will become more evident.

Babies who are underweight at birth (less than 5.5 pounds), even if they're full-term, may also be less responsive than other newborns. At first they may be very sleepy and not seem very alert. After a few weeks they seem to wake up, eating eagerly but still remaining irritable and hypersensitive to stimulation between feedings. This irritability may last until they grow and mature further. The more they are protected from overstimulation and comforted through this fussy period, the more quickly it will pass.

From the very beginning your baby's temperamental traits will influence the way you treat him and feel about him. If you had specific ideas about child rearing before he was born, reevaluate them now to see if they're really in tune with his character. The same goes for expert advice—from books, articles, and especially from well-meaning relatives and friends—about the "right way" to raise a child. The truth is, there is no right way that works for every child. You have to create your own guidelines based on your child's unique personality, your own beliefs, and the circumstances of your family life. The important thing is to remain responsive to your baby's individuality. Don't try to box him into some previously set mold or pattern. Your baby's uniqueness is his strength, and respecting that strength from the start will help lay the best possible foundation for his high self-esteem and for loving relationships with others.

Toys Appropriate for Your Baby's First Month

- Mobile with highly contrasting colors and patterns
- Unbreakable mirror attached securely to inside of crib
- Music boxes and record or tape players with soft music
- Soft, brightly colored and patterned toys that make gentle sounds

---

BASIC CARE

Feeding and Nutrition
(see Chapter 4 for additional information)

Breast milk or formula should be your child's basic source of nutrition for the first twelve months. But while you don't have to worry much about his diet, you need to establish a regular pattern of feedings and make sure that he's getting enough calories for growth.

Establishing a pattern of feedings does not mean setting a rigid timetable and insisting that he eat a full four ounces at each feeding. It's much more important to listen to your baby's signals and work around his needs. If he is bottle-fed, he probably will cry at the end of his feeding if he is not getting enough. On the other hand, if he is getting an adequate amount in the first ten minutes, he may stop and fall asleep. Breast-fed babies behave a little differently in that they do not always cry when they are hungry, and the only way to be sure yours is getting enough milk is to watch his weight gain. Also, he should be fed at least every three to four hours and not be allowed to sleep through a feeding until at least four weeks of age.

At the beginning of the second week and again between three and six weeks, your baby will go through growth spurts that may make him hungrier than usual. Even if you don't notice any outward growth, his body is changing in important ways and needs extra calories during these times. Be prepared to feed him more often if he's breast-fed, and if he's bottle-fed, try giving him slightly more at each feeding.

If your baby has a nutritional problem, he's likely to start losing weight. There are some signals that may help you detect such a problem before a great deal of weight loss occurs.

If he's breast-feeding, one warning signal is a lack of fullness in your breasts after one week. If they don't drip milk at the start of each feeding, the baby may not be providing enough stimulation when he sucks. Some other trouble signs are listed below. These also may be signs of medical problems that are unrelated to your baby's nutrition. You should call your pediatrician if they persist.

Too Much Feeding:

- If bottle-fed, the baby stops feeding after ten minutes or less, or after consuming more than 3 to 4 ounces (90 to 120 cc).

- He vomits most or all the food after a complete feeding.

- Stools are loose and very watery, eight or more times a day.

Too Little Feeding:

- If breast-fed, the baby stops feeding after ten minutes or less.

- He wets fewer than four diapers.

- His skin remains wrinkled beyond the first week.

- He does not develop a rounded face by about three weeks.

- He appears hungry, searching for something to suck shortly after feedings.

- He becomes more yellow, instead of less, after the first week.

Feeding Allergy or Digestive Disturbance:

- Your baby vomits most or all food after a complete feeding.

- He produces loose, very watery stools eight or more times a day.

- If breast-feeding, he becomes more yellow, instead of less, after the first week.

Most babies this age begin to spit up occasionally after feedings. That's because the muscular valve between the esophagus (the passage between throat and

A very young infant who has not developed head control needs to be carried in a way that keeps his head from flopping from side to side or snapping from front to back.

stomach) and the stomach is immature. Instead of closing tightly, it remains open enough to allow the contents of the stomach to come back up and gently spill out of the mouth. This is normal and won't harm your baby.

Carrying Your Baby

A newborn or very young infant who has not developed head control needs to be carried in a way that keeps his head from flopping from side to side or snapping from front to back. This is done by cradling the head when carrying the baby in a lying position, and supporting the head and neck with your hand when carrying the baby upright.

Pacifiers

Many parents have strong feelings about pacifiers. Some oppose their use because of the way they look, or they resent the notion of "pacifying" a baby with an object. Others believe—incorrectly—that using a pacifier can harm a baby. Pacifiers do not cause any medical or psychological problems. If your baby wants to suck beyond what nursing or bottle-feeding provides, a pacifier will satisfy that need.

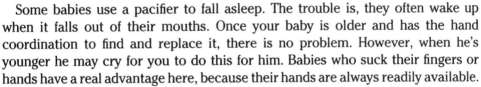

A pacifier is meant to satisfy your baby's non-eating sucking needs, not to replace or delay meals. So offer a pacifier to your baby only after or between feedings, when you are sure he is not hungry. If he is hungry, and you offer a pacifier as a substitute, he may become so angry that it interferes with feeding. Remember, the pacifier is for your baby's benefit, not your convenience, so let him decide whether and when to use it.

Some babies use a pacifier to fall asleep. The trouble is, they often wake up when it falls out of their mouths. Once your baby is older and has the hand coordination to find and replace it, there is no problem. However, when he's younger he may cry for you to do this for him. Babies who suck their fingers or hands have a real advantage here, because their hands are always readily available.

When shopping for a pacifier, look for a one-piece model that has a soft nipple (some models can break into two pieces). It should be dishwasher-safe so you can either boil it or run it through the dishwasher before your baby uses it. Until he's six months old the pacifier should be cleaned this way frequently, so he's not exposed to any increased risk of infection, as his immune system is still maturing. After that, the likelihood of his picking up an infection in that way is minimal, so you can just wash it with soap and rinse it in clear water.

Pacifiers are available in two sizes, one for the first six months and another for children after that age. You'll also find a variety of nipple shapes, from squarish "orthodontic" versions to the standard bottle type. Once you decide which your baby prefers, buy some extras. Pacifiers have a way of disappearing or falling on the floor or street when you need them most. However, *never* try to solve this problem by fastening the pacifier with a cord around your baby's neck. That could interfere with his breathing or choke him. Also, for safety reasons, do not make your own pacifiers out of a bottle nipple. Babies have pulled the nipple out of such homemade pacifiers and choked on them.

Going Outside

Fresh air and a change of surroundings are good for both you and your baby, even in his first month, so take him out for walks when the weather is nice. Be careful to dress him properly for these outings, however. His internal temperature control isn't fully mature until the end of his first year. This makes it difficult for him to regulate his body temperature when he's exposed to excessive heat or cold. His clothing must do some of this work for him by keeping heat in when he is in a cold location and letting heat escape when he's in a very warm place. In general, he should wear one more layer than you do.

Your infant's skin also is extremely susceptible to sunburn during the first six months, so it's important to keep him out of direct and reflected sunlight (off of water, sand, or concrete, for example) as much as possible. If you must take him out in the sun, use sun block with a sun protective factor (SPF) of 15 or more to protect his skin. Also dress him in lightweight and light-colored clothing, with a bonnet or hat to shade his face. If he is lying or sitting in one place, make sure it is shady, and adjust his position to keep him in the shade as the sun moves.

Another warning for the hot-weather months: Do not let baby equipment (car seats, strollers) sit in the sun. When that happens, the plastic and metal parts can get hot enough to burn your child. Check the temperature of the surface of any such equipment before you allow your baby to come in contact with it.

In uncomfortably cold or rainy weather, keep your baby inside as much as possible. If you have to go out, bundle him up in warm sweaters or bunting bags over his other clothes, and use a warm hat to cover his head and ears. You can shield his face from the cold with a blanket when you're outside.

To check whether he's clothed well enough, feel his hands and feet and the skin on his chest. His hands and feet should be slightly cooler than his body, but not cold. His chest should feel warm. If hands, feet, and chest feel cold, take him to a warm room, unwrap him, and feed him something warm or hold him close so the heat from your body warms him. Until his temperature is back to normal, extra layers of clothing will just trap the cold, so use these other methods to warm his body before wrapping him in additional blankets or clothing.

Finding Temporary Child-Care Help

Most mothers need some help when they bring a new baby home. If Dad can take a few days off from work during the first week or two, the problem is usually solved. If he cannot, and the family finances won't allow you to hire help, the next best choice is a close relative or friend. It is wise to make these arrangements in advance rather than waiting until after the delivery to seek help.

Some areas have a visiting nurse or homemaking service. This will not solve your middle-of-the-night problems, but it will give you an hour or two during the day to catch up on work or simply rest a little. These arrangements, too, should be made in advance.

Be selective about the help you seek. Look for assistance from those who will really support you. Don't forget, your goal is to reduce the stress level in your home, not add to it.

Before you start interviewing or asking friends or family for assistance, decide exactly what kind of help will work best for you. Ask yourself the following questions:

- Do you want someone who can help you tend the baby, or do the housework, or cook meals—or a little bit of everything?

- During what hours do you want help?

- Do you need someone who can drive (to pick up other children at school, shop for groceries, run errands, and the like)?

Once you know what you need, make sure the person you choose to help out understands and agrees to your requests.

Your Baby's First Sitter. Sometime in the first month or two, you'll probably need to leave your baby for the first time. The more confidence you have in your babysitter, the easier this experience will be for you, so you may want to have your first sitter be someone very close and trusted—a grandparent, close friend, or relative who's familiar with both you and the child.

After you've survived the first separation, you may want to look for a regular babysitter. Start by asking your friends for recommendations. If they have no suggestions, ask your pediatrician if he knows of any local child-care agencies or referral services. If that still doesn't yield any names, contact the placement services at local colleges for a listing of students who babysit. You can also find the names of babysitters in community newspapers, telephone directories, and church and grocery store bulletin boards, but remember that no one screens the people in these listings.

Interview every candidate in person and with your baby present. You should be looking for someone who is affectionate, capable, and supports your views about child care. If you feel comfortable with the individual after you've talked awhile, let her hold the baby so you can see how she handles him. Although experience, references, and good health are important, the best way to judge a babysitter is by giving her a trial run while you're home. It will give your baby and the babysitter a chance to get to know each other before they're alone together, and it will give you an opportunity to make sure you feel comfortable with the sitter.

Whenever you leave your child with a sitter, give her a list of all emergency phone numbers, including those where you or other close family members can be contacted if problems arise. Establish clear guidelines about what to do in an

When traveling by automobile, make sure your child is safely strapped into his car seat. At this age he should ride in the rear-facing position.

emergency. Make sure the sitter knows how to treat a child who is choking or not breathing (see *Choking,* page 452; *Cardiopulmonary Resuscitation and Mouth-to-Mouth Resuscitation,* page 449). Ask the sitter to jot down any notes or questions she has about your child during the day. Let friends and neighbors know about your arrangement so they can help if there's an emergency, and ask them to tell you if they suspect any problems in your absence.

Traveling with Your Baby

Traveling with your baby during his infancy is probably the easiest traveling the two of you will ever do. For the first few months, all he cares about is his own comfort, which amounts to a full stomach, a clean diaper, and a comfortable place to sit or lie. If you can satisfy these basic needs, your baby probably will travel with minimum protest. The key is to maintain his normal patterns as much as possible.

Long trips involving a change of time zones can disturb your baby's sleep schedule, so try to plan your activities according to the schedule your child is on, and allow several days for him to adjust to a time change. For instance, if you've just traveled from New York to California (where it is three hours earlier), and he is waking very early in the morning, plan to start your own activities earlier. Be ready to stop earlier, too, because your little one will be getting tired and cranky long before the clock says it's time to go to bed. To avoid problems, let your baby's signals set the limits for each day.

If you're going to remain in a new time zone for more than two or three days, your baby's internal time clock will gradually shift to coincide with the time zone you're in. You'll have to adjust mealtimes to match the times when his body is telling him he's hungry. Mom and Dad—and even older children—may be able to postpone meals to fit the new time zone, but a baby isn't able to make those adjustments.

Your baby will adapt to his new environment more quickly if you bring some familiar things from home. If he has a favorite blanket that he always sleeps with, make sure it goes with you on your trip. A few familiar rattles and toys will provide some comfort and reassurance too. Use his regular soap, a familiar towel, and bring along one of his tub toys to make him more at ease during baths. At meals give him his normal foods. This is not the time to try out a new formula or introduce him to strange tastes.

When packing for a trip with your baby, it's usually best to use a separate bag for his things. This makes it easier to find items quickly when you want them, and reduces the chance that you'll forget an important one. You'll also need a large diaper bag for such things as bottles, small toys, snacks, lotion, diapers, and baby wipes. Keep this bag with you at all times.

When traveling by automobile, make sure your child is safely strapped into his car seat. If you're renting an automobile, reserve a car seat ahead of time or bring your own with you. If a rented car seat seems too large, you can use rolled-up diapers to center your baby. If you're not sure how to secure him safely on a plane or train, ask a flight attendant or a conductor to help you. Unless you buy a ticket for the baby, you'll be expected to carry the baby on your lap. When there is extra room on board, you may be able to get a separate seat for the baby without paying for it.

If your baby is bottle-fed, bring not only enough formula for the expected travel time, but some extra in case any unexpected delays occur. The attendant or conductor will help you refrigerate the formula until it is needed. If you're nursing and you are concerned about privacy, ask the attendant for some blankets you can use as a screen.

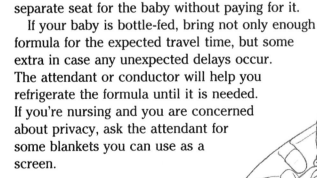

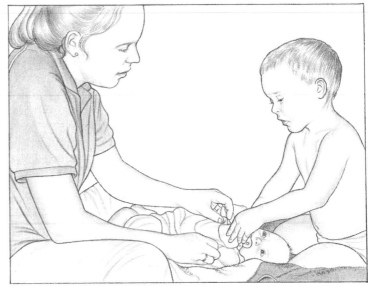

Once the infant arrives, you can expect your older child to be very proud and protective.

THE FAMILY

A Special Message to Mothers

One reason why this first month can be especially difficult is that you are still recovering physically from the stress of pregnancy and delivery. It may take weeks before your body is back to normal; your incisions (if you had an episiotomy or C-section) have healed, and you're able to resume everyday activities. You may also experience strong mood swings due to changes in the amount of hormones in your body. These changes can prompt sudden crying episodes for no apparent reason, or feelings of mild depression for the first few weeks. These emotions may be intensified by the exhaustion that comes with waking up every two or three hours at night to feed and change the baby.

If you experience these so-called "postpartum blues," they may make you feel a little "crazy," embarrassed, or even that you're a "bad mother." Difficult as it may be, try to keep these emotions in perspective by reminding yourself that they're *normal* after pregnancy and delivery. Even fathers sometimes feel sad and unusually emotional after a new baby arrives (possibly a response to the psychological intensity of the experience). To keep the blues from dominating your life—and your enjoyment of your new baby—avoid isolating yourself in these early weeks. Try to nap when your baby does, so you don't get overtired. If these feelings persist past a few weeks or become severe, consult your pediatrician or your own physician about getting extra help.

Visitors can often help you combat the blues by celebrating the baby's arrival with you. They may bring welcome gifts for the baby or—even better during these early weeks—offer food or household help. But they can also be exhausting for you, overwhelming for the baby, and may expose him to infection. So strictly limit the number of visitors during the first couple of weeks, and keep anyone with a cough, cold, or contagious disease away from your newborn. Ask all visitors to call in advance, and keep the visits brief until you're back to a regular schedule. If the baby seems unsettled by all the attention, don't let anyone outside the family hold or come close to him.

If you become overwhelmed with phone calls, and you have a telephone answering machine, use it to give yourself a little peace. Record a message that gives the baby's sex, name, birth date, time, weight, and length. Then turn on the machine and turn off the ringing mechanism on your phone. That allows you to return the calls on your own schedule without feeling stressed or guilty every time the bell rings. If you don't have an anwering machine, leave your phone off the hook or muffle the sound of the bell with a pillow.

With a new baby, constant visitors, an aching body, unpredictable mood swings, and, in some cases, other siblings demanding attention, it's no wonder the housework gets neglected. Resign yourself ahead of time to knowing that the wash may not get done as often as it should, the house will get dustier than usual, and a lot of meals will be frozen or takeout. You can always catch up next month. For now, concentrate on recuperating and enjoying your new baby.

A Special Message to Fathers

This can be a very stressful time for parenting couples. It's almost impossible to find time—much less energy—for each other, between the seemingly constant demands of the baby, the needs of other children, household chores, the father's work schedule (in our society, few fathers have the option of taking paternity leaves, which can help reduce these tensions). Nights spent feeding, diapering, and walking the floor with a crying baby quickly take their toll in fatigue. If both parents don't make up for this by relieving each other and taking naps, exhaustion can drive a large and unnecessary wedge between them.

At this time, some fathers also feel shut off from the child and from the mother's attention and affections, especially if the baby is breast-fed. The problem is not helped by the fact that sexual intercourse is usually prohibited by the obstetrician for these first few weeks. Even if it were allowed, many women simply aren't interested in sexual activity for a while after delivery because of the physical exhaustion and emotional stress they may be experiencing at this time.

This conflict and the jealous feelings that may arise at this time are temporary. Life soon settles into a fairly regular routine that will once again give you some time to yourselves, and restore your sex life and social activities to normal.

Become as involved as possible in caring for and playing with the new baby. You'll get just as emotionally attached to him as his mother will.

Meanwhile, make an effort for just the two of you to spend some time together each day, and remember, you're entitled to hold, hug, cuddle, and kiss each other as well as the baby!

A positive way for men to deal with these issues is to become as involved as possible in caring for and playing with the new baby. When you spend this extra time with your baby, you'll get just as emotionally attached to him as his mother will.

This is not to say that moms and dads play with babies the same way. In general, fathers play to arouse and excite their babies, while mothers generally concentrate on more low-keyed stimulation such as gentle rocking, quiet interactive games, singing, and soothing activities. Fathers tend to roughhouse more, making lots of noise, and move the baby about more vigorously. The babies respond in kind, laughing and moving more with Dad than they do with Mom. From the baby's viewpoint, both play styles are equally valuable and complement each other beautifully, which is another reason why it's so important to have *both* of you involved in the care of the baby.

Siblings

With all the excitement over the new baby's arrival, siblings often feel neglected. They may still be a little upset over their mother's hospitalization, especially if this was their first prolonged separation from her. Even after Mom returns home, they may have trouble understanding that she's tired and cannot play with them as much as they're used to. Compound this with the attention she's now devoting to the baby—attention which just a couple of weeks ago belonged to them!—and it's no wonder that they may feel jealous and left out. It's up to both parents to find ways to reassure the siblings that they're still very much loved and valued, and help them come to terms with their new "competition."

Here are some suggestions to help soothe your older children and make them feel more involved during the first month home with your new baby.

1. If possible, have the siblings visit mother and baby in the hospital.

2. When Mom comes home from the hospital, bring each sibling a special gift to celebrate.

3. Set aside a special time to spend alone with each sibling every day. Make sure that both Mom and Dad have time with each child, individually and together.

4. While you're taking pictures of the new baby, take some of the older children—alone and with the baby.

5. Ask the grandparents or other close relatives to take the older children on a special outing—to the zoo, a movie, or just to dinner. This special attention may help them through moments when they feel abandoned.

6. Especially during the first month, when the baby's feedings are so frequent, older children can get very jealous of the intimacy you have with the baby during feedings. Show them that you can share this intimacy by turning feeding times into story times. Reading stories that specifically deal with issues of jealousy encourages a toddler or preschooler to voice his feelings so that you can help him become more accepting.

HEALTH WATCH

The following medical problems are of particular concern to parents during the first month. (For problems that occur generally throughout childhood, check the listings in Part II.)

Breathing Difficulties. Normally, your baby should take from twenty to forty breaths per minute. This pattern is most regular when he is asleep and healthy. When awake, he may occasionally breathe rapidly for a short period, then take a brief pause (less than 10 seconds) before returning to normal breathing. If he has a fever, his breathing may increase by about two breaths per minute for each degree of temperature elevation. A runny nose may interfere with breathing because his nasal passages are narrow and fill easily. This condition is eased by using a cool-mist humidifier and gently suctioning the nose with a rubber aspirating bulb (ordinarily given to you by the hospital; for its use, see page 513). Occasionally, mild salt-solution nose drops are used to help thin the mucus and clear the nasal passages.

Diarrhea. A baby has diarrhea if he produces loose, very watery stools more than six to eight times a day. This is usually caused by a viral infection. The danger, especially at this young age, is of losing too much water and becoming dehydrated. The first signs of dehydration are a dry mouth and a significant decrease in the number of wet diapers. But don't wait for dehydration to occur. Call your pediatrician if the stools are very loose or occur more often than after each feeding (six to eight per day).

Excessive Sleepiness. Since each infant requires a different amount of sleep, it's difficult to tell when a baby is excessively drowsy. If your infant starts sleeping much more than usual, it might indicate the presence of an infection, so notify your pediatrician. Also, if you are nursing and your baby sleeps more than five hours without a feeding in the first month, you must consider the possibility that he is not getting enough milk or perhaps is being affected, through the breast milk, by a medication that you are taking.

Eye Infections. (See also *Tear Production Problems,* page 560.) Some babies are born with one or both tear ducts partially or totally blocked. They typically open by about two weeks, when tear production begins. If they don't, the blockage may cause a watery or mucus tearing. In this case, the tears will back up and flow over the eyelids instead of draining through the nose. This is not harmful, and the ducts generally will open without treatment. You may also help open them by gently massaging the inner corner of the eye and down the side of the nose. However, do this only at the direction of your pediatrician.

If the ducts remain blocked, thus keeping the tears from draining properly, infection can easily occur. These infections produce a white discharge in the corner of the eye. The eyelashes become sticky and may dry together at night so the eyelid can't open. Such infections usually are treated with special drops or ointment that your doctor will prescribe after examining the eye. Sometimes all that's needed is a gentle cleansing with sterile water. When the lashes are sticky, dip a cotton ball in sterile water, and use it to gently wipe from the part of the lid nearest the nose to the outside. Use each cotton ball just once, and then discard it. Use as many cotton balls as you need to clean the eye thoroughly.

Although this type of mild infection may recur several times during your baby's first months, it will not damage the eye and he probably will outgrow it, even without more serious treatment. Only rarely does this tear-duct blockage require surgical care.

If the eye itself is bloodshot or pinkish, there probably is a more serious infection, called conjunctivitis, and you should notify your pediatrician at once.

Fever. Whenever your child is unusually cranky or feels warm, take his temperature. (See *Taking a Rectal Temperature,* page 58.) If his rectal temperature reads higher than 100 degrees F. (37.8 degrees C.) on two separate readings, and he's not overly bundled up, call your pediatrician at once. Fever in these first few weeks can signal an infection, and babies this age can quickly become seriously ill.

Floppiness. Newborn infants all seem somewhat floppy because their muscles are still developing, but if your baby feels exceptionally loose or *loses* muscle tone, it could be a sign of a more serious problem, such as an infection. Consult your pediatrician immediately.

Hearing. Pay attention to the way your baby responds to sounds. Does he startle at loud or sudden noises? Does he become quiet or turn toward you when you talk to him? If he does not respond normally to sounds around him, ask your pediatrician about formal hearing testing. This testing might be particularly appropriate if your infant was extremely premature, if he was deprived of oxygen or had a severe infection at birth, or if your family has a history of hearing loss in early childhood. If there is any suspicion of hearing loss, your infant should be tested as early as possible, as a delay in diagnosis and treatment is likely to interfere with normal language development.

Jaundice. Jaundice, the yellow color that often appears in the skin shortly after birth, sometimes persists into the second week of life in a baby who is breastfed (see page 130). It occurs because some individual's breast milk interferes with the liver's ability to break down bilirubin, the blood product that causes the yellow color. Sometimes breast-feeding must be stopped for twenty-four to forty-eight hours in order to clear the jaundice. Once it disappears, you may resume breast-feeding, because this type of jaundice rarely recurs. If it does, a second interruption of breast-feeding might be recommended, or the baby might be changed to formula-feeding. Your pediatrician will help you make this decision.

Jitters. Many newborns have quivery chins and shaky hands, but if your baby's whole body seems to be shaking, it could be a sign of low blood sugar or calcium levels, or some type of seizure disorder. Notify your pediatrician so he can determine the cause.

Rashes and Infections. Common newborn rashes include the following:

   1. Cradle Cap (seborrheic dermatitis) appears as scaly patches on the scalp. Washing the hair and brushing out the scales daily helps control this condition.

Sudden Infant Death Syndrome (SIDS)

Approximately two or three newborns out of every one thousand die in their sleep, for no apparent reason, between the fourth and sixteenth weeks of life. These babies generally are well cared for and show no obvious symptoms of illness. Their autopsies turn up no identifiable cause of death, so the terms *Sudden Infant Death Syndrome (SIDS)* or *crib death* are used.

SIDS occurs most often in winter among males who had a low birthweight. Premature infants and babies with a family history of SIDS, and babies of mothers who smoke and those who sleep in the prone (stomach) position (see page 37) also appear to be at increased risk. There are many theories about the cause of SIDS, but none has been proven. Infection, milk allergy, pneumonia, suffocation, and child abuse all have been disproven as causes. The most believable theory at this time is that prolonged periodic pauses in breathing, known as apnea, interfere with normal respiration and lead to death.

If your baby occasionally stops breathing or turns blue, your pediatrician probably will want to hospitalize him to make sure there are no treatable causes for the episodes and to assess the severity of the condition. If the apnea is severe, you may be advised to learn cardiopulmonary resuscitation (CPR) and use a home monitor while the baby sleeps. This device measures his respiration rate and sounds an alarm if it goes too low. If your baby was born prematurely, the pediatrician may choose to control the apnea with medications such as caffeine or theophylline, which stimulate respiration.

Along with the normal feelings of grief and depression, many parents who lose a child to SIDS feel guilty, and become extremely protective of older siblings or any babies born afterward. Help for parents is available through local groups or through the National SIDS Alliance in Maryland. Ask your pediatrician about resources in your area.

It usually disappears on its own within the first few months, but may have to be treated with a special shampoo. (See *Cradle Cap and Seborrheic Dermatitis,* page 630.)

2. Fingernail or Toenail Infections will appear as a redness around the edge of the toenail or fingernail, which may seem to hurt when touched. These infections may respond to warm compresses, but usually need to be examined by a doctor.

3. Umbilical Infections often appear as redness around the umbilical stump. They should be examined by your pediatrician.

4. Diaper Rash. See instructions for handling this problem on page 46.

Thrush. White patches in the mouth may indicate that your baby has thrush, a common yeast infection. This condition is treated with an oral antifungal medication prescribed by your pediatrician.

Vision. Watch how your baby looks at you when he is alert. When you're about 8 to 15 inches from his face, do his eyes follow you? Will he follow a light or small toy passing before him at the same distance? At this age, the eyes may appear crossed, or one eye may occasionally drift inward or outward. This is because the muscles controlling eye movement are still developing. Both eyes should be able to move equally and together in all directions, however, and he should be able to track slowly moving objects at close range. If he can't, or if he was born severely premature or needed oxygen as a newborn, your pediatrician may refer you to an eye specialist for further examination.

Vomiting. If your baby starts forcefully vomiting (shooting out several inches rather than dribbling from the mouth), contact your pediatrician at once to make sure the baby does not have an obstruction of the valve between the stomach and the small intestine (pyloric stenosis). Any vomiting that persists for more than twelve hours or is accompanied by diarrhea or fever also should be evaluated by your pediatrician.

Weight Gain. Your baby should be gaining weight rapidly (½ to 1 ounce per day) by the middle of this month. If he isn't, your pediatrician will want to make sure that he's getting adequate calories in his feedings and that he is absorbing them properly. Be prepared to answer the following questions:

- How often does the baby eat?

- How much does he eat at a feeding, if bottle-feeding? How long does he nurse, if breast-feeding?

- How many bowel movements does the baby have each day?

- What is the amount and thinness or thickness of the stools?

- How often does the baby urinate?

If your baby is eating well and the contents of his diapers are normal in amount and consistency, there is probably no cause for alarm. Your baby may just be getting off to a slow start, or his weight could even have been measured wrong. Your pediatrician may want to schedule another office visit in two or three days to reevaluate the situation.

SAFETY CHECK

Car Seats

- Your baby should ride in a properly installed, federally approved car seat *every time* he is in the car. At this age, he should ride in the rear-facing position.

Bathing

- When bathing the baby in the sink, seat him on a washcloth to prevent slipping, and hold him under the arms.

- Adjust the temperature of your water heater to less than 120 degrees so the hot water can't scald him.

Changing Table

- Never leave your baby unattended on any surface above the floor. Even at this young age, he can suddenly extend his body and flip over the edge.

Suffocation Prevention

- If you use baby powder, shake it out away from your infant's face so he doesn't inhale it.

- Keep the crib free of all small objects (safety pins, small parts of toys, etc.) that he could swallow.

- Never leave plastic bags or wrappings where your baby can reach them.

Fire Prevention

- Dress your baby in clothing treated with flame-retardant chemicals.

- Install smoke detectors in the proper places throughout your home.

Supervision

- Never leave your baby alone in the house, yard, or car.

Necklaces and Cords

- Don't attach pacifiers, medallions, or other objects to the crib or body with a cord.

- Don't place a string or necklace around the baby's neck.

Jiggling

- Be careful not to jiggle or shake the baby's head too vigorously.

- Always support the baby's head and neck when moving his body.

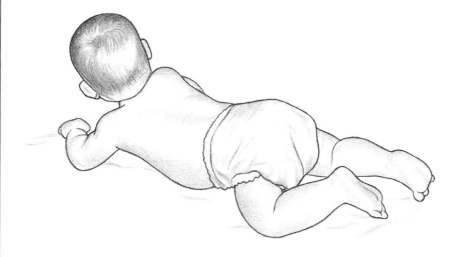

7

AGE ONE MONTH THROUGH THREE MONTHS

*B*y the beginning of your baby's second month, much of the awe, exhaustion, and uncertainty that you felt immediately after his birth has given way to self-confidence. You probably have settled into a fairly routine (if still grueling) schedule around his feedings and naps. You've adjusted to having a new member of the family and are beginning to understand his general temperament. And you probably have already received the crowning reward that makes all the sacrifice worthwhile: his first true smile. This smile is just a glimmer of the delights in store over the next three months.

Between one and four months, your baby will undergo a dramatic transformation from a totally dependent newborn to an active and

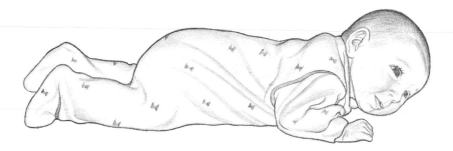

responsive infant. He'll lose many of his newborn reflexes while acquiring more voluntary control of his body. You'll find him spending hours inspecting his hands and watching their movements. He'll also become increasingly interested in his surroundings, especially the people close to him. He'll quickly learn to recognize your face and voice, and will often smile when he sees or hears you. Sometime during his second or third month, he'll even begin "talking" back to you in gentle but intentional coos and gurgles. With each of his new discoveries or achievements, you'll see a new part of your child's personality emerging.

Occasionally there will be moments in which your baby's development seems to be going backward. For example, he may have been sleeping through the night for several weeks—and then suddenly starts waking up every three hours again. What should you make of this? It's probably a sign that he's about to take a major developmental leap forward. In a week or two he'll probably be sleeping through the night again and taking fewer naps, and he'll be considerably more alert and responsive to people and events around him. Developmental progress like this is often preceded by what appears to be a slight setback. As frustrating as it may be at first, you'll soon learn to read the signals, anticipate, and appreciate these periods of change.

GROWTH AND DEVELOPMENT

Physical Appearance and Growth

From months one through four, your baby will continue growing at the same rate he established during his first few weeks of life. Each month he'll probably gain between 1½ and 2 pounds (0.7 to 0.9 kg) and grow 1 to 1½ inches (2.5 to 4 cm). His head size will probably increase in diameter by about ½ inch (1.25 cm) each month. These figures are only averages, however, so you shouldn't be concerned as long as your child's development matches one of the normal curves on the growth charts on pages 118–121.

At two months the soft spots on your baby's head should still be open and flat, but by four months the soft spot at the back should be closed. Also, his head

By his fourth-month
birthday, your baby
will be able to
hold up his head
and chest as he
supports himself
on his elbows.

may seem out of proportion, because it is growing faster than the rest of his body. This is quite normal; his body will soon catch up.

At two months your baby will look round and chubby, but as he starts using his arms and legs more actively, muscles will develop and fat will begin to disappear. His bones also will grow rapidly, and as his arms and legs "loosen up," his body and limbs will seem to stretch out, making him appear taller and leaner.

Movement

Many of your baby's movements will still be reflexive at the beginning of this period. For example, he may assume a "fencing" position every time his head turns (tonic neck reflex; see page 137) and throw out his arms if he hears a loud noise or feels that he's falling (Moro reflex, page 136). But as we've mentioned, most of these newborn reflexes will peak and begin to fade by the second or third month. He may temporarily seem less active after the reflexes have diminished, but now his movements, however subtle, are intentional ones and will build steadily toward mature activity.

One of the most important developments of these early months will be your baby's increasing neck strength. Try placing him on his stomach, and see what happens. Before two months he'll struggle to raise his head to look around. Even if he succeeds for only a second or two, that will at least allow him to turn for a slightly different view of the world, and move his nose and mouth away from any pillows or blankets that might be in the way. These momentary "exercises" also

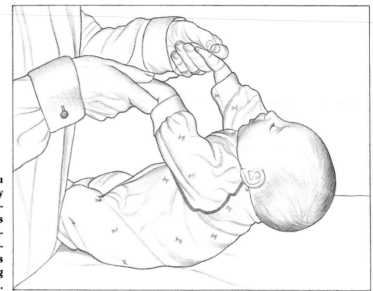

At one month, if you gently pull your baby by the arms to a sitting position, his head will flop backward (so always support your baby's head when picking him up).

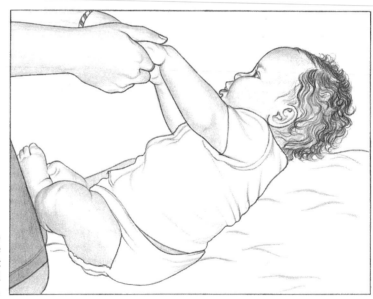

By four months, however, he'll be able to hold it steady in all directions.

will strengthen the muscles in the back of his neck so that, by his four-month birthday, he'll be able to hold up his head and chest as he supports himself on his elbows. This is a major accomplishment, giving him the freedom and control to look all around at will, instead of just staring at his crib mattress or the mobile directly overhead.

For you, it's also a welcome development because you no longer have to support his head quite so much when carrying him. If you use a front or back carrier,

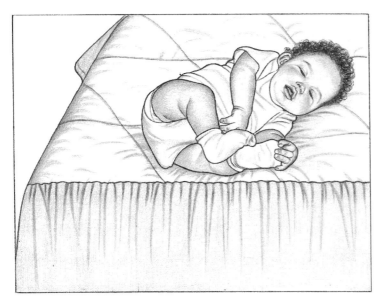

Since you can't predict when he'll begin rolling over, you'll need to be especially vigilant.

he'll now be able to hold his own head up and look around as you walk.

A baby's control over the front neck muscles and abdominal muscles develop more gradually, so it will take a little longer for your baby to be able to raise his head when lying on his back. At one month, if you gently pull your baby by the arms to a sitting position, his head will flop backward; by four months, however, he'll be able to hold it steady in all directions.

Your child's legs also will become stronger and more active. During the second month they'll start to straighten from their inward-curving newborn position. Though his kicks will remain mostly reflexive for some time, they'll quickly gather force, and by the end of the third month he might even kick himself over from front to back. (He probably won't roll from back to front until he's about six months old.) Since you cannot predict when he'll begin rolling over, you'll need to be especially vigilant whenever he's on the changing table or any other surface above floor level.

The newborn stepping reflex will disappear at about six weeks, and you may not see your baby step again until he's ready to walk. By three or four months, however, he'll be able to flex and straighten his legs at will. Lift him upright with his feet on the floor and he'll push down and straighten his legs so that he's virtually standing by himself (except for the balance you're providing). Then he'll try bending his knees and discover that he can bounce himself.

Your baby's hand and arm movements also will develop rapidly during these three months. In the beginning his hands will be tightly clenched with his thumb curled inside his fingers; if you uncoil the fingers and place a rattle in his palm, he'll grasp it automatically, yet he won't be able to shake it or bring it to his

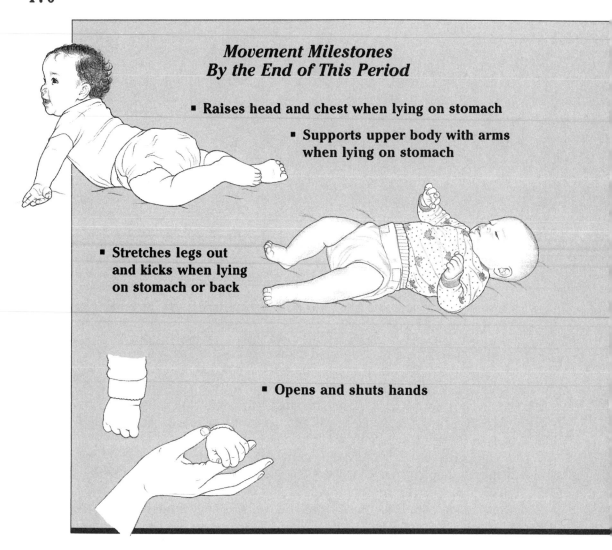

Movement Milestones
By the End of This Period

- Raises head and chest when lying on stomach

  - Supports upper body with arms when lying on stomach

- Stretches legs out and kicks when lying on stomach or back

- Opens and shuts hands

mouth. He'll gaze at his hands with interest when they come into view by chance or because of reflexive movements, but he probably won't be able to bring them to his face on his own.

However, many changes will occur within just a month or two. Suddenly your baby's hands will seem to relax and his arms will open outward. During the third month his hands will be half open most of the time, and you'll notice him carefully opening and shutting them. Try placing a rattle in his palm and he'll grip it, perhaps bring it to his mouth, and then drop it only after he's explored it fully. (The more lightweight the toy, the better he'll be able to control it.) He'll never seem to grow bored with his hands themselves; just staring at his fingers will amuse him for long stretches of time.

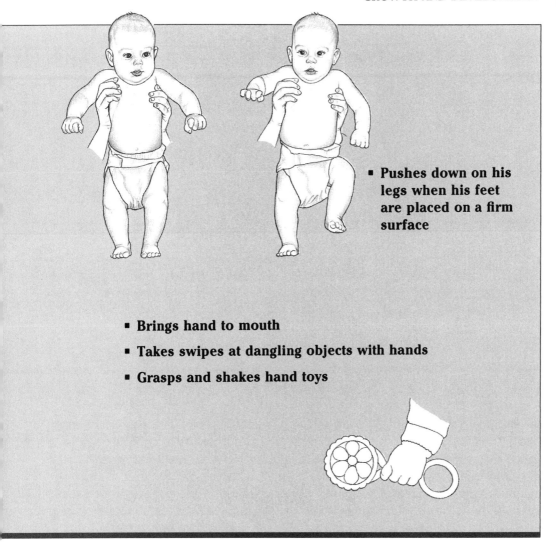

- **Pushes down on his legs when his feet are placed on a firm surface**

- **Brings hand to mouth**
- **Takes swipes at dangling objects with hands**
- **Grasps and shakes hand toys**

Your baby's attempts to bring his hands to his mouth will be persistent, but mostly in vain at first. Even if his fingers occasionally reach their destination, they'll quickly fall away. By four months, however, he'll probably have finally mastered this game and be able to get his thumb to his mouth and keep it there whenever he wishes. Put a rattle in his palm now and he'll clench it tightly, shake it, mouth it, and maybe even transfer it from hand to hand.

Your baby also will be able to reach accurately and quickly—not only with both hands but with his entire body. Hang a toy overhead and he'll reach up eagerly with arms and legs to bat at it and grab for it. His face will tense in concentration and he may even lift his head toward his target. It's as if every part of his body shares in his excitement as he masters these new skills.

By two months, your baby's eyes are more coordinated and can work together to move and focus at the same time.

Vision

At one month your baby still can't see very clearly beyond 12 inches or so, but he'll closely study anything within this range: the corner of his crib, the play of lights, the shadows on the wall, the shapes of his mobile. The human face is his favorite image, however. As you hold him in your arms his attention is drawn automatically to your face, particularly your eyes. Often the mere sight of your eyes will make him smile. Gradually his visual span will broaden so that he can take in your whole face instead of just a single feature like your eyes. As this happens he'll be much more responsive to facial expressions involving your mouth, jaw, and cheeks. He'll also love flirting with himself in the mirror. Buy an unbreakable mirror that's specially made to attach inside cribs and playpens, so he can entertain himself when you're not nearby.

In his early weeks your baby will have a hard time tracking movement. If you wave a ball or toy quickly in front of him, he'll seem to stare through it, or if you shake your head, he'll lose his focus on your eyes. But this will change dramatically by two months, when his eyes are more coordinated and can work together to move and focus at the same time. Soon he'll be able to track an object moving through an entire half-circle in front of him. This increased visual coordination also will give him the depth perception he needs to track objects as they move toward and away from him. By three months he'll also have the arm and hand control needed to bat at objects as they move above or in front of him; his aim

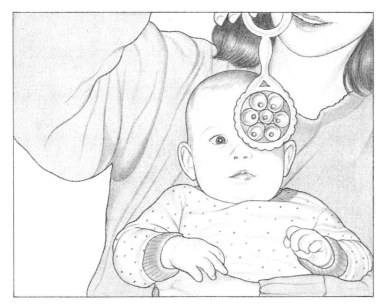

Soon he'll be able to track an object moving through an entire half-circle in front of him.

won't be very good for a long time to come, but the practice will help him develop his hand-eye coordination.

Your baby's distance vision is also developing at this time. You may notice at three months that he's smiling at you halfway across the room, or studying a toy several feet away. By four months you'll catch him staring at the distant television screen or looking out the window. These are clues that his distance vision is fully developed.

Visual Milestones
By the End of This Period

- **Watches faces intently**

- **Follows moving objects**

- **Recognizes familiar objects and people at a distance**

- **Starts using hands and eyes in coordination**

Your infant's color vision will mature at about the same rate. At one month he'll be quite sensitive to the brightness or intensity of color; consequently, he'll prefer to look at bold patterns in sharply contrasting colors or in black-and-white. The soothing pastels we usually associate with a newborn's nursery, in fact, are not appreciated by young infants because of their limited color vision. By about four months your baby will finally be responsive to the full range of colors and their many shades.

As his eyesight develops, your infant naturally will seek out more stimulating things to see. Around one month his favorite patterns will be simple linear images such as big stripes or a checkerboard. By three months he'll be much more interested in circular patterns (bull's-eyes, spirals). This is one reason why faces, which are full of circles and curves, are so appealing to him.

Hearing and Making Sounds

Just as your baby naturally prefers the human face over any other visual pattern, he also prefers the human voice to other sounds. His mother's voice is his absolute favorite, because he associates it with warmth, food, and comfort. Babies like the high-pitched voices of women in general—a fact that most adults seem to understand intuitively and respond to accordingly, without even realizing it.

Just listen to yourself the next time you talk to your baby. You'll probably notice that you raise the pitch of your voice, slow your rate of speech, exaggerate certain syllables, and widen your eyes and mouth more than normal. This dramatic approach is guaranteed to capture almost any baby's attention—and usually make him smile.

By listening to you and others talk to him, your baby will discover the importance of speech long before he understands or repeats any specific words himself. By one month he'll be able to identify you by voice, even if you're in another room, and as you talk to him he'll be reassured, comforted, and entertained. When he smiles and gurgles back at you, he'll see the delight on your face and realize that talk is a two-way process. These first conversations will teach him many of the subtle rules of communication, such as turn-taking, vocal tone, imitation and pacing, and speed of verbal interaction.

At about two months you may begin hearing your infant repeat some vowel sounds (ah-ah-ah, ooh-ooh-ooh), especially if you've been talking to him often with clear, simple words and phrases. Along the way, it's easy to fall into a habit of baby talk, but you should try to mix your conversations with adult language and phase out the baby talk after he's six months old.

By four months your infant will babble routinely, often amusing himself for long periods by producing strange new sounds (muh-muh, bah-bah). He'll also be more sensitive to your tone of voice and the emphasis you put on certain words or phrases. As you move through each day together he'll learn from your voice when you're going to feed him, change his diapers, go out for a walk, or put him down to sleep. The way you talk will tell him a great deal about your mood and personality, and the way he responds will tell you a lot about his. If you speak in an upbeat or comforting way, he may smile or coo. Yell or talk angrily, and he'll probably startle or cry.

*Hearing and Speech Milestones
By the End of This Period*

- **Smiles at the sound of your voice**

- **Begins to babble**

- **Begins to imitate some sounds**

- **Turns head toward direction of sound**

Emotional and Social Development

By the second month your baby will spend much of each day watching and listening to the people around him. He learns that they will entertain and soothe him, feed him, and make him comfortable. He feels good when they smile at him, and he seems to know instinctively that he can smile too. Even during his first month he'll experiment with primitive grins and grimaces. Then, during the second month, these movements will turn to genuine signals of pleasure and friendliness.

Have you experienced his first true smile yet? It's a major turning point for both you and your infant. In case there was any doubt in your mind, all the sleepless nights and erratic days of these first weeks suddenly seem worthwhile at the sight of that first grin, and you'll do everything in your power to keep those smiles coming. For his part, your baby will suddenly discover that just by moving his lips he can have two-way "conversations" with you, as his grins bring him even more attention than usual and make him feel good. Smiling will also give him another way besides crying to express his needs and exert some control over what happens to him.

At first your baby may actually seem to smile past you without meeting your gaze, but don't let this disturb you. Looking away from you gives him some control and protects him from being overwhelmed by you. It's his way of taking in the total picture without being "caught" by your eyes. This way, he can pay equal attention to your facial expressions, the sound of your voice, the warmth of your body, and the way you're holding him. As you get to know each other he'll gradually

As you get to know each other he'll gradually hold your gaze for longer and longer periods.

hold your gaze for longer and longer periods, and you'll find ways to increase his "tolerance"—perhaps by holding him at a certain distance, adjusting the level of your voice, or modifying your expressions.

By three months your baby will be a master of "smile talk." Sometimes he'll start a "conversation" by aiming a broad smile at you and gurgling to catch your attention. At other times he'll lie in wait, watching your face until you give the first smile and then beaming back his enthusiastic response. His whole body will participate in these dialogues. His hands will open wide, one or both arms will lift up, and his arms and legs will move in time with the rhythms of your speech. His facial movements may also mirror yours. As you talk he may open his mouth and widen his eyes, and if you stick out your tongue, he may do the same!

Of course your baby probably won't act this friendly with everyone. Like adults, your infant will prefer certain people to others. And his favorites, naturally, will be his parents. Then, at about three or four months, he'll become intrigued by other children. If he has brothers or sisters, you'll see him beaming as soon as they start talking to him. If he hears children's voices down the street or on television, he may turn to find them. This fascination with children will increase as he gets older.

Grandparents or familiar sitters may receive a hesitant smile at first, followed by coos and body talk once they've played with him awhile. By contrast, strangers may receive no more than a curious stare or a fleeting smile. This selective behavior tells you that even at this young age, he's starting to sort out who's who in his life. Although the signals are subtle, there's no doubt that he's becoming very attached to the people closest to him.

This unspoken give-and-take may seem like no more than a game, but these early exchanges play an important part in his social and emotional development. By responding quickly and enthusiastically to his smiles and engaging him often in these "conversations," you'll let him know that he's important to you, that he can trust you, and that he has a certain amount of control in his life. By recognizing his cues and not interrupting or looking away when he's "talking," you'll also show him that you are interested in him and value him. This contributes to his developing self-esteem.

As your baby grows, the way the two of you communicate will vary with his needs and desires. On a day-to-day basis you'll find that he has three general levels of need, each of which shows a different side of his personality:

1. When his needs are urgent—when he's very hungry or in pain, for instance—he'll let you know in his own special way, perhaps by screaming, whimpering, or using desperate body language. In time you'll learn to recognize these signals so quickly that you can usually satisfy him almost before he himself knows what he wants.

2. While your baby is peacefully asleep, or when he's alert and entertaining himself, you'll feel reassured that you've met all his needs for the moment. This will give you a welcome opportunity to rest or take care of other business. The times when he's playing by himself provide you with wonderful opportunities to observe—from a distance—how he is developing new skills such as reaching, tracking objects, or manipulating his hands.

3. Each day there will be periods when your baby's obvious needs are met but he's still fussy or fitful. He may let you know this with a whine, agitated movements, or spurts of aimless activity between moments of calm. He probably won't even know what he wants, and any of several responses might help calm him. Playing, talking, singing, rocking, and walking may work sometimes; on other occasions, simply repositioning him or letting him "fuss it out" may be the most successful strategies. You also may find that while a particular response calms him down momentarily, he'll soon become even fussier and demand more attention. This cycle may not break until you either let him cry a few minutes or distract him by doing something different—for example, taking him outside or feeding him. As trying as these spells can be, you'll both learn a lot about each other because

Social/Emotional Milestones
By the End of This Period

- Begins to develop a social smile

- Enjoys playing with other people, and may cry when playing stops

- Becomes more communicative and expressive with face and body

- Imitates some movements and facial expressions

of them. You'll discover how your baby likes to be rocked, what funny faces or voices he most enjoys, and what he most likes to look at. He'll find out what he has to do to get you to respond, how hard you'll try to please him, and where your limits of tolerance lie.

Over time your baby's periods of acute need will decrease, and he'll be able to entertain himself for longer stretches. In part, this is because you're learning to anticipate and care for many of his problems before he's uncomfortable. But also, his nervous system will be maturing, and as a result, he'll be better able to cope with everyday stresses by himself. With greater control over his body, he'll be able to do more things to amuse himself and he'll experience fewer frustrations. The periods when he seems most difficult to satisfy probably won't disappear entirely for a few years, but as he becomes more active it will be easier to distract him. Ultimately, he should learn to overcome these spells on his own.

During these early months, don't worry about spoiling him with too much attention. Observe your baby closely and respond promptly when he needs you. You may not be able to calm him down every time, but it never hurts to show him that you care. In fact, the more promptly and consistently you comfort your baby's fussing in the first six months, the less demanding he's likely to be when he's older. At this age he needs frequent reassurance in order to feel secure about himself and about you. By helping him establish this sense of security now, you're laying a foundation for the confidence and trust that will allow him gradually to separate from you and become a strong, independent person.

Developmental Health Watch

Although each baby develops in his own individual way and at his own rate, failure to reach certain milestones may signal medical or developmental problems requiring special attention. If you notice any of the following warning signs in your infant at this age, discuss them with your pediatrician.

- Still has Moro reflex after four months
- Doesn't seem to respond to loud sounds
- Doesn't notice his hands by two months
- Doesn't smile at the sound of your voice by two months
- Doesn't follow moving objects with his eyes by two to three months
- Doesn't grasp and hold objects by three months
- Doesn't smile at people by three months
- Cannot support his head well at three months
- Doesn't reach for and grasp toys by three to four months
- Doesn't babble by three to four months
- Doesn't bring objects to his mouth by four months
- Begins babbling, but doesn't try to imitate any of your sounds by four months
- Doesn't push down with his legs when his feet are placed on a firm surface by four months
- Has trouble moving one or both eyes in all directions
- Crosses his eyes most of the time. (Occasional crossing of the eyes is normal in these first months.)
- Doesn't pay attention to new faces, or seems very frightened by new faces or surroundings
- Still has the tonic neck reflex at four to five months

Toys and Activities Appropriate for a One- to Three-Month-Old

- Images or books with high-contrast patterns

- Bright, varied mobile

- Unbreakable mirror attached to inside of crib

- Rattles

- Sing to your baby.

- Play varied music from music boxes, records, or tapes.

BASIC CARE

Feeding

Ideally, your baby will continue on his diet of breast milk or formula without any additions from ages one month to four months. The amount he consumes at each feeding should gradually increase from about 4 or 5 ounces during the second month, to 5 or 6 ounces by four months. His daily intake should reach about 30 ounces by four months. Ordinarily, this will supply all his nutritional needs at this age.

If your baby seems persistently hungry after what you think are adequate feedings, consult your pediatrician for advice. When a breast-feeding infant is not gaining weight, your milk supply may have decreased and a supplemental bottle or two may be the answer. If it's clear that he's getting enough milk but is still hungry, the doctor may advise you to start solid foods. Solids should be introduced only near the end of this period, however, because younger babies don't have much control over the muscles in the tongue and mouth, which makes spoon-feeding difficult. Also, young infants may not be able to tolerate certain solid foods. If you do need to introduce solids, start with the least allergenic food, which is rice cereal, and thin it as much as possible with breast milk or formula. (For more information about introducing solids, see Chapter 8.)

Even if you don't make any additions to your baby's diet, you'll probably notice a change in his bowel movements during these months. His intestines can now hold more and absorb a greater amount of nutrients from the milk, so the stools will tend to be more solid. The gastrocolic reflex is also diminishing, so he should no longer have a bowel movement after each feeding. (See *Bowel Movements,* page 45.) In fact, between two and three months, the frequency of stools in both breast-fed and bottle-fed babies may decrease dramatically; some breast-fed babies have only one bowel movement every three or four days, and a few perfectly healthy breast-fed infants have just one a week. As long as your baby is eating well, gaining weight, and his stools are not too hard or dry, there's no reason to be alarmed by this drop in frequency.

Sleep

By two months your baby will be more alert and social, and will spend more time awake during the day. This will make him a little more tired during the dark, quiet hours when no one is on hand to entertain him. Meanwhile, his stomach capacity will be growing, so that he needs less frequent feedings; as a result he may start skipping one middle-of-the-night feeding and sleep from around 10:00 P.M. through to daylight. By three months, most (but not all) infants consistently sleep through the night (seven or eight hours without waking).

If your child does not start sleeping through the night by three months, you may need to give him some encouragement by keeping him awake longer in the afternoon and early evening. Play with him actively at these times, or let him join the rest of the family in the kitchen or living room so he's not tempted to drift to sleep before bedtime. Increase the amount of his feeding right before bed as well (if he's breast-feeding, increase the amount of time he nurses), so he doesn't wake up too early because he's hungry.

Even after your baby has established a fairly regular and reasonable sleep pattern, problems can develop. For example, it's common for babies at this age to get their days and nights mixed up so that they're doing most of their sleeping during the day. Although this situation may seem to occur without warning, it usually develops over several days. The baby begins by sleeping more during the day, which causes him to sleep less at night. If he's fed and comforted when he wakes up at night, he'll adopt this new sleep cycle quite naturally. To prevent or break this habit, induce your baby to go back to sleep as quickly as possible during the night. Don't turn up the lights, talk, or play with him. If you need to feed and change him, try to disturb him as little as possible when doing so. Then keep him awake as much as possible during the day, and don't put him down for the night before 10:00 or 11:00 P.M. If you're patient and consistent, his sleep pattern will soon start to respond. (See *Helping Your Baby Sleep,* page 37.)

Many infants also wake up too early in the morning to suit their parents. Sometimes this problem can be solved by putting shades on the windows to block

After three months, most (but not all) infants consistently sleep through the night.

out the morning sun; then when the baby awakens, perhaps after a few minutes of fussing, he may fall back to sleep. If this doesn't work, however, it may help to keep him up an extra hour at night. Unfortunately, not all infants are able to sleep late in the morning; some wake up automatically, and are ready to start the day at dawn. If that's your own baby's pattern, you really have little choice but to adapt to his schedule. As he gets older (age six to eight months) having favorite toys in his crib may keep him occupied so you can have a few more minutes to sleep.

Sometimes you may think your baby is waking up when he's actually going through a phase of very light slumber. He could be squirming, startling, fussing, or even crying—and still be asleep. Or he may be awake but on the verge of drifting off again if left alone. Don't make the mistake of trying to comfort him during these moments; you'll only awaken him further and delay his going back to sleep. Instead, if you let him fuss and even cry for a few minutes, he'll learn to get himself to sleep without relying on you. Some babies actually need to let off energy by crying in order to settle into sleep or rouse themselves out of it. As much as fifteen to twenty minutes of fussing won't do your child any harm. Just be sure he's not crying out of hunger or pain, or because his diaper is wet. Though it may be difficult just to let him cry for even a minute or two, you and he will be much better off in the long run.

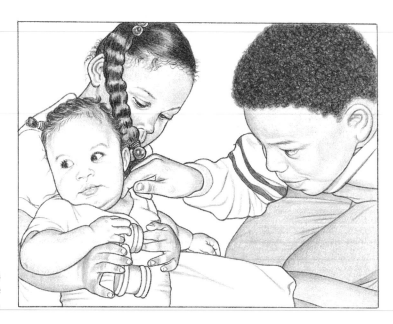

Invite older siblings to play with the baby.

Siblings

By the second month, although you may be used to having a new baby in the house, your older children may still be having a hard time adjusting. Especially if the baby is your second child, your first probably resents giving up the central place in the household. No longer the primary focus of the family, he may do everything in his power to recapture that position—and that usually involves misbehaving.

Sometimes your older child might display his frustration by talking back, doing something he knows is forbidden, or literally shouting for attention. He might also regress, suddenly wetting his bed or having daytime accidents even though he's been toilet-trained for months. Having each parent take time with him alone each day should help resolve these problems.

However, if the older child takes out his anger on the baby—pulling away his bottle or even hitting him—you'll need to take more direct action. Sit down and talk with him, and be prepared to hear things such as "I wish that baby had never come here." Try to keep these and his other feelings in mind as you confront him. Reassure him that you still love him very much, but explain firmly that he must not hurt the baby. Make an extra effort to include him in all family activities, and invite him to play with the newborn. Make him feel like an important "big kid" by giving him specific baby-related jobs, such as carrying the diaper bag, putting away toys, or helping dress the baby. At the same time, set clear and consistent rules, such as never picking up the baby without permission.

Set clear and consistent rules, such as never picking up the baby without permission.

HEALTH WATCH

The following medical problems are common between the ages of two months and four months. Check Part II of this book for other illnesses and conditions that occur throughout childhood.

Diarrhea. (See also *Diarrhea*, page 476.) If your baby has a vomiting spell followed a day or two later by diarrhea, he probably has a viral infection in his intestinal tract. If you're breast-feeding, your pediatrician will probably suggest that you continue nursing him as usual. If you're bottle-feeding, he may advise you to limit the baby's intake to plain water or a special solution containing electrolytes (such as salt and potassium) and sugar. When milk-feeding is restarted, you may be advised to use a soy formula for a few days. This is because diarrhea washes out the enzymes needed to digest the sugar in cow's milk.

Ear Infections. (See also *Ear Infection,* page 537.) Although ear infections are more common in older babies, they occasionally occur in infants under three months. Babies are prone to ear infections because the tube that connects the nasal passages to the middle ear is very short, making it easy for a cold in the nose to spread to the ear. If the infection becomes severe or is not treated, the eardrum may break and the infected fluid will pass through it and out the ear canal. With proper treatment, however, the eardrum will heal with no permanent damage.

The first sign of an ear infection is usually irritability, especially at night. Your baby also may use his hand to pull or swipe at his ear. As the infection advances, it may produce a fever. If you suspect that your child has an ear infection, call the doctor as soon as possible. If an ear examination confirms that an infection is present, the doctor will prescribe a course of antibiotics.

Rashes and Skin Conditions. Many of the rashes seen in the first month may persist through the second or third. In addition, eczema may occur any time after one month. Eczema, or atopic dermatitis (see also *Eczema,* page 631), produces dry, scaly, and often red patches, usually on the face, in the bends of the elbows, and behind the knees. In young infants, elbows and knees are the most common locations. The patches are extremely itchy, which may make your baby irritable. Ask your pediatrician to prescribe treatment. Don't use any over-the-counter lotions or creams unless he specifically recommends them. To prevent a recurrence of the rash, make sure you use only the mildest of soaps to wash your baby and his clothes, and dress him only in soft clothing (no wool or rough weaves). Bathe him no more than three times a week, since frequent baths may further dry his skin.

Upper Respiratory Infections (URI). (See also *Colds/Upper Respiratory Infection,* page 535.) Many babies have their first cold during these months. Breast-feeding provides some immunity, but it is not complete protection by any means, especially if another member of the family has a respiratory illness. The infection can spread easily through droplets in the air or by hand contact. (Exposure to cold temperatures or drafts does *not* cause colds.) Washing hands, covering mouths while sneezing or coughing, and refraining from kissing when you have a cold will help prevent the infection from spreading to others.

Most respiratory infections in young babies are mild, producing a cough, runny nose, and slightly elevated temperature, but rarely a high fever. A runny nose, however, can be troublesome for an infant. He cannot blow his nose, so the mucus blocks the nasal passages. Before three or four months of age, an infant doesn't breathe well through his nose, so this blockage of his nose causes more discomfort for him than for older children. A congested nose also often disturbs his sleep because he wakes up when he's not able to breathe. It can interfere with feeding, too, since he must interrupt sucking in order to breathe through his mouth.

To help reduce this problem, use a cool-mist humidifier in his room. If congestion does occur, use a bulb syringe to suction the mucus from his nose, especially before feedings and when it's obviously blocked. If you put a few drops of normal saline (prescribed by your pediatrician) into his nose first, this will thin the mucus, making it easier to suction. Squeeze the bulb first; *then* insert the tip gently into the nostril and slowly release the bulb. Although acetaminophen will lower an elevated temperature and calm him if he's irritable, you should give it to a baby this age *only* on your pediatrician's advice. *Do not use aspirin.* (See *Reye Syndrome,* page 490; *Medication,* page 659.)

Ordinarily, you won't need to take your baby to the doctor when he has an upper respiratory infection. You should call, however, if any of the following occurs:

- He develops a persistent cough.

- He loses his appetite and refuses several feedings.

- He runs a fever: *Anytime your baby has a rectal temperature higher than 101 degrees, you should contact your pediatrician.*

- He seems excessively irritable.

- He seems unusually sleepy or hard to awaken.

IMMUNIZATION ALERT

At birth, and again at one to two months, your baby should receive:

- Hepatitis B vaccine

At two months, and again at four months, your baby should receive:

- DTP vaccine
- Oral polio vaccine
- Hib Conjugate vaccine. (This may cause a slight fever and some soreness where it's infected. The vaccine helps prevent meningitis, pneumonia, and joint infection caused by *Haemophilus influenzae* bacteria.

(For detailed information, see page 63 and Chapter 27, "Immunizations.")

SAFETY CHECK

Falls
- Never place the baby in an infant seat on a table, chair, or any other surface above floor level.

- Never leave your baby unattended on a bed, couch, table, or chair.

Burns

- Never hold your baby while smoking, drinking a hot liquid, or cooking by a hot stove or oven.

- Never allow anyone to smoke around your baby.
- Before placing your baby in the bath, always test the water temperature with the inside of your wrist or forearm.

- Never heat your baby's milk (or, later on, food), in a microwave oven.

Choking

- Routinely check all toys for sharp edges or small parts that could be pulled or broken off.

- If you use a crib gym or other suspended toys for the crib, make sure they are fastened securely and tightly so the baby cannot pull them down or entangle himself in them.

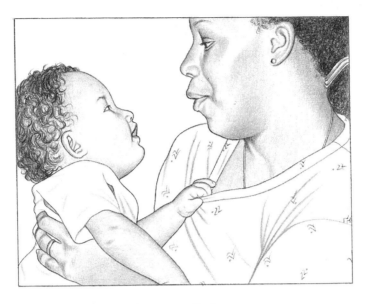

8

AGE FOUR MONTHS THROUGH SEVEN MONTHS

*B*y your infant's four-month birthday you'll probably have a daily routine for his feeding, napping, bathing, and going to sleep at night. This routine will provide a predictability that will help your baby feel secure while allowing you to budget your time and activities. The schedule should be flexible, however, to allow for spur-of-the-moment fun. Short strolls when the sun finally appears on a dreary day, an unexpected lunch visit from grandparents, or a family excursion to the zoo or park are all wonderful excuses to break the routine. Being open to impulse will make your life together more enjoyable and help your baby learn to adapt to all the changes facing him in his life ahead.

For the time being, the most important changes are taking place within him. This is the period when he'll learn to coordinate his emerging perceptive abilities (the use of senses like vision, touch, and hearing) and his increasing motor abilities to develop skills like grasping, rolling over, sitting up, and possibly even crawling. The control that's evident in his budding motor skills will extend to every part of his life. Instead of reacting primarily by reflex, as he did during his earlier months, he'll now choose what he will and won't do. For example, as a newborn he sucked on almost anything placed in his mouth, but now he has definite favorites. Though in the past he merely looked at a strange new toy, now he mouths, manipulates, and explores every one of its qualities.

Your baby will be better able to communicate his emotions and desires now, and he'll voice them frequently. For example, he'll cry not only when he's hungry or uncomfortable, but also when he wants a different toy or a change in activity.

You may find that your five- or six-month-old also occasionally cries when you leave the room or when he's suddenly confronted by a stranger. This is because he's developing a strong attachment for you and the other people who regularly care for him. He now associates you with his own well-being and can distinguish you from other people. Even if he doesn't cry out for you, he will signal this new awareness by curiously and carefully studying a stranger's face. By eight or nine months, he may openly object to strangers who come too close. This signals the start of a normal developmental stage known as "stranger anxiety."

During these months before stranger anxiety hits full force, however, your child will probably go through a period of delightful "show-offmanship," smiling and playing with everyone he meets. His personality will be coming out in full bloom, and even people meeting him for the first time will notice many of his unique character traits. Take advantage of his sociability to acquaint him with people who will help care for him in the future, such as babysitters, relatives, or child-care workers. This won't guarantee clear sailing through the stranger-anxiety period, but it may help smooth the waters.

You'll also learn during these months, if you haven't before, that there is no formula for raising an ideal child. You and your baby are each unique, and the relationship between the two of you is unique as well. So what works for one baby may not for another. You have to discover what succeeds for *you* through trial and error. While your neighbor's child may fall asleep easily and sleep through the night, your baby may need some extra holding and cuddling to settle him down at bedtime and again in the middle of the night. While your first child might have needed a great deal of hugging and comforting, your second might prefer more time alone. These individual differences don't necessarily indicate that your parenting is "right" or "wrong"; they just mean that each baby is unique. Over these first months and years you will get to know your child's individual traits and you'll develop patterns of activity and interaction that are designed especially for him. If you remain flexible and open to his special traits, he'll help steer your actions as a parent in the right direction.

GROWTH AND DEVELOPMENT

Physical Appearance and Growth

Between four and seven months your baby will continue to gain approximately 1 to 1¼ pounds (.45 to .56 kilograms) a month. By the time he reaches his eight-month birthday, he probably will weigh about two and a half times what he did at birth. His bones also will continue to grow at a rapid rate, and as a result during these months his length will increase by about 2 inches (5 centimeters) and his head circumference by about 1 inch (2.5 centimeters).

Your child's specific weight and height are not as important as his *rate* of growth. By now you should have established his position on the growth curve on page 121. Continue to plot his measurements at regular intervals to make sure he keeps growing at the same rate. If you find that he's beginning to follow a different curve or gaining weight or height unusually slowly, discuss it with your pediatrician.

Movement

In his first four months your baby established the muscle control he needed to move both his eyes and his head so he could follow interesting objects. Now he'll take on an even greater challenge—sitting up. He'll accomplish this in small steps as his back and neck muscles gradually strengthen and he develops better balance in his trunk, head, and neck. First he'll learn to raise his head and hold it up while lying on his stomach. You can encourage this by placing him on his stomach and extending his arms forward; then hold a rattle or other attractive toy in front of him to get his attention and coax him to hold his head up and look at you. This also is a good way to check his hearing and vision.

Once he's able to lift up his head, your baby will start pushing up on his arms and arching his back to lift his chest. This strengthens his upper body so he can remain steady and upright when sitting. At the same time he may rock on his stomach, kick his legs, and "swim" with his arms. These abilities, which usually appear at about five months, are necessary for rolling over and crawling. By the end of this period he'll probably be able to roll over in both directions. Most children are able to roll first from the stomach to the back and later in the opposite direction, though doing it in the opposite sequence is perfectly normal too.

Once your baby is strong enough to raise his chest, you can help him "practice" sitting up. Hold him up or support his back with pillows or a couch corner as he learns to balance himself. Soon he'll learn to "tripod," leaning forward as he extends his arms to balance his upper body. Bright, interesting toys placed in front of him will give him something to focus on as he gains his balance. It will be some time before he can maneuver himself into a sitting posture without your assistance, but by six to eight months, if you position him upright, he'll be able to remain sitting without leaning forward on his arms. Then he can discover all the wonderful things that can be done with his hands as he views the world from this new vantage point.

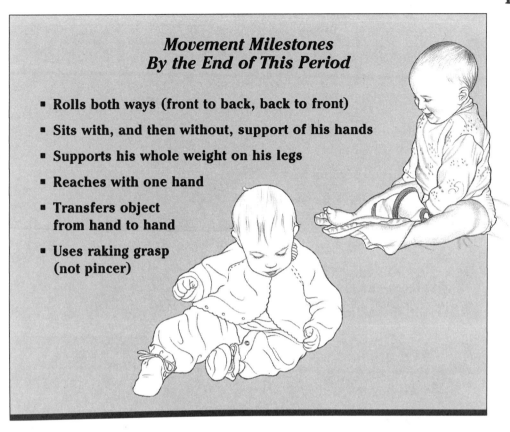

Movement Milestones
By the End of This Period

- **Rolls both ways (front to back, back to front)**

- **Sits with, and then without, support of his hands**

- **Supports his whole weight on his legs**

- **Reaches with one hand**

- **Transfers object from hand to hand**

- **Uses raking grasp (not pincer)**

By the fourth month your baby can easily bring interesting objects to his mouth. During his next four months he'll begin to use his fingers and thumbs together in a mitten or clawlike grip or raking motion, and he'll manage to pick up many things. He won't develop the pincer grasp using his index finger and thumb until he's about nine months old, but by the sixth to eighth month he'll learn how to transfer objects from hand to hand, turn them from side to side, and twist them upside down.

As his physical coordination improves, your baby will discover parts of his body that he never knew existed. Lying on his back he can now grab his feet and toes and bring them to his mouth. While being diapered, he may reach down to

Toys Appropriate for a Four- to Seven-Month-Old

- Unbreakable mirror attached to inside of crib or playpen

- Soft balls, including some that make soft, pleasant sounds

- Textured toys that make sounds

- Toys that have fingerholds

- Musical toys, such as bells, maracas, tambourines (make sure none of the parts can become loose)

- See-through rattles that show the pieces making the noise

- Old magazines with bright pictures for you to show him

- Baby books with board, cloth, or vinyl pages

touch his genitals. When sitting up he may slap his knee or thigh. Through these explorations he'll discover many new and interesting sensations. He'll also start to understand the function of each body part. For example, when you place his newly found feet on the floor, he may first curl his toes and stroke the carpet or wood surface, but soon he'll discover he can use his feet and legs to practice "walking" or just to bounce up and down. Watch out! These are all preparations for the next major milestones: crawling and standing.

Vision

As your baby works on his important motor skills, have you noticed how closely he watches everything he's doing? The concentration with which he reaches for a toy may remind you of a scientist engrossed in research. It's obvious that his good vision is playing a key role in his early motor and cognitive development. Conveniently, his eyes become fully functional just when he needs them most.

By four months your baby will begin noticing not only the way you talk but the individual sounds you make.

Although your baby was able to see at birth, his total visual ability has taken months to develop fully. Only now can he distinguish subtle shades of reds, blues, and yellows. Don't be surprised if you notice that he prefers red or blue to other colors; these seem to be favorites among many infants this age. Most babies also like increasingly complex patterns and shapes as they get older—something to keep in mind when you're shopping for picture books or posters for your child's nursery.

By four months your baby's range of vision has increased to several feet or more, and it will continue to expand until, at about seven months, his eyesight will be more mature. At the same time, he'll learn to follow faster and faster movements with his eyes. In the early months, when you rolled a ball across the room he couldn't coordinate his eyes well enough to track it, but now he'll easily follow the path of moving objects. As his hand-to-eye coordination improves, he'll be able to grab these objects as well.

A mobile hung over the crib or in front of the infant seat is an ideal way to stimulate a *young* baby's vision. However, by about five months your baby will quickly get bored and search for other things to watch. Also by this age, he may be sitting up and might pull down or tangle himself in a mobile. *For this reason, mobiles should be removed from cribs or playpens as soon as your baby is able to pull or hold himself upright.*

Still another way to hold your baby's visual interest is to keep him moving—around your home, down the block, to the store, or out on special excursions. Help him find things to look at that he's never seen before, and name each one out loud for him.

A mirror is another source of endless fascination for babies this age. The reflected image is constantly changing, and even more important, it responds directly to your child's own movements. This is his clue that the person in the mirror is actually himself. It may take your baby a while to come to this realization, but it probably will register during this period.

In general, then, your child's visual awareness should clearly *increase* during these four months. Watch how he responds as you introduce him to new shapes, colors, and objects. If he doesn't seem to be interested in looking at new things, or if one or both eyes turn in or out, inform your pediatrician. (See also Chapter 21, "Eyes.")

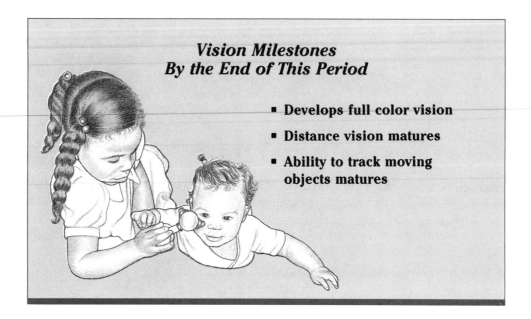

Vision Milestones By the End of This Period

- Develops full color vision
- Distance vision matures
- Ability to track moving objects matures

Language Development

Your baby learns language in stages. From birth he *receives* information about langauge by hearing people make sounds and watching how they communicate with one another. At first he is most interested in the pitch and level of your voice. When you talk to him in a soothing way, he'll stop crying because he hears that you want to comfort him. By contrast, if you shout out in anger he probably will cry, because your voice is telling him something is wrong. By four months he'll begin noticing not only the way you talk but the individual sounds you make. He'll listen to the vowels and consonants, and begin to notice the way these combine into syllables, words, and sentences.

As well as receiving sounds, your baby also has been producing them from the very beginning, first in the form of cries and then as coos. At about four months he'll start to babble, using many of the rhythms and characteristics of his native language. Though it may sound like gibberish, if you listen closely you'll hear him raise and drop his voice as if he were making a statement or asking a question. Encourage him by talking to him throughout the day. When he says a recognizable syllable, repeat it back to him and then say some simple words that contain that sound. For example, if his sound of the day is "bah," introduce him to "bottle," "box," "bonnet," and "Baa, Baa, Black Sheep."

Your participation in your child's language development will become even more important after six or seven months when he begins actively imitating the sounds of speech. Up to that point he might repeat one sound for a whole day or even days at a stretch before trying another. But now he'll become much more responsive to the sounds he hears you make, and he'll try to follow your lead. So introduce him to simple syllables and words like "baby," "cat," "dog," "go," "hot," "cold," and "walk," as well as "Mama" and "Dada." Although it may be as much as a year before you can interpret any of his babbling, your baby can understand many of your words well before his first birthday.

If he doesn't babble or imitate any sounds by his seventh month, it could mean a problem with his hearing or speech development. A baby with a partial hearing loss still can be startled by loud noises or will turn his head in their direction, and he may even respond to your voice. But he will have difficulty imitating speech. If your child does not babble or produce a variety of sounds, alert your pediatrician. If he has had frequent ear infections he might have some fluid remaining in his inner ear, and this could interfere with his hearing.

Language Milestones By the End of This Period

- **Responds to own name**
- **Begins to respond to "no"**
- **Distinguishes emotions by tone of voice**
- **Responds to sound by making sounds**
- **Uses voice to express joy and displeasure**
- **Babbles chains of consonants**

A very young baby's hearing can be checked by using special equipment, but your observations are the early warning system that tells whether such testing is needed. If you suspect a problem, you might ask your pediatrician for a referral to a children's hearing specialist.

Cognitive Development

During your baby's first four months did you have doubts that he really understood much that was happening around him? This parental reaction is not surprising. After all, although you knew when he was comfortable and uncomfortable, he probably showed few signs of actually *thinking*. Now, as his memory and attention span increase, you'll start to see evidence that he's not only absorbing information but also applying it to his day-to-day activities.

During this period, one of the most important concepts he'll refine is the principle of cause and effect. He'll probably stumble upon this notion by accident somewhere between four and five months. Perhaps while kicking his mattress, he'll notice the crib shaking. Or maybe he'll realize that his rattle makes a noise when he hits or waves it. Once he understands that he can *cause* these interesting reactions, he'll continue to experiment with other ways to make things happen.

Your baby will quickly discover that some things, like bells and keys, make interesting sounds when moved or shaken. When he bangs certain things on the

When he bangs certain things on the table or drops them on the floor, he'll start a chain of responses from his audience.

table or drops them on the floor, he'll start a chain of responses from his audience, including funny faces, groans, and other reactions that may lead to the reappearance—or disappearance—of the object. Before long, he'll begin intentionally dropping things to see you pick them up. As annoying as this may be at times, it's one important way for him to learn about cause and effect and his personal ability to influence his environment.

It's important that you give your child the objects he needs for these experiments and encourage him to test his "theories." But make sure that everything you give him to play with is unbreakable, lightweight, and large enough that he can't possibly swallow it. If you run out of the usual toys or he loses interest in them, plastic or wooden spoons, unbreakable cups, and jar or bowl lids and boxes are endlessly entertaining and inexpensive.

Another major discovery that your baby will make during this period is that objects continue to exist when they're out of his sight—a principle called *object permanence*. During his first few months he assumed that the world consisted only of things that he could see. When you left his room, he assumed you vanished; when you returned you were a whole new person to him. In much the same way, when you hid a toy under a cloth or a box, he thought it was gone for good and wouldn't bother looking for it. But sometime after four months he'll begin to realize that the world is more permanent than he thought. You're the same person who greets him every morning. His teddy bear on the floor is the same one that was in bed with him the night before. The block that you hid under the can did not actually vanish after all. By playing hiding games and observing the comings and goings of people and things around him, your baby will continue to learn about object permanence for many months to come.

Cognitive Milestones
By the End of This Period

- **Finds partially hidden object**

- **Explores with hands and mouth**

- **Struggles to get objects that are out of reach**

Developmental Health Watch

Because each baby develops in his own particular manner, it's impossible to tell exactly when or how your child will perfect a given skill. The developmental milestones listed in this book will give you a general idea of the changes you can expect, but don't be alarmed if your own baby's development takes a slightly different course. Alert your pediatrician, however, if your baby displays any of the following signs of possible developmental delay for this age range.

- Seems very stiff, with tight muscles
- Seems very floppy, like a rag doll
- Head still flops back when body is pulled up to a sitting position
- Reaches with one hand only
- Refuses to cuddle
- Shows no affection for the person who cares for him
- Doesn't seem to enjoy being around people
- One or both eyes consistently turn in or out
- Persistent tearing, eye drainage, or sensitivity to light

Emotional Development

Between four and seven months your baby may undergo a dramatic change in personality. At the beginning of this period he may seem relatively passive and preoccupied with getting enough food, sleep, and affection. But as he learns to sit up, use his hands, and move about, he's likely to become increasingly assertive and more attentive to the world outside. He'll be eager to reach out and touch everything he sees, and if he can't manage on his own, he'll demand your help by yelling, banging, or dropping the nearest object at hand. Once you've come to his rescue, he'll probably forget what he was doing and concentrate on you—smiling, laughing, babbling, and imitating you for many minutes at a stretch. While he'll quickly get bored with even the most engaging toy, he'll never tire of your attention.

- Does not respond to sounds around him
- Has difficulty getting objects to his mouth
- Does not turn his head to locate sounds by four months
- Doesn't roll over in either direction (front to back or back to front) by five months
- Seems inconsolable at night after five months
- Doesn't smile spontaneously by five months
- Cannot sit with help by six months
- Does not laugh or make squealing sounds by six months
- Does not actively reach for objects by six to seven months
- Doesn't follow objects with both eyes at near (1 foot) and far (6 feet) ranges by seven months
- Does not bear some weight on legs by seven months
- Does not try to attract attention through actions by seven months
- Does not babble by eight months
- Shows no interest in games of peekaboo by eight months

The more subtle aspects of your baby's personality are determined largely by his constitutional makeup or temperament. Is he rambunctious or gentle? Easygoing or easily upset? Headstrong or compliant? To a large extent these are inborn character traits, and they'll become increasingly apparent during these months. You won't necessarily find all of these characteristics enjoyable all the time— especially not when your determined six-month-old is screaming in frustration as he lunges for the family cat. But in the long run, adapting to his natural personality is best for both of you.

Strong-willed and high-strung babies require an extra dose of patience and gentle guidance. They often don't adapt to changing surroundings as easily as calmer babies, and will become increasingly upset if pushed to move or perform before they're ready. For an irritable child, language and cuddling will sometimes do wonders to calm his nerves. Distracting him can also often help refocus his energy. For instance, if he screams because you won't retrieve the toy he dropped for the tenth time, move him to the floor so he can reach the toy himself.

The shy or "sensitive" child also requires special attention, particularly if you have more boisterous children in the household who overshadow him. When a baby is quiet and undemanding, it's easy to assume he's content, or if he doesn't laugh or smile a lot, you may lose interest in playing with him. But a baby like this often needs personal contact even more than other children. He may be easily overwhelmed and needs you to show him how to be assertive and become involved in the activities around him. How should you do this? Give him plenty of time to warm up to any situation, and make sure that other people approach him slowly. Let him sit on the sidelines before attempting to involve him directly with other children. Once he feels secure, he'll gradually become more responsive to the people around him.

Also let your pediatrician know if you have any concerns about your baby's emotional development. Your pediatrician can help if he knows there are problems, but they can be difficult to detect in a routine office visit. That's why it's important for you to call the doctor's attention to your concerns, and describe your day-to-day observations. Write them down so you don't forget them.

Social/Emotional Milestones
By the End of This Period

- **Enjoys social play**

- **Interested in mirror images**

- **Responds to other people's expressions of emotion**

BASIC CARE

Introducing Solid Foods

At four months your baby's diet still consists mainly of breast milk and/or formula (with added fluoride, vitamins, or iron if your pediatrician recommends it), but by four to six months you can begin adding solid foods. Some babies are ready for solids as early as three months, but most have not lost their tongue-thrust reflex at that age. Because of this reflex, the young infant will push his tongue against a spoon or anything else inserted into his mouth, including food. Most babies lose this reflex at about four months. Coincidentally, the baby's energy needs increase around this age, making it an ideal time to start adding different calories through solids.

You may start solid food at whichever feedings during the day are most acceptable to you and your baby. However, remember that as he gets older he will want to eat with the other family members. To minimize the chances of choking, make sure your baby is sitting up, either in your lap or in an infant seat, when you introduce solids. If he cries or turns away when you try to feed him, don't force the issue. It's more important that you both enjoy his mealtimes than for him to start these foods by a specific date. Go back to nursing or bottle-feeding exclusively for a week or two; then try again.

Always use a spoon to feed your baby solids. Some parents try putting solid foods in a bottle or infant feeder with a nipple, but feeding a baby this way can drastically increase the amount of food he takes in at each feeding and lead to excessive weight gain. Besides, it's important for your baby to get used to the process of eating—sitting up, taking bites from a spoon, resting between bites, and stopping when he's full. This early experience will help lay the foundation for good eating habits throughout his life.

Even standard baby spoons may be too wide for a child this young, but a small coffee spoon will work well. Start with half a spoonful or less (about a quarter of a teaspoonful) and talk your baby through the process ("Mmm, see how good this is"). He probably won't know what to do the first time or two. He may look confused or insulted, wrinkle his nose, and roll the food around his mouth or reject it entirely. This is an understandable reaction, considering how different his feedings have been up to this point.

One way to ease the transition to solids is to give your infant a little milk first, then switch to very small half-spoonfuls of food, and finally finish off with more milk. This will prevent him from being overly frustrated when he's very hungry, and it will link the satisfaction of nursing with this new experience of spoon-feeding.

No matter what you do, most of the first few solid-food feedings are sure to wind up outside his mouth on his face and bib, so increase the size of his feedings

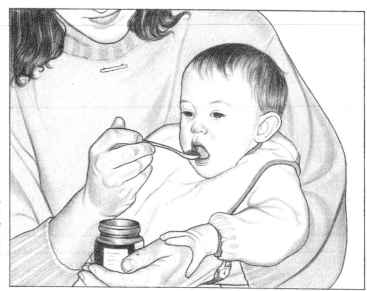

Start with half a spoonful or less (about a quarter of a teaspoonful) and talk your baby through the process.

very gradually, starting with just a teaspoonful or two, until he gets the idea of swallowing solids.

For most babies the first solid food is rice cereal, followed by oatmeal and barley. Generally, it's a good idea to introduce wheat and mixed cereals last, since they may cause allergic reactions in very young babies.

You may use premixed baby cereals in a jar or dry varieties to which you add formula, breast milk, or water. The prepared products are convenient, but the dry ones are richer in iron and can be varied in consistency to suit your baby. Whichever you choose, make sure that it's made for babies. This assures you that it contains the extra nutrients your child needs at this age.

Once your baby has accepted cereal, slowly start introducing him to other foods. One possible order is strained vegetables (except corn, which is difficult for most infants to digest before six months), fruit, and meat. Give your baby just one new food at a time, and wait at least two to three days before starting another. After each new food, watch for allergic responses such as diarrhea, rash, or vomiting. If any of these occur, eliminate the suspect food from his diet until you've consulted your pediatrician. Within two or three months your baby's daily diet should include breast milk or formula, cereal, vegetables, meats, and fruits, distributed among three meals. Because it frequently is associated with allergy, egg is started last.

Once your baby sits up, you can give him finger foods to help him learn to feed himself. Make sure anything you give him is soft, easy to swallow, and breaks down into small pieces that can't possibly choke him. Well-cooked cut-up green beans, peas, potatoes, and small pieces of wafer-type cookies or crackers are good examples. Don't give him any food that requires chewing at this age.

At each of his three daily meals, he should be eating about four ounces, or the amount in one small jar of strained baby food. (Because canned adult-type foods generally contain added salt and preservatives, they should not be fed to babies.)

You may start juice at this time also. However, because many young babies are sensitive to orange juice, it is a good idea to delay introducing it and other citrus fruits until about the sixth month. Fruit juices—or large amounts of fruit in general—can make the stool acidic and irritating to the skin. This can cause a rash that is bright-red and painful when the baby is wiped during his diaper change. Contact with air and the application of a heavy, protective diaper ointment usually will heal the rash, but you may also want to decrease the fruit and/or juice intake for a while.

If your child seems to be thirsty between feedings, give him extra water. During the hot months when he's losing fluid through perspiration, offer him water two or more times a day. If you live in an area where the water is fluoridated, these feedings will also help prevent future tooth decay. (See *Water,* page 105.)

What if you want your baby to have fresh food instead of canned or dehydrated? In that case, use a blender or food processor, or just mash softer foods with a fork. Everything should be soft, unsalted, well cooked, and unseasoned. Cooked fresh vegetables and stewed fruits (see box for exceptions) are the easiest to prepare. Though you can feed your baby mashed raw bananas, all other fruits should be cooked. Refrigerate any food you don't use immediately, and then inspect it carefully for signs of spoilage before giving it to your baby. Unlike commercial foods, your own are not bacteria-free, so they will spoil more quickly.

By the time your baby is six or seven months old he'll probably sit up well enough to use a highchair during mealtime. To ensure his comfort, the seat of the chair should be covered with a pad that's removable and washable, so you can clean out the food that will probably accumulate there. Also, when shopping for a highchair, look for one with a detachable tray with raised rims. (See page 389, for safety recommendations.) The rims will help keep dishes and food from sliding off during your baby's more rambunctious feeding sessions. The detachable tray can be carried straight to the sink for cleaning, a feature you're bound to appreciate in the months to come (although there still may be days when the only solution is to put the entire chair in the shower for a complete wipe-down!).

As your child's diet expands and he begins feeding himself more regularly, discuss his personal nutritional needs with your pediatrician. The latest evidence indicates that obesity in adulthood is largely the result of hereditary influences, but if your child establishes poor eating habits in infancy, they could lead to health problems later on. He was not born with a taste for salt or saturated fats

---

Do Not Home-Prepare These Foods

Beets, Turnips, Carrots, Collard Greens. In some parts of the country, these vegetables contain large amounts of nitrates, a chemical that can cause an unusual type of anemia (low blood count) in young infants. Baby-food companies are aware of this problem and screen the produce they buy for nitrates; they also avoid buying these vegetables in parts of the country where nitrates have been detected. Since you cannot test for this chemical yourself, it's safer to use commercially prepared forms of these foods, especially while your child is an infant. If you choose to prepare them at home anyway, serve them fresh and don't store them. Storage of these foods may actually increase the amount of nitrates in them.

(fatty meats, butter, fried foods, and eggs, for example), but if given these foods, he'll acquire a taste for them. By continuing to eat them in later life, he'll have a greater risk of developing hardening of the arteries (atherosclerosis) and high blood pressure. Also, if he learns to overeat in infancy, he may continue to do so as he grows up, and eventually develop a permanent weight problem.

Your pediatrician will help you determine whether your baby is overfed, not eating enough, or eating too many of the wrong kinds of foods. By familiarizing yourself with the caloric and cholesterol contents of what he eats, you can make sure he's eating a proper diet. Since prepared infant foods contain no added salt, don't worry about salt intake at this age, but beware of the habits of others in your family. As your baby eats more and more "table foods" (this usually starts at eight to ten months in quantities similar to those used for baby foods), he'll imitate the way you eat—including using the salt shaker and nibbling on salty snacks and processed foods. For his sake as well as your own, cut your salt use to a minimum.

What if you're concerned that your baby is *already* overweight? Get your pediatrician's advice before making any dietary adjustments. During these months of rapid growth, your infant needs the proper balance of fat, carbohydrates, and protein. So it's not wise to switch a baby this age to skim milk, for example, or to other low-fat substitutes for breast milk or formula. A better solution might be to slightly reduce the portions of the things he eats. This way, he'll continue to receive the variety of nutrients he needs.

As soon as you start giving your child solid foods, his stools will become more solid and variable in color. Due to the added sugars and fats, they'll have a much stronger odor too. Peas and other green vegetables may turn the stool deep-green; beets may make it red. (Beets sometimes make urine red as well.) If his meals aren't strained, his stools may contain undigested particles of food, especially hulls of peas or corn, and the skin of tomatoes or other vegetables. All of this is perfectly normal. His digestive system is still immature and needs time before it can fully process these new foods. If the stools are extremely loose, watery, or full of mucus, however, it may mean the digestive tract is irritated. In this case, reduce the amount of solids, particularly those you suspect of causing the problem, and let him build a tolerance for them a little more slowly.

Dietary Supplements

In formula-fed infants, the formula supplies all the vitamins that are necessary, and thus no vitamin supplements are required. Breast-fed babies should continue receiving supplemental vitamin D.

For the first four months your breast-fed baby needed no additional iron. The iron he had in his body at birth was enough to see him through his initial growth. But now the reserves will be running low and his need for iron will increase as his growth speeds up. Fortunately, once you start him on solid foods, he'll receive sufficient iron from iron-fortified baby cereals, green vegetables, and meat. Four level tablespoons of fortified cereal, diluted with milk or formula, provides 7 mg of iron. (See also *Supplementation for Breast-Fed and Bottle-Fed Infants,* page 104.)

Weaning from Breast to Bottle

Many nursing mothers begin to wean their babies between four and seven months so they can return to work or resume other activities away from the child. But even if you don't plan to stop breast-feeding until much later, you still may want to start giving your baby an occasional bottle of either breast milk or formula so you can spend more than a few hours away from him at a stretch, and so that his father, grandparents, or siblings have a chance to feed him every now and then. Bottle-feeding also gives you more flexibility when you take him out or travel.

In any event, you should continue to breast-feed or provide infant formula until your baby is one year old. After that, whole cow's milk can be given.

Don't expect smooth sailing if your baby has never been given a bottle before. He probably will object to it the first few times, especially if his mother tries to give it to him. By this age he associates his mother with nursing, so it's understandable if he's confused and annoyed when there's a sudden change in the routine. Things may go more smoothly if his father or another family member feeds him—and Mom stays out of the room. After he's gotten used to the idea, then she can take over, but he should get lots of cuddling, stroking, and encouragement to make up for the lost skin-to-skin contact.

Once your baby has learned to take an occasional bottle, it should be relatively easy to wean him from the breast. The time needed to wean him, however, will vary, depending on the emotional and physical needs of both child and mother. If your baby adapts well to change and you're ready for the transition, you can make a total switch in one or two weeks. For the first two days, substitute one bottle of formula for one breast-feeding per day. (Don't express milk during this time.) On the third day, use a bottle for two feedings. By the fifth day, you can jump to three or four bottle-feedings.

Once you've stopped breast-feeding entirely, breast milk production will cease very quickly. In the meantime, if your breasts should become engorged, you may need to express milk for the first two or three days to relieve the discomfort. Mild fluid restriction or wearing a breast binder can also help. Within a week the discomfort should subside.

Many women prefer to wean more slowly, even when their babies cooperate fully. Breast-feeding provides a closeness between mother and child that's hard to duplicate any other way, and, understandably, you may be reluctant to give up such intimacy. In this case you can continue to offer a combination of the breast and the bottle for up to one year, or slightly beyond. Don't force him to keep breast-feeding if he resists, however. Many babies lose interest between nine and twelve months, or when they learn to drink from a cup. It's important for you to remember that this is not a personal rejection, but a sign of your child's growing independence.

Sleeping

Most babies this age still need at least two naps a day, of from one to three hours each, one in the morning and the other in the afternoon. In general it's best to let your baby sleep as long as he wants, unless he has trouble falling asleep at his normal nightly bedtime. If this becomes a problem, wake him up earlier from his afternoon nap.

By four months your baby should be sleeping through at least one nighttime feeding, and perhaps through the entire night. "Through the night" could mean from 7:00 P.M to 7:00 A.M., or from 10:00 P.M. to 6:00 A.M., depending on your baby's own internal clock; but at this age he should be able to go at least eight hours without being fed.

Because your child is more alert and active now, he may have trouble winding down at the end of the day. A consistent bedtime routine will help. Experiment to see what works best, taking into consideration both the activities in the rest of the household and your baby's temperament. A warm bath, a massage, rocking, a story or lullaby, soft music, and a breast- or bottle-feeding will all help relax him and put him in a bedtime mood. Eventually, he'll associate these activities with going to sleep, and that will help relax and soothe him.

Instead of letting your baby fall asleep during this ritual, settle him in his crib while he's still awake so he learns to fall asleep on his own. Gently put his head down, whisper your goodnight, and leave the room. If he cries, don't rush back in. He may calm down after a few minutes and fall asleep on his own.

But what if he's still crying lustily at the end of five minutes? Go in and comfort him for about a minute, without picking him up, and then leave. Let him know that you love him and are available if he needs you, but don't stay in the room. If he continues to cry, wait a little longer than five minutes before going back in again to repeat the sequence. Be consistent and firm. As hard as this is on you, it's harder on your baby if he senses you are wavering. The real reward will come when he awakens in the middle of the night and goes back to sleep without your help.

Many babies cry some every night, leading parents to wonder if the prolonged crying can hurt him psychologically. If you actually time your baby's crying, you may find that it doesn't last that long—it just *seems* forever. If parents are steadfast, most babies will cry less each night until they finally go to sleep with only a token protest. But even if your child cries for a long time (twenty to thirty minutes), there is no evidence that he'll be hurt by it.

Crying that goes on for more than twenty minutes may need to be checked to see if there is not some problem (such as an open diaper pin), but such interruptions should be short. Do not stop to play. The important thing is for you to keep your perfectly natural feelings of frustration and, perhaps, anger in check, so you can be firm in a calm and loving way when your baby resists sleep.

When your child awakens in the middle of the night, give him a few minutes to fall back to sleep before you go to him. If he continues to cry, talk to him and comfort him, but don't bring him to your bed. Also, unless you have reason to believe he's really hungry (for example, if he fell asleep earlier than usual and missed a feeding), don't feed him. As tempting as it may be to calm him down with food or cuddling in your bed, he'll soon come to expect these responses when he wakes up at night, and he won't go back to sleep without them.

When a baby wakes up more than once a night, there may be something disturbing his sleep. If the child is still sleeping in your room by six months, it's time to move him out; he may be waking up because he hears you or senses your presence when you're nearby. If he's still in a bassinet, he's probably feeling cramped; by this age he needs room to stretch and move in his sleep, and he should be in a full-size crib with bumpers to cushion him when he rolls to the sides. Still another problem may be a room that's too dark. He needs enough light to reassure himself that he's in familiar surroundings, and a simple night-light can solve this problem.

Teething

Teething usually starts during these months. The two bottom front teeth (central incisors) usually appear first, followed about four to eight weeks later by the four upper teeth (central and lateral incisors), and then about one month later by the two lower incisors. The first molars come in next, followed by the canine or eye teeth.

If your child doesn't show any teeth until much later, don't worry. This may be determined by heredity, and it doesn't mean that anything is wrong.

Teething *occasionally* may cause mild irritability, crying, low-grade temperature (but not over 100 degrees), excessive drooling, and a desire to chew on something hard. More often, the gums around the new teeth will swell and be tender. To help your baby's discomfort try gently rubbing or massaging the gums with one of your fingers. Teething rings are helpful, too, but they should be made of firm rubber (the teethers that you freeze tend to get too hard, and thus can cause more harm than good). Pain relievers and medications that you rub on the gums are not necessary or useful, either, since they wash out of the baby's mouth within minutes. If your child seems particularly miserable or has a fever higher than 100 degrees, it's probably not because he's teething, and you should consult your pediatrician.

How should you clean the new teeth? Simply brush them with a soft child's toothbrush, or wipe them with gauze at the end of the day. To prevent cavities, never let your baby fall asleep with a bottle, either at nap time or at night. By avoiding this situation, you'll keep milk from pooling around the teeth and creating a breeding ground for decay.

Swings and Playpens

Many parents find that mechanical swings, especially those with cradle attachments, can calm a crying baby when nothing else seems to work. If you use one of these devices, don't put your baby in the seat of the swing until he can sit on his own (usually between seven and nine months). Use only swings that stand firmly on the floor, not the ones that hang suspended from door frames. Also, don't use a swing more than half an hour, twice a day; while it may quiet your baby, it is no substitute for your attention.

Once your baby starts to move about, you may need to start using a playpen (also called a play yard). But even before he crawls or walks, a playpen offers a protected place where he can lie or sit outdoors as well as in rooms where you have no crib or bassinet. (See *Playpens,* page 391, for specific recommendations.) If the baby gets used to it now, he may be more willing to stay in it as he gets older. Don't count on this, though; while some babies don't mind being enclosed, others resist it vigorously.

BEHAVIOR

Discipline

As your baby becomes more mobile and inquisitive, he'll naturally become more assertive as well. This is wonderful for his self-esteem, and should be encouraged as much as possible. When he wants to do something that's dangerous or disrupts the rest of the family, however, you'll need to take charge.

For the first six months or so, the best way to deal with such conflicts is to distract him with an alternative toy or activity. Standard discipline won't work until his memory span increases around the end of his seventh month. Only then can you use a variety of techniques to discourage undesired behavior.

When you finally begin to discipline your child, it should never be harsh. Often, the most successful approach is simply to reward desired behavior and withhold rewards when he does not behave as desired. For example, if he cries for no apparent reason, make sure there's nothing wrong physically; then when he stops, reward him with extra attention, kind words, and hugs. If he starts up again, wait a little longer before turning your attention to him, and use a firm tone of voice as you talk to him. This time, don't reward him with extra attention or hugs.

The main goal of discipline is to teach a child limits, so try to help him understand exactly what he's doing wrong when he breaks a rule. If you discover him doing something that's not allowed, like pulling the trash out of the wastebasket, let him know that it's wrong by calmly saying "no," stopping him, and redirecting his attention to an acceptable activity.

If your child is touching or trying to put something in his mouth that he shouldn't, gently pull his hand away as you tell him this particular object is off limits. But since you do want to encourage him to touch *other* things, avoid saying "Don't touch." More pointed phrases, like "Don't eat the flowers" or "No eating leaves," will convey the message without confusing him.

Because it's still relatively easy to modify his behavior at this age, this is a good time to establish your authority. Be careful not to overreact, however. He's still not old enough to misbehave intentionally, and won't understand if you punish him or raise your voice. So instead, remain calm, firm, consistent, and loving in your approach. If he learns now that you have the final word, it may make life much more comfortable for both of you later on, when he naturally becomes more headstrong.

Siblings

If your baby has a big brother or sister, you may start to see increasing signs of rivalry at about this time. Earlier, the baby was more dependent, slept a lot, and didn't require your constant attention. But now that he's becoming more demanding, you'll need to ration your time and energy so you have enough for each child individually as well as all of them together. This is even more important—and more difficult—if you go back to work.

One way to give some extra attention to your older child is to set aside special "big brother" or "big sister" chores that don't involve the baby. This allows you to spend some time together and get the housework done. Be sure to show the child how much you appreciate this help.

You might also help sibling relations by including the older child in activities with the baby. If the two of you sing a song or read a story, the baby will enjoy listening. The older child can also help take care of the baby to some extent, assisting you at bathtime or changing time. But unless the child is at least ten, don't leave him alone with the baby, even if he's trying to be helpful. A youngster this age can easily drop or injure an infant without realizing what he's doing.

HEALTH WATCH

Don't be surprised if your baby catches his first cold or ear infection soon after his four-month birthday. Now that he can actively reach for objects, he'll come into physical contact with many more things and people, so he'll be much more likely to contract contagious diseases.

The first line of defense is to keep your child away from anyone you know is sick. Be especially careful of infectious diseases like chicken pox, measles, or mumps (see *Chicken Pox,* page 629; *Measles,* page 640; *Mumps,* page 600). If someone in your play group has caught one of these diseases, keep your child out of the group until you're sure no one else is infected.

No matter how you try to protect your baby, of course, there will be times when he gets sick. This is an inevitable part of growing up, and will happen more frequently as he has more direct contact with other children. It's not always easy to tell when a baby is ill, but there are some signs that will tip you off. Does he look pale or have dark circles under his eyes? Is he acting less energetic or more irritable than usual? If he has an infectious disease he'll probably have a fever (see Chapter 23, "Fever") and he may be losing weight due to loss of appetite, diarrhea, or vomiting. Some difficult-to-detect infections of the kidneys or lungs also can prevent weight gain in babies. At this age, weight loss could also mean that the baby has some digestive problem such as an allergy to wheat or milk protein (see *Milk Allergy,* page 487; *Celiac Disease,* page 474) or lacks the digestive enzymes needed to digest certain solid foods. If you suspect that your child may be ill but can't identify the exact problem, or you have any concerns about what is happening, call your pediatrician and describe the symptoms that worry you.

The most common illnesses that occur at this age include the following (all are described in Part II of this book).

Bronchiolitis	Diarrhea	Viral Infections
Colds (URIs)	Earache/Ear Infection	Vomiting
Conjunctivitis	Fever	
Croup	Pneumonia	

IMMUNIZATION ALERT

At four months your baby should receive:

- Second DTP vaccine

- Second oral polio vaccine

- Second Hib Conjugate vaccine

And at six months:

- Third DTP vaccine

- Third oral polio vaccine (only in high-risk areas)

- Third Hib Conjugate vaccine

- Third Hepatitis B vaccine can be given between 6 and 18 months.

SAFETY CHECK

Car Seats
- Buckle the baby into an approved, properly installed car seat before you start the car. Keep the seat in backward-facing position until the child is able to sit independently.

Drowning

- Never leave a baby alone in a bath or near a pool of water, no matter how shallow it is. Infants can drown in just a few inches of water.

Falls
- Never leave the baby unattended in high places, such as on a tabletop or in a crib with the sides down. If he does fall, and seems to be acting abnormally in any way, call the pediatrician immediately.

Burns
- Never smoke, eat, drink, or carry anything hot while holding a baby.
- Prevent scalding by reducing the water heater setting to 120 degrees or lower.

Choking
- Never give a baby any food or small object that could cause choking. All foods should be mashed, ground, or soft enough to swallow without chewing.

9

AGE EIGHT MONTHS
THROUGH TWELVE MONTHS

*D*uring these months, your baby is becoming increasingly mobile, a development that will thrill and challenge both of you. Being able to move from place to place gives your child a delicious sense of power and control—his first real taste of physical independence. And while this is quite exhilarating for him, it's also frightening, since it comes at the time when he's most likely to be upset by separation from you. So, as eager as he is to move out on his own and explore the farthest reaches of his domain, he may wail if he wanders out of your sight or you move too far from him.

From your point of view, your baby's mobility is a source of considerable concern as well as great pride. Crawling and walking are signals that he's developing right on target, but these achievements also mean that you'll have your hands full keeping him safe. If you haven't already fully child-proofed your home, do it now. (Read Chapter 13, on safety.) At this age your baby has no concept of danger and only a limited memory for your warnings. So the only way to protect him from the hundreds of hazards in your home is to secure cupboards and drawers, place dangerous and precious objects out of his reach, and make perilous rooms like the bathroom inaccessible unless he's supervised.

By child-proofing your home, you'll also give your baby a greater sense of freedom. After all, fewer areas will be off limits, and thus you can let him make his own discoveries without your intervention or assistance. These personal accomplishments will promote his emerging self-esteem; you might even think of ways of facilitating them, for example:

1. Fill a low kitchen cupboard with safe objects and let your baby discover it himself.

2. Place some kiddie gardening tools in a corner of the garden for him to find when he's in the yard with you.

3. Equip your home with cushions of assorted shapes and sizes and let him experiment with the different ways he can move over and around them.

Knowing when to guide a child and when to let him do things for himself is part of the art of parenting. At this age your child is extremely expressive and will give you the cues you need to decide when to intervene. When he's acting frustrated rather than challenged, for instance, don't let him struggle alone. If he's crying because his ball is wedged under the sofa out of his reach, or he's climbed up the stairs and can't get down, he needs your help. At other times, however, it's important to let him solve his own problems. Don't let your own impatience cause you to intervene any more than absolutely necessary. You may be tempted to feed your nine-month-old, for instance, because it's faster and less messy than letting him feed himself. However, that also deprives him of a chance to learn a valuable new skill. The more opportunities you can give him to discover, test, and strengthen his new capabilities, the more confident and adventuresome he'll be.

GROWTH AND DEVELOPMENT

Physical Appearance and Growth

Your baby will continue to grow rapidly during these months. The typical eight-month-old boy weighs between 14½ and 17½ pounds (6½ to 8½ kg). Girls tend to weigh half a pound less. By his first birthday, the average child has tripled his birthweight and is 28 to 32 inches (71 to 81 cm) tall. Head growth between eight

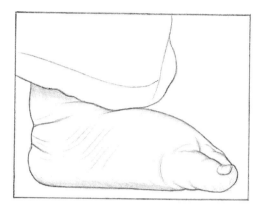

At this age your child's feet will seem flat because the arch is hidden by a pad of fat. But in two to three years this fat will disappear and his arch will be evident.

and twelve months slows down a bit from the first six months. Typical head size at eight months is 17½ inches in diameter (45 cm); by one year it's 18 inches (47 cm). Each baby grows at his own rate, however, so you should check your child's height and weight curves on the growth chart on page 121 to make sure he's following the pattern established in his first eight months.

When your child first stands, you may be surprised by his posture. His belly will protrude, his rear end will stick out, and his back will have a forward sway to it. It may look unusual, but this stance is perfectly normal from the time he starts to stand until he develops a confident sense of balance sometime in the second year.

Your child's feet also may look a little odd to you. When he lies on his back, his toes may turn inward so that he appears pigeon-toed. This common condition usually disappears by eighteen months. If it persists, your pediatrician may show you some foot or leg exercises to do with your baby. If the problem is severe, your pediatrician may recommend casts and refer you to a pediatric orthopedist. (See *Pigeon Toes,* page 623.)

When your child takes his first teetering steps, you may notice quite a different appearance—his feet may turn *out*ward. This occurs because the ligaments of his hips are still so loose that his legs naturally rotate outward. During the first six months of his second year, the ligaments will tighten and his feet should then point nearly straight.

At this age your child's feet will seem flat because the arch is hidden by a pad of fat. But in two to three years this fat will disappear and his arch will be evident.

Movement

At eight months your baby probably will be sitting without support. Though he may topple over from time to time, he'll usually catch himself with his arms. As the muscles in his trunk grow stronger he'll also start leaning over to pick up

toys. Eventually he'll figure out how to roll down onto his stomach and get back up to a sitting position.

When he's lying on a flat surface your baby is now in constant motion. When on his stomach he'll arch his neck so he can look around, and when on his back he'll grab his feet (or anything else nearby) and pull them to his mouth. But he won't be content to stay on his back for long. He can turn over at will now, and flip without a moment's notice. This can be especially dangerous during diaper changes, so you may want to retire his changing table, using instead the floor or a bed from which he's less likely to fall. Never leave him alone for an instant at any time.

All this activity strengthens muscles for crawling, a skill that usually is mastered between seven and ten months. For a while he may simply rock on his hands and knees. Since his arm muscles are better developed than his legs, he may even push himself backward instead of forward. But with time and pratice he'll discover that, by digging with his knees and pushing off, he can propel himself forward across the room toward the target of his choice.

A few children never do crawl. Instead, they use alternative methods such as scooting on their bottoms or slithering on their stomachs. As long as your baby is learning to coordinate each side of his body and is using each arm and leg equally, there's no cause for concern. The important thing is that he's able to explore his surroundings on his own and is strengthening his body in preparation for walking. If you feel your child is not moving normally, discuss your concern with the pediatrician.

How can you encourage your child to crawl? Try presenting him with intriguing objects placed just beyond his reach. As he becomes more agile, create miniature obstacle courses using pillows, boxes, and sofa cushions for him to crawl over and between. Join in the game by hiding behind one of the obstacles and surprising him with a "peekaboo!" Don't ever leave your baby unsupervised among these props, though. If he falls between pillows or under a box, he might not be able to pull himself out. This is bound to frighten him, and he could even smother.

Stairs are another ready-made—but potentially dangerous—obstacle course. While your baby needs to learn how to go up and down stairs, you should not allow him to play on them alone during this time. If you have a staircase in your home he'll probably head straight for it every chance he gets, so place sturdy gates at both the top and the bottom to close off his access. The gates should have small openings and a solid piece across the top; old-fashioned accordion gates can strangle children who get their heads caught in the openings. (See illustration in Chapter 13, page 387.)

As a substitute for real stairs, let your baby practice climbing up and down steps constructed of heavy-duty foam blocks or sturdy cardboard cartons covered in fabric. At about a year of age, when your baby has become a competent crawler, teach him to go down real stairs backward. He may take a few tumbles before he understands the logic of going feet first instead of head first, so practice on carpeted steps and let him climb only the first few. If your home doesn't have

While your baby needs to learn how to go up and down stairs, you should not allow him to play on them alone during this time.

Soon he'll manage to keep himself up and moving until you catch him several steps later.

carpeted stairs, let him perfect this skill when you visit a home that does.

Although crawling makes a huge difference in how your baby sees the world and what he can do in it, don't expect him to be content with that for long. He'll see everyone else around him walking, and that's what he'll want to do too. In preparation for this big step, he'll pull himself to a standing position every chance he gets—although when he first starts, he may not know how to get down. If he cries for your help, physically show him how to bend his knees so he can lower himself to the floor without falling. Teaching him this skill will save you many extra trips to his room at night when he's standing in his crib and crying because he doesn't know how to sit down.

Once your baby feels secure standing, he'll try some tentative steps while holding on to a support. For instance, when your hands aren't available he'll "cruise" alongside furniture. Just make sure that whatever he uses for support has no sharp edges and is properly weighted or securely attached to the floor so it won't fall on him.

Movement Milestones
By the End of This Period

- Gets to sitting position without assistance

- Crawls forward on belly

- Assumes hands-and-knees position

- Creeps on hands and knees

- Gets from sitting to crawling or prone (lying on stomach) position

- Pulls self up to stand

- Walks holding on to furniture

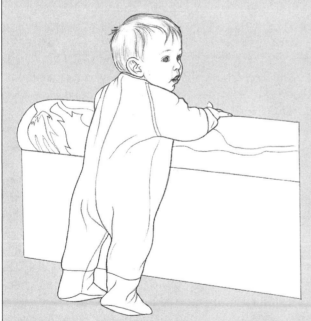

- Stands momentarily without support

- May walk two or three steps without support

As his balance improves he may occasionally let go, only to grab for support when he feels himself totter. The first time he continues forth on his own, his steps will be shaky. At first he may take only one step before dropping, either in surprise or relief. Soon, however, he'll manage to keep himself up and moving until you catch him several steps later. As miraculous as it may seem, most children advance from these first steps to quite confident walking in a matter of days.

Although both of you will feel excited over this dramatic development, you'll also find yourself unnerved at times, especially when he stumbles and falls. But even if you take pains to provide a safe and soft environment, it's almost impossible to avoid bumps and bruises. Just be matter-of-fact about these accidents. Offer a quick hug or a reassuring word and send your little one on his way again. He won't be unduly upset by these falls if you're not.

At this stage, or even earlier, many parents start using a baby walker. Contrary to what the name suggests, these devices actually *hinder* the process of learning to walk. While they strengthen the muscles in the lower legs, they don't do a good job of strenghtening muscles in the *upper* legs and hips, which are used most in walking and need the workout. These walkers actually eliminate the desire to walk, since they allow the baby to get around too easily. To make matters worse, they present a serious safety hazard because they can easily tip over when the child bumps into an obstacle such as a small toy or a throw rug. Children in walkers also are more likely to fall down stairs and get into dangerous places that would otherwise be beyond their reach. *For these reasons, the American Academy of Pediatrics strongly urges parents not to use baby walkers.*

A sturdy wagon or a "kiddie push car" is a better choice. Be sure the toy has a bar he can push, and that it's weighted so it won't tip over when he pulls himself up on it.

As your child begins to walk he'll need shoes to protect his feet. Wedges, inserts, high backs, reinforced heels, special arches, and other features designed to shape and support the feet make shoes more expensive but have no proven benefit for the average child. So look instead for comfortable shoes with nonskid soles that will help your baby avoid slipping on smooth floors; sneakers are fine. His feet will grow rapidly during these months, and his shoes will have to keep pace. His first pair of shoes probably will last two to three months, but you should check the fit of his shoes as often as monthly during this formative period.

Many babies' first steps are taken around their first birthday, though it's perfectly normal for children to start walking a little earlier or later. At first your child will walk with feet wide apart to improve his shaky sense of balance. During those initial days and weeks, he may accidentally get going too fast and fall when he tries to stop. As he becomes more confident he'll learn how to stop and change directions. Before long he'll be able to squat to pick something up and then stand again. When he reaches this level of accomplishment he'll get enormous pleasure from push-pull toys—the noisier the better.

Hand and Finger Skills

Your baby's mastery of crawling, standing, and walking are bound to be his most dramatic accomplishments during these months, but don't overlook all the wonderful things he's learning to do with his hands. At the beginning of this period he'll still clumsily "rake" things toward himself, but by the end he'll grasp accurately with his thumb and first or second finger. You'll find him practicing this pincer movement on any small object, from dust balls to cereal, and he may even try to snap his fingers if you show him how.

Milestones in Hand and Finger Skills
By the End of This Period

- **Uses pincer grasp**
- **Bangs two cubes together**
- **Puts objects into container**
- **Takes objects out of container**
- **Lets objects go voluntarily**

- **Pokes with index finger**
- **Tries to imitate scribbling**

As your baby learns to open his fingers at will, he'll delight in dropping and throwing things. If you leave small toys on the tray of his highchair or in his playpen, he'll fling them down and then call loudly for someone to retrieve them so he can do it again. If he throws hard objects such as blocks, he might do some damage and probably will increase the noise level in your household considerably. Your life will be a little calmer if you redirect him toward softer objects such as balls of various sizes, colors, and textures. (Include some with beads or chimes inside so they make a sound as they roll.) One activity that not only is fun but allows you to observe your child's developing skills is to sit on the floor and roll a large ball toward him. At first he'll slap randomly at it, but eventually he'll learn to swat it so it rolls back in your direction.

With his improved coordination, your baby can now investigate the objects he encounters more thoroughly. He'll pick them up, shake them, bang them, and pass them from hand to hand. He'll be particularly intrigued by toys with moving parts—wheels that spin, levers that can be moved, hinges that open and close. Holes also are fascinating because he can poke his fingers in them and, when he becomes a little more skilled, drop things through them.

Blocks are another favorite toy at this age. In fact, nothing motivates a baby to crawl quite as much as a tower waiting to be toppled. Toward the end of this period your child may even start to build towers of his own by stacking one block on top of another.

Language Development

Toward the end of the first year, your baby will begin to communicate what he wants by pointing, crawling, or gesturing toward his target. He'll also imitate many of the gestures he sees adults make as they talk. This nonverbal communication is only a temporary measure, however, while he learns how to phrase his messages in words.

Do you notice the coos, gurgles, and screeches of earlier months now giving way to recognizable syllables, like "ba," "da," "ga," and "ma"? Your child may even stumble on words such as "mama" and "bye-bye" quite accidentally, and when you get excited he'll realize he's said something meaningful. Before long he'll start using "mama" to summon you or attract your attention. At this age, he may also say "mama" throughout the day just to practice saying the word. Ultimately, however, he'll use words only when he wants to communicate their meanings.

Even though you've been talking to your baby from birth, he now understands more language, and thus your conversations will take on new signifcance. Before he can say many, if any, words, he'll probably be comprehending more than you suspect. For example, watch how he responds when you mention a favorite toy

> ## *Language Milestones By the End of This Period*
>
> - **Pays increasing attention to speech**
> - **Responds to simple verbal requests**
> - **Responds to "no"**
> - **Uses simple gestures, such as shaking head for "no"**
> - **Babbles with inflection**
> - **Says "dada" and "mama"**
> - **Uses exclamations, such as "Oh-oh!"**
> - **Tries to imitate words**

across the room. If he looks toward it, he's telling you he understands. To help him increase his understanding, just keep talking to him as much as possible. Tell him what's happening around him, particularly as you bathe, change, and feed him. Make your language simple and specific: "I'm drying you with the big blue towel. How soft it feels!" Verbally label familiar toys and objects for him, and try to be as consistent as possible—that is, if you call the family pet a cat today, don't call it a kitty tomorrow.

Picture books can enhance this entire process, too, by reinforcing his budding understanding that everything has a name. Choose books with large board, cloth, or vinyl pages that he can turn himself. Also look for simple but colorful illustrations of things your child will recognize.

Whether you're reading or talking to him, give him plenty of opportunities to join in. Ask questions and wait for a response. Or let him take the lead. If he says "Gaagaagaa," repeat it back and see what he does. Yes, these exchanges may seem meaningless, but they tell your baby that communication is two-way and that he's a welcome participant. Paying attention to what he says also will help you identify the words he understands and make it more likely that you'll recognize his first spoken words.

These first words, incidentally, often aren't proper English. For your child a "word" is any sound that consistently refers to the same person, object, or event. So if he says "mog" every time he wants milk, then "mog" should be treated with all the respect of a legitimate word. When you speak back to him, however, use "milk," and eventually he'll make the correction himself.

There's a tremendous variance in the age at which children begin to say recognizable words. Some have a vocabulary of two to three words by their first birthday. More likely, your baby's speech at twelve months will consist of a sort of gibberish that has the tones and variations of intelligible speech. As long as he's experimenting with sounds that vary in intensity, pitch, and quality, he's getting ready to talk. The more you respond to him as though he were speaking, the more you'll stimulate his urge to communicate.

Cognitive Development

An eight-month-old is curious about everything, but he also has a very short attention span and will move rapidly from one activity to the next. Two to three minutes is the most he'll spend with a single toy, and then he'll turn to something new. By twelve months he may be willing to sit for as long as fifteen minutes with a particularly interesting plaything, but most of the time he'll still be a body in motion, and you shouldn't expect him to be any different.

Ironically, although toy stores are brimming with one expensive plaything after another, the toys that fascinate children most at this age are ordinary household objects like wooden spoons, egg cartons, and plastic containers of all shapes and sizes. Your baby will be especially interested in things that differ just a bit from what he already knows, so if he's bored with the oatmeal box he's been playing with, you can renew his interest by putting a ball inside or turning it into a pull toy by tying a string to it. These small changes will help him learn to detect small differences between the familiar and the unfamiliar. Also, when you choose playthings, remember that objects too much like what he's seen before will be given a quick once-over and dismissed, while things that are too foreign may be confusing or frightening. Look instead for objects and toys that gradually help him expand his horizons.

Often your baby won't need your help to discover objects that fall into this middle ground of newness. In fact, as soon as he can crawl he'll be off in search of new things to conquer. He'll rummage through your drawers, empty out wastebaskets, ransack kitchen cabinets, and conduct elaborate experiments on everything he finds. (Make sure there's nothing that can hurt him in those containers, and keep an eye on him whenever he's into these things.) He'll never tire of dropping, rolling, throwing, submerging, or waving objects to find out how they behave. This may look like random play to you, but it's your child's way of finding out how the world works. Like any good scientist he's observing the properties of objects, and from his observations he'll develop ideas about shapes (some things roll and others don't), textures (things can be scratchy, soft, or smooth), and sizes (some things fit inside each other). He'll even begin to understand that

Variations of Peekaboo

The possible variations of peekaboo are almost endless. As your child becomes more mobile and alert, create games that let him take the lead. Here are some suggestions.

1. Drape a soft cloth over his head and ask, "Where's the baby?" Once he understands the game he'll pull the cloth away and pop up grinning.

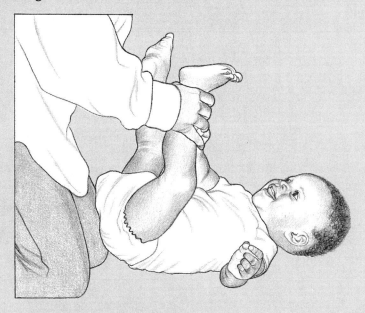

2. With baby on his back facing toward you, lift both his legs together—"Up, up, up"—until they conceal your face from him. Then open them wide—"Peekaboo!" As he gets the idea, he'll move his legs himself. (This is a great game at diaper-changing time.)

3. Hide yourself behind a door or a piece of furniture, leaving a foot or arm in his view as a clue. He'll be delighted to come find you!

4. Take turns with your baby "hiding" your head under a large towel and letting him pull the towel off and then putting it over his head and pulling it off.

Cognitive Milestones
By the End of This Period

- **Explores objects in many different ways (shaking, banging, throwing, dropping)**

- **Finds hidden objects easily**

- **Looks at correct picture when the image is named**

- **Imitates gestures**

- **Begins to use objects correctly (drinking from cup, brushing hair, dialing phone, listening to receiver)**

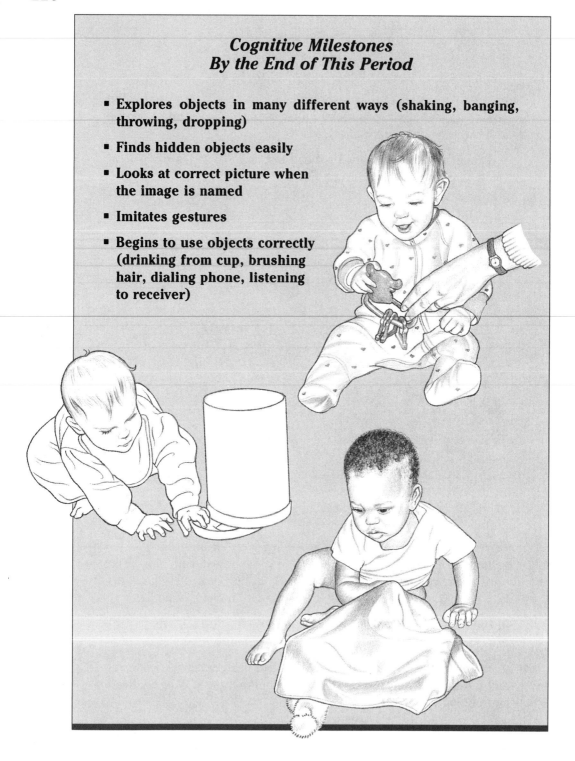

some things are edible and others aren't, though he'll still put everything into his mouth just to be sure. (Again, make sure there's nothing dangerous lying around that he can put in his mouth.)

His continuing observations during these months also will help him understand that objects continue to exist even when they're out of his sight. This concept is called "object permanence." At eight months, when you hide a toy under a scarf, he'll pick up the scarf and search for the toy underneath—a response that wouldn't have occurred three months earlier. Try hiding the toy under the scarf and then removing it when he's not looking, however, and your eight-month-old will be puzzled. By ten months he'll be so certain that the toy still exists that he'll continue looking for it. To help your baby learn object permanence, play peekaboo with him. By switching from one variation of this game to another, you'll maintain his interest almost indefinitely.

As he approaches his first birthday your child will become increasingly conscious that things not only have names but that they also have particular functions. You'll see this new awareness weave itself into his play as a very early form of fantasy. For example, instead of treating a toy telephone as an interesting object to be chewed, poked, and banged, he'll put the receiver to his ear just as he's seen you do. You can encourage important developmental activities like this by offering him suggestive props—a hairbrush, toothbrush, cup, or spoon—and by being an enthusiastic audience for his performances.

Emotional Development

During these four months your child may sometimes seem like two separate babies. First there's the one who's open, affectionate, and outgoing with you. But then there's another who's anxious, clinging, and easily frightened around unfamiliar people or objects. Some people may tell you that your child is fearful or shy because you're "spoiling" him, but don't believe it. His widely diverse behavior patterns aren't caused by you or your parenting style; they occur because he's now, for the first time, able to tell the difference between familiar and unfamiliar situations. If anything, the predictable anxieties of this period are evidence of his healthy relationship with you.

Anxiety around strangers is usually one of the first emotional milestones your baby will reach. You may think something is wrong when this child of yours who, at the age of three months, interacted calmly with people he didn't know is now beginning to tense up when strangers come too close. This is normal for this age, and you need not worry. Even relatives and frequent babysitters with whom your baby was once comfortable may prompt him to hide or cry now, especially if they approach him hastily.

At about the same time, he'll become much more "clutchy" about leaving you. This is the start of separation anxiety. Just as he's starting to realize that each

The predictable anxieties of this period are evidence of your child's healthy relationship with you.

object is unique and permanent, he'll also discover that there's only one of you. When you're out of his sight he'll know you're *somewhere,* but not with him, and this will cause him great distress. He'll have so little sense of time that he won't know when—or even whether—you'll be coming back. Once he gets a little older his memory of past experiences with you will comfort him when you're gone and he'll be able to anticipate a reunion. But for now he's only aware of the present, so every time you leave his sight—even to go to the next room—he'll fuss and cry. When you leave him with someone else he may scream as though his heart will break. At bedtime he'll refuse to leave you to go to sleep, and then he may wake up searching for you in the middle of the night.

How long should you expect this separation anxiety to last? It usually peaks between ten and eighteen months, and then fades during the last half of the second year. In some ways this phase of your child's emotional development will be especially tender for both of you, while in others it will be painful. After all, his desire to be with you is a sign of his attachment to his first and greatest love— namely you. The intensity of his feeling as he hurtles into your arms is irresistible, especially when you realize that no one—including your child himself—will ever again think you are quite as perfect as he does at this age. On the other hand, you may feel suffocated by his constant clinging, while experiencing guilt whenever you leave him crying for you. Fortunately, this emotional roller coaster eventually will subside along with his separation anxiety. But in the meantime, try to down-play your leave-taking as much as possible. Here are some suggestions that may help.

Social/Emotional Milestones By the End of This Period

- Shy or anxious with strangers

- Cries when mother or father leaves

- Enjoys imitating people in his play

- Shows specific preferences for certain people and toys

- Tests parental responses to his actions during feedings. (What do you do when he refuses a food?)

- Tests parental responses to his behavior. (What do you do if he cries after you leave the room?)

- May be fearful in some situations

- Prefers mother and/or regular care-giver over all others

- Repeats sounds or gestures for attention

- Finger-feeds himself

- Extends arm or leg to help when being dressed

1. Your baby is more susceptible to separation anxiety when he's tired, hungry, or sick. If you know you're going to go out, schedule your departure after he's napped and eaten. And try to stay with him as much as possible when he's sick.

2. Don't make a fuss over your leaving. Instead, have the person staying with him create a distraction (a new toy, a visit to the mirror, a bath). Then say goodbye and slip away quickly.

3. Remember that his tears will subside within minutes of your departure. His outbursts are for your benefit, to persuade you to stay. With you out of sight, he'll soon turn his attention to the person staying with him.

4. Help him learn to cope with separation through short practice sessions at home. Separation will be easier on him when *he* initiates it, so when he crawls to another room (one that's baby-proofed), don't follow him right away; wait for one or two minutes. When *you* have to go to another room for a few seconds, tell him where you're going and that you'll return. If he fusses, call to him instead of running back. Gradually he'll learn that nothing terrible happens when you're gone and, just as important, that you always come back when you say you will.

Acquainting Your Baby with a Sitter

Is your baby about to have a new babysitter for a few hours? Whenever possible, let your child get to know this new person while you're there. Ideally, have the sitter spend time with him on several successive days before you leave them alone. If this isn't possible, allow yourself an extra hour or two for this get-acquainted period before you have to go out.

During this first meeting, the sitter and your baby should get to know each other very gradually, using the following steps.

1. Hold the baby on your lap while you and the sitter talk. Watch for clues that your child is at ease before you have the sitter make eye contact with him. Wait until the baby is looking at her or playing contentedly by himself.

2. Have the sitter talk to the baby while he stays on your lap. She should not reach toward the child or try to touch him yet.

3. Once the baby seems comfortable with the conversation, put him on the floor with a favorite toy, across from the sitter. Invite the sitter to slowly come closer and play with the toy. As the baby warms up to her, you can gradually move back.

4. See what happens when you leave the room. If your baby doesn't notice you're missing, the introduction has gone well.

5. If you take your child to a sitter's home or a child-care center, don't just drop him off and leave. Spend a few extra minutes playing with him in this new environment. When you do leave, reassure him that you'll be back later.

If your child has a strong, healthy attachment to you, his separation anxiety probably will occur earlier than in other babies, and he'll pass through it more quickly. Instead of resenting his possessiveness during these months, maintain as much warmth and good humor as you can. Through your actions, you're showing him how to express and return love. This is the emotional base he'll rely on in years to come.

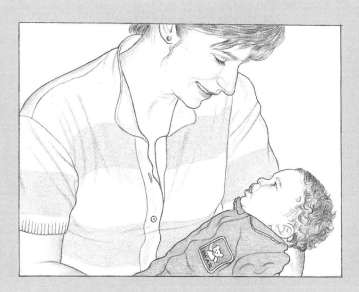

This leisurely introduction can be used with anyone who hasn't seen the child within the past few days, including relatives and friends. Adults often overwhelm babies of this age by coming close and making funny noises or, worse yet, trying to take them from their mothers. You have to intervene when this occurs. Explain to these well-meaning people that your baby needs time to warm up to strangers and that he's more likely to respond well if they go slowly.

From the beginning you've considered your baby to be a unique person with specific character traits and preferences. He, however, has had only a dim notion of himself as a person separate from you. But now his sense of identity is coming into bloom. As he develops a growing sense of himself as an individual, he'll also become increasingly conscious of you as a separate person.

One of the clearest signs of his own self-awareness is the way your baby watches himself in the mirror at this age. Up to about eight months, he treated the mirror as just another fascinating object. Perhaps, he thought, the reflection was another baby, or maybe it was a magical surface of lights and shadows. But now his

Transitional Objects

Almost everyone knows about the cartoon character Linus and his blanket. He drags it around wherever he goes, nibbling on its corner or curling up with it when the going gets tough. Security objects such as blankets are part of the emotional support system every child needs in his early years.

Your child may not choose a blanket, of course. He may prefer a soft toy or even the satin trim on Mom's bathrobe. Chances are, he'll make his choice between months eight and twelve, and he'll keep it with him for years to come. When he's tired, it will help him get to sleep. When he's separated from you, it will reassure him. When he's frightened or upset, it will comfort him. When he's in a strange place, it will help him feel at home.

These special comforts are called "transitional objects," because they help children make the emotional transition from dependence to in-dependence. They work, in part, because they feel good: They're soft, cuddly, and nice to touch. They're also effective because of their fa-miliarity. This so-called "lovey" has your child's scent on it and it reminds him of the comfort and security of his own room. It makes him feel that everything is going to be okay.

Despite myths to the contrary, transitional objects are not a sign of

responses will change, indicating he understands that one of the images belongs to him. While watching the mirror, for example, he may touch a smudge on his own nose or pull on a stray lock of his hair. You can reinforce his sense of identity by playing mirror games. When you're looking in the mirror together, touch different body parts: "This is Johnny's nose. . . . This is Mommy's nose." Or move in and out of the mirror, playing peekaboo with the reflections. Or make faces and verbally label the emotions you are conveying.

As the months pass and your child's self-concept becomes more secure, he'll have less trouble meeting strangers and separating from you. He'll also become more assertive. Before, you could count on him to be relatively compliant as long as he was comfortable. But now, more often than not, he'll want things his own particular way. For instance, don't be surprised if he turns up his nose at certain foods or objects when you place them in front of him. Also, as he becomes more weakness or insecurity, and there's no reason to keep your child from using one. In fact, a transitional object can be so helpful that you may want to help him choose one and build it into his nighttime ritual. From early infancy you might try keeping a small, soft blanket or toy in his crib. He may ignore it at first, but if it's always there he'll probably take to it eventually.

You can also make things easier for yourself by having two *identical* security objects. This will allow you to wash one while the other is being used, thus sparing your baby (and yourself) a potential emotional crisis and a very bedraggled "lovey." If your baby chooses a large blanket for his security object, you can easily turn it into two by cutting it in half. He has little sense of size, and won't notice the change. If he's chosen a toy instead, try to find a duplicate as soon as possible. If you don't start rotating them early, your child may refuse the second one because it feels too new and foreign.

Parents often worry that transitional objects promote thumb sucking, and in fact they sometimes (but not always) do. But it's important to remember that thumb or finger sucking is a normal, natural way for a young child to comfort himself. He'll gradually give up both the transitional object and the sucking as he matures and finds other ways to cope with stress.

mobile, you'll find yourself frequently saying no, to warn him away from things he shouldn't touch. But even after he understands the word, he may touch anyway. Just wait—this is only a forerunner of power struggles to come.

Your baby also may become afraid of objects and situations that he used to take in stride. At this age, fears of the dark, thunder, and loud appliances like vacuum cleaners are common. Later you'll be able to subdue these fears by talking about them, but for now, the only solution is to eliminate the source of the fears as much as possible: Put a nightlight in his room, or vacuum when he's not around. And when you can't shield him from something that frightens him, try to anticipate his reaction and be close by so he can turn to you. Comfort him, but stay calm so he understands that you are not afraid. If you reassure him every time he hears a clap of thunder or the roar of a jet overhead, his fear gradually will subside until all he has to do is look at you to feel safe.

Toys Appropriate for an Eight- to Twelve-Month-Old

- Stacking toys in different sizes, shapes, colors
- Cups, pails, and other unbreakable containers
- Unbreakable mirrors of various sizes
- Bath toys that float, squirt, or hold water
- Large building blocks
- "Busy boxes" that push, open, squeak, and move

- Squeeze toys
- Large dolls and puppets
- Cars, trucks, and other vehicle toys made of flexible plastic, with no sharp edges or removable parts
- Balls of all sizes (but not small enough to fit in the mouth)
- Cardboard books with large pictures
- Records, tapes, music boxes, and musical toys
- Push-pull toys
- Toy telephones
- Paper tubes, empty boxes, old magazines, egg cartons, empty plastic soda/juice/milk bottles (well-rinsed)

Developmental Health Watch

Each baby develops in his own manner, so it's impossible to tell exactly when your child will perfect a given skill. Although the developmental milestones listed in this book will give you a general idea of the changes you can expect as your child gets older, don't be alarmed if his development takes a slightly different course. Alert your pediatrician if your baby displays any of the following signs of *possible* developmental delay in the eight- to twelve-month age range.

- Does not crawl

- Drags one side of body while crawling (for over one month)

- Cannot stand when supported

- Does not search for objects that are hidden while he watches

- Says no single words ("mama" or "dada")

- Does not learn to use gestures, such as waving or shaking head

- Does not point to objects or pictures

BASIC CARE

Feeding

At this age your baby needs between 750 and 900 calories each day, about 400 to 500 of which should come from breast milk or formula (approximately 24 ounces a day). But don't be surprised if his appetite is less robust now than it was during the first eight months. This is because his rate of growth is slowing, and he also has so many new and interesting activities to distract him.

At about eight months you may want to introduce "junior" foods. These are slightly coarser than strained foods and are packaged in a larger jar—usually 6 to 8 ounces. They require more chewing than baby foods. You can also expand your baby's diet to include soft foods such as puddings, mashed potatoes, yogurt, and gelatin. Eggs are an excellent source of protein, but feed him only the yolks at first, since their nutritional value is higher and they're less likely to cause allergies than the whites. In one or two months you can give him the whole egg. As always, introduce one food at a time, then wait two or three days before trying something else to be sure your child doesn't develop an allergic reaction.

At about eight to nine months, as your baby's ability to use his hands improves, give him his own spoon and let him play with it at mealtimes. Once he's figured out how to hold it, dip it in his food and let him try to feed himself. But don't expect much in the beginning, when more food is bound to go on the floor and highchair than into his mouth. A plastic cloth under his chair will help minimize some of the cleanup.

Be patient, and resist the temptation to grab the spoon away from him. He needs not only the practice but also the knowledge that you have confidence in his ability to feed himself. For a while you may want to alternate bites from his spoon with bites from a spoon that you hold. Once he consistently gets his own spoon to his mouth (which might not be until after his first birthday), you may keep filling his spoon for him to decrease the mess and waste, but leave the actual feeding to him.

In the early weeks of self-feeding, things may go more smoothly when he's really hungry and is more interested in eating than playing. Although your baby now eats three meals, just like the rest of the family, you may not want to impose his somewhat disorderly eating behavior upon everyone else's dinnertime. Many families compromise by feeding the baby most of his meal in advance, and then letting him occupy himself with finger foods while the others eat their meal.

Finger foods for babies include crunchy toast, well-cooked pasta, small pieces of chicken, scrambled egg, cereals, and chunks of banana. Try to offer a selection

In the early weeks of self-feeding, things may go more smoothly when he's really hungry and is more interested in eating than playing.

of flavors, shapes, colors, and textures, but always watch him for choking in case he bites off a piece too big to swallow (see *Choking,* page 452). Also, because he's likely to swallow without chewing, never offer a young child spoonfuls of peanut butter, large pieces of raw carrot, nuts, grapes, popcorn, uncooked peas, celery, hard candies, or other hard round foods. Choking can also happen with hot dogs or meat sticks (baby-food "hot dogs"), so these should always be cut lengthwise and then into smaller pieces before being fed to a child of this age.

Weaning to a Cup

Once your baby is feeding himself more often, it's a natural time to introduce him to drinking from a cup. To get started, give him a trainer cup that has two handles and a snap-on lid with a spout, or use small plastic juice glasses. Either option will minimize spillage as he experiments with different ways to hold (and most likely to throw) the cup.

In the beginning, fill the cup with water and offer it to him at just one meal a day. Show him how to maneuver it to his mouth and tip it so he can drink. Don't become dismayed, however, if he treats the cup as a plaything for several weeks;

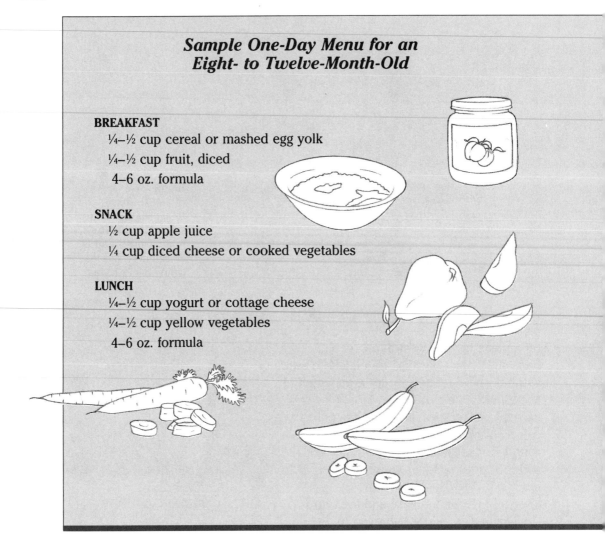

Sample One-Day Menu for an Eight- to Twelve-Month-Old

BREAKFAST
¼–½ cup cereal or mashed egg yolk
¼–½ cup fruit, diced
4–6 oz. formula

SNACK
½ cup apple juice
¼ cup diced cheese or cooked vegetables

LUNCH
¼–½ cup yogurt or cottage cheese
¼–½ cup yellow vegetables
4–6 oz. formula

most babies do. Just be patient until he's finally able to get most of the liquid down his throat—not dribbling down his chin or flying around the room—before you fill the cup with juice or milk or give it to him at other meals.

There are advantages to drinking from a cup: It will improve your child's hand-to-mouth coordination, and it will begin to prepare him for the weaning process, which frequently occurs around this age. Your baby's readiness for this will be signaled by his:

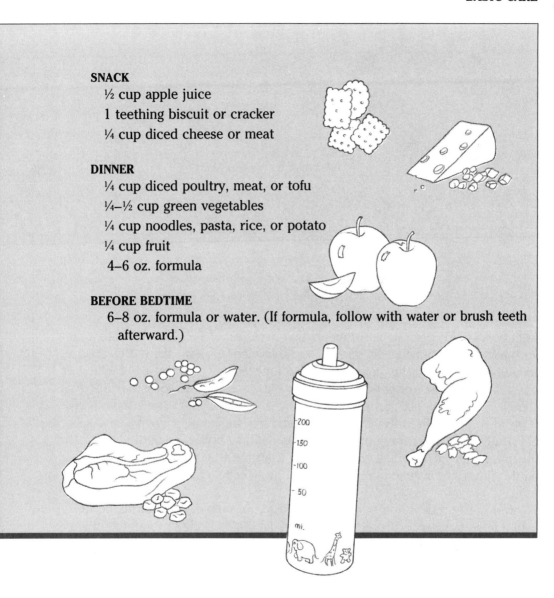

SNACK

½ cup apple juice

1 teething biscuit or cracker

¼ cup diced cheese or meat

DINNER

¼ cup diced poultry, meat, or tofu

¼–½ cup green vegetables

¼ cup noodles, pasta, rice, or potato

¼ cup fruit

4–6 oz. formula

BEFORE BEDTIME

6–8 oz. formula or water. (If formula, follow with water or brush teeth afterward.)

1. Looking around while nursing or taking the bottle

2. Mouthing the nipple without sucking

3. Trying to slide off your lap before the feeding is finished

Even under the best of circumstances, weaning may not take place overnight. Six months may pass before your baby is willing to take all his liquid from a cup. Even so, you can start the process and proceed gradually, letting his interest and

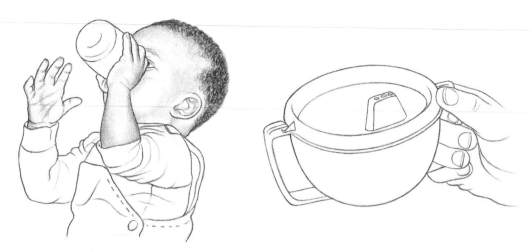

**Six months may pass before your baby is
willing to take all his liquid from a cup.**

willingness guide you. You'll probably find it easiest at first to substitute a cup
for the bottle or breast at the midday feeding. Once he's adjusted to this change,
try doing the same in the morning. The bedtime feeding probably will be the last
one abandoned, and for good reason: Your baby has become accustomed to this
source of nighttime comfort and calming, and it will take him some time to give
it up. If he's sleeping through the night and not waking up hungry, he doesn't
physically need the extra nourishment from bedtime breast- or bottle-feeding. In
this case, you might break the habit in stages, first by substituting a bedtime
bottle with water instead of milk, and then by switching to a drink of water from
a cup.

During this process you may be tempted to put milk or juice in his bottle to
help him go to sleep, but don't do it. If he falls asleep while feeding, the milk or
juice will pool around his teeth, and this can cause his incoming teeth to decay—
a condition known as nursing-bottle syndrome. To make matters worse, drinking
while lying flat on his back can also contribute to middle-ear infections, since the
liquid may actually flow through the eustachian tube into the middle ear.

There's still one more disadvantage to prolonged bottle feeding: The bottle can
become a security object, particularly if your baby keeps it beyond about age
one. To avoid this, don't let him carry or drink from a bottle while playing. Restrict
the use of a bottle to feedings when he's sitting down or being held. At all other
times, give him a cup. If you never allow him to take the bottle with him, he won't
realize that bringing it along is even an option. Don't relent once this decision
has been made, or it could prompt him to demand a bottle again long after he
has "officially" been weaned.

Sleeping

At eight months your baby probably still takes two regular naps, one in the morning and one in the afternoon. He's also likely to sleep as much as twelve hours at night without needing a middle-of-the-night feeding. But be aware of some possible problems ahead: As his separation anxieties intensify in the next few months, he may start to resist going to bed, and he may wake up more often looking for you.

During this difficult period you may need to experiment with several strategies to find those that help your baby sleep. For example, some children go to sleep more easily with the door open (so they can hear you); others develop consoling habits such as sucking their thumbs or rocking. As previously mentioned, your child might also adopt a special blanket or stuffed animal as a transitional object, which comforts him when you're not nearby. Anything that's soft and huggable and can be stroked or sucked will serve this purpose. You can encourage your child to use a transitional object by providing him with an assortment of small blankets or soft toys. But avoid resorting to a pacifier; if he depends on it to fall asleep, he'll cry for you to retrieve it each time it falls out of his mouth during the night.

Once your baby dozes off, his sleep patterns will be quite predictable. After one or two hours of deep sleep, he'll move into a stage of lighter snoozing, and he may partially awaken before returning to deeper sleep. For the rest of the night, there will be alternating periods of deeper and then lighter sleep. During the lighter periods, which may occur four to six times a night, he may even open his eyes, look around, and cry for you. This can be an exasperating experience, particularly if you've just become used to getting a full night's sleep. However, take comfort in the fact that most babies go through this stage, largely because of separation anxiety. He just needs to be reassured that you're still there when he wakes up. He also must learn to put himself back to sleep, and it's up to you to teach him. To do so, use the same techniques you relied on to get him to sleep in the first place (see *Sleeping,* page 38). Handled properly, this period of nighttime awakenings should last no more than a few weeks.

Here are some additional suggestions to help this stage pass more quickly. First of all, don't do anything that will reward your baby for calling you in the middle of the night. Go to his side to make sure he's all right, and tell him that you're nearby if he really needs you; but don't turn on the light, rock him, or walk with him. You might offer him a drink of water, but don't feed him, and certainly don't bring him to your bed. If he's suffering from separation anxiety, taking him in your bed will only make it harder for him to return to his own crib.

When you do check on him, try to make him as comfortable as possible. If he's gotten tangled in his blanket or stuck in a corner of his crib, rearrange him. Also make sure he isn't sick. Some problems, such as ear infections or the croup, can come on suddenly in the night. Once you're sure there's no sign of illness, then check his diaper, changing him only if he's had a bowel movement or if his diaper is uncomfortably wet. Do the change as quickly as possible in dim light and then settle him back in his crib under his blanket. Before leaving the room, whisper a few comforting words about how it's time to sleep. If he continues to cry, wait five minutes, then come back in and comfort him for a short time. Continue to return briefly every five to ten minutes until he's asleep.

To repeat, this period can be extremely difficult for parents. After all, it's emotionally and physically exhausting to listen to your child cry, and you'll probably respond with a combination of pity, anger, worry, and resentment. But remember, his behavior is not deliberate. Instead, he's reacting to anxieties and stresses that are natural at his age. If you stay calm and follow a consistent pattern from one night to the next, he'll soon be putting himself to sleep. Keep this objective in sight as you struggle through the "training" nights. It will ultimately make life much easier for both of you.

BEHAVIOR
Discipline

Your baby's desire to explore is almost impossible to satisfy. As a result, he'll want to touch, taste, and manipulate everything he can get into his hands. In the process, he's bound to find his way into places and situations that are off limits. So although his curiosity is vital to his overall development and shouldn't be discouraged unnecessarily, he can't be allowed to jeopardize his own safety or to damage valuable objects. Whether he's investigating the burners on your stove or pulling up plants in your flower bed, you need to help him stop these activities.

Keep in mind that the way you handle these early incidents will lay the foundation for future discipline. Learning *not* to do something that he very much wants to do is a major first step toward self-control. The better he learns this lesson now, the less you'll have to intervene in years to come.

So what's your best strategy? As we suggested earlier, distraction usually can deal effectively with undesirable behavior. Your baby's memory is still short, and thus you can shift his focus with minimal resistance. If he's headed for something he shouldn't get into, you don't necessarily have to say no. Overusing that word will blunt its effect in the long run. Instead, pick him up and direct him toward something he *can* play with. Look for a compromise that will keep him interested and active without squelching his natural curiosity.

You should reserve your serious discipline for those situations where your child's activities can expose him to real danger—for example, playing with electric cords. This is the time to say no firmly, and remove him from the situation. But don't expect him to learn from just one or two incidents. Because of his short memory, you'll have to repeat the scene over and over before he finally recognizes and responds to your directions.

To improve the effectiveness of your discipline, consistency is absolutely critical. So make sure that everyone responsible for caring for your baby understands what the child is and isn't allowed to do. Keep the rules to a minimum, preferably limited to situations that are potentially dangerous to the child. Then make sure he hears "no" *every time* he strays into forbidden territory.

Immediacy is another important component of good discipline. React as soon as you see your baby heading into trouble, not five minutes later. If you delay your reprimand, he won't understand the reason you're angry and the lesson will be lost. Likewise, don't be too quick to comfort him after he's been scolded. Yes, he may cry, sometimes as much in surprise as distress; but wait a minute or two before you reassure him. Otherwise, he won't know whether he really did something wrong.

As you refine your own disciplinary skills, don't overlook the importance of responding in a positive way to your baby's *good* behavior. This kind of reaction is equally important in helping him learn self-control. If he hesitates before reaching for the stove, notice his restraint and tell him how pleased you are. And give him a hug when he does something nice for another person. As he grows older his good behavior will depend, in large part, on his desire to please you. If you make him aware now of how much you appreciate the good things he does, he'll be less likely to misbehave just to get your attention.

Some parents worry about spoiling a child this age by giving him too much attention, but you needn't be concerned about that. At eight to twelve months your baby still has a limited ability to be manipulative. You should assume that when he cries, it's not for effect but because he has real needs that aren't being met.

These needs will gradually become more complex, and as they do you'll notice more variation in your baby's cries—and in the way you react to them. For example, you'll come running when you hear the shattering wail that means something is seriously wrong. By contrast, you may finish what you're doing before you answer the shrill "come-here-I-want-you" cry. You'll also probably soon recognize a whiny, muffled cry that means something like "I could fall alseep now if everyone would leave me alone." By responding appropriately to the hidden message behind your baby's cries, you'll let him know that his needs are important, but you'll only respond to deserving calls for attention.

Incidentally, there probably will be times when you won't be able to figure out exactly why your baby is crying. In these cases, he himself may not even know what's bothering him. The best response is some comfort from you, combined with consoling techniques that he chooses for himself. For instance, try holding him while he cuddles his favorite stuffed animal or special blanket, or take time to play a game or read a story with him. Both of you will feel better when he's cheered up. Remember that his need for attention and affection is just as real as his need for food and clean diapers.

A baby this age can be a wonderful playmate to his siblings.

Siblings

As your baby becomes more mobile, he'll be better able to play with his siblings, and those brothers and sisters usually will be glad to cooperate. Older children, particularly six- to ten-year-olds, often love to build towers for an eight-month-old to destroy. Or they'll lend a finger to an eleven-month-old just learning to walk. A baby this age can be a wonderful playmate to his siblings.

However, while the baby's mobility can turn him into a more active participant in games with his brothers and sisters, it will also make him more likely to invade their private territory. This may violate their budding sense of ownership and privacy, and it can present a serious safety hazard for the baby, since the toys of older children often contain small, easily swallowed pieces. You can ensure that everyone is protected by giving older siblings an enclosed place where they can keep and play with their belongings without fear of a "baby invasion."

Also, now that the baby can reach and grab just about everything in sight, sharing is another issue that must be dealt with. Children under three just aren't capable of sharing without lots of adult prodding and, in most cases, direct intervention. As much as possible, try to sidestep the issue by encouraging both children to play with their own toys, even if they're doing so side by side. When they do play together, suggest looking at books or listening to music, rolling a ball back and forth, or playing hide-and-seek games—in other words, activities requiring limited cooperation.

SAFETY CHECK

Car Seats

- Buckle the baby into an approved, properly installed car seat before you start the car. Since he sits up without assistance at this age, he can be facing forward.

Falls

- Use gates at the top and bottom of stairways, and to doors of rooms with furniture or other objects that the baby might climb on or that have sharp or hard edges against which he might fall.

Burns

- Never carry hot liquids or foods near your baby or while you're holding him.

- Never leave containers of hot liquids or foods near the edges of tables or counters.

- Do not allow your baby to crawl around hot stoves, floor heaters, or furnace vents.

Drowning

- Never leave your baby alone in a bath or around containers of water, such as buckets, wading pools, sinks, or open toilets.

Poisoning and Choking

- Never leave small objects in your baby's crawling area.

- Do not give your baby hard pieces of food.

- Store all medicines and household cleaning products up and out of his reach.

- Use safety latches on drawers and cupboards that contain objects that might be dangerous to him.

10

THE SECOND YEAR

*Y*our baby enters his second year and becomes a toddler, crawling vigorously, starting to walk, even talking a little. As he becomes more and more independent, the days of his unquestioning adoration and dependency on you are becoming numbered.

This realization probably makes you feel both sad and excited—not to mention a little nervous as you think about the coming clashes between his will and yours. In fact, you may already be getting some glimpses of these struggles. For instance, try to take something away from him and he may scream in protest. Or pull him away from a dangerous swinging door and he may quickly return to it, ignoring your warnings. Or offer him his favorite meal of cereal and bananas and he may unexpectedly reject it. These are his early experiments with control—testing your limits and discovering his own.

Exploring the boundaries established by your rules and his own physical and developmental limits will occupy much of his time for the next few years. Fortunately, this testing will begin slowly, giving both of you time to adjust to his emerging independence. As a toddler just learning to walk he'll be most interested in finding out what the world looks like from an upright position. This curiosity, however, is bound to lead him into some forbidden situations. Remember, he's not consciously trying to be mischievous. He still very much counts on you to show him what's okay and what's not, and he'll look to you frequently for reassurance and security.

But as he becomes more confident on his feet, he'll also start showing more signs of assertiveness. By eighteen months he'll probably have chosen "no" as his favorite word, and as he nears age two he may throw a tantrum when you ask him to come with you against his will.

Your toddler also may be showing more signs of possessiveness with belongings and people close to him. Upon seeing you pick up another baby he may react with an outpouring of tears, or if another child grabs an attractive toy, he may engage in a strenuous tug of war for possession. In a few months, as his vocabulary grows, "mine" will become another of his favorite words.

For now, his vocabulary is still limited, although expanding rapidly. He understands much of what you say to him, provided you speak in clear, simple words, and you can probably decipher some of what he says to you. Hard as it may be to believe, in a year you'll be having running conversations.

GROWTH AND DEVELOPMENT

Physical Appearance and Growth

By the end of his first year your baby's growth rate will begin to slow. From now until his next growth spurt (which occurs during early adolescence) his height and weight should increase steadily, but not as rapidly as during those first months of life. As an infant he may have gained 4 pounds (1.8 kg) in four months or less, but during the entire second year, 3 to 5 pounds (1.4 to 2.3 kg) probably will be his total weight gain. Continue to plot his measurements every few months on the growth chart on pages 118–121 to make sure he's generally following the normal growth curve. As you'll see, there's now a much broader range of what's "normal" than there was at earlier ages.

At fifteen months, the average girl weighs about 22 pounds (10 kg) and is almost 31 inches (77.5 cm) tall; the average boy weighs about 23 pounds (10.4 kg) and is 31 inches (77.5 cm) tall. Over the next three months they'll each gain approximately 1½ pounds (0.7 kg) and grow about an inch (2.5 cm). By two, she'll be about 34 inches (86.4 cm) tall and weigh 27 pounds (12.2 kg); he'll reach 34 inches (86.4 cm) and almost 28 pounds (12.7 kg).

Your baby's head growth also will slow dramatically during the second year. Although he'll probably gain only about 1 inch (2.5 cm) in circumference this entire year, he'll have attained about 90 percent of his adult head size by age two.

Your toddler's looks, however, will probably change more than his size. At twelve months he still looked like a baby, even though he may have been walking and saying a few words. His head and abdomen were still the largest parts of his body, his belly stuck out when he was upright, and his buttocks, by comparison, seemed small—at least when his diaper was off! His arms and legs were still relatively short and soft, rather than muscular, and his face had softly rounded contours.

All this will change as he becomes more active, developing his muscles and trimming away some of his baby fat. His arms and legs will lengthen gradually, and his feet will start to point forward as he walks, instead of out to the sides. His face will become more angular and his jawline better defined. By his second birthday it will be hard to remember how he looked as an infant.

Movement

If your baby hasn't started walking before his first birthday, he should within the next six months. In fact, perfecting this skill will be the major physical accomplishment of his second year. Even if he's already begun walking, it may take another full month or two before he can stand up and start moving smoothly without support. However, don't expect him to get up the way you would. Instead, his technique may be to spread his hands on the floor, straighten his arms, and lift his bottom in the air as he pulls his legs under him. Finally, while straightening his legs he'll unbend at the waist and be off.

In the beginning he really is toddling, which is quite different from mature walking. Instead of striding, he'll plant his legs wide apart, toes pointing outward, and lurch from side to side as he moves forward. As slow and painstaking as the process may seem in the beginning, he'll quickly pick up speed. In fact, don't be surprised if very soon you're running to keep up with him.

An inevitable part of this toddling, of course, is falling. In particular, walking on uneven surfaces will remain a challenge for some time. At first he'll trip on even small irregularities, like a wrinkle in the carpet surface or

Movement Milestones
By the End of This Period

- Walks alone

- Pulls toys behind him while walking

- Carries large toy or several toys while walking

- Begins to run

- Stands on tiptoe

- Kicks a ball

- Climbs onto and down from furniture unassisted

- Walks up and down stairs holding on to support

an incline into another room. It will be months before
he can walk up and down stairs, or turn corners
without falling.

Also, at the beginning, don't expect him to use
his hands during walking. While he'll use his arms for
balance (bent and held at shoulder level in the "high
guard" position), using his hands to carry, play with, or
pick up a toy will be out of the question for a time. After
he's been walking for two to three months, however, he'll
have the entire process under control: Not only will he be
stooping to pick up and carry a toy across the room, but
he'll be able to push or pull a toy wagon, step sideways or
backward, and even throw a ball while walking.

About six months after he takes his first steps, your
baby's walking style will become much more mature. He'll
keep his feet close together as he moves, making his gait
much smoother. With your help he may even walk up and
down stairs. However, when he tries this on his own, he'll
crawl up on his hands and knees and back down one stair
at a time on his stomach. Soon he'll take his first short, stiff
runs straight ahead, though he probably won't run well
until his third year. By his second birthday your child will
be moving with great efficiency. To think—just a year ago
he could barely walk!

Hand and Finger Skills

Given all the large motor skills your one-year-old is mastering, it's easy to overlook the more subtle changes in his ability to use his hands, both alone and in
coordination with his eyes. These developments will allow him much more control
and precision as he examines objects and tries new movements. They also will
greatly expand his ability to explore and learn about the world around him.

At twelve months it's still a challenge for him to pick up very small objects
between his thumb and forefinger, but by the middle of his second year this task
will be simple. Watch how he'll manipulate small objects at will, exploring all the
ways they can be combined and changed. Some of his favorite games might
include:

- Building towers of up to four blocks, then knocking them down

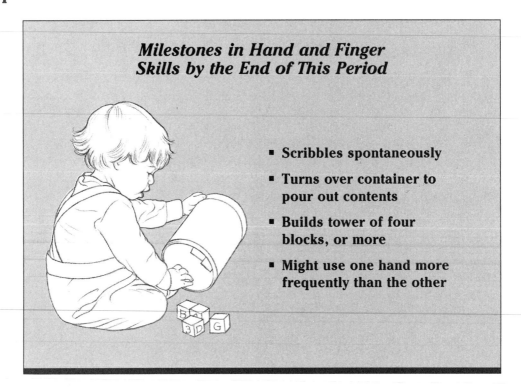

Milestones in Hand and Finger Skills by the End of This Period

- **Scribbles spontaneously**
- **Turns over container to pour out contents**
- **Builds tower of four blocks, or more**
- **Might use one hand more frequently than the other**

- Covering and uncovering boxes or other containers
- Picking up balls or other objects in motion
- Turning knobs and pages
- Putting round pegs into holes
- Scribbling and painting

These activities will not only help him develop hand skills but will also teach him spatial concepts, like "in," "on," "under," and "around." As he nears two years and his physical coordination improves, he'll be able to try more complex games, such as:

- Folding paper (if you show him how)
- Putting large square pegs into matching holes (which is more difficult than it is with round pegs, because it involves matching angles)
- Stacking up to five or six blocks

- Taking toys apart and putting them back together

- Making shapes from clay

By his second birthday, your toddler may demonstrate a clear tendency toward right or left-handedness. However, many children don't show this preference for several years. Other children are ambidextrous, being able to use both hands equally well. They may never establish a clear preference. There's no reason to pressure your toddler to use one hand over the other, or to rush the natural process that leads him to this preference.

Language Development

Early in the second year, your toddler will suddenly seem to understand everything you say. You'll announce lunchtime and he'll be waiting by his highchair. You'll tell him you've lost your shoe and he'll find it. At first, his rapid response may seem a little unusual. Did he really understand, or is this just a dream? Rest assured, it's not your imagination. He's developing his language and comprehension skills right on schedule.

This giant developmental leap probably will alter the way you now talk to him and converse with others when he's around. For example, you may edit conversations held within his earshot, perhaps spelling out words you'd rather he didn't understand (as in, "Should we stop for I-C-E-C-R-E-A-M?"). At the same time you'll probably feel more enthusiastic about talking to him, because he's so responsive.

You may find yourself using less baby talk, no longer needing high-pitched singsong monologues to get his attention. Instead, try speaking slowly and clearly, using simple words and short sentences. Teach him the correct names of objects and body parts, and stop using cute substitutes such as "piggies" when you really mean "toes." By providing a good language model, you'll help him learn to talk with a minimum of confusion.

Most toddlers master at least fifty spoken words by the end of the second year and can talk in sentences, although there are differences among children. Even with normal hearing and intelligence, some don't talk much during the second year. Also, boys generally develop language skills more slowly than girls. Whenever your own child begins to speak, his first few words probably will include the names of familiar people, his favorite possessions, and parts of his body. You may be the only person who understands these early words, since he'll omit or change certain sounds. For example, he might get the first consonant (b, d, t) and vowel (a, e, i, o, u) sounds right, but drop the end of the word. Or he may substitute sounds he can pronounce, like d or $b,$ for more difficult ones.

You'll learn to understand what he's saying over time and with the help of his gestures. By all means don't ridicule his language mistakes at this age. Give him as much time as he needs to finish what he wants to say without hurrying, and then answer with a correct pronunciation of the word ("That's right, it's a *ball*!"). If you're patient and responsive, his pronunciation will gradually improve.

By midyear he'll use a few active verbs, such as "go" and "jump," and words of direction such as "up," "down," "in," and "out." By his second birthday he'll have mastered the words "me" and "you" and use them all the time.

At first he'll make his own version of a whole sentence by combining a single word with a gesture or grunt. He might point and say "ball"—his way of telling you he wants you to roll him the ball. Or he might shape a question by saying "Out?" or "Up?"—raising his voice at the end. Soon he'll begin to combine verbs or prepositions with nouns, to make statements like "Ball up" or "Drink milk," and questions like "What that?" By the end of the year, or soon thereafter, he'll begin to use two-word sentences.

Language Milestones
By the End of This Period

- **Points to object or picture when it's named for him**

- **Recognizes names of familiar people, objects, and body parts**

- **Says several single words**
  (by fifteen to eighteen months)

- **Uses phrases (by eighteen to**
  twenty-four months)

- **Uses two- to four-word sentences**

- **Follows simple instructions**

- **Repeats words overheard in conversation**

Cognitive Development

As you watch your toddler at play, have you noticed how hard he concentrates on everything he does? Each game or task is a learning proposition, and he'll gather all sorts of information about the way things work. He'll also now be able to draw on facts he's already learned in order to make decisions and find solutions to play-related challenges. However, he'll be interested in solving only those problems that are appropriate for his developmental and learning level, so hand him a toy that fascinated him at eleven months and he may walk away bored. Or suggest a game that's slightly too advanced and he'll object. He'll be especially attracted to mechanical devices, such as wind-up toys, switches, buttons, and knobs. It may be difficult for you to judge exactly what he can and can't handle at this age, but it's not hard for him to decide. So provide him with a range of activities, and he'll select the ones that are challenging but not completely beyond his abilities.

Imitation is a big part of his learning process at this age. Instead of simply mauling household objects, as he did during his first year, he'll actually use a brush on his hair, babble into the phone, turn the steering wheel of his toy car, and push it back and forth. At first he'll be the only one involved in these activities, but gradually he'll include other players. He might brush his doll's hair, "read" to you from his book, offer a playmate a pretend drink, or hold his toy phone to your ear.

Well before his second birthday your toddler will excel at hiding games, re-membering where hidden objects are long after they leave his sight. If you pocket his ball or cracker while he's playing, you may forget all about it, but he won't!

As he masters hide-and-seek, he'll also become more understanding about separations from you. Just as he knows that a hidden object is *somewhere,* even when he can't see it, he'll now recognize that you always come back, even when you're away from him a whole day. If you actually show him where you go when you leave him—to work or to the grocery store, for example—he'll form a mental image of you there. This may make the separation even easier for him.

At this age, your toddler is very much the director; he lets you know what role he wants you to play in his activities. Sometimes he'll bring you a toy so you can help him make it work; other times he'll pull it away from you to try it by himself. Often, when he knows he's done something special, he'll pause and wait for your applause. By responding to these cues you'll provide the support and encour-agement he needs to keep learning.

You must also supply the judgment that he still lacks. Yes, he now understands how certain things behave, but—because he can't see how one thing affects another—he doesn't yet grasp the full notion of consequences. So even though he may understand that his toy wagon will roll downhill, he can't predict what will happen when it lands in the middle of the busy street below. Though he

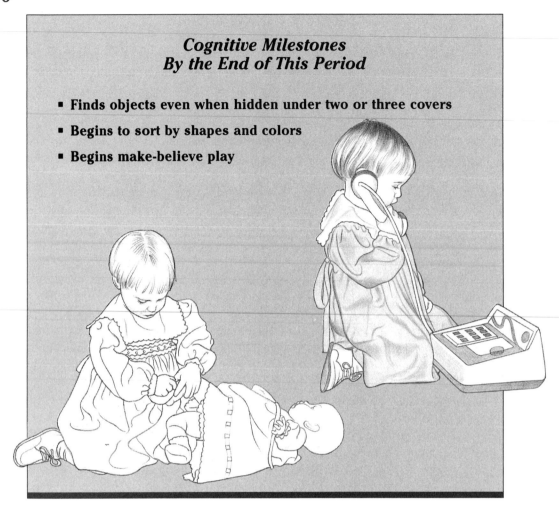

Cognitive Milestones By the End of This Period

- Finds objects even when hidden under two or three covers

- Begins to sort by shapes and colors

- Begins make-believe play

knows that a door swings open and shut, he doesn't know that he has to keep his hand from getting caught in it. And even if he's found out the hard way once, don't assume he's learned his lesson. Chances are he doesn't associate his pain with the chain of events that led up to it, and he almost certainly won't remember this sequence the next time. Until he develops his own common sense, he'll need your vigilance to keep him safe.

Social Development

During his second year your toddler will develop a very specific image of his social world, friends, and acquaintances. He is at its center, and while you may be close at hand, he is most concerned about where things are in relation to himself. He knows that other people exist, and they vaguely interest him, but he has no idea how they think or what they feel. As far as he's concerned, everyone thinks as he does.

As you can imagine, his view of the world (technically, some experts call it egocentric or self-centered) makes it impossible for him to play with other children in a truly social sense. He'll play alongside and compete for toys, but he doesn't easily play cooperative games. He'll enjoy watching and being around other children, especially if they're slightly older. He may imitate them or treat them the way he does dolls—for example, trying to brush their hair—but he's usually surprised and resists when they try to do the same thing to him. He may offer them toys or things to eat, but may get upset if they respond by taking what he's offered them.

Sharing is a meaningless term to a child this age. Every toddler believes that he alone deserves the spotlight. Unfortunately, most are also as assertive as they are self-centered, and competition for toys and attention frequently erupts into hitting and tears. How can you minimize the combat when your child's "friends" are over? Try providing plenty of toys for everyone—and be prepared to referee.

Gender Identification

If you were to take a group of one-year-olds, dress them alike, and let them loose on a playground, could you tell the boys from the girls? Probably not, because—except for minor variations in size—there are very few differences between the sexes at this age. Boys and girls develop skills at about the same rate (although girls tend to talk earlier than boys) and they enjoy the same activities. Some studies have found boys to be more active than girls, but the differences in these first years are negligible.

Although parents generally treat boys and girls this age very similarly, they often encourage different toys and games for each sex. But aside from tradition, there's no basis for pushing girls toward dolls and boys toward trucks. Left to their own devices, both sexes are equally attracted to all toys, and they'll benefit developmentally if allowed to play with both "boy" *and* "girl" toys.

Incidentally, young children learn to identify themselves as boys or girls by associating with other members of their own sex. But this process takes years. Dressing your girl exclusively in frills or taking your boy to baseball games won't make much of a difference at this age. What does matter is the love and respect you give your child as a *person,* regardless of sex. This will lay the foundation for high self-esteem.

As we've suggested earlier, your child may also start to show possessiveness over toys that he knows belong to him. If another child even touches the plaything, he may rush over and snatch it away. Try reassuring him that the other child is "only looking at it" and that "it's okay for him to have a turn with it." But also acknowledge that "yes, it's your toy, and he's not going to take it away from you." It may help to select a couple of particularly prized items and make them off limits to everyone else. This sometimes helps toddlers feel they have some control over their world, and makes them less possessive about other belongings.

Because children this age have so little awareness of the feelings of others, they can be very physical in their responses to the children around them. Even when just exploring or showing affection, they may poke each other's eyes or pat a little too hard. (The same is true of their treatment of animals.) When they're upset, they can hit or slap without realizing they are hurting the other child. For

Masturbation

As your toddler explores the many parts of his body, he'll naturally discover his genitals. Since touching them will produce pleasant sensations, he'll do it often when his diaper is off. Although this may look like mature masturbation, and may be accompanied by penile erections in boys, it's neither a sexual nor emotional experience for toddlers. It just feels good. There's no reason to discourage it, worry, or call any attention to it. If you show a strong negative reaction when he touches his genitals, you're suggesting to him that there is something wrong or bad about these body parts. He may even interpret this to mean there's something wrong or bad about *him*. Wait until he's older to teach him about privacy and modesty. For now, accept his behavior as normal curiosity.

Social Milestones
By the End of This Period

- **Imitates behavior of others, especially adults and older children**

- **Increasingly aware of himself as separate from others**

- **Increasingly enthusiastic about company of other children**

this reason, be alert whenever your toddler is among playmates, and pull him back as soon as this physical aggressiveness occurs. Tell him: "Don't hit," and redirect all the children to friendlier play.

Fortunately, your toddler will show his self-awareness in less aggressive ways as well. By eighteen months he'll be able to say his own name. At about the same time, he'll identify his reflection in the mirror and start showing a greater interest in caring for himself. As he approaches age two, he may be able to brush his teeth and wash his hands if shown how to do it. He'll also help dress and, especially,

The Aggressive Child

Some children are naturally aggressive in ways that begin to show during the second year. They want to take charge and control everything that goes on around them. When they don't get what they want, they may turn their energy toward violent behavior like kicking, biting, or hitting.

Does your toddler fit this description? If so, you'll need to watch him closely and set firm, consistent limits. Give him plenty of positive outlets for his energy through physical play and exercise. But when he's with other children, supervise him carefully to prevent serious trouble, and be sure to praise him when he gets through a play session without a problem.

In some families aggressiveness is encouraged, especially in boys. Parents proudly call their little child "tough," which he may take to mean that he has to kick and bite in order to win their approval. In other families a toddler's aggressive outbursts are considered an omen of future delinquency. Believing they have to come down hard on this behavior as soon as it appears, the parents spank or hit the child as punishment. However, a child treated this way can begin to believe that this is the correct way to handle people when you don't like their behavior, so this reaction may just reinforce his aggressiveness toward others. The best way to teach your child how to hold his aggressive impulses in check is to be firm and consistent when he misbehaves. Also, give him a good example to imitate with your own behavior and that of his siblings.

(See also *Anger, Aggression, and Biting,* page 495.)

undress himself. Many times a day you may find him busily removing his shoes and socks—even in the middle of a store or the park.

Because your toddler is a great imitator, he will eagerly participate in anything you're doing around the house. Whether you're reading the paper, sweeping the floors, mowing the lawn, or making dinner, he'll want to "help." Even though it may take longer with him doing so, try to turn it into a game. If you're doing something he can't help with—because it's dangerous or you're in a hurry—look for another "chore" he *can* do. By all means don't discourage these wonderful impulses to be helpful. Helping, like sharing, is a vital social skill, and the sooner he develops it, the more pleasant life will be for everyone.

Emotional Development

Throughout his second year your child will constantly swing back and forth between fierce independence and clinging to you. Now that he can walk and do things for himself physically, he has the power to move away from you and test his new skills. But at the same time, he's not yet entirely comfortable with the idea that he's an individual, separate from you and everyone else in the world. Especially when he's tired, sick, or scared, he'll want you there to comfort him and fend off loneliness.

It's impossible to predict when he'll turn his back on you and when he'll come running for shelter. He may seem to change from one moment to the next, or he may seem mature and independent for several whole days before suddenly regressing. You may feel mixed reactions to this as well: While there are moments

The Shy Child

Some children are naturally fearful about new people and situations. They hold back, watching and waiting before joining a group activity. If pushed to try something different, they resist, and when faced with someone new, they cling. For a parent trying to encourage boldness and independence, this behavior can be very frustrating. But challenging or ridiculing it will only make a shy child more insecure.

The best solution is to allow your child to move at his own individual pace. Give him the time he needs to adapt to new situations and let him hold your hand when he needs some extra assurance. If you take his behavior in stride, outsiders will be less likely to ridicule him, and he'll develop self-confidence much more quickly. If he continues this kind of behavior, discuss it with your pediatrician. He will be able to give you some individual advice and can, if necessary, refer you to a pediatric psychologist or child psychiatrist.

Developmental Health Watch

Because each child develops at his own particular pace, it's impossible to tell exactly when yours will perfect a given skill. The developmental milestones listed in this book will give you a general idea of the changes you can expect as your child gets older, but don't be alarmed if he takes a slightly different course. Alert your pediatrician, however, if he displays any of the following signs of possible developmental delay for this age range.

- Cannot walk by eighteen months

- Fails to develop a mature heel-toe walking pattern after several months of walking, or walks exclusively on his toes

- Does not speak at least fifteen words by eighteen months

- Does not use two-word sentences by age two

- By fifteen months does not seem to know the function of common household objects (brush, telephone, bell, fork, spoon)

- Does not imitate actions or words by the end of this period

- Does not follow simple instructions by age two

- Cannot push a wheeled toy by age two

when it feels wonderful to have your baby back, there are bound to be other times when his fussing and whining is the last thing you need. Some people call this period "the first adolescence." It reflects some of your child's mixed feelings about growing up and leaving you—and it's absolutely normal. Remember that the best way to help him regain his composure is to give him attention and reassurance when he needs it. Snapping at him to "act like a big boy" will only make him feel—and act—more insecure and needy.

Brief separations from you may help your toddler become more independent. He'll still suffer some separation anxiety and, perhaps, put up a fuss when you leave him—even if it's just for a few minutes. But the protest will be brief. Chances are, you may be more upset by these separations than he is, but try not to let him know that. Instead, leave him with a kiss and a promise to return. And when

***Emotional Milestones
By the End of This Period***

- **Demonstrates increasing independence**
- **Begins to show defiant behavior**
- **Episodes of separation anxiety increase toward midyear, then fade.**

you do come back, greet him enthusiastically and devote your full attention to him for a while before moving on to other chores or business. When your child understands that you always return and continue to love him, he'll feel more secure.

BASIC CARE

Feeding and Nutrition

You'll probably notice a sharp drop in your toddler's appetite after his first birthday. Suddenly he's picky about what he eats, turns his head away after just a few bites, or resists coming to the table at mealtimes. It may seem as if he should be eating *more* now that he's so active, but there's a good reason for the change. His growth rate has slowed, and he really doesn't require as much food now.

Your toddler needs about 1,000 calories a day to meet his needs for growth, energy, and good nutrition. If you've ever been on a 1,000-calorie diet, you know it's not a lot of food. But your child will do just fine with it, divided among three small meals and two snacks a day. Don't count on his always eating it that way, however, because the eating habits of toddlers are erratic and unpredictable from one day to the next. He may eat everything in sight at breakfast but almost nothing else for the rest of the day. Or he may eat only his favorite food for three days in a row, then reject it entirely.

As a general rule, it's a real mistake to turn mealtimes into sparring matches to get him to eat a balanced diet. He's not rejecting *you* when he turns down the food you prepared, so don't take it personally. Besides, the harder you push him to eat, the less likely he is to comply. Instead, offer him a selection of nutritious

Toys Appropriate for
the Second Year

- Board books with large pictures, simple stories
- Books and magazines with photographs of babies
- Blocks
- Nesting toys
- Simple shape sorters and pegboards
- Beginner's jigsaw puzzles
- Toys that encourage make-believe play (child lawn mower, kitchen sets, brooms)
- Digging toys (bucket, shovel, rake)
- Dolls of all sizes
- Cars, trucks, trains
- Unbreakable containers of all shapes and sizes

- Bath toys (boats, containers, floating squeak toys)

- Balls of all shapes and sizes

- Push and pull toys

- Outdoor toys (slides, swings, sandbox)

- Beginner's tricycle

- Connecting toys (links, large stringing beads, S-shapes)

- Stuffed animals

- Child keyboard and other musical instruments

- Large crayons

- Toy telephone

- Unbreakable mirrors of all sizes

- Dress-up clothes

- Wooden spoons, old magazines, baskets, cardboard boxes and tubes, other similar safe, unbreakable items he "finds" around the house (such as pots and pans)

Adult eating preferences are developed now.

foods at each sitting, and let him choose what he wants. Vary the tastes and consistencies as much as you can.

If he rejects everything, you might try saving the plate for later when he's hungry. However, don't allow him to fill up on cookies or sweets after refusing his meal, since that will just fuel his interest in empty-calorie foods (those that are high in calories but relatively low in important nutrients such as vitamins and minerals) and diminish his appetite for nutritious ones. Hard as it may be to believe, your child's diet will balance out over several days if you make a range of wholesome foods available and don't pressure him to eat a particular one at any given time.

Your toddler needs foods from the same four basic nutrition groups that you do:

1. Meat, fish, poultry, eggs

2. Dairy products

3. Fruits and vegetables

4. Cereal grains, potatoes, rice, breads, pasta

When planning your child' menu, remember that cholesterol and other fats are very important for his normal growth and development, so they should not and need not be restricted during this period.

By his first birthday, your child should be able to handle most of the foods you serve the rest of the family—but with a few precautions. First, be sure the food is cool enough so that it won't burn his mouth. Test the temperature yourself, because he'll dig in without considering the heat. Also, don't give him foods that are heavily spiced, salted, buttered, or sweetened. Young children seem to be more sensitive than adults to these flavorings, and may reject foods prepared in these ways. These flavorings also prevent your child from experiencing the natural taste of foods, and they can be harmful to his long-term good health.

Your little one can still choke on chunks of food that are hard and large enough to plug his airway, so make sure anything you given him is mashed or cut into small, easily chewable pieces. Never offer him peanuts, grapes, carrots, hot dogs, meat sticks, or hard candies. Hot dogs and carrots in particular should be quartered lengthwise and then sliced into small pieces. Also make sure your toddler eats only while seated and supervised by an adult. "Eating on the run" increases his risk of choking.

By his first birthday or soon thereafter, your toddler should drink his liquids from a cup. He'll need less milk now, since he'll get most of his calories from solid foods.

Cutting Down on Sweets

Almost everyone naturally enjoys sweets, and your toddler is no different. Like other human beings he was born with a taste for sugar, and he's already quite sensitive to different concentrations of sweetness. Offer him a yam and a baked potato, and he'll take the yam every time. Give him a choice between the yam and a cookie, and the cookie will win. Rest assured, it's not your fault if he makes a beeline for the candy and ice cream when you'd rather he take a piece of cheese. But it is your responsibility to limit his access to sweets, and to provide a diet made up primarily of more nutritious foods that promote growth, not tooth decay.

Fortunately, when sweets are out of your toddler's sight they won't be on his mind, so either don't bring them into the house, or keep them hidden. Also avoid adding sugar to his food, and don't make dessert an everyday event. As for snacks, instead of giving him sweet ones, let him have small portions of fruit, bread, crackers, and cheese. In other words, start encouraging good eating habits that can last a lifetime.

Sample One-Day Menu for a One-Year-Old

This menu is planned for a one-year old child who weighs approximately 21 pounds.

1 tablespoon = ½ ounce (15 cc)

1 teaspoon = ⅓ tablespoon (5 cc)

1 cup = 8 ounces (240 cc)

BREAKFAST

½ cup iron-fortified breakfast cereal or 1 cooked egg (not more than 3 eggs per week)

¼ cup whole milk (with cereal)

½ cup orange juice

Add to cereal one of the following:

½ banana, sliced

2–3 large sliced strawberries

SNACK

1 slice toast or whole wheat muffin

1–2 tablespoons cream cheese or peanut butter (spread)

1 cup whole milk

LUNCH

½ sandwich—tuna, egg salad, peanut butter, or cold cuts

½ cup cooked green vegetables

½ cup apple juice

SNACK

1–2 ounces cubed cheese, or 2–3 tablespoons pitted and diced dates

1 cup whole milk

DINNER

2–3 ounces cooked meat, ground or diced

½ cup cooked yellow or orange vegetables

½ cup pasta, rice, or potato

½ cup whole milk

Discontinuing the Bottle

Most pediatricians recommend that the bottle be given up entirely at around age one and almost certainly by eighteen months. As long as your baby is drinking from a cup, he doesn't need to take liquids from a bottle anymore. Unfortunately, weaning your baby from the bottle is not as easy as it sounds. To help things along, eliminate the midday bottle first, then the evening and morning ones; save the bedtime bottle for last, since it's often the most difficult for your youngster to give up.

For a child who has trouble falling asleep or who wakes up at night, it's easy to get into the habit of using food or a bottle to comfort him. But at this age he no longer needs anything to eat or drink during the night. If you are still feeding him at that time, you should stop. Even if he demands a bottle and drinks thirstily, midnight feedings are still a comfort rather than a nutritional necessity. The bottle soon turns into a crutch and prevents his learning to fall back to sleep on his own. If he cries for only a short time, try letting him "cry himself back to sleep." After a few nights he'll probably forget all about the bottle. If this doesn't happen, consult your pediatrician and read the other sections on sleep in this book (see, for example, page 243 and page 275).

Incidentally, giving your toddler a drink or other snack *before* bedtime is perfectly fine. In fact, it may help him fall asleep. A short breast-feeding, a drink of cow's milk or other liquid, or even some fruit or another nutritious food will do. If the snack is a bottle, you can gradually phase it out by substituting a cup.

Whatever the snack, have your child finish it before brushing his teeth. Otherwise the food or liquid will remain in his mouth all night, promoting tooth decay. If he needs some comfort to get to sleep, let him use a cuddly toy, blanket, or his thumb—but not a bottle.

Make sure your toddler eats only while seated and supervised by an adult.

Dietary Supplements. Preschool children don't need vitamin supplements. If you provide your child with selections from each of the four basic food groups, and let him experiment with a wide variety of tastes, colors, and textures, he should be eating a balanced diet with plenty of vitamins. However, he may need some vitamin and/or mineral supplementation if your family's dietary practices limit the food groups available to him. For example, if your household is strictly vegetarian, with no eggs or dairy products (which is not recommended for children), he may need supplements of vitamins B-12 and D as well as riboflavin and calcium. Consult your pediatrician about which supplements are needed and the amounts.

Iron deficiency does occur among some young children, and can lead to anemia (a condition that limits the ability of the blood to carry oxygen). In some cases the problem is dietary. Toddlers need to receive at least 15 mg of iron a day in their food, but many fail to do so. (See table of iron-rich foods.) Some also drink large quantities of milk, which can interfere with the absorption of iron.

Drinking large quantities of pasteurized cow's milk each day also can cause intestinal irritation, which may produce some bleeding into the bowel and thus result in anemia. (Evaporated cow's milk does not cause this problem.) The loss of blood is so small that it can be detected only by a chemical test of the bowel movement. However, it can still cause anemia unless the child consumes a great deal of iron in his diet.

If your child is drinking 24 to 32 ounces of milk or less each day, there's little cause for concern. If he drinks much more than that and you can't get him to eat more iron-rich foods, consult your pediatrician about adding an iron supplement

SOURCES OF IRON

EXCELLENT

Liver	Oysters	Blackstrap molasses
40% bran flakes	Clams	

GOOD

Hamburger	Shrimp	Potato, baked in skin	Dried apricots
Lean beef	Frankfurter	Navy beans	Raisins
Chicken	Egg, egg yolks	Kidney beans	Prunes, prune juice
Tuna	Spinach, mustard greens	Soybeans	Strawberries
Ham	Asparagus	Split peas	Tomato juice

ADEQUATE

Enriched rice	Avocado	Broccoli	Green peas
Enriched pasta, noodles	Cranberry juice	Tomato	Bacon
Enriched bread	Orange	Carrots	Peanut butter
Banana	Apple	Green beans	

to his diet. In the meantime, decrease his milk intake and keep offering him a wide variety of iron-rich foods so that, eventually, supplementation won't be necessary.

Self-Feeding. At twelve months your baby was just getting used to drinking from a cup and feeding himself with a spoon and his fingers. By fifteen months he'll be much more in control, getting food into his mouth with relative ease when he wants to, and flinging it about the room when that seems like more fun. He'll be able to fill his spoon and get it to his mouth consistently, though it will occasionally tip the wrong way and spill at the last second. Unbreakable dishes, cups, and glasses are essential, since they, too, may go flying when he's bored with their contents. Such behavior should be discouraged by a firm reprimand and replacement of the utensils in the proper location.

By eighteen months your toddler can use a spoon, fork, and unbreakable glass or cup when he wants to—but he may not always want to. There will be times when he'd rather fingerpaint with his pudding or turn his plate into a soaring airplane. Fortunately, some children get over this chaotic eating behavior by their second birthday, at which time they may actually become upset when they spill or get even a little smudge of food on their hands. Others, however, will remain very messy eaters well into their third year.

Getting Ready for Toilet Training

As your child approaches age two, you'll begin to think about toilet training. Perhaps the grandparents will urge you to start, or you may be considering a day-care or preschool program that requires him to be trained. Before you launch your campaign, however, be forewarned that toilet training generally becomes easier and is accomplished more quickly when your child is older. Yes, early training is possible—but not necessarily preferred. It may even place unnecessary pressure on your young toddler. He may not have the necessary bowel or bladder control, or the motor skills needed to remove his clothes quickly and reliably before using the toilet.

Many children are ready to be toilet trained after their second birthday (boys often slightly later than girls), but your toddler might be ready earlier. If so, you'll see the following signals:

1. His bowel movements occur on a fairly predictable schedule.

2. His diaper is not always wet, which indicates that his bladder is able to store urine.

3. He can and will follow instructions.

4. He shows an interest in imitating other family members or friends in the bathroom.

5. Through words, facial expressions, or a change in activity, he shows you that he knows when his bladder is full or when he's about to have a bowel movement.

If your toddler is ready to be toilet trained, turn to page 309 for complete details. Even if he's not quite ready, you can still familiarize him with the process by keeping his potty chair handy and, in very simple terms, explaining how it works. The more familiar he is with the process, the less scary and confusing it will seem when you begin training him.

Sleeping

No toddler looks forward to going to sleep. After all, it means missing out on the action, separating from you, and facing the nighttime on his own. If you let him, your youngster will probably spend the entire evening putting off bedtime. One more story, one more kiss, one more drink of water—he'll use any trick he can think of to keep you with him. As he becomes more verbal, his requests and delaying tactics will become more contrived and elaborate. And once he becomes bigger and stronger, he may even climb out of his crib and come to get you himself.

It's sometimes tempting just to give up and let your child "fall asleep in his tracks" when he's overcome by exhaustion. But that will only make the problem worse. Instead, watch the clock to see when he shows signs of sleepiness, and then make that his regular bedtime. Devise a quiet bedtime ritual and discuss it with your toddler. Whether you include a bath, story, or song, the routine should end with him quiet, but awake, in his crib, ready for your goodnight kiss before you leave the room. If he cries continuously, use the method described in Chapter 9 to teach him to fall asleep on his own.

Unfortunately, resistance at bedtime isn't the only sleep struggle you'll have with your youngster. Remember the first time he slept through the night as a baby and you thought sleep problems were over? As the parent of a toddler, you now know the unhappy truth: You can *never* depend on your child to sleep through the night—at least not in these early years. He may go for a few days, weeks, or even months sleeping like an angel, then begin waking up almost as frequently as a newborn.

A change in routine is a common cause of nighttime awakening. Changing rooms or beds, losing a favorite cuddly toy or blanket, or taking a trip away from home may all disrupt his sleep. If he's ill or cutting a tooth, he might wake up more often. Also, between twelve and fourteen months he'll begin actively dreaming, which can startle or frighten him awake. These are all valid reasons for him to wake up—but not for you to pick him up or bring him to your room. He needs to put himself back to sleep, even if it means crying a bit first. The strategies outlined in Chapter 9 still apply.

But what if your toddler is used to getting lots of nighttime attention? In this case, you'll need to retrain him gradually. Let's say you've been giving him milk when he wakes up. It's time to change first to diluted milk or water, and then to stop it entirely. If you've been turning on the light and playing with him, try to soothe him in the dark instead. If you've been picking him up, restrict yourself to calming him with only your voice from a distance. Above all, don't get angry with him if he continues to protest. You'll need to show him some compassion, even as you remain firm. It's not easy, but in the long run it will improve your sleep as well as his.

BEHAVIOR
Discipline

Having a toddler is a humbling experience. Before your child was born, or even when he was a baby, it was easy for you to watch someone else's toddler throwing a temper tantrum and say, "*My* child will *never* do that." Now you realize there are times when *any* child acts up unexpectedly. You can guide your child and teach him what's right, and that will work most of the time. But you can't force him to act exactly as you want. So face the facts: There are bound to be times when the unruly child everyone is staring at is yours!

At this age your toddler has a limited idea of what "good" or "bad" mean, and he does not fully understand the concept of rules or warnings. You may say "if you pull the cat's tail, she'll bite you," but it may make no sense to him at all. Even "Be nice to kitty" may not be clear to him. So whether he's running into the street or turning his face away from Grandma's kiss, he's not deliberately behaving badly, nor do his actions mean that you've failed as a parent. He's simply acting on the impulses of the moment. It will take years of firm but gentle guidance before he fully understands what you expect from him and has the self-control to meet those expectations.

Many people think of discipline as punishment. While punishment is part of it, a much more important aspect of discipline is love. Affection and caring form the core of your relationship with your child, and they play a powerful role in shaping his behavior. Your love and respect will teach him to care about others as well as himself. Your own daily example of honesty, dedication, and trust will teach him to become honest, trustworthy, and hardworking himself. Also, the control you show in helping him to learn right from wrong will serve as a model for the self-discipline he develops later on. In short, if you want him to behave well, you need to act that way toward him.

If you were keeping a running tally, you'd want displays of affection to greatly outnumber punishments and criticisms. Even a quick hug or kiss, or a bit of good-natured roughhousing, will reassure your child that you love him. And on a day when your toddler is getting into everything and you find yourself being especially snappy with him, make sure you go out of your way when he *does* behave well to give him a hug and tell him he's doing a good job. Especially during this second year, pleasing you is very important to your toddler, so praise and attention are powerful rewards that can motivate him to obey the reasonable rules you set for him.

It's important to have realistic expectations for your child's behavior. They should reflect his own temperament and personality, not your fantasies. He may be much more active and inquisitive than you would like him to be, but insisting that he spend long stretches in the playpen or confined in his highchair will only make him more nervous and frustrated.

Even if your toddler *is* a "model" child, he still has to learn what you expect. No matter how obvious it may seem to you, he won't automatically know that it's wrong to eat dirt or run into the street or pull his friend's hair. And telling him once won't get the message across. He'll have to learn by trial and error (often, several errors) before he understands the rule.

One other important reminder. If you load too much on your child at this early age you'll be frustrated, and he'll be hurt and bewildered. So make things easier for both of you by establishing some priorities and then building your list of rules gradually. Give precedence to limits that keep him safe, as well as to prohibitions against hitting, biting, and kicking. Once he masters these rules, you can then turn your attention to nuisance behavior such as screaming in public, throwing food, writing on the wall, and removing his clothing at unexpected moments. Plan to save the finer points of polite social behavior for the next few years. It's too much to ask an eighteen-month-old to be nice when Grandma's kissing him at a time he'd rather be outside playing.

At this age, since your toddler can't understand everything that you say, it's also only fair to eliminate as many temptations as possible. He needs freedom to explore. Cluttering your home with "no-nos" will deprive him of this freedom and create more restrictions than he can possibly absorb. It also will frustrate him. So while you can't get rid of the oven, you can lock away the china and place your house plants out of reach.

To prevent further unwanted behavior, pay extra attention to your toddler when he's tired, hungry, sick, or in an unfamiliar setting—in other words, when he's most likely to be stressed. Also try to keep your own daily routine as flexible as possible so he doesn't feel extra pressure. If the two of you are at the grocery store during his nap time, don't be surprised if he acts up.

Despite all your attempts at prevention, your toddler will sometimes violate one or more of your top ten rules. When that happens, alert him with your facial expression and the displeased sound of your voice. Then move him to a different place. Sometimes this will be enough, but just as often, other measures may still be required. It's best to decide upon these responses now, while your toddler is young. Otherwise, when he becomes naturally more mischievous in the next few years, you may be more prone to lose your temper and do something you'll regret.

Here's an important pact to make with yourself. *Never* resort to punishments that physically or emotionally hurt your child. While you need to let him know that he's done something wrong, this doesn't mean you have to inflict pain. Spanking, slapping, beating, and screaming at children of any age does far more harm than good. Here are some of the main reasons why this is true:

1. Even if it stops the child from misbehaving at the moment, it also teaches him that it's okay to hit and yell when he's upset or angry. Think of the mother busily whacking her child as she yells at him: "I told you not to hit!" It's absurd, isn't it? But it's also tragically common, and has an equally tragic result: Children who are hit often become hitters themselves.

2. Physical punishment can harm your child. If a little spank doesn't work, many parents will slap even harder as they become angrier and more frustrated.

3. Physical punishment makes the child angry at the parent. So instead of developing self-discipline, the youngster is much more likely to try to get back at the parent by continuing to misbehave, but without getting caught.

4. Physical punishment gives a child a very extreme form of attention. Although it's unpleasant—even painful—it tells the child that he's gotten through to his parent. If the mother or father is usually too busy or preoccupied to pay much attention to him, this type of punishment may actually promote bad behavior.

So if spanking and yelling are wrong, what approach should you take? As difficult as it may be, the best way to deal with your misbehaving toddler is to isolate him briefly. No attention. No toys. No fun. This strategy, known as "timeout," works like this:

1. You've told your toddler not to open the oven door, but he persists.

2. Without raising your voice, again say firmly, "No. Don't open the oven door," and pick him up with his back toward you.

3. Put him in his playpen and empty it of everything else. Then leave the room.

4. Wait a minute or two, or until his crying subsides, before returning to him.

The keys to this form of discipline—or to any other, for that matter—are consistency and calmness. As hard as it may be, try to respond immediately every time your child breaks an *important* rule, but don't let your irritation get the better of you. If you're like most parents, you won't succeed 100 percent of the time, but an occasional slip-up won't make much difference. Just try to be as consistent as you can.

When you do feel yourself losing your temper, take a few deep breaths, count to ten, and if possible, get someone else to watch your child while you leave the room. Remind yourself that you are older and should be wiser than your toddler. You *know* that at his age he's not deliberately trying to annoy or embarrass you, so keep your own ego out of it. In the end, the more self-discipline you exercise, the more effective you'll be at disciplining your child.

Coping with Temper Tantrums

While you're busily planning the rules and regulations by which your toddler must live, he's attempting to master his own destiny, and it's inevitable that you'll clash from time to time. Your first sign of this collision course will come when your one-year-old shakes his head and emphatically says "No!" after you've asked him to do something. By year's end, his protests may have escalated to screaming fits or full-blown tantrums in which he throws himself onto his back on the floor, clenches his teeth, kicks and screams, pounds his fists on the floor, and perhaps even holds his breath. As difficult as these performances may be for you to tolerate, they are a normal (even healthy) way for your toddler to deal with conflict at this age.

Look at the situation from his point of view. Like all young toddlers, he believes that the world revolves around him. He's trying hard to be independent, and most of the time you're encouraging him to be strong and assertive. Yet every now and then, when he's trying to do something he very much wants to do, you pull him away or ask him to do something else. He can't understand why you're getting in his way, nor can he verbally tell you how upset he is. The only way he can express his frustration is by acting it out.

Outbursts, then, are all but inevitable, and your child's general temperament will set the tone for most of them. If he's very adaptable, easygoing, generally positive, and easily distracted, he may never kick and scream. Instead, he might pout, say no, or simply head in an opposite direction when you try to guide him. The negativism is there, but it's low-key. On the other hand, if your child has been very active, intense, and persistent from infancy, he'll probably channel the same intensity into his tantrums. You'll need to remind yourself over and over that this is neither good nor bad, and it has nothing to do with your skill as a parent. Your child is not consciously trying to thwart you, but is simply going through a normal stage of development that soon (though perhaps not soon enough to suit you) will pass.

You may have an easier time coping with your toddler's outbursts if you think of them as performances. This will help remind you of what you have to do to stop them: namely, eliminate the audience. Since you are the only audience that matters to your child, leave the room. If he follows, call timeout and put him in his playpen. Also, if he kicks or bites at any time during the tantrum, call timeout immediately. While it's normal for him to try out this kind of superaggressive behavior, you shouldn't let him get away with it.

Of course, when a tantrum takes place away from home, it's much more difficult to remain calm. Especially when you're out in public, you can't just leave him and go to another room. And because you're trapped and embarrassed, you're much more likely to spank or snap at him. But that's not going to work any better here than it does at home, and it has the added disadvantage of making *you* look

Preventing Temper Tantrums
(See also *Temper Tantrums*, page 502)

When it comes to discipline, you have several distinct advantages over your child. First of all, because you *know* that there will inevitably be conflicts between you (you can probably even predict which issues are likely to spark them), you can plan your strategy in advance to prevent friction as much as possible.

Use the following guidelines to help you minimize your child's temper tantrums, both in number and in intensity. Make sure everyone who takes care of him understands and follows these policies consistently.

1. When you ask your toddler to do something, use a friendly tone of voice and phrase your request like an invitation instead of a command. It also helps to say "please" and "thank you."

2. Don't overreact when he says no. For quite some time, he may automatically say no to *any* request or instruction. He'll even say no to ice cream and cake at this stage! What he really means is something like "I'd like to be in control here, so I'll say no until I think it through or until I see if you're serious." Instead of jumping on him, answer his hidden challenge by repeating your request calmly and clearly. Don't punish him for saying no.

3. Choose your battles carefully. He won't throw a temper tantrum unless you push him first, so don't push unless there's something worth fighting for. For example, keeping him safely buckled into his car seat while the automobile is moving is a priority item. Making sure he eats his peas before his applesauce is not. So while he's

even worse than your child. So rather than lashing out or letting him have his way—either of which will only encourage his tantrums—calmly carry him to a rest room or out to the car, so he can finish his performance away from onlookers. Also, sometimes in public a big, immobilizing hug and calming voice will soothe and quiet such a child.

When the tantrum or the timeout is over, don't dwell on it. Instead, if a request from you had initially triggered his outburst, calmly repeat it. Remain composed and determined, and he'll soon realize that acting out is a waste of his time as well as yours.

saying no to everything all day long, you should be saying no only the few times a day when it's absolutely necessary.

4. Don't offer choices where none exist, and don't make deals. Issues like bathing, bedtime, and staying out of the street are nonnegotiable. He doesn't deserve an extra cookie or trip to the park for cooperating with these rules. Bribery will only teach him to break the rule whenever you forget to give him the agreed-upon reward.

5. *Do* offer limited choices whenever possible. Let him decide which pajamas to wear, which story to read, which toys to play with. If you encourage his independence in these areas, he'll be much more likely to comply when it counts.

6. Avoid situations that you know will trigger a tantrum. If he always makes a scene in the grocery store, arrange to leave him with a sitter the next few times you go shopping. If one of his playmates always seems to get him keyed up and irritable, separate the children for a few days or weeks and see if the dynamics improve when they're older.

7. Reward his good behavior with plenty of praise and attention. Even if you just sit with him while he looks at his books, your companionship shows him you approve of this quiet activity.

8. Keep your sense of humor. While it's not a good idea to laugh at your toddler as he kicks and screams (that just plays to his performance), it can be very therapeutic to laugh and talk about it with friends or older family members when he's out of earshot.

Incidentally, he may hold his breath during a severe temper tantrum. Sometimes this might last long enough to cause him to faint for a very short period of time. This can be very frightening when it occurs, but he will awaken in thirty to sixty seconds. Just keep him safe and protected during this brief episode and try not to overreact yourself, since this tends to reinforce tantrum breath-holding behavior. If not reinforced, this type of activity will usually disappear after a short period of time.

Family Relationships

Because your toddler is so self-centered, his older brothers and sisters might find him very taxing. Not only does he still consume the bulk of your time and attention, but with increasing frequency he will deliberately invade his siblings' territory and possessions. When they throw him out, he may respond with a tantrum. Even if the older siblings were tolerant and affectionate toward him as an infant, they're bound to display some antagonistic feelings toward him now—at least occasionally.

It will help keep the peace if you enforce off-limits rules to protect the older children's privacy, and you set aside time to spend just with them. No matter how old they are, *all* your children want your affection and attention. Whether they're preparing for the preschool picnic, planning a second-grade science project, trying out for the junior high soccer team, or fretting over a date for the junior prom, they need you as much as your toddler does.

If your toddler *is* the older sibling, the rivalry may be much more intense. (See *Sibling Rivalry*, page 574.) The normal feelings of jealousy are heightened by his self-centeredness, and he doesn't have the reasoning abilities to cope with them. Despite his drive for independence, there are many times each day when he'll want to be the baby, and he isn't about to wait his turn.

It's important to begin preparing your toddler before the new baby arrives. He'll recognize the changes quite early in pregnancy, so don't try to hide anything from him. When he asks, tell him that a new baby is coming, but don't stress that it will be a brother or sister. Otherwise he'll expect a playmate instead of an infant. Also, try not to overemphasize the arrival of the new brother or sister far in advance of your delivery; your toddler is concerned only with events that happen in the immediate future.

As tempting as it may be to have him toilet trained before the new baby arrives—so you don't have two in diapers at the same time—it's not worth it if you have to pressure him to make it happen. (See Chapter 1, page 20.) Such efforts will probably backfire, and the added stress may make him resent the new baby. If there are major changes that must be made, like moving him to a new room, make them well in advance of the baby's due date. The less pressure you place on your toddler at this time, the better everyone will fare.

After the new baby comes home, include your toddler as much as possible in your activities with the infant. Though he definitely can't be trusted alone with the infant, invite him to "help" as you feed, bathe, change, and dress his new sibling. Take advantage of the baby's naps to spend time alone with your toddler, and stress his importance to you and to the baby.

It's also essential to recognize that you can't satisfy the needs of both of them all the time—especially not by yourself. When you're feeling especially overwhelmed, "divide and conquer" by handing one child to your spouse, relative, or a close friend while you attend to the other. If possible, arrange for your toddler to go on special outings during this time, even if just to a park or the zoo. If the children get these occasional breaks from each other, everyone will feel less competitive—and a little more comfortable.

IMMUNIZATION ALERT

Between twelve and fifteen months, your toddler may need a booster dose of the Hib Conjugate vaccine. (This may cause a slight fever and some soreness where it's injected.) The vaccine helps prevent meningitis, pneumonia, and joint infection caused by *Haemophilus influenzae* bacteria.

At fifteen months:

- Measles, mumps, rubella vaccine (MMR)

Between twelve and eighteen months:

- Chicken pox vaccine

And at eighteen months:

- The fourth dose of the DTP vaccine
- The third dose of oral polio vaccine

SAFETY CHECK

Sleeping Safety

- Keep crib mattress at lowest setting.

- Keep the crib free of any objects that your toddler could stack and climb on to get out.

- If your toddler can climb out of his crib, move him to a low bed.

- Keep the crib away from all drapery and electrical cords.

- Be sure all cradle gyms and hanging toys have been removed from the crib.

Toy Safety

- Do not give your toddler any toy that has to be plugged into an electrical outlet.

- Do not give him a motorized riding toy.

Water Safety

- Never leave your toddler, *even for a few seconds,* in or near any body of water without supervision. This includes a bathtub, wading pool, swimming pool, fish pond, whirlpool, hot tub, lake, or ocean.

Auto Safety

- Never let your toddler climb out of his car seat while the car is moving.
- Never leave him alone in the car, even if it is locked and in your driveway.

Home Safety

- Protect any open windows with screens or barriers that your toddler cannot possibly push out.
- Make sure all electrical outlets have caps on them and all cabinets that contain cleaning fluids or other dangerous items have safety locks on them.
- If you have guns (which are not recommended to be kept in a house occupied by children), keep them unloaded and locked out of sight. Lock ammunition in a separate location.

Outdoor Safety

- Hold on to your toddler whenever you're near traffic.
- Set up fences or other barriers to make sure he stays within his outside play area and away from the street, pools, and other hazards.
- Make sure there is grass, sand, wood chips, or other soft surfaces under outdoor play equipment.

11

AGE TWO TO THREE YEARS

*Y*our baby is now advancing from infancy into the preschool years. During this time his physical growth and motor development will slow, but you can expect to see some tremendous intellectual, social, and emotional changes. His vocabulary will grow, he'll try to increase his independence from the other members of his family, and—upon discovering that society has certain rules that he is expected to observe— he'll begin to develop some real self-control.

These changes will present an emotional challenge for both you and your child. After all, these are the "terrible twos," when his every other word seems to be "no." This period will seem like a constant tug-of- war between his continuing reliance on you and his need to assert his

GIRLS: 2 TO 18 YEARS
PHYSICAL GROWTH
NCHS PERCENTILES*

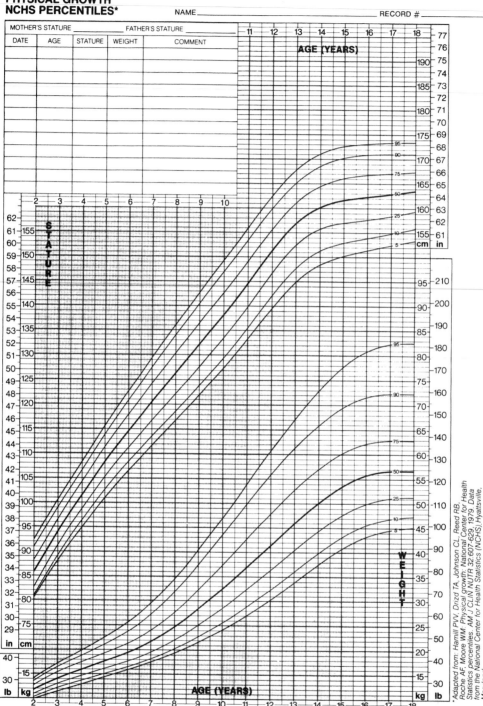

*Adapted from: Hamill PVV, Drizd TA, Johnson CL, Reed RB, Roche AF, Moore WM. Physical growth: National Center for Health Statistics percentiles. AM J CLIN NUTR 32:607-629, 1979. Data from the National Center for Health Statistics (NCHS), Hyattsville, Maryland.

© 1982 Ross Laboratories

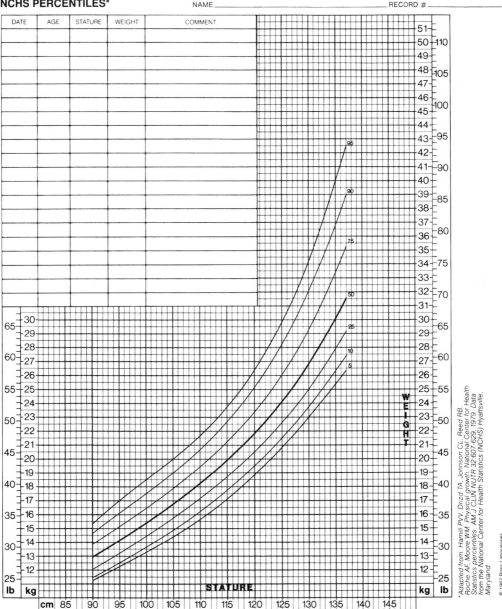

GIRLS: PREPUBESCENT
PHYSICAL GROWTH
NCHS PERCENTILES*

NAME _____ RECORD # _____

DATE	AGE	STATURE	WEIGHT	COMMENT

independence. He may flip-flop between these extremes, clinging to you when you try to leave him and running in the opposite direction when you want him to obey you. You may find yourself longing for the cuddly infant he used to be while at the same time pushing him to behave like a "big kid." It's no wonder you occasionally lose patience with each other!

By acknowledging and accepting these changes, you'll make it easier for both

BOYS: 2 TO 18 YEARS
PHYSICAL GROWTH
NCHS PERCENTILES*

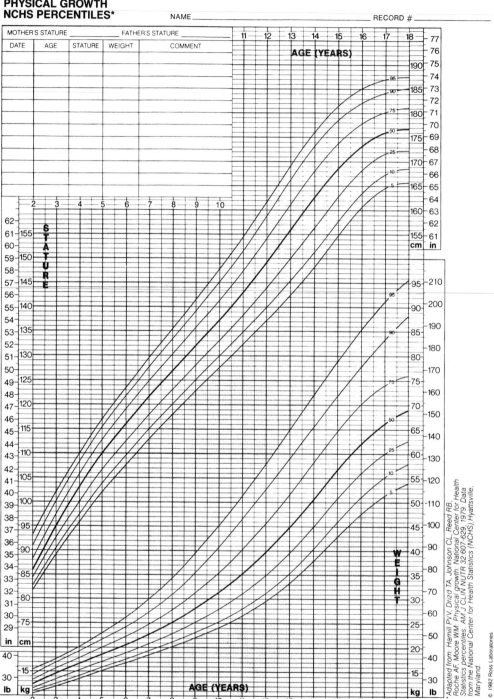

*Adapted from: Hamill PVV, Drizd TA, Johnson CL, Reed RB, Roche AF, Moore WM. Physical growth National Center for Health Statistics percentiles. AM J CLIN NUTR 32:607-629, 1979 Data from the National Center for Health Statistics (NCHS), Hyattsville, Maryland.

NAME _____ RECORD # _____

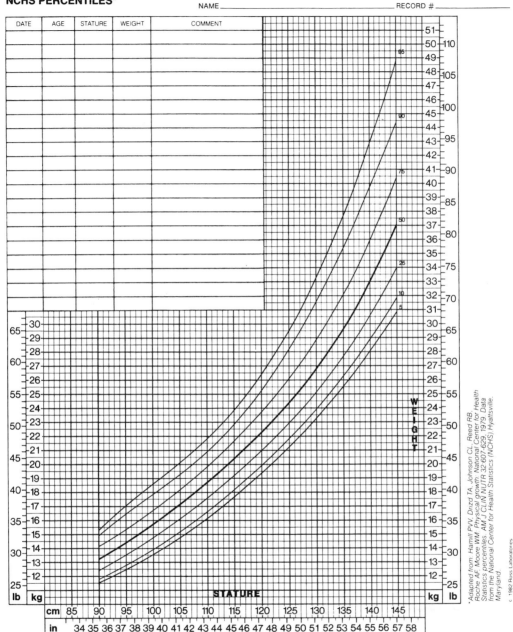

*Adapted from: Hamill PVV, Drizd TA, Johnson CL, Reed RB, Roche AF, Moore WM. Physical growth: National Center for Health Statistics percentiles. AM J CLIN NUTR 32:607-629, 1979. Data from the National Center for Health Statistics (NCHS) Hyattsville, Maryland

c 1982 Ross Laboratories

of you through the next few hectic years. Largely through your responses to him—the encouragement and respect you show him, your appreciation for his accomplishments, the warmth and security you offer him—he'll learn to feel comfortable, capable, and special. These feelings will help in later years as he goes to school and meets new people. Most important, they'll make him proud of himself as a person.

GROWTH AND DEVELOPMENT

Physical Appearance and Growth

Although your toddler's growth rate will slow between his second and third birthdays, he will nevertheless continue his remarkable physical transformation from baby to child. The most dramatic change will occur in his bodily proportions. As an infant he had a relatively large head and short legs and arms; but now his head growth will slow, from ¾ inch (2 cm) in his second year alone to ¾ to 1¼ inches (2–3 cm) over the next ten years. At the same time, his height will increase, primarily because his legs and, to some degree, his trunk will be growing quickly. With these changes in the rates of growth, his body and legs will look much more in proportion. By measuring his "sitting height" you'll get a good sense of these proportional changes.

"Sitting height" is the distance from the top of a child's head to the surface on which he's seated. It accounts for about 70 percent of a newborn's total body length, mainly because of his proportionately large head. But by age two, sitting height declines to about 60 percent of total body length, decreasing further to 57 percent by age three, and 52 percent by age thirteen or fourteen.

The baby fat that seemed to make your infant so cuddly in the first months of life gradually will disappear during the preschool years. The percentage of fat, which reached a peak of 22 percent at age one, will steadily decrease to between 12 and 16 percent by his fifth birthday. Notice how his arms and thighs become more slender, and his face less round. Even the pads of fat under the arches, which have until now given the appearance of flat feet, will disappear.

His posture will change as well during this time. His pudgy, babyish look as a toddler has been partly due to his posture, particularly his protruding abdomen and inwardly curving lower back. But as his muscle tone improves and his posture becomes more erect, he'll develop a longer, leaner, stronger appearance.

Though it will happen more slowly now, your child will continue to grow steadily. Preschoolers grow an average of 2½ inches (6 cm) annually, and gain about 4 pounds (2 kg) each year. Plot your child's height and weight on the growth chart on pages 286–289 to compare his rate of growth to the average for this age. If you should notice a *pronounced* lapse in growth, discuss it with your pediatrician. He probably will tell you there is no need to become overly concerned, as some healthy children just may not grow as quickly during these second and third years as their playmates seem to do. By age three their growth rate usually does return to normal, although they may not reach normal height for their age until adolescence. Also, because of this slowdown in growth, such youngsters often enter puberty at a later age. Even though their adolescent growth spurt may come later than usual, most of these children eventually achieve normal adult height.

Less commonly, this pause in growth during the toddler or preschool years may signal something else—perhaps a chronic health problem such as kidney or liver disease or a recurrent infection. In rare cases slow growth may be due to a disorder of one of the hormone glands or to gastrointestinal complications of some chronic illnesses. Your pediatrician will take all of these things into consideration when he examines your child.

Remember that after age two, children of the same age begin to vary much more in size and weight, so try not to spend too much time comparing your child's measurements with those of his playmates. As long as he's maintaining his own individual rate of growth, there's no reason to worry.

Don't be surprised if your child is eating less than you think he should. Children need fewer calories at this time because they're growing more slowly. Even though he's eating less, he can still remain well-nourished as long as you make a variety of healthy food available to him.

Movement

At this age your child will seem to be continually on the go—running, kicking, climbing, jumping. His attention span, which was never particularly lengthy, may now seem even shorter. Try starting a game with him, and he'll immediately change to a different one. Head in one direction and he'll quickly detour to another. This yearlong energy spurt between ages two and three will certainly keep you on the go. But take heart—his activity level will strengthen his body and develop his coordination.

In the months ahead, his running will become smoother and more coordinated. He'll also learn to kick and direct the motion of a ball, walk up and down steps by himself while holding on, and seat himself confidently in a child-size chair. With a little help he'll even be able to stand on one leg.

Watch your two-year-old walk, and you'll see how he has cast aside the stiff, spread-legged gait of a young toddler, replacing it with a more adult, heel-to-toe motion. In the process he's become much more adept at maneuvering his body, capable of walking backward and turning corners that are not too sharp. He also can do other things as he moves, such as using his hands, talking, and looking around.

Don't worry about finding activities that will help your child develop his motor skills. He'll probably be able to do that himself. When you are able to join in the fun, bear in mind that children this age love piggyback rides, rolling on mats, going down small slides, and climbing with help on the floor-level balance beam. The more running and climbing your games involve, the better.

If you can, set aside specific times during the day when he can go outside to run, play, and explore. This will help minimize wear and tear on the inside of the house—as well as on your nerves. It's also safer for him to run around in the open than to bump into walls and furniture inside. While outdoors, let him use the yard, playground, or park—whichever is most available and safe for him. But be aware that since his self-control and judgment lag considerably behind his motor skills, you must remain vigilant and keep safety and injury prevention high on your priority list at all times.

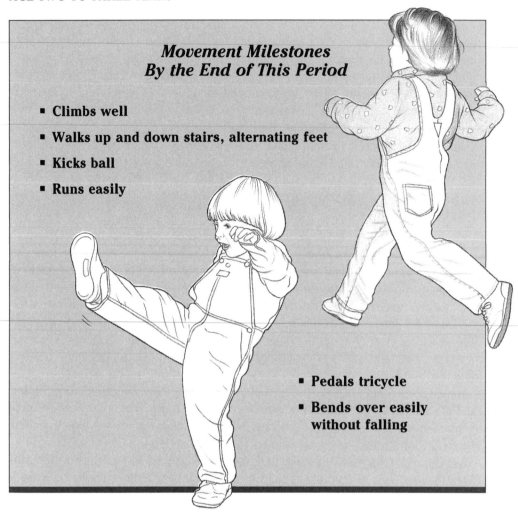

**Movement Milestones
By the End of This Period**

- Climbs well
- Walks up and down stairs, alternating feet
- Kicks ball
- Runs easily
- Pedals tricycle
- Bends over easily without falling

Hand and Finger Skills

At age two your child will be able to manipulate small objects with ease. He'll turn the pages of a book, build a tower six blocks high, pull off his shoes, and unzip a large zipper. He'll also coordinate the movements of his wrist, fingers, and palm so well that he can turn a doorknob, unscrew a jar lid, use a cup with one hand, and unwrap paper from a candy.

One of his major accomplishments this year will be learning to "draw." Hand him a crayon and watch what happens: He'll place his thumb on one side of it and his fingers on the other, then awkwardly try to extend his index or middle finger toward the point. Clumsy as this grip may seem, it will give him enough control to create his first artistic masterpieces, using sweeping vertical and circular strokes.

Fortunately your child's quiet play at this age will be much more focused than it was at eighteen months, when he was "into everything." His attention span is longer, and now that he can turn pages he'll be an active participant as you look at books or magazines together. He'll also be interested in activities such as drawing, building, or manipulating objects, so blocks and interlocking construction sets may keep him entertained for long periods. And if you let him loose with a box of crayons or a set of fingerpaints, his creative impulses will flourish.

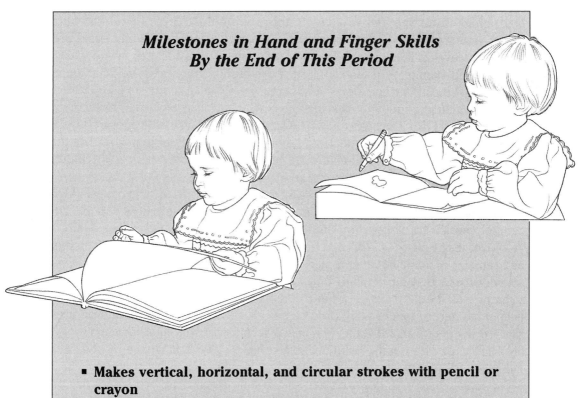

Milestones in Hand and Finger Skills By the End of This Period

- **Makes vertical, horizontal, and circular strokes with pencil or crayon**
- **Turns book pages one at a time**
- **Builds a tower of more than six blocks**
- **Holds a pencil in writing position**
- **Screws and unscrews jar lids, nuts and bolts**
- **Turns rotating handles**

Language Development

Your two-year-old not only understands most of what you say to him, but also speaks with a rapidly growing vocabulary of fifty or more words. Over the course of this year, he'll graduate from two- or three-word sentences ("Drink juice," "Mommy want cookie") to those with four, five, or even six words ("Where's the ball, Daddy?" "Dolly sit in my lap"). He's also beginning to use pronouns (I, you, me, we, they), and understands the concept of "mine" ("I want my cup," "I see my mommy"). Pay attention to how he is also using language to describe ideas and information, and to express his physical or emotional needs and desires.

It's human nature to measure your toddler's verbal abilities against those of other children his age, but you should try to avoid this. There's more variation at this time in language development than in any other area. While some pre-schoolers develop language skills at a steady rate, others seem to master words in an uneven manner. And some children are naturally more talkative than others. This doesn't mean that the more verbal children are necessarily smarter or more advanced than the quieter ones, nor does it even mean that they have richer vocabularies. In fact, the quiet child may know just as many words but be choosier about speaking them. As a general rule, boys start talking later than girls, but this variation—like most others mentioned above—tends to even out as children reach school age.

Without any formal instruction, just by listening and practicing, your child will master many of the basic rules of grammar by the time he enters school. You can help enrich his vocabulary and language skills by making reading a part of your everyday routine. At this age he can follow a story line and will understand and remember many ideas and pieces of information presented in books. Even so, because he may have a hard time sitting still for too long, the books you read to him should be short. To keep his attention, choose activity-oriented books that encourage him to touch, point, and name objects, or to repeat certain phrases. Toward the end of this year, as his language skills become more advanced, he'll also have fun with poems, puns, or jokes that play with language by repeating funny sounds or using nonsense phrases.

For some youngsters, however, this language-development process does not run smoothly. In fact, about one in every ten to fifteen children has trouble with language comprehension and/or speech. For some the problem is caused by hearing difficulty, low intelligence, or lack of verbal stimulation at home. In most cases, though, the cause is unknown. If your pediatrician suspects your child has difficulty with language, he'll conduct a thorough physical exam and hearing test and, if necessary, refer you to a speech/language or early-childhood specialist for further evaluation. *Early* detection and identification of language delay or hearing impairment is critically important, so that treatment can begin before the problem interferes with learning in other areas. Without identifying the difficulty and doing something about it, the child may have continuous trouble with classroom learning.

*Language Milestones
By the End of This Period*

- Follows a two- or three-component command

- Recognizes and identifies almost all common objects and pictures

- Understands most sentences

- Understands physical relationships ("on," "in," "under")

- Uses four- and five-word sentences

- Can say name, age, and sex

- Uses pronouns (I, you, me, we, they) and some plurals (cars, dogs, cats)

- Strangers can understand most of his words

Cognitive Development

Think back to your child's infancy and the early toddler months. That was a time when he learned about the world by touching, looking, manipulating, and listening. But now the learning process has become more thoughtful. His grasp of language is increasing and he's beginning to form mental images for things, actions, and concepts. He also can solve some problems in his head, performing *mental* trial-and-error instead of having to manipulate objects *physically*. And as his memory and intellectual abilities develop, he'll begin to understand simple time concepts, such as "You can play *after* you finish eating."

Your toddler also is starting to understand the relationship between objects. For instance, he'll be able to match similar shapes when you give him shape-sorting toys and simple jigsaw puzzles. He'll also begin to recognize the purpose of numbers in counting objects—especially the number 2. And as his understanding of cause and effect develops, he'll become much more interested in winding up toys and turning lights and appliances on and off.

You'll also notice your toddler's play growing more complex. Most noticeably, he'll start stringing together different activities to create a logical sequence. Instead of drifting randomly from one toy to another, he may first put a doll to bed and then cover it up. Or he may pretend to feed several dolls, one after the other. Over the next few years he'll put together longer and more elaborate sequences

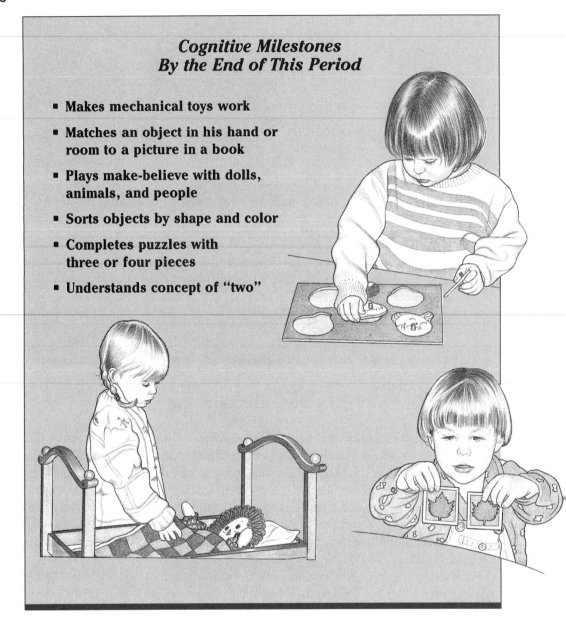

Cognitive Milestones
By the End of This Period

- Makes mechanical toys work
- Matches an object in his hand or room to a picture in a book
- Plays make-believe with dolls, animals, and people
- Sorts objects by shape and color
- Completes puzzles with three or four pieces
- Understands concept of "two"

of make-believe, acting out much of his own daily routine, from getting up in the morning to taking a bath and going to bed at night.

If we were to single out the major intellectual limitation at this age, it would be your child's feeling that everything that happens in his world is the result of something he has done. With a belief like this, it becomes very difficult for him to understand correctly such concepts as death, divorce, or illness, without feeling that he played some role in it. So if parents separate or a family member gets sick, children often feel responsible. (See discussion in Chapter 22, "Family Issues.")

Reasoning with your two-year-old is often difficult. After all, he views everything in extremely simple terms. He still often confuses fantasy with reality unless he's actively playing make-believe. For example, a wonderful story from Selma Fraiberg's *The Magic Years* talks about parents telling their two-and-a-half-year-old that they would soon be flying to Europe. With a worried look on his face, the little boy said, "But my arms aren't strong enough to fly." Therefore, during this stage, be sure to choose your own words carefully: Comments that you think are funny or playful—like "If you eat more ice cream, you'll explode"—may actually panic him, since he won't know you're joking.

Social Development

By nature, children this age are selfish and self-centered. They may refuse to share anything that interests them, and they do not easily interact with other children, even when playing side by side, unless it's to snatch a toy or to quarrel over one that someone else has grabbed from them. There may be times when your child's behavior makes you want to disown him, but if you take a close look, you'll notice that all the other toddlers in the play group are probably acting the same way.

At age two, children view the world almost exclusively through their own needs and desires. Because they can't yet understand how others might feel in the same situation, they assume that everyone thinks and feels exactly as they do. And on those occasions when they realize they're out of line, they may not be able to control themselves. For these reasons, it's quite useless to try to shape your child's behavior using statements such as "How would you like it if he did that to you?" Save these comments until your child is about seven; then he'll be able to really understand how other people think and feel, and be capable of responding to such reasoning.

Because your two-year-old's behavior is so self-centered, you may also find yourself worrying that he's spoiled or out of control. In all likelihood your fears are unfounded, and he'll pass through this phase in time. Highly active, aggressive children who push and shove are usually just as "normal" as quiet, shy ones who never seem to act out their thoughts and feelings.

Ironically, despite your child's self-centeredness, much of his playtime will be spent imitating other peoples' mannerisms and activities. Imitation and "pretend" are favorite games at this age. So, as your two-year-old puts his teddy to bed or feeds his doll, you may hear him use exactly the same words and tone of voice you use when telling him to go to sleep or eat his vegetables. No matter how he resists your instructions at other times, when he moves over into the parent role,

Social Milestones
By the End of This Period

- Imitates adults and playmates
- Spontaneously shows affection for familiar playmates
- Can take turns in games
- Understands concept of "mine" and "his/hers"

he imitates you exactly! These play activities help him learn what it's like to be in someone else's shoes, and they serve as valuable rehearsals for future social encounters. They'll also help you appreciate the importance of being a good role model, by demonstrating that children often do as we do, not as we say.

The best way for your child to learn how to behave around other people is to be given plenty of trial runs. So don't let his relatively antisocial behavior discourage you from getting play groups together. At first it may be wise to limit the groups to two or three children. And although you'll need to monitor their activities closely to be sure that no one gets hurt or overly upset, you should let the children guide themselves as much as possible. They need to learn how to play with *one another,* not with one another's parents.

Emotional Development

It's so difficult to follow the ups and downs of a two-year-old. One moment he's beaming and friendly; the next he's sullen and weepy—and for no apparent reason. These mood swings, however, are just part of growing up. They are signs of the emotional changes taking place as your child struggles to take control of actions, impulses, feelings, and of his body.

At this age your child wants to explore the world and seek adventure. As a result, he'll spend most of his time testing limits—his own, yours, and his environment's. Unfortunately, he still lacks many of the skills required for the safe accomplishment of everything he needs to do, and he often will need you to protect him.

When he oversteps a limit and is pulled back, he'll react with anger and frustration, possibly with a temper tantrum or sullen rage. He may even strike back by hitting, biting, or kicking. At this age, he just doesn't have much control over his emotional impulses, so his anger and frustration tend to erupt suddenly in the form of crying, hitting, or screaming. It's his only way of dealing with the difficult realities of life. He may even act out in ways that unintentionally harm himself or others. It's all part of being two.

Have sitters or relatives ever told you that your child never behaves badly when they're caring for him? It's not uncommon for toddlers to be angels when you're not around, because they don't trust these other people enough to test their limits. But with you, your toddler will be willing to try things that may be dangerous or difficult, because he knows you'll rescue him if he gets into trouble.

Whatever protest pattern he has developed around the end of his first year will probably persist for some time. For instance, when you're about to leave him with a sitter, he may become angry and throw a tantrum in anticipation of the separation. Or he may whimper, or whine and cling to you. Or he could simply become subdued and silent. Whatever his behavior, try not to overreact by scold-

Holding the Line on Tantrums

Frustration, anger, and an occasional tantrum are inevitable for all two-year-olds. As a parent you should allow your toddler to express his emotions but, at the same time, try to help him channel his anger away from violent or overly aggressive behavior. Here are some suggestions:

1. When you see your child starting to get worked up, try to turn his energy and attention to a new activity that is more acceptable.

2. If you can't distract your toddler, ignore him. Every time you react to one of his outbursts in any way, you're rewarding his negative behavior with extra attention. Even scolding, punishing, or trying to reason with him may encourage him to act up more.

3. If you're in a public place where his behavior is embarrassing you, simply remove him without discussion or fuss. Wait until he's calmed down before you return or continue with your activities.

4. If the tantrum involves hitting, biting, or some other potentially harmful behavior, you can't ignore it. But it still won't help your child if you overreact. Instead, tell him immediately and clearly that he is not to behave this way, and move him off by himself for a few minutes. He can't understand complicated explanations, so don't try to reason with him. Just make sure he understands what he was doing wrong, and dole out your punishment then and there. If you wait an hour, he won't connect the punishment with the "crime." (See *Temper Tantrums*, page 502.)

ing or punishing him. The best tactic is to reassure him before you leave that you will be back and, when you return, to praise him for being so patient while you were gone. Take solace in the fact that separations should be much easier by the time he's three years old.

The more confident and secure your two-year-old feels, the more independent and well-behaved he's likely to be. And you can help him develop these positive feelings, by encouraging him to behave more maturely. To do this, *consistently* set reasonable limits that allow him to explore and exercise his curiosity, but

5. Don't use physical punishment to discipline your child. If you do, he may assume that aggression is an acceptable way to respond when he doesn't get his way.

6. Monitor his television viewing. (See *Television,* page 500.) Preschool children may behave more aggressively if they watch violent programs on TV.

which draw the line at dangerous or antisocial behavior. With these guidelines he'll begin to sense what's acceptable and what's not. To repeat, the key is consistency. Praise him every time he plays well with another child, or whenever he feeds, dresses, or undresses himself without your help. As you do, he'll start to feel good about these accomplishments and himself. With his self-esteem on the rise, he'll also develop an image of himself as someone who behaves a certain way—the way that you have encouraged—and negative behavior will fade.

Hyperactivity

By adult standards, many two-year-olds seem "hyperactive." But it's perfectly normal for a child this age to prefer running, jumping, and climbing to walking slowly or sitting still. He may also speak so fast that it's hard to understand him and you may worry about his short attention span, but be patient. This excess energy usually subsides by the time he reaches school age.

While the energy level is high, it makes more sense for parents to adjust than to try to force the child to slow down. If your toddler is a "mover," adjust your expectations accordingly. Don't expect him to stay seated through a long community meeting or restaurant meal. If you take him shopping, be prepared to move at his pace, not yours. In general, avoid putting him in confining situations where you know you'll both be frustrated, and give him plenty of opportunities to release his excess energy through games involving running, jumping, climbing, and throwing or kicking a ball.

Without strong guidance, a very active child's energy can easily turn toward aggressive or destructive behavior. To avoid this, you need to establish clear and logical rules and enforce them consistently. You also can encourage more low-keyed behavior by praising him whenever he plays quietly or looks at a book for more than a few minutes at a time. It helps, too, to keep his routine of bedtime, mealtimes, baths, and naps as regular as possible so that he has a sense of structure to his day.

A small number of preschool children have problems with hyperactivity and short attention spans that persist beyond the preschool years. Only if these problems interfere with school performance or social behavior do they warrant special treatment. (See *Hyperactivity and the Distractible Child,* page 497.) If you suspect that your child may be having difficulties in these areas, ask your pediatrician to evaluate him to determine if a medically treatable problem exists.

Emotional Milestones
By the End of This Period

- **Expresses affection openly**

- **Expresses a wide range of emotions**
- **By three, separates easily from parents**
- **Objects to major changes in routine**

Since two-year-olds normally express a broad range of emotions, be prepared for everything from delight to rage. However, you should consult your pediatrician if your child seems very passive or withdrawn, perpetually sad, or highly demanding and unsatisfied most of the time. These could be signs of depression, caused either by some kind of hidden stress or biological problems. If your doctor suspects depression, he'll probably refer your child to a mental health professional for a consultation.

Developmental Health Watch

The developmental milestones listed in this book give you a general idea of the changes you can expect as your child gets older, but don't be alarmed if his development takes a slightly different course. Each child develops at his own pace. Do consult your pediatrician, however, if your child displays any of the following signs of possible developmental delay for this age range.

- Frequent falling and difficulty with stairs

- Persistent drooling or very unclear speech

- Inability to build a tower of more than four blocks

- Difficulty manipulating small objects

- Inability to copy a circle by age three

- Inability to communicate in short phrases

- No involvement in "pretend" play

- Failure to understand simple instructions

- Little interest in other children

- *Extreme* difficulty separating from mother

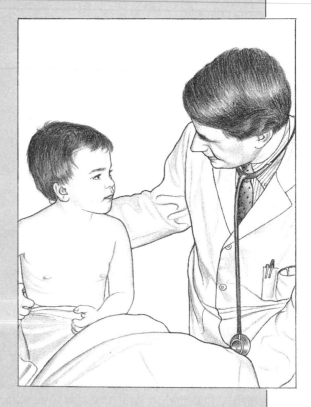

BASIC CARE

Feeding and Nutrition

By age two your toddler should be eating three meals a day, plus one or two snacks. He can eat the same food as the rest of the family. With his improved language and social skills, he'll become an active participant at mealtimes if given the chance to eat with everyone else.

Fortunately, your child's feeding skills have become relatively "civilized" by now. At age two he can use a spoon, drink from a cup with just one hand, and feed himself a wide variety of finger foods. By three he should also be able to use a fork and feed himself independently, spilling only occasionally between the plate and his mouth. But while he *can* eat properly, he's still learning to chew and swallow efficiently, and may gulp his food when he's in a hurry to get on with playing. For that reason, the risk of choking is high, so avoid the following foods that could be swallowed whole and block the windpipe.

hot dogs (unless sliced lengthwise, then across)	spoonfuls of peanut butter
	whole raw carrots
nuts (especially peanuts)	raw cherries with pits
round, hard candies	raw celery
whole grapes	

Sample One-Day Menu for a Two-Year-Old

This menu is planned for a two-year-old child who weighs approximately 27 pounds (12.5 kg).

1 tablespoon = ½ ounce (15 cc)
1 teaspoon = ⅓ tablespoon (5 cc)
1 cup = 8 ounces (240 cc)

BREAKFAST
¾ cup 2% milk
½ cup iron-fortified cereal or 1 egg
½ cup citrus or tomato juice or ⅓ cup cantaloupe or strawberries
½ slice toast
½ teaspoon margarine
1 teaspoon jelly

SNACK
1 ounce cream cheese
4 crackers
½ cup juice

Ideally, your child will eat from each of the basic four food groups each day:

1. Meat, fish, poultry, eggs

2. Milk, cheese, and other dairy products

3. Fruits and vegetables

4. Cereals, potatoes, rice, flour products

Don't be alarmed, however, if he doesn't meet this ideal. Many toddlers resist eating certain foods, or for long periods of time insist on eating only one or two favorite foods. The more you struggle with your child over his eating preferences, the more determined he'll be to defy you. As we suggested earlier, if you offer him a variety of foods and leave the choices to him, he'll eventually consume a

LUNCH

½ cup 2% milk

½ sandwich—1 slice whole wheat bread, 1 teaspoon margarine or 2 teaspoons salad dressing, and 1 ounce meat

2–3 carrot sticks or 2 tablespoons other dark yellow or dark green vegetable

1 small (½ ounce) oatmeal cookie

SNACK

½ cup 2% milk

½ apple (sliced), 3 dates, ⅓ cup grapes, or ½ orange

DINNER

½ cup 2% milk

2 ounces meat

⅓ cup pasta, rice, or potato

2 tablespoons vegetable

1 teaspoon margarine or 2 teaspoons salad dressing

balanced diet on his own. He may be more interested in healthful foods if he can feed them to himself. So, whenever possible, offer him finger foods (such as fruits or raw vegetables other than carrots and celery) instead of cooked ones that require a fork or spoon to eat.

Dietary Supplements. For toddlers who have a varied diet, vitamin supplements are rarely necessary. However, supplemental iron may be needed if your child eats very little meat, iron-fortified cereal, or vegetables rich in iron. Large quantities of milk (more than a quart per day) also may interfere with the proper absorption of iron, thus increasing the risk of iron deficiency. Your child should drink between 16 and 32 ounces of milk each day. This will provide most of the calcium he needs for bone growth and still not interfere with his appetite for other foods, particularly those that provide iron.

Teething and Dental Hygiene

By age two and a half your child should have all his primary (or baby) teeth, including the second molars, which usually erupt between twenty and thirty months. His secondary (or permanent) teeth probably won't start coming in until he's six or seven, though it's quite normal for them to arrive a little earlier or later than this.

As you might guess, the number-one dental problem among preschoolers is tooth decay. Approximately 8 percent of two-year-olds already have one or more cavities, and by age three that number increases to nearly 60 percent. Many parents assume that cavities don't matter in baby teeth because they'll be lost anyway. But that's a risky assumption. If primary teeth are lost too early because of decay or infection, the secondary teeth won't be ready to replace them. When that happens, the other primary teeth shift position to fill in the gap, so by the time the permanent teeth finally break through, there's no room for them.

The best way to protect your child's teeth is to teach him good dental habits. With the proper coaching he'll quickly adopt good oral hygiene as a part of his daily routine. By age two he should have his teeth brushed at least once a day, preferably at bedtime. However, while he may be an enthusiastic participant, he won't yet have the control or concentration to brush his teeth all by himself. You'll need to supervise and help him so that the brush removes all the plaque— the soft, sticky, bacteria-containing deposits that accumulate on the teeth, causing tooth decay.

Be sure to use a soft, multitufted nylon-bristle brush. Use only a small amount of toothpaste; *too* much fluoride could cause permanent tooth stains, and it's difficult to keep him from swallowing some of the toothpaste. If he doesn't like the taste of one type of paste, try another or just use plain water for a while. The brushing and rinsing are more important than the toothpaste.

You'll hear all kinds of advice on whether the best brushing motion is up and down, back and forth, or around in circles. The truth is that the direction really doesn't matter. What's important is to clean each tooth thoroughly, top and bottom, inside and out. This is where you'll encounter resistance from your child, who probably will concentrate on only the front teeth he can see. It may help to turn it into a game of "find the hidden teeth."

Aside from regular toothbrushing, your child's diet will play a key role in his dental health. And, of course, sugar is the big villain. The longer and more frequently his teeth are exposed to sugar, the greater the risk of cavities. This means that a giant piece of cake will do virtually no harm if he brushes his teeth immediately after eating it; but sticky caramel, toffee, gum, and dried fruit—which stay in his mouth and bathe his teeth in sugar for hours—could do serious damage. You should discourage these "sticky sugar" foods, especially as between-meal snacks.

By the end of this year, or when all twenty baby teeth are present, your child should make his first visit to the dentist. During this first appointment his teeth will be examined and he'll receive a basic lesson in oral hygiene. The dentist will make sure his teeth are coming in normally, and that there are no dental problems. He also may apply a topical fluoride solution to provide extra protection against cavities. If you live in an area where the water is not fluoridated, he may suggest a prescription of fluoride drops or chewable tablets for your toddler.

Toilet Training

By the time your toddler is two years old, you can probably hardly wait for him to be toilet trained. The pressure to reach that goal may be particularly intense if you want him to enter a nursery school or child-care program that requires the children to be trained. Be forewarned, though, that pushing him too early, before *he* is ready, may actually prolong the process. Studies indicate that many children who begin training before eighteen months are not completely trained until after age four. By contrast, most of those who start around age two are completely trained before their third birthdays.

Chances are, toilet training won't be very successful until your child is past the extreme negativism and resistance to it that occurs in early toddlerhood. He must *want* to take this major step. He'll be ready when he seems eager to please and imitate you, but also wants to become more independent. Most children reach this stage sometime between eighteen and twenty-four months, but it's also normal for it to occur a little later.

Once your toddler is ready to begin this process, things should proceed smoothly as long as you maintain a relaxed, unpressured attitude. Praise him for his successes, while not even mentioning his mistakes along the way. Punishing him or making him feel bad when he has an "accident" will only add an unnecessary element of stress, which is bound to hinder his progress.

How should you introduce your toddler to the concept of using the toilet? The best way is to let him watch other family members of his sex. (Watching people of the opposite sex may simply confuse him.) The first goal is bowel training.

For the first few weeks, let him sit on the potty fully clothed while you tell him about the toilet, what it's for, and when to use it.

Urination usually occurs with the bowel movement, so at first it is difficult for the child to separate the two acts. Once bowel training is established, however, most children (especially girls) will quickly relate the two. Boys usually learn to empty their bladders in the sitting position but gradually transfer to the standing one, particularly after watching the "older boys" do it that way.

The first step in training is to obtain a potty chair and place it in your child's room or in the nearest or most convenient bathroom. Then do the following:

1. For the first few weeks, let him sit on the potty fully clothed while you tell him about the toilet, what it's for, and when to use it.

2. Once he sits on it willingly, let him try it with his diaper off. Show him how to keep his feet planted solidly on the floor, since this will be important when he's having a bowel movement. Make the potty part of his routine, gradually increasing from once to several times each day.

3. When he's comfortable with this pattern, try changing his diaper while he's seated, and actually drop the contents of the dirty diaper into the pot under him to let him know that this is the chair's real purpose.

4. Once your child grasps how this process works, he'll probably be more interested in using the potty properly. To encourage this, let him play near the chair without a diaper and remind him to use the potty when he needs to. He's bound to forget or miss at first, but don't show your disappointment. Instead, wait until he succeeds and reward him with excitement and praise.

5. After he's using the potty chair regularly, gradually switch over from diapers to training pants during the day. At this point, most boys quickly learn to urinate into an adult toilet by imitating their fathers or older boys. Both girls and boys may also be able to use adult toilets outfitted with training seats.

Like most children, your own toddler probably will take a little longer to complete nap- and nighttime toilet training. Even so, these steps should be encouraged along with daytime training, and stressed even more after he's routinely using the potty. The best approach is to encourage your toddler to use the potty immediately before going to bed and as soon as he wakes up. Using training pants rather than diapers at nap time and bedtime may also help. Yes, there will be a few accidents, but a plastic sheet under the cloth one will minimize the cleanup. Reassure your toddler that all children have these accidents, and praise him whenever he makes it through the nap or night without wetting. Also tell him that if he wakes up in the middle of the night and needs to use the toilet, he can either go by himself or call for you to help him.

Your goal is to make this entire process as positive, natural, and nonthreatening as possible so he's not afraid to make the effort on his own. If nap- or nighttime wetting is still a consistent problem one year after daytime training is complete, discuss the situation with your pediatrician.

Sleeping

Between ages two and three your child may sleep from nine to thirteen hours a day. Most toddlers take a two- to three-hour nap around lunchtime, but some continue to take two shorter naps instead. Others give up napping entirely during this period. Unless he routinely becomes irritable and overtired from lack of sleep, there's no reason to force a nap schedule on your child.

At bedtime your toddler may become downright rigid about his going-to-sleep ritual. He now knows that at a certain time each day he changes into his nightclothes, brushes his teeth, listens to a story, and takes his favorite blanket, doll, or stuffed animal to bed. If you change this routine, he may complain or even have trouble going to sleep.

However, even with a completely predictable bedtime routine, some children between the ages of two and three resist going to sleep. If they're still in a crib, they may cry when left alone or even climb out to look for Mom and Dad. If they've graduated to a bed, they may get up again and again, insisting that they're not tired (even when they're clearly exhausted) or asking to join in whatever else is going on in the household. Part of this pattern is due to the typical negativism of this age—that is, the refusal to do anything Mom and Dad want them to do—and part is due to lingering separation anxiety. Despite their insistence on independence, they still feel uneasy when Mom or Dad is out of their sight—especially if they're left alone in the dark.

At bedtime, put your toddler in a good frame of mind for sleep by playing quietly or reading a pleasant story.

To give a child like this a feeling of control, let him make as many of the choices as possible at bedtime—for example, which pajamas to wear, what story he wants to hear, and which stuffed animals to take to bed. Also, leave a night-light on (he may even be more comfortable with the room light on), and let him sleep with his security objects (see *Transitional Objects,* page 234), to help take the edge off his separation anxiety. If he still cries after you leave, give him ten minutes or so to stop on his own before you go in to settle him down again; then leave for another ten minutes, and repeat the process. Don't scold or punish him, but also don't reward his behavior by feeding or staying with him.

For some children, this bedtime battle is actually an attempt to attract attention. If your toddler climbs out of bed night after night and comes looking for you, immediately return him to bed and tell him: "It's time to go to sleep." Don't reprimand or talk to him any further, and leave as soon as he's lying down again. He'll probably push you to your limits, getting up over and over for many nights in a row; but if you keep calm and remain consistent, he'll eventually realize he has nothing to gain by fighting you, and he'll start going to sleep more willingly.

Occasionally, your child may wake up from a nightmare. Bad dreams are common among toddlers, who still cannot distinguish between imagination and reality. Often if they hear a scary story or see violence on television, the images will stay in their minds, later cropping up as nightmares. And if they remember dreaming about a "monster," they may believe the monster is real.

When a nightmare awakens your toddler, the best response is to hold and comfort him. Let him tell you about the dream if he can, and stay with him until he's calm enough to fall asleep.

Your child will have nightmares more frequently when he's anxious or under stress, so try to keep the tension in his life to a reasonable level. If he has bad dreams often, see if you can determine what's worrying him in order to ease his anxiety. For example, if he's having nightmares during the period when he's being toilet trained, relax the pressure to use the potty and give him more opportunities to be messy through fingerpainting or playing with his food. Also try talking with him (to the extent he can) about issues that might be bothering him. Some of his anxieties may involve his separation from you, time spent in day care, or changes at home. Talking can sometimes help prevent these stressful feelings from building up.

As a general precaution against nightmares, carefully select television programs for your toddler, and don't allow him to watch TV right before bed. Even programs you consider innocent may contain images that are frightening to him. During the rest of the day, restrict his viewing to educational or nature programs geared to his age level. And don't let him watch violent programs of any kind, including cartoons.

At bedtime, put your toddler in a good frame of mind for sleep by playing quietly with him or by reading him a pleasant story. Soothing music may also help calm him as he falls asleep, and a night-light will help reassure him if he wakes up.

Discipline

What's the greatest challenge facing you as a parent during this and the next few years? Without a doubt, it's discipline. As you'll see, your child will develop the ability to control his impulses very gradually. At two and three he'll still be very physical, using temper tantrums, pushing, shoving, and quarreling to get his own way. Most of these reactions are very impulsive; although he doesn't plan to behave this way, he cannot yet control himself. Whether or not he consciously understands it, the whole point of his misbehavior is to find not only his limits but yours as well.

How you choose to establish and enforce these limits is a very personal issue. Some parents are quite strict, punishing their children whenever they violate a household rule; others are more lenient, preferring reason to punishment. Whatever approach you choose, if it's going to work, it must suit your child's temperament, and *you* must also feel comfortable enough with it to use it consistently. You'll find other helpful suggestions in *Some Golden Rules of Preschool Discipline,* on page 314.

Preparing for School

Kindergarten is usually considered the "official" start of school. But many children actually get a taste of school much earlier, through preschool, nursery school,

Some Golden Rules of Preschool Discipline

Whether you're a strict disciplinarian or use a more easygoing approach, the following guidelines should help you shape a strategy of discipline that ultimately will benefit both you and your child.

1. Always encourage and reward good behavior, as well as punishing the bad. Whenever you have a choice, take the positive route. For example, let's say your two-year-old is moving toward the stove; you should try to distract him with a safe activity instead of waiting for him to get into trouble. And when you notice that he has independently chosen to do something acceptable instead of misbehaving, congratulate him on making the right decision. By showing that you're proud of him, you'll make him feel good about himself and encourage him to behave the same way in the future.

2. Map out rules that help your child learn to control his impulsiveness and behave well socially without impairing his drive for independence. If your rules are overly restrictive, he may be afraid to explore on his own or try out new skills.

3. Always keep your child's developmental level in mind when you set limits, and don't expect more than he's capable of achieving. For example, a two- or three-year-old can't control the impulse to touch things that attract him, so it's unrealistic for you to expect him not to touch displays at the grocery or toy store.

4. Set the punishment to your child's developmental level. For example, if you decide to send your toddler to his room for misbehaving,

or group child-care programs that may accept children as young as two or three. These programs generally are not designed to begin your child's academic or "book-learning" education, but they will help him get used to the idea of leaving home for a period of time each day, and introduce him to the idea of learning in a group. They'll also give him a chance to improve his social skills by meeting and playing with other children and adults, as well as introducing him to more formal rules than you may have established at home. A preschool program may be especially beneficial if your child doesn't have many opportunities to meet don't keep him there for more than about five minutes; any longer, and he'll forget why he's there. If you prefer to reason with him, keep the discussion simple and practical. Never use hypothetical statements such as "How would you like it if I did that to you?" No preschooler can understand this kind of reasoning.

5. Don't change the rules or the punishments at random. That will only confuse your child. As he grows older you naturally will expect more mature behavior, but when you change the rules at that time, tell him why. For example, you may tolerate his pulling on your clothes to get your attention when he's two, but by the time he's four you may want him to find more grown-up ways of approaching you. Once you make the decision to change a rule, explain it to him before you start to enforce it.

6. Make sure that all the adults in the house and other care-givers agree to and understand the limits and punishments used to discipline your child. If one parent says something is okay and the other forbids it, the child is bound to be confused. Eventually he'll figure out that he can get his way by playing one adult against the other, which will make your lives miserable now and in the future. You can prevent this game-playing by presenting a united front.

7. Remember that you are a key role model for your child. The more even-handed and controlled your behavior, the more likely your child will be to pattern himself after you. If, on the other hand, you hit or spank him every time he breaks a rule, you're teaching him that it's okay to solve problems through violence.

other youngsters or adults, or if he has unusual talents or developmental problems that might benefit from special attention.

Aside from these advantages for your child, a preschool or child-care program may help you meet some of your own needs. Perhaps you're going back to work now, or have a new baby at home. Maybe you just want a few hours to yourself each day. At this stage of your child's development, the separation can be good for both of you.

If you've never regularly spent much time apart from your child, you may feel

Extinction

Extinction is a disciplinary technique that is most effective with two- and three-year-olds, though it may continue to be useful into the school years. The idea is to *systematically* ignore the child whenever he breaks a certain rule. As you might guess, this method should be used for misbehavior that's annoying or undesirable but not dangerous or destructive; the latter needs the more direct, immediate approach already discussed.

Here's how "extinction" works:

1. Define exactly what your child is doing wrong. Does he scream for attention in public? Does he cling to you when you're trying to do something else? Be very specific about the behavior and the circumstances in which it occurs.

2. Keep track of how often your child does this, and what you do in response. Do you try to pacify him? Do you stop what you're doing to pay attention to him? If so, you're unwittingly encouraging him to keep misbehaving over and over.

3. Keep recording the frequency of his misbehavior as you begin to ignore it. Remember, the key is consistency. Even if every person in the grocery store is glaring at you, do *not* show your child that you hear him screaming. Just keep doing what you're doing. At first, he'll probably act out more intensely and more frequently to test your will, but eventually he'll realize that you mean business.

4. When your child acts properly in a situation where he usually misbehaves, be sure to compliment him. If, instead of screaming when you refuse to buy him a candy bar, he talks to you in a normal voice, praise him for acting so grown up.

5. If you manage to extinguish the misbehavior for a while and then it reappears, start the process over again. It probably won't take as long the second time.

A preschool program may be especially beneficial if your child doesn't have many opportunities to meet other youngsters or adults.

sad or guilty about this new separation. You may also feel a little jealous if he becomes attached to his preschool teacher, especially if—in a moment of anger—he insists he likes his teacher better than you. But face it: You know very well that his teacher can't replace you, any more than preschool can replace your child's home life. These new relationships help him learn that there's a world of caring people in *addition* to his family. This is an important lesson for him to learn as he gets ready for the much larger world of primary school.

When you're hit by pangs of sadness, guilt, or jealousy, remind yourself that these structured separations will help your child become more independent, experienced, and mature, as well as giving you valuable time to pursue your own interests and needs. In the end, this time apart will actually strengthen the bond between the two of you.

Ideally, every preschool or nursery school program should offer children a safe and stimulating environment supervised by attentive, supportive adults. Unfortunately, not all programs meet these basic requirements. How can you distinguish the good from the bad? Here are some things to look for:

1. The school should have stated goals with which you agree. A good preschool tries to help children gain self-confidence, become more independent, and develop interpersonal skills. Be wary of programs that claim to teach academic skills or "speed up" children's intellectual development. From a developmental standpoint, most preschoolers are not yet ready to begin formal education, and pushing them will only prejudice them against learning. If you suspect that your child *is* ready to take on more educational challenges, ask your pediatrician to evaluate him or refer him to a child development specialist. If testing supports your suspicions, look for a program that will nurture his natural curiosity and talents without pressuring him to perform.

2. For a child with special needs—such as language or hearing impairment, behavioral or developmental problems—contact the director of special education in your local school system for a referral to appropriate programs in your area. Most neighborhood programs are not equipped to provide special therapy or counseling, and may do more harm than good by making your child feel "behind" or out of place among the other children.

3. Look for programs with a relatively small class size. Two- to three-year-olds do best in classes of ten children or fewer, with close adult supervision. By age four, your child will need slightly less direct supervision and thus may enjoy a group of up to twenty.

4. Teachers and aides should be trained in early-childhood development or education. Be suspicious of schools with an extremely high turnover rate among the teachers. Not only does this reflect poorly on the school's appeal to good teachers, but also makes it difficult to find people who know anything about the teachers who are now there.

5. Make sure you agree with the disciplinary methods used. Limit-setting should be firm and consistent without discouraging each child's need to explore. Rules should reflect the developmental level of the children in the program, and teachers should be supportive and helpful without stifling creativity and independent learning.

6. You should be welcome to observe your child at any time. While it may disrupt the daily routine to have parents coming and going, this openness reassures you that the program is consistent and the school has nothing to hide.

7. The school and grounds should be thoroughly child-proofed. (See Chapter 13 on safety.) Make sure there's an adult present at all times who knows basic first aid, including cardiopulmonary resuscitation (CPR—emergency breathing and heart stimulation techniques to revive a person who has stopped breathing or whose heart has stopped beating) and how to care for a child who's choking.

8. There should be a clear policy about illness among the children. It's best to isolate any child who becomes feverish. Also, whenever a child shows symptoms of an infectious illness, he should be sent home as soon as possible.

9. Hygiene is very important to minimize the spread of infectious illness among the children. Make sure there are child-height sinks and that children are encouraged to wash their hands when appropriate, especially after using the toilet. If the school accepts youngsters who are not yet toilet trained, a completely

Programs for Children with Potential Learning Difficulties

Some children who regularly fail to meet the developmental milestones for their age will have trouble learning in school unless they get special help. Delays in early development may point to a later learning disability. Early identification and intervention may prevent later problems in school and may help you deal with the day-to-day difficulties you might have been experiencing. (See *Hyperactivity and the Distractible Child,* page 497.)

If your pediatrician shares your concern, and the teacher (an invaluable source of information) also agrees, an additional professional evaluation may be suggested. But don't be alarmed. A learning disability is just a difficulty that any child could experience while trying to learn new information. It may only mean a problem with reading or understanding what is said to him.

A recent federal law (Public Law 99-457) encourages the establishment of state-supported services for infants and preschoolers who need special help to promote their early development and prepare them for school. While the actual way in which this law has been put into action varies from state to state, most states provide services for children who are at least three years old, and some provide programs beginning in early infancy. Children may be referred to these programs by their parents, pediatricians, preschool teachers, or any concerned adult. Recommendations for assistance are based on the child's needs and the available programs. Most of these services involve some form of nursery school or specialized preschool. (See also Chapter 19, "Developmental Disabilities.")

separate diaper-changing area is absolutely necessary to control the spread of infectious disease.

10. Be certain you agree with the program's overall philosophy. Find out ahead of time how the school's philosophy affects the curriculum, and decide whether this is right for your family. Many preschools are connected with churches, synagogues, or other religious organizations. Children do not generally have to be members of the congregation in order to attend the program, but they may be exposed to certain rituals of faith.

For more information about child-care and preschool programs, see Chapter 14.

FAMILY RELATIONSHIPS

A New Baby

During this year, if you decide to have another baby, you can expect your toddler to greet this news with considerable jealousy. After all, at this age he doesn't yet understand the concept of sharing time, possessions, or your affection. Nor is he eager to have someone else become the center of the family's attention.

The best way to minimize his jealousy is to start preparing him several months before the new baby is born. Let him help shop for clothes and equipment for the infant. If your hospital offers a sibling preparation class, take him there during the last month of pregnancy so he can see where the baby will be born and where he can visit you. Discuss what it will be like having a new member of the family and how he can help his little brother or sister. (See *Preparing Your Other Children for the Baby's Arrival,* page 18.)

Once the baby is home, encourage your toddler to help and play with the newborn, but don't force him. If he shows an interest, give him some tasks that will make him feel like a big brother, such as disposing of dirty diapers and picking

If he shows an interest, give the older sibling some tasks that will make him feel like a big brother.

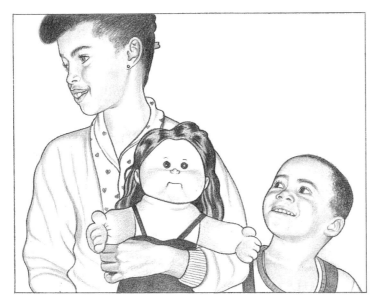

In the young child's eyes, his older brother or sister can do no wrong.

out the baby's clothes or bath toys. And when you're playing with the baby, invite him to join you and show him how to hold and move the baby. Make sure he understands, however, that he's not to do these things unless you or another adult is present. Remember to reserve special time for older siblings.

Hero Worship

Does your preschooler have older siblings? If so, you'll probably start seeing signs of hero worship around age two. In the young child's eyes, his older brother or sister can do no wrong. They are perfect role models—someone who's strong and independent, but still plays like a kid.

This kind of relationship has both benefits and drawbacks. Your preschooler will probably follow his older sibling around like a lapdog. This will give you some freedom and it's usually fun for both children for a while. But before long your older youngster will want his freedom back, which is bound to cause some disappointment—and perhaps tears or misbehavior—from your little one. Nevertheless, it's up to you to make sure that he doesn't overstay his welcome with big brother or sister. If you don't step in, their relationship will become very strained.

If the older child is eight or more, he probably already has a fairly independent life, with friends and activities outside the home. Given the chance, your preschooler will tag along with him everywhere he goes. But you shouldn't allow this unless the older child desires it or you, too, are going along and can keep the little one from becoming a pest. If the older child is of babysitting age, compensating him for taking care of your preschooler when you're out will help prevent resentment.

Pressures and rivalries are inevitable between siblings, but if there's a healthy balance between comradeship and independence, the bond between your children should grow and contribute to the self-esteem of both of them. Through his older sibling, your preschooler will get a sense of family values as well as a preview of what it's like to be a "big kid." The older child, meanwhile, will discover what it means to be a hero in his own home.

Being a role model for a younger brother or sister is a big responsibility, of course, and if you point this out to your older child it may prompt an improvement in behavior. If you feel he's a bad influence on his younger sibling, however, and he doesn't improve, you have no choice but to separate the two whenever he's misbehaving. Otherwise, your preschooler will mimic him and soon pick up bad habits. Don't embarrass the older child by punishing him in front of the preschooler, but make sure the younger one understands the difference between "good" and "bad" behavior.

VISIT TO THE PEDIATRICIAN

Beginning at twenty-four months, your child should see the pediatrician for a routine examination once a year. In addition to the screening tests performed during his earlier examinations, he may undergo the following laboratory tests.

- *A blood test:* to check for lead poisoning.

- *A urinalysis:* to check for infection and kidney and metabolic diseases. If the results of the first urinalysis are normal, it may not be repeated at future visits unless there are symptoms of a urinary-tract infection or related problems. However, some pediatricians do "dipstick" tests for sugar and protein at each regular checkup.

- *A skin test for tuberculosis:* may be given annualy, depending upon the risk of possible exposure.

IMMUNIZATION ALERT

By age two your child should have received the Hib Conjugate vaccine series against *Haemophilus influenzae B.* If not, consult your pediatrician.

SAFETY CHECK

Your preschooler is now able to run, jump, and ride a tricycle. His natural curiosity will drive him to explore many new things, including some dangerous places. Unfortunately, his self-control and ability to rescue himself are not yet fully developed, so he still needs careful supervision.

Falls
- Lock doors to any dangerous areas and hide the keys.
- Install stairway gates and window guards.

Burns
- Keep him away from kitchen appliances, irons, and wall or floor heaters.
- Place plug covers on all outlets.

Poisonings
- Keep all medicines in child-resistant containers and locked up out of reach.
- Store only those household products and medicines that are used regularly, and keep them in a locked cabinet.
- Post the phone number of your local poison control center or emergency room next to every telephone.
- Keep syrup of ipecac accessible. (See Chapter 13 on safety.)

Car Safety

- Supervise your child closely whenever he's playing in the driveway or near the street.

- Use approved and properly installed car seats for every ride.

12

AGE THREE TO FIVE YEARS

With your child's third birthday, the "terrible twos" are officially over and the "magic years" of three and four begin—a time when your child's world will be dominated by fantasy and vivid imagination. No longer a toddler, he is becoming more independent and, at the same time, more responsive to other children. This is a perfect age to introduce him to nursery school or an organized play group, where he can stretch his skills while learning to socialize.

During the next two years he'll mature in many areas, including toilet training and learning how to take proper care of his body. Since he can control and direct his movements now, he'll be able to play more organized games and sports. He also has mastered the basic rules of language and has built an impressive vocabulary that will increase daily as he experiments with words. Language will play an important role in his behavior, too, as he learns to express his desires and feelings verbally instead of through physical actions such as grabbing, hitting, or crying. Helping him put all his new skills together so he feels confident and capable is one of the most important ways you can guide his self-discipline during this period.

Your relationship with your child will change dramatically during this time. Emotionally, he is now able to view you as a separate person, with feelings and needs he's beginning to understand. When you're sad he may render some sympathy or offer to solve your problems. If you become angry at another person, he may announce that he, too, "hates" that individual. He wants very much to please you at this age, and knows that he must do certain things and behave in certain ways to do so. At the same time, though, he wants to please himself, so he'll often try to bargain with you: "If I do this for you, will you do that for me?" At times when you simply want him to behave as you desire, this attempt at bargaining may be irritating, but it's a healthy sign of independence, and it shows that he has a clear sense of justice.

By his fifth birthday your "baby" will be ready to tackle real school—the major occupation of childhood. This enormous step demonstrates that he's able to behave within the limits expected by school and society, and has the skills to take on increasingly complex learning challenges. It also means that he's able to separate comfortably from you and move out on his own. Not only can he now share and show concern for others, but also he has learned to value friends—both children and adults—outside his own family.

GROWTH AND DEVELOPMENT

Physical Appearance and Growth

Your child's body should continue to lose baby fat and gain muscle during this time, giving him a stronger and more mature appearance. His arms and legs will become more slender and his upper body more narrow and tapered. In some children, gains in height occur so much quicker than gains in weight and muscle that they may begin to look quite skinny and fragile. But this doesn't mean they are unhealthy or that anything is wrong; such children fill out gradually as their muscles develop.

Your preschooler's growth will gradually slow from about 5 pounds (2.3 kg) and 3½ inches (8.9 cm) during the third year to about 4½ pounds (2 kg) and 2½ inches (6.4 cm) during the fifth. Measure your child twice a year and record his measurements on his growth chart on pages 286–289. If his weight seems to be rising much faster than his height, he may be getting too fat, or if his height does not

How to Measure Your Child

Although your child may visit the doctor only once a year during the preschool period, you might want to measure and weigh him every six months. But you'll need his cooperation to get an accurate measurement of his height, so make it a special event. Start by establishing a special place where you can record the height. For example, you may want to make or buy a measuring scroll that can be fastened to the wall or the back of a door. Such a scroll usually is illustrated and has measurements marked up to about five feet. Space is available to note the child's height along with his age and the date. Alternatively, you can use a doorframe or wall. If you record the measurements there over a period of years, however, you'll have to be careful not to paint over it during remodeling. It's great fun for both you and your child to look back and see how he's grown!

To take the measurement, have him back up against the wall, bare feet flat on the floor. His head should be straight so that he's looking directly in front of him. Then use a ruler, book, or other firm, flat device to accurately line up the top of his head before making the mark on the wall.

increase at all in six months, he may have a growth problem. In either case, discuss this with your pediatrician.

Your child's face also will mature during these years. The length of his skull will increase slightly, and the lower jaw will become more pronounced. At the same time, the upper jaw will widen to make room for his permanent teeth. As a result, his face actually will become larger and his features more distinct.

AGE THREE TO FOUR YEARS

Movement

At age three your preschooler no longer has to concentrate on the mechanics of standing, running, jumping, or walking. His movements are now quite agile, whether he's going forward, backward, or up and down stairs. While walking he stands erect, shoulders pulled back and belly held in by firm abdominal muscles. He uses a regular heel-toe motion, taking steps of the same length, width, and speed. He can also ride a tricycle with great ease.

However, not everything comes easily yet. Your child may still need to make a conscious effort while standing on tiptoes or on one foot, while getting up from a squatting position, or while catching a ball. But if he keeps his arms extended and stiffly forward, he can catch a large ball as well as throw a smaller one overhand quite smoothly.

Your three-year-old still may be as active as he was at two, but he'll probably be more interested in structured games at this age. So instead of running aimlessly or flitting from one activity to another, he'll probably ride his tricycle or play in the sandbox for long periods at a time. He also may enjoy active games like tag, catch, or playing ball with other children.

Your preschooler may seem to be in constant motion much of the time. This is because he uses his body to convey thoughts and emotions that he still can't describe through language. Moving his body also helps him better understand many words and concepts that are new to him. For example, if you start talking about an airplane, he may spread his wings and "fly" around the room. While this level of activity may at times be annoying and distracting for you, it's a necessary part of his learning process and his fun.

Movement Milestones
By the End of This Period

- **Hops and stands on one foot up to five seconds**

- **Goes upstairs and downstairs without support**

- **Kicks ball forward**

- **Throws ball overhand**

- **Catches bounced ball most of the time**

- **Moves forward and backward with agility**

Because your child's self-control, judgment, and coordination are still developing, adult supervision remains essential to prevent accidents and injuries. However, it's a mistake to fuss too much over him. A few bumps and bruises are inevitable and even necessary to help him discover his limits in physical activity. As a general rule, you usually can leave him alone when he's playing by himself in his room. He'll play at his own pace, attempting only tasks within his abilities. Your concern and attention should be reserved for situations when he's around other children, hazardous equipment or machinery, and especially traffic. Other children may tease or tempt him to do things that are dangerous, while machines, equipment, and traffic defy his ability to predict their actions or speed. And he still cannot anticipate the consequences of actions such as chasing a ball into traffic or sticking his hand into the spokes of his tricycle, so you'll have to protect him in these situations.

Hand and Finger Skills

At age three your child is developing both the muscular control and the concentration he needs to master many precision finger and hand movements. You'll notice that he now can move each of his fingers independently or together, which means that instead of grasping his crayon in his fist he can hold it like an adult, with thumb on one side and fingers on the other. He will now be able to trace a square, copy a circle, or scribble freely.

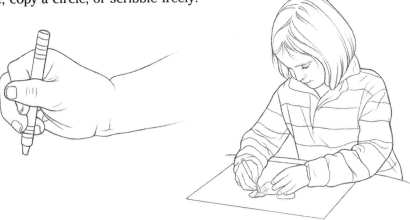

Because his spatial awareness has developed quite a bit, he's now more sensitive to the relationships between objects, so he'll position his toys with great care during play, and control the way he holds utensils and tools to perform specific tasks. This increased sensitivity and control will allow him to build a tower of nine or more cubes, feed himself without spilling very much, pour water from a pitcher into a cup (using two hands), unbutton clothes, and possibly put large buttons into buttonholes.

He's also extremely interested in discovering what he can do with tools such as a paper scissors, and with materials such as clay, paint, and crayons. He now has the skill to manipulate these objects and is beginning to experiment with using them to make other things. At first he'll play randomly with craft materials, perhaps identifying the end product only after it's completed. Looking at his scribbles, for example, he might decide they look like a dog. But soon this will change, and he'll decide what he wants to make *before* starting to work on it. This change in approach will motivate him to develop even more precision in moving and using his hands.

Quiet time activities that can help improve your child's hand abilities include:

- Building with blocks

- Simple jigsaw puzzles (four or five large pieces)

- Pegboards

- Stringing large wooden beads

- Coloring with crayons or chalk

- Building sand castles

- Pouring water into containers of various sizes

- Dressing and undressing dolls in clothing with large zippers, snaps, and laces

You can also encourage your child to use his hands by teaching him to use certain adult tools. He'll be thrilled to progress to a real screwdriver, a lightweight hammer, an eggbeater, or gardening tools. You'll need to supervise closely, of course, but if you let him help as you work you may be surprised how much of the job he can do himself.

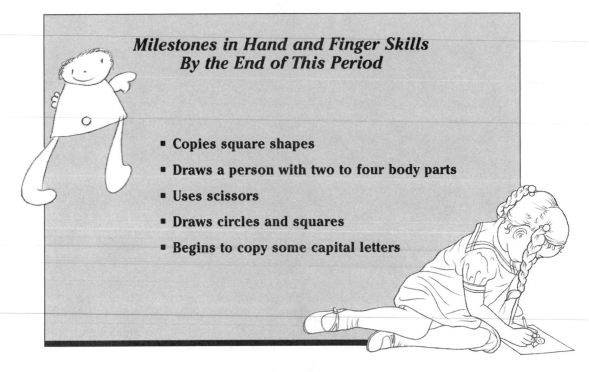

**Milestones in Hand and Finger Skills
By the End of This Period**

- Copies square shapes
- Draws a person with two to four body parts
- Uses scissors
- Draws circles and squares
- Begins to copy some capital letters

Language Development

At three your child should have an active vocabulary of about three hundred to one thousand words. He'll be able to talk in sentences of five or six words, and imitate most adult speech sounds. At times he'll seem to be chattering constantly—a phenomenon that may sometimes disturb you but which is essential to his learning of new words and gaining experience in using and thinking with them. Language allows him to express his thoughts, and the more advanced he is in speaking and understanding words, the more tools he'll have for thinking, creating, and telling you about it.

You should be able to see how your child uses language to help him understand and participate in the things going on around him. For instance, he can name most familiar objects, and he'll freely ask "What's this?" when he can't call something by name. You can help him expand his vocabulary by providing additional words that he might not even request. For example, if he points to a car and says, "Big car," you might answer, "Yes, that's a big gray car. Look how shiny the surface is." Or if he's helping you pick flowers, describe each one he collects: "That's a beautiful white-and-yellow daisy, and that's a pink geranium."

You also can help him use words to describe things and ideas he can't see. When he's describing the "monster" in his dream, for example, ask him if the monster is angry or friendly. Ask him about the monster's color, where he lives,

Stuttering

Many parents experience anxiety over their child's stuttering, even though such concern is usually unnecessary. After all, it's quite common for children to repeat sounds occasionally or to hesitate between words at around age two or three. Most of them never realize they're talking incorrectly, and they grow out of it without any special help. Only when this pattern persists over a long period of time (greater than two to three months) and interferes with communication is it considered actual stuttering.

About one in twenty preschool children stutter at some point, with a greater incidence in boys than in girls. The cause is unknown. Some children may have trouble learning the normal timing and rhythm of speech, but most have no medical or developmental problems. Stuttering may increase when a child is anxious, tired, ill, or when he gets excited and tries to talk too rapidly. Some children stutter when learning too many new words at once. At other times the child's thoughts are running ahead of his speech and he loses track of what he is saying in midsentence. Repeating a sound or word allows him to catch up.

The more frustrated a child becomes about his stuttering, the more trouble he will have. Thus, the best approach for parents is simply to ignore the stuttering. Listen when he speaks, but don't correct him. At the same time, you can set a good example by talking calmly and correctly and using simple language when addressing the child. If your child stutters, it may also help him if you slow down the entire pace of your household, including the speed at which *you* speak. You should set aside some relaxed time each day to play and talk quietly with him. You can build his self-esteem by praising him for all the activities he's doing *correctly,* while not drawing attention to his speech difficulties. With this kind of support, children who develop true stuttering can usually overcome their problem before entering school.

When a child's stuttering is severe, speech therapy may be necessary to help avoid a long-term problem. If your child frequently repeats sounds or parts of words, is very self-conscious, and shows obvious signs of tension (such as facial twitches or grimaces), let your pediatrician know. Also inform him of any family history of serious stuttering. He'll probably refer you to a speech and language specialist.

If the question is, "Why can't the dog talk to me?" you can invite your child to look into the question further by finding a book about dogs.

whether he has friends. Not only will this help your child use words to express his thoughts, but also it may help him overcome his fear of such strange and frightening images.

Your three-year-old is still learning to use pronouns such as "I," "me," "mine," and "you." As simple as these words seem, they're difficult ideas to grasp because they indicate where his body, possessions, or authority ends and someone else's begins. And to complicate matters, the terms change depending on who's talking. Often he may use his name instead of saying "I" or "me." Or when talking to you, he may say "Mommy" instead of "you." If you try to correct him (for example, by suggesting "Say 'I would like a cookie' ") you'll only confuse him more, because he'll think you're talking about yourself. Instead, use these pronouns correctly in your own speech. So, for instance, say "I would like you to come" instead of "Mommy would like you to come." Not only will this help him learn the correct use of these words, but also it will help him establish a sense of you as an individual apart from your role as Mommy.

At this age, your child's speech should be clear enough that even strangers can understand most of what he says. Even so, he still may mispronounce as many as half the speech sounds he uses. For example, he may use *w* for *r* ("wabbit," "wice," "wose"), *d* for *th* ("dis," "dat," "den"), or *t* for any sounds he has trouble with ("tee" for *three*, "tik" for *six*). The sounds *b, p, m, w,* and *h* will only begin to emerge midway through this year, and it may take months after that for him to perfect his use of them.

Language Milestones
By the End of This Period

- **Understands the concepts of "same" and "different"**

- **Has mastered some basic rules of grammar**

- **Speaks in sentences of five to six words**

- **Speaks clearly enough for strangers to understand**

- **Tells stories**

Cognitive Development

Your three-year-old will spend most of his waking hours questioning everything that happens around him. He loves to ask "Why do I have to . . . ?" and he'll pay close attention to your answers as long as they're simple and to the point. Don't feel that you have to explain your rules fully; he can't yet understand such reasoning and isn't interested in it anyway. If you try to have this kind of "serious" conversation, you'll quickly see him stare into space or turn his attention to more entertaining matters, like a toy across the room or a truck passing outside the window. Instead, telling him to do something "because it's good for you" or "so you don't get hurt" will make more sense to him than a detailed explanation.

Your child's more abstract "why" questions may be more difficult, partly because there may be hundreds of them each day, and also because some of them have no answers—or none that you know. If the question is "Why does the sun shine?" or "Why can't the dog talk to me?" you can answer that you don't know, or invite him to look into the question further by finding a book about the sun or about dogs. Be sure to take these questions seriously. As you do, you help broaden your child's knowledge, feed his curiosity, and teach him to think more clearly.

When your three-year-old is faced with specific learning challenges, you'll find his reasoning still rather one-sided. He can't yet see an issue from two angles, nor can he solve problems that require him to look at more than one factor at the same time. For example, if you take two equal cups of water and pour one into a short fat container and the other into a tall skinny one, he'll probably say the tall container holds more water than the short. Even if he sees the two equal

Cognitive Milestones
By the End of This Period

- Correctly names some colors
- Understands the concept of counting and may know a few numbers
- Approaches problems from a single point of view
- Begins to have a clearer sense of time
- Follows three-part commands
- Recalls parts of a story
- Understands the concept of same/different
- Engages in fantasy play

cups to start with and watches you pour, he'll come up with the same answer. By his logic, the taller container is "bigger" and therefore must hold more. At around age seven, children finally understand that they have to look at all the possible aspects of a problem before arriving at an answer.

At about three years of age your child's sense of time will become much clearer. He'll now know his own daily routine and will try hard to figure out the routines of others. For example, he may eagerly watch for the mail carrier who arrives every day, but be perplexed that the garbage man comes only one day out of seven. He'll understand that certain special events, like holidays and birthdays, occur every once in a while, but even if he can tell you how old he is, he'll have no real sense of the length of a year.

Although it's almost human nature to try to measure your child's intellectual progress, beware of over- or underestimating his reasoning or thinking ability without formal testing. It's easy to convince yourself that a friendly, happy, highly verbal three-year-old is brilliant, while the quieter, more laid-back youngster playing next to him is not as bright. This may or may not be true, but the only way to know for sure is to have both children professionally tested. All pediatricians are familiar with these developmental evaluations, and some actually perform the tests themselves. Many pediatricians prefer to refer children to testing specialists. So, if you believe your child is either gifted or lagging behind, ask your doctor about such testing. If your suspicions prove true, you may want to enter him in a special program geared to his individual needs and abilities.

Social Development

At age three your child will be much less selfish than he was at two. He'll also be less dependent on you, a sign that his own sense of identity is stronger and more secure. Now he'll actually play *with* other children, interacting instead of just playing side by side. In the process, he'll recognize that not everyone thinks exactly as he does, and that each of his playmates has many unique qualities, some attractive and some not. You'll also find him drifting toward certain children and starting to develop friendships with them. As he creates these friendships, he'll discover that he, too, has special qualities that make him likable—a revelation that will give a vital boost to his self-esteem.

There's some more good news about your child's development at this age: As he becomes more aware of and sensitive to the feelings and actions of others, he'll gradually stop competing and will learn to cooperate when playing with his friends. In small groups he'll be capable of taking turns and sharing toys, even if he doesn't always do it. Instead of grabbing, whining, or screaming for something, he'll actually ask politely much of the time. As a result, you can look forward to less aggressive behavior and calmer play sessions. Often, three-year-olds are able to work out their own solutions to disputes by taking turns or trading toys.

However, particularly in the beginning, you'll need to encourage this type of cooperation. For instance, you might suggest that he "use his words" to deal with problems instead of violent actions. Also, remind him that when two children are sharing a toy, each gets an equal turn. Suggest ways to reach a simple solution when he and another child want the same toy, perhaps drawing for the first turn or finding another toy or activity. This doesn't work all the time, but it's worth a try. Also, help him with the appropriate words to describe his feelings and desires so that he doesn't feel frustrated. Above all, show him by your own example how to cope peacefully with conflicts. If you have an explosive temper, try to tone down your reactions in his presence. Otherwise, he'll mimic your behavior whenever he's under stress.

No matter what you do, however, there probably will be times when your child's anger or frustration becomes physical. When that happens, restrain him from hurting others, and if he doesn't calm down quickly, move him away from the other children. Talk to him about his feelings and try to determine why he's so upset. Let him know that you understand and accept his feelings, but make it clear that physically attacking another child is *not* a good way to express these emotions.

Help him see the situation from the other child's point of view by reminding him of a time when someone hit or screamed at him, and then suggest more peaceful ways to resolve his conflicts. Finally, once he understands what he's done wrong—but not before—ask him to apologize to the other child. However, simply saying "I'm sorry" may not help your child correct his behavior; he also needs to know *why* he's apologizing. He may not understand right away, but by age four these explanations will begin to mean something to him.

Actually, the normal interests of three-year-olds will help keep fights to a minimum. They spend much of their playtime in fantasy activity, which tends to be more cooperative than play that's focused on toys or games. As you've probably already seen, your preschooler and his playmates enjoy assigning different roles to one another and then launching into an elaborate game of make-believe using imaginary or household objects. This type of play helps them develop important social skills, such as taking turns, paying attention, communicating (through actions and expressions as well as words), and responding to one another's actions. And there's still another benefit: Because pretend play allows children to slip into any role they wish—including He-Man, Wonder Woman, Superman, or the Fairy Godmother—it also helps them explore more complex social ideas, such as power, wealth, compassion, cruelty, and sexuality.

By watching the role-playing that goes on during your child's make-believe games, you'll also see that he's beginning to identify with his own sex. So while playing house, boys will naturally adopt the father's role and girls the mother's, reflecting whatever differences they've noticed in their own families and in the world around them. At this age, your son may also be fascinated by his father, older brothers, or other boys in the neighborhood, while your daughter will be drawn to her mother, older sisters, and other girls.

Research shows that a few of the developmental and behavioral differences that typically distinguish boys from girls are *biologically* determined. For instance, the average preschool boy tends to be more aggressive, while girls generally are more verbal. However, most gender-related characteristics at this age are more likely to be shaped by cultural and family influences. Even if you try to run a so-called nontraditional household, with both parents working and sharing family responsibilities, your child will still find conventional male and female role models in television, magazines, books, billboards, and the families of friends and neighbors.

Social Milestones
By the End of This Period

- **Interested in new experiences**
- **Cooperates with other children**
- **Plays "Mom" or "Dad"**
- **Increasingly inventive in fantasy play**
  - **Dresses and undresses**

- **Negotiates solutions to conflicts**
- **More independent**

Your daughter, for example, may be encouraged to play with dolls by advertisements, gifts from well-meaning relatives, and the approving comments of adults and other children. Boys, meanwhile, are generally guided away from dolls (though most enjoy them during the toddler years) in favor of more rough-and-tumble games and sports. The girl who likes to roughhouse is called a tomboy, but the boy who plays that way is called tough or assertive. Not surprisingly, children sense the approval and disapproval in these labels, and adjust their behavior accordingly. Thus, by the time they enter kindergarten, children's sexual identities are well established.

Children this age will often take this identification process to an extreme. Girls will insist on wearing dresses, nail polish, and makeup to school or to the playground. Boys will strut, be overly assertive, and carry pretend guns wherever they go. This behavior reinforces their sense of being male or female.

As your child develops this identity during these early years, he's bound to experiment with attitudes and behaviors of both sexes. There's rarely any reason to discourage such impulses, except when the child is resisting or rejecting strongly established cultural standards. For instance, if your son wanted to wear dresses every day, you should gently persuade him to take a more conventional course. If he persists, however, discuss the issue with your pediatrician.

Your child may also imitate certain types of behavior that adults consider sexual, such as flirting. If he's very dramatic and expressive, you may be put off by these "suggestive" looks and movements, but the suggestions are all in *your* head, not his. At this age he has no mature sexual intentions, and his mannerisms are merely playful mimicry, so don't worry. If, however, his imitation of sexual behavior is very explicit or otherwise indicates that he may have been personally exposed to sexual acts, you should discuss this with your pediatrician, as it could be a sign of sexual abuse.

Emotional Development

Your three-year-old's vivid fantasy life will help him explore and come to terms with a wide range of emotions, from love and dependency to anger, protest, and fear. He'll not only take on various identities himself, but also he'll often assign living qualities and emotions to inanimate objects, such as a tree, a clock, a truck, or the moon. Ask him why the moon comes out at night, for example, and he might reply, "To say hello to me."

From time to time, expect your preschooler to introduce you to one of his imaginary friends. Some children have a single make-believe companion for as long as six months; some change "pretend playmates" every day, while still others never have one at all or prefer imaginary animals instead. Don't be concerned, incidentally, that these phantom friends may signal loneliness or emotional upset;

Emotional Milestones By the End of This Period

- **Imagines that many unfamiliar images may be "monsters"**
- **Views self as a whole person involving body, mind, and feelings**
- **Often cannot distinguish between fantasy and reality**

they're actually a very creative way for your child to sample different activities, lines of conversation, behavior, and emotions.

You'll also notice that, throughout the day, your preschooler will move back and forth freely between fantasy and reality. At times he may become so involved in his make-believe situation that he can't tell where it ends and reality begins. His play experience may even spill over into real life. One night he'll come to the dinner table convinced he's Prince Charming; another day he may come to you sobbing after hearing a ghost story that he believes is true.

While it's important to reassure your child when he's frightened or upset by an imaginary incident, be careful not to belittle or make fun of him. This is a normal and necessary stage in emotional development and thus should not be discouraged. Above all, never joke with him about "locking him up if he doesn't eat his dinner" or "leaving him behind if he doesn't hurry up." He's liable to believe you and feel terrified the rest of the day—or longer!

From time to time, try to join your child in his fantasy play. By doing so you can help him find new ways to express his emotions and even work through some problems. For example, you might suggest "sending his doll to school" to see how *he* feels about going to nursery school. Don't insist on participating in these fantasies, however. Part of the joy of fantasy for him is being able to control these imaginary dramas, so if you plant an idea for make-believe, stand back and let him make of it what he will. If he then asks you to play a part, keep your performance low-key. Let the world of pretend be the one place where *he* runs the show.

Back in real life, let your preschooler know that you're proud of his new independence and creativity. Talk with him, listen to what he says, and show him that his opinions matter. Give him choices whenever possible—in the foods he eats, the clothes he wears, the games you play together. This will give him a sense of importance and help him learn to make decisions. Keep his options simple, however. When you go to a restaurant, for example, narrow the menu to two or three items from which he is allowed to choose. Otherwise he may be overwhelmed

Developmental Health Watch

Because each child develops in his own particular manner, it's impossible to tell exactly when or how he'll perfect a given skill. The developmental milestones listed in this book will give you a general idea of the changes you can expect as your child gets older, but don't be alarmed if his development takes a slightly different course. Alert your pediatrician, however, if your child displays any of the following signs of possible developmental delay for this age range.

- Cannot throw a ball overhand
- Cannot jump in place
- Cannot ride a tricycle
- Cannot grasp a crayon between thumb and fingers
- Has difficulty scribbling
- Cannot stack four blocks
- Still clings or cries whenever his parents leave him
- Shows no interest in interactive games
- Ignores other children
- Doesn't respond to people outside the family
- Doesn't engage in fantasy play
- Resists dressing, sleeping, using the toilet
- Lashes out without any self-control when angry or upset
- Cannot copy a circle
- Doesn't use sentences of more than three words
- Doesn't use "me" and "you" appropriately

and unable to decide. (A trip to an ice cream store that sells twenty flavors can be agonizing if you don't limit his choices!)

What's the best approach? Despite what we've already said, one of the best ways to nurture his independence is to maintain fairly firm control over all parts of his life, while at the same time giving him some freedom. Let him know that you're still in charge, and that you don't expect him to make the big decisions. When his friend is daring him to climb a tree, and he's afraid, it will be comforting to have you say no, so that he doesn't have to admit his fears. As he conquers many of his early anxieties and becomes more responsible in making his own decisions, you'll naturally give him more control. In the meantime, it's important that he feels safe and secure.

AGE FOUR TO FIVE YEARS

Before you know it, the somewhat calm child of three becomes a dynamo of energy, drive, bossiness, belligerence, and generally out-of-bounds behavior. You may be reminded of the earlier trials and tribulations you went through when he was two, but your child is now taking different directions. Though he may seem to be chasing off in all directions at the same time, he is actually learning from all these experiences. Eventually this will let up (just when you thought you couldn't take it for another day), and gradually a more confident, calm child will emerge around his fifth birthday.

Meanwhile, this is a difficult age to handle. Each day, there are new challenges to deal with. The emotional highs and lows will have him appearing secure and bragging one minute, and insecure and whining the next. In addition, four-year-olds become set in some of their routines, not wanting to change for fear they will not know what to do. This fixation reveals some of the insecurity they are feeling during these months.

Their out-of-bounds behavior is also seen in the language they use. They enjoy using four-letter words, and they love to watch your expression when they say them. They use these words more to get a response out of you than for any other reason, so don't overreact to them.

This energy machine of yours still has little sense of property. To him, all things appear to be his. Four-year-olds are not thieves or liars, though. They simply believe that possession means ownership.

Also obvious during this year is the tremendous spurt of imaginative ideas that spring from children's minds and mouths. The "monsters" they talked with at school, or the "dragon" who helped them across the street, represent the normal tall tales told by four- to five-year-olds. They reflect the fact that children of this age are trying to distinguish fact from fantasy, and their fantasies sometimes get a bit out of control. All of this kind of behavior and thinking will help your youngster build a secure foundation as he emerges into the world of the kindergarten.

Movement

Your preschooler now has the coordination and balance of an adult. Watch him walk and run with long, swinging, confident strides, go up and down stairs without holding the handrail, stand on his tiptoes, whirl himself in a circle, and pump himself on a swing. He also has the muscular strength to perform challenging activities such as turning somersaults and doing a standing broad jump. It will be a tossup as to who is excited more by his progress—him or you.

In your child's eagerness to prove just how capable and independent he is, he'll often run ahead of you when out on a walk. His motor skills are still way ahead of his judgment, however, so you'll need to remind him frequently to wait and hold your hand when crossing the street. The need for vigilance is just as important when he is anywhere near water. Even if he can swim, he probably can't swim well or consistently. And should he accidentally go under, he may get frightened and forget how to keep himself afloat. So *never* leave him alone in a pool or in the water at the beach.

Movement Milestones By the End of This Period

- **Stands on one foot for ten seconds or longer**
- **Hops, somersaults**
- **Swings, climbs**
- **May be able to skip**

Hand and Finger Skills

Your four-year-old's coordination and ability to use his hands are almost fully developed. As a result he's becoming able to take care of himself. He now can brush his teeth and get dressed with little assistance, and he may even be able to lace his shoes.

Notice how he uses his hands with far more care and attention when he draws now. He'll decide in advance what he wants to create and then go ahead with it. His figures may or may not have a body, and the legs may be sticking out of the head. But now they'll have eyes, a nose, and a mouth, and most important to your child, they are people.

Because of this growing control over his hands, arts and crafts in general are becoming more exciting for him now. His favorite activities may include:

- Writing and drawing, holding the paper with one hand and the pencil or crayon in the other

- Tracing and copying geometric patterns, such as a star or diamond

- Card and board games

- Painting with a brush and fingerpainting

- Clay modeling

- Cutting and pasting

- Building complex structures with many blocks

These kinds of activities will not only permit him to use and improve many of his emerging skills, but he'll also discover the fun of creating. In addition, because of the success he'll feel with these activities, his self-esteem will grow. You may even notice certain "talents" emerging through his work, but at this age it's not advisable to push him in one direction over another. Just be sure to provide a broad range of opportunities so he can exercise all his abilities. He'll take the direction he enjoys most.

Milestones in Hand and Finger Skills By the End of This Period

- Copies triangle and other geometric patterns
- Draws person with body
- Prints some letters
- Dresses and undresses without assistance
- Uses fork, spoon, and (sometimes) a table knife
- Usually cares for own toilet needs

Language Development

At about age four your child's language skills will blossom. He'll now be able to pronounce most of the sounds in the English language, with the following exceptions: *f, v, s,* and *z* probably will remain difficult for him until midway through age five, and he may not fully master *sh, l, th,* and *r* until age six or later.

Your preschooler's vocabulary will have expanded to around 1,500 words by now, and it will grow by another 1,000 or so over the course of this year. He can now tell elaborate stories using relatively complex sentences of up to eight words. And he will tell you not only about things that happen to him and things he wants but also about his dreams and fantasies.

Don't be surprised, however, if some of the words he uses are *not* ones you want to hear. After all, by now he's learned how powerful words can be, and he'll enthusiastically explore this power, for better and for worse. Thus, if your four-year-old is like most others, he'll be very bossy at times, perhaps commanding you and your spouse to "stop talking" or his playmates to "come here *now.*" To help counteract this, teach your child how to use "please" and "thank you." But also review the way you and other adults in the family address him and each other. Chances are, he's repeating many of the commands he most often hears.

Your child will also probably pick up many swear words at this age. From his point of view, these are the most powerful words of all. He hears adults say them when they are most angry or emotional, and whenever he uses them himself, he gets quite a reaction. What's the best way to stop this behavior? Be a good role model and make a conscious effort not to use these words, even when you are stressed. In addition, try to minimize your child's using these words without drawing too much attention to them. He probably has no idea what these words really mean; it's just the energy of them that he enjoys.

When your child's upset, you may find he'll use words as insults. Of course this is certainly preferable to physical violence, although it can be quite disturbing to you. Remember, though, that when your child uses these words, he's disturbed too. If he says "I hate you!" what he really means is "I am very angry, and I want you to help me sort out my feelings." By getting angry and shouting back at him you'll only make him feel more hurt and confused. So instead, remain calm and tell him you know he doesn't really hate you. Then let him know that it's okay to feel angry, and talk about the events leading up to his outburst. Try giving him the words that will allow him to tell you how he feels.

If the insults he chooses are mild ones, the best response may be a joke. For example, let's presume he calls you a "wicked witch"; you might laugh and respond: "And I'm just boiling up a pot of bat's wings and frog's eyes. Care to join me for supper?" This kind of humor is an excellent way to take the edge off his anger as well as your own.

Of course, sometimes your preschooler doesn't have to say anything offensive to try your patience—his constant chatter can do it just as quickly. One solution at these moments is to redirect his verbal energy. For instance, instead of allowing him to chant mindless sound rhymes, teach him some limericks or songs, or take time out to read some poems. This will help him learn to pay more attention to the words he speaks, and will boost his appreciation for the written language as well.

Language Milestones By the End of This Period

- **Recalls part of a story**
- **Speaks sentences of more than five words**
- **Uses future tense**
- **Tells longer stories**
- **Says name and address**

Learning to Read

Is your child interested in learning the names of letters? Does he look through books and magazines on his own? Does he like to "write" with a pencil or pen? Does he listen attentively during story time? If the answer is yes, he may be ready to learn some of the basics of reading. If not, he's like most preschoolers, and will take another year or two to develop the language skills, visual perception, and memory he needs to begin formal reading.

While a few four-year-olds sincerely want to learn to read, and will begin to recognize certain familiar words, there's no need to push your child to do so. Even if you succeed in giving him this head start, he may not maintain it once school begins. Most early readers lose their advantage over other children during the second or third grade, when the other students acquire the same basic skills.

The crucial factor that determines whether a student will do well or poorly in school is *not* how aggressively he was pushed early on, but rather his own enthusiasm for learning. This passion cannot be forced on a child by teaching him to read at age four. To the contrary, many

Cognitive Development

By age four your child is beginning to explore many basic concepts that will be taught in greater detail in school. For example, he now understands that the day is divided into morning, afternoon, and night, and that there are different seasons. By the time he enters kindergarten he may know some days of the week, and that each day is measured in hours and minutes. He also may comprehend the essential ideas of counting, the alphabet, size relationships (big versus small), and the names of geometric shapes.

There are many good children's books that illustrate these concepts, but don't feel compelled to rush things. There's no advantage to his learning them this early, and if he feels pressured to perform now, he may actually resist learning when he gets to school.

The best approach is to offer your child a wide range of learning opportunities. For instance, this is the perfect age to introduce him to zoos and museums, if so-called early learning programs *interfere* with the child's natural enthusiasm by forcing him to concentrate on tasks for which he's not yet ready.

So what's the most successful approach to early learning? Let your child set his own pace and have fun at whatever he's doing. Don't drill him on letters, numbers, colors, shapes, or words. Instead, encourage his curiosity and tendencies to explore on his own. Read him books that he enjoys, but don't push him to learn the words. Provide him with educational experiences, but make sure they're also entertaining.

When your child is ready to learn to read, there are plenty of valuable tools to help him—educational television, games, songs, and even some of the latest computer teaching programs. But don't expect them to do the job alone. You need to be involved too. If he's watching *Sesame Street* or other educational television programs, for example, sit with him and talk about the concepts and information being presented. If he's playing with a computer program, do it with him so you can make sure it's appropriate for his abilities. If the game is too frustrating for him, it may diminish some of his enthusiasm and defeat the whole purpose. Active learning in a warm, supportive environment is the key to success.

you haven't already. Many museums have special sections designed for children, where he can actively experience the learning process.

At the same time, you should respect his special interests and talents. If your child seems very artistic, take him to art museums and galleries, or let him try a preschool art class. Also, if you know an artist, take him for a visit so he can see what a studio is like. On the other hand, if he's most interested in machines and dinosaurs, take him to the natural history museum, help him learn to build models, and provide him with construction kits that allow him to create his own machines. Whatever his interests, you can use books to help answer his questions and open his horizons even further. At this age, then, your child should be discovering the joy of learning so that he will be self-motivated when his formal education begins.

You'll also find that, in addition to exploring practical ideas, your four-year-old probably will ask many "universal" questions about subjects such as the origin of the world, death and dying, and the composition of the sun and the sky. Now, for example, is when you'll hear the classic question "Why is the sky blue?" Like

***Cognitive Milestones
By the End of This Period***

- **Can count ten or more objects**

- **Correctly names at least four colors**

- **Better understands the concept of time**

- **Knows about things used every day in the home (money, food, appliances)**

so many other parents, you may have trouble answering these questions, particularly in simple language your child will understand. As you grapple with these issues, don't make up answers but rely instead on children's books that deal with them. Your local library should be able to recommend age-appropriate books to help you.

Social Development

By age four your child should have an active social life filled with friends, and he may even have a "best friend" (usually, but not always, of his own sex). Ideally, he'll have friends in the neighborhood or in his nursery school or preschool whom he sees routinely. But what if your child is not enrolled in preschool and doesn't live near other families? And what if the neighborhood children are too old or too young for him? In these cases, you'll want to arrange play sessions with other preschoolers. Parks, playgrounds, and preschool activity programs all provide excellent opportunities to meet other children.

Once your preschooler has found playmates he seems to enjoy, you need to take some initiative to encourage their relationships. More than anything, encourage him to invite these friends to your home. It's important for him to "show off" his home, family, and possessions to other children. This will help him establish a sense of self-pride. Incidentally, to generate this pride, his home needn't be luxurious or filled with expensive toys; it needs only to be warm and welcoming.

It's also important to recognize that at this age his friends are not just playmates. They also actively influence his thinking and behavior. He'll desperately want to be just like them, even during those times when their actions violate rules and standards you've taught him from birth. He now realizes that there are other values and opinions besides yours, and he may test this new discovery by demanding things that you've never allowed him—certain toys, foods, clothing, or permission to watch adult TV programs.

Don't despair if your child's relationship with you changes dramatically in light of these new friendships. For instance, he may be rude to you for the first time in his life. When you tell him to do something that he objects to, he may occasionally tell you to "shut up" or even swear at you. Hard as it may be to accept, this sassiness is actually a positive sign that he's learning to challenge authority and test the limits of his independence.

Once again, the best way to deal with it is to express disapproval, and you might want to discuss with him what he really means or feels. The more emotionally you react, the more you'll encourage him to continue behaving badly. But if the subdued approach doesn't work, and he persists in talking back to you, a "timeout" is the most effective form of punishment (see page 365).

Bear in mind that even though your child is exploring the concepts of good and bad at this age, he still has an extremely simplified sense of morality. Thus,

Social Milestones By the End of This Period

- **Wants to please friends**

- **Wants to be like his friends**

- **More likely to agree to rules**

- **Likes to sing, dance, and act**

- **Shows more independence and may even visit a next-door neighbor by himself**

Developmental Health Watch

Because each child develops in his own particular manner, it's impossible to predict exactly when or how your own preschooler will perfect a given skill. The developmental milestones listed in this book will give you a general idea of the changes you can expect as your child gets older, but don't be alarmed if his development takes a slightly different course. Alert your pediatrician, however, if your child displays any of the following signs of possible developmental delay for this age range.

- Exhibits extremely fearful or timid behavior

- Exhibits extremely aggressive behavior

- Is unable to separate from parents without major protest

- Is easily distracted and unable to concentrate on any single activity for more than five minutes

- Shows little interest in playing with other children

- Refuses to respond to people in general, or responds only superficially

- Rarely uses fantasy or imitation in play

- Seems unhappy or sad much of the time

when he obeys rules rigidly, it's not necessarily because he understands or agrees with them, but more likely because he wants to avoid punishment. In his mind, consequences count but not intentions. So when he breaks something of value, for instance, he probably assumes he's bad, whether or not he did it on purpose. But he needs to be taught the difference between accidents and misbehaving.

To help him learn this difference, you need to separate him—as a person—from his behavior. When he does or says something that calls for punishment, make sure he understands that he's being punished for a particular act that he's done, and not because *he's* "bad." Instead of telling him that *he* is bad, describe specifically what he did wrong, clearly separating the person from the behavior. For example, if he is picking on a younger sibling, explain that it's wrong to make

- Doesn't engage in a variety of activities

- Avoids or seems aloof with other children and adults

- Doesn't express a wide range of emotions

- Has trouble eating, sleeping, or using the toilet

- Can't differentiate between fantasy and reality

- Seems unusually passive

- Cannot understand two-part commands using prepositions ("Put the cup on the table"; "Get the ball under the couch.")

- Can't correctly give his first and last name

- Doesn't use plurals or past tense properly when speaking

- Doesn't talk about his daily activities and experiences

- Cannot build a tower of six to eight blocks

- Seems uncomfortable holding a crayon

- Has trouble taking off clothing

- Cannot brush his teeth efficiently

- Cannot wash and dry his hands

someone else feel bad, rather than just saying, "You're bad." When he accidentally does something wrong, comfort him and tell him you understand it was unintentional. Try not to get upset yourself, or he'll think you're angry at *him* rather than about what he did.

It's also important to give your preschooler tasks that you know he can perform—and then praise him when he does them well. He's quite ready for simple responsibilities like helping to set the table or cleaning his room. When you go on family outings, explain that you expect him to behave well, and congratulate him when he does so. Along with the responsibilities, give him ample opportunities to play with other children, and tell him how proud you are when he shares or is helpful to another youngster.

Emotional Development

Just as it was when he was three, your four-year-old's fantasy life will remain very active. However, he's now learning to distinguish between reality and make-believe, and he'll be able to move back and forth between the two without confusing them as much.

As his games of pretend become more advanced, don't be surprised if he experiments with make-believe games involving some form of violence. War games, "cowboys and Indians," dragon-slaying, and even games like tag all fall into this category. Some parents forbid their children to play with store-bought toy guns, only to find them cutting, pasting, and using cardboard guns, or simply pointing a finger and shouting "bang bang." But parents shouldn't panic over these activities. This is *not* evidence that these youngsters are "violent." A child has no idea what it is to kill or die. For him, toy guns are an innocent and entertaining way to be competitive and boost his self-esteem.

If you want a gauge of your own child's developing self-confidence, listen to the way he talks to adults. Instead of hanging back, as he may have done at two or three, he now is probably friendly, talkative, and curious. He is also likely to be especially sensitive to the feelings of others—adults and children alike—and to enjoy making people happy. When he sees they're hurt or sad, he'll show sympathy and concern. This probably will come out as a desire to hug or "kiss the hurt," because this is what *he* most wants when he's in pain or unhappy.

At about this age, your preschooler also may begin to show an avid interest in basic sexuality, both his own and that of the opposite sex. He may ask where babies come from and about the organs involved in reproduction and elimination. He may want to know how boys' and girls' bodies are different. When confronted with these kinds of questions, answer in simple but correct terms. Don't go into a long explanation, and try not to appear overly embarrassed or serious about the matter. Your four-year-old doesn't need to know the details about intercourse, but he should feel free to ask questions, knowing he'll receive direct and accurate answers.

Along with this increased interest in sexuality, he'll probably also play with his own genitals and may even demonstrate an interest in the genitals of other children. These are not adult sexual activities but signs of normal curiosity and don't warrant scolding or punishment.

At what point should parents set limits on such exploration? This really is a family matter. It's probably best not to overreact to it at this age, since it's normal if done in moderation. On the other hand, children need to learn what's socially appropriate and what's not. So, for example, you may decide to tell your child:

- Interest in genital organs is healthy and natural.

- Nudity and sexual play in public are not acceptable.

- No other person, including even close friends and relatives, may touch his "private parts." The exceptions to this rule are doctors and nurses during physical examinations, and his own parents when they are trying to find the cause of any pain or discomfort he's feeling in the genital area.

At about this same time, your child may also become fascinated with the parent of the opposite sex. A four-year-old girl can be expected to compete with her mother for her father's attention, just as a boy may be vying for his mother's attention. This so-called Oedipal behavior is a normal part of personality development at this age, and will disappear in time by itself if the parents take it in stride. There's no need to feel either threatened or jealous because of it.

Emotional Milestones
By the End of This Period

- **Aware of sexuality**

- **Able to distinguish fantasy from reality**

- **Sometimes demanding, sometimes eagerly cooperative**

BASIC CARE

Feeding and Nutrition

As a preschooler your child should have a healthy attitude toward eating. Ideally, by this age he no longer uses eating—or not eating—to demonstrate defiance, nor does he confuse food with love or affection. Generally (though almost certainly not always), he'll now view eating as a natural response to hunger, and meals as a pleasant social experience.

Your child should also be good company at meals now, and be ready to learn basic table manners. By age four he'll no longer grip his fork or spoon in his fist, because he's now able to hold them like an adult. With instruction, he also can learn the proper use of a table knife. You can now teach him other table manners as well, such as not talking with his mouth full, using his napkin instead of his sleeve to wipe his mouth, and not reaching across another person's plate. While it's necessary to explain these rules, it's much more important to model them; he'll behave as he sees the rest of the family behaving. He'll also develop better

How Much Is Enough?

Many parents worry whether their children are getting "enough" to eat. Here are some guidelines to help you make sure your child gets enough, but not too much.

1. Offer him small portions, with seconds only if he asks for them. Here are some acceptable "child-sized" portions:

4–6 ounces milk or juice	4 tablespoons vegetables
½ cup cottage cheese or yogurt	½ cup cereal
2 ounces hamburger	2 ounces chicken
1 slice toast	1 teaspoon margarine

2. Limit snacks to two a day, stressing healthful items in place of such foods as soft drinks, candy, pastries, or salty and greasy items. Not only will additional snacks decrease his appetite for proper meals, but also they'll expose his teeth to cavity-causing foods over an extended period of time. To minimize the risk of cavities and excess calories, encourage nutritious snack foods such as:

fruit and fruit juices	finger sandwiches
carrot, celery,	oatmeal cookies
or cucumber sticks	bran muffins
yogurt	cheese
toast or crackers	

3. Don't use food as a reward for good behavior.

table manners if you have a family custom of eating together. So make at least one meal a day a special and pleasant family time, and have your child set the table or help in some other way in the meal preparation.

Despite your four-year-old's general enthusiasm for eating, he may still have very specific preferences in food, some of which may vary from day to day. As irritating as it may be to have him turn up his nose at a dish he devoured the

4. Make sure your child is actually hungry or thirsty when he asks for food or drink. If what he really wants is attention, talk or play with him, but don't use food as a pacifier.

5. Don't allow him to eat while playing, listening to stories, or watching television. This will lead to "unconscious" eating well past the point when he's full.

6. Learn the calorie counts for the foods he eats most often and monitor how many calories he consumes on an average day. The total for a child aged four to five should be 900 to 1,800, or about 40 calories per pound of body weight.

7. Don't worry if your child's food intake is inconsistent. One day he may seem to eat anything he can get his hands on, and the next he'll grimace at the sight of everything. When he refuses to eat, he may not be hungry because he's been less active than the day before. Also consider the possibility that he's using food as a means of exercising control. Especially during the period when he's being negative about nearly everything, he's bound to resist your efforts to feed him. When that happens, don't force him to eat. Rest assured that even at the height of this negativism, he will not starve himself, and he'll seldom, if ever, lose weight. If, however, a markedly decreased appetite persists for more than one week, or there are other signs of illness such as fever, nausea, diarrhea, or weight loss, consult your pediatrician.

8. Limit his milk intake. Milk is an important food, mainly because of its calcium content. Too much milk, however, may reduce his appetite for other important foods. Your child needs to drink approximately one pint (16 ounces) of milk a day to meet his calcium requirement.

day before, it's best not to make an issue of it. Let him eat the other foods on his plate or select something else to eat. As long as he chooses foods that aren't overly sugary, fatty, or salty, don't object. However, encourage him to try new foods by offering him very small amounts to taste, not by insisting that he eat a full portion of an unfamiliar food.

Television advertising, incidentally, can be a serious obstacle to your pre-

Sample One-Day Menu
for a Preschooler

This menu is planned for a four-year-old child who weighs approximately 36 pounds (16.5 kg).

1 tablespoon = ½ ounce (15 cc)

1 teaspoon = ⅓ tablespoon (5 cc)

1 cup = 8 ounces (240 cc)

BREAKFAST

½ cup 2% milk

½ cup cereal

½ cup citrus or tomato juice or ½ cup cantaloupe or strawberries

SNACK

½ cup 2% milk

½ cup banana

1 slice whole wheat bread

1 teaspoon margarine

1 teaspoon jelly

LUNCH

¾ cup 2% milk

1 sandwich—2 slices whole wheat bread, 1 teaspoon margarine or 2 teaspoons salad dressing, and 1 ounce meat or cheese

¼ cup dark yellow or dark green vegetable

SNACK

1 teaspoon peanut butter

1 slice whole wheat bread or 5 crackers

½ cup fruit juice

DINNER

¾ cup 2% milk

2 ounces meat, fish, or chicken

½ cup pasta, rice, or potato

¼ cup vegetable

1 teaspoon margarine or 2 teaspoons salad dressing

schooler's good nutrition. Children this age are extremely receptive to ads for sugary cereals and sweets, especially after they've visited other homes where these foods are served. To combat these outside influences, keep your own home as "clean" as possible. Stock up on low-sodium, low-sugar, low-fat products, and reserve sweets for special occasions. Also monitor your child's television viewing and exposure to advertisements. Eventually he'll become accustomed to healthy foods, and that may make him less susceptible to the temptation of the more sugary, salty, or greasy ones. (See *Television,* page 500.)

Dietary Supplements. Ordinarily, preschool children don't need any vitamin supplements. However, if your child is extremely selective and refuses to eat a balanced diet, you should consult your pediatrician concerning the need for a multivitamin.

Beyond Toilet Training

By about age three most children are already fully toilet trained, although as a toddler your child may have used a potty chair rather than a toilet. But now, in preparation for school, he must get used to using toilets both at home and away.

The first step in this process is to position the potty next to the toilet so that your child gets used to "going to the bathroom." When he has fully adjusted to the potty seat, get a child-size toilet seat for the toilet, and provide a sturdy box or stool so he can climb up and down by himself. This will also give him a surface on which to plant his feet while using the toilet. Once he has completely and voluntarily made the transition from potty to toilet, remove the potty.

Little boys generally sit down to urinate during early toilet training, but as preschoolers they'll begin to copy their fathers, friends, or older brothers, and stand up while urinating. As your son learns to do this, make sure he also lifts the toilet seat beforehand. You'd better be prepared to do some extra cleaning around the toilet bowl for a while, since he probably won't have perfect aim for some time. (Note: Make sure the toilet seat stays in the raised position when put there; injuries have been caused by falling seats.)

Away from home, teach your child to recognize rest room signs, and encourage him to use public bathrooms whenever necessary. You'll need to accompany and

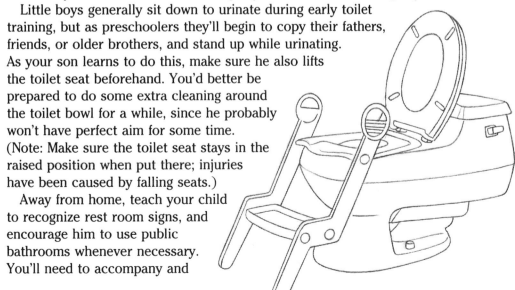

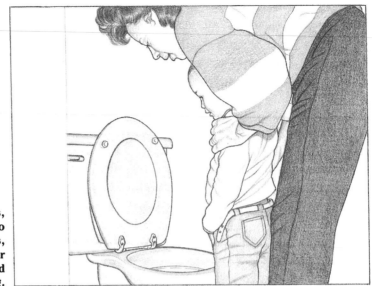

As preschoolers, little boys begin to copy their fathers, friends, or older brothers, and stand up while urinating.

assist him in the beginning, but he should become comfortable enough to manage by himself during his fifth year. Whenever possible, however, an adult or older child should accompany him or at least wait outside the door.

He'll also need to learn that, at times, he'll have to use facilities when they're available, even *before* he feels a strong need. This will make outings and especially car trips much more pleasant. Sometimes, however, a bathroom will not be available when it's really needed, so you may have to teach your child to urinate outdoors. This isn't a problem for boys, but little girls must learn to squat so their feet and clothing are out of the way. You can help your daughter by showing her the appropriate position and physically supporting her as she squats.

During the entire process described above, you'll need to help your child in the bathroom at first—whether at home or away. Plan not only on wiping, but also on helping him dress and undress. Before he goes to school, however, you must teach him to manage entirely on his own. For a girl, that means teaching her to wipe from front to back, particularly after bowel movements, because contact between feces and the urethra or vagina can lead to urinary-tract or vaginal infections. A boy must learn to pull down his pants (if elastic-waisted) or use the fly front. To make this procedure as simple as possible, dress your child in clothes that can easily be undone without help. Although overalls, for example, may be practical in other ways, they're very difficult for a child to get into and out of without help. For children of both sexes, elastic-waisted pants or shorts are generally the most practical clothing at this age. A dress with elastic-waisted underpants will work equally well for girls.

Bed-Wetting

All young children occasionally wet their beds while going through nighttime toilet training. Also, even after your preschooler is able to stay dry at night for a number of days or weeks, he may start wetting at night again, perhaps in response to stress or changes occurring around him. When this happens, don't make an issue of it. Simply put him back in training pants at night for a while, and as the stress decreases, he should stop wetting. If it persists, however, check with your pediatrician.

Most children with an ongoing bed-wetting pattern have never been consistently dry at night. Some may have unusually small bladders, even by age four or five, so they can't last a whole night without urinating. In other cases, the processes required for successful bladder control take longer to develop.

If your preschooler persistently wets his bed, the problem probably will gradually disappear as he matures. Medication is not advisable during the preschool years, nor should he be punished or ridiculed. He is not wetting the bed on purpose. Limiting his fluid intake and waking him up to use the bathroom probably won't help the situation much either, but reassuring him that these mishaps are "no big deal" may help him feel less ashamed. Also, make sure he understands that the bed-wetting is not his fault, and that it will probably stop as he gets older. If there's a family history of bed-wetting, let him know that, too, further taking the burden off his shoulders.

Should the bed-wetting continue after age five, your pediatrician may recommend one of several treatment programs. See *Wetting Problems,* page 593.

For a child who has been completely toilet trained for six months or longer, and who suddenly begins wetting his bed again, there may be an underlying physical or emotional cause. If he has frequent accidents during the day as well as at night, "dribbles" urine constantly, or complains of burning or pain while urinating, he may have a urinary-tract infection or other medical problem. In any of these cases, see your pediatrician as soon as possible.

Sleeping

For many parents, their child's bedtime is the most dreaded part of the day, and often for good reason: Unless a preschooler is very tired, he may resist going to sleep. This is even more likely to be a particular problem if he has older brothers or sisters who stay up later. The younger one is bound to feel left out and afraid of "missing something" if the rest of the family is up after he's asleep. These feelings are understandable, and there's no harm in granting him some flexibility in his bedtime. But remember that he needs at least ten to twelve hours of sleep each night.

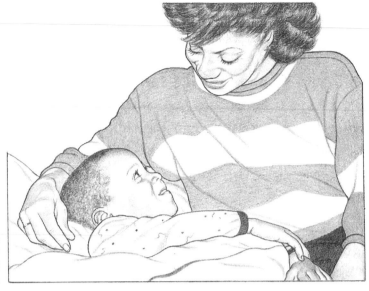

Unless a preschooler is very tired, he may resist going to sleep.

The best way to prepare your preschooler for sleep is by reading him a story. Once the story is over and you've said your goodnights, don't let him stall further, and don't let him talk you into staying with him until he falls asleep. He needs to get used to doing this on his own. Also, don't let him roughhouse or get involved in a lengthy play project right before bedtime. The calmer and more comforting the activity, the better and the more easily he'll go to sleep.

Most preschoolers sleep through the night, but often rouse several times to check their surroundings before falling back to sleep. There may be nights, however, when your child's very active dreams awaken him. These vivid dreams often represent the way he viewed some of the events of the day. They may reflect some impulse, aggressive feeling, or inner fear that only comes to the surface by way of these frightening images or dreams.

By the time he's five or a little older, he'll be better able to understand that these images are only dreams, but as a preschooler he may still need to be reassured that they're not real. So, when he wakes up in the middle of the night, afraid and crying, try holding him, talking about the dream, and staying with him until he's calm. For your own peace of mind, don't forget that these are only nightmares and not a serious problem.

To further help your child overcome his nighttime fears, you might read him stories about dreams and sleep. As you talk about these stories together, he'll better understand that everyone has dreams and that he needn't be frightened of them. Some classic children's books on these topics include Maurice Sendak's *In the Night Kitchen,* Russell Hoban's *Bedtime for Frances,* Mercer Mayer's *There's a*

Nightmare in My Closet, and Chris van Allsberg's *Ben's Dream.* But always make sure that these books aren't themselves frightening to him.

Occasionally, your preschooler will be in bed, appearing to be awake and desperately upset, perhaps screaming and thrashing, eyes wide open and terrified, but he won't respond to you. In this case, he's neither awake nor having a nightmare. Rather, you're witnessing something called a "night terror"—a mysterious and, to parents, distressing form of sleep behavior common during the preschool and early school years. Typically, the child falls asleep without difficulty, but wakes up an hour or so later, wide-eyed and terrified. He may have hallucinations, point to imaginary objects, kick, scream, and generally be inconsolable. The only thing you can really do in this situation is hold the child to protect him from hurting himself. Reassure him: "You're fine. Mommy and Daddy are here." After ten to thirty minutes of this, he'll settle down and go back to sleep. The next morning, he'll remember nothing about the occurrence.

Some children may have just one episode of night terrors, while others experience them several times. It's rare, however, for them to recur frequently or for a prolonged period. In cases of very frequent night terrors, sleep medications prescribed by your pediatrician may be helpful, but the best strategy seems to be to wait them out. They'll disappear naturally as the child grows older.

But what about those instances in which you're sure your child is having neither a nightmare nor a night terror but is nevertheless waking up and calling for you? Give him about ten minutes to put himself back to sleep before you go to him. Then merely reassure him that everything is all right, and leave. Don't reward him for waking up by giving him food or by bringing him to your room.

How to Tell a Nightmare from a Night Terror

Sometimes it's difficult to tell the difference between a nightmare and a night terror. This chart should help.

	NIGHTMARE	NIGHT TERROR
What is it?	A scary dream followed by complete awakening	A partial arousal from very deep sleep
When do you become aware of it?	After it's over, when your child wakes up and tells you	During the terror itself, as he screams and thrashes. Afterward he is calm.
Time of occurrence	In the second half of the night, when dreaming is most intense	Usually one to four hours after falling asleep
Appearance and behavior	Crying and fearful after waking	Sitting up, thrashing, bizarre movements. Crying, screaming, moaning, talking. Bulging eyes, racing heart, sweating. The apparent fear and confusion disappear after awakening.
Responsiveness	After waking, child is aware of and reassured by your presence	Child is not very aware of you, and may physically push you away, screaming and thrashing more if you try to restrain him.
Return to sleep	May have trouble falling back to sleep because of fear	Returns to sleep rapidly without fully awakening
Memory of experience	Often remembers dream and may talk about it	No memory of a dream or of yelling or thrashing

Adapted from *Solve Your Child's Sleep Problems,* by Richard Ferber, M.D.

Timeout

Although you can't ignore dangerous or destructive behavior, you can call a timeout. This technique is most successful with three- and four-year-olds, who generally know when they've done something seriously wrong and understand that this is why they're being punished.

Here's how the timeout works:

1. Define the behavior you want to stop, and keep track of how frequently it occurs. Punishment of any kind should be used only when your child is *intentionally* doing something he knows is forbidden.

2. Warn him that if he continues to do this, he'll be punished.

3. Identify a timeout area, preferably a room that's empty of toys, television, or other attractions—in other words, one that's as boring as possible for the child. If such a room isn't available, use a chair facing the wall in a hall or unoccupied room.

4. When the child does something he knows will result in timeout, send him immediately to the area you have selected and tell him how long he has to stay there. Five minutes is usually sufficient. Place a timer or a clock within view so he can keep track of the time.

5. If he cries or screams, reset the timer for another five minutes. If he leaves the timeout area, return him there and reset the timer.

6. Use a timeout each and every time he violates this particular rule. Also, any time you notice that he's observing the rule, congratulate him for behaving so well.

Discipline

By age four your preschooler will have his unpredictable emotional responses somewhat under control, but still won't be able to manage his feelings of defiance. Thus, at this age, he may openly disobey family rules, talk back, or even swear at you. He'll often behave badly just to annoy you. As irritating and embarrassing as this behavior may be, it's rarely a sign of emotional illness and usually disappears by school age if you take a relaxed approach to it.

This doesn't mean letting your child control or intimidate you. Believe it or not, even *he* doesn't want that. On the contrary, he expects you to restrain him when he gets too far out of line, just as he assumes you'll protect him when he does something dangerous. So you must teach him what is acceptable behavior and what isn't. The only way he'll learn to set his own limits later is by having you set reasonable limits for him now.

In deciding what limits to set, keep in mind that many of the strategies you used when he was younger are also suitable now. It's still important to reward good behavior more often than punishing bad, and to avoid physical punishments. And it's still essential to deal with misbehavior promptly and fairly, not waiting so long that your child forgets why he's being disciplined.

At this age his misconduct tends to be more conscious than it once was. As a toddler your child acted out of curiosity, trying to find and test his limits; now that he's a preschooler his misbehavior tends to be less innocent. A three-year-old whose mother is pregnant or whose parents are separated, for example, may react by doing something that he well knows is forbidden. He may not understand the emotions that are driving him to break the rules, but he certainly realizes that he is breaking them.

To discourage such behavior, help your child learn to express his emotions through words instead of violent or obnoxious actions. The mother whose son hits her might say, "Stop it! You are very angry. Please tell me why." If he refuses to stop, a "timeout" may be necessary.

Sometimes your child won't be able to explain his anger, and it will be up to you to help him. This can be a real test of skill and patience, but is well worth it. Usually, however, the problem will be fairly obvious if you examine the situation from his viewpoint. The pregnant mother described above, for example, can suggest, "You're angry about the baby, aren't you?" This approach is most successful if you encourage your child to talk about his problems and feelings on an ongoing basis.

Preparing for Kindergarten

Kindergarten is a major turning point for your child. Even if he has attended nursery school, he'll be expected to be much more grown up as he enters elementary school, and he'll be given more responsibilities and more independence. "Regular" school is also a much larger and more confusing social setting than any he's known before. Even though his class may be no larger than the one in nursery school, he may spend part of each day mixing with children from older classes. So he must be prepared emotionally not only for the tasks of kindergarten but also for the challenge of being one of the youngest in a big school.

As your child nears school age, you can start the preparations by talking to him about going to kindergarten. Explain how his routine will change when he

Lying

Lying at this age is very common. Preschoolers lie for a variety of reasons. Sometimes it's because they're afraid of punishment, or it may be because they've gotten carried away with their fantasies, or perhaps they're imitating behavior they see among adults. Before you punish your child for not telling the truth, make sure you understand his motives.

When he's lying to avoid punishment, he may have broken one of the household rules. For instance, he may have damaged something he shouldn't have been handling. Or maybe he was too rough and he hurt one of his playmates. In any case, he's concluded that what he did is more serious an offense than lying. If you want him to confess, you must make him understand that lying is the greater misdeed. So save your anger and punishment for times when he conceals the truth, and instead of accusing him when you suspect he's done something wrong, say something like "This is broken. I wonder how it happened?" If he confesses, remain calm and even-tempered, and make the punishment less severe than if he persisted in the lie. This way he may be less afraid to divulge the truth next time.

Telling tall tales is entirely different from lying. This usually is just an expression of your child's imagination at work, and does no harm to anyone. It becomes a problem only if you—or your child—can no longer distinguish truth from fantasy. Although a tall tale doesn't require punishment, it does call for a lesson. Tell him the story of the "Boy Who Cried Wolf" and explain how it could be dangerous for him to keep making up falsehoods. (For example, what if he were hurt or ill, and you didn't know whether or not to believe him?) Make it clear that it's in his own best interests to tell the truth.

When your child's lying is just a copy of your behavior, you can best stop it by eliminating the model. When your child hears you telling "white lies," he may not understand that you're doing it to be tactful or in an effort to avoid hurting another person's feelings. All he knows is that you're not telling the truth—so he feels free to lie as well. You can try teaching him the difference between outright lies and white lies, but he probably won't understand most of it. You're more likely to succeed by changing your behavior.

Kindergarten is a
major turning point
for your child.

starts school, and get him involved in choosing his back-to-school clothes. It will also help to drive or walk him by the school occasionally, and even go in and show him the classroom so he'll see firsthand what to expect. Many schools open their classrooms before school begins so you can take your child in and introduce him to his teacher. All this preparation will help build his enthusiasm and lessen his anxietey about taking his next big step away from home.

Prior to beginning school, your child also should have a thorough physical examination (many states require it). Your doctor will evaluate your child's vision, hearing, and overall physical development, make sure he has had the necessary immunizations, and give him any boosters he needs. (See Chapter 27, "Immunizations," especially the immunization schedule on page 613.) Depending on state law and the likelihood of exposure, he may also administer a test for tuberculosis and he may send you to a laboratory for other tests.

In most school systems, children are accepted for kindergarten based on their age, often with a very rigid cutoff date as a guideline. For example, if your child turns five years old by December 31, he may be allowed to start school at age four, but if his birthday is January 1, he probably will have to wait until the following fall. While this approach works well for most children, it's not perfect. Developmental rates vary so widely that one child may be prepared for school at four while another is not mature enough until late in his fifth year.

For these reasons, if your child's birthday falls between October and late December, you might consider keeping him in nursery school for another year. If in doubt, and your child is attending nursery school, his teacher may be able to

help you. She's seen him in action with other children and should be able to tell you if he's ready for a more structured classroom experience. Developmental testing of your child may also help determine whether he has the necessary skills to do well in kindergarten. Your pediatrician can help you make arrangements for such testing. These tests can also be helpful if you feel your child is advanced for his age, and you wish him to start school earlier than normal.

Travel Activities

If you make car trips fun, your child is less likely to resist the confinement. Here are some suggestions to help pass the time.

- Talk about the passing sights. Ask your child what he sees out his window. Point out interesting sights. When he begins to learn colors, letters, and numbers, ask him to identify them in signs and billboards. Remember to keep *your* eyes on the road, however!

- Keep a variety of picture books and small toys in the car within reach of his car seat.

- Keep several cassettes of children's songs or stories in the car. Encourage your child to sing along with his favorite tunes.

- For longer trips, bring along a small box filled with age-appropriate acitivity materials, such as coloring or activity books, crayons, paper, stickers, paper dolls, pop-beads, a Viewmaster®, or an Etch-A-Sketch®. (Do not allow scissors in the car; they could be hazardous in the event of a sudden stop.)

- Stop at least every two hours to break up the trip. This will allow your child a chance to stretch, perhaps eat a snack, and have a diaper change or use the toilet.

- If your child is prone to motion sickness, it may help to give him an appropriate dose of Dramamine® one half hour before getting in the car. (See *Motion Sickness,* page 599.)

The trip will be more pleasant and comfortable for everyone if you follow several additional rules consistently, wherever you are.

- Don't allow yelling, hitting, biting, or loud noisemaking.

- Don't allow children to touch door handles.

- Never let a child play alone in the car.

- Remind children to be considerate of other people in the car.

Many public school systems conduct preschool screening tests for all kindergarten-age children to assess their readiness for school. This testing of developmental skills is generally held at the school during the summer before the child is scheduled to enter kindergarten. At the same time, school administrators may also collect information about the child's health, making sure he's been fully immunized, and perhaps examining his hearing and vision as well.

Unless there's evidence that your child will do very poorly, however, the best test may be a trial run when school opens. If there is a serious question about his progress at the end of the year, a decision will have to be made concerning his promotion. This will be based largely on his ability to learn, follow directions and routines, and relate to the other children as well as the teacher.

Traveling with Your Preschooler

As your child gets older and more active, traveling will become more challenging. He will be restless when confined to a seat and, with his increasing willfulness, may protest loudly when you insist that he stay put. For safety's sake you will need to be firm, but if you provide enough distractions he may actually forget his restlessness. The specific tricks of traveling will vary somewhat with your mode of transportation.

Traveling by Car. Even on the shortest trips, your child must stay in his car seat or booster seat. (See *Car Seats,* page 395, for guidelines on selection and instal-

Even on the shortest trips, your child must stay in a car seat or booster seat.

lation of car seats.) Most automobile accidents occur within five miles of home and at speeds under twenty-five miles per hour, so there can be no exceptions to the rule. If your youngster protests, refuse to start the car until he's fastened in. If you are driving and he escapes from his seat, pull over until he is secured again.

Traveling by Plane. When flying with a young child, always let the airlines know in advance. Special seating arrangements may be possible, and there may be a selection of "kiddie" meals available if you inquire when making your reservations.

One advantage of air travel is that you and your child can take walks when the "Fasten Seat Belt" sign is off. This is the best antidote to restlessness, especially if you should meet another preschooler in the aisles!

To amuse your child in his seat, bring along an assortment of books and toys similar to those you would pack for a car trip. Also, many airlines offer assortments of activity materials for children. Check with your flight attendant about this.

VISIT TO THE PEDIATRICIAN

Your preschooler should be examined by the pediatrician once a year. Now that he is better able to follow instructions and communicate, some screening procedures are possible that previously weren't. In particular, his maturity will allow more accurate testing of his hearing and vision.

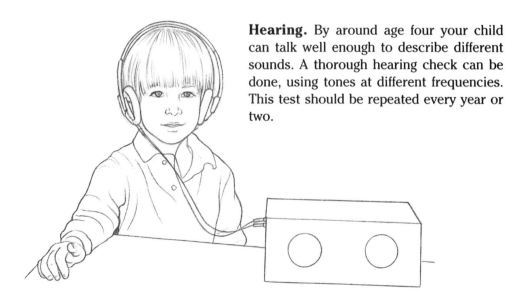

Hearing. By around age four your child can talk well enough to describe different sounds. A thorough hearing check can be done, using tones at different frequencies. This test should be repeated every year or two.

Vision: By age three or four your child is able to understand directions and cooperate well enough to have a formal vision test. At this age his visual acuity should be 20/40 or better, improving to 20/30 by age five. If it's not at that level, he'll need to be seen by a pediatric ophthalmologist.

IMMUNIZATION ALERT

The preschool DTP is given during these years. The preschool DTP booster is due two and one-half to three and one-half years after the first booster was given. As the first booster is usually given at around eighteen months of age, the next should be due around age four to five years. For the fourth and fifth doses, the acellular (DTaP) vaccine may be substituted for the DTP vaccine. Some states now require an MMR booster, for school entry, so you must check your child's school requirements with your pediatrician.

SAFETY CHECK

Guard Against Falls From

- Play equipment such as slides and monkey bars
- Tricycles: Avoid unstable tricycles, and use the kind that allow the child to be low to the ground.
- Stairs: Continue to use gates at the top and bottom of staircases.
- Windows: Continue to use window guards.

Burns

- Keep matches and cigarette lighters out of your child's reach.

Auto Accidents

- Do not allow children to ride tricycles in the street or near traffic; do not allow them to ride down driveways into the street.
- Keep your child in a booster seat with seat belt properly attached.

Drowning

- Never leave your preschooler unattended near water, even if he supposedly knows how to swim.

KEEPING YOUR CHILD SAFE

*E*veryday life is full of well-disguised dangers for children: sharp objects, shaky furniture, reachable hot water faucets, pots on burning stoves, hot tubs, swimming pools, and busy streets. By adulthood we've learned to navigate this mine field so well that we no longer think of things like scissors and stoves as hazards. And that's the problem. To protect your child from the dangers he'll encounter in and out of your home, you have to see the world as he does, and you must recognize that he cannot yet distinguish hot from cold or sharp from dull.

Keeping your child physically safe is your most basic responsibility—and a never-ending one. Today, unintentional injuries are the number-one cause of death in children under five. Each year, one million children seek medical care because of unintentional injury. Forty to fifty thousand suffer permanent damage—and four thousand die.

As might be expected, automobile crashes account for a large number of the injuries and deaths. But many children are injured and killed by equipment designed specifically for their use. In one recent twelve-month period, falls from highchairs sent 7,000 children to the hospital. Each year, toys cause more than 120,000 injuries serious enough to require treatment in hospital emergency rooms. Even cribs account for 150 to 200 deaths annually.

These are grim statistics, but they are not inevitable. In the past, injuries were called "accidents" because they seemed unpredictable and unavoidable. Today, we know that accidents are not random; instead, they follow distinct patterns. By understanding these patterns, parents can take the precautions that will prevent most, if not all, injuries.

WHY CHILDREN GET INJURED

Every childhood injury involves three elements: the child, the object that causes the injury, and the environment in which it occurs. To keep your child safe, you must be aware of all three.

Let's start with your child. His age makes a tremendous difference in the kind of protection he needs. The three-month-old who sits cooing in an infant seat requires quite different supervision from that needed by the ten-month-old who's started walking or the toddler who has learned to climb. So at each stage of your child's life you must think again about the hazards that are present and what you can do to eliminate them. Repeatedly, as your child grows, you must ask: How far can he move? How high can he reach? What objects attract his attention? What can he do today that he couldn't do yesterday? What will he do tomorrow that he can't do today?

During the first six months of life you can guarantee your child's safety by never leaving him alone in a dangerous situation. But once he begins to move, he'll create dangers of his own—first by rolling off the bed, then by creeping into places he shouldn't be, and finally by actively seeking out things to touch and taste.

As your child begins to move about, you will certainly tell him "No" whenever he approaches something potentially hazardous, but he may not really understand the significance of your message. Many parents find the ages between six months and eighteen months extremely frustrating, because the child doesn't seem to learn from these reprimands. Even if you tell him twenty times a day to stay away from the toilet, he's still in the bathroom every time you turn your back. At this age your child is not being willfully disobedient; his memory just isn't developed enough for him to recall your warning the next time he's attracted by the forbidden

His curiosity may take him to the top shelf of the refrigerator, into the medicine cabinet, and under the sink.

object or activity. What looks like naughtiness is actually the testing and retesting of reality—the normal way of learning for a child of this age.

The second year is also risky for children because their physical abilities exceed their capacities to understand the consequences of their actions. Although your child's judgment will improve, his sense of danger won't be intense enough and his self-control won't be developed enough to make him stop once he's spotted something interesting. At this point, even the things he can't see will interest him, so his curiosity may take him to the top shelf of the refrigerator, into the medicine cabinet, and under the sink—to touch things, perhaps taste.

Young children are extraordinary mimics, so they may try to take medicine just as they've seen Mom doing, or they may play with a razor just like Dad. Unfortunately, their notions of cause and effect aren't as advanced as their motor skills. Yes, your child may realize that tugging on the cord pulled the iron down on his head *after* it falls, but his ability to *anticipate* many similar consequences is still months away.

Gradually, between the ages of two and four, your child will develop a more mature sense of himself as a person who makes things happen—he flips a switch, for instance, and the light goes on. Although this thinking eventually will help children avoid dangerous situations, at this age they are so self-involved that they are likely to see only their own part in the action. A two-year-old whose ball rolls into the street will think only about retrieving the ball, not about the danger of being hit by a car.

The risks of this kind of thinking are obvious. And the risks are compounded by something the experts call "magical thinking," which means that at this age a child behaves as though his wishes and expections actually control what happens. A four-year-old, for example, may light a match because he wants to create the beautiful bonfire he saw on television last night. It probably won't occur to him that the fire could get out of control; but even if it did, he might discount the idea because it isn't his idea of what *should* happen.

This type of self-centered, magical thinking is entirely normal at this age. But because of it, you must be twice as careful about your child's safety until he outgrows this stage. You can't expect your two- to four-year-old to understand fully that his actions can have harmful consequences for himself or for others. He may, for example, throw sand at a playmate partly because it amuses him and partly because he *wants* it to be fun. Either way, he will find it difficult to understand that his friend is not enjoying the game.

For all these reasons, you must establish and consistently enforce rules related to safety during the early preschool years. Explain the reasons behind the rules: "You can't throw stones, because you'll hurt your friend"; "Never run into the street, because you could be hit by a car." But don't expect these reasons to persuade your child. Repeat the rule itself every time your child is on the edge of breaking it until he understands that unsafe actions are *always* unacceptable. For most children, it takes dozens of repetitions before even the most fundamental safety rules are remembered. So be patient.

Your child's temperament also may determine his vulnerability. Studies suggest that children who are extremely active and unusually curious have more than their share of accidents. At certain stages of development your child is likely to be stubborn, easily frustrated, aggressive, or unable to concentrate—all characteristics associated with accidental injury. So when you notice that your child is having a bad day, or is going through a difficult phase, be especially alert: That's when he's most likely to test safety rules, even those he ordinarily follows.

Since you can't change your child's age, and you have little influence over his basic temperament, most of your efforts to prevent injury should focus on objects and surroundings. By designing an environment in which the obvious hazards have been removed, you can allow your young child the freedom he needs to explore.

Some parents feel they don't need to "child-proof" their homes because they intend to supervise their children closely. And in fact, with constant vigilance, most injuries *can* be avoided. But even the most conscientious parents can't watch a child every moment. Most injuries occur not when parents are alert and at their best, but when they are under stress. The following situations are often associated with accidents:

- Hunger and fatigue (i.e., the hour or so before dinner)

- Mother's pregnancy

- Illness or death in the family

- Changes in the child's regular care-giver

- Tension between parents

- Sudden changes in the environment, such as moving to a new home or going on vacation

All families experience at least some of these stresses some of the time. Child-proofing eliminates or reduces the opportunities for injury so that even when you are momentarily distracted—for example, by the ring of the telephone or door-bell—your child is less likely to encounter situations and objects that can cause him harm.

The pages that follow include advice about how to minimize dangers in and out of the home. The intention is not to frighten you, but to alert you to hazards—particularly those that, on the surface, might seem harmless—so you can take the sensible precautions that will keep your child safe *and* allow him the freedom he needs to grow up happy and healthy.

SAFETY INSIDE YOUR HOME

Room to Room

Your life-style and the layout of your home will determine which rooms should be child-proofed. Examine every room in which your child spends any time (for most families, that means the entire house). It's tempting to exclude a formal dining or living room that remains behind closed doors when not in use; but remember, the rooms that are forbidden to your child are the ones he'll want most to explore as soon as he's old enough. Any areas not child-proofed will require extra vigilance on your part, even if their entrances are normally locked or blocked.

At the very least, your child's room should be a place where everything is as safe as it can be.

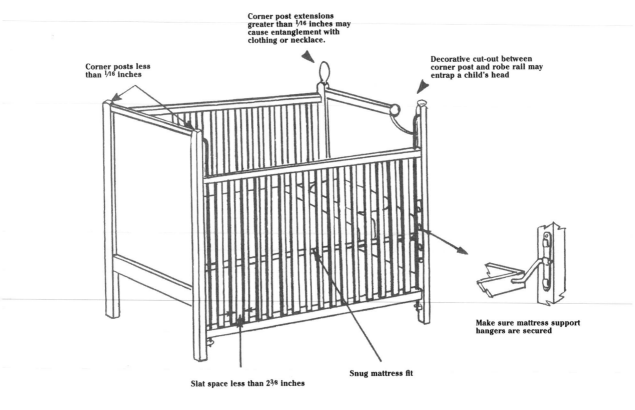

Corner post extensions greater than ¹⁄₁₆ inches may cause entanglement with clothing or necklace.

Corner posts less than ¹⁄₁₆ inches

Decorative cut-out between corner post and robe rail may entrap a child's head

Make sure mattress support hangers are secured

Snug mattress fit

Slat space less than 2³⁄₈ inches

Nursery

Cribs. Your baby usually will be unattended when in his crib, so this should be a totally safe environment. Falls are the most common injury associated with cribs, even though they are the easiest to prevent. Children are most likely to fall out of the crib when the mattress is raised too high for their height, or when the side rail is left down.

If you use a new crib or one manufactured since 1985, it will meet current safety standards. If you plan to use an older crib, inspect it carefully for the following features.

- Slats should be no more than 2⅜ inches apart so a child's head cannot become trapped between them.

- There should be no cutouts in the headboard or footboard, as your child's head could become trapped in them.

- If the crib has corner posts (sometimes called finials), unscrew them or cut them off. Loose clothing can become snagged on these and choke your baby.

Many older cribs were painted with lead-based paint, which can poison children if they gnaw on the crib rails (it does happen). As a precaution, strip the old paint and then repaint the crib using high quality, new enamel. Let it dry thoroughly in a well-ventilated room. Then place plastic strips (available at most children's furniture stores) over the top of the side rails.

You can prevent other crib hazards by observing the following guidelines:

1. If you purchase a new mattress, remove and destroy all plastic wrapping material that comes with it, because it can suffocate a child. If you cover the mattress with heavy plastic, be sure the cover fits tightly; zippered covers are best.

2. As soon as your baby can sit, lower the mattress of the crib to the level where he cannot fall out either by leaning against the side or by pulling himself over it. Set the mattress at its lowest position by the time your child learns to stand. The most common falls occur when a baby tries to climb out, so move your child to another bed when he is thirty-five inches tall, or the height of the side rail is less than three quarters of his height.

3. When fully lowered, the top of the side rail of the crib should be at least four inches above the mattress, even when the mattress is set at its highest position. Be sure the locking latch that holds the side up is sturdy and can't accidentally be released by your child. Always leave the side up when your child is in the crib.

4. The mattress should fit snugly so your child cannot slip into the crack between it and the crib side. If you can insert more than two fingers between the mattress and the sides or ends of the crib, replace the mattress with one that fits snugly.

5. Periodically check the crib to be sure there are no rough edges or sharp points on the metal parts, and no splinters or cracks in the wood. If you notice tooth marks on the railing, cover the wood with a plastic strip (available at most children's furniture stores).

6. Use a crib bumper when your child is an infant. Be sure the pad goes all the way around the crib and is secured with at least six straps or ties, to keep the bumper from falling away from the sides. To prevent strangulation, the ties should be no more than six inches long.

7. As soon as your child can pull to a standing position, remove crib bumpers as well as any toys, pillows, or stuffed animals that are large enough to be used as a step for climbing out.

8. If you hang a mobile over your child's crib, be sure it is securely attached to the side rails. Hang it high enough so your baby cannot reach it to pull it

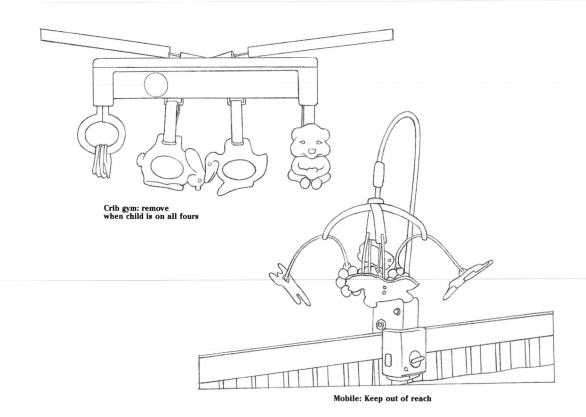

**Crib gym: remove
when child is on all fours**

Mobile: Keep out of reach

down, and remove it when he is able to get up on his hands and knees, or when he reaches five months, whichever comes first.

9. Crib gyms should be removed as soon as your child can get up on all fours. Even though these gyms are designed to withstand a child's grabbing and tugging, he could fall forward onto the gym and become entangled.

10. To prevent the most serious of falls, don't place a crib—or any other child's bed—beside a window.

Bunk Beds. Although children love them, bunk beds pose two dangers: The child on the top bunk can fall out, and the child on the lower bunk can be injured if the top bunk collapses. If, despite these warnings, you choose to use bunk beds, take the following precautions.

1. Place the beds in a corner of the room so there are walls on two sides. This provides extra support and blocks two of the possible four sites for falling out.

2. Don't allow a child under six to sleep in the upper bunk. He won't have the coordination he needs to climb safely, or to stop himself from falling out.

3. Be sure the top mattress fits snugly and cannot possibly slip over the edge of the frame.

4. Attach a ladder to the top bunk bed. Use a night-light so your child can see the ladder.

5. Install a guardrail on the top bunk. The gap between the side rail and guardrail should be no more than 3½ inches. Be sure your child can't roll under the guardrail when the mattress on the top bunk is compressed by the weight of his body. You may need a thicker mattress to prevent this.

6. Check the supports under the upper mattress. Wires or slats should run directly under the mattress and be fastened in place at both ends. A mattress that is supported only by the frame of the bed or unsecured slats could come crashing down.

7. If you separate bunks into two individual beds, make sure all dowels or connectors are removed.

8. To prevent falls and collapse of the bed, don't allow children to jump or roughhouse on either bunk.

Changing Tables. Although a changing table makes it easier to dress and diaper your baby, falls from such a high surface can be serious. Don't trust your vigilance alone to prevent falls, but also consider the following recommendations.

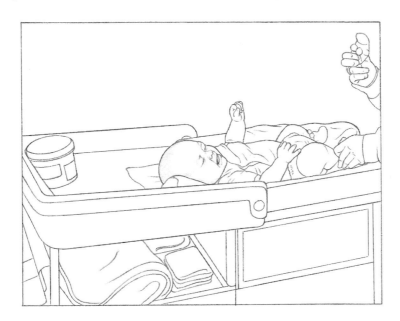

1. Choose a sturdy, stable changing table with a two-inch guardrail around all four sides.

2. The top of the changing table should be concave, so that the middle is slightly lower than the sides.

3. Don't depend on a safety strap alone to keep your child secure. *Never leave a child unattended on a dressing table, even for a moment, whether strapped or not.*

4. Keep powder and other diapering supplies within your reach, so you don't have to leave your baby's side to get them. Never let him play with the powder container while you change him. If he accidentally opens and shakes it, he's likely to inhale particles of powder, which can injure his lungs.

5. If you use disposable diapers, store them out of your child's reach and cover them with clothing when he wears them. Children can suffocate if they tear off pieces of the plastic liner and swallow them.

Kitchen

The kitchen is such a dangerous room for young children that some experts recommend they be excluded from it. That's a difficult rule to enforce, because parents spend so much time there and most young chldren want to be where the action is. It's probably more realistic to eliminate the most serious dangers by taking the following precautions.

1. Store strong cleaners, lye, furniture polish, dishwasher soap, and other dangerous products in a high cabinet and out of sight. If you must store some items under the sink, buy a "kiddy lock" that refastens automatically every time you close the cupboard (most hardware and department stores have them). Never transfer dangerous substances into containers that look as if they might hold food.

2. Keep knives, forks, scissors, and other sharp instruments separate from "safe" kitchen utensils, and in a latched drawer. Store sharp cutting appliances such as food processors out of reach or in a locked cupboard.

3. Unplug appliances when they are not in use so your child cannot accidentally turn them on. Don't allow electrical cords to dangle where your child can reach and tug on them, possibly pulling a heavy appliance down on himself.

4. Always turn pot handles toward the back of the stove so your child can't reach up and grab them. Whenever you have to walk with hot liquid—a cup of coffee, a pot of soup—be sure you know where your child is so you don't trip over him.

5. If you have a gas stove, turn the dials firmly to the off position, and if they're easy to remove, do so when you aren't cooking so that your child can't accidentally turn the stove on. If they cannot be removed easily, block the access to the stove as much as possible.

6. Keep matches out of reach and out of sight.

7. Don't warm baby bottles in a microwave oven. The liquid heats unevenly, so there may be pockets of milk hot enough to scald your baby's mouth when he drinks. Also, there have been incidents in which overheated baby bottles have exploded when they were removed from the microwave.

8. Keep a fire extinguisher in your kitchen. (If your home has more than one story, mount an extinguisher in a conspicuous place on each floor.)

Bathroom

The simplest way to avoid bathroom accidents is to make this room inaccessible unless your child is accompanied by an adult. This may mean installing a latch on the door at adult height so the child can't visit when you aren't around. Also be sure any lock on the door can be unlocked from the *outside,* just in case your baby accidentally locks himself in.

The following suggestions will prevent accidents when your child is using the bathroom.

1. Children can drown in only a few inches of water, so *never leave a young child alone in the bath, even for a moment.* If you can't ignore the doorbell or the phone, wrap your child in a towel and take him along when you go to answer them.

2. Install no-slip strips on the bottom of the bathtub. Put a cushioned cover over the water faucet so your child won't be hurt if he bumps his head against it.

3. Get in the habit of closing the lid of the toilet. A curious toddler who tries to play in the water can lose his balance and fall in.

4. To prevent scalding, don't set your hot water heater higher than 120 degrees Fahrenheit (48 degrees Celsius). When your child is old enough to turn the faucets, teach him to start the cold water before the hot.

5. Keep all medicines in containers with safety caps. Remember, however, that these caps are child-*resistant,* not child-proof, so store all medicines and cosmetics in a *locked* cabinet. Don't keep toothpaste, soaps, shampoos, and other frequently used items in the same cabinet. Instead, store them in a hard-to-reach cabinet equipped with a safety latch or locks.

6. If you use electrical appliances in the bathroom, particularly hair dryers and razors, be sure to unplug them when they aren't in use. Better yet, use them in another room where they cannot possibly come in contact with water. Your electrician can install special bathroom wall sockets (ground fault circuit interrupters) that can lessen the likelihood of electrical injury when an appliance falls into the sink or bathwater.

Garage and Basement

Garages and basements tend to be places where potentially lethal tools and chemicals are stored. In almost all homes, these areas should be locked and strictly off limits to children. To minimize the risk on those occasions when children do gain access to the garage and basement:

1. Keep paints, varnishes, thinners, pesticides, and fertilizers in a locked cabinet or locker. Be sure these substances are always kept in their original, labeled containers.

2. Store tools in a safe area out of reach. Be sure power tools are unplugged when you finish using them.

3. Do not allow your child to play near the garage or driveway where cars may be coming and going.

4. If you have an automatic garage door opener, be sure your child is nowhere near the door before you open or close it. Keep the opener out of reach and out of sight. Make sure the automatic reversing mechanism is properly adjusted.

5. If, for some reason, you must store an unused refrigerator or freezer, remove the door so that a child cannot become trapped if he crawls inside.

All Rooms

Certain safety rules and preventive actions apply to *every* room. The following safeguards against commonplace household dangers will protect not only your small child, but your entire family.

1. Install smoke detectors throughout your home, check them monthly to be sure they are working, and change the batteries annually. Develop a fire escape plan and practice it so you'll be prepared if an emergency does occur. (See *Burns*, page 448.)

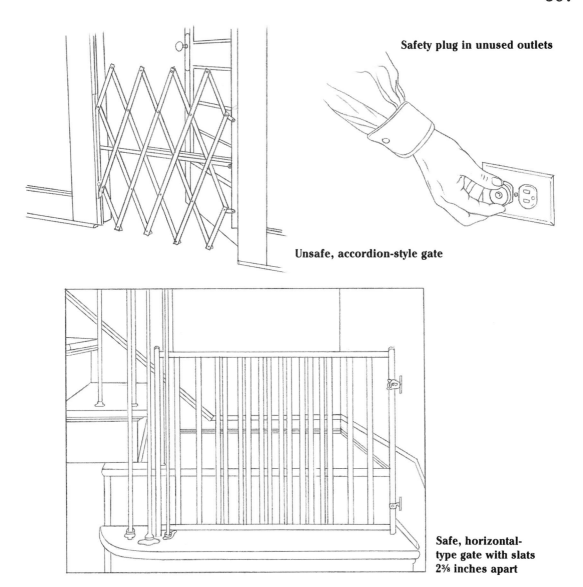

Safety plug in unused outlets

Unsafe, accordion-style gate

Safe, horizontal-type gate with slats 2⅜ inches apart

2. Put safety plugs in all unused electrical outlets so your child can't stick his finger or a toy into the holes. If your child won't stay away from outlets, buy the plastic covers that block unused sockets and make it impossible for him to pull plugs out of sockets that are in use.

3. To prevent slipping, carpet your stairs where possible. Be sure the carpet is firmly tacked down at the edges. When your child is just learning to crawl and walk, install safety gates at both top and bottom of stairs. Avoid accordion-style gates, which can trap an arm or a neck.

4. Certain houseplants may be harmful. Your regional Poison Control Center will have a list or description of plants to avoid. (See *Poisoning,* page 464.)

5. Check your floors constantly for small objects that a child might swallow, such as coins, buttons, beads, pins, and screws. This is particularly important if someone in the household has a hobby that involves small items.

6. If you have hardwood floors, don't let your child run around in stocking feet. Socks make slippery floors even more dangerous.

7. Attach cords for Venetian blinds and drapes to floor mounts that hold them taut, or wrap these cords around wall brackets to keep them out of reach. Children can strangle on them if they are left loose.

8. Pay attention to the doors between rooms. Glass doors are particularly dangerous, because a child may run into them, so fasten them open if you can. Swinging doors can knock a small child down, and folding doors can pinch little fingers, so if you have either, consider removing them until your child is old enough to understand how they work.

9. Check your home for furniture pieces with hard edges and sharp corners that could injure your child if he fell against them (coffee tables are a particular hazard). If possible, move this furniture out of traffic areas, particularly when your child is learning to walk. You also can buy cushioned corner- and edge-protectors that stick onto the furniture.

10. Test the stability of tall pieces of furniture such as floor lamps and book-shelves. If they seem unsteady, anchor the bookcases to the wall and put floor lamps behind other furniture so your child can't pull them over.

11. Open windows from the top if possible. If you must open them from the bottom, install window bars or screens that only an adult or older child can push out from the inside. Never put chairs, sofas, low tables, or anything else a child might climb on in front of a window. This gives him access to the window and creates an opportunity for a serious fall.

12. Never leave plastic bags lying around the house, and don't store children's clothes or toys in them. Bags from the dry cleaner are particularly dangerous. Knot them before you throw them away so that it's impossible for your child to crawl into them or pull them over his head.

13. Think about the potential hazard to your child of anything you put into the trash. Any trash container into which dangerous items will go—for example, spoiled food, discarded razor blades, or batteries—should have a child-resistant cover.

14. To prevent burns, check your heat sources. Fireplaces, woodstoves, and kerosene heaters should be screened so that your child can't get near them. Check electric baseboard heaters, radiators, and even vents from hot-air furnaces to see how hot they get when the heat is on. They, too, may need to be screened.

15. If you elect to have a firearm in the house (this should be avoided whenever possible), keep it unloaded and locked up. Lock ammunition in a separate cupboard.

16. Alcohol can be very toxic to a young child. Keep all alcoholic beverages in a locked cabinet and *remember to empty* any unfinished drinks immediately.

BABY EQUIPMENT

During the past fifteen years, the Consumer Product Safety Commission has taken an active role in setting standards to assure the safety of equipment manufactured for children and infants. Because many of these rules went into effect in the early 1970s, you must pay special attention to the safety of used furniture made before then. The following guidelines will help you select the safest possible baby equipment, whether used or new, and utilize it properly.

Highchairs

Falls are the most serious danger associated with highchairs. To minimize the risk of your child falling:

1. Select a chair with a wide base, so it can't be tipped over if someone accidentally bumps against it.

2. If the chair folds, be sure the locking device is secure each time you set it up.

3. Strap your child in with the safety strap whenever he sits in the chair. Never allow him to stand in the highchair.

4. Don't place the highchair near a counter

or table. Your child may be able to push hard enough against these surfaces to tip the chair over.

5. Don't leave a young child unattended in a highchair and don't allow older children to climb or play on it, as this could tip it over.

6. A cantilevered highchair that hooks on to a table is not a substitute for a more solid one. But if you plan to use such a model when you eat out or when you travel, look for one that locks on to the table. Be sure the table is heavy enough to support your child's weight without tipping. Also, check to see whether his feet can touch a table support. If he can push against it, he may be able to dislodge the seat from the table.

Infant Seats

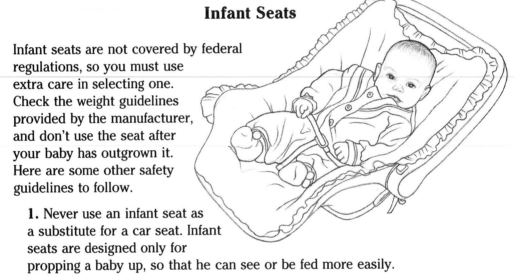

Infant seats are not covered by federal regulations, so you must use extra care in selecting one. Check the weight guidelines provided by the manufacturer, and don't use the seat after your baby has outgrown it. Here are some other safety guidelines to follow.

1. Never use an infant seat as a substitute for a car seat. Infant seats are designed only for propping a baby up, so that he can see or be fed more easily.

2. Always use the strap and harness when your baby is in the seat.

3. Choose a seat with an outside frame that allows the infant to sit deeply inside. Be sure the base is wide, so it is difficult to tip over.

4. Look at the bottom of the infant seat to see whether it's covered with a nonskid material. If it isn't, cut thin pieces of rubber, and glue them to the base so that the seat is less likely to slip when it's on a smooth surface.

5. Always carry your baby securely strapped into the seat, and use both your arms *under* the frame to hold it. Although some infant seats have carrying handles, using them alone will allow the seat to tip if the baby's weight is distributed unevenly. Even with the strap on, the weight of his head could pull him down and out.

6. The most serious injuries associated with infant seats occur when a baby falls from a high surface. Therefore, it's not wise to put the seat above floor level. Even there, an active, squirming baby can tip the seat over, so place the seat on a carpeted area near you and away from sharp-edged furniture.

Playpens

Most parents depend on playpens (sometimes called play yards) as a safe place to put a baby when Mom or Dad isn't available to watch him every moment. Yet playpens, too, can be dangerous under certain circumstances. To prevent mishaps:

1. Never leave the side of a mesh playpen lowered. An infant who rolls into the pocket created by the slack mesh can become trapped and suffocate.

2. Once your child is able to sit, remove any toys that have been tied across the top of the playpen, so he cannot become entangled in them.

3. When your child can pull himself to a standing position, remove all boxes and large toys that he could use to help him climb out.

4. Children who are teething often bite off chunks of the vinyl or plastic that cover the top rails, so you should check them periodically for tears and holes. If the tears are small, repair them with heavy-duty cloth tape; if they are more extensive, you may need to replace the rails.

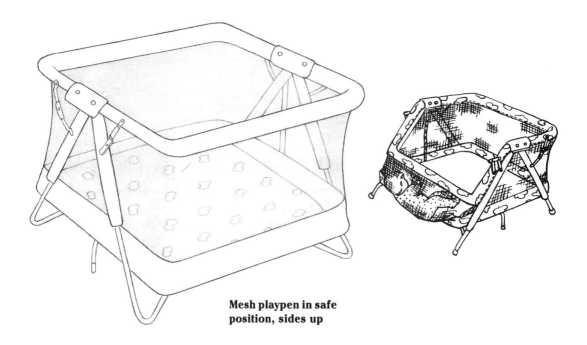

Mesh playpen in safe position, sides up

5. If you use a playpen built before 1974, be sure the mesh is free of tears and that the openings are less than ¾ of an inch across, so that your child cannot get caught in it. Slats on wooden playpens should be no more than 2⅜ inches apart, so your child's head cannot become trapped between them.

6. Circular enclosures made from accordion-style fences are extremely dangerous, because children can get their heads caught in the diamond-shaped openings and the V-shaped border at the top of the gate. Never use such an enclosure, either indoors or out.

Walkers

Baby walkers are advertised for use when a child is old enough to sit securely, yet not steady enough to walk; *but the American Academy of Pediatrics does not recommend using them.* They are involved in more than 28,000 injuries in the United States every year. If you decide to use a walker anyway, take note of the following precautions, and remember injuries will occur even in the best of circumstances.

1. If you select a walker with an X-frame, be aware that the frame can trap small fingers. Look for spacers between the collapsing components, and for locking devices that prevent this action. Also be sure that coil springs, if present, have protective covers.

2. To prevent tipping, which is the most common cause of injury, all walkers should have at least six wheels. For maximum stability, the wheel base should be wider and longer than the seat height.

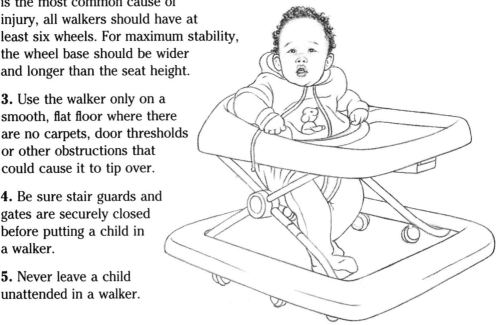

3. Use the walker only on a smooth, flat floor where there are no carpets, door thresholds or other obstructions that could cause it to tip over.

4. Be sure stair guards and gates are securely closed before putting a child in a walker.

5. Never leave a child unattended in a walker.

Pacifiers

Pacifiers that are improperly constructed can choke an infant if they come apart. For maximum safety:

1. Do not use the top and nipple from a baby bottle as a pacifier, even if you tape them together. If the baby sucks hard, the nipple may pop out of the ring and choke him.

2. Purchase pacifiers that cannot possibly come apart. Those molded of one solid piece of plastic are particularly safe. Pacifiers with little animals on the side opposite the nipple are usually made of several pieces and are especially likely to come apart. If you are in doubt, ask your pediatrician for a recommendation.

3. The shield between the nipple and the ring should be at least 1½ inches across, so the infant cannot take the entire pacifier into his mouth. Also, the shield should be made of firm plastic with ventilation holes.

4. After retrieving your child's pacifier for the thousandth time, you may think about tying it to his hand or around his neck. Don't. The danger of strangulation is too great.

5. Pacifiers deteriorate over time. Inspect them periodically to see whether the rubber is discolored or torn. If so, replace them.

Toy Boxes and Toy Chests

A toy box can be dangerous for two reasons: Its hinged lid can fall on your child's head while he's searching for a toy, and he could be trapped inside. If possible, store toys on open shelves so that your child can get them easily. If you must use a toy box:

1. Look for one with no top, or choose one that has a lightweight removable lid or sliding doors or panels.

2. If you use a toy box with a hinged lid, be sure it has a support that holds the lid open at any angle to which the lid is opened. If your toy box didn't come with such a support, install one yourself—or remove the lid.

3. Look for a toy box with rounded or padded edges and corners, so your child won't be injured if he falls against it.

4. Children occasionally get trapped inside toy boxes, so be sure your box has ventilation holes or a gap between the lid and the box. Don't block the holes by pushing the box tight against a wall. Be sure the lid doesn't latch.

Toys

Most toy manufacturers are conscientious in trying to produce safe toys, but they cannot always anticipate the way a child might use—or abuse—their products. If your child is injured by a toy or if you discover any toys that seem unsafe, call the toll-free number of the Consumer Product Safety Commission: 1-800-638-CPSC. The Commission keeps a record of complaints and initiates recalls of dangerous toys, so your phone call may protect not only your child but others. When selecting or using toys, always observe the following safety guidelines:

1. Match all toys to your child's age and abilities. Manufacturers' guidelines can help, but in the end you must decide whether your child is mature and skilled enough to use a plaything safely. Remember, the age on toy packaging is for educational, not safety purposes.

2. Rattles—probably your child's first toys—should be at least 1⅝ inches across. An infant's mouth and throat are very flexible, so one that's smaller than that could cause choking.

3. All toys should be constructed of sturdy materials that won't break or shatter even when a child throws or bangs them.

4. Check squeeze toys to be sure the squeaker can't become detached from the toy.

5. Before giving your child a stuffed animal or a doll, be certain the eyes and nose are firmly attached. Remove all ribbons. Don't allow your child to suck on a pacifier or any other accessory that comes packaged with a doll and is small enough to be swallowed.

6. Swallowing and/or inhaling small parts of toys are serious dangers to young children. Inspect toys carefully for small parts that could fit in your child's mouth and throat. Look for toys labeled for children three and under, because they must meet federal guidelines requiring that they have no small parts likely to be swallowed or inhaled.

7. Toys with small parts that are purchased for older children should be stored out of the reach of younger ones. Impress upon your child the importance of picking up all the pieces from such toys when he's finished playing with them.

8. Don't let a child under age five play with balloons: he may inhale a balloon if he tries to blow it up. If a balloon pops, be sure to pick up and discard all the broken pieces.

9. To prevent both burns and electrical shocks, don't give young children (under age ten) a toy that must be plugged into an electrical outlet. Instead, buy toys that are battery-operated.

10. Toys with mechanical parts should be inspected carefully for springs, gears, or hinges that could trap a child's fingers, hair, or clothing.

11. To prevent cuts, check toys before you purchase them to be sure they don't have sharp edges or pointed pieces. Avoid toys with parts made of glass or rigid plastic that could shatter.

12. Don't allow your child to play with very noisy toys, including squeeze toys with unexpectedly loud squeakers. Noise levels at or about 100 decibels—the sound of the typical cap gun at close range—can damage hearing.

13. Projectile toys are not suitable for children, because they can so easily cause eye injuries. Never give your child a toy gun that actually fires anything except water.

SAFETY OUTSIDE THE HOME

Even if you create the perfect environment for your child inside your home, he'll also be spending a lot of time outside, where surroundings are somewhat less controllable. Obviously, your personal supervision will remain the most valuable protection. However, even a well-supervised child will be exposed to many hazards. The information that follows will show you how to eliminate many of these hazards and reduce the risk that your child will ever be injured.

Car Seats

Each year, more children between one and fourteen are killed in car crashes than by any other cause. Many of these deaths could be prevented if the children were properly restrained. Contrary to what many people believe, a parent's lap is actually the most perilous place for a child to ride. In case of an accident, you probably wouldn't be able to hold on to your child. But even if you could, your

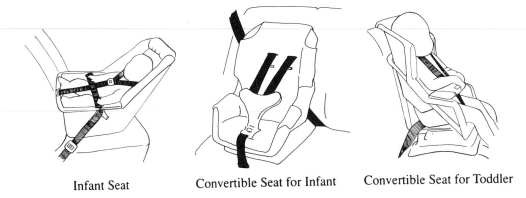

Infant Seat   Convertible Seat for Infant   Convertible Seat for Toddler

body would crush his as you were thrown against the dashboard and windshield. The single most important thing you can do to keep your child safe in the car is to buy, install, and use a federally approved car seat.

Car seats are required by law in all fifty states. Unfortunately, recent studies show that many parents are not properly using them. The most common mistakes are threading seat belts through the wrong slots, not using top tethers when they are required, and failing to harness the child into the seat. Also, some parents don't use the seat on short trips. They are not aware that most fatal crashes occur within five miles of home and at speeds of less than twenty-five miles per hour. For all these reasons, children continue to be at risk. It's not enough to have a car seat—you must use it correctly, every time.

Choosing a Car Seat

Here are some guidelines you can use to help you select a car seat.

1. All new car seats sold today must meet federal safety guidelines. Don't use a seat made before 1982, the year these regulations went into effect. The abbreviated table on page 397 lists some of the seats that are available. For a more complete up-to-date list, including prices, ask your pediatrician or write to the American Academy of Pediatrics, Shopping Guide, 141 Northwest Point Road, P.O. Box 927, Elk Grove Village, Illinois 60009.

2. Buy the seat before your baby is born, so he can use it on his first ride home from the hospital. If you haven't purchased the seat in advance, you may be able to rent one from the hospital or through a "loaner" program in your community.

3. The most effective restraint is a five-point harness that consists of two shoulder straps, a lap belt, and a crotch strap. A padded armrest in front of

1995 Shopping Guide to Car Seats

All products listed meet current Federal Motor Vehicle Safety Standard 213. New models in italics.

Manufacturer/name	Harness type	Safety Features	Price range
INFANT SEATS		**(Birth to 20 lbs unless noted)**	
Century 565 series	3-pt harness	Correct recline indicator	$39–49
Century 590 series	3-pt harness	Detachable base; correct recline indicator	$59–65
Cosco Arriva	3-pt harness	Some models have detachable base; correct recline indicator	$39–79
Cosco Dream Ride	3-pt harness	To 17–20 lbs (depending on mfg. date); use as car bed side-lacing; use as car seat rear-facing	$59
Cosco TLC	3-pt harness		$25–35
Evenflo Dyn-O-Mite	3-pt harness	Shoulder belt wraps around front of seat	$25
Evenflo Joy Ride	3-pt harness	Shoulder belt wraps around front of seat	$25–45
Evenflo On My Way	3-pt harness	Detachable base; can use without base	$35–65
Evenflo Travel Tandem	3-pt harness	Detachable base; used without base in second car	$35–65
Gerry Guard with Glide	3-pt harness	Use as glider in house; must be converted to in-car position	$50–70
Gerry Secure Ride	3-pt harness	Correct recline indicator	$39–49
Infant Rider Car Seat (Kolcraft)	3-pt harness	To 18 lbs only	$59–69
Kolcraft Rock 'N Ride	3-pt harness	To 18 lbs only; no harness height adjustment; optional detachable base; used without base in second car	$30–50
Convertible Seats		**(Birth to approximately 40 lbs)**	
Babyhood Mfg Baby Sitter	5-pt harness		$89
Century 1000 STE	5-pt harness	One-strap harness adjustor; adjustable crotch buckle position	$49–75
Century 2000 STE	T-Shield	One-strap harness adjustor; adjustable crotch buckle position	$59–85
Century 3000 and 5000 STE	Tray Sheild	One-strap harness adjustor; adjustable crotch buckle position	$69–99
Century Smart Move	5-pt harness	Reclines 47 degrees when rear-facing; moves to upright position for more protection in a frontal collision	$119–129
Cosco Soft Shield	T-shield	One-strap harness adjustor	$69–99
Cosco Touriva 5-pt	5-pt harness	Overhead shield/harness with 2-piece harness retainer	$49–79
Cosco Touriva LXS	T-Shield	2-piece harness retainer	$59–99
Evenflo Champion	Tray Shield	Optional tether available; one-strap harness adjustor	$50–70
Evenflo Scout	T-Shield/5-pt harness	Comes in either 5-pt or T-Shield; optional tether available; one-strap harness adjustor	$39–60
Evenflo Trooper	Tray Shield		$40–70
Evenflo Ultara I Premier	Tray Shield	One-strap harness adjustor; adjustable shield	$60–110
Evenflo Ultara V Premier	5-pt harness	One-strap harness adjustor	$65–110
Gerry Pro-Tech	5-pt harness	Automatic harness adjustment	$70
Kolcraft Auto-Mate	5-pt harness		$50–70
Kolcraft Traveler 700	Tray Shield		$79–89
Safeline Sit 'N Stroll	5-pt harness	Converts to stroller	$149–169
Vests and Integral Seats		**(20–25 lbs and up)**	
E-Z-On Vest	4-pt harness	For 25+ lbs; tether strap must be installed in vehicle	$62
Little Cargo Travel Vest	5-pt harness	For 25–40 lbs; simplified strap-buckle system	$39–49
Chrysler Integral Child Seat	5-pt harness	For 20–40 lbs; Booster 40+ lbs; two built-in seats optional in minivans	$100–200
Ford Built-In Child Seat	5-pt harness	For 1 yr–60 lbs; two built-in sets optional in minivan	$224
Booster Seats*		**(Use after convertible/toddler seat is outgrown)**	
Century Breverra Premiere		Removable shield; high-back style	$59–69
Century Brevarra Sport		Must use with vehicle lap/shoulder belt; high-back type	$44–49
Cosco Explorer		Shield for use with lap belt; two seat heights	$25–29
Downunder Design Kangaroo		Must use with vehicle lap/shoulder belt; high-back style	$80–90
Evenflo Sidekick		Must use shield if vehicle has only lap belts	$20–40
Fisher-Price T-Shield Car Seat		Removable shield	$45–50
Gerry Double Guard		Removable shield	$50–55
Kolcraft Tot Rider II		Removable shield	$29–39

*Belt-positioning boosters without shields for children over 50 lbs not listed.

your child may make him more comfortable, but it does not provide extra protection. Whether you use such an armrest or not, your child must still be fastened into the harness.

4. Be sure the seat fits easily in your car, particularly if you'll be taking it in and out frequently.

5. Look for a restraint that's easy to fasten and unfasten; you're more likely to use the seat if it's convenient.

6. For information on the special travel needs of premature and small infants, the American Academy of Pediatrics has endorsed a video called *Special Delivery: Safe Transportation of Premature and Small Infants.* To order, send $50 to Automotive Safety for Children Program, Riley Hospital for Children, 702 Barnhill Drive, Room 1601, Indianapolis, Indiana, 46202-5225, or call (800) 543-6227.

Installing a Car Seat

1. The center of the back seat is the safest place for a seat to be installed, but if you need to use the seat up front so that you can watch your baby, that is OK.

2. Be sure to follow the manufacturer's installation instructions precisely.

3. Thread the lap belt in your car through the correct spaces or holes in the car seat. Be sure the belt stays tight. With seat belts in some cars a special clip, available at baby stores and some auto supply stores, may be required to prevent the belt from slipping and loosening on the car seat. When you rock the seat back and forth, there should be almost no movement.

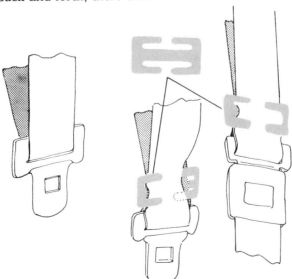

Locking clip placed to keep straps snug

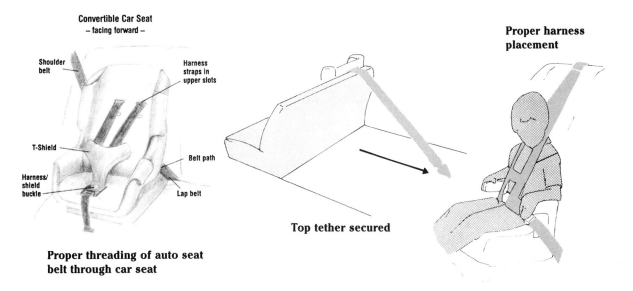

Convertible Car Seat
– facing forward –

Shoulder belt

Harness straps in upper slots

T-Shield

Belt path

Harness/ shield buckle

Lap belt

Proper threading of auto seat belt through car seat

Top tether secured

Proper harness placement

4. If the seat is equipped with a top tether strap, be sure it is secured correctly. A seat that requires a top tether is not safe if the tether isn't used, because the seat itself will fly forward in a crash or even if you just stop abruptly. Again, follow the manufacturer's instructions precisely.

5. A seat for an infant should be installed facing backward. When your child sits well by himself and weighs at least 18 pounds or is eight to nine months old, he can move into a properly secured, forward-facing toddler seat or a "convertible seat" used in the forward-facing position.

6. Adjust the straps in the car seat to your baby's size. The shoulder straps should come through slots level with or just above his shoulders. The straps should be flat, not twisted, and should be adjusted to fit snugly. The crotch strap should be kept short.

Use of the Car Seat

1. A car seat can protect your child only if he sits in it every time he rides in the car—no exceptions. If you have two cars, buy two seats or transfer the seat to the car in which your child will be traveling. When renting cars, reserve a car seat at each destination on your trip. If you will be using a car that belongs to family or friends, ask them to rent a seat ahead of time from the loaner program in their community. (Most hospitals have loaners available or can tell you where to get one.)

2. Most children go through a stage when they protest every time you put them

Keeping Your Child Happy and Safe on the Road

As hard as you may try to enforce car-seat and seat-belt use, your child may resist these constraints as he gets older. Here are some tips to keep him occupied and content—and also safe—while the car is in motion.

Birth to Nine Months

- Ensure your newborn's comfort by padding the sides of his car seat with rolled towels to prevent slouching.

- Place a small rolled towel between the crotch strap and your baby to prevent his lower body from sliding too far forward.

Nine Months to Twenty-four Months

- Children this age love to climb, and may want desperately to get out of the car seat. If this describes your child, remind yourself that this is only a phase, and in a calm but stern voice insist that he stay in his seat whenever the car is on the road.

- Entertain your toddler by talking or singing with him as you drive. However, never do this to the point that it distracts you from paying attention to your driving.

in the seat. Explain firmly that you cannot drive until everyone is buckled up. Then back up your words with action.

3. Be sure the harness straps are snug against your child's body.

4. In hot weather, drape a towel over the seat when you leave the car in the sun. Before putting your child in the seat, touch the vinyl and the metal buckle with your hand to be sure they aren't hot.

5. No matter how short your errand is, never leave an infant or child alone in a car. He might get overheated or too cold, if the outside temperature is extreme, or he may become frightened and panicky when he realizes he's alone. Any child alone in a car is a target for abduction, and an older child may be tempted to play with things such as a cigarette lighter or the gear shift, which could cause him serious injury.

Twenty-four Months to Thirty-six Months

- Make driving a learning experience by talking about the things your child sees out the window, as long as this doesn't distract the driver.

- Encourage your child to buckle his toy animals or dolls into a seat belt and talk about how safe the toy is now that it's buckled up.

Preschoolers

- Talk about safety as "grown-up" behavior, and praise your child whenever he voluntarily buckles up.

- Encourage your child to accept the seat belts by suggesting make-believe roles, such as astronaut, pilot, or race car driver.

- Explain why the safety seat is important: "If we have to stop suddenly, the straps keep you from bumping your head."

- Show him books and pictures with safety messages.

- *Always* wear your seat belt, and make sure everyone else in the car buckles up, too.

6. Always use your own seat belt. In addition to setting a good example, you'll reduce your own risk of injury or death in an accident by 60 percent.

7. Let your child use his car seat until he outgrows it, usually around age four. He may then want a booster seat, so he can see out the window. The boosters that provide the best protection are those that hold the child with a harness or the combination lap-shoulder belts. Raised seats with only a padded barrier in front of the child but no harness are convenient but provide less protection.

8. When your child outgrows the booster seat (when his ears extend above the seat back), make sure he uses the seat belt *at all times*. Don't use the shoulder harness unless it rides across his shoulder rather than his throat, where it might cause injury. If your child is too short to use the shoulder belt, place the shoulder harness behind his back, using the lap belt only. Do not place the shoulder strap across the rib cage and under the arm.

Baby Carriers—Backpacks
and Front Packs

Back and front carriers for infants are very popular, although most babies outgrow front carriers by the age of three months. For your baby's—and your own—comfort and safety, follow these guidelines when purchasing and using baby carriers.

1. Take your baby with you when you shop for the carrier so that you can match it to his size. Make sure the carrier supports his back, and that the leg holes are small enough so he can't possibly slip through. Look for sturdy material.

2. If you buy a backpack, be sure the aluminum frame is padded, so that your baby won't be hurt if he bumps against it.

3. Check the pack periodically for rips and tears in the seams and fasteners.

4. When using a back carrier, be sure to bend at the knees, not the waist, if you need to pick something up. Otherwise, the baby may tip out of the carrier and you may hurt your back.

5. Babies over five months may become restless in the back carrier, so be sure the restraining straps are always used. Some children will brace their feet against the frame, changing their weight distribution. You should insist that your child be seated properly before you walk.

Strollers and Baby Carriages

Because children outgrow baby carriages so quickly, many manufacturers now make low carriages that can be converted into strollers when the baby is bigger. Unfortunately, neither strollers nor carriages are regulated by the federal government, so it's up to you to look for safety features and take the following precautions.

1. If you use bumpers in your baby carriage, or if you string toys across it, fasten them securely so they can't fall on top of the baby. Remove such toys as soon as the baby can sit or get on all fours.

2. If the carriage is collapsible, be sure your child cannot reach the release mechanism. This mechanism should always be locked upright before you put your baby in the carriage.

3. Once your child is able to sit alone, stop using the carriage, because falls from them are very common after this point. If you must continue to use the

carriage for some reason, or if you have an extremely active baby, harness him and attach the harness to the side of the carriage so he cannot lean out while you're walking.

4. Both carriages and strollers should have brakes that are easy to operate. Use the brake whenever you are stopped, and be sure your child can't reach the release lever. A brake that locks two wheels provides an extra measure of safety.

5. Select a stroller with a wide base, so it won't tip over.

6. Children's fingers can become caught in the hinges that fold the stroller, so keep your child at a safe distance when you open and close it.

7. Don't hang bags or other items from the handles of your stroller—they can make it tip backward. If the stroller has a basket for carrying things, be sure it is placed low and near the rear wheels.

8. The stroller should have a seat belt and harness, and it should be used whenever your child goes for a ride. For infants, roll up baby blankets to be used as bumpers on either side of the seat.

9. Never leave your child unattended in a baby carriage or stroller.

10. If you purchase a twin stroller, be sure the footrest extends all the way across both sitting areas. If there are separate footrests, a child's foot can become trapped between them.

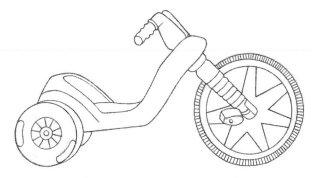

Bicycles and Tricycles

If you like to ride a bicycle, you'll probably consider getting a child carrier that attaches to the back of the bike. You should be aware that even with the best carrier and safety helmet, your child is at risk for serious injury. This can occur when you lose control on an uneven road surface, or if you should happen to strike or be struck by another vehicle. It is wiser to wait to enjoy bicycling together until your child is old enough to ride with you on his own two-wheeler.

As your child outgrows babyhood, he will want a tricycle of his own, and when he gets one, he'll be exposing himself to a number of hazards. For example, a child on a tricycle is so low to the ground that he can't be seen by a motorist who is backing up. But riding trikes and bikes is almost an essential part of growing up. Here are some safety suggestions that will help you reduce the risk to your child.

1. Don't buy a tricycle until your child is physically able to handle it. Most children are ready around age three.

2. Buy a tricycle that is built low to the ground and has big wheels. This type is safer because it is less likely to tip over.

3. Tricycles should be used only in protected places. Don't allow your child to ride near automobiles.

4. In general, children don't have the balance and muscle coordination to ride a two-wheel bicycle until around age seven. Most children can safely begin to ride a two-wheeler with training wheels after age six, but not before. *To protect your child from injury, make sure he is wearing an approved bicycle helmet. Look for a "Snell Approved" or "Meets ANSI Z90.4 Standard" sticker inside or on the box.*

Playgrounds

Whether it's a swing set in the backyard or the more elaborate apparatus in the park, there are many positive things to say about playground equipment. The use of this equipment encourages children to test and expand their physical abilities. However, there are some inevitable dangers. The risks can be minimized when equipment is well designed and children are taught basic playground manners. Here are some guidelines you can use in selecting playground equipment and sites for your child.

1. Make sure there is sand, wood chips, or rubberized matting under swings, seesaws, and jungle gyms. On concrete or asphalt, a fall directly on the head can be fatal—even from a height of just one foot.

2. Wooden structures should be made from all-weather wood, which is less likely to splinter. Examine the surfaces periodically to be sure they are smooth.

3. Conduct a periodic inspection of equipment, looking especially for loose joints, open chains that could come loose, and rusted cotter pins. On metal equipment, check for rusted or exposed bolts as well as sharp edges and points. At home, cover them with protective rubber. In a public playground, report the hazard to the appropriate authorities.

4. Be sure swings are made of soft and flexible material. Insist that your child sit in the middle of the seat, holding on with both hands. Don't allow two children to share the same swing. Teach your child never to walk in front of or behind a swing while another youngster is on it.

5. Be sure children on slides use the ladder instead of climbing up the sliding surface. Don't permit pushing and shoving on the ladder, and have children go up one at a time. Teach your child to leave the bottom of the slide as soon as he reaches it. If a slide has been sitting in the sun for a long time, check the sliding surface to see if it's too hot before letting him use it.

6. Don't allow children under four to use climbing equipment that is taller than they (such as a jungle gym) without close supervision.

7. Between the ages of three and five, your child should use a seesaw only with other children of comparable age and weight. Children under three don't have the arm and leg coordination to use the equipment.

8. Children under five should play on equipment separate from older children.

Your Backyard

Your backyard can be a sanctuary for your child if you eliminate potential hazards. Here are some suggestions for keeping your yard safe.

1. If you don't have a fenced yard, teach your child the boundaries within which he should play. Always have a responsible person supervise outdoor play.

2. Check your yard for dangerous plants. Among preschoolers, plants are a leading cause of poisoning. If you are unsure about any of the plants in your yard, call your local poison control center and request a list of poisonous plants common in your area. If you find any, either replace them or securely fence and lock that area of the yard away from your child.

3. Teach your youngster never to pick and eat anything from a plant, no matter how good it looks, without your permission. This is particularly important if you let him help out in a vegetable garden where there's produce that could be eaten.

4. If you use pesticides or herbicides on your lawn or garden, read the instructions carefully. Don't allow children to play on a treated lawn for at least forty-eight hours.

5. Don't use a power mower to cut the lawn when young children are around. The mower may throw sticks or stones with enough force to injure them. Never have your child on a riding mower even when you are driving.

6. When you cook food outdoors, screen the grill so that your child cannot touch it, and explain that it is hot like the stove in the kitchen. Store propane grills so your child cannot reach the knobs. Be sure charcoal is cold before you dump it.

7. Children under five should not be allowed to cross streets by themselves and should never play unattended near traffic.

Water Safety

Water is one of the most ominous hazards your child will encounter. Young children can drown in only a few inches of water, even if they've had swimming instruction. Though swimming classes for young children are widely available, the American Academy of Pediatrics does not recommend them for children under three. There are two reasons:

1. You may be lulled into being less cautious because you think your child can swim.

2. Young children who are repeatedly immersed in water may swallow so much of it that they develop water intoxication. This can result in convulsions, shock, and even death.

If you do enroll a child under three in a swimming program, particularly a "mommy-and-me" class, think of it primarily as an opportunity to enjoy playing in the water together. Be sure the class you choose adheres to guidelines established by the national YMCA. Among other things, these guidelines forbid submersion of young children and encourage parents to participate in all activities. When your child reaches three, you may want to teach him to swim so he'll feel more comfortable in and around water. But remember that even a child who knows how to swim needs to be watched constantly. Whenever your child is near water, follow these safety rules:

1. Be aware of small bodies of water your child might encounter, such as fishponds, ditches, fountains, rain barrels, watering cans—even the bucket you use when you wash the car. Children are drawn to places and things like these and need constant supervision to be sure they don't fall in.

2. Children who are swimming—even in a shallow toddler's pool—should be watched by an adult, preferably one who knows CPR. (See *Cardiopulmonary Resuscitation and Mouth-to-Mouth Resuscitation,* page 449.) Inflatable pools should be emptied and put away after each play session.

3. Enforce safety rules: no running near the pool and no pushing others underwater.

4. Don't allow your child to use inflatable toys or mattresses to keep him afloat. These toys may deflate suddenly or your child may slip off them into water that is too deep for him.

5. Be sure the deep and shallow ends of any pool your child swims in are clearly marked. Never allow your child to dive in the shallow end.

6. If you have a swimming pool at home, it should be completely surrounded with a tall fence that has a self-locking gate. Keep the gate closed and locked *at all times.* Be sure your child cannot manipulate the lock or climb the fence.

7. If your pool has a cover, remove it completely before swimming. Also, never allow your child to walk on the pool cover; water may have accumulated on it, making it as dangerous as the pool itself. Your child could also fall through it and become trapped underneath.

8. Keep a safety ring with a rope beside the pool at all times. If possible, have a phone in the pool area with emergency numbers clearly marked.

9. Spas and hot tubs are dangerous for young children, who can easily drown or become overheated in them. Don't allow young children to use these facilities.

10. Your child should always wear a life preserver when he swims in deep water or rides in a boat. A life preserver fits properly if you can't lift it off over your child's head after he's been fastened into it. For the child under age five, particularly the nonswimmer, it also should have a flotation collar to keep the head upright and the face out of the water.

11. Adults should not drink alcohol when they are swimming. It presents a danger for them as well as for any children they might be supervising.

Safety Around Animals

Children are more likely than adults to be bitten by domesticated animals, including your own family pet. This is particularly true when a new baby is brought into the home. At such times the pet's response should be observed carefully, and he should not be left alone with the infant. After the two- or three-week "get acquainted" period, the animal usually ignores or actually enjoys the baby. However, it is always wise to be cautious when the animal is around, regardless of how much your pet seems to enjoy the relationship.

If you are getting a pet as a companion for your child, wait until he is mature enough to handle and care for the animal—usually around age five or six. Younger children have difficulty distinguishing an animal from a toy, so they may inadvertently provoke a bite through teasing or mistreatment. Remember that you have ultimate responsibility for your child's safety around any animal, so take the following precautions.

1. Look for a pet with a gentle disposition. An older animal is often a good choice for a child, because a puppy or kitten may bite out of sheer friskiness. Avoid older pets raised in a home without children, however.

2. Treat your pet humanely so he will enjoy human company. Don't, for example, tie a dog on a short rope or chain, since extreme confinement may make him anxious and aggressive.

3. Never leave a young child alone with an animal. Many bites occur during periods of playful roughhousing, because the child doesn't realize when the animal gets overexcited.

4. Teach your child not to put his face close to an animal.

5. Don't allow your child to tease your pet by pulling its tail or taking away a toy or a bone. Make sure he doesn't disturb the animal when it's sleeping or eating.

6. Have all pets—both dogs and cats—immunized against rabies.

7. Obey local ordinances about licensing and leashing your pet. Be sure your pet is under your control at all times.

8. Find out which neighbors have dogs, so your child can meet the pets with which he's likely to have contact. Teach your child how to greet a dog: The child should stand still while the dog sniffs him; then he can slowly extend his hand to pet the animal.

9. Warn your child to stay away from yards in which dogs seem high-strung or unfriendly. Teach older children the signs of an unsafe dog: rigid body, stiff tail at "half mast," hysterical barking, crouched position, staring expression.

10. Instruct your child to stand still if he is approached or chased by a strange dog. Tell him not to run, ride his bicycle, kick, or make threatening gestures. Your child should face the dog and back away slowly until he's out of reach.

11. To avoid bites by wild creatures, notify the health department whenever you see an animal that seems sick or injured, or one that is acting strangely. Don't try to catch the animal or pick it up. Teach your child to avoid all undomesticated animals.

When planning ways to keep your child safe, remember that he is constantly changing. Strategies that successfully protect him from danger when he's one year old may no longer be adequate as he becomes stronger, more curious, and more confident in later months and years. Review your family's home and habits often to make sure your safeguards remain appropriate for your child's age.

14

PART-TIME CARE FOR
YOUR CHILD

*W*ho will care for your child during the hours when you are away?
Sooner or later you're bound to face this question. Whether you need
someone to care for him a few hours a week or nine hours a day, you'll
want to feel confident about the person who does it. But finding the
right person to care for your baby can be a big challenge. This chapter
provides suggestions to make your search easier. It also contains guidelines for preventing, recognizing, and resolving problems once you've
made your choice.

The most difficult and crucial part of finding good part-time care is
judging the character and abilities of the caregiver. If she (most, though
not all, caregivers are women) is not a member of your family, chances

Never entrust your child to anyone until you've taken time to watch her with your child and other children.

are you'll meet this person only once or twice before entrusting your child to her. Even so, you'll want to feel as confident about her as if she were a member of your family. While it's impossible to be 100 percent sure about anyone under these circumstances, you can tell a great deal about caregivers by observing them at work for a day or two and carefully checking references. Never entrust your child to anyone until you've taken time to watch her with your child and other children, and you feel confident in her abilities and dedication.

WHAT TO LOOK FOR IN A CAREGIVER: GUIDELINES FOR THE TODDLER AND PRESCHOOL CHILD

(For infants, see Chapter 6, page 153.)

Most children thrive when they're cared for by supportive adults who help them make their own decisions, let them solve their own problems, and allow them to do things for themselves as much as possible. The following list describes many things you should look for when you're observing someone who might take care of your child. These guidelines apply not only to child-care workers but also to babysitters and teachers during the preschool and early primary school years. They're also good to keep in mind as you play with your child yourself or supervise small groups of children.

A good caregiver should:

- set reasonable limits for children and maintain those limits consistently.

- tell children why certain things are not allowed, and offer acceptable activities.

- deal with difficult situations as they arise and before they get out of control.

- live up to promises made to the children.

- join children at play without disrupting their activity.

- encourage children to think of their own ideas before offering suggestions.

- reward children's efforts and relieve their "hurts" with a physical gesture, such as a hug or a pat.

- talk naturally and conversationally with the children about what they are doing.

- help children encourage each other by asking them to share their accomplishments.

- encourage children to complete projects, even if they take longer than the time originally scheduled.

- limit adult conversations in the children's presence.

- show respect for the children's ideas and decisions.

- avoid offering children choices when there is no choice.

- allow children to make mistakes and learn from them (as long as there is no danger involved in doing so).

CHOICES IN PART-TIME CARE

In addition to the *general* suggestions mentioned above, you need to identify your *specific* needs and desires. Your list of questions should include:

- Where do I want my child to be during the day: at home? in someone else's home? in a child-care center? If away from home, in what part of town?

- What days and hours do I need part-time care each week?

- How will I handle my child's transportation to and from the program (if it's away from home)?

- What backup arrangements can I make? How will I handle sick days, holidays, summertime, vacations?

- What can I realistically afford?

- How large a program would I like for my child?

- What qualifications would I like the caregiver(s) to have?

- How do I want my child disciplined?

- What other basic conditions would make me feel comfortable about leaving my child with someone else?

About half of all parents keep the part-time care of their children within their own families, either by sharing the responsibility between the parents or by letting the child stay with relatives during work hours. Usually this is one of the better arrangements, because the child is familiar with the people caring for him and there's little uncertainty about the quality of care he'll receive. So if you have family members or friends whom you would like to care for your child and who live nearby, you should ask if they'd be willing to provide part-time care either on a regular basis or as a backup if other arrangements fail. Consider also, when possible, that offering payment for these services makes the arrangement fairer and creates an additional incentive for a member of your family to help you.

Your next decision is whether to bring someone into your own home or to take your child to another person's home or a child-care center. Your financial resources, the age and needs of your child, and your own preferences about child rearing will help you decide which choice is best.

In-Home Care

If you are returning to work while your child is still an infant, your first choice for child care may be to bring someone into your own home who can look after him and perhaps help with the housework. This person may come to your home on a regular basis, or live with you. You can find such a person by asking your friends for recommendations, scanning ads in the paper (especially local publications for parents), and checking with agencies that specialize in child care.

In-home caregivers are not required to be licensed, so you'll have to check references very carefully. When you have a candidate, ask for her work record during the past four or five years and talk to each of her former employers. Don't be afraid to ask detailed and personal questions about whether she's reliable and capable. Also, ask about her approach to discipline, scheduling, feeding, and comforting, to try to determine if she is right for your child and your style of child rearing.

The person you ultimately choose will quickly become part of your family, so make sure you hire someone who respects your values, beliefs, and life-style. To the extent possible, involve the whole family in the decision, and arrange for a trial period before you make a final commitment.

Arranging for child care at home has the following advantages and disadvantages.

ADVANTAGES

1. Your child stays in familiar surroundings and receives individualized care and attention.

2. He isn't exposed to the illnesses and negative behavior of other children.

3. When your child is sick, you don't have to stay home from work or make different arrangements to take care of him.

4. Your caregiver may do some light housework as well. (If this is one of your expectations, make that clear from the start.)

5. You needn't worry about transportation for your child (unless you allow the caregiver to take him on outings).

DISADVANTAGES

1. You may have difficulty finding someone who is wiling to accept the wages, benefits, and confinement of working in the home or you may find the costs of qualified in-home care (such as a trained nanny) prohibitive.

2. Since you will be considered an employer, you must meet minimum-wage, Social Security, and tax-reporting requirements. (If you use a part-time care agency, your costs may be higher, but you won't have to manage the government reporting and tax payments yourself.)

3. The presence of a caregiver may infringe on your family's privacy, especially if she lives in your home. Furthermore, she may bring her own needs and problems with her, which could involve more of your own time and energy than you bargained for.

4. Rivalry may develop between you and the caregiver for your child's affection and control of his behavior. For example, you may hear "Funny, he never does that for me" when he misbehaves. (Don't take this seriously—children usualy save their worst behavior for the people they trust most.)

5. Because the caregiver is alone with your child most of the time, you have no way of knowing exactly how she is performing her job.

6. You are dependent on your caregiver's reliability. If she gets sick, has a family crisis, finds a better job, or wants to take a vacation without warning you, you'll be left frantically searching for a replacement.

Family Child Care

Many people provide informal care in their homes for small groups of preschool-age children, often looking after their own children or grandchildren at the same time. Some offer evening care or care for children with special needs. Family day care generally is less expensive and more flexible than that offered by formal child-care centers.

Some of these so-called family child-care arrangements are formally licensed and registered. Licensing regulations vary from state to state, and can be obtained from your local health department. Also, the American Academy of Pediatrics can provide general information on the basic requirements and the new national standards for an acceptable child-care center. (Send request for information to the American Academy of Pediatrics, 141 Northwest Point Road, P.O. Box 927, Elk Grove Village, Illinois 60009.)

However, the majority of family child-care homes do not meet these requirements. For that reason you must be careful to check caregiver references and certification before making a decision about such care for your child.

Family child care has the following advantages and disadvantages:

ADVANTAGES

1. In good family child-care settings, there is a favorable adult/child ratio. The number of children is usually no more than about four if some of the children are infants.

2. Your child has all the comforts of being in a home, and can be involved in many of the same household activities he'd find at your own house.

3. There will be playmates. This provides more opportunities for social stimulation than if your child were cared for alone at home.

4. Family child care is very flexible, so special arrangements usually can be made to meet your child's individual interests and needs.

DISADVANTAGES

1. There is no way for you to observe what happens to your child in your absence. While some providers carefully organize activities that are appropriate and stimulating for children, others use TV as a babysitter—even letting the children watch shows that are inappropriate for them—while they do housework. (Be aware that the same thing could be true of people who care for your child in your own home.)

2. Because children often do not stay in the same family child-care homes very long, it may be difficult for you to get satisfactory references for a particular caregiver.

In family child care, your child can be involved in many of the same household activities he'd find at your own house.

3. Most family child-care providers work without supervision or advice from other adults.

For the names of family child-care homes in your area, contact the local agency that licenses or registers them, or use a local referral agency that lists them. Check with these agencies about homes advertised in the paper or on neighborhood bulletin boards, since these may not be licensed. References from parents of children the same age as yours can also be very helpful.

Before committing to a particular family child-care home:

- Check references, licensing, accreditation, and inspection status (if any).

- Call the parents of children who are in, or recently were in, child care there, and ask about their impression and experiences.

- Find out how many children (inlcuding the caregiver's children) are actually cared for in the home at various times of the day.

- Ask about substitute arrangements in case the caregiver (or someone in her family) becomes ill.

- Ask how the caregiver would handle an emergency situation involving the children.

- Make sure the caregiver and facility (if licensed) complies with standard health and safety requirements such as those endorsed by the American Academy of Pediatrics and the new national standards. Your pediatrician will have these available in his office or help you get them. (Also see discussion in *Making a Final Selection,* page 419.)

Child-Care Centers

More formal part-time care programs are available through child-care centers (also called day care, child-development centers, and extended-day nursery schools) Child-care centers generally are open from 6:00 or 7:00 A.M. to 6:00 P.M., thus meeting the needs of most working parents. These facilities usually care for groups of ten or more children, often in a church, community center, or school. Most are licensed for children from two and a half to six years, though some offer care for infants. A growing number of centers participate in accreditation programs. For more information about accreditation of centers, contact The National Association for the Education of Young Children, 1834 Connecticut Avenue NW, Washington, D.C., 20009-5786.

Child-care centers are the fastest-growing form of part-time care in the United States. They can be found in several different versions, each with its own characteristics, strengths, and weaknesses.

Chain Centers have become a thriving national industry. Many of the larger ones have a wide variety of activities and programs that appeal to both parents and children (child-development programs, structured curricula, and so on). Because of their size, however, they may be less flexible in addressing the individual needs of each child within the program. And they may be less likely to open early or to stay open later if you have an emergency.

Independent For-Profit Centers usually are small operations run by a small staff. They generally have no agency, church, or other support, so they must depend on enrollment fees to pay the overhead and earn a narrow profit for the owners. Because many of these programs are built around one or two dedicated people, they can be quite excellent—as long as those individuals remain on the staff. Unfortunately, such programs do not always maintain their high standards, because of staff turnovers or ownership changes.

Nonprofit Centers often are linked with churches, synagogues, community centers, universities, or organizations like the YMCA or YWCA. They may have access to public funding, permitting discounted fees for lower-income families. Any profits earned from enrollment are put back into the project, thus directly benefiting the children. However, these programs are also subject to undesirable changes in order to meet the demands of the sponsoring organization. Many also rely on parent involvement for fund-raising events such as bake sales and children's fairs.

There are several advantages and disadvantages to child-care centers:

ADVANTAGES

1. Because local child-care centers are easier to regulate and observe, more information is generally available about them than about other part-time care choices.

2. Many centers have structured programs designed to meet children's developmental needs.

3. Most centers have several caregivers, so you are not dependent on the availability of just one person.

4. Because workers are less isolated and often better paid in these centers, they tend to be better trained and supervised than caregivers in less formal settings.

5. You can often arrange shorter hours or fewer days of care if you work only part-time.

DISADVANTAGES

1. Regulations for child-care centers vary widely: Strict standards applied to publicly funded centers may not apply to privately financed ones, and many states exempt church-run facilities from even minimum requirements. Because older children require less observation, the center may provide less supervision for them than they do for infants and toddlers.

2. Good programs may have waiting lists for admission because they are in such demand.

3. Because these arrangements serve more children and have larger staffs, your child may receive less personalized attention than in smaller programs.

Child-care centers generally are listed in the phone book or can be identified by calling your local health or welfare agency. Ask your pediatrician or other parents with children in child care to recommend a center from these lists.

MAKING A FINAL SELECTION

When considering a particular child-care setting, you need to know all of the rules and practices that would affect your child. If the program is formal enough to

The younger the child, the more adults there should be in each group.

have a printed handbook, this may answer many of your questions. Otherwise, ask the program director about the following (some of which apply to in-home or family child-care as well):

1. What are the hiring requirements for staff members? In most good programs, caregivers must have at least two years of college, pass minimum health requirements, and receive basic immunizations. Ideally, they will have some background in early child development and perhaps have children themselves. Directors generally must have a college degree or many years of experience qualifying them as experts in both child development and administration.

2. How many staff members are available per child? Although some children need highly personalized attention and others do well with less direct supervision, the general rule to follow is: the younger the child, the more adults there should be in each group. Each child should be assigned to one caregiver as the primary person responsible for that child's care.

Here are ideal ratios for each age category:

Infants and toddlers (up to age two)—3 children per adult

Age two to three—4 children per adult

Age three to six—8 children per adult

3. How many children are in each group? Generally, smaller groups offer children a better chance to interact with and learn from one another. The maximum group size for each age category should be:

Infants and toddlers—6 per group (2 care-givers)

Age two to three—12 per group (3 care-givers)

Age three to five—16 per group (2 care-givers)

4. Is there any problem with frequent staff changes? This may suggest that there may be problems with the center. Ideally, most caregivers should have been with the program for several years. Unfortunately, a high turnover rate is common.

5. What are the goals of the program? Some are very organized and try to teach children new skills, or attempt to change or mold their behavior. Others are very relaxed, with an emphasis on helping children develop at their own pace. Still others fall somewhere in between. Decide what you want for your child, and make sure the program you choose meets your desires. Avoid those that are simply "babysitters" and offer no personalized attention or support for your child. Generally, these care for large groups of children with very few staff members.

6. What are the admission procedures? Quality child-care programs require some background information on each child. Be prepared for very specific questions about your child's individual needs, developmental level, and health status. You may also be asked about your own child-rearing desires and any other children in your family. Be concerned if the center has no interest in any of this information.

7. Does the care-provider have a valid license and recent health certificate, and what are the health and immunization requirements for children in the program? Standard immunizations and regular checkups should be required for all children and staff members.

8. How are illnesses handled? Parents should be notified if a staff member or child contracts a significant communicable disease (not just a cold, but problems like chicken pox, measles, or hepatitis). The program also should have a clear policy regarding sick children. You should know when to keep your youngster home and how the center will respond if he becomes ill during the day.

9. What are the costs? How much will you have to pay to start, and how often will you make installment payments? What do the payments specifically cover?

10. What happens on a typical day? Ideally, there should be a mix of physical activity and quiet times. Some activities should be group oriented and others individualized. There should be set times for meals and snacks. While a certain amount of structure is desirable, there should also be room for free play and special events.

11. How much parental involvement is expected? Some programs rely heavily on parent participation while others request very little. At the least, quality programs should welcome your opinions and allow you to visit your child during the day. Do *not* consider any program that is closed to parents for part or all of the day.

12. What are the general procedures? A well-organized program should have clearly-defined rules and regulations regarding:

- Hours of operation

- Transportation of children

- Field trips

- Meals and snacks

- Administration of medication and first aid

- Emergency evacuations

- Notification of child's absence

- Weather cancellations

- Withdrawal of children from the program

- Supplies or equipment that parents must provide

- Special celebrations

- How parents may contact the staff during the day and at night

Once you've received the basic information, you should inspect the building and grounds during operating hours to see how the care-givers interact with the children. Your first impressions are especially important, since they'll influence all your future dealings with the program. If you sense warmth and a loving approach to the children, you'll probably feel comfortable placing your own child there. If you see a worker spank one of the youngsters, you should reconsider sending your own child, even if that's the only sign of abusiveness you notice.

Try to observe the daily routine, paying attention to how the day is organized and what activities are planned for the children. Watch how food is prepared and find out how often the children are fed. Check how frequently the children are taken to the toilet and/or diapered. While touring the child-care home or center, also check to see if the following basic health and safety standards are being met.

- The premises are clean and reasonably neat (without discouraging play by the children.)

- There is plenty of play equipment, and it is in good repair.

- The equipment is appropriate for the developmental skills of the children in the program.

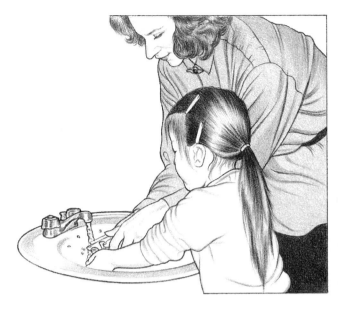

While touring the child-care home or center, also check to see if basic health and safety standards are being met.

- Children are closely supervised when climbing on playthings, roughhousing, or playing with blocks (which are sometimes thrown) and other potentially dangerous toys.

- There is a safe outdoor area where the children play each day with cushioning material under climbing equipment.

- Areas where food is handled are clearly separate from toilets and diaper-changing areas.

- Diaper-changing areas are cleaned and sanitized after each child's use.

- Handwashing sinks are available to the children and staff next to the toilets and changing areas.

- Potty (or training) chairs should be avoided because they increase the risk of spreading germs that cause diarrhea.

- Children are supervised at all times, even when napping.

- Caregivers who handle diaper changing or toileting wash their hands carefully after diapering and toileting, and before handling food.

Once you're satisfied that a particular program will provide your child with the safe, loving, healthy environment that he needs in your absence, let him test it out while you're present. Watch how the caregivers and your child interact, and make sure that all of you are comfortable with the situation.

A Child-Care Checklist

The following checklist can be used to help you evaluate care-givers and child-care programs. Ideally, the answer to every question will be yes, but realistically there are bound to be a few no's. Look carefully at the questions that receive "no" responses, and decide how important these issues are to you personally.

For All Children

Does the care-giver:

1. feel like someone with whom you can develop an open relationship?

2. impress you as someone your child will enjoy, and who enjoys working with children?

3. agree with your beliefs about child rearing and discipline, and respect your family's cultural and religious values?

4. provide the right activities, materials, and equipment to help children learn and grow?

5. encourage good health habits, such as washing hands before eating?

6. know basic first aid?

7. have enough time for each child in her care?

8. help each child to feel good about himself?

9. take time to discuss your child with you regularly?

10. have a regular medical examination and TB test?

Does the child-care home or center have:

1. an up-to-date license?

2. a convenient location near your home or work?

3. an open-door policy allowing parents to visit at any time?

4. enough indoor and outdoor space so children can move freely and safely?

5. an adequate number of caregivers to meet the needs of all the children?

6. equipment that is safe, clean, and suitable for the ages of the children in the program?

7. enough heat, light, and ventilation?

8. a clear policy for the care of sick children, and a separate area to care for sick children? (An isolated area is not necessary, but a quiet place to rest should be available.)

9. acceptable safety standards? These should include:

- Cushioning material in the fall zone of any climbing equipment, indoors or out

- A first-aid kit

- Smoke detectors and enough exits in case of fire

- Covered radiators and protected heaters

- Strong screens or bars on windows above the first floor

- Safety caps on all electrical outlets

- Medicines and poisonous substances stored out of children's reach and locked if possible

Are there opportunities:

1. to play both quietly and actively, indoors and out?

2. to play both alone and in groups?

3. to use materials and equipment that help develop new skills and abilities?

4. to learn to get along and share with others?

5. to learn about different cultures through art, music, and games?

If Your Child Is an Infant or Toddler (Through Age Three)

Does the caregiver:

1. enjoy cuddling your baby?

2. properly care for your child's physical needs, such as feeding and diapering?

3. spend plenty of time holding, talking, and playing with your child?

4. help your child find interesting things to look at, touch, and hear?

5. cooperate with you in toilet training your toddler?

6. provide a safe environment for children who are beginning to crawl and walk?

Does the child-care home or center have:

1. gates at the top and bottom of stairs?

2. special toilet seats or toilets designed for children, and which can be easily cleaned after each use? (Potty or training chairs should not be used, since they are difficult to keep clean and may spread infection.)

3. a clean, safe place to change diapers?

4. cribs with firm mattresses covered in heavy plastic?

5. separate cribs and linens for each baby?

Are there opportunities:

1. to crawl and explore safely?

2. to play with objects and toys that help develop the senses of touch, sight, and hearing (such as mobiles, rattles, crib gyms, nesting toys, balls, and blocks)?

If Your Child Is a Preschooler (Ages Three to Five)

Does the caregiver:

1. plan a variety of activities for your child?

2. join in activities herself?

3. set consistent and reasonable limits that encourage your child's independence?

4. recognize the value of play and creativity?

5. seem patient and accepting of your child's individuality?

Does the child-care home or center have:

1. easy-to-reach handwashing facilities near the toilets?

2. safe, sturdy play equipment inside and outside?

3. a fenced outdoor play area with a gate that can be locked?

4. adequate room for play?

5. educational toys and equipment?

Are there opportunities:

1. to play make-believe using costumes and props?

2. for each child to choose his own activities for part of the day?

3. to take short field trips?

After completing this checklist, if you still are uncertain about your child's care arrangement, discuss your concerns with your pediatrician.

BUILDING A RELATIONSHIP WITH YOUR CHILD'S CAREGIVERS

For your child's sake, you need to develop a good relationship with the person or people who care for him in your absence. The better you get along with his caregiver, the more comfortable your child will feel as he interacts with both of you. The better you communicate with each other about him, the more continuity there will be in his care throughout the day.

One way to build this relationship is by talking with the caregiver—even briefly—each time you leave or return for your child. If something exciting or upsetting happened during the early morning, it might affect your child's behavior during the rest of the day, so the caregiver should know about it. When you take him home, you should be told about any important events that occurred in your absence, from a change in bowel movements or eating patterns to a new way of playing or his first steps. Also, if he's showing symptoms of a developing illness, you and the caregiver should discuss the situation and agree on what to do if these symptoms get worse.

If you treat caregivers as partners, they will feel that you respect them and probably will be more enthusiastic about looking after your child. Here are some ways to build this sense of partnership on a daily basis.

- Show the caregiver something that your child has made at home, or talk about things he's done that are particularly funny or interesting. Explain that sharing this kind of information is important to you, and encourage two-way communication.

- Extend basic courtesy to your child's caregivers by inquiring about their lives, offering small gifts on their birthdays or at appropriate holidays, and including them in special events centering on your child (such as his birthday celebrations).

- Provide materials and suggestions for special projects the caregivers can do with your child and/or the group.

- Help out before you leave your child by spending a few minutes getting him settled. If he's in a child-care center, help him put away his things and join an activity. If he is being cared for at home, get him involved in an activity before you depart. Make sure your child always knows you are leaving. Say goodbye before you disappear, but leave without prolonging your departure. Don't just "slip away."

- If your child is in a child-care program, invite his caregivers to your home for a visit. This might give them a better understanding of this part of his life.

The better you get along with his caregiver, the more comfortable your child will feel as he interacts with both of you.

- Help plan and carry out special activities with the caregiver.

Periodically, the two of you also should have longer discussions to review any problems and plan for future changes in your child's care. Try to schedule these extended conversations at a time when you won't be rushing to get somewhere and at a place where there won't be distractions. If possible, arrange for someone else to care for your child while you are talking. Allow enough time to discuss all the facts and opinions that both of you have on your minds, and agree on specific objectives and plans.

Most parents find that this discussion goes more smoothly if they've made a list of important topics beforehand. You should also start the conversation on a positive note by talking about some of the things the caregiver is doing that please you. Then move on to your concerns. After presenting your own thoughts, ask for her opinions and listen carefully. Remember, there is little that's strictly right or wrong when it comes to child rearing, and most situations have several "right" approaches. So try to be open-minded and flexible in your discussions. Close the conversation with a specific plan of action and a date to meet again. Both of you will be more comfortable if something concrete comes out of the meeting, even if it's only a decision to stay on the same course for another month or two.

Tips to Make It Easier When You Leave Your Child

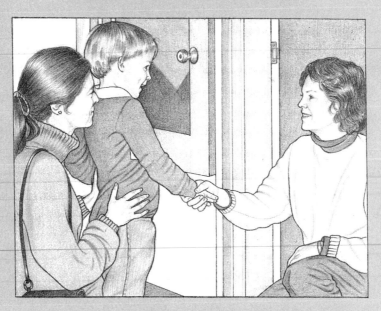

Leaving a young child is never easy for any parent, but for the working mom or dad who must do this each morning, separation can become a daily test of strength and determination. Just getting the day started is challenging enough: You have to get the whole family dressed and fed, leaving enough time to get to the child-care center and then to work on schedule. The biggest struggle in all of this comes the moment you leave your child. Separating is hard, whatever your child's age, but especially difficult during the first two years of life. Here are some suggestions to make this morning ritual a little easier for both of you.

YOUR CHILD'S DEVELOPMENTAL STAGE	YOUR RESPONSE
0 to 7 months In early infancy your baby primarily needs love, comforting, and good basic care to satisfy his physical needs.	Though this period may be a difficult time of separation for you, young infants generally will accommodate well to a consistent child-care worker in almost any setting. After the initial break-in period, your presence should last for up to one hour. This can be shortened by the end of one to two weeks.
7 to 12 months This is when stranger anxiety normally occurs. Your baby may suddenly be reluctant to stay with anyone outside his family. The unfamiliar setting of a child-care center may also upset him.	If possible, do not start child care during this period. If your child is already in such a program, take a little extra time each day before you say goodbye. Create a short goodbye ritual, perhaps involving a favorite toy. Above all, be consistent from day to day.
12 to 24 months This is when separation anxiety peaks and your child has the most difficulty with your leaving. He may not believe you will really return, and may weep and cling to you as you try to get out the door.	Be understanding but firm and persistent. Once you have left, do not reappear unless you are prepared to stay or to take your child with you.

RESOLVING CONFLICTS THAT ARISE OVER YOUR CHILD'S CARE

Let's presume that you've chosen a child-care setting carefully. Does that mean your problems are over? Hardly.

Whenever two or more people share responsibility for a child, some conflicts eventually are bound to arise. In many cases you can resolve a disagreement about child care simply by talking through the problem. You may find that the conflict is nothing more than a misunderstanding or a misreading of the situation. Other times, especially when several people are involved in the care of your child, you may need a more organized approach to resolving problems. The following step-by-step strategy can help.

1. Define the problem clearly. Make sure you understand who is involved, but avoid blaming anyone. For example, what if your child has been biting other children in his child-care program? Find out whom he's bitten and which caregivers were on hand at the time. Ask what they observed before you decide whether the problem is solely your child's. Perhaps he was provoked. Maybe you can suggest an alternate way in which the caregivers can respond if the incident recurs.

2. Listen to everyone's ideas, in order to find other possible solutions.

3. Agree on a specific plan of action with clearly defined time limits and assignments to each of the caregivers—including you.

4. Consider everything that could go wrong with the plan you've devised, and decide how these problems might be avoided or handled if they occur.

5. Put the plan into action.

6. Meet again at a specified time to decide whether the plan is working. If it's not, go through the process again to decide what changes need to be made.

WHAT TO DO WHEN YOUR CHILD IS SICK

If your child is like most others, he'll get his share of illnesses, whether or not he's in a child-care program. In most cases these illnesses will be colds or other respiratory infections, which tend to occur more often between early fall and late spring. At times he may get one infection right after another, and be sick for weeks. If both parents have full-time jobs, this can be a big problem.

Even children who are only mildly ill are generally sent home from child-care programs, and for good reason. A sick child may be contagious and risks giving his illness to another child. Also, a sick child may be more susceptible to contracting other illnesses; and he needs extra care and attention, which most programs are poorly equipped to provide.

Some states have regulations that actually require child-care programs to send sick children home. This makes sense, particularly when a child has fever, is sneezing or coughing, is vomiting, or has diarrhea, since it is under those circumstances that contagious diseases are spread to others.

Respiratory diseases, however, are contagious well before any symptoms appear. By the time anyone realizes the child is sick, he's probably already spread the infection, and excluding him won't do much to contain it at that point. Nevertheless, few child-care workers want to accept the responsibility of caring for a sick child with anything more than a very minor illness.

Ideally, you'll be able to stay home when your child is sick. However, if you work full time, this may be difficult. Talk to your employer ahead of time to see if arrangements can be made for you to be home when your child is sick. You might suggest bringing your work home with you, or try to identify in advance co-workers who can substitute for you when this situation arises.

If your job and your spouse's require full-time attendance, you'll have to make other arrangements for a sick child. These are days when you might arrange alternate care for him, preferably where both the caregiver and the setting are familiar. If you rely on a relative or hire a sitter to stay with him, make sure she understands the nature of the illness and how it should be treated.

If your child requires medication, write out detailed instructions. Tell the caregiver why it's being given, how it should be stored and administered (in what doses and at what intervals), what side effects to look for, and what to do if they occur. Explain that medicine should not be disguised as food or described as candy; instead, the child should be told what the medicine is and why he needs to take it. Ask the care-giver to record the time each dose is given. If your child is in a child-care center, you might be asked to sign a consent for the care-giver to administer the medication.

In a few communities there are services that specialize in care for mildly ill children. These include:

Home-based Programs

1. Family child-care homes that are equipped to care for both sick and well children. If a child becomes ill in such a program, he can continue attending in a segregated area if possible.

2. Family child-care homes that care only for sick children. Some of these are associated with well-child care centers.

3. Agencies or child-care centers that provide caregivers who can work in your home.

Part-time Care and Child Abuse

The media sometimes publicize frightening stories about child abuse in child-care settings. As a result, many parents are reluctant to leave their child in the hands of anyone outside their families. The truth is that child abuse in child-care settings is extremely rare. More often, child-care homes and centers are places where children who are abused *elsewhere* can get help.

Still, for your own peace of mind, you can minimize any chance of abuse by inspecting your child's program fully before enrolling him, and making unannounced visits after he starts going there. (If parental visits are restricted, don't enroll your child.) However, because parental visits can be disruptive and distracting, stay in the background as much as possible. If you yourself are unable to visit, you might ask other adults (relatives, close friends) to drop in and observe from time to time. Also get to know other parents with children in the program and share your observations and concerns.

How will you know if your child is being physically abused, in child care or elsewhere? You might be alerted by changes in his behavior or appearance. Pay special attention to the following.

- Any injury that does not have a reasonable explanation

- Repeated injuries, even if apparently accidental

- Changing accounts from the care-giver about injuries to a child

- Hand-shaped bruises; burns in patterns that don't look accidental; marks in the shape of a cord, belt, or other object

Center-based Programs

1. Regular child-care centers that have trained staff members to care for sick children in the usual child-care setting, but apart from the main group of well children.

2. Centers that offer a separate "get-well room" for sick children, staffed by a caregiver.

3. Sick-child care centers that are set up specifically to care for ill children.

- Bruises, infections, and bleeding around the genital or anal area

- A child who has been toilet trained for a long time who suddenly starts having accidents without any other logical explanation

- Open, inappropriate sexual behavior by the child. (Be careful not to confuse normal experimentation and curiosity with something more sinister; three-to-four-year-olds, for example, normally masturbate and develop a heightened interest in sexuality; see page 261.)

As a general guideline, if your child has been comfortable in his child-care program for a while but then suddenly starts to protest, look for explanations—but don't automatically assume the worst. This shift of attitude may simply reflect a developmental change. Between seven and nine months, for example, most babies suddenly become afraid of "strangers," which could include anyone other than mom and dad. Between thirteen and eighteen months most toddlers go through separation anxiety, clinging to parents whenever they leave. If you can't reasonably explain your child's change in behavior, consult your pediatrician for advice before launching an investigation of the child-care program.

Finally, pay attention to the way your child plays and talks. The stories he makes up, the pictures he draws, and the fantasies he acts out all reflect his recent experiences, interests, and fears. If something unpleasant has happened to him, it may come through in his play, even if he can't tell you any other way. Learn to read this special language.

In sick-child programs, the activity level of the youngsters is kept to a minimum, and they receive a lot of cuddling and personal attention. These programs should pay extra attention to hygiene for both caregivers and children. The premises and equipment, especially toys, should be cleaned thoroughly and often. Disposable toys may be necessary in some situations, depending on the nature of the illnesses involved. A pediatrician and public health consultant should be on call at every sick-child care facility.

CONTROLLING INFECTIOUS DISEASES IN CHILD-CARE PROGRAMS

Whenever chiildren gather in groups, their risk of getting sick increases. Infants and toddlers are particularly affected, since they tend to place their hands and play objects in their mouths, making it even easier to spread infectious diseases.

It's impossible for adults to keep toys and other objects in the child-care center in perfect sanitary condition. However, there are many precautions and practices that can help control the spread of infection. Immunizations, for example, can greatly reduce outbreaks of serious infectious diseases. Centers should require children to be immunized (at appropriate ages) against diphtheria, tetanus, pertussis, polio, measles, mumps, rubella, *Haemophilus influenzae B,* Hepatitis B, and possibly viral influenza. The immunity of caregivers should be checked, and if there is any doubt, they should receive appropriate immunizations as well.

In addition to requiring immunizations, child-care programs should be extremely careful about maintaining good hygiene. Children should have easy access to sinks. Like the adults in charge, they should be reminded, and assisted if necessary, to wash their hands after using toilets. For the staff this should also be done after changing diapers, blowing noses, and before touching food. If a center cares for infants, toddlers, and toilet trained youngsters, each group should have a separate area, each with its own accessible sink for handwashing. The facility and all equipment should be cleaned at least daily. Changing tables, toilets, and anything that goes in the children's mouths should be washed, then wiped with a sanitizing solution and allowed to air-dry.

As a parent, you also can help control the spread of disease in your child's center by keeping him home when he has an illness that's contagious or requires extra attention. (Your center should issue guidelines to help you determine when to do this.) Also notify his caregiver as soon as *anyone* in your family is diagnosed as having a serious communicable disease, and request that all parents be alerted when any child in the program has an infectious illness.

Teach your youngster proper hygiene and handwashing habits so that he's less likely to spread illnesses himself. And finally, educate yourself about the illnesses that are most common in child-care settings, so you know what to expect and how to respond if they occur in your child's program. These include the following:

Colds, Flu, and Other Respiratory Infections

The most common infections are caused by viruses that produce the symptoms of a cold or the "flu," or result in ear infections. Because infants in child care are exposed to many people while they're so young, they often get these infections at an earlier age than do infants cared for at home. However, after infancy the risk begins to decrease for children in stable child-care arrangements. Infections caused by the bacteria *Haemophilus influenzae B* are an important exception to this. They are two or three times more common among children in child care. Fortunately, the chances of contracting this illness can be decreased by immunizing children with the HBCV vaccine starting at two months of age.

Diarrheal Diseases

Gastrointestinal diseases are less common than respiratory infections. The average child has one or two episodes of diarrhea a year. These illnesses can spread easily in day-care homes and centers that have poor handwashing practices, careless handling of diapers, or unsanitary food practices. Even when the staff is vigilant, however, a single infected child can pass the disease to others.

If your child has diarrhea, check with your pediatrician or the staff at the center before leaving him that day. If he has a mild, viral form of the illness, then several days away from the center should minimize the chances that he'll transmit it to other children. But if a more serious case is suspected, then further tests to identify the responsible agent (bacteria or virus) will need to be done before the child returns. (See *Diarrhea,* page 476.)

Skin and Eye Infections

Impetigo, lice, scabies, cold sores, and conjunctivitis (pinkeye) are common problems in young children. These afflictions of the skin and mucous membranes can be spread simply by touching a person on the affected area. Fortunately, these are not serious illnesses, but they are uncomfortable and inconvenient. The child-care staff should notify you if this kind of problem occurs in any child in the program, so you can watch for symptoms in your own child. If these symptoms do appear, contact your pediatrician for early diagnosis and treatment. (See *Eye Infections,* page 559; *Scabies,* page 643; *Impetigo,* page 637; *Herpes Simplex,* page 544; *Head Lice,* page 635.)

Hepatitis

If a youngster in a child-care program gets hepatitis A, a viral infection of the liver, it can spread easily to other children and care-givers. The infected children may have only mild fever, nausea, vomiting, diarrhea, or jaundice (a yellowish skin color). However, the adults who contract this illness usually experience these problems to a much greater degree. The spread of hepatitis can be controlled by

Car Pool Safety

If you drive children in a car pool, you must be as responsible for every child in the car as you are for your own. This means making sure that everyone buckles up, not overloading the car, disciplining children who disobey safety rules, and checking that your insurance covers everyone on board. In addition, make sure that you and other drivers observe the following precautions.

- Pick up and drop off children only at the curb or driveway.

- If possible, have each child's own parents or another responsible adult buckle him into the car and take him out when he returns home.

- Turn all children over to the direct supervision of a child-care staff member.

- Place all hard objects, such as lunch boxes or toys, on the floor.

- Close and lock all car doors, but only after checking that fingers and feet are inside.

- Open passenger window only a few inches, and lock all power window and door controls from the driver's seat if possible.

- Remind children about safety rules and proper behavior before starting out.

- Plan your routes to minimize travel time and avoid hazardous conditions.

- Pull over if any child in the group gets out of control or misbehaves. If any child presents a problem consistently, exclude him from the car pool until his conduct improves.

- Have available emergency contact information for each child who rides in the car.

- Ideally, equip each vehicle with a fire extinguisher and first-aid kit.

giving injections of gamma globulin, but several staff members and parents may be infected before anyone realizes there's a problem. For this reason, whenever hepatitis A is diagnosed in anyone even remotely connected with the program, parents and staff should be alerted and a doctor consulted to decide how best to stop the disease from spreading. (See *Hepatitis,* page 482.)

Cytomegalovirus (CMV) Infection

Cytomegalovirus usually causes only mild illness in children and adults, and children often show no symptoms at all. However, this virus is dangerous to any pregnant woman who is not immune to it, because infection can cause serious defects in her unborn child. The infection is transmitted easily through direct contact with body fluids (tears, urine, saliva). Fortunately, most adult women are already immune to this disease, but if you are pregnant, have a child in child care, or work in a child-care home or center yourself, you have an increased risk of exposure to CMV and should discuss the problem with your obstetrician.

HIV (AIDS Virus) and Hepatitis B

Hepatitis B virus and HIV (AIDS virus) produce serious chronic infections. HIV infection, when it develops into full blown AIDS, is a fatal illness. Children usually first get these infections from their infected mother during pregnancy or birth. Both diseases are transmitted from one child to another only by passage of blood from an infected child into the body of someone not infected. Because this does not occur in the usual child-care activities, children with these infections are not a danger to others. In order to be sure that no transmission of these serious illnesses can occur, all bloody injuries should be handled with protective gloves and all blood contaminated surfaces or clothing should be washed and disinfected.

PREVENTING AND DEALING WITH INJURIES IN CHILD-CARE PROGRAMS

Many injuries that occur at home or in child-care settings are predictable and preventable. While the staff is largely responsible for your child's safety, you can contribute to the prevention of injuries by helping them to identify potential hazards in the facility and by observing the safety practices of caregivers when you leave or return for your child. For instance, you can take "safety walks" through the center, to make sure all equipment is in proper working condition, and to find other ways to reduce risks.

Safety for children (and adults) in and around cars is a special concern. The

Safety Walk Checklist

Next time you walk through your child's child-care home or center, use the following checklist to make sure the facility is safe, clean, and in good repair. If there is a problem with any item on the list, bring it to the attention of the director or care-giver and follow up later to be sure it was corrected.

Indoors in All Programs

- Floors are smooth, clean, and have a nonskid surface.

- Climbers are mounted over impact-absorbent surfaces.

- Medicines, cleaning agents, and tools are out of children's reach.

- First-aid kit is fully supplied and out of children's reach.

- Walls and ceilings are clean and in good repair, with no peeling paint or damaged plaster.

- Children are never left unattended.

- Electrical outlets are covered with child-proof caps.

- Electric lights are in good repair, with no frayed or dangling cords.

- Heating pipes and radiators are out of reach or covered so children cannot touch them.

- Hot water is set at or below 120 degrees Fahrenheit (92 degrees Celsius) to prevent scalding.

- There are no poisonous plants or disease-bearing animals (such as water turtles).

- Trash containers are covered.

- Exits are clearly marked and easy to reach.

- No smoking is allowed in the child-care facility.

- Windows are securely screened.

Outdoors in All Programs

- Grounds are free of litter, sharp objects, and animal droppings.

- Play equipment is smooth, well-anchored, and free of rust, splinters, or sharp corners. All screws and bolts are capped or concealed.

- No play equipment is higher than six feet.

- Swing seats are lightweight and flexible, and there are no open or S-shaped hooks.

- Slides have wide, flat, stable steps with good treads, rounded rims along the sides to prevent falls, and a flat area at the end of the slide to help children slow down.

- Metal slides are shaded from the sun.

- Sandboxes are covered when not in use.

- Child-proof barriers keep children out of hazardous areas.

- Playground surfaces are made of 12 inches of wood chips, shredded tires, or other impact-absorbing material in areas where falls are more likely to occur (under monkey bars, slides).

Infant and Toddler Programs

- Toys do not contain lead or have any signs of chipping paint, rust, or small pieces that could break off. (The weight or softness of the material may provide clues that the toys are made of lead.)

- Highchairs have wide bases and safety straps.

- Toddlers are not allowed to walk around with bottles or to take bottles to bed.

center should have large, sheltered, and well-marked pickup and drop-off points. Parents should be protected from stormy weather as they get their children into and out of car seats and seat belts, and the children should be shielded as they walk to and from the building. CHILDREN AT PLAY or similar signs should be placed along the street near the center. If your child shares a ride to and from child care, be sure the other drivers are using seat belts on all the children. Also, care should be taken that the children are released only to recognized adults at the child-care facility or at day's end at the child's home.

If your child-care program includes swimming, make sure appropriate safety precautions are followed. Any pool, lake, creek, or pond used by children should first be checked by public health authorities. If the pool is at or near the child-care center itself, it should be surrounded by a child-proof fence with a locked gate. For hygienic reasons, portable wading pools should be avoided.

PART-TIME CARE FOR CHILDREN WITH SPECIAL NEEDS

If your child has a developmental disability or a chronic illness, don't let that keep him out of child care. In fact, quality part-time care may be extremely good for him. He may actually benefit more than other children from the social contact, physical exercise, and variety of experiences of a group program.

The time he spends in a child-care program will be good for you too. Tending a disabled child can be extremely demanding of time, energy, and emotions. It can also be expensive, requiring both parents to work. The challenge is to find an excellent program that encourages normal childhood activities and at the same time meets his special needs.

Since the passage of the Amendments to the Education for All Handicapped Children Act in 1986, all states are required to develop special education programs for preschool (3–5 years old) children with developmental disabilities. Another part of this Act also gives states the option to develop special education programs for infants and toddlers with developmental disabilities or delays. Parents should check with their pediatrician or their State Education or Health Department regarding the availability of these programs.

Start your search with your pediatrician by asking if your child is capable of participating in a group program, and requesting referrals to suitable centers. Sometimes there will be only one choice available, but often, especially in larger communities, you will have several from which to choose. The one you select should meet the same basic requirements outlined earlier for other child-care programs, plus the following.

If your child has a developmental disability or a chronic illness, don't let that keep him out of child care.

1. The program should include children with and without disabilities, to the extent possible. Having normal relationships with nondisabled playmates helps a disabled child feel more relaxed and confident socially, and helps build his self-esteem. The arrangement also benefits the nondisabled child by teaching him to look past the surface differences, and helping him develop sensitivity and respect for *all* people.

2. The staff should be specially trained to provide the specific care your child requires.

3. The program should have at least one physician consultant who is active in the development of policies and procedures affecting the disabled in the group.

4. Disabled children should be encouraged to be as independent as their abilities allow, within the bounds of safety. They should be restricted only in activities that might be dangerous for them or that have been prohibited by doctor's orders.

5. The program should be flexible enough to adapt to slight variations in the children's abilities. For example, this may include altering some equipment or facilities for visually or hearing-impaired children.

6. The program should offer special equipment and activities to meet the needs of disabled children. The equipment should be in good repair, and the staff should be trained to operate it correctly.

7. The staff should be familiar with each child's medical and developmental status. If a child has a chronic disease, the staff should be able to recognize its symptoms and determine when the child needs medical attention.

8. The staff should know how to reach each child's physician in an emergency, and should be qualified to administer any necessary medications.

These are very general recommendations. Because disabilities vary so widely, it's impossible to tell you more precisely how to determine the best program for your own child. If you're having trouble deciding among the programs your pediatrician has suggested, go back and discuss your concerns with him. Your pediatrician will work with you to make the right choice.

Whatever your child's special needs, how he will be cared for in your absence is one of the most difficult decisions you will have to make as a parent. The information you have just read should help you. However, remember that you know your child better than anyone, so rely most heavily on your needs and impressions when choosing or changing a child-care arrangement.

PART II

15

EMERGENCIES

The information and policies in this section, such as first aid procedures for the choking child and CPR, are constantly changing. Ask your pediatrician or other qualified health professional for the latest information on these procedures.

Animal Bites

Many parents assume that children are most likely to be bitten by strange or wild animals, but in fact most bites are inflicted by animals the child knows, including the family pet. Although the injury often can be minor, biting does at times cause serious wounds, facial damage, and emotional problems.

Treatment

If your child is bleeding from an animal bite, apply firm continuous pressure to the area for five minutes or until the blood flow stops. Then wash the wound gently with plenty of soap and water, and consult your pediatrician.

If the wound is very large, or you cannot stop the bleeding, continue to apply pressure and call your pediatrician to find out where your child should be taken for treatment. If the wound is so large that the edges won't come together, it will probably need to be sutured (stitched). This will help reduce scarring but, in an animal bite, increases the chance of infection, so your doctor may prescribe preventive antibiotics.

Contact your pediatrician whenever your child receives an animal bite that breaks the skin, no matter how minor the injury appears. The doctor will need to check whether your child has been adequately immunized against tetanus (see immunizations schedule on page 613) or might require protection against rabies. Both of these diseases can be spread by animal bites.

Rabies is a viral infection that can be transmitted by an infected animal. It causes high fever, difficulty in swallowing, convulsions, and ultimately death. Fortunately, rabies is so rare today that no more than five cases have been reported in the United States each year since 1960. Nevertheless, because the disease is so serious and the incidence has been increasing in animals, your pediatrician will carefully evaluate the bite for the risk of contracting this disease. The risk probably depends a great deal on the animal and the circumstances surrounding the bite. Bites from wild animals such as bats, skunks, raccoons, and foxes are much more dangerous than those from tame, immunized (against rabies) ones such as dogs and cats. The health of the animal also is important, so if possible, the animal should be captured and confined for later examination by a veterinarian. *Do not destroy the animal.* If it *has* been killed, however, the brain can still be examined for rabies, so call your pediatrician immediately for advice on how to handle the situation.

If the risk of rabies is high, your pediatrician immediately will give injections of medications to prevent it. If the biting animal is a healthy dog or cat, he will have you observe the bite for ten days, initiating your child's treatment only if the animal shows signs of rabies. If the animal is a wild one, commonly identified as a rabies risk, it usually is sacrificed immediately so that its brain can be examined for signs of rabies infection.

Like any other wound, a bite can become infected. Notify your pediatrician immediately if you see any of the following signs of infection.

- Pus or drainage coming from the bite

- The area immediately around the bite becoming swollen and tender (It normally will be red for two or three days, so this is not cause for alarm.)

- Red streaks that appear to spread out from the bite

- Swollen glands above the bite

(See also *Safety Around Animals,* page 408.)

Burns

Burns are divided into three categories, according to their severity. First-degree burns are the mildest and cause redness and perhaps slight swelling of the skin. Second degree causes blistering and considerable swelling. Third degree may appear white or charred, and causes serious injury not just to the surface but also to the deeper skin layers.

There are many different causes of serious burns in children, including sunburn, hot water scalds, and those due to fire, electrical contact, or chemicals. All of these can cause permanent injury and scarring to the skin.

Treatment

Your *immediate* treatment of a burn should include the following.

1. As quickly as possible, soak the burn in cool water. Don't hesitate to run cool water over the burn long enough to cool the area and relieve the pain immediately after the injury. *Do not use ice.*

2. Remove any clothing from the burned area unless it is stuck firmly to the skin. In that case, cut away as much as possible.

3. If the injured area is not oozing, cover the burn with a sterile gauze pad.

4. If the burn is oozing, cover it lightly with sterile gauze if available (if not, leave open) and immediately seek medical attention.

5. Do not put butter, grease, or powder on a burn. All of these so-called home "remedies" can actually make the injury worse.

For anything more serious than a superficial burn, or if redness and pain continue for more than a few hours, consult a physician. *All* electrical burns, and burns of the hands, mouth, or genitals should receive immediate medical attention.

If your physician thinks the burn is not too serious, he or she may show you how to clean and care for it at home using medicated ointments and dressings. Under the following circumstances, however, hospitalization may be necessary.

- If the burns are third degree

- If 10 percent or more of the body is burned

- If the burn involves the face, hands, feet, or genitals

- If the child is very young or fussy, and therefore too difficult to treat at home

When treating a burn at home, watch for any increase in redness or swelling, or the development of a bad odor or discharge. These can be signs of infection, which will require medical attention.

Prevention

Chapter 13, "Keeping Your Child Safe," provides ways to safeguard your child against fire and scalding at home. For added protection, here are a few more suggestions:

- Install smoke detectors in all sleeping rooms, hallways outside sleeping rooms, kitchen, and living rooms, with *at least* one on every floor of the house. Test them regularly.

- Practice home fire drills. Make sure every family member knows how to leave any area of the home safely in case of fire.

- Have several working fire extinguishers readily available.

- Teach your children to crawl to the exits if there's smoke in the room. (They will avoid inhaling the smoke by staying below it.)

- Purchase a safety ladder if your home has a second story. If you live in a high-rise, teach your children the locations of all exits and make sure they understand that the elevator should never be used in a fire. (It can become trapped between floors or open on a floor where the fire is burning.) Also, agree on a family meeting point outside the house or apartment so you can make certain everyone has gotten out of the burning area.

- Teach your children to **stop, drop,** and **roll** on the ground if their clothing catches fire.

- Lock up flammable liquid in the home.

- Lower the temperature of your hot water heater to below 120° F, 48.8° C.

- Don't use inadequate extension cords or old, questionably unsafe electrical equipment.

- Keep matches and lighters away from children.

- Avoid fireworks.

Cardiopulmonary Resuscitation (CPR) and Mouth-to-Mouth Resuscitation

Reading about CPR is not enough to teach you how to perform it. *The Academy strongly recommends that all parents and anyone who is responsible for the care of children should complete a course in basic CPR and treatment for choking.* This training is vital if you own a swimming pool or live near water. Contact your local chapter of the American Heart Association or Red Cross to find out where and when certified courses are given in your community.

CPR can save your child's life if his heart stops beating or he has stopped breathing for any reason—an accident, drowning, poisoning, suffocation, smoke inhalation, choking, infections of the respiratory tract, or suspected sudden infant death syndrome (SIDS). This procedure is most likely to be successful if it is begun immediately after the heart or breathing stops. The following danger signs can alert you that CPR may be needed.

- Unresponsiveness, with no evidence of effective respirations

- Extreme difficulty in breathing (such as with chest pain or obstruction from an aspirated foreign body)

- Blue lips or skin associated with extreme difficulty in breathing

- Rapid or labored breathing (grunting or pushing with respirations)

- Severe wheezing

- Drooling, or difficulty in swallowing

- Extreme paleness

If your child displays any of these signs and you are with someone else, have that person call for emergency help while you begin the steps below. If you are alone, go ahead and follow these steps immediately after shouting or **calling for help.**

Step 1. Rapidly evaluate your child's condition.

Is he unconscious? Firmly shake, tap, or shout as though trying to awaken him. Assume he is unconscious if he doesn't respond after three attempts.

Is he breathing? Place your ear directly over his mouth and listen for breathing. If he is breathing with difficulty, arrange to get him immediately to an emergency medical facility. If you don't hear breathing, look to see whether his chest is moving up and down.

Step 2. If your child is not breathing, position him on his back on a firm flat surface.

If you suspect that he has injured his neck or spine (a possibility in a fall or automobile accident) move him carefully so that his neck does not bend. If you find your child facedown, support his head to keep his neck from twisting while you roll him over.

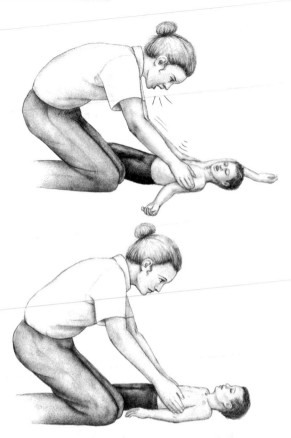

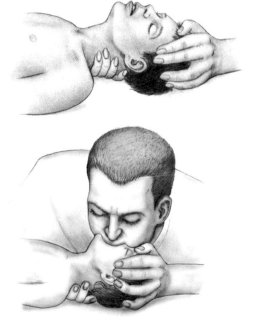

Step 3. Open your child's airway by tilting his head back so his nose is in the air.

Be careful not to push the head back too far, because that could block the airway in an infant or small child. To clear the tongue from the back of the throat, lift the chin up gently with one hand while pushing down on the forehead with the other hand. In some cases, simply opening the airway will allow your child to breathe on his own. If it doesn't, look into the throat to see whether it is blocked by a foreign object or a piece of food. If so, follow the instructions under *Choking* (see page 452).

Step 4. If your child still is not breathing, and he does not appear to be choking, give mouth-to-mouth resuscitation.

1. Take a deep breath.

2. If your child is an infant, place your mouth over his nose and mouth, making as tight a seal as possible. If your child is older, pinch his nostrils and place your mouth over his.

3. Give two rescue breaths, blowing enough air into your child so you can see his chest rise slightly. Then pause, removing your mouth from his so the air can escape, and take another deep breath. *With an infant, be careful not to exhale with too much force, because this can be dangerous.* If *no* air seems to be getting into the chest, the airway is still blocked, and you will need to repeat Step 3.

4. If your child's chest does rise as you breathe into his mouth, continue to breathe for him at a rate of approximately one breath every three seconds (twenty per minute), until he is breathing on his own.

Step 5. Check your child's pulse after the two rescue breaths.

With an infant under one year, find the artery in the front of the elbow. With an older child, feel for the artery in the neck under the ear and just below the jawbone. If the heart is beating, you should feel a pulse with your fingers gently touching these points. Do not press hard.

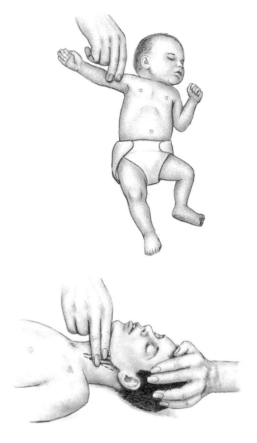

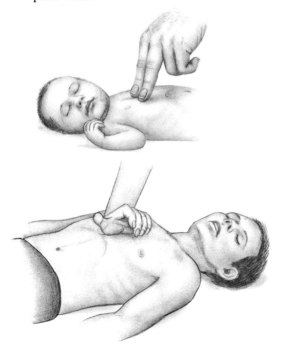

Step 6. If you can't feel a pulse, assume the heart has stopped, and begin chest compressions (CPR) to keep the blood circulating to the vital organs.

Proceed as follows:

1. With an infant, place two or three fingers on the breastbone one finger width below the nipple line. Press down ½ to 1 inch, at a rate of about one hundred times per minute. *Be careful not to apply too much pressure.*

With an older child, place the heel of one of your hands over the lower third of the breastbone. Press down 1 to 1½ inches at a rate of eighty to one hundred times per minute.

2. After five compressions, give the child one breath, as described in Step 4. Continue five-compressions/one-breath, five-compressions/one-breath until you feel a pulse in the artery indicating that the heart is pumping once again.

Step 7. Get emergency medical help.
If you are alone with your child, call immediately for emergency help after he begins breathing. Be sure to give your location and the number of the phone from which you are calling. The paramedics who arrive on the scene will determine his condition and treat him appropriately.

Choking

Choking occurs whenever a person inhales something other than air into his windpipe. Among children, choking often is caused by liquid that "goes down the wrong way." The child will cough, wheeze, gasp, and gag until the windpipe is cleared, but this type of choking is not usually harmful.

Choking becomes life-threatening when a child swallows or inhales an object—often food—that blocks the flow of air to the lungs. If this happens, your child will not be able to talk or make normal sounds, and his face will turn from bright-red to blue. This is an emergency that calls for immediate first aid. There is no time to call the doctor; you must deal with it immediately. However, if the situation appears critical, have someone else call for medical assistance while you continue your first-aid efforts.

How to Respond

The way to handle a choking incident depends upon the condition and age of the child.

Child of Any Age—Coughing but Able to Breathe and Talk

Coughing is the natural mechanism for expelling an object from the throat. Instead of trying some other maneuver that might make the obstruction worse, let your child cough.

In particular, don't try to remove the object with your fingers; that could push it farther into the throat and totally block the windpipe.

Baby Under Age One—Cannot Breathe and Is Turning Blue

This requires immediate first aid. Because the child's internal organs are fragile, *be gentle,* and use the following steps. (Do not use the Heimlich maneuver recommended for older children and adults.)

1. Place the infant face-down on your forearm in a head-down position with the head and neck stabilized. Rest your forearm firmly against your body for additional support.

For a large infant, you may instead lay the baby face-down over your lap, with his head lower than his trunk and firmly supported.

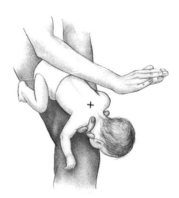

2. Give four back blows rapidly with the heel of the hand between the shoulder blades.

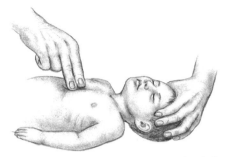

3. If he still cannot breathe, turn the infant over onto his back, resting on a firm surface, and deliver four rapid chest thrusts over the breastbone, *using only two fingers*.

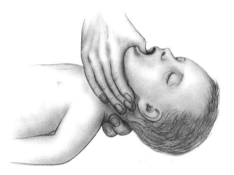

4. If he is still not breathing, open the airway using the tongue-jaw lift technique, and attempt to see the foreign body. Do not try to pull out the object unless you can see it. But if you see it, sweep it out with your finger.

5. If he doesn't start breathing on his own, try to start him breathing by giving two breaths by mouth-to-mouth, or mouth-to-mouth-and-nose, technique (see Step 4, page 450).

6. Continue to repeat steps 1 through 5 as you call for emergency medical help (from other family members, neighbors, or your local emergency service).

Child Over One Year—Cannot Breathe or Talk and Is Turning Blue:

Step 1. Apply a series of up to six-to-ten abdominal thrusts (Heimlich maneuver) as follows, until the foreign body comes out.

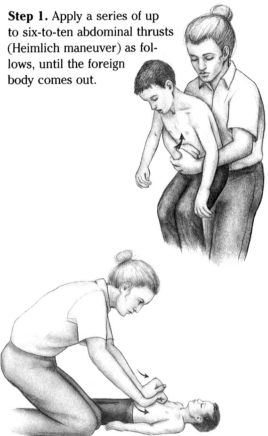

- If the child is small, place him on his back. An older, larger child can be treated while standing, sitting, or lying down.

- Kneel at the child's feet if he is on the floor; or stand at his feet if he is on a table..

- Place the heel of one hand in the center of his body between the navel and the rib cage, your second hand on top of your first.

- Press into the abdomen with a rapid inward and upward thrust. In a small child the thrusts must be applied *gently*.

Step 2. If the object does not come out with the Heimlich maneuver, open the child's mouth using the tongue-jaw lift; this draws the tongue away from the back of the throat and may help relieve the obstruction. If you can see the object, you may try to sweep it out with your finger. However, blind sweeps may cause further obstruction, so don't attempt this unless you can see the blockage.

Step 3. If your child doesn't start breathing, give mouth-to-mouth resuscitation (see Step 4, page 450). If unsuccessful, repeat a series of six to ten abdominal thrusts.

Step 4. Continue to repeat steps 1 to 3 as you call for emergency medical help.

If the emergency team arrives before your child has started breathing, they will repeat the steps described above. If this is not successful, he will be taken to the hospital so that further treatment (such as insertion of a breathing tube) can be performed.

A child who begins to breathe by himself two or three minutes after a choking incident probably will not suffer any long-term damage. The longer he is deprived of oxygen, however, the greater the risk of brain damage or death. Fortunately, most choking incidents do not cause long-term damage, and are not even severe enough to require medical attention.

Occasionally a choking episode is followed by persistent coughing, gagging, wheezing, excessive salivation, or difficulty in swallowing or breathing. If this occurs, it may mean that an object is still partially blocking the airway—possibly in the lower breathing tubes. In this case, the object can cause continued breathing difficulty, irritation, and possibly pneumonia. Your pediatrician should be notified if any symptoms persist, so that further tests such as chest X-rays can be done. If they show that your child has inhaled something, he probably will need to be admitted to the hospital for an operation to remove the object. (This generally is done under anesthesia by inserting a special instrument through the mouth and into the lungs.)

Prevention

Choking is the most common cause of accidental death in children under age one, and the danger remains significant until the age of five. Ask your pediatrician for information about preventing choking and what to do if it should occur. Also see Chapter 13, "Keeping Your Child Safe."

In the past, objects such as safety pins and coins were the primary cause of choking, but today food is responsible for most incidents. You must be particularly watchful when your child is sampling new foods, around the age of one. Here are some additional suggestions for preventing choking.

- Don't give young children hard, smooth foods (such as peanuts) that must be chewed with a grinding motion. Children don't master that kind of chewing until age four. Peanuts should not be given to children until age seven or older.

- Cut or break food into bite-size pieces and encourage your child to chew thoroughly.

- Don't let your child eat while playing or running. Teach him to chew and swallow his food before talking or laughing.

- Avoid giving your child round foods such as meat sticks, hot dogs, carrot sticks, celery sticks, grapes, and hard candies. All of these can lodge easily in his throat.

Because young children put everything into their mouths, small nonfood objects are also responsible for many choking incidents. Look for age guidelines in selecting toys, but use your own judgment concerning your child. Government regulations specify that toys for children under age three cannot have parts less than 1¼ inches in diameter and 2¼ inches long. If older siblings have toys with small parts, keep them out of the reach of your younger children. Also, be aware that the following objects have been associated with choking:

- Uninflated balloons and pieces of broken balloon. Children may inhale the rubber when they try to blow them up.

- Baby powder. Don't allow your baby to play with the powder container when you change his diaper.

- Items from the trash. Be especially alert for eggshells and pop tops from beverage cans.

- Safety pins. Be sure they are closed and out of reach when not in use.

- Coins. Don't give small children coins or other small objects as a reward or treat.

Despite these precautions, choking can occur at any time. You must familiarize yourself with the procedures for dealing with it, so that you can act quickly in an emergency. If you feel unsure, seek out an approved first-aid course such as those sponsored by the American Heart Association or the American Red Cross, or view a videotape such as those available from the American Academy of Pediatrics. To order the *Baby Alive* video or book ($19.95 video, $4.95 book plus $4.25 shipping and handling) contact:

American Academy of Pediatrics
P.O. Box 927
Elk Grove Village, Illinois 60009-0927
800-433-9016

Cuts and Scrapes

Your child's natural curiosity and eagerness is likely to produce some scrapes and cuts along the way. The shrieks and cries that accompany these injuries may bring terror to your heart, but his reaction usually will be far more severe than the actual damage. In most cases, good treatment will require little more than cleansing the injury and providing plenty of reassurance (and perhaps a kiss on the minor bump or bruise).

Scrapes

Most minor injuries in young children are scrapes, or abrasions, which means that the outer layers of skin have literally been scraped off. If the abrasion covers a large area, it may appear to be very bloody, although the actual amount of blood lost usually is very small. The only treatment required is cleansing, since dirt can lead to infection. The area should be rinsed first with water to flush away debris, and then washed vigorously with warm water and soap. Iodine and other antiseptic solutions generally should be avoided. They have little protective value, but can add to the pain and discomfort.

Most abrasions "scab" over quickly without treatment, and this is the best natural remedy. Scrapes that are large or oozing should be covered with a sterile (germ-free) dressing. These can be obtained at your local pharmacy either in the form of an adhesive bandage or a separate gauze pad that is held in place by roller gauze or adhesive tape. The sterility of the dressing is guaranteed as long as the covering envelope is not opened or has not become wet. Care should be taken to be sure dressings around such areas as the fingers or toes are not so tight as to interfere with circulation.

Some dressings are made of materials such as Telfa, which are less likely to adhere to the raw surface of a wound, but the best way to prevent sticking is to apply an antibiotic cream (such as bacitracin ointment) to the wound before covering it with the dressing. The wound should be examined daily and the dressing changed at that time or whenever it becomes dirty or wet. If a bandage sticks when you try to remove it, soak it off with warm water.

Once a firm scab has formed, a covering usually is not necessary or recommended. Most wounds will require a dressing for only two or three days, but your child may be reluctant to give his up that quickly, because small children regard bandages as badges or medals. There is no harm in leaving the area loosely covered as long as the bandage is kept dry and clean and the wound is checked daily.

Call your pediatrician if you can't get a wound clean, or if you notice drainage of pus, increasing tenderness or redness around the site, or fever. These are signs that the wound may be infected. If necessary, the doctor can use a local anesthetic to prevent severe pain while cleaning out dirt and debris that you are not able to remove. If the wound is infected, he may prescribe antibiotics orally or in the form of an ointment or cream.

Cuts, Lacerations, and Bleeding

A cut or laceration is a wound that breaks through the skin and into the tissues beneath. Because the injury is deeper than a scrape, there are more likely to be problems such as bleeding, and there is the possibility of damage to nerves and tendons. The following simple guidelines will help you prevent serious bleeding and other problems such as scarring when your child gets a cut.

1. Apply pressure. Almost all active bleeding can be stopped by applying direct pressure with clean gauze or cloth over the site for five minutes. The most common mistake is interrupting the pressure too early in order to peek at the wound. This may result in more bleeding or in the buildup of a clot that can make it harder to control the problem with further pressure. If bleeding starts again after five minutes of continuous pressure, reapply pressure and call your doctor for help. Do not use a tourniquet on an arm or leg unless you are trained in its use, since this can cause severe damage if left on too long.

2. Stay calm. The sight of blood frightens most people, but this is an important time to stay in control. You'll make better decisions if you are calm, and your child will be less likely to get upset by the situation. Remember, with direct pressure you will be able to control bleeding from even the most severe lacerations until help can arrive.

3. Seek medical advice for serious cuts. No matter how much (or how little) bleeding occurs, call your doctor if the laceration is deep (through the skin) or more than ½ inch (1.2 cm) long. Deep cuts can severely damage underlying nerves and tendons, even if the wound on the surface does not appear serious. Long lacerations and those located on the face, chest, and back are more likely to leave disfiguring scars. In these situations, if the wound is properly sutured (stitched), the scar probably will be much less apparent. If in doubt about whether sutures are needed, call your doctor for advice. To reduce unsightly scarring, sutures should be placed within eight hours after injury occurs.

You should be able to treat short, minor cuts yourself, as long as the edges come together by themselves or with the aid of a "butterfly" bandage, and if there is no numbness beyond the wound. However, have your doctor examine your child if there is any possibility that foreign matter such as dirt or glass is trapped in it. Your child may not like to let you examine a laceration thoroughly because of the pain involved. The pediatrician, however, can use a local anesthetic, if necessary, to ensure a thorough exam.

4. Cleanse and dress the wound. If you feel comfortable handling the problem, wash the wound with plain water and examine it carefully to be sure it is clean; then cover it with a sterile dressing. It's easy to underestimate the extent or severity of a laceration, so even if you choose to treat it yourself, don't hesitate to call your pediatrician for advice. If any redness, swelling, or pus appears around the wound, or if bleeding recurs, consult your physician as soon as possible.

Antiseptics such as iodine, Mercurochrome, and alcohol are not necessary and increase the discomfort for your child, so do not use them on cuts. Tetanus shots are not necessary after most abrasions and lacerations, if your child's immunizations are current. If your child has not had a tetanus booster within five years, however, your pediatrician may recommend that one be given.

Prevention

It is almost impossible for a curious and active child to get by without some scrapes and minor cuts, but there are things you can do to decrease the number your child will have and to minimize their severity. Keep potentially dangerous objects like sharp knives, easily breakable glass objects, and fire arms out of his reach. When he gets old enough to use knives and scissors himself, teach him how to handle them properly and insist that they be used that way. At regular intervals make a safety check of your house, garage, and yard. If you find objects that are potentially dangerous because your child is older and can "get into them," store them securely out of his reach.

See also Chapter 13, "Keeping Your Child Safe."

Drowning

Children drown either because they get into water that is too deep or they get trapped while their faces are submerged. With very young children, this can happen even in only a few inches of water. The natural response in either situation is for the child to panic and struggle, stop breathing, or try to hold his breath. When he finally does breathe, he inhales water and suffocates. Drowning refers to death that occurs in this way. When a child is rescued before death occurs, we refer to the episode as near-drowning.

What You Should Do

As soon as your child is out of the water, check to see if he is breathing on his own. If he is not, begin CPR immediately. (See page 449.) If someone else is present, send him or her to call for emergency medical help, but don't spend precious moments looking for someone, and don't waste time trying to drain water from your child's lungs. Concentrate instead on giving him artificial respiration and CPR until he is breathing on his own and has a pulse of between 80 and 100 beats per minute. Only then should you stop and seek emergency help. Once the paramedics arrive, they will administer oxygen and continue CPR if necessary. You can then call your pediatrician for further instructions.

Any child who has come close to drowning should be given a complete medical examination, even if he seems all right. If he stopped breathing, inhaled water, or lost consciousness, he should remain under medical observation for at least twenty-four hours to be sure there is no damage to his respiratory or nervous system.

A child's recovery from a near-drowning depends upon how long he was deprived of oxygen. If he was underwater only briefly, he is likely to recover completely. Longer periods without oxygen can cause damage to the lungs, heart, or brain. A child who doesn't respond quickly to CPR may have more serious problems, but it's important to keep trying, because sustained CPR has revived children who have appeared lifeless or who have been immersed in very cold water for lengthy periods.

Prevention

Toddlers, mentally retarded youngsters, and children with seizure disorders are particularly vulnerable to drowning, but all youngsters are in danger if they play unsupervised in or near water. Even a child who knows how to swim may drown a few feet from safety if he becomes frightened or confused. Therefore, never allow youngsters of any age to swim alone or unsupervised, and watch constantly when small children are near a body of water such as a swimming pool, lake, or river.

Swimming is not the only opportunity for drowning, however. A toddler's innocent exploration of the toilet or a bucket of water can lead to tragedy. Never leave water standing where your toddler can get to it. Empty or cover plastic wading pools when not in use. Drain wash water promptly from basins. Keep the lid down on the toilet, and, if your toddler is very active and curious, close and latch the bathroom door. Never leave a child under four standing beside a tub while the water is running, or alone in a tub filled with water. (For more information on water safety, see page 406).

Electric Shock

When the human body comes in direct contact with a source of electricity, the current passes through it, producing what's called an electric shock. Depending upon the voltage of the current and the length of contact, this shock can cause anything from minor discomfort to serious injury to death.

Young children, particularly toddlers, most often experience electric shock when they bite into electrical cords or poke metal objects like forks or knives into unprotected outlets or appliances. These accidents also can take place when electric toys, appliances, or tools are used incorrectly, or when electric current makes contact with water in which a child is sitting or standing. Lightning accounts for about one fifth of the cases that occur. Christmas trees and their lights are a seasonal hazard.

What You Should Do

If your child comes in contact with electricity, *always* try to turn the power off first. In many cases you'll be able to pull the plug or turn off the switch. If this isn't possible, consider an attempt to remove the live wire—*but not with your bare hands,* which would bring you in contact with the current yourself. Instead, try to cut the wire with a wood-handled ax or well-insulated wire cutters or move the wire off the child using a dry stick, a rolled-up magazine or newspaper, a rope, a coat, or another thick, dry object that won't conduct electricity, such as a piece of wood.

If you can't remove the source of the current, try to pull the child away. Again, *do not touch the child with your bare hands* when he's attached to the source of the current, since his body will transmit the electricity to you. Instead, use a nonconducting material such as rubber (or those described above) to shield you while freeing him. (*Caution:* None of these methods can be guaranteed safe unless the power can be shut off.)

As soon as the current is turned off (or the child is removed from it), check the child's breathing, pulse, skin color, and ability to respond to you. If his breathing or heartbeat has stopped, or seems very rapid or irregular, immediately use CPR (see page 449) to restore it, and have someone call for emergency medical help. At the same time, avoid needlessly moving the child, since a spinal fracture may have occurred with such a severe electrical shock.

If the child is conscious and it seems the shock was minor, check him for burned skin, especially if his mouth was the point of contact with the current. Then call your pediatrician. Electric shock can cause internal organ damage that may be difficult to detect without a medical examination. For that reason *all* children who receive a significant electric shock should see a doctor.

In the pediatrician's office, any minor burns resulting from the electricity will be cleansed and dressed. The doctor may order laboratory tests to check for signs of damage to internal organs. If the child has severe burns or any sign of brain or heart damage, he will need to be hospitalized.

Prevention

The best way to prevent electrical accidents is to cover all outlets, make sure all wires are properly insulated, and provide adult supervision whenever children are in an area with potential electrical hazards. Small appliances are a special hazard around bathtubs or pools. (See also Chapter 13, "Keeping Your Child Safe.")

Fingertip Injuries

Children's fingertips get smashed frequently, usually getting caught in closing doors. Too often, those doors are shut by parents unaware that little fingers are in danger. The child is either unable to recognize the potential danger, or he fails to remove his hand quickly enough. Fingers also sometimes get crushed when youngsters play with a hammer or other heavy object.

Because fingertips are exquisitely sensitive, your child will let you know immediately that he's been injured. Usually the damaged area will be blue and swollen, and there may be a cut or bleeding around the cuticle. The skin, tissues below the skin, and the nail bed—as well as the underlying bone and growth plate—may all be affected. If bleeding occurs underneath the nail, it will turn black or dark-blue, and the pressure from the bleeding may be painful.

Home Treatment

When the fingertip is bleeding, wash it with soap and water, and cover it with a soft, sterile dressing. An ice pack or a soaking in cold water may relieve the pain and minimize swelling.

If the swelling is mild and your child is comfortable, you can allow the finger to heal on its own. But be alert for any increase in pain, swelling, redness, or drainage from the injured area, or a fever beginning twenty-four to seventy-two hours after the injury. These may be signs of infection, and you should notify your pediatrician.

When there's excessive swelling, a deep cut, blood under the fingernail, or the finger looks as if it may be broken, call your doctor immediately. And by all means, do not attempt to straighten a fractured finger on your own.

Professional Treatment

If your doctor suspects a fracture, he may order an X-ray. If the X-ray confirms a fracture—or if there's damage to the nail bed where nail growth occurs—an orthopedic consultation may be necessary. A fractured finger can be straightened and set under local anesthesia. An injured nail bed also must be repaired surgically to minimize the possibility of a nail deformity developing as the finger grows. If there's considerable blood under the nail, the pediatrician may drain it by making a small hole in the nail, which should relieve the pain.

Although deep cuts may require stitches, often all that's necessary is sterile adhesive strips (thin adhesive strips similar to butterfly bandages). If there's a fracture underneath a cut, this is considered an "open" fracture and is susceptible to infection in the bone. In this case, antibiotics will be prescribed. Depending on your child's age and immunization status, the doctor also may order a tetanus booster.

(See also *Fractures/Broken Bones,* below.)

Fractures/Broken Bones

Although the term *fracture* may sound serious, it is just another name for a broken bone. As you probably remember from your own childhood, fractures are *very* common. In fact, they are the fourth most common injury among children under age six. Falls cause most of the fractures in this age group, but the most serious bone breaks usually result from car accidents.

A broken bone in a child is different from one in an adult, because young bones are more flexible and have a thicker covering, which makes them better able to absorb shock. Children's fractures *rarely* require surgical repair. They usually just need to be kept free of movement, most often through the use of a molded cast.

Most broken bones in youngsters are either "greenstick" fractures, in which the bone bends like green wood and breaks only on one side, or "torus" fractures, in which the bone is buckled, twisted, and weakened but not completely broken. A "bend" fracture refers to a bone that is bent but not broken, and is also relatively common among youngsters. "Complete" fractures, in which the bone breaks all the way through, also occur in young children.

Because your child's bones are still growing, he is vulnerable to an additional type of fracture that does not occur in adults. This involves damage to the growth plates at the ends of the bones. These regulate future growth. If this part of the bone does not heal properly after the fracture, the bone may grow at an angle, or more slowly than the other bones in the body. Unfortunately, the impact on the bone's growth may not be visible for a year or more after the injury, so these fractures must be followed carefully by the pediatrician for twelve to eighteen months to make sure no growth damage has occurred.

Fractures are also classified as "nondisplaced," when the broken ends are still in proper position, or "displaced," when the ends are separated or out of alignment. In an "open" or "compound" fracture, the bone sticks through the skin. If the skin is intact, the fracture is "closed."

Signs and Symptoms

It's not always easy to tell when a bone is broken, especially if your child is too young to describe what he's feeling. Ordinarily with a fracture, you will see swelling and your child will clearly be in pain and unable—or unwilling—to move the injured limb. However, just because your child can move the bone doesn't necessarily rule out a fracture. Any time you suspect a fracture, notify your pediatrician immediately.

Home Treatment

Until your child can be seen in the pediatrician's office, emergency room, or urgent-care center, use an improvised sling or rolled-up newspaper or magazine as a splint to protect the injury from unnecessary movement.

Don't give the child anything by mouth to drink or to relieve pain without first consulting the doctor, but if yours is an older child, you can use an ice bag or a cold towel, placed on the injury site, to decrease pain. Extreme cold can cause injury to the delicate skin of babies and toddlers, so ice should not be used with children this young.

If your child has broken his leg, do not try to move him yourself. Call an ambulance, make the child as comfortable as possible, and let the paramedics supervise his transportation.

If part of the injury is open and bleeding, or if bone is protruding through the skin, place firm pressure on the wound or use a tourniquet to stop the bleeding (see *Cuts, Lacerations, and Bleeding,* page 456); then cover it with clean (preferably sterile) gauze. Do not try to put the bone back underneath the skin. After this injury has been treated, be alert to any fever, which may indicate that the wound has become infected.

Professional Treatment

After examining the break, the doctor will order X-rays to determine the extent of the damage. If the doctor suspects that the bone's growth plate is affected, or if the bones are out of line, an orthopedic consultation will be necessary.

Because children's bones heal rapidly and well, a plaster or Fiberglas cast, or sometimes just an immobilizing splint, is all that is needed for most minor fractures. For a displaced fracture, an orthopedic surgeon may have to realign the bones. This may be done as a "closed reduction," in which the surgeon uses local or general anesthesia, manipulates the bones until they're straight, and then applies a cast. An "open reduction" is a surgical procedure done in an operating room, but this is rarely necessary for children. After the surgical reduction, a cast will be used until the bone has healed, which usually takes about half the time that adult bones require, or less, depending on the child's age. The nice thing about young bones is that they don't have to be in perfect alignment. As long as they are more or less in the right place, they will remodel as they grow. Your pediatrician may order periodic X-rays while the bone is healing, just to make sure they are aligning properly.

Usually, casting brings rapid relief or at least a decrease in pain. If your child has an increase in pain, numbness, pale or blue fingers or toes, call your doctor immediately. These are signs that the extremity has swollen and requires more room within the cast. If the cast is not adjusted, the swelling may press on nerves, muscles, and blood vessels, which can produce permanent damage. To relieve the pressure, the doctor may split the cast, open a window in it, or replace it with a larger one.

Also let the doctor know if the cast breaks, becomes very loose, or if the plaster gets wet and soggy. Without a proper, secure fit, the cast will not hold the broken bone in position to mend correctly.

Bones that have been broken often will form a hard knot at the site of the break during the healing process. Especially with a broken collarbone, this may look unsightly, but there is no treatment for this, and the knot will not be permanent. The bone will remodel and resume its normal shape in a few months.

Head Injury/Concussion

It's almost inevitable that your child will hit his head every now and then. Especially when he's a baby, these collisions may upset you, but your anxiety is usually worse than the bump. Most head injuries are minor, causing no serious problems. Even so, it's important to know the difference between a head injury that warrants medical attention and one that needs only a comforting hug.

If your child suffers a brief, temporary loss of consciousness after a hard blow to the head, he is said to have had a concussion. If a child has a concussion, it doesn't necessarily mean that his brain has been damaged, but it does indicate that the brain centers for consciousness have been momentarily disturbed.

Treatment

If a child's head injury has been mild, he'll remain alert and awake after the incident, and his color will be normal. He may cry out due to momentary pain and fright, but the crying should last no more than ten minutes and then he'll go back to playing as usual.

Occasionally, a minor head injury also will cause slight dizziness, nausea, and headache, and the child might vomit once or twice. Even so, if the injury seems minor and there's not a significant cut (one that's deep and/or actively bleeding) which might require medical attention or possibly stitches (see *Cuts and Scrapes,* page 455), you can treat your child at home. Just wash the cut with soap and water. If there's a bruise, apply a cold compress. This will help minimize the swelling if you do it in the first few hours after the injury.

Even after a minor head injury, you should observe your child for twenty-four to forty-eight hours to see if he develops any signs of more severe damage. Although it's *very rare,* children can develop serious brain injury after a seemingly minor bump on the head that causes no immediate obvious problems. When brain injury does occur, it's usually due to internal bleeding and almost always shows up within one to two days of the original incident. If your child develops any of the following symptoms, consult your pediatrician immediately.

- He seems excessively sleepy or lethargic during his usual wakeful hours, or you cannot awaken him while he's asleep at night. (You should try to awaken him once or twice during the first night if he's had a hard blow to the head.)

- He has a headache that won't go away (even with acetaminophen), or vomits more than once or twice. Headache and vomiting occur commonly after head trauma, but they are usually mild and last only a few hours.

- He's persistently and/or extremely irritable. With an infant who cannot tell you what he's feeling, this may indicate a severe headache.

- Any significant change in your child's mental abilities, coordination, sensation, or strength warrants immediate medical attention. Such changes would include weakness of arms or legs, clumsy walking, slurred speech, crossed eyes, or difficulty with vision.

- He becomes unconscious again after being awake for a while, or he has a seizure (convulsion) or starts to breathe irregularly. These are signs of disturbed brain activity and, possibly, a serious head injury.

If your child loses consciousness *at any time* after hitting his head, the pediatrician should be notified. If he doesn't awaken within a few minutes, he needs *immediate medical attention.* Call for help while you follow these steps.

1. Move your child as little as possible. *If you suspect that he might have injured his neck, do not attempt to move him. Changing the position of his neck might make his injuries worse.* One exception: Move him only if he's in danger of being injured further where he is (for example, on a ledge or in a fire).

2. Check to see if he's breathing. If he isn't, perform CPR (see page 449).

3. If he's bleeding severely from a scalp wound, apply direct pressure with a clean cloth over the wound.

4. If trained ambulance personnel are readily available, it's safer to await their arrival than to try taking your child to the hospital yourself.

Loss of consciousness following a head injury may last only a few seconds or as long as several hours. If you find the child after the accident happened, and you are not sure if he lost consciousness, notify the pediatrician. (An older child who has had a concussion may say that he can't remember what happened just prior to and just after the accident.)

Most children who lose consciousness for more than a few minutes will be hospitalized overnight. Hospitalization is essential for youngsters with severe brain injury and irregular breathing or convulsions. Fortunately, with modern pediatric intensive care, many children who have suffered serious head injury—and even those who have been unconscious for several weeks—may eventually recover completely.

Lead Poisoning

During the first two or three years of life your child is bound to go through a phase of putting things other than food into his mouth. He'll chew on his toys, taste the sand in the playground, and sample the cat's food if given the opportunity. As annoying as this can be for you, few of these things will cause him any serious harm, as long as you keep poisons and sharp objects out of his reach. Lead is one dangerous substance, however, that your child can consume without your knowledge.

Contrary to popular belief, lead poisoning is not caused by chewing on a pencil or being stabbed with its point. The so-called "lead" in a pencil actually is harmless graphite, and there is no lead in the paint coating the outside. Lead poisoning *is* most often caused by eating lead contained in bits of old paint or in dirt that has been contaminated by lead, by breathing lead in the air, or by drinking water from pipes lined or soldered with lead.

Lead was an allowable ingredient in house paint before 1977, and therefore may be present on the walls, door jambs, and window frames of many older homes. As the paint ages, it chips, peels, and comes off in the form of dust. Toddlers are tempted by such bite-size pieces and will taste or eat them out of curiosity. Even if they don't intentionally eat the material, the dust can get on hands and into food. Sometimes the lead-containing finish has been covered over with layers of newer, safer paints. This can give a false sense of reassurance, however, since the underlying paint may still chip or peel off with the newer layers and fall into the hands of toddlers.

About 4 million children in the United States have unacceptably high lead levels in their blood. Living in a city, being poor, and being black or hispanic are all risk factors that increase the chances of having an elevated blood-lead level. But even children living in the country or who are in well-to-do families can still be at risk.

As the child continues consuming lead, it accumulates in the body. Though it may not be noticeable for some time, it ultimately will affect many of the organs in the body, including the brain. Slight lead poisoning can can cause mild learning disabilities. More severe lead poisoning may produce permanent mental and physical retardation. Lead also can cause stomach and intestinal problems, anemia, hearing loss, and even short stature. (See *Abdominal Pain*, page 469.)

Prevention

You can make certain that your child doesn't eat lead by removing any sources of leaded paint. There is little cause for worry if your home was built after 1977, when federal regulations restricted the amount of lead permitted in paint. If you live in an older home that has not been painted recently, it would be wise to repaint now. Make sure to repair all wall and ceiling cracks, and scrape off all traces of old paint before applying the new. The process of repairing and repainting your home should be done carefully, preferably by workers experienced in lead paint removal. All surfaces with leaded paint should either be sealed over with plaster board or paneling or the paint removed. If it is to be removed, then each room as it's being worked on, should be closed off from the rest of the house to prevent the spread of leaded dust. The safest thing to do is to move out while the renovation is ongoing and until the final cleaning has been completed.

If for some reason you are unable to repaint, keep your home as clean as possible and try to control the amount of dust in the air by wet-mopping all bare floors and surfaces with a high phosphate containing detergent. Such detergents can be found in hardware stores.

In a rented home the landlord is responsible for all maintenance, and this includes necessary repainting and repairs. If you suspect unhealthy levels of lead in the building, and your landlord is unresponsive, notify your community's department of health. A representative will inspect the house, and if unhealthy levels of lead are found, you can legally compel the landlord to correct the situation.

You also can make your child less susceptible to lead poisoning by making sure he has a well-balanced, low-fat diet. Calcium and iron in particular reduce the amount of lead absorbed and retained from the intestine.

Treatment

Children who have lead poisoning often show no symptoms until they reach school age, when they begin to have difficulty keeping up with classwork. Some may even seem overly active, due to the physical effects of the lead. For this reason, the only sure way to know if your child has been exposed to excessive lead is to have him tested annually during these early years, particularly if he is in the high-risk groups mentioned earlier.

The most common screening test for lead poisoning uses a drop of blood from a finger prick. If this test result indicates that a child has been exposed to excessive lead, a second test will be done using a larger sample of blood obtained from a vein in the arm. This test is more accurate and can measure the precise amount of lead in the blood.

Children who have lead poisoning may require treatment with a drug that binds the lead in the blood and greatly increases the ability of the body to eliminate it. The treatment usually involves hospitalization and a series of injections. New medicines that can be given orally are being developed.

Some children with lead poisoning require more than one course of treatment, and all require months of close follow-up. If the damage is severe, the child may require special schooling and therapy. No one yet knows whether treatment can reverse the effects of mild lead poisoning, but it certainly can prevent further damage.

Poisoning

Most children who swallow poison are *not* permanently harmed, particularly if they receive immediate treatment. If you think your child has been poisoned, stay calm and act quickly.

You should suspect poisoning if you ever find your child with an open or empty container of a toxic substance, especially if he is acting strangely in any way. Be alert for these other signs of possible poisoning.

- Unexplained stains on his clothing

- Burns on his lips or mouth

- Unusual drooling, or odd odors on his breath

- Unexplained nausea or vomiting

- Abdominal cramps without fever

- Difficulty in breathing

- Sudden behavior changes, such as unusual sleepiness, irritability, or jumpiness

- Convulsions or unconsciousness (only in very serious cases)

Treatment

Any time your child has ingested a poison of any kind, your pediatrician should be notified. However, your regional poison control center will provide the *immediate* information and guidance you need when you first discover that your child has been poisoned. These centers are staffed twenty-four hours a day with experts who can tell you what to do without delay. The number of your regional poison control center should be listed on the inside cover of your telephone book. You also should write that number on a piece of paper that is attached to or located near every phone in your home, along with other emergency numbers. *If an emergency exists and you cannot find the number, dial 911 or Information and ask for poison control.*

The immediate action you need to take will vary with the type of poisoning. The poison control center can give you specific instructions if you know the particular substance your child has swallowed. However, carry out the following instructions before calling them.

Swallowed Poison

First, get the poisonous substance away from your child. If he still has some in his mouth, make him spit it out, or remove it with your fingers. Keep this material along with any other evidence that might help determine what he swallowed.

Next, check for these signs:

- Severe throat pain

- Excessive drooling

- Breathing difficulty

- Convulsions

- Excessive drowsiness

If any of these are present, get emergency medical help immediately by calling for an ambulance or having someone drive you to the nearest emergency center. Take the poison container and remnants of material with you to help the doctor determine what was swallowed. *Do not make your child vomit,* as this may cause further damage, and *do not follow instructions about poisoning on the label* of the container, as these are often out of date or incorrect.

If your child is not showing these serious symptoms, call your regional poison control center. They will need the following information in order to help you:

- Your name and phone number.

- Your child's name, age, and weight. Also be sure to mention any serious medical conditions he may have.

- The name of the substance your child swallowed. Read it off the container, and spell it if necessary. If ingredients are listed on the label, read them too. If your child has swallowed a prescription medicine, and the drug is not named on the label, give the center the name of the pharmacy and its phone number, the date of the prescription and its number. Try to describe the tablet or capsule, and mention any imprinted numbers on it. If your child swallowed another substance, such as a part of a plant, provide as full a description as possible to help identify it.

- The time your child swallowed this poison (or when you found him), and the amount you think he swallowed.

If the poison is extremely dangerous, or if your child is very young, you may be told to make him vomit and/or take him directly to the nearest emergency room for medical evaluation. Otherwise, you will be given instructions to follow at home.

If you are advised to make your child vomit, give him syrup of ipecac *(keep this on hand)* in the recommended dose (see page 466). Encourage him to drink a glass of water as well. If he doesn't vomit within twenty minutes, repeat the dose *once.* Get a large basin or bowl, and when your child starts to vomit, place him over your lap, with his face down and his head lower than his hips. Catch the vomit in the basin so it can be inspected. Save it until your pediatrician or the poison control center tells you to discard it. If your child continues to vomit for more than two hours after being given syrup of ipecac, or shows any of the symptoms described earlier, again contact your pediatrician.

In some cases vomiting may be dangerous, so never make a child vomit unless the poison control center instructs you to do so. Strong acids (such as toilet bowl cleaner) or strong alkalis (such as lye, drain or oven cleaner, or dishwasher detergent) can burn the throat— and vomiting will only increase the damage. In such cases you probably will be advised to have the child drink milk or water. Also, sometimes induction of vomiting may interfere with administration of activated charcoal or oral antidote.

Poison on the Skin

If your child spills a dangerous chemical substance on his body, remove his clothes and rinse the skin with lukewarm—not hot— water. If the area shows signs of being burned, continue rinsing for at least fifteen minutes, no matter how much your child may protest. Then call the poison control center for further advice. Do not apply ointments or grease.

Poison in the Eye

Flush your child's eye by holding his eyelid open and pouring a steady stream of luke-

Poison-Proofing Your Home

- Store drugs and medications in a medicine cabinet that is locked or out of reach. Do not keep toothpaste in the same cabinet.

- Buy and *keep* medication in containers with child-proof caps. Discard prescription medicines when the illness for which they were prescribed has passed.

- Do not take medicine in front of small children; they may try to imitate you later. Never coax a child into taking medicine by calling it candy.

- Check the label every time you give medication, to be sure you are giving the right medicine in the correct dosage. Mistakes are most likely to occur in the middle of the night, so always turn on the light when handling any medication.

- Read labels on all household products before you buy them. Try to find the least toxic ones for the job, and buy only what you need to use immediately.

- Store hazardous products in locked cabinets that are out of your child's reach. Do not keep detergents and other cleaning products under the kitchen or bathroom sink unless they are in a cabinet with a safety lock.

- Never put poisonous or toxic products in containers that were once used for food.

- Never run your car in a closed garage. Be sure that coal, wood, or kerosene stoves are properly maintained. If you smell gas, turn off the stove or gas burner, leave the house, and then call the gas company.

- Keep a small bottle of syrup of ipecac on hand. (Store it with your other medicines, out of children's reach.) This is available without prescription at most pharmacies. Use it only when and as directed by Poison Control or your pediatrician. **Recommended dosage schedule: one month to one year— consult your pediatrician; one year to ten years—½ ounce (1 tablespoon or 3 teaspoons or 15 milliliters) followed by two glasses of water.**

- Post the Poison Control number near every telephone in your home, along with other emergency numbers. Be sure that your babysitter knows how to use these numbers.

warm water into the inner corner. A young child is sure to object to this treatment, so get another adult to hold him while you rinse the eye. If that's not possible, wrap him tightly in a towel and clamp him under one arm so you have one hand free to hold the eyelid open and the other to pour in the water. Continue flushing the eye for fifteen minutes. Then call poison control for further instructions. Do not use an eyecup, eyedrops, or ointment. If there is any question of continued pain or severe injury, seek emergency assistance immediately.

Poison Fumes

In the home, poisonous fumes are most likely to be produced by an idling automobile in a closed garage; leaky gas vents; and wood, coal, or kerosene stoves that are improperly vented or maintained. If your child is exposed to fumes or gases from these or other sources, get him into fresh air immediately. If he is breathing, call poison control for further instructions. If he has stopped breathing, start CPR (see page 449) and don't stop until he breathes on his own or someone else can take over. If you can, have someone call for emergency medical help immediately; otherwise, wait until your child is breathing and then call for emergency assistance.

Prevention

Young children, especially those between ages one and three, are poisoned most commonly by things in the home such as drugs and medications, cleaning products, plants, cosmetics, pesticides, paints, and solvents. This happens because tasting and mouthing things is a natural way for children to explore their surroundings, and because they imitate adults without understanding what they are doing.

Most poisonings occur when parents are distracted. If you are ill or under a great deal of stress, you may not watch your child as closely as usual. The hectic routine of getting dinner on the table at the end of the day causes so many lapses in parental attention that late afternoon is known as "the arsenic hour" by poison control personnel.

The best way to prevent poisonings is to store all toxic substances, locked, where your child cannot possibly get to them, even when you are not directly watching him. Also, supervise him even more closely whenever you're visiting a store or home that has not been child-proofed.

(See also Chapter 13, "Keeping Your Child Safe.")

16

ABDOMINAL/GASTROINTESTINAL TRACT

Abdominal Pain

Children of all ages experience abdominal pain occasionally, but the causes of such pain in infants tend to be quite different than they are in older children. So, too, is the way children of different age groups react to the pain. An older youngster may rub his abdomen and tell you he's having a "bellyache" or "tummyache," while a very young infant will show his distress by crying and pulling up his legs or by passing gas. Vomiting or excessive burping may also accompany the crying in babies.

Fortunately, most stomachaches disappear on their own, and are not serious. However, if your child's complaints continue or worsen over a period of three to five hours, or if he has a fever, severe sore throat, or extreme change in appetite or energy level, you should notify your pediatrician immediately. These symptoms may indicate that a more serious disorder is causing the pain.

Common Causes of Abdominal Pain in Infancy

1. Colic usually occurs in infants under three months of age. While no one knows exactly what causes it, colic seems to produce rapid and severe contractions of the intestine which probably are responsible for the baby's pain. The discomfort often is more severe in the late afternoon and early evening, and may be accompanied by inconsolable crying, pulling up of the legs, frequent passage of gas, and general irritability. (See Chapter 7, "Age One Month Through Three Months.")

How should you respond? You may need to try a variety of approaches (detailed on page 139).

2. Intussusseption. Another cause of abdominal pain in young infants is due to something called intussusseption. This particular problem is due to one part of the intestine telescoping on itself. This creates a blockage

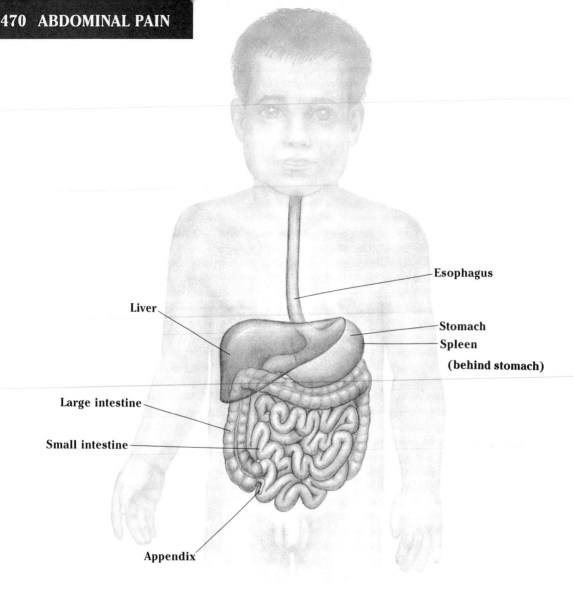

Esophagus

Liver

Stomach

Spleen

(behind stomach)

Large intestine

Small intestine

Appendix

Abdomen/Gastrointestinal Tract

that causes severe pain. The child will intermittently cry and pull his legs toward his stomach.

It is important to recognize this cause of abdominal pain and to talk to your pediatrician immediately. He will want to see your child and perhaps order an X-ray called a barium enema. Sometimes doing this test will not only make the diagnosis but also unblock the intestine.

3. Constipation often is blamed for abdominal pain, but it's rarely a problem in younger

infants. Older babies who have started solid foods, however, do sometimes become constipated, and may experience abdominal discomfort while having a bowel movement. If this appears to be your child's problem, try the following:

- Add extra water to the diet.

- Decrease constipating foods, such as rice, banana, or cereal.

If these simple measures don't seem to help, consult the section on *Constipation* (page

474), and talk to your pediatrician. Never give a child laxatives or other types of stool loosening or softening medications without first consulting your pediatrician.

Causes of Abdominal Pain in Older Children

1. Urinary tract infection (UTI) can occur during infancy, but it rarely produces abdominal pain at that age. UTI is much more common among three- to five-year-old girls, when it produces discomfort in the bladder area as well as some pain and burning when urinating. These children may also urinate more frequently and possibly wet the bed. However, the infection usually does not produce a fever.

If your child complains of these symptoms, take her to the pediatrician, who will examine the child and her urine. If an infection is present, an antibiotic will be prescribed. This will eliminate both the infection and the abdominal pain. (See *Urinary Tract Infections,* page 592.)

2. Strep throat is a throat infection caused by bacteria called *streptococci.* It occurs frequently in children over two. The symptoms and signs include a sore throat and a fever. There may be some vomiting and headache as well. The pediatrician will want to examine your child and take a throat culture. If the culture is positive for strep—it usually takes twenty-four hours for results, though some doctors are now using a test that provides results in less than an hour—your child will need to be treated with an antibiotic. (See *Sore Throat,* page 547.)

3. Appendicitis is very rare in children under age three, and uncommon under the age of five. When it does occur, the first sign is often a complaint of *constant* stomachache in the center of the abdomen. Later, the pain moves down and over to the right side, and the child may feel nauseous, have a slight fever, and even vomit. If your child has pain and other symptoms that occur in this pattern, notify your pediatrician at once. The doctor will want to see your child immediately, and may even ask you to come to the emergency room at the hospital for blood tests and X-rays. If the diagnosis turns out to be appendicitis, an operation will be performed as quickly as possible to remove the appendix. (See *Appendicitis,* page 472, for more detailed information.)

4. Lead poisoning most often occurs in toddlers living in an older house where lead-based paint has been used. Children in this age group may eat small chips of paint off the walls and woodwork. The lead is then stored in their bodies and can create many serious health problems. Symptoms of lead poisoning include

- Abdominal pain
- Constipation
- Irritability (The child is fussy, crying, difficult to satisfy.)
- Lethargy (He is sleepy, doesn't want to play, has a poor appetite.)
- Convulsions

If your child is exposed to lead paint, or if you know he has eaten paint chips and has any of the above symptoms, call your pediatrician. He can order a blood test for lead, and advise you as to what else needs to be done. (See *Lead Poisoning,* page 462.)

5. Intestinal infection (gastroenteritis): Viruses are the most frequent cause of intestinal infection and the abdominal pain that results from such infection. However, intestinal infection can be caused by bacteria or parasites, organisms—larger than bacteria or viruses—that are frequently found in unsanitary water or food supplies. When infection occurs, there are usually abdominal cramps, diarrhea, and/or vomiting. (See *Diarrhea,* page 476, and *Vomiting,* page 491.) The pain generally lasts one or two days and then disappears. One exception is an infection caused by the *Giardia lamblia* parasite. This infestation may produce periodic recurrent pain not localized to any one part of the abdomen. The pain may persist for a week or more, and can lead to a marked loss of appetite and weight. Treatment with appropriate medication can cure this infestation and the abdominal pain that accompanies it.

6. Milk allergy or milk intolerance is a reaction to the protein in milk which results in cramping abdominal pain. (See *Milk Allergy,* page 487.)

7. Emotional upset sometimes causes recurrent abdominal pain which has no other obvious cause. Although this rarely occurs before age five, it can happen to a younger child who is under unusual stress. The first clue is pain that tends to come and go, over a period of more than a week. Second, there are no other associated findings or complaints (fever, vomiting, diarrhea, coughing, lethargy or weakness, urinary tract symptoms, sore throat, or flulike symptoms). There may also be a family history of this type of illness. Finally, your child will probably act either quieter or noisier than usual, and have trouble expressing his thoughts or feelings. If this type of behavior occurs with your child, find out if there's something troubling him at home or school, or with siblings, relatives, or friends. Has he recently lost a close friend or a pet? Has there been a death of a family member, or the divorce or separation of his parents?

Your pediatrician can suggest ways to help your child talk about his troubles. For example, he may advise you to use toys or games to help the youngster act out his problems. If you need additional assistance, the pediatrician may refer you to a child psychologist or psychiatrist.

Appendicitis

The appendix is a narrow, finger-shaped, hollow structure attached to the large intestine. While it serves no purpose in humans, it can cause serious problems when it becomes inflamed. Because of its location, this can happen quite easily; for instance, a piece of food or stool can get trapped inside, causing the appendix to swell, become infected and painfully inflamed. This inflammation—called appendicitis—is most common in youngsters over the age of six, but can occur in younger children as well.

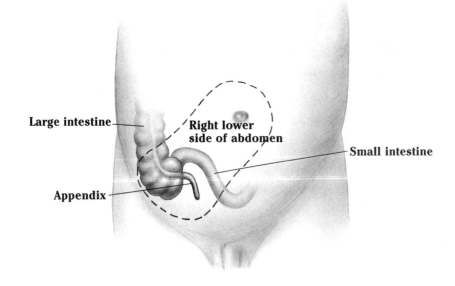

Large intestine

Right lower side of abdomen

Small intestine

Appendix

Once infected, the appendix must be removed. Otherwise it may burst, allowing the infection to spread within the abdomen. Since this problem is potentially life-threatening, it's important to know the symptoms of appendicitis so you can call your pediatrician at the first sign of trouble. In order of appearance, the symptoms are

1. Abdominal pain: This usually is the first complaint the child will have. Almost always, the pain is felt first around the umbilicus (belly button). After several hours, as the infection worsens, the pain may intensify in the lower right side. Sometimes, if the appendix is not located in the usual position, the discomfort may occur elsewhere in the abdomen or in the back, or there may be urinary symptoms such as increased frequency or burning. Even when the appendix lies in its normal position and the pain is in the right lower abdomen, it may also irritate one of the muscles that leads toward the leg, causing the child to limp or walk bent over.

2. Vomiting: After several hours of pain, vomiting may occur. It is important to remember that *stomachache comes* before *the vomiting with appendicitis, not after.* Abdominal pain that *follows* vomiting is very commonly seen in viral illnesses such as the flu.

3. Loss of appetite: The absence of hunger occurs shortly after the onset of the pain.

4. Fever: There may be a low-grade fever (100–101 degrees Fahrenheit; 38–38.5 degrees Celsius).

Unfortunately, the symptoms associated with appendicitis sometimes may be hidden by preceding viral or bacterial infections. Diarrhea, nausea, vomiting, and fever may appear before the typical pain of appendicitis, making the diagnosis much more difficult.

Also, your child's discomfort may suddenly vanish, thus persuading you that all is well. Unfortunately, this disappearance of pain could also mean that the appendix has just broken open! Though the pain may leave for several hours, this is exactly when appendicitis becomes dangerous. The infection will spread to the rest of the abdomen, causing your child to become much more ill, develop a higher fever, and require hospitalization for surgery and intravenous antibiotics. Recovery may take much longer, and there may be more complications than with appendicitis diagnosed and treated earlier.

Treatment

Detecting the signs of appendicitis is not always easy. This is particularly the case in a child under the age of two, who cannot tell you where it hurts or that the pain is moving to the right side. This is why it's better to act sooner rather than later if you have any suspicion that your child's pain or discomfort seems "different," more severe than usual, or out of the ordinary. While most children with abdominal pain don't have appendicitis, only a physician should diagnose this serious problem. So if the abdominal pain persists for more than an hour or two, and if your child also has nausea, vomiting, loss of appetite, and fever, notify your pediatrician immediately. If the doctor is not certain the problem is appendicitis, he may decide to observe your child closely for several hours, either in or out of the hospital. During this time, he will have performed additional laboratory or X-ray examinations to see if more conclusive signs develop. If there is a strong probability that appendicitis is present, surgery usually will be done as soon as possible.

In almost all cases the treatment of appendicitis is surgical removal of the appendix. In rare instances the tissue covering the intestines may enclose the appendix, thus containing the infection. This makes it more difficult to remove the appendix without spreading the infection, so antibiotics may be used, either alone or combined with drainage of the infection by a small tube. But because inflammation can recur even after the initial infection is gone, the appendix usually is removed later on.

Celiac Disease

Celiac disease is a problem that causes malabsorption—that is, a failure of the bowels to absorb nutrients. It's caused by an immune reaction to gluten (the protein found in wheat) that takes place in the intestine and stimulates the body's immune system to attack and damage the lining of the intestine, preventing nutrients from being absorbed into the system. As a result, food simply passes through the intestines, only partially digested. The result is crampy abdominal pain, foul-smelling stools, diarrhea, weight loss, irritability, and a continuous feeling of being sick.

Treatment

Once the physician has ruled out all other possible digestive problems, he may recommend an intestinal biopsy—that is, the removal of a small piece of the intestine for laboratory examination. This procedure usually is done by passing a small tube through the mouth and into the small intestine, where the biopsy is obtained. This doesn't usually require a general anesthetic.

If the intestinal lining turns out to be damaged, your child will be placed on a gluten-free diet. This means staying away from wheat, rye, barley, or oat products. Your pediatrician will give you a complete list of foods to avoid, but you also need to carefully check the labels of any foods you purchase, since wheat flour is a hidden ingredient in many items. Because rice and rice products do not contain gluten, they'll probably become a major part of your child's diet.

Once your child's condition seems back to normal, a second sample of the intestine will be taken. If the lining appears normal, a small amount of gluten may be reintroduced into the diet temporarily, after which a third tissue sample might be taken. If any signs of gluten sensitivity have reappeared, it is a confirmation of celiac disease.

Incidentally, your child may not be able to tolerate milk sugar for as long as several months after each tissue sample is taken from his intestine. In this case, milk as well as gluten products will be eliminated temporarily from his diet. During this time he might be given milk treated with enzymes, so that it will be predigested before reaching the intestine. Extra vitamins and minerals also might be necessary.

If your child does have celiac disease, he must remain on the gluten-free diet for his entire life, avoiding completely wheat, rye, barley, and oats.

(See also: *Malabsorption,* page 486; *Diarrhea,* page 476; *Anemia,* page 649; *Milk Allergy,* page 487.)

Constipation

Bowel patterns vary in children just as they do in adults. Because of this, it is sometimes difficult to tell if your child is truly constipated. One child may go two or three days without a bowel movement and still not be constipated, while another might have relatively frequent bowel movements but have difficulty passing the stool. In general, it is best to watch for the following signals before suspecting constipation:

- In a newborn, firm stools less than once a day

- In an older child, stools that are hard and compact, with three or four days between bowel movements

- At any age, stools that are hard and dry and associated with painful bowel movements

- Episodes of abdominal pain relieved after having a large bowel movement

- Blood in or on the outside of the stools

- Soiling between bowel movements

Constipation generally occurs when the muscles at the end of the large intestine tighten, preventing the stool from passing normally. The longer the stool remains there, the firmer and drier it becomes, making it even more difficult to pass without discomfort. Then, because the bowel movement is painful, your child may consciously try to hold it back, making the problem still worse.

The tendency to constipation seems to run in families. It may start in infancy and remain as a lifetime pattern, becoming worse if the child does not establish regular bowel habits, or withholds stool. Stool retention most commonly occurs between the ages of two and five, at a time when the child is coming to terms with independence, control, and toilet training. Older children may resist having bowel movements away from home because they don't want to use an unfamiliar toilet. This, too, can cause constipation or make it worse.

If your child does withhold, he may produce such large stools that his rectum stretches. He may no longer feel the urge to defecate until the stool is too big to be passed without the help of an enema, laxative, or other treatment. In some of these cases, soiling occurs when liquid waste leaks around the solid stool. This looks like diarrhea on the child's underpants or diaper. In these severe cases, the rectum must be emptied under a physician's supervision, and the child must be retrained to establish normal bowel patterns.

Treatment

Mild or occasional episodes of constipation may be helped by the following suggestions:

If your constipated child is between six months and twelve months of age and recently has started cow's milk, return to his previous formula. This may be helpful, since infant formula tends to be less constipating than unmodified cow's milk. Constipation due to breast milk is unusual, but if your breast-fed infant is constipated it is probably due to a reason other than diet. Do *not* substitute formula for breast milk unless your doctor tells you to do so.

If your child is eating solid foods and has problems with constipation, you may need to add high-fiber foods to his daily diet. These include prunes, apricots, plums, raisins, high-fiber vegetables (such as peas, beans, broccoli), and whole-grain cereals and bread products. Increasing the daily consumption of water may also help.

In more severe cases the pediatrician may prescribe a mild laxative or enema. Follow such prescriptions exactly. Never give your child a laxative without your doctor's advice.

Prevention

Parents should become familiar with their children's normal bowel patterns and the typical size and consistency of their stools. This is helpful in determining when constipation occurs and how severe the problem is. If the child does not have regular bowel movements each day or two, or is uncomfortable when they are passed, he may need help in developing proper bowel habits. This may be done by providing a proper diet and establishing a regular bowel routine.

In a child who is not yet toilet trained, the best way to guard against constipation is to provide a high-fiber diet. The amount of fiber should be increased as he gets older.

Once the child is mature enough to be toilet trained, he should be urged to sit on the toilet after breakfast every day. A book, puzzle, or toy can occupy him during this time so that he feels relaxed. He should be encouraged to stay on the toilet until he has a bowel movement or for about fifteen minutes. If he is successful, he should be praised; if not, he should be encouraged with positive statements. Eventually he should be able to toilet himself without parental guidance.

If the combination of a high-fiber diet and a daily toilet routine does not result in regular bowel movements, the child may consciously be withholding stool. In this case the pediatrician should be consulted. He can supervise the use of stool softeners, laxatives, or suppositories, should they be necessary. Occasionally stool withholding becomes so severe that both the child and the family become upset by the symptoms. Much of each day's interactions focus on bowel movements. Programs have been devised to deal effectively with this problem.

Usually the withholding begins around toilet training. The child is reluctant to move his bowels on the potty or toilet and withholds. The next bowel movement is painful. The child associates pain with bowel movements, and now withholds stool because of that. The situation can progress to an all-consuming fear. With such severe symptoms the rectum must be cleansed with enemas or rectal suppositories. Following this, a stool softener such as mineral oil is given in amounts large enough to prevent the child from voluntarily withholding stool. Because the bowel movements are now no longer painful, the child will start to go on the potty without fear. This treatment may go on for several months while the mineral oil is slowly withdrawn. A diet high in fiber and regular toileting are also part of the routine.

Diarrhea

Your child's bowel movements normally will vary in number and consistency, depending on his age and diet. Breast-fed newborns may have up to twelve small bowel movements a day, but by the second or third month may have some days without any. Most babies under one year of age produce less than 5 ounces of stool per day, while older children can produce up to 7 ounces. By age two, most children will have only one or two large bowel movements a day, but your child can have several smaller ones and still be normal, especially if his diet includes juices and fiber-containing foods, such as prunes or bran.

An occasional loose stool is not cause for alarm. If, however, the bowel pattern *suddenly changes* to loose, watery stools that occur more frequently than usual, your child has diarrhea.

Diarrhea occurs when the inner lining of the intestine is injured. The stools become loose because the nutrients that your child eats and drinks are not properly digested or absorbed by the intestine. Also, the injured lining tends to leak fluid. Minerals and salt are lost along with the fluid. This loss can be made even worse if your child is fed food or beverages that contain large amounts of sugar, since unabsorbed sugar draws even more water into the intestine, increasing the diarrhea.

When the body loses too much water and salt, dehydration results. This can be prevented by replenishing the diarrhea losses with adequate amounts of fluid and salt, as described under *Treatment.*

The medical term for intestinal inflammation is *enteritis.* When the problem is accompanied by or preceded by vomiting, as it often is, there is usually some stomach inflammation as well and the condition is called *gastroenteritis.*

Children with viral diarrheal illnesses (see the box on page 477) often have vomiting, fever, and irritability as well. (See *Vomiting,* page 491; Chapter 23, "Fever.") Their stools tend to be greenish-yellow in color, and have a significant amount of water with them. (If they occur as often as once an hour, they usually won't have any solid material at all.) If the stools appear red or blackish, they might contain blood. Bleeding may arise from the injured lining of the intestine or, more likely, may simply be due to irritation of the rectum by frequent, loose bowel movements. In any event, if you notice this or any other unusual stool color, you should mention it to your pediatrician.

Treatment

There are no effective medications for treating viral intestinal infections, the cause of most cases of diarrhea in infants. Antibiotics

Causes of Diarrhea

In young children, the intestinal damage that produces diarrhea is most often caused by viruses called *enteroviruses.*
Other causes are:

- Bacteria (salmonella, shigella, E. coli, campylobacter)

- Parasitic infections *(Giardia)*

- Food or milk allergy

- Side effects from oral medications (most commonly antibiotics)

Food poisoning (from things such as mushrooms, shellfish, or contaminated food)

- Infections outside the gastrointestinal tract, including the urinary tract, the respiratory tract, and even the middle ear. (If your child is taking an antibiotic for such an infection, the diarrhea may become more severe.)

- Rotavirus infections

should be used only to treat certain types of bacterial or parasitic intestinal infections, which are much less common. When these other conditions are suspected, your pediatrician will ask for stool specimens to test in the laboratory. Other tests also may be done.

Over-the-counter antidiarrheal medications are not recommended for children under age two, and should be used with caution in older children. They often worsen the intestinal injury, and they do not stop the body's loss of water and salt if an infection is present. Instead, they cause the fluid and salt to remain *within* the intestine. When this occurs, the child can become dehydrated without your being aware of it, because the diarrhea *appears* to stop. For this reason, always consult your pediatrician before giving your child any medication for diarrhea.

Mild Diarrhea

If your child has a small amount of diarrhea, but is not dehydrated (see the box on page 478 for signs of dehydration), does not have a high fever, and is active and hungry, the diet need not be changed and breast milk or formula can be continued. You should *not* give a "clear liquid diet" consisting solely of

sweetened beverages (juices, Jell-O, water, or soda pop), because their high sugar content may make the diarrhea worse.

If your child has mild diarrhea and is vomiting, substitute a commercially available electrolyte solution for his normal diet. These solutions will be recommended by your pediatrician, to maintain normal body water and salt levels until the vomiting has stopped. In most cases, they're needed for only one to two days. Once the vomiting has subsided, gradually restart the normal diet.

Never give boiled milk (skimmed or otherwise) to any child with diarrhea. Boiling the milk allows the water to evaporate, leaving the remaining part dangerously high in salt and mineral content. (In fact, you should not even give a well child boiled milk.)

Significant Diarrhea

If your child has a watery bowel movement every one to two hours, or more frequently, and/or has signs of dehydration (see the box on page 478), consult his pediatrician. He may advise you to withhold all solid foods for at least twenty-four hours and to avoid liquids that are high in sugar (Jell-O, soft drinks, full-strength fruit juices, or artificially sweetened

Signs and Symptoms of Dehydration
(Loss of Significant Amounts of Body Water)

The most important part of treating diarrhea is to prevent your child from becoming dehydrated. Be alert for the following warning signs of dehydration, and notify the pediatrician immediately if any of them develop.

Mild to Moderate Dehydration:

- Plays less than usual

- Urinates less frequently (wets fewer than six diapers per day)

- Parched, dry mouth

- Fewer tears when crying

- Sunken soft spot of the head in an infant or toddler

Severe Dehydration (in addition to the symptoms and signs listed above):

- Very fussy

- Excessively sleepy

- Sunken eyes

- Cool, discolored hands and feet

- Wrinkled skin

- Goes several hours without urinating

---

beverages), high in salt (packaged broth), or very low in salt (water and tea). He probably will have you give him only commercially prepared electrolyte solutions, which contain the ideal balance of salt and minerals. (See the table on page 479.) Breast-fed babies usually are treated in a similar fashion except in very mild cases, where breast-feeding may be continued.

If your child has diarrhea and you are concerned that he may be becoming dehydrated, call your pediatrician and withhold all foods and milk beverages until he gives you further instructions. *Take your child to the pediatrician or nearest emergency room immediately if you think he is moderately to severely dehydrated.* A commercially prepared electrolyte solution should be given in the meantime.

For severe dehydration, hospitalization is sometimes necessary so that your child can be rehydrated intravenously. In milder cases all that may be necessary is to give your child an electrolyte replacement solution according to your pediatrician's directions. The table on page 479 indicates the approximate amount of this solution to be used.

Once your child has been on an electrolyte solution for twenty-four to forty-eight hours and the diarrhea is decreasing, you gradually may expand the diet to include foods such as applesauce, pears, bananas, and flavored gelatin. Milk can be withheld for one to two days except in the case of young, bottle-fed babies, who can be given half-strength formula to start (add an equal volume of water to your child's usual full-strength formula). If the infant is breast-fed, you can continue breast-feeding while giving the electrolyte solution. As the diarrhea improves, an older child may be able to eat bland foods such as rice, toast, potatoes, and cereal in small quantities. The electrolyte replacement solution can continue to be given.

It is usually unnecessary to withhold food for longer than forty-eight hours, as your child will need some normal nutrition to start to regain lost strength. After you have started

ESTIMATED ORAL FLUID AND ELECTROLYTE REQUIREMENTS BY BODY WEIGHT

Body Weight, in pounds	Minimum Daily Fluid Requirements, in ounces*	Electrolyte Solution** Requirements for Mild Diarrhea, in ounces for 24 hours
6–7	10	16
11	15	23
22	25	40
26	28	44
33	32	51
40	38	61

*NOTE: This is the *smallest* amount of fluid that a normal child requires. Most children drink more than this.
**Commercially available electrolyte solutions include Pedialyte® and Rehydralyte®.

giving your child food again, the stools may remain loose, but that does not necessarily mean that things are not going well. Look for increased activity, better appetite, more frequent urination, and the disappearance of any of the signs of dehydration. When you see these, you will know your child is getting better.

Diarrhea that lasts longer than two weeks (chronic diarrhea) may signify a more serious type of intestinal problem. When diarrhea persists this long, the pediatrician will want to do further tests to determine the cause, and to make sure your child is not becoming malnourished. If malnutrition is becoming a problem, the pediatrician may recommend a special diet or special type of formula.

If your child drinks too much fluid, especially too much juice or sweetened beverages, a condition commonly referred to as "toddler's diarrhea" could develop. This causes ongoing loose stools but shouldn't affect appetite or growth, or cause dehydration. Although toddler's diarrhea is not a dangerous condition, the pediatrician may suggest that you limit the amounts of juice and sweet-

ened fluids your child drinks. Plain water can be given to children whose thirst does not seem to be satisfied by their normal dietary and milk intake.

When diarrhea occurs in combination with other symptoms, it could mean that there is a more serious medical problem. Notify your pediatrician immediately if the diarrhea is accompanied by any of the following:

- Fever that lasts longer than twenty-four to forty-eight hours

- Bloody stools

- Vomiting that lasts more than twelve to twenty-four hours

- Vomited material that is green-colored, blood-tinged, or like coffee grounds in appearance

- A distended (swollen-appearing) abdomen

- Refusal to eat or drink

- Severe abdominal pain

- Rash or jaundice (yellow color of skin and eyes)

If your child has another medical condition, or is taking medication routinely, it is best to tell your pediatrician about any diarrheal illness that lasts more than twenty-four hours without improvement, or anything else that really worries you.

Prevention

The following guidelines will help lessen the chances that your child will get diarrhea.

1. Most forms of infectious diarrhea are transmitted from direct hand-to-mouth contact following exposure to contaminated fecal (stool) material. This happens most often in children who are not toilet trained. Promote personal hygiene (such as hand washing after using the toilet or changing diapers and before handling food) and other sanitary measures in your household and in your child's day-care center or preschool.

2. Avoid drinking raw milk and eating foods that may be contaminated. (See *Food Poisoning,* below.)

3. Avoid the unnecessary use of medications, especially antibiotics.

4. If possible, breast-feed your child through early infancy.

5. Do not give your child unlimited amounts of sweetened beverages or juice.

(See also *Milk Allergy,* page 487; *Vomiting,* page 491; *Celiac Disease,* page 474; *Abdominal Pain,* page 469; *Malabsorption,* page 486.)

Food Poisoning

Food poisoning occurs after eating food contaminated by bacteria. The symptoms of food poisoning are basically the same as those of "stomach flu": abdominal cramps, nausea, vomiting, diarrhea, and fever. But if your child and other people who have eaten the same food all have these same symptoms, the problem is more likely to be food poisoning than the flu. The bacteria that cause food poisoning cannot be seen, smelled, or tasted, so your child won't know when he is eating them. These organisms include:

Staphylococcus aureus (Staph)

Staph contamination is the leading cause of food poisoning. These bacteria ordinarily cause skin infections such as pimples or boils, and is transferred when foodstuffs are handled by an infected person. If the food temperature is right (100 degrees Fahrenheit [37.5 Celsius] is ideal), the staph bacteria multiply and produce a poison (toxin) that ordinary cooking will not destroy. The symptoms begin one to six hours after eating the contaminated food, and the discomfort usually lasts about one day.

Salmonella

Salmonella bacteria (there are many types) are another major cause of food poisoning in the United States. The most commonly contaminated foods are raw meat (including chicken), eggs, and unpasteurized milk. Fortunately, salmonella are killed when the food is thoroughly cooked. Symptoms caused by salmonella poisoning start sixteen to forty-eight hours after eating, and may last two to seven days.

Clostridium perfringens

Clostridium perfringens (C. perfringens) is a bacterium frequently found in soil, sewage, and the intestines of man and animals. It usually is transferred by the handler to the food, where it multiplies and produces its toxin. C. perfringens often is found in school cafeterias because it thrives in food that is served in quantity and left out for long periods at room temperature or on a steam table. The foods most often involved are cooked beef, poultry, gravy, fish, casseroles, stews, and bean burritos. The symptoms of this type of poisoning start eight to twenty-four hours after eating, and can last from one to several days.

Botulism

This is the deadly food poisoning caused by the bacteria *Clostridium botulinum*. Although these bacteria normally can be found in soil and water, illness from them is extremely rare because they need very special conditions in order to multiply and produce poison. *Clostridium botulinum* grows best without oxygen and in certain chemical conditions, which explains why improperly canned food is most often contaminated and the low-acid vegetables, such as green beans, corn, beets, and peas, are most often involved. Honey also can be contaminated and frequently causes severe illness, particularly in children under one year of age.

Botulism attacks the nervous system and causes double vision, droopy eyelids, and difficulty in swallowing and breathing. It also can cause vomiting, diarrhea, and abdominal pain. The symptoms develop in eighteen to thirty-six hours and can last weeks to months. Without treatment, botulism can cause death. Even with treatment, it can cause nerve damage.

Other sources of food poisoning include poisonous mushrooms, contaminated fish products, and foods with special seasonings. Young children do not care for most of these foods, and so will eat very little of them. However, it still is very important to be aware of the risk. If your child has unusual gastrointestinal symptoms, and there is *any* chance he might have eaten contaminated or poisonous foods, call your pediatrician.

Treatment

In most cases of food poisoning, all that's necessary is to limit eating and drinking for a while. The problem then will usually resolve itself. Infants can tolerate three to four hours

without food or liquids; older youngsters, six to eight. If your child is still vomiting or his diarrhea has not decreased significantly during this time, call your pediatrician.

Also notify the doctor if your child

- Shows signs of dehydration: dry lips; no tears when he cries; sunken eyes; doughy-feeling skin; decreased appetite; decreased urination; sleepiness; irritability.

- Has bloody diarrhea.

- Has continuous diarrhea with a large volume of water in the stool, or diarrhea alternating with constipation.

- Was poisoned by mushrooms.

- Suddenly becomes weak, numb, confused, restless, and feels tingling, acts drunken, or has hallucinations or difficulty breathing.

Tell the doctor the symptoms your child is having, what foods he has eaten recently, and where they were obtained. The treatment your pediatrician gives will depend upon your child's condition and the type of food poisoning. If there is dehydration, fluid replacement will be prescribed. Sometimes antibiotics are helpful, but only if the bacteria are known. Antihistamines help if the illness is due to an allergic reaction to a food, toxin, or seasoning. If your child has botulism, he will require hospitalization and intensive care.

Prevention

Most food poisoning is preventable if you observe the following guidelines.

Cleanliness

- Be especially careful when preparing raw meats and poultry. After you have rinsed the meat thoroughly, wash your hands and all surfaces with hot, sudsy water before continuing your preparation.

- Always wash your hands before preparing

meals and after going to the bathroom or changing your child's diaper.

- If you have open cuts or sores on your hands, wear gloves while preparing food.

- Do not prepare food when you are sick, particularly if you have nausea, vomiting, abdominal cramps, or diarrhea.

Food Selection

- Carefully examine any canned food (especially home-canned goods) for signs of bacterial contamination. Look for milky liquid surrounding vegetables (it should be clear), cracked jars, loose lids, and swollen cans or lids. *Don't use canned goods showing any of these signs. Do not even taste them. Throw them away so that nobody else will eat them.* (Wrap them first in plastic and then in a heavy paper bag.)

- Buy all meats and seafood from reputable suppliers.

- Do not use raw milk, or cheese made from raw milk.

- Do not eat raw meat.

- Do not give honey to a baby under one year of age.

Food Preparation and Serving

- Do not let prepared foods (particularly starchy ones), cooked and cured meats, or cheese and meat salads stay at room temperature for more than two hours.

- Do not interrupt the cooking of meat or poultry to finish the cooking later.

- Do not prepare food one day for the next unless it will be frozen or refrigerated right away. (Always put hot food right into the refrigerator. Do not wait for it to cool first.)

- Make sure all foods are thoroughly cooked. Use a meat thermometer for large items like roasts or turkeys, and cut into other pieces of meat to check if they are done.

- When reheating meals, cover them and reheat thoroughly.

You also may want to write to the U.S. Department of Agriculture, Washington, D.C. 20250. The department has a number of extremely helpful pamphlets and newsletters, including special ones about cooking on a grill and preparing holiday turkeys.

Hepatitis .

Hepatitis is an inflammation of the liver that, in children, is almost always caused by one of several viruses. In some children it may cause no symptoms, while in others it can provoke fever, jaundice (yellow skin), loss of appetite, nausea, and vomiting. There are four forms of hepatitis, each categorized according to the type of virus that causes it:

1. Hepatitis A, also called infectious hepatitis or epidemic jaundice

2. Hepatitis B, also known as serum hepatitis or transfusion jaundice

3. Non-A, non-B hepatitis, also known as Hepatitis C

4. Hepatitis D, or delta virus hepatitis

5. Hepatitis E, caused by a recently recognized virus.

Approximately 400,000 cases of hepatitis occur in the United States each year. About half of these are caused by hepatitis B, forty out of every hundred by hepatitis A, and nearly all of the remainder are of the non-A, non-B variety.

Children, especially those in low socioeconomic groups, have the highest incidence of hepatitis A infection. However, because they often have no symptoms, their illness may go unrecognized.

Hepatitis A can be transmitted from person

to person, or through contaminated food or water. Commonly, human feces are infected with the virus, so in a day-care or household setting, the infection can be spread when hands are not washed after having a bowel movement or changing the diaper of an infected infant. Drinking water contaminated with infected human feces, or eating raw shellfish taken from polluted areas may also result in infection. A child infected with hepatitis A virus will become ill from two to six weeks after the virus is transmitted. The illness usually disappears within one month after it begins.

While hepatitis A is rarely transmitted via contaminated blood, semen, or saliva, hepatitis B is sometimes spread through these body fluids. The incidence of hepatitis B infection is now greatest among adolescents, young adults, and in the newborns of women who are infected with the virus. When a pregnant woman has hepatitis B, she may transmit the infection to her newborn at the time of delivery.

The use of sterile disposable needles and the screening of all blood and blood products has essentially eliminated the risk of transmission of hepatitis B in hospitals and doctors' offices.

Most cases of transfusion-related hepatitis are now due to non-A, non-B infection.

There are at least two non-A, non-B hepatitis viruses. Infection with these viruses commonly produces mild symptoms, with a gradual onset of fatigue and jaundice. In many cases this form of hepatitis may last for several months, even years, and can occasionally result in severe liver disease and even death. More common in adults than children, this form of hepatitis has become the most frequent type of hepatitis acquired after a transfusion.

The delta virus appears to be a defective or incomplete virus that is transmitted by routes similar to those of hepatitis B. Delta virus infection only occurs in the presence of acute or chronic hepatitis B infection.

Signs and Symptoms

Your child could have hepatitis without your even being aware of it, since many affected children have few, if any, symptoms. In some children the only signs of disease may be malaise and fatigue for several days. In others there will be a fever followed by the appearance of jaundice (the sclera, or whites of the eyes, develop noticeable yellowish color). This jaundice is due to an abnormal increase in bilirubin (a yellow pigment) in the blood, caused by the liver inflammation.

With hepatitis B, fever is less likely to occur, although the child may suffer loss of appetite, nausea, vomiting, abdominal pain, and malaise, in addition to jaundice.

If you suspect that your child has jaundice, notify your pediatrician. He will order blood tests to determine if hepatitis is causing the problem, or if it is due to another condition. You should contact your doctor any time vomiting and/or abdominal pain persist beyond a few hours, or if appetite loss, nausea, or malaise continue for more than a few days. These all may be indicators of hepatitis.

Treatment

There is no specific treatment for hepatitis. As with most viral infections, the body's own defense mechanisms usually will overcome the infecting agent. Although you do not need to rigidly restrict the diet or activity of your child, you may need to make adjustments depending on his appetite and energy levels. Avoid aspirin and acetaminophen, because of the risk of toxicity due to inadequate liver function. Also, children on certain medications for long-term illnesses should have their dosages carefully reviewed by the pediatrician, again to avoid the toxicity that might result because the liver is unable to handle the usual medication load.

Most children with hepatitis do not need to be hospitalized. However, if loss of appetite or vomiting is interfering with your child's fluid intake and posing a risk of dehydration, your pediatrician may recommend that he be hospitalized. You should contact your doctor immediately if your youngster appears very lethargic, unresponsive, or delirious, as these may indicate that his illness is worsening and hospitalization is indicated.

The great majority of children with hepatitis recover uneventfully. Cirrhosis (scarring of the liver) occasionally follows recovery, but only in severe cases. Death occurs very rarely. There is no chronic infection following hepatitis A, but about 10 of every 100 people infected with hepatitis B become chronic carriers of the virus. Infants born to mothers with acute or chronic hepatitis B become chronic carriers if not properly immunized with the vaccine developed for protection against the hepatitis B virus. As chronic hepatitis B carriers, they would be at risk for the development of liver cancer many years later.

Prevention

Thorough handwashing before eating and after using the toilet is the most important preventive measure against hepatitis, and children should be taught as young as possible to wash their hands at these times. If your child is in day care, you should check to be sure that members of the staff wash their hands after handling diapers and before feeding the children.

Hepatitis is not transmitted by simply being in the same school or room with an infected person, or by talking to him, shaking his hand, or playing a board game with him. It can occur only if there has been a direct or indirect exposure to the blood, bodily fluids, or excretions of a person with hepatitis. This could happen during kissing, mouthing of toys, or sharing food or utensils.

If you find out that your child has been exposed to a person with hepatitis, you should immediately contact your pediatrician, who will determine if the exposure has placed your youngster at risk. If there's a chance of infection, the doctor may administer an injection of gamma globulin or a hepatitis vaccine, depending on which hepatitis virus was involved.

Prior to foreign travel with your child, consult your physician to determine the risk of exposure to hepatitis in the countries you plan to visit. In certain situations, gamma globulin and/or a hepatitis vaccine may be indicated.

It is now recommended that all newborn infants, children, and adolescents be immunized against Hepatitis B (see immunization schedule on page 63).

Hydrocele (Communicating Hydrocele, Infant Hernia)

The testicles of the developing male grow inside his abdominal cavity, moving down through a tube (the inguinal canal) into the scrotum as he nears birth. When this movement takes place, the lining of the abdominal wall (peritoneum) is pulled along with the testes to form a sac connecting the testicle with the abdominal cavity. The opening into the abdominal space usually closes. If it does not, and the passage remains open, the fluid which normally surrounds the abdominal organs will flow through it and collect in the scrotal area. This is called a communicating hydrocele (pronounced hy-dro-seal).

As many as half of all newborn boys have this problem; however, it often disappears

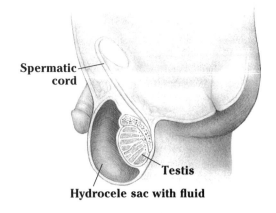

Spermatic cord

Testis

Hydrocele sac with fluid

within one year without any treatment. Although most common in the newborn, hydroceles also can develop later in childhood, most often in association with a hernia (see below).

If your son has a hydrocele, he probably will not complain, but you or he will notice that one side of his scrotum is swollen. In an infant or young boy this swelling decreases at night or when he is resting or lying down. When he gets more active or is crying, it increases, then subsides when he quiets again. Your pediatrician will make the final diagnosis by shining a bright light through the scrotum, to show the fluid surrounding the testicle.

If your baby is born with a hydrocele, your pediatrician will examine it at each regular checkup until around one year of age. During this time your child should not feel any discomfort in the scrotum or the surrounding area. If he seems to be tender in this area or has unexplained discomfort, nausea, or vomiting, call the doctor at once. These are signs that a piece of intestine may have entered the scrotal area along with abdominal fluid. (See *Inguinal Hernia,* below.) If this occurs and the intestine gets trapped in the scrotum, your son probably will require immediate surgery to release the trapped intestine and close the opening between the abdominal wall and scrotum.

If the hydrocele persists beyond one year without causing pain, a similar surgical procedure may be recommended. In this relatively minor operation, the excess fluid is removed and the opening into the abdominal cavity closed.

Inguinal Hernia

If you notice a small lump or bulge in your child's groin area or an enlargement of the scrotum, you may have discovered an inguinal hernia. This condition, which is present in five of every hundred children (most commonly in boys), occurs when an opening

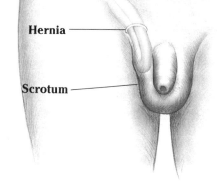

Opening is inside, leading into the scrotum in boys, allowing abdominal contents to slide downward. In girls, the hernia may simply appear as a bulge in the groin area.

Hernia

Scrotum

in the lower abdominal wall allows the child's intestine to squeeze through.

A hernia in a child is due to a failure of normal protrusions from the peritoneum to close properly before birth. The peritoneum is a large, balloonlike sac which surrounds all the organs within the abdomen. Before birth, this sac has two fingerlike projections through the muscle walls which, in boys, lead into the scrotum alongside the testicles and, in girls, lead into the labia. Normally, these projections separate from the rest of the peritoneum before birth, producing in boys protective sacs for the testicles inside the scrotum. When these extensions do not close properly, a small portion of the bowel may push through into the groin or scrotum, producing a hernia. If the opening is very small and only abdominal fluid comes down into the sac, it is called a hydrocele (see page 484).

Most hernias do not cause any discomfort, and you or the pediatrician will discover them only by seeing the bulge. While this kind of hernia must be treated, it is not an emergency condition. You should, however, notify your doctor, who may instruct you to have the child lie down and elevate his legs. Sometimes this will cause the bulge to disappear.

However, your doctor will still want to examine the area as soon as possible.

Rarely, a piece of the intestine gets trapped in the hernia, causing swelling and pain. (If you touch the area, it will be tender.) This condition is called an incarcerated (trapped) hernia, and does require immediate medical attention.

Treatment

Even if the hernia is not incarcerated, it still needs to be surgically repaired as soon as possible. The surgeon also may check the other side to see if it, too, needs to be corrected, since it is very common for the same defect to be present there.

If the hernia is causing pain, it may indicate that a piece of intestine has become trapped or incarcerated. In that case, your pediatrician will want to be consulted immediately. He may try to move the trapped piece of intestine out of the sac. Even if this can be done, the hernia still needs to be surgically repaired soon thereafter. If the intestine remains trapped despite the physician's efforts, emergency surgery must be performed to prevent permanent damage to the intestine.

Malabsorption

Sometimes children who eat a balanced diet suffer from malnutrition. The reason for this may be malabsorption, the body's inability to absorb nutrients from the digestive system into the bloodstream.

Normally, the digestive process converts nutrients from the diet into small units that pass through the wall of the intestine and into the bloodstream, where they are carried to other cells in the body. If the intestinal wall is damaged by a virus or bacterial infection or by parasites, its surface may change so that digested substances cannot pass through. When this happens, the nutrients will be eliminated through the stool.

Malabsorption commonly occurs in a normal child for a day or two during severe cases of stomach or intestinal flu. It rarely lasts much longer. However, if two or more of the following signs or symptoms seem to persist, notify your pediatrician.

Signs and Symptoms

Possible signs and symptoms of malabsorption include the following:

- Abdominal pain and vomiting
- Frequent, loose, bulky, foul-smelling stools
- Increased susceptibility to infection
- Loss of fat and muscle
- Increase in bruises and bone fractures
- Dry, scaly skin rashes
- Personality changes
- Slowing of growth and weight gain (may not be noticeable for several months)

Not all children who have absorption problems display these symptoms. Some simply consume more food to make up for the nutrients they're losing. In others, the digestive surface of the intestine heals so quickly there is no significant discomfort or damage. In these cases, malabsorption is no cause for concern.

Treatment

When a child suffers from malnutrition, malabsorption is just one of the possible causes. He might be undernourished because he's not getting enough of the right types of food, or has digestive problems that prevent his body from digesting them. He also might have a combination of these problems. Before prescribing a treatment, the pediatrician must determine the cause. This can be done in one or more of the following ways.

- You may be asked to list the amount and type of food your child eats.

- The pediatrician may test the child's ability to digest and absorb specific nutrients. For example, the doctor might have him drink a solution of milk sugar (lactose) and then measure the level of hydrogen in the breath afterward. This is known as a lactose hydrogen breath test.
- The pediatrician may collect and analyze stool samples. In healthy people, only a small amount of the fat consumed each day is lost through the stool. If too much is found in the stool, it is an indication of malabsorption.
- A "sweat test" may be performed to see if cystic fibrosis (see page 651) is present. This is a disease in which there are insufficient amounts of certain enzymes necessary for proper digestion.
- In some cases the pediatrician might request a specialist to take a small piece of the wall of the small intestine (a biopsy) and have it examined under the microscope for signs of infection, inflammation, or other injury.

Ordinarily, these tests are performed before any treatment is begun, although a seriously sick child might be hospitalized in order to receive special feedings while his problem is being evaluated.

Once the physician is sure the problem is malabsorption, he will try to identify a specific reason for its presence. When the reason is infection, the treatment usually will include antibiotics. If malabsorption occurs because the intestine is too active, certain medications may be used to counteract this, so that there's time for the nutrients to be absorbed.

Sometimes there's no clear cause for the problem. In this case, the diet may be changed to include foods or special nutritional formulas that are more easily tolerated and absorbed.

Milk Allergy

Everyone has heard of children who are allergic to ordinary cow's milk. It's actually a rare occurrence. Only 1 to 3 children in 100 develop a true intolerance to milk. It usually appears in the first few months of life, when an infant's digestive system is still quite immature.

If other family members have allergies, your baby may be more likely to develop a milk allergy. This likelihood will increase further if he's fed cow's milk formula from birth. Very few breast-fed babies develop milk allergy. Once in a while a very sensitive breast-fed baby may develop this condition because milk products consumed by the mother may be passed to the baby through the breast milk.

The symptoms of milk allergy may appear anywhere from a few minutes to a few hours after the baby consumes the product, but the most severe symptoms usually occur within half an hour. The most common symptoms are

- Colic: inconsolable crankiness or fussiness, often interfering with normal sleep. (See *Colic,* page 469.)

- Vomiting and/or diarrhea. (See pages 491 and 476.)

Less common symptoms are

- Constipation (See page 474.)

- Bleeding in the digestive tract

If the respiratory system is affected by the milk allergy, the baby also may have chronic nasal stuffiness, a runny nose, cough, wheezing, or difficulty in breathing. The allergy can also cause eczema, hives, swelling, itching, or a rash around the mouth and on the chin due to contact with milk. (See *Eczema,* page 631; *Hives,* page 636; *Cough,* page 512.)

If you suspect your baby has an allergy to milk, tell your pediatrician, and be sure to mention whether there's a family history of allergy. Take your child to the doctor's office or emergency room *immediately* if he

- Has difficulty breathing

- Turns blue

- Is extremely pale or weak

- Has generalized hives

- Develops swelling in the head and neck region

- Has bloody diarrhea

Treatment

If your pediatrician suspects that a milk allergy is present, he will first try eliminating milk and milk products completely for a period of time to see if there is any improvement. If there is, your child may then be given a milk trial—that is, a controlled introduction of milk to the diet. This will reveal whether the symptoms decrease or disappear when milk is avoided, and if they reappear when it's introduced again. *This trial of milk should be carried out cautiously and under the supervision of a physician.* Infants who are allergic to milk can become quickly sick, even if exposed to only a small amount.

Your pediatrician can use several appropriate medications to treat the symptoms of milk allergy. These include antihistamines, decongestants, and anti-asthma medication (if wheezing is among your child's allergy symptoms). The most important treatment, however, is to eliminate milk and milk products from your child's diet (or from yours if you're breast-feeding). When milk is avoided completely for a long enough period of time, most children will eventually outgrow the allergy. Your child has about a 50 percent chance of outgrowing it by age one; 75 percent by age two; and 85 percent by three to four years. This allergy seldom lasts until adolescence.

In the meantime, children with milk allergy must avoid cheese, yogurt, ice cream, and cow's milk formula as well as any food that contains milk. You must also check all processed food labels for *casein, caseinate,* and *whey*—they are all milk products and must be avoided too. A bottle-fed infant will need a milk substitute such as a soybean formula.

If he's also sensitive to soy protein (some infants and children are allergic to both soy and milk), your doctor will suggest still another milk substitute. Some milk-sensitive children can tolerate diluted evaporated milk, because the heating process used in making this product alters some of the milk protein. Goat's milk should not be used as a substitute because of its similarity to cow's milk. Older children, who can eat a wide variety of calcium-containing foods, usually don't need a milk substitute.

If your breast-fed infant develops a milk allergy, you'll have to have a milk-free diet yourself. (You'll also need to start taking calcium and vitamin supplements.) When you wean your baby, delay feeding him cow's milk as long as possible, and give it very cautiously at first, at the direction of your doctor.

You may be tempted to "cheat" on the milk-free diet once your child's symptoms lessen or disappear. Don't! If you give your child even small quantities of milk or its products, he may continue to have mild symptoms or an ongoing hidden reaction and he may even develop other food allergies. In the process, you also may prolong the milk allergy and reduce his chance of outgrowing it.

We can't overemphasize the importance of a milk-free diet for a child with milk allergy. If it's ignored, his allergy may lead to potentially serious complications, including dehydration due to severe vomiting or diarrhea; loss of weight from chronic diarrhea; anemia caused by gastrointestinal bleeding; infected eczema; severe difficulty breathing; and occasionally an inflammation of the lungs resembling recurrent pneumonia. The very worst complication, acute shock, is rare but can be fatal.

Prevention

In general, breast-feeding a baby is the best way to prevent milk allergy. Particularly if anyone in the immediate family is allergy-prone, you should plan to breast-feed your baby for as long as possible, preferably for six months or more. While doing so, you'll need to minimize or perhaps eliminate your own intake of milk products. And when you eventually introduce other foods to your baby, you'll want to do it gradually (a new one at one- or two-week intervals), watching for the signs of allergy mentioned previously.

If you cannot breast-feed, ask your pediatrician to guide you in selecting an appropriate formula.

Pinworms

The most common type of worm infesting children, pinworms are essentially harmless. They are unpleasant to look at and may cause itching and, in girls, vaginal discharge, but they rarely cause more serious problems. Pinworms cause more social than medical problems in affected children and their families.

Pinworms are spread easily from one child to another by the transfer of eggs. The mature pinworm, which lives in the intestinal tract and around the anal area, lays its eggs on the skin around the anus and buttocks. An infested child may get the tiny eggs on his hand when scratching the area or while wiping after a bowel movement, or the eggs may be left on the toilet seat, to be picked up by the next person who uses it. If the child does not wash the eggs off his hands, he may transfer them to his mouth or to other objects he touches, including the hands or mouth of another person.

Another child picks up the eggs by touching the infested child's hands or objects he handled. He then transfers them to his own mouth by putting his hands in his mouth or mouthing contaminated material.

After the eggs are swallowed they remain in the small intestine until they hatch, and the small worms travel to the end of the intestine, where they mature and mate. The female then deposits eggs around the anus, and the thirty-five-day life cycle is ready to be repeated. If the new eggs are not ingested,

however, the infestation ends at this time.

Your child probably will become aware that he has pinworms at night, when the adult worms move from the rectum to the anus. This movement causes irritation and, sometimes, intense itching. If the worms crawl into the vaginal area, they may cause pain and a slight discharge. In some children, however, pinworms cause absolutely no discomfort, and may be detected only if the mature worms are seen while depositing their eggs.

The adult worms are whitish-gray and threadlike, measuring about ¼ to ½ inch long. You might see them on the skin around the anus, or you or your pediatrician might collect some of the worms and eggs by applying the sticky side of a strip of special cellophane tape to the skin around the anus. This then can be examined under a microscope to confirm the presence of the parasite.

Treatment

Pinworms can be treated easily with an oral prescription, taken in a single dose and then repeated in one to two weeks. This medication causes the mature pinworms to be expelled through the bowel movements. Some pediatricians may recommend treating the other family members as well, since one of them may be a carrier without having any symptoms.

Prevention

It is very difficult to prevent pinworms, but here are some hints that might be helpful.

- Encourage your child to wash his hands after using the bathroom.

- Encourage his sitter or day-care provider to wash the toys frequently, particularly if pinworms have been detected in one or more of the children.

- Encourage your child to wash his hands after playing with a house cat or dog, since these pets can carry the eggs in their fur.

Reye Syndrome

Reye syndrome (often referred to as Reye's syndrome) is a rare but very serious illness that usually occurs in children between the ages of three and twelve. It can affect all organs of the body, but most often injures the brain and the liver. Most children who survive an episode of Reye syndrome do not suffer any lasting consequences. However, this illness can lead to permanent brain damage or death.

Reye syndrome is always preceded by a viral infection, such as chicken pox or influenza. However, it only affects an extremely small number of the children who have these infections. Therefore, there must be another cause in addition to the infection. While no one knows exactly what this second cause is, there are three major theories:

1. An unusual reaction to common medications, such as aspirin, which are taken during a viral illness

2. A toxin or poison that is released from inside the body while the susceptible child has a viral illness

3. Chemical changes within the body caused by viral illness in a child who is particularly susceptible

Because there have been so many children who were given aspirin during the viral illness preceding Reye syndrome, the first theory currently is the most widely accepted.

Signs and Symptoms

Whenever your child has a viral illness, be alert for the following pattern, which is typical of Reye syndrome.

1. Your child has had a viral infection, such as influenza, an upper respiratory illness, or chicken pox, and he seems to be improving; his fever is decreasing.

2. Then he abruptly starts to vomit repeatedly and frequently—every one or two hours— over a twenty-four- to thirty-six-hour period.

3. During that twenty-four- to thirty-six-hour period, he shows variations in the level of his *consciousness.* He may be lethargic or sleepy, and then become agitated, delirious, or angry. Then he may become confused or even go into a light coma.

4. If the disease progresses, there is a strong chance he will have seizures and go into a deep coma.

Call your pediatrician as soon as you suspect that your child's illness is following this pattern. If your doctor is not available, take your child to the nearest emergency room. It is very important to diagnose this illness as early as possible. Children with Reye syndrome must be hospitalized. In some cases it may be necessary to transfer the child to a center that specializes in the treatment of this condition. The diagnosis is made by testing the blood and spinal fluid. Sometimes it is necessary to examine a specimen of liver tissue under a microscope. If so, a liver biopsy will be performed by inserting a needle through the anesthetized skin into the liver.

Prevention

Since we do not know the exact cause of Reye syndrome, it is difficult to prevent it. However, since the medical community issued a public warning against the use of aspirin during viral illnesses, the number of cases of Reye syndrome has decreased greatly. Therefore, we strongly advise you, *do not give your child or teenager aspirin or any medications containing aspirin when he has any viral illness, particularly chicken pox or influenza.* If he needs medication for mild fever or discomfort, give him acetaminophen instead.

Vomiting

Since many common childhood illnesses can cause vomiting, you should expect your child to have this problem several times during these early years. Usually, it ends quickly without treatment, but this doesn't make it any easier for you to watch. That feeling of helplessness—combined with the fear that something serious might be wrong and the desire to do something to make it better—may make you tense and anxious. To help put your mind at ease, learn as much as you can about the causes of vomiting and what you can do to treat your child when it occurs.

First of all, there's a difference between real vomiting and just spitting up. Vomiting is the forceful throwing up of stomach contents through the mouth. Spitting up (most commonly seen in infants under one year of age) is the easy flow of stomach contents out of the mouth, frequently with a burp.

Vomiting occurs when the abdominal muscles and diaphragm contract vigorously while the stomach is relaxed. This reflex action is triggered by the "vomiting center" in the brain after it has been stimulated by

- Nerves from the stomach and intestine when the gastrointestinal tract is either ir-

ritated or swollen by an infection or blockage

- Chemicals in the blood (drugs, for example)

- Psychological stimuli from disturbing sights or smells

- Stimuli from the middle ear (as in vomiting caused by motion sickness)

The common causes of spitting up or vomiting vary according to age. During the first few months, for instance, most infants will spit up small amounts of formula, usually within the first hour after being fed. This "cheesing," as it is often called, is simply the occasional movement of food from the stomach, through the tube (esophagus) leading to it, and out of the mouth. It will occur less often if a child is burped frequently and if active play is limited right after meals. This spitting up tends to decrease as the baby becomes older, but may persist in a mild form until ten to twelve months of age. Spitting up is not serious and doesn't interfere with normal weight gain. (See *Spitting Up,* page 107.)

Occasional vomiting may occur during the first month. If it appears repeatedly, or is unusually forceful, call your pediatrician. It may be just a mild feeding difficulty, but could also be a sign of something more serious.

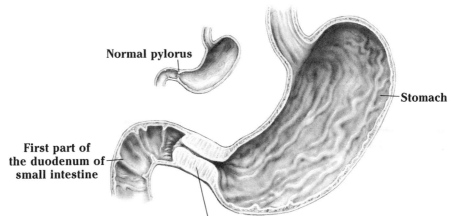

Normal pylorus

Stomach

First part of the duodenum of small intestine

Hypertrophied (enlarged) pylorus muscle with narrowed stomach outlet

Between two weeks and four months of age, persistent forceful vomiting may be caused by a thickening of the muscle at the stomach exit. This prevents food from passing into the intestines, and is known as *pyloric stenosis.* It requires immediate medical attention. Surgery usually is required to open the narrowed area. The important sign of this condition is forceful vomiting occurring approximately fifteen to thirty minutes or less after every feeding. Any time you notice this, call your pediatrician as soon as possible.

Occasionally, the spitting up in the first few weeks to months of life gets worse instead of better—that is, even though it's not forceful, it occurs all the time. This happens when the muscles at the lower end of the esophagus become overly relaxed and allow the stomach contents to back up. This condition usually can be controlled by the following:

1. Thicken the milk with small amounts of baby cereal.

2. Avoid overfeeding.

3. Burp the baby frequently.

4. Leave the infant in a quiet, upright position for at least thirty minutes following feeding. If this is not effective, you may want to put the child in a prone or prone-elevated position (prone with head elevated).

After the first few months of life, the most common cause of vomiting is a stomach or intestinal infection. Viruses are by far the most frequent infecting agents, but occasionally bacteria and even parasites may be the cause. The infection also may produce fever, diarrhea, and sometimes nausea and abdominal pain. The infection is usually contagious, so if your child has it, chances are some of his playmates also will be affected.

Occasionally, infections outside the gastrointestinal tract will cause vomiting. These include infections of the respiratory system, infections of the urinary tract (see page 592), otitis media (see page 537), and pneumonia (see page 516), as well as meningitis (see page 597), appendicitis (see page 472), and Reye syndrome (see page 490). Some of these conditions require immediate medical treatment, so be alert for the following trouble signs, whatever your child's age, and call your pediatrician if they occur.

- Blood or bile (a green-colored material) in the vomitus

- Severe abdominal pain

- Strenuous, repeated vomiting

- Swollen abdomen

- Lethargy or severe irritability

- Convulsions

- Signs or symptoms of dehydration, including dry mouth, absent tears, depression of the "soft spot," and decreased urination

- Inability to drink adequate amounts of fluid

- Vomiting continuing beyond twenty-four hours

Treatment

In most cases, vomiting will stop without specific medical treatment. You should never use over-the-counter or prescription remedies unless they've been specifically prescribed by your pediatrician for your child and this particular illness.

When your infant or young child is vomiting, keep him lying on his stomach or side as much as possible. This will minimize the chances of vomit being inhaled into the upper airway and lungs.

When there is continued vomiting, you need to make certain that dehydration doesn't occur. (*Dehydration* is a term used when the body loses so much water that it can no longer function efficiently.) If allowed to reach a severe degree, it can be serious and life-threatening. To prevent this from happening, make sure your child consumes enough extra fluids to restore what has been lost through throwing up. If he vomits these, notify your pediatrician.

For the first twenty-four hours or so of any illness that causes vomiting, keep your child off solid foods, and encourage him to suck or drink clear fluids, such as water, sugar water (½ teaspoon [2.5 cc] sugar in 4 ounces [120 cc] of water), popsicles, gelatin water (1 teaspoon [5 cc] of flavored gelatin in 4 ounces of water), or preferably an electrolyte solution (ask your pediatrician which one), instead of eating. Liquids not only help to prevent dehydration, but also are less likely than solid foods to stimulate further vomiting.

Here are some guidelines to follow for giving your child fluids *after* he has vomited:

1. Wait for two to three hours after the last vomiting episode, and then give 1 to 2 ounces of cool water every half hour to one hour for four feedings.

2. If he retains this, give 2 ounces of electrolyte solution alternated with 2 ounces of clear liquids every half hour.

3. If this is retained for two feedings, add half-strength formula or milk (depending upon age), and continue increasing the quantity slowly to 3 to 4 ounces every three or four hours.

4. After twelve to twenty-four hours with no additional vomiting, gradually return your child to his normal diet, but continue to give him plenty of clear fluids.

In most cases, your child will just need to stay at home and receive a liquid diet for twelve to twenty-four hours. Your pediatrician usually won't prescribe a drug to treat the vomiting.

If your child also has diarrhea (see page 476), ask your pediatrician for instructions on giving liquids and restoring solids to his diet.

If he can't retain any clear liquids or the symptoms become more severe, notify your pediatrician. He will examine your child and may order blood and urine tests or X-rays to make a diagnosis. Occasionally, hospital care may be necessary.

17

Behavior

Anger, Aggression, and Biting

We all have feelings of anger and aggression, and so does your child. These impulses are normal and healthy. They can also be dangerous, however, if not controlled. As a toddler or preschooler, your youngster still lacks the self-control to express his anger peacefully. Instead, he naturally lashes out, perhaps hitting or biting in frustration. When this happens, he needs you to take control for him and to help him develop judgment, self-discipline, and the other tools he needs in order to express his bad feelings in more acceptable ways.

While occasional violent outbursts are normal in youngsters, especially during temper tantrums, it is not normal for a child to have frequent rages in which he attacks others or himself. Most children get angry at others only when they are provoked. Unless they are very tired or overstressed, they usually can be distracted or consoled, and will quickly forget their anger. They may cry, argue, or yell, but they resort to violence only when they are extremely frustrated.

Some children are supersensitive, easily offended, and easily angered. Many of these youngsters have been tense and unusually active since birth. They are often more difficult to sooth and settle as infants. Beginning in the preschool years, they show signs of becoming violent toward other children, adults, even animals. They often lash out suddenly and for no apparent reason, and may seem to be touchy or irritable most of the time. Even if they hurt someone in their anger, they rarely are sorry, and never feel responsible for the incident. Instead, they blame the other child for "making me angry," as if this excuses their own actions.

Your child might go through a brief period of this kind of behavior if he's particularly worried, tired, or overstressed, but if it continues for more than a few weeks, consult your pediatrician. If it becomes a routine daily pattern for more than three to six months, it should be viewed as a serious problem.

This extreme form of aggressive behavior can lead to serious social and emotional problems if allowed to continue. The child eventually loses all his friends, which makes him even more tense and irritable, and seriously damages his self-esteem. There is always the danger that he will seriously injure himself or others, and the problems will multiply when he reaches school age. Then his violent behavior may cause him to be suspended or expelled from school, and may even lead to lawsuits against him. Because he has so little self-esteem, he may later become self-destructive, abuse drugs or alcohol, become accident-prone, or even attempt suicide.

No one knows exactly what causes conduct disorder. The problem may lie in the child's biological makeup, the relationships within the family, or a combination of the two. In many cases other members of the child's family behave violently and the atmosphere within the family is tense and stressful. In some cases, however, there is no clear explanation for the child's behavior.

What You Can Do

The best way to prevent violent behavior is to give your child a stable, secure home life with firm, loving discipline and full-time supervision during the toddler and preschool years. Everyone who cares for your child should agree on the rules he's expected to observe as well as the type of punishment to use if he disobeys. Whenever he breaks an important rule, he should be reprimanded *immediately* so that he understands exactly what he's done wrong.

Your youngster has little natural self-control. He needs you to teach him not to kick, hit, or bite when he is angry, but instead to express his feelings through words. It's important for him to learn the difference between real and imagined insults, and between appropriately standing up for his rights and attacking out of anger.

The best way to teach these lessons is to supervise your child carefully when he's involved in disputes with his playmates. As long as a disagreement is minor, you can keep your distance and let the youngsters solve it on their own. However, you must intervene when children get into a physical fight which continues even after they're told to stop, or when one child seems to be in an uncontrollable rage and is assaulting or biting the other. Pull the children apart and keep them separate until they have calmed down. If the fight is extremely violent, you may have to end the play session. They probably will accuse each other in an attempt to excuse themselves, but don't take sides. Make it clear that it doesn't matter who "started it." There is no acceptable excuse for trying to hurt each other.

Help your child find ways to deal with his anger without resorting to violence. Teach him to say no in a firm tone of voice, to turn his back, or to find compromises instead of fighting with his body. Through example, teach him that settling differences with words is more effective—and more civilized—than with physical violence. Praise him and tell him how "grown-up" he is acting whenever he uses these tactics instead of hitting, kicking, or biting.

Always watch your own behavior around your child. One of the best ways to teach him nonviolence is to control your own temper. If you express your anger in quiet, peaceful ways, he probably will follow your example. If you must punish him, do not feel guilty about it and certainly don't apologize. If he senses your mixed feelings, he may convince himself that he was in the right all along and *you* are the "bad" one. While punishing your child is never pleasant, it is a necessary part of parenthood and there is no reason to feel guilty about it. Your child needs to understand when he is in the wrong so that he will take responsibility for his actions and be willing to accept the consequences.

When to Call the Pediatrician

If your child seems to be unusually aggressive for longer than a few weeks, and you cannot cope with his behavior on your own, consult your pediatrician. Other warning signs include:

- Physical injury to himself or others (teeth marks, bruises, head injuries)

- Attacks on you or other adults

- Being sent home or barred from play by neighbors or school

- Your own fear for the safety of those around him

The most important warning sign is the frequency of outbursts. Sometimes children with conduct disorders will go for several days or a week or two without incident, and may even act quite charming during this time, but few can go an entire month without getting into trouble at least once.

Your pediatrician can suggest ways to discipline your child and will help you determine if he has a true conduct disorder. If this is the problem, you probably will not be able to resolve it on your own, and your pediatrician will refer you to a child health professional.

This specialist will interview both you and your child and may observe your youngster in different situations (home, preschool, with adults and other children). A behavior management program will be outlined. Not all methods work on all children, so there will be a certain amount of trial and error. Once several effective ways are found to reward good behavior and discourage bad, they can be used in establishing an approach that works both at home and away. The progress may be slow, but such programs usually are successful if started when the disorder is just beginning to develop.

(See also *Temper Tantrums,* page 502, and the sections on *Discipline* in Chapters 9 through 12.)

Hyperactivity and the Distractible Child

Almost every child has days when he seems "hyperactive," but true hyperactivity is a condition that affects only about one in twenty children under age twelve. Children who are hyperactive move about a great deal, have trouble sleeping, and cannot sit still for more than a few minutes at a time. They usually are easily distracted, often act on impulse, and have difficulty paying attention when listening or watching events around them. Physicians call this condition of combined hyperactivity and distractibility "attention deficit hyperactivity disorder," or ADHD.

Particularly when your child is a toddler, you may worry that he shows signs of hyperactivity, but if you compare him with others his age you probably will discover that he's normal. Around ages two and three, children naturally are very active and impulsive and have a short attention span. All children occasionally seem overactive or easily distractible—for example when they're very tired, excited about doing something "special," or anxious about being in a strange place or among strangers.

Truly hyperactive children, however, are noticeably *more* active, *more* easily distracted, and *more* excitable than their peers. Most important of all, these children never seem to be calm from one day to the next, nor does their behavior improve as they get older.

Although most have normal intelligence, they may seem like slow learners, because they can't pay attention or follow instructions through to completion. They also are slower to develop control over their impulses and emotions, and slower in developing the ability to concentrate and pay attention. They tend to be more talkative, emotional, demanding, and disobedient than others their age. Their behavior often remains immature throughout childhood and adolescence, and leads to problems in school, among friends, and in some cases with the law. Without support and treatment, children who are truly hyperactive have difficulty developing the self-esteem they need to lead healthy, productive lives.

No one knows exactly what causes hyperactivity. Sometimes the condition can be traced to illnesses affecting the brain or nervous system, such as meningitis, encephalitis, fetal alcohol syndrome, or severe prematurity. Most hyperactive children have never had such an illness, however, and most children who do suffer these ailments do *not* become hyperactive. Many children with this disorder do have close relatives with similar problems, which suggests that it may be at least partially inherited. Also, boys are four to seven times more likely than girls to develop this problem. In part, this is because boys naturally tend to mature more slowly in these areas of behavior, but no one knows precisely why these differences exist. Although there has also been much speculation that certain foods and food additives might be linked to ADHD, extensive research has failed to conclusively show any such link.

Whatever the source of hyperactivity, the way a child is raised and disciplined seems to determine how severe the disorder will become and how well the child will cope with it. Youngsters whose parents are mentally disturbed or abusive generally have more severe problems than those whose parents are emotionally healthy and who discipline with gentle firmness, consistency, and love.

When to Call the Pediatrician

Observing your child alongside others his age over a period of days or weeks is the best way to determine if he is hyperactive. For this reason, those who care for him at nursery school or day care may be your best source of information. They can tell you how he behaves in a group and whether he is acting normally for his age.

Specific signs of hyperactivity include:

- Difficulty paying attention to activities that interest other children his age

- Difficulty following simple instructions

- Repeated running into the street, interrupting other children's play, racing through off-limits areas without considering consequences

- Unnecessarily hurried activity, such as running, touching, and jumping without periods of rest

- Sudden emotional outbursts, such as crying, angry yelling, hitting, or frustration that seems inappropriate

- Persistent misbehavior despite being told "no" many times

If you and others observe three or more of these warning signs on a continuing basis, consult your pediatrician. The doctor will examine your child to rule out any medical cause for the behavior and then either conduct a further evaluation or refer you to a psychologist or child psychiatrist. The evaluation of hyperactivity ordinarily consists of three parts. The doctor or therapist will ask questions about past behavior and may consult the nursery school or child-care providers to see if there's a pattern of behavior over time and in different settings. Developmental testing will determine whether your child is maturing normally mentally and physically. Finally, a play session will reveal whether his emotional development is normal for his age.

If this evaluation suggests that your preschooler is hyperactive, the doctor or therapist probably will recommend some specific disciplinary strategies for managing his behavior, and may refer you to a special nursery school. Unless the behavior is extremely unmanageable, medication probably won't be prescribed because of possible side effects in a child this young and because many diagnoses of hyperactivity made before age five are uncertain. Toddlers and preschoolers change so rapidly and so dramatically that what might seem like a behavioral problem at one point could disappear a few months later. For this reason, most physicians prefer to watch the child's development over a period of months or even years before prescribing medical treatment.

Medications are used in severe cases of

Effective Discipline

Child's Behavior	Your Responses	
	Effective	Constructive
Temper tantrum	Walk away.	Discuss the incident when child is calm.
Overexcitement	Distract with another activity.	Talk about his behavior when he's calm.
Hitting or biting	Immediately remove him from situation.	Discuss consequences of his actions (pain, damage, bad feelings) to himself and others.
Not paying attention	Establish eye contact to hold his attention.	Lower your expectations (ask him to listen to a story for 3 minutes instead of 10; don't insist he sit through a full church service).
Refuses to pick up toys	Don't let him play until he does his job.	Show him how to do the task and help him with it; praise him when he finishes.

attention deficit disorder among older children. The only medication approved for use with preschoolers is dextroamphetamine (Dexedrine), and no medications are recommended for hyperactivity among children under age three.

As a parent of a hyperactive child you may hear about alternative treatments, some of which are still unproven and some of which have been proven ineffective. Controversial therapies which may be useful in some cases include:

- Play therapy. This approach helps the child to overcome inhibitions and anxieties, but these are not the key problems among most hyperactive children.

- Special physical exercises. These generally are intended to improve motor coordination and increase the child's tolerance for stimulation. Most hyperactive children do

have difficulty in these areas, but this is not the *cause* of the disorder. While such exercises may benefit a hyperactive child, they seem to work mostly because they cause the parents to pay more attention to the child, and this increases his self-esteem.

- Special diets. These are based on the assumption that certain foods produce undesirable behavior. Each diet targets a different group of foods or substances, such as artificial additives, sugar, or common allergenic foods (corn, nuts, chocolate, shellfish, wheat). While there is no scientific evidence to support such diets, many parents strongly believe they help. Most of these food plans are healthy and will not cause harm unless the child's eating habits become a source of conflict within the family, or unless they are used *instead* of other methods for modifying his behavior. No special diet alone can solve the problem of hyperactivity.

Treatments that have been disproven and may be dangerous include:

- Megavitamin therapy

- Special vitamin and mineral supplements

How to Respond

If your child shows signs of hyperactivity, it means that he cannot control his behavior on his own. In his hurry and excitement, he is exceptionally accident-prone and may be quite destructive to property and other people. You will have to help him learn to control himself and to pay attention to what he is doing.

To discipline a hyperactive child you need to respond both "effectively" and "constructively." If your actions are "effective," your child's behavior will improve as a result. If they are "constructive," they also will help develop his self-esteem and make him more personable. Here are some examples of effective and constructive responses to common problems among hyperactive children.

It is important to respond immediately whenever your child misbehaves, and to make sure that everyone caring for him responds to these incidents in the same way. Punishment that hurts, such as spanking or slapping, may stop him temporarily but does not encourage him to control himself. To the contrary, this approach tells him that it's okay to hurt other people. Loving, nonviolent discipline is far more effective in the long run.

True hyperactivity does not disappear with treatment, but the basic traits of the disorder usually do become milder as the child grows up. Loving support and discipline, along with formal treatment if necessary, make it possible for him to cope with his condition and develop into a productive and healthy adult.

Television

Your child will probably view his first television program during infancy, and by his third year will have several favorite ones. If you own a TV set, it will become an important part of his life and will teach him many lessons, some good and some bad.

During the preschool years your youngster can benefit a great deal from watching educational programming such as *Sesame Street, Mister Rogers' Neighborhood,* nature programs, and broadcasts of concerts or dance. Educational television is not a substitute for reading or playing, but it can enrich your child's life. Such viewing introduces young children to letters, numbers, and experiences they could not have any other way.

Unfortunately, most television programming is not good for youngsters. Even if your child watches only cartoons, he'll see characters hitting, shooting, or otherwise harming each other at a rate of about twenty times per hour. This violence usually occurs without any reasonable explanation, and the victims rarely seem to suffer any pain or have any permanent injuries. Both the heroes and the villains attack one another with lethal weapons, then reappear to fight again. The message to children is that violence is an acceptable way to deal with problems, and that it does no real harm. This encourages them to behave more violently, and discourages them from objecting when they see others in physical fights.

Television also exposes children to sexuality, drugs, and alcohol use at a time when they are far too young to understand these issues. Soap operas, prime time television, music videos, and many other programs inevitably expose your child to people engaged in or talking about sex, using or selling drugs, and drinking alcohol. Often, these actions are portrayed as if they were exciting, fun things that all adults do. Your child will not see people getting sick, pregnant, or dying as a result of these actions, and will come away with a distorted view of how to handle these issues in his own life.

Children tend to believe what they're told, and they do not understand the concept of a sales pitch. Just as a child believes that the cartoon characters are real creatures, he believes the children in the ads really love the sugar-coated cereals they eat and that the toys shown on TV will be as big and lifelike as they appear. Cartoon programs based on toy products are specifically intended to be attractive, increasing a child's desire to have the full range of characters and equipment.

Furthermore, because your child will see commercials for so many products, he may assume he is deprived if he isn't constantly acquiring new possessions. You will feel this pressure keenly every time you take him shopping and he begs for something that he "has to have" because he's seen it on TV.

Food commercials also can have an undesirable impact on your child's eating habits. Many of these ads push heavily sugared or salted products such as cereals, soft drinks, and snack foods. Less than 5 percent of food ads during the daytime are for more nutritious foods such as fruits and vegetables. As a result, your child gets a very distorted view of what he should be eating. The more commercial television he watches, the more he will demand snack items and the less interested he'll be in healthy foods.

Children who watch a great deal of television are more likely to become obese than are children who tend to be more physically active. One reason is that advertising tends to encourage them to eat more frequently, and to select more fattening foods. Another is that much of the time they spend sitting in front of TV would otherwise be spent actively playing and burning up calories.

All children need active play, not only for the physical exercise but also for proper mental and social development. Watching TV is passive. It does not help your child acquire the most important skills and experiences he needs at this age, such as communication, fantasy, judgment, and experimentation. The more time your child spends in front of a TV set, the less he'll have left for other, more worthwhile activities.

What You Can Do

If you do not make a conscious effort to control your child's television viewing, it could become one of the most important influences in his life.

For many youngsters, TV serves as a substitute for friends, babysitters, teachers, and even parents. It is the easiest way to be entertained, and quickly becomes habit-forming unless limits are set.

As a general policy your child should watch no more than one to two hours of television a day. It is easy to enforce this rule when he is a toddler, but it becomes more difficult as he grows older and more independent, so you should start early. If your child never gets used to watching a lot of TV, he won't develop a habit that may be difficult to break later in life.

Distraction is the best way to get your child away from television. Invite him to join you in enjoyable but constructive activities such as reading, playing board or outdoor games, coloring, cooking, building, or visits with playmates. Praise him when he entertains himself without relying on television, and present a good model by restricting your own viewing. Do not use television as a reward or withhold it as a punishment. This will only make it seem more enticing.

If these tactics are not effective and your child "sneaks" TV time behind your back, you may need more forceful measures, such as removing the television or installing a lockout device so he cannot view certain channels.

Even an hour or two of television can be harmful if your child chooses to watch programs that are violent or otherwise inappropriate for him. Teach him to plan his viewing so you both know in advance what he'll be watching. Help him find programs that encourage positive behavior instead of violence. If you forbid him to watch a particular show, give him a clear explanation so he understands why. Then make sure the set goes off as soon as his chosen program is over, so he doesn't get involved in the show that follows. Never allow the television set to become a babysitter.

To help your youngster get the most out of the programs he does watch, view them with him. Even "bad" shows can be educational if you discuss them with him. Help him understand that the violence he sees on the screen is not actually happening, and that if it were, the characters would be severely injured. Explain that TV shows are "made up" and that the characters are really actors playing imaginary roles. Criticize the characters that drink alcohol, smoke, use drugs, or ride in cars without wearing seat belts. If he knows that you disapprove of these characters he will start to think about their behavior and question it instead of automatically accepting it.

When watching television with your child you can also educate him about advertising. Teach him that commercials are not the same as programs, and that their sole purpose is to make him want something he doesn't have. This is not an easy lesson for a preschooler, but if you explain the difference between "healthy" and "unhealthy" foods and toys, it will help him become a more critical viewer. Pointing out any advertised products that he's tried and rejected will help him realize how misleading commercials can be.

You also can help improve television programming for children by contacting the networks, commercial sponsors, or local broadcasters. Voice your complaints and your preferences. If there is a program you especially like, be sure to let the local station manager know, because quality programs often have low ratings, and your support can help keep them on the air.

Temper Tantrums

Temper tantrums are not fun for you or your child, but they are a normal part of life with most preschoolers. The first time your child screams and kicks because he can't have his way, you may feel angry, frustrated, humiliated, or frightened. You may wonder where you've gone wrong as a parent to produce such a miserable child. Rest assured, you are not responsible for this behavior, and tantrums are not ordinarily a sign of severe emotional or personality disorders. Almost all youngsters have these episodes occasionally, especially around ages two and three. If handled successfully, they usually diminish in intensity and frequency by age four or five.

In the developmental stage of separating from their parents, the "no" is a perfectly understandable and normal expression of childen's emerging need for some autonomy. Tantrums are often an expression of frustration. Preschoolers are very eager to take control. They want to be more independent than their skills and safety allow, and they don't appreciate their limits. They want to make decisions, but they don't know how to compromise, and they don't deal well with disappointment or restraint. They also can't express their feelings well in words, so instead they act out their anger and frustration by crying or withdrawing, and sometimes by having temper tantrums. While these emotional displays are unpleasant, they rarely are dangerous.

You often can tell when a temper tantrum is coming. For some time before it begins, the child may seem more sullen or irritable than usual, and neither gentle affection nor playing with him will change his moodiness. Then he tries to do something beyond his capabilities, or asks for something he can't have. He begins to whimper or whine, and becomes more demanding. Nothing will distract or comfort him, and finally he starts to cry. As the crying increases, he begins to flail his arms and kick his legs. He may fall to the ground or hold his breath—some children actually hold their breath until they turn blue or faint. As frightening as it is to watch these so-called *breath-holding spells,* the child's breathing normally resumes as soon as he faints, and he will recover quickly and completely. (Also see the box on page 499.)

Don't be surprised if your child has tantrums only when you are present—most children act up only around their parents or other family members, seldom when with outsiders. He is also testing your rules and limits, whereas he wouldn't dare do this with someone he knows less well. When his challenge goes too far and you restrain him, he may respond with a tantrum. He's not consciously trying to make your life miserable, and he certainly doesn't prefer strangers to you. Ironically, his occasional outbursts are actually a sign that he trusts you.

This emotional explosion serves as a kind of energy release, which often exhausts the child so that he falls asleep soon afterward. When he awakens he usually is calm and his behavior quiet and pleasant. If he is ill or there is a great deal of tension among the people around him, however, the frustration may start building all over again. Children who are anxious, ill, or temperamental, get too little rest, or live in very stressful households tend to have tantrums more frequently.

Prevention

You can't prevent every tantrum, but you may be able to decrease the number by making sure your child does not get overtired, overly anxious, or unnecessarily frustrated. Your child's temper may become very short if he doesn't have enough "quiet time," particularly when he is sick, anxious, or has been unusually active. Even if he doesn't sleep, lying down for fifteen or twenty minutes can help restore his energy and reduce the likelihood of those tantrums caused by exhaustion. Children who do not nap may be particularly prone to tantrums and often need

such a quiet period on a daily, scheduled basis. If your child resists, you might lie down with him or read him a story, but do not allow him to play or talk excessively.

Children whose parents fail to set limits or are overly strict tend to have more frequent and severe tantrums than children whose parents take a moderate approach. As a rule it's best to set very few limits but to be firm about those that are set. Expect your child to tell you "no" many times each day. He needs to assert himself this way and would not be normal if he never challenged you. You can allow him to have his way when the issue is minor—for example, if he wants to wander around slowly instead of walking quickly to the park, or if he refuses to get dressed before breakfast. But when he starts to run into the street, you must stop him and insist that he obey you, even if you have to hold him back physically. Be loving but firm, and respond the same way *every time* he violates the rule. He won't learn these important lessons immediately, so expect to repeat these scenes many times before his behavior changes. Also, make sure that every adult who cares for him observes the same rules and disciplines him in the same way.

How to Respond

When your child has a temper tantrum, it's important that you try to remain calm yourself. If you have loud angry outbursts, your child naturally will imitate your behavior. If you shout at him to calm down, you probably will make the situation worse. Maintaining a peaceful atmosphere will reduce the general stress level and make both you and your child feel better and more in control. In fact, sometimes gentle restraint, holding, or distracting comments such as "Did you see what the kitty is doing?" or "I think I heard the doorbell" will interrupt behavior such as breath-holding before it reaches the point of fainting. (See also the box on page 499.)

Sometimes, if you feel yourself losing control, humor will save the day. Turn a dispute over taking a bath into a race to the bathroom. Soften your command to "eat your dinner" by making a funny face. Unless your child is extremely irritable or overtired, he is more likely to be distracted into obedience if you temper discipline with a bit of fun or whimsy. This will also make *you* feel better.

Some parents feel guilty every time they say no to their children. They try too hard to explain their rules, or apologize for them. Even at age two or three, children can detect uncertainty in a tone of voice and they will try to take advantage of it. If the parent sometimes gives in, the child becomes even more outraged on those occasions when he doesn't get his way. There is no good reason to be apologetic about enforcing your rules. It only makes it more difficult for your child to understand which of them are firm and which can be questioned. This does not mean that you should be unfriendly or abusive when you say no, but state your position clearly. As your child gets older you can offer brief, simple reasons for your rules, but do not go into long, confusing explanations.

When you ask your child to do something against his will, follow through on the order with him. If you've asked him to put away his toys, offer to help him. If you've told him not to throw his ball against the window, show him where he *can* throw it. If you've reminded him not to touch the hot oven door, either remove him from the kitchen or stay there with him to make sure that he minds you. (Never issue a safety order to a two- or three-year-old and then leave the room.)

When to Call the Pediatrician

While occasional temper tantrums during the preschool years are normal, they should become less frequent and less intense by the middle of the fourth year. Between tantrums, the child should seem normal and healthy. At no time should the behavior cause the child to harm himself or others, or destroy property. When the outbursts are very severe, fre-quent, or prolonged, they may be an early sign of emotional disturbance.

Consult your pediatrician if your child shows any of the following warning signs.

- Tantrums persist or intensify after age four.

- Your child injures himself or others, or destroys property during tantrums.

- Tantrums are accompanied by frequent nightmares, extreme disobedience, reversal of toilet training, development of headaches or stomachaches, refusal to eat or go to bed, extreme anxiety, constant grumpiness, or clinging to parents.

- Your child holds his breath and faints during tantrums.

Also call the pediatrician the first time your child faints during a tantrum, especially if he falls. The doctor may want to examine him and possibly check for other causes of "fainting" such as seizures (see page 601). The pediatrician also can offer suggestions for disciplining the child, and suggest parent education groups that might provide additional support and guidance. If the doctor feels the tantrums indicate a severe emotional disturbance, he will refer you to a child psychiatrist, psychologist, or mental health clinic.

Thumb and Finger Sucking

Do not be upset if your baby begins sucking his thumb or fingers. This habit is very common and has a soothing and calming effect. Some experts feel that nine out of every ten children engage in this activity at some time in their early life. It is largely the result of the normal rooting and sucking reflexes present in all infants. There actually is evidence that some infants suck their thumbs and fingers even before delivery, and some, particularly finger suckers, will show that behavior immediately after being born.

Because sucking is a normal reflex, thumb

and finger sucking can be considered a normal habit. The only time it might cause you concern is if it continues too long or affects the shape of your child's mouth or the alignment of his teeth. Since over half of thumb or finger suckers stop by age six or seven months, your child stands a good chance of stopping before problems begin to appear at around age five. At that time you might see changes in the roof of the mouth (palate) or in the way the teeth are lining up. It is then that you and your dentist might become concerned. It is also at that time that your child might begin to be affected by the negative comments of his playmates, siblings, and relatives. If these factors become worrisome, consult your pediatrician about treatment.

Treatment

Severe emotional or stress-related problems that might cause this habit to be prolonged should be ruled out before any treatment program is begun. Also, your child should want to stop the habit and should be directly involved with the treatment chosen.

The techniques used usually begin with gentle reminders, particularly during the daytime hours. Friends or relatives might suggest that you use a pacifier, but there is no evidence that this is effective. It only substitutes one sucking habit for another.

If these measures are ineffective and your child is still interested in breaking the habit, your pediatrician might recommend trying some type of "aversive" (unpleasant) treatment. These are designed to serve as a reminder when your child begins to suck. They include coating the finger or thumb with a bitter substance, covering it with a band-aid or "thumb guard" (an adjustable plastic cylinder that can be taped to the thumb), or using an elbow restraint to prevent the elbow from bending and thus keeping the fingers and thumb from being brought up close to the mouth. Before any of these methods are employed they should be explained to your child. If they cause undue anxiety or tension, they should be discontinued. In rare cases where there is severe tooth misalignment and the techniques described above have all failed, some dentists will install a device in the mouth that prevents the fingers or thumb from putting pressure on the palate or teeth. In fact, this apparatus usually makes placement of the thumb or finger into the mouth unpleasant enough that your child will withdraw it.

It is important to remember that your child may be one of the very few who for one reason or another cannot seem to stop thumb and finger sucking. Be assured that all of these children stop daytime sucking habits before they progress very far along in school. This is because of the peer pressure that is exerted. These same children might still tend to use sucking as a way of going to sleep or calming themselves when they are particularly upset. This is usually done away from the observation of strangers and causes no harm either emotionally or physically. Exerting excessive pressure on your child to stop this type of behavior probably would cause more harm than good, and even these children will eventually stop the habit on their own.

18

CHEST AND LUNGS

Asthma

If your child is coughing and/or making a high-pitched wheezing or whistling sound as he breathes, he may have asthma, a lung disorder affecting the bronchial tubes.

The bronchial tubes are small airways that connect the main air passages (bronchi) to the place in the lung where the oxygen and carbon dioxide exchange takes place during normal breathing. These tubes are surrounded by smooth muscles that are very sensitive. When stimulated they go into spasm, making the small breathing passages even narrower. In addition, the lining (mucous membrane) of the breathing tubes becomes swollen and inflamed, and produces more of its protective fluid, called mucus. The airway inflammation is the most important aspect of the disease. The inflammation leads to the airway reactivity, which causes the airway smooth muscles to go into spasm. This results in narrowing of these airways, which in turn causes the whistling or wheezing sound heard particularly when the child exhales.

Many things can trigger an attack of asthma, but in children under five an attack most commonly occurs after a viral respiratory infection goes on to inflame the lining of the bronchial tubes and stimulates the muscles surrounding them.

Other common triggers of asthma attacks include:

- Air pollutants such as cigarette smoke or paint fumes

- Allergens such as pollens, mold spores, and animal danders

- Exercise, in some children

- Inhaling cold air

- Certain medications

  Some less common triggers are:

- Stress and emotional upset

- Sinus infections

- Allergic reactions to certain foods

- Injury to the airways

Signs and Symptoms

When your child has an asthma attack that is set off by an upper respiratory infection, the major symptom will be a cough that gets worse at night, with exercise, or after contact

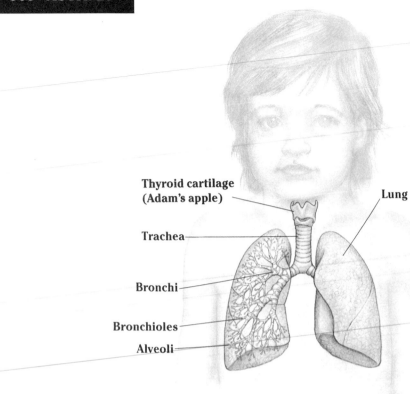

Chest and Lungs

Thyroid cartilage (Adam's apple)

Lung

Trachea

Bronchi

Bronchioles

Alveoli

with an irritant (such as cigarette smoke) or an allergen (such as animal hair or dander). He will make a wheezing sound as he breathes out. As the attack progresses the wheezing may actually decrease, as less air is able to move in and out.

If the asthma is severe, he will breathe very rapidly, his heart rate will increase, and he might vomit. In very severe cases, his chest wall seems to pull inward with each breath, his fingernails and lips turn blue, he becomes very tired and slow-moving, and he coughs all the time. *Such an attack requires immediate medical attention.*

Most children with asthma have chronic disease. This may be daily (or nightly) cough, cough with exercise, cough with certain daily exposures; or, the physician may hear wheezes (especially when the child blows out hard) even in the absence of symptoms. In the older child, abnormalities may be detected by pulmonary function testing.

When to Call the Pediatrician

If your child has asthma, you should know the situations that require immediate medical attention. As a rule, call your pediatrician immediately if:

- Your child has *severe* trouble breathing and seems to be getting worse, especially if he is breathing rapidly and there is pulling in of the chest wall when he inhales and forceful grunting when he exhales.

- Your child's eyes or fingertips appear blue, his skin seems darkened, or he acts agitated, extremely lethargic, or confused.

- He has chest, throat, or neck pain.

Although it may not be as urgent, you also should call your pediatrician without delay if:

- Your child has a fever and persistent coughing or wheezing that is not responding to the prescribed medications.

- He is vomiting, and cannot take oral medication.

- He has difficulty speaking or sleeping because of wheezing, coughing, or troubled breathing.

- He is receiving the drug theophylline and is experiencing side effects such as nausea, vomiting, loss of appetite, headaches, hyperactivity, or shakiness.

- He is missing school.

Treatment

Asthma should always be treated under your pediatrician's supervision. The goals of treatment are to:

1. If possible, eliminate the things that are triggering attacks, including irritants such as cigarette, cigar, or pipe smoke and substances to which the child is allergic (allergens).

2. Gain control of the wheezing and return lung function to normal.

3. With your pediatrician, develop a sensible "plan of response" for any major asthma attack in order to reduce the need for emergency medical treatment and hospitalization.

4. Allow your child to grow and develop normally, and take part in normal childhood activities as fully as possible.

With these goals in mind, your pediatrician will prescribe medication and may refer you to a specialist who can evaluate your child's lung function. Your doctor also will help you plan your child's specific home treatment program. This probably will include learning how to use the medicines and treatments that are prescribed and developing a plan for the elimination of irritants and allergens from your home.

If your child's asthma seems to be triggered by severe allergies, your pediatrician may refer you to a pediatric allergist for skin testing. The allergist also may recommend giving your child vaccines to lessen his sensitivity to the allergens that are triggering his attacks. This involves regular injections of a dilute form of the allergenic materials, which commonly include dust, molds, mites, and pollens.

The medication prescribed will depend on the nature of the asthma:

- If your child's symptoms occur on a sporadic basis, the pediatrician might prescribe a short-acting medication to open the airways (a bronchodilator) at those times. These drugs are given orally or by inhalation.

- If the asthma is recurrent or chronic, your doctor may prescribe medications for regular daily use. These might include theophylline, usually given every eight to twelve hours in liquid or pill form, or a drug such as cromolyn sodium, which is inhaled either by mist or in a fine powder, or inhaled corticosteroids. (It may take several weeks for either of these inhaled drugs to have a full effect.) The cromolyn and inhaled corticosteroids reduce the airway inflammation and reactivity. The theophylline has little to none of this activity.

- During severe attacks additional medication, such as corticosteroids (cortisone), may be prescribed.

Prevention

The most important and successful ways to keep your child from having asthma attacks are:

- Give medications according to your pediatrician's directions. *Do not stop medicines too soon,* give them less often than recommended, or switch to other drugs or treatments without first discussing the change with the doctor. If you do not understand why something is being done to your child, or why a particular medication is being given, ask for an explanation.

- Keep your child away from the things that trigger his attacks, such as house dust, smoke, heavy pollen exposure, certain pets, and certain foods. Keeping a diary of when the attacks occur and what preceded them may help you identify the triggering substances. Whenever possible, learn to anticipate the attacks. If your child has asthma with viral infections, begin medication at the start of the viral infection. This should consist of antiinflammatory therapy, possibly with a bronchodilator. Don't wait for the cough and wheeze to start treating. The easiest and best time to treat the attack is before it begins.

Bronchiolitis

Bronchiolitis is an infection of the small breathing tubes (bronchioles) of the lungs. It occurs most often in infants. (Note: The term *bronchiolitis* is sometimes confused with bronchitis, which is an infection of the larger, more central airways.)

Bronchiolitis is almost always caused by a virus, most commonly the respiratory syncytial virus (RSV). Other viruses that can cause this condition are parainfluenza, influenza, measles, and adenovirus. The infection causes inflammation and swelling of the bronchioles, which in turn causes blockage of air flow through the lungs.

Most adults and many children who are infected by RSV get only a cold. In infants, however, the infection is more likely to lead to bronchiolitis. This is because their airways are smaller and are more easily blocked when infection and inflammation occur.

Almost half the infants who develop bronchiolitis go on to develop asthma later in life. We do not know why these youngsters are more susceptible, but it is likely that the RSV infection is the first trigger for the airway reaction.

RSV infection is the most likely cause of bronchiolitis from October through March. During the other months, bronchiolitis is usually caused by other viruses.

The RSV is spread by contact with secretions from an infected person. It often spreads through families, day-care centers, and hospital wards. Careful hand washing can help prevent this.

Signs and Symptoms

If your infant has bronchiolitis, it will start with signs of an upper respiratory infection (a cold): runny nose, mild cough, and sometimes fever. After a day or two the cough becomes more pronounced, the child begins to breathe more rapidly, and with more difficulty:

- He may dilate his nostrils and squeeze the muscles under his rib cage in efforts to get more air in and out of his lungs.

- He will use the muscles between the ribs and above the collarbone to help him breathe.

- When he breathes he may grunt and tighten his abdominal muscles.

- He will make a high-pitched whistling sound, called a wheeze, each time he exhales.

- He may not take fluids well because he is working so hard to breathe that he has difficulty sucking and swallowing.

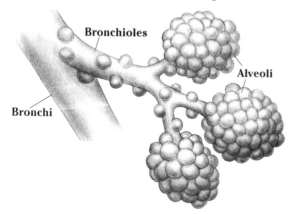

Bronchioles

Alveoli

Bronchi

- As his breathing difficulty increases you may notice a bluish tint around the lips and fingertips. This indicates that his airways are so blocked that an inadequate amount of oxygen is getting into the blood.

If your baby shows any of these signs of breathing difficulty, or if his fever lasts more than three days (or is present at all in an infant under three months), call your pediatrician immediately.

Also call the pediatrician if your child develops any of the following signs or symptoms of dehydration, which also can be present with bronchiolitis.

- Dry mouth

- Taking less than his normal amount of fluids

- Shedding no tears when he cries

- Urinating less often than normal

If your child has any of the following conditions, notify your pediatrician as soon as you suspect that he has bronchiolitis.

- Cystic fibrosis

- Congenital heart disease

- Bronchopulmonary dysplasia (seen in some infants who have been on a respirator as newborns)

- Low immunity

- Organ transplant

- A cancer for which he is receiving chemotherapy

Home Treatment

There are no medications you can use to treat RSV infections at home. All you can do during the early phase of the illness is ease your child's cold symptoms. You can relieve some of the nasal stuffiness with a humidifier, nasal aspirator, and perhaps some mild salt-solu-

tion nasal drops prescribed by your pediatrician. (See the treatment for *Colds/Upper Respiratory Infection,* page 535.) Also make sure your baby drinks lots of fluid during this time so he does not become dehydrated. (See *Diarrhea,* page 476.) He may prefer clear liquids rather than milk or formula. Because of the breathing difficulty, he also may feed more slowly and may not tolerate solid foods very well.

Professional Treatment

If your baby is having mild to moderate breathing difficulty, your pediatrician may try using a bronchodilating drug (one that opens up the breathing tubes) before considering hospitalization. These drugs seem to help a small number of patients.

Unfortunately, some children with bronchiolitis need to be hospitalized, either for breathing distress or dehydration. The breathing difficulty is treated with oxygen and bronchodilating drugs, which are inhaled periodically. Occasionally, another medicine, called theophylline, is used. The dehydration will be treated with a special liquid diet or by fluids given intravenously.

An antiviral drug called ribavirin is sometimes used to treat RSV infections, especially in infants who have serious lung disease. This medicine has to be administered by aerosol and is quite expensive, but its use is seldom necessary if the baby is otherwise normal and healthy.

Very rarely an infant will not respond to any of these treatments and might have to be assisted by a breathing machine (respirator). This usually is only a temporary measure to help him until his body is able to overcome the infection.

Prevention

The best way to protect your baby from bronchiolitis is to keep him away from the viruses that cause it. When possible, especially while he's an infant, avoid close contact with children or adults who are in the early (contagious) stages of respiratory infections. If he is in a day-care center where other children might have the virus, make sure that those who care for him wash their hands thoroughly and frequently.

Cough

Coughing is almost always an indication of an irritation in your child's air passages. When the nerve endings in the throat, windpipe, or lungs sense the irritation, a reflex causes air to be ejected forcefully through the passageways.

Coughs usually are associated with respiratory illnesses such as colds/upper respiratory infection, (see page 535), bronchiolitis (see page 510), croup (see page 513), flu (see page 515) or pneumonia (see page 516). If your child's cough is accompanied by fever, irritability, or difficulty in breathing, he probably has such an infection.

To a large extent, the location of the infection determines the sound of the cough: An irritation in the larynx (voice box), such as croup, causes a cough that sounds like the bark of a dog or seal; irritation of the larger airways such as the trachea (windpipe) or bronchi is characterized by a deeper, raspy cough that gets worse in the morning.

A chronic or long-lasting cough without fever may indicate that your child has accidentally inhaled a small object such as a peanut into his windpipe or lungs (see *Choking*, page 452). Allergies can cause chronic cough, too, because mucus drips down the back of the throat, producing a dry, hard-to-stop cough, particularly at night. A child who coughs only at night also may have a mild form of asthma (see page 507).

Occasionally a cough is caused by a temporary irritation, such as breathing strong fumes from drying paint, tobacco smoke, or insecticide sprays. In this case, the cough will go away when the child gets into fresh air. In rare situations, the child may continue to have a dry, periodic cough long after the physical cause has been cleared. Though this can be bothersome (more to you than to your child), the cough usually will eventually disappear. If it becomes a habit, however, your physician will be able to recommend ways of discouraging it.

When to Call the Pediatrician

An infant under two months of age who develops a cough should be seen by the doctor. For older infants and children, consult your physician if:

- The coughing makes it difficult for your child to breathe.

- The coughing is painful, persistent, and accompanied by whooping, vomiting, or turning blue.

- The cough lasts longer than one week.

- The cough appears suddenly and is associated with fever.

- The coughing begins after your child chokes on food or any other object. (See *Choking,* page 452.)

Your pediatrician will try to determine the cause of your child's cough. Most often, it will be a symptom of a cold or flu, and he will recommend lots of rest. He also may suggest an over-the-counter or prescription cough medicine if the symptoms are severe enough to warrant it.

When the cough is caused by another medical problem, such as a bacterial infection or asthma, it will be necessary to treat that condition before the cough will clear. Occasionally, when the cause of a chronic cough is not clear, further tests such as chest X-rays or tuberculosis (see page 518) skin tests may be necessary.

Treatment

The treatment for a cough depends upon its cause. But, whatever the cause, it is always a good idea to give your child extra fluids. Adding moisture to the air with a humidifier or vaporizer also may make your child more comfortable, especially at night.

A cold-water humidifier is just as effective as a hot-water vaporizer and is considerably safer if accidentally knocked over. However, be sure to clean the device thoroughly with detergent and water each morning, so it doesn't become a breeding ground for harmful bacteria or fungi.

Nighttime coughs, particularly those associated with allergies or asthma, can be especially annoying, because they occur when everyone is trying to sleep. In some cases it may help to elevate the head of the child's bed. A cough medicine containing an antihistamine or decongestant may also bring relief. If the night cough is due to asthma, bronchodilators should be used.

Although cough medicines can be purchased without a prescription, they vary widely in their ingredients, so ask your pediatrician to recommend a brand and specify the appropriate dosage and frequency for your child. Most cough syrups contain a combination of the following ingredients.

- Expectorants: These medications thin the secretions within the breathing passages so that they can be coughed up more easily. The one most commonly used is guaifenesin.

- Decongestants: These medications shrink the blood vessels in the walls of breathing passages, which decreases the amount of mucus produced. Phenylephrine and pseudoephedrine are generic names for two of the most common.

- Antihistamines: These decrease the secretions and swelling of the mucous membranes when the cause is an allergy. Chlorpheniramine and brompheniramine are two of the most widely used.

- Cough suppressants: These medications inhibit the cough reflex.

Although the amounts of decongestants and antihistamines in over-the-counter medicines are usually safe for adults, in young children they may cause adverse reactions such as drowsiness, irritability, hallucinations, and high blood pressure. They should be given only with your doctor's approval.

Croup

Croup is an inflammation of the larynx and trachea which narrows the airway just below the vocal cords and makes breathing noisy and difficult.

There are different types of croup:

Spasmodic croup is often most frightening because it comes on suddenly in the middle of the night. Your child will go to bed with a mild cold and awaken within one to three hours, gasping for breath. He also will be hoarse and have a distinctive cough (see page 512) that sounds like the bark of a seal. This type of croup is usually caused by a mild upper respiratory infection (see page 535) or allergy (see page 541).

Viral croup results from a more severe viral infection in the larynx and trachea. This condition usually starts with a cold, which gradually develops into croup's barky cough. As

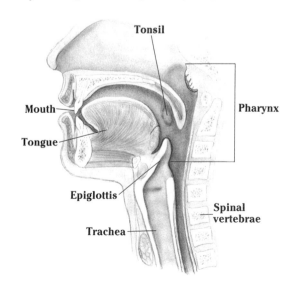

your child's airway swells and secretions increase, his breathing will become noisy and labored, a condition called "stridor." Some children have a fever as high as 104 degrees Fahrenheit (40 degrees Celsius), but others do not.

The greatest danger is that the trachea will continue to swell, further narrowing your child's windpipe and making it first difficult and then impossible to breathe. As your child tires from the effort of breathing, he may stop eating and drinking. He also may become too fatigued to cough, though the stridor will become more audible with each breath.

Croup can occur at any time of the year, but it is more common between October and March. Some youngsters are particularly prone and seem to get croup whenever they have a respiratory illness. Children generally are most susceptible to it between six months and three years. After three, the condition is uncommon because the windpipe is larger, so swelling is less likely to interfere with breathing.

Treatment

If your child awakens in the middle of the night with spasmodic croup, take him into the bathroom and steam it up by turning on the shower with the hottest available water. Close the door and sit in the steamy bathroom with your child. Inhaling the warm, humidified air should ease his breathing within fifteen to twenty minutes, but he will still have a croupy cough.

For the rest of that night and the three nights that follow, use a cold-water vaporizer or humidifier in your child's room. Sometimes another episode of spasmodic croup will occur the same night or the next. If it does, repeat the steam treatment in the bathroom. Steam is almost always effective, but if it doesn't seem to be working, take your child outdoors for a few minutes. Inhaling the cold, moist night air will loosen up his air passages so he can breathe more freely.

Steam also may make your child feel better if he has viral croup, but the results won't be as dramatic.

Do *not* try to open the airway with your finger. Breathing is being obstructed by swollen tissue beyond your reach, so you can't clear it away. Besides, putting your finger in your child's throat will make him even more agitated, which will make his breathing even more difficult. For similar reasons, don't make your child vomit. If he does happen to throw up, hold his head down and then quickly sit him back up in the steamy room.

With either type of croup, call your pediatrician right away—even if it's the middle of the night. Also, pay attention to your child's breathing. Take him to the nearest emergency room *immediately* if:

- He makes a whistling sound that gets louder with each breath.

- He can't speak for lack of breath.

- He seems to be struggling to get a breath.

For spasmodic croup, the doctor will ask whether the child is breathing comfortably after the steam treatment. Some doctors recommend decongestants for spasmodic croup, because they feel they will minimize the problem on subsequent nights.

For viral croup, some doctors prescribe cortisone medications to reduce swelling in the throat or to shorten the illness. Although its effectiveness has not been firmly established, treatment with cortisone for five days or less should do no harm.

Antibiotics are not helpful for croup, because the problem is caused by a virus. Cough syrups are of little use, because they do not affect the larynx or trachea, where the infection is located. They also may interfere with your child's ability to cough up the secretions produced by the infection.

In the most serious cases, which are quite rare, your child will not get enough oxygen into his blood. Your doctor may then hospitalize him so that he can receive oxygen in a croup tent. He also will be fed intravenously and given appropriate medicines by aerosol. Sometimes, to bypass the swelling in the larynx and trachea, a tube will be inserted through the nose or mouth into the windpipe. This treatment may leave your child temporarily hoarse when the tube is removed, but usually has no long-lasting consequences.

Flu/Influenza

Influenza is an illness caused by a respiratory virus. There are three different influenza viruses, types A, B, and C; the usual epidemics of the flu are caused by either A or B. Each of these viruses also has different subgroups or strains, so that each year, the flu virus that causes the majority of the cases of the flu is slightly different. That's why individuals at high risk for serious or complicated influenza infection should receive a flu shot every year.

You can suspect that your child has the flu if you observe the following signs or symptoms:

- Sudden onset of fever (usually above 101 degrees Fahrenheit, or 38.3 degrees Celsius)

- Chills and shakes accompanying the fever

- Extreme tiredness or fatigue

- Muscle aches and pains

- Dry, hacking cough

After the first few days of these symptoms, a sore throat, stuffy nose, and continuing cough become most evident. The flu can last a week or even longer. A child with a common cold (see *Colds/Upper Respiratory Infection,* page 535) usually has a lower degree of fever, a runny nose, and only a small amount of coughing. Children with the flu—or adults for that matter—usually feel much more sick, achy, and miserable.

Influenza is spread from person to person by direct contact, by virus particles being passed through the air (by coughing, for example), or by a person with the flu contaminating objects with virus-containing nasal secretions. When there is an outbreak or epidemic, usually during the winter months, the spread tends to be most pronounced in preschool or school-age children. Adult caretakers are then easily exposed and can contract the disease. The virus is usually transmitted in the first several days of the illness.

Fortunately, there are usually no serious complications for otherwise healthy children. You might suspect such a complication if your child says that his ear hurts or that he feels all congested in his face and head or if his cough and fever persist. Occasionally, an ear infection (see page 537), a sinus infection (see page 603), or pneumonia (see page 516) might develop, in which case you should notify your pediatrician.

Very rarely, there is a risk of developing Reye syndrome (see page 490), though the incidence of this disorder seems to have diminished significantly with the awareness that it may be associated with aspirin use during viral illnesses and the consequent decrease in the use of aspirin to treat symptoms of the flu or chicken pox.

Children who appear to be at greatest risk for complications from the flu are those with an underlying chronic medical condition, such as heart disease, lung disease, an immune problem, some blood diseases, or malignancy. As these children may have more severe disease or complications, they should, when possible, be kept away from children with the flu and additional precautions should be taken for them. They should be immunized each fall, as should others in their household.

Treatment

For all children who don't feel so well, lots of tender loving care is in order. Children can benefit from extra bed rest, extra fluids, and light, easy-to-digest meals. A cold-water vaporizer in the room may add additional moisture to the air and make breathing through inflamed mucous membranes of the nose a little easier.

If your child is uncomfortable because of fever, acetaminophen in proper doses for age and weight (see Chapter 23, "Fever") will help him feel better. *It is extremely important that aspirin not be given to a child who has the flu or is suspected of having the flu. An increased risk of developing Reye syndrome is associated with aspirin use during bouts of influenza.*

Prevention

Since the flu virus is transmitted from person to person, a first step you can take to decrease the chances of family members getting the flu is to practice and teach good hygiene. If, for example, you have a child with the flu, do the following to prevent its spread.

- Avoid kissing your infected child on or around the mouth, though he will need plenty of hugs during the illness.

- Teach your child not to cough or sneeze without covering his nose and mouth with a tissue, and make sure the tissue is disposed of properly.

- Make sure you and other caretakers wash hands both before and after caring for your child.

- Wash your child's utensils in hot, soapy water or in the dishwasher.

- Don't allow others to share drinking glasses or utensils and never share toothbrushes.

- Use disposable paper cups in the bathroom and kitchen.

There are vaccines to protect against the flu; the current vaccines are considered safe, effective, and associated with minimal side effects. However, since the majority of children tolerate the flu quite well, the vaccine is generally recommended for those children (or adults) who are at greater risk for serious disease or complications. Those children, six

months or older, for whom yearly influenza vaccination is recommended include:

- Children with chronic pulmonary disease

- Children with significant heart disease

- Children receiving therapy that suppresses their immune system (for treatment of a malignancy)

- Children with sickle-cell disease or other hemoglobinopathies

There are other high-risk children who may benefit, including those with diabetes, chronic renal and metabolic disease, symptomatic HIV infection, and those receiving long-term aspirin therapy, such as children with rheumatoid arthritis.

Even though there appear to be few side effects to the vaccine, it must be noted that production of the vaccine involves the use of eggs. If a child or an adult has had a serious allergic reaction to eggs or egg products, he should be skin tested before receiving the vaccine. If skin testing confirms hypersensitivity, the influenza vaccine should not be given.

Pneumonia

The word *pneumonia* means "infection of the lung." While such infections were extremely dangerous in past generations, most children today can easily recover from them if they receive proper medical attention.

Most pneumonias follow a viral upper-respiratory-tract infection. Typically, the viruses that cause these infections (respiratory syncytial virus [RSV], influenza, parainfluenza, adenovirus) spread to the chest and produce pneumonia there. Other viruses—such as those related to measles, chicken pox, herpes, infectious mononucleosis, and rubella—may travel from various parts of the body to the lungs, where they also can cause pneumonia.

Pneumonia can also be caused by bacterial

infections. Some of these are spread from person to person by coughing or by direct contact with the infected person's saliva or mucus. Also, if a viral infection has weakened a child's immune system, bacteria that ordinarily are harmless may begin to grow in the lung, adding a second infection to the original one.

Children whose immune defenses or lungs are weakened by other illnesses such as cystic fibrosis, asthma, or cancer (as well as by the chemotherapy used to treat cancer) are more likely to develop pneumonia, as are children whose airways or lungs are abnormal in any other way.

Because most forms of pneumonia are linked to viral or bacterial infections that spread from person to person, they're most common during the fall, winter, and early spring, when children spend more time indoors in close contact with others. The likelihood that a child will develop pneumonia is *not* affected by how he is dressed, by the temperature of the air he is in, or by whether he is exposed to fresh air when ill.

Signs and Symptoms

Like many infections, pneumonia usually produces fever, which in turn may cause sweating, chills, flushed skin, and general discomfort. The child also may lose his appetite and seem less energetic than normal. If he's a baby or toddler, he may seem pale and limp, and cry more than usual.

Because pneumonia can cause breathing difficulties, you may notice these other, more specific symptoms, too:

- Cough (see page 512)

- Fast, labored breathing

- Increased activity of the breathing muscles below and between the ribs and above the collarbone

- Flaring (widening) of the nostrils

- Wheezing

- Bluish tint to the lips or nails, caused by decreased oxygen in the bloodstream

Although the diagnosis of pneumonia can usually be made on the basis of the signs and symptoms, a chest X-ray is sometimes necessary to make certain and to determine the extent of lung involvement.

Treatment

When pneumonia is caused by a virus, there is no specific treatment other than rest and the usual measures for fever (see Chapter 23). Cough suppressants containing codeine or dextromethorphan should not be used, because coughing is necessary to clear the excessive secretions caused by the infection. Viral pneumonia usually disappears after a few days, though the cough may linger up to several weeks. Ordinarily, no medication is necessary.

Because it is often difficult to tell whether the pneumonia is caused by a virus or by bacteria, your pediatrician may prescribe an antibiotic. All antibiotics should be taken for the full prescribed course and at the specific dosage recommended. You may be tempted to discontinue them early, since your child will feel better after just a few days, but if you do this, some bacteria may remain and the infection might return.

Your child should be checked by the pediatrician as soon as you suspect pneumonia. You should check back with the doctor if your youngster shows any of the following warning signs that the infection is worsening or spreading.

- Fever lasting more than two or three days despite the use of antibiotics

- Breathing difficulties

- Evidence of infection elsewhere in the body: red, swollen joints, bone pain, neck stiffness, vomiting

(See also: Chapter 23, "Fever"; *Colds/Upper Respiratory Infection,* page 535; *Asthma,* page 507.)

Tuberculosis

Tuberculosis (TB) is a chronic bacterial infection that usually affects the lungs. While it is much less common today than several decades ago, a resurgence has occurred over the past few years due to the AIDS epidemic and influx of various immigrant groups. Babies under age two are the most susceptible to this infection. Vulnerability then decreases until age thirteen, when it seems to return again, but to a lesser degree.

Tuberculosis usually is spread when an infected adult coughs the bacteria into the air. These germs are inhaled by the child, who then becomes infected. (Children with TB of the lungs rarely infect other people, because they tend to have very few bacteria in their mucus secretions and also have a relatively ineffective cough.)

Fortunately, most children exposed to tuberculosis don't become ill. When the bacteria reach their lungs, the body's immune system attacks them and prevents further spread. Many of these children will develop a chronic condition indicated by a positive skin test. This does not mean the child has active tuberculosis, but that he must be treated, as noted below, to prevent an active disease from ever occurring. Occasionally, in a small number of children, the infection does progress, causing fever, fatigue, irritability, a persistent cough, weakness, heavy and fast breathing, night sweats, swollen glands, weight loss, and poor growth.

In a very small number of children (mostly babies), the tuberculosis infection spreads through the bloodstream, affecting virtually any organ in the body. This requires much more complicated treatment, and the earlier it is started, the better the outcome.

The signs and symptoms of childhood tuberculosis can be difficult to detect. Often, the only way you can tell for sure that a child has been exposed to this infection is by a positive skin test. Your pediatrician will perform this test if either of you suspects that your youngster has been exposed to the disease, or if your child has any symptoms that suggest it. Also, a routine test will be given at one year of age and repeated annually.

The test is done by injecting killed, inactive TB germs into the skin. If there has been an infection, your child's skin will swell and redden in the area of the injection. You'll be asked to check for this two days after the test is administered, since the reaction takes about forty-eight hours to appear. This skin test will reveal past exposure to the bacteria, even if the child has had no symptoms and even if his body has successfully fought the disease. If your child's skin test for TB turns positive, or even if it is negative but your child has symptoms suggestive of current (active) infection with tuberculosis, a chest X-ray will be ordered to determine if there is evidence of active or past infection in the lungs. If the X-ray does indicate the possibility of active TB, the pediatrician also will search for the TB bacteria in your child's cough secretions or in his stomach contents (obtained with a tube inserted into the stomach). This is done in order to determine the type of treatment to be given.

Treatment

If your child's skin test turns positive, but he does not have symptoms or signs of active tuberculosis infection (typical X-ray finding or TB bacteria in saliva or stomach contents), he can still be harboring the infection or germ. In order to prevent the infection from becoming active, your pediatrician will prescribe a medication called isoniazid (INH). This must be taken orally once a day for a year.

For an *active* tuberculosis infection, your physician may prescribe two or sometimes three medications. You'll have to give these for six months to one and one-half years, depending upon the response and extent of the disease. The child may have to be in the hospital initially, although most of the treatment can be carried out at home. In severe cases of TB of the lung, or when it strikes other organs, the child may have to stay in the hospital longer and take additional medications.

Prevention

If your child has been infected with TB, regardless of whether he develops symptoms, it's *very* important to identify the person from whom he caught the disease. This usually is done by looking for symptoms of TB in everyone who came in close contact with him, and having TB skin tests performed on all family members, babysitters, and housekeepers. Anyone who has a positive skin test should receive a physical examination and a chest X-ray.

When an actively infected adult is found, he'll be isolated as much as possible—especially from young children—until treatment is under way. All family members who have been in contact with that person usually are also treated with INH, regardless of the results of their own skin tests. (In a person with a negative skin test, the medication can be discontinued after repeated tests remain negative for three months.) But if the test is or becomes positive, INH will be prescribed once a day for a year. Anyone who becomes ill or develops an abnormality on a chest X-ray should be treated as an active case of tuberculosis.

Tuberculosis is much more common in an underprivileged population, which has a greater susceptibility to disease due to crowded living conditions, poor nutrition, and the probability of inadequate medical care. AIDS patients, too, are at a greater risk of getting TB, because of their lowered resistance. To prevent your child's acquiring this disease, keep his resistance high through good health habits, including regular medical care and proper nutrition. Also, never use unpasteurized (raw) milk for yourself or for your family, since it can contain the bacteria that cause tuberculosis in addition to other infectious agents.

If untreated, tuberculosis can lie dormant for many years, only to surface during adolescence, pregnancy, or later adulthood. At that time, not only can the individual become quite ill but he can also spread the infection to those around him. Thus, it's very important to have your child tested for TB if he comes in close contact with any adult who has the disease, and to get prompt and adequate treatment for him if he tests positive.

Whooping Cough (Pertussis)

Pertussis, or whooping cough, is seen very rarely now, as the pertussis vaccine has made most children immune. (This is the "P" part of the DTP vaccine given to all infants beginning at two months of age; the other parts are for the prevention of diphtheria and tetanus.) Before the vaccine was developed, there were several hundred thousand cases of whooping cough each year in the United States. Now there are approximately four thousand.

This illness is called pertussis because it is caused by the pertussis bacterium, which attacks the lining of the breathing passages (bronchi and bronchioles) producing severe inflammation and narrowing of the airways. Severe coughing is a prominent symptom. If not treated properly, the bacteria may spread to other parts of the body, causing further infection.

Infants under one year of age are at greatest risk of developing severe breathing problems and life-threatening illness from whooping cough. Because the child is short of breath, he inhales deeply and quickly between coughs. These breaths (particularly in older infants) frequently make a "whooping" sound—which is how this illness got its common name. The intense coughing scatters the pertussis bacteria into the air, spreading the disease to other susceptible persons.

Pertussis often acts like a common cold for a week or two. Then the cough gets worse, and the older child may start to have the characteristic "whoops." During this phase (which can last two weeks or more) the child often is short of breath and can look bluish around the mouth. He also may tear, drool, and vomit. Infants with pertussis become exhausted, susceptible to other infections such as pneumonia, and may have seizures. Pertussis can be fatal in some infants, but the usual course is for recovery to begin after two to four more weeks. The cough may not disappear for months, and may return with subsequent respiratory infections.

When to Call the Pediatrician

Pertussis infection starts out acting like a cold. You should consider the possibility of whooping cough if the following conditions are present.

- The child is a very young infant who has not been fully immunized and/or has had exposure to someone with the disease.

- The child's cough becomes more severe and frequent, or his lips and fingertips become dark or blue.

- He becomes exhausted after coughing episodes, eats poorly, and looks "sick."

Treatment

If your pediatrician determines that your infant has whooping cough, he may admit him to the hospital. (If your child is older, he is more likely to be treated at home.) Depending upon the age of the child and the severity of the illness, treatment will include

- Antibiotics (If given during the active coughing stage, this will not shorten the length of the illness, but will make the child less contagious.)

- Close observation, sometimes in an intensive-care setting

- Oxygen and intravenous fluids

Prevention

The best way to protect your child against pertussis is with DTP immunizations at two months, four months, and six months of age, and booster shots at eighteen months and before entering school. For the fourth and fifth dose, the acellular (DTaP) vaccine may be substituted for the DTP vaccine. (See Chapter 27, "Immunizations.") Pertussis vaccine has been the subject of much controversy because of its possible association with irritability, convulsions, high fever, and brain injury. The risk to your child is much greater if he does not receive the vaccination, however. In countries that have stopped giving pertussis immunization to all children, there has been an increase in the number of cases of the disease, as well as all the problems that result from it (one child dies for every thousand who get whooping cough). Therefore, the *American Academy of Pediatrics urges parents to continue immunizing their infants against pertussis but to be aware of the following reactions that can occur, and the conditions under which the vaccine should not be used.*

Severe reactions to the DTP vaccine that should alert you and your pediatrician not to give another pertussis immunization:

- Allergic reaction (rash, convulsion, shock)

- Fever of 105 degrees Fahrenheit (40.6 degrees Celsius) or greater

- Prolonged, continuous crying

- An episode of limpness or paleness

- Unusual high-pitched cry

- Convulsions

In addition to the above, there are certain children who probably should never get the "P" part of the injection in the first place: Any child with a seizure disorder or a neurologic (nervous system) condition that increases the likelihood of developing a seizure.

Fortunately, the number of children to whom these rules apply is very small. Do not make the mistake of refusing to immunize your child if he is normal and healthy. The benefits of the vaccine far outweigh the risks. It is hoped that there will be an even more effective but less reactive vaccine in the next few years.

19

DEVELOPMENTAL DISABILITIES

It's natural to compare your child with others his age. When the neighbor's baby walks at ten months, for example, you may worry if yours does not crawl until thirteen months. And if your toddler is using words at an earlier age than his playmates, probably you'll be very proud. Usually, however, such differences are not significant. Each child has his own unique rate of development, so some learn certain skills faster than others.

Only when a baby or preschooler lags far behind, or fails altogether to reach the developmental milestones outlined in Chapters 5 through 12 of this book, or loses a previously acquired skill is there reason to suspect a mental or physical problem serious enough to be considered a developmental disability. Disabilities that can be identified during childhood include mental retardation, language and learning disorders, cerebral palsy, autism, and sensory impairments such as vision and hearing loss. (Some pediatricians include seizure disorders in this category, but a large percentage of children who have seizures develop normally.)

Each of these disabilities can vary greatly in severity. For example, one child with mild cerebral palsy may have no obvious handicap other than a slight lack of coordination, while another with a severe form may be unable to walk or feed himself. Also, some children have more than one disability, each requiring different care.

If your child does not seem to be developing normally, he should have a complete medical and developmental evaluation, perhaps including a consultation with a specialist in this field. This will give your pediatrician the information needed to determine whether a real disability exists and, if so, how it should be managed. Depending on the results of the evaluation, the doctor may recommend physical, speech and language, or occupational therapy. Educational intervention or psychological counseling also might be necessary. A child development center affiliated with a medical school should be able to help you arrange these consultations. In some states and cities these evaluations are offered free of charge, or are partially paid for by local government. Your local board of education can tell you if this is the case in your area.

Today, every child over the age of three years who has a developmental disability is entitled by federal law to special education in a preschool or school program. A new federal law has mandated that states also offer special programs for infants and toddlers who

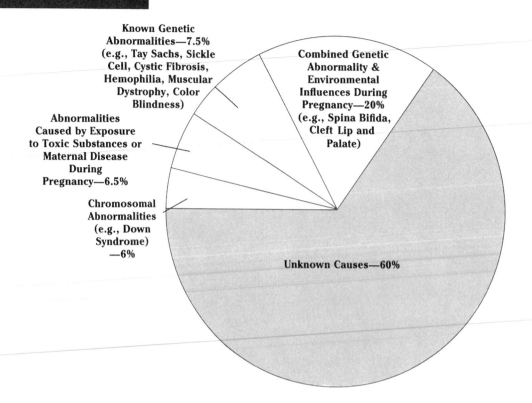

Known Genetic Abnormalities—7.5% (e.g., Tay Sachs, Sickle Cell, Cystic Fibrosis, Hemophilia, Muscular Dystrophy, Color Blindness)

Combined Genetic Abnormality & Environmental Influences During Pregnancy—20% (e.g., Spina Bifida, Cleft Lip and Palate)

Abnormalities Caused by Exposure to Toxic Substances or Maternal Disease During Pregnancy—6.5%

Chromosomal Abnormalities (e.g., Down Syndrome)—6%

Unknown Causes—60%

have developmental delays or disabilities, or who are at risk for these difficulties.

The families of children with disabilities also need special support and education. It's not so easy to accept the fact that a loved one is disabled. To understand what the child is facing and how he can be helped to realize his full potential, each member of the family should be educated about the specific problem and counseled about how to deal with it.

Birth Defects

Thanks to improved medical care during pregnancy, and the progress in early detection of chromosomal and other genetic abnormalities through amniocentesis, chorionic villus sampling, or other newer diagnostic tests, there are fewer and fewer newborns with congenital problems. About three of every hundred babies born in the

United States have birth defects that will affect the way they look, develop, or function—in some cases for the rest of their lives.

Birth defects are caused by abnormalities in the development of the infant before birth. There are five categories, grouped according to the cause of the abnormality.

Chromosome Abnormalities

Chromosomes are the structures that carry the genetic material inherited from one generation to the next. Normally, twenty-three chromosomes come from the father and twenty-three from the mother, and all are found in the center of every cell in the body except the red blood cells. The genes carried on the chromosomes determine how the baby will grow, what he will look like, and to a large extent how he will function.

When a child does not have the normal forty-six chromosomes, or when pieces of the chromosomes are missing or duplicated, he may look and behave differently from others his age, and he may develop serious health problems as well. *Down syndrome* is an example of a condition that can occur when a child is born with an extra chromosome.

Single Gene Abnormalities

Sometimes the chromosomes are normal in number but one or more of the genes on them is abnormal. Some of these genetic abnormalities can be passed on to the child if one of the parents is affected with the same abnormality. This is known as autosomal dominant inheritance.

Other genetic problems can be passed to the child only if both parents carry the same defective gene. (Cystic fibrosis, Tay-Sachs disease, and sickle-cell anemia are all examples of this type of abnormality.) In these cases both parents are normal but one in four of their children would be expected to be affected. This is known as autosomal recessive inheritance.

A third type of genetic defect is called sex-linked, and generally is passed on to boys only. Girls may carry the abnormal gene that causes these disorders. (Examples of this problem include hemophilia, color blindness, and the common forms of muscular dystrophy.)

Damaging Conditions During Pregnancy

Certain illnesses during pregnancy, particularly during the first nine weeks, can cause serious birth defects—German measles and diabetes, for example. Excess alcohol consumption and the use of certain drugs during pregnancy significantly increase the risk that a baby will be born with abnormalities. Certain medications, if taken during pregnancy, also can cause permanent damage to the unborn child, as can certain chemicals that can pollute air, water, and food. Before using any medication during pregnancy, women should check with their doctors.

Combination of Genetic and Environmental Problems

Spina bifida and cleft lip and palate are types of birth defects that may occur when there is a genetic tendency for the abnormality combined with exposure to certain environmental conditions within the womb during critical stages of the pregnancy.

Unknown Causes

The vast majority of birth defects have no known cause. This is particularly troubling for parents who plan to have more children, because there is no way to predict if the problem will occur again. If you and your family have experienced such a situation, ask your pediatrician for a referral to a genetic counselling service. These individuals or groups have expertise with a variety of genetic abnormalities and may be able to advise you as to the proper course of action.

Learning to Live with the Problem

If your newborn has a birth defect, the first hours and days of his life will be very difficult for you. At the same time that you are learning about your child as he is, you probably will be mourning the perfect baby you'd imagined he would be. Meanwhile, all your relatives and friends are calling to hear the "good news." One way to relieve the social pressure you're bound to feel is to appoint one family member and one friend to inform other friends and relatives about your newborn's condition.

If you have other children, you'll need to explain the situation to them as soon as possible. It is difficult to predict how siblings will react to such news; but, whether they show it or not, many feel guilty. They may have felt jealous and resentful about the baby during the pregnancy—perhaps even wished secretly that the baby would never come. If so, when they learn that their new brother or sister has a problem, they may feel that their wishes were responsible. Encourage them to ask questions, answer them in terms that they can understand, and be sure to explain that the problem is no one's fault.

Try not to blame yourself for what's happened, either. Except in cases where the birth defect is caused by the mother's use of drugs or alcohol during pregnancy, there is nothing that could have been done to cause an abnormality of this kind. Don't allow yourself to feel guilty or responsible. Guilt will only get in the way of the love and affection that are especially vital in these special circumstances.

As overwhelmed as you may be by the problems facing your family and your newborn, this child needs to receive all the nurturing and affection you would give any baby. It's easy to forget this during the first days of his life, when you are confronting many difficult decisions and feeling anxious, fearful, and disappointed. Yet this is precisely the time when touching, holding, and comforting are especially critical to the child and to you.

Coping with the Medical Necessities

Birth defects are so diverse, and require such different types of treatment, that it would be impossible to discuss them all in this section. Instead, we will look only at the medical management of the two most common problems, Down syndrome and spina bifida.

Down Syndrome

Approximately one out of every eight hundred babies is born with Down syndrome. Fortunately, with the use of amniocentesis, Down syndrome can be detected prenatally. This problem—which is caused by the presence of an extra chromosome—results in a number of physical abnormalities, including up-slanted eyes with extra folds of skin at the inner corners, flattening of the bridge of the nose, a large tongue, and a decrease in the muscle and ligament tone of the body.

A major serious effect of Down syndrome is mental retardation. All but a very small number of these children develop more slowly than average, though the extent of the delay can vary widely from one youngster to the next. Some seem to border on normal development, while others are severely retarded. However, even though children with Down syndrome may be retarded in development as children and young adults, most eventually are able to feed and dress themselves and to be toilet trained. Many, with special education, can learn job skills.

Early detection of Down syndrome is very important, since many babies with the disorder have related abnormalities of the heart, intestinal tract, and/or blood which require prompt treatment. Early detection also allows parents to adjust to the situation and gather support and information. Once suspected, the condition is confirmed by a blood test (it takes a few days to produce results). Since newborns with Down syndrome usually have no medical problems that require immediate treatment, most can leave the hospital after the normal newborn stay.

If you have a newborn with Down syndrome, your pediatrician may recommend a special early intervention program for you and your baby. If so, you should begin it as soon as possible. These programs apply specially designed therapies to help your child make the most of his developmental and physical capabilities.

You will probably hear about other types of "therapy" that are *not* proven or recommended, such as multivitamin ("orthomolecular") treatments and a system known as "patterning," which focuses on the child's behavior. These approaches receive a lot of media attention because they claim to have great success, but no long-term benefits have ever been proven for them. They also may delay proven methods of treatment and be very expensive. If you hear of any treatments that you think may help your child, always discuss them first with your pediatrician to see if they are valid before spending your money or trying them.

In addition to developmental delay, Down syndrome can result in physical problems as your child gets older. His growth should be closely watched, since extremely slow growth in height and/or excessive weight gain may indicate a lack of thyroid hormone, a problem that affects many youngsters with Down syndrome. Even without thyroid problems, chances are that he'll be shorter and weigh less than average for his age. Some children with Down syndrome also have heart problems that may require medication or surgery.

Another problem, which affects fifteen of every hundred of these children, is an abnormality in the ligaments of the neck that can cause serious spinal injury if the neck is extended (bent backward) during exercise. For this reason, consult your pediatrician for advice regarding the need for your child's neck to be X-rayed before he's allowed to participate in vigorous athletic activities (especially tumbling and gymnastics). If X-rays show this abnormality, his physical activities should be limited to movements that cannot cause injury.

For all its difficulties, raising a child with Down syndrome can be deeply rewarding. Children with this condition are usually loving and openly affectionate, and will thrive if nurtured and loved in return. Each small achievement they make is a triumph shared by everyone in the family.

Spina Bifida

Spina bifida occurs when the spinal bones fail to close properly during early formation. Spina bifida occurs less often than Down syndrome, or in about one in one thousand births. It is, however, the most common of the *physically* disabling birth defects. A parent who has one child with spina bifida has a greater chance (one out of a hundred) of having another. This increased frequency appears to be due to some combined effect of heredity and the environment. There are now tests available to screen for spina bifida early in pregnancy.

A newborn with spina bifida appears at first glance to be normal, except for a small sac protruding from the spine. However, the sac contains spinal fluid and defective nerves that lead to the lower body. Within the first few days, surgery must be performed to remove the sac and close the opening in the spine. Unfortunately, little can be done to repair the defective nerves.

Most babies with spina bifida develop further problems later on, including:

Hydrocephalus. Approximately seventy of every hundred children with spina bifida eventually develop hydrocephalus, or "water on the brain," caused by an excessive increase in the fluid that normally cushions the brain from injury. The increase occurs because the spina bifida defect blocks the path through which the fluid ordinarily flows. This condition is serious and, if not treated, may lead to death.

The pediatrician should suspect hydrocephalus if the baby's head is growing more rapidly than expected. The condition is confirmed by a computerized X-ray of the head, called a CT scan. If hydrocephalus is present, surgery will be necessary to relieve the fluid buildup.

Muscle weakness or paralysis. Because the nerves leading to the lower part of the body are defective, the muscles in the legs may be very weak or even paralyzed in children with spina bifida. Their joints also tend to be very stiff, and many babies with this disorder are born with deformities of the hips, knees, and feet. Surgery can be performed to correct some of these deformities, and the muscle weakness can be treated with physical therapy and special equipment such as braces and walkers. Many children with spina bifida eventually can stand and walk, though the learning process is often long and extremely frustrating.

Bowel and bladder problems. Often the nerves that control bowel and bladder function are destroyed or defective in children with spina bifida. As a result, these children are more likely to develop urinary tract infections and damage to the kidneys due to abnormal urine flow.

Bowel control also is a problem but usually can be accomplished by children with this disorder. It may, however, take a great deal of time, patience, careful dietary management (to keep stool soft), and the occasional use of suppositories or other bowel stimulants.

Infection. Parents of children who have spina bifida and hydrocephalus or urinary tract problems must be ever alert for signs of infection. Fortunately, the types of infections that occur in these cases usually can be treated effectively with antibiotics.

Educational and social problems. Seven out of ten children with spina bifida have developmental and learning disabilities requiring some sort of special education. Many need psychological counseling and tremendous emotional support in order to deal with their medical, educational, and social problems.

Parents of a child with spina bifida need more than one physician to manage their child's medical care. In addition to the basic care your pediatrician delivers, this disorder requires a team approach that involves neurosurgeons, orthopedic surgeons, urologists, rehabilitation experts, physical therapists, psychologists, and social workers. Many medical centers run special spina bifida clinics, which offer the services of all these health professionals in one location. Having all members of the team together makes it easier for everyone to communicate, and usually provides better access to information and assistance when parents need it.

Resources

Information and support for parents are available from various organizations.

The National Down Syndrome Congress
1800 Dempster Street
Park Ridge, Illinois 60068-1146
(1-800-232-NDSC)

The Spina Bifida Association of America
1700 Rockville Pike, Suite 540
Rockville, Maryland 20852

For information about birth defects, write:

The March of Dimes
1275 Mamaroneck Avenue
White Plains, New York 10605

Cerebral Palsy

Children with cerebral palsy have an abnormality in the area of the brain that controls movement and muscle tone. Many of these youngsters have normal intelligence, even though they have difficulty with motor control and movement. The condition causes different types of motor disability in each child. Depending on the severity of the problem, a child with cerebral palsy may simply be a little clumsy or awkward, or he may be unable to walk. Some children have weakness and poor motor control of one arm and one leg on the same side of the body (this is called hemiparesis). Many have problems in all four extremities, with the legs mostly involved: this is called diplegia. In some children the muscle tone generally is increased (called spasticity or hypertonia), while others are abnormally limp (called hypotonia). Speech may be affected as well.

Cerebral palsy frequently is caused by malformation or damage to the brain during pregnancy, delivery, or immediately after birth. Premature birth is associated with an increased risk of cerebral palsy. A baby can also get cerebral palsy from *severe* jaundice after birth, or later on in infancy from a brain injury or an illness affecting the brain. In most cases the cause is unknown.

Signs and Symptoms

The signs and symptoms of cerebral palsy vary tremendously because there are many different types and degrees of disability. The main clue that your child might have cerebral palsy is a delay in achieving the motor milestones listed in Chapters 5 through 12 of this book. Here are some specific warning signs.

In a Baby Over Two Months

- Head lags when you pick him up while he's lying on his back.

- He feels stiff.

- He feels floppy.

- When held cradled in your arms, he seems to overextend his back and neck—constantly acts as if he is pushing away from you.

- When you pick him up and hold him by the trunk with his legs down, his legs get stiff and they cross or "scissor" (after two to three months).

In a Baby Over Six Months

- He continues to have the asymmetrical tonic neck reflex (see page 137).

- He reaches out with only one hand while keeping the other fisted.

In a Baby Over Ten Months

- He crawls in a lopsided manner, pushing off with one hand and leg while dragging the opposite hand and leg.

- He scoots around on buttocks or hops on knees, but does not crawl on all fours.

If you have any concerns about your child's development, talk to your pediatrician at your routine visit. Because children's rates of development do vary so widely, it is sometimes difficult to make a definite diagnosis of mild cerebral palsy in the first year or two of life. As a result, there is the possibility that some young children may be identified inappropriately as having this problem though they later develop normally. Even when a firm diagnosis is made during these early years, it often is difficult to predict how severe the disability will be in the future. However, usually by three to four years of age there is enough information to predict accurately how a child will function in years to come.

Treatment

If your pediatrician suspects that your child has cerebral palsy, you will be referred to an early-intervention program. These programs are staffed by early childhood educators; physical, occupational, and speech and language therapists; nurses; social workers; and medical consultants. In such a program you'll learn how to become your child's own teacher and therapist. You will be taught what exercises to do with your infant, what positions are most comfortable and beneficial to him, and how to help with specific problems such as feeding difficulties. Through these programs you can also meet parents of other children with similar disabilities, and share experiences, concerns, and solutions.

The most important thing you can do for your child is to help him grow up feeling good about himself. When he is old enough to ask or understand, explain to him that he has a disability, and reassure him that he'll be able to make adjustments in order to succeed in life. Encourage him to perform the tasks he is ready for, but do not push him to do things at which you know he will fail. The professionals at early intervention centers can help you evaluate your child's abilities and teach you how to reach appropriate goals.

Do not make the mistake of searching for magical cures or undertaking controversial treatments. They will waste your time, energy, and money. Instead, ask your pediatrician, or contact the United Cerebral Palsy Association for information about resources and programs available in your area.

Associated Problems

Mental Retardation

It has been estimated that more than one half of children with cerebral palsy have problems with intellectual functioning (thinking, problem solving). Many are classified as mentally retarded, while others have average abilities with some learning disorders. Some have perfectly normal intelligence. (See also page 531.)

Seizures

One out of every three people with cerebral palsy has or will develop seizures. (Some start having them years after the brain is damaged.) Fortunately, these seizures can usually be controlled with anticonvulsant medications. (See also page 601.)

Vision Difficulties

Because the coordination of the eye muscles is often affected by the brain damage, more than three out of four children with cerebral palsy have strabismus, a problem with one eye turning in or out, with or without nearsightedness. If this problem is not corrected early, the vision in the affected eye will get worse and eventually will be lost permanently. This makes it extremely important to have your child's eyes checked regularly by your pediatrician. (See also *Strabismus,* page 558.)

Limb Shortening and Scoliosis

Of those children with cerebral palsy affecting only one side of the body, over half will develop a shortening of the involved leg and arm. The difference between the legs is rarely more than two inches, but an orthopedic surgeon should be consulted if shortening is noticed. Depending on the degree of difference between the legs, a heel or sole lift may be prescribed to fit into the shoe on the shorter side. This is done to prevent a tilt of the pelvis, which can lead to curvature of the spine (scoliosis) when standing or walking. Sometimes surgery is required to correct a serious degree of scoliosis.

Dental Problems

Many children with cerebral palsy have more than the average number of cavities. One reason may be that it is difficult for them to brush their teeth. However, they also have enamel defects more frequently than normal children, which make their teeth more susceptible to decay.

Hearing Loss

More than one fifth of children with cerebral palsy have a complete or partial hearing loss. This most often happens when the cerebral palsy is a result of *severe* jaundice at birth. If you find that your baby does not blink to loud noises or is not turning his head toward a sound by three to four months, or is not saying words by eighteen months, discuss it with your pediatrician. (See also page 529.)

Joint Problems

In children with spastic forms of cerebral palsy, it is often difficult to prevent "contracture," an extreme stiffening of the joints caused by the unequal pull of one muscle over the other. A physical therapist or physiatrist (doctor of physical medicine) can teach you how to stretch the muscles to try to prevent the onset of contracture.

Problems with Spatial Awareness

Over half the children with cerebral palsy affecting one side of the body cannot sense the position of their arm or hand on the affected side. (For example, when his hands are relaxed, the child cannot tell whether his fingers are pointing up or down without looking at them.) When this problem is present, the child rarely will attempt to use the involved hand, even if the motor disability is minimal. He acts as if it is not there! Physical or occupational therapy can help him learn to use the affected parts of his body, despite this disability.

Hearing Loss

Most children experience mild hearing loss when fluid accumulates in the middle ear in response to allergies or colds. This hearing loss is temporary. In many children, perhaps one in ten, fluid stays in the middle ear because of *ear infection* (see page 537). They don't hear as well as they should during the infections, and sometimes have delays in talking. Much less common is the permanent kind of hearing loss that always endangers normal speech and language development. This difficulty varies from mild or partial to complete or total.

Although they can occur at any age, the most serious effects come from hearing losses that are present from birth or develop during infancy and the toddler years. Hearing loss during this time demands immediate attention, because it directly affects the child's ability to understand and produce spoken language. Even a temporary severe hearing loss during infancy or early in the preschool years can make it very difficult for the child to learn proper oral language.

There are two main kinds of hearing loss:

Conductive hearing loss. When a child has a conductive hearing loss, there may be an abnormality in the structure of the outer ear canal or middle ear, or there may be fluid in the middle ear that interferes with the conduction of sound.

Sensorineural hearing loss (also called nerve deafness). This type of hearing impairment is caused by an abnormality of the inner ear or the nerves that carry sound messages from the inner ear to the brain. The loss can be present at birth or occur shortly thereafter. If there is a family history of deafness, the cause is likely to be inherited (genetic). If the mother had rubella (German measles), cytomegalovirus (CMV), or another infectious illness that affects hearing during pregnancy, the fetus could have been infected and lost hearing at that time. The problem also may be due to a malformation of the inner ear. The cause of severe sensorineural hearing loss is most often unknown. In such cases the probability that the hearing loss is genetic is high even when no other family members are affected. Future brothers and sisters of the child have a greatly increased risk of also being hearing impaired.

Hearing loss must be diagnosed as soon as possible, so that the child isn't delayed in learning language—a process that begins the day he is born. If you and/or your pediatrician suspect that your child has a hearing loss, insist that a formal hearing evaluation be performed promptly. Although some family doctors, pediatricians, and well-baby clinics can test for fluid in the middle ear—a common cause of hearing loss—they cannot measure hearing precisely. Your child should go to an audiologist, who can perform this service. He should also be seen by an ear, nose, and throat doctor (an otolaryngologist).

If your child is under age two, or is uncooperative during his hearing examination, he may be given a test called brain-stem evoked response audiometry. This allows the doctor to test your child's hearing without having to rely on his cooperation. This test may not be available in your immediate area because it is relatively new, but the consequences of undiagnosed hearing loss are so serious that your doctor may advise you to travel to where it can be done.

Treatment

The treatment of a hearing loss will depend on its cause. If it is a mild conductive hearing loss due to fluid in the middle ear, the doctor may simply recommend that your child be retested in a few weeks to see whether the fluid has cleared by itself. Use of antihistamines or decongestants is rarely an effective treatment for fluid in the middle ear, but it is often tried first. Antibiotics are of limited value unless the ear is infected (see *Ear Infection,* page 537) or unless your pediatrician is using them in a prophylactic (preventive) fashion.

If there is no improvement in hearing over a three-month period, the doctor may recommend drainage of the fluid through ventilating tubes, which are surgically inserted through the eardrum. This is a minor operation and takes only a few minutes, but the child must receive a general anesthetic for it to be done properly. Even with the tubes in place, future infections can occur, but the tubes help reduce the amount of fluid and decrease your child's risk of repeated infection. They also improve the hearing.

If a conductive hearing loss is due to a malformation of the outer or middle ear, a hearing aid may restore hearing to normal or near-normal levels. However, a hearing aid will work only when it's being worn. You must make sure it is on and functioning at all times, particularly in the very young child. Reconstructive surgery may be considered when the child is much older.

Hearing aids will not restore hearing completely to those with significant sensorineural

---

When to Call the Pediatrician

Hearing Loss—What to Look For

Here are the signs and symptoms that should make you suspect that your child has a hearing loss, and alert you to call your pediatrician.

- Your child doesn't startle at loud noises or turn to the source of a sound by three to four months of age.

- He doesn't notice you until he sees you.

- He concentrates on gargles and other vibrating noises that he can feel, rather than experimenting with a wide variety of vowel sounds and consonants. (See *Language Development* in Chapters 8 and 9.)

- Speech is delayed or hard to understand, or he doesn't say single words such as *dada* or *mama* by one year of age.

- He doesn't always respond when called. (This usually is mistaken for inattention or resistance, but could be the result of a partial hearing loss.)

- He seems to hear some sounds but not others. (Some hearing loss affects only high-pitched sounds; some children have hearing loss in only one ear.)

- He seems not only to hear poorly but also has trouble holding his head steady, or is slow to sit or walk unsupported. (In some children with sensorineural hearing loss, the part of the inner ear that provides information about balance and movement of the head is also damaged.)

hearing loss, but may help. There is no surgical treatment for children with sensorineural hearing loss.

Implantation of an electronic replacement for the inner ear in children and adults with hearing impairments has attracted a lot of publicity recently, but this procedure still is considered experimental. At best, these "cochlear implants" help a person to become aware of extremely loud sounds. They do not restore hearing nearly well enough for the child to learn spoken language without additional help, including hearing aids to amplify sounds, as well as special education, and parent counseling.

Parents of children with sensorineural hearing loss usually are most concerned about whether their child will learn to talk. The answer is that all children with a hearing impairment can be taught to speak, but not all will learn to speak clearly. Some children learn to lip-read well, while others never fully master the skill. But speech is only one form of language. Most learn a combination of spoken and sign language. Written language also is very important because it is the key to educational and vocational success. Learning excellent oral language is highly desirable, but not all people who are born deaf can master this. Sign language is the primary way deaf people communicate with one another, and the way many express themselves best.

If your child is learning sign language, you and your immediate family must also learn it. How else can you share life with your child? You must be able to teach him, discipline him, praise him, comfort him, and laugh with him. You should encourage friends and relatives to learn signing too. It is a lot of work, but it is also fun.

Today there is no reason for hearing impaired children to be isolated from people because of their hearing loss. With proper treatment, education, and support, these children will grow to be full participants in the world around them.

Mental Retardation

The term *mental retardation* is used when a child's intelligence and abilities to adjust to his surroundings are significantly below average and affect the way he learns and develops new skills. The more severe the retardation, the more immature a child's behavior will be for his age.

Intelligence in children over age two years generally is measured in terms of IQ (intelligence quotient). To determine IQ, the child is given tasks in a variety of areas to assess his problem-solving skills and other specific abilities. An average IQ score is 100, which is achieved when the child's mental age score is identical to the average score for his age group.

In some cases standard IQ tests are not accurate or reliable, because cultural or language differences or a physical handicap affect a child's understanding of the questions or his ability to respond appropriately. In such cases, different tests which measure the ability to function and reason in areas other than language, or which rely less on motor skills, should be used.

Signs and Symptoms

Generally, the more severe the degree of mental retardation, the earlier the signs are noticeable. However, even though such signs may be present, it may still be difficult to predict in young children the ultimate *degree* of retardation that will be present as the child grows. Children born with Down syndrome, for example (see page 524), can vary greatly in their ultimate level of mental retardation, from mild to severe.

When a baby is late in developing basic motor skills (such as holding his head up by himself by three to four months or sitting unsupported by seven to eight months), there also may be some associated mental disability. However, this is by no means always the case. Nor does normal motor development guarantee normal intelligence. Some children with mild to moderate degrees of mental retardation appear to have normal physical development during the first few years of life. In such cases the first sign of mental retardation may be a delay in language development or in learning simple imitation skills such as waving bye-bye or playing pat-a-cake.

In many cases of mild retardation, except for delays in speech, the young child may otherwise appear to be developing normally. Later, when he begins preschool or school, he may have difficulty performing academic skills at his grade level. He might have trouble completing puzzles, recognizing colors, or counting when his classmates already have mastered these tasks. Remember, however, children do develop at very different rates, and problems in school certainly are not always a sign of retardation. Developmental delays also can be caused by disorders such as hearing loss, vision problems, learning disabilities, or emotional difficulties.

When to Call the Pediatrician

If you are concerned about a delay in your child's development (see the sections on *Development* in Chapters 6 through 12), call your pediatrician, who will review your child's overall development and determine whether it is appropriate for his age. If the pediatrician is concerned, he will probably refer you to a pediatric developmental specialist, a pediatric neurologist, or a multidisciplinary team of professionals for further assessment. With older children, referral for formal psychological testing may be helpful. However, your pediatrician may suggest waiting awhile, to see if your child's rate of development improves or speeds up. This is more likely to happen if the child has been seriously ill, or if his pattern of development does not seem significantly delayed. If you remain worried despite your pediatrician's reassurances, ask for a referral to an appropriate specialist.

If you take your child to a developmental pediatrician or a pediatric neurologist, a variety of tests will be performed to determine the nature and cause of the problem. In addition to identifying what is wrong, these tests should help you discover some of your child's physical and intellectual strengths. Once the testing is completed, you should be given a full explanation of the problem, what (if anything) is known about its cause, what can be done to help your child, and generally what to expect in the future. Remember, especially when there are related physical disabilities such as those caused by cerebral palsy, it can be very difficult to make accurate predictions about how a young child with delayed development will function later in life.

Treatment

The main treatment for children with mental retardation is education and training. With proper instruction, a child who is classified as having *borderline* intelligence can be educated up to about a sixth-grade level; should be able to perform independently all activities of daily living, such as dressing, feeding, bathing, and toileting; can travel on his own; and can be employed, although he may need specialized vocational training. Most individuals with *mild* retardation can be educated to a fourth- or fifth-grade level and can learn to read and write, be relatively independent in daily activities, learn to travel, and hold a job. Adults with *moderate* retardation may read or write on a first- or second-grade level, can be trained to perform the activities of daily living , but need special transportation and employment in a sheltered setting. Although people with *severe* or *profound* retardation do not read or write, except in rare cases, and often are very dependent, they can be partially trained to dress, feed, and toilet themselves with assistance.

One of the most common questions parents ask is, "Will my child be able to function independently when he is older?" The answer to that question varies, depending on the degree of disability, the level of mental retardation, and whether the child has any additional problems.

Today, many adults with mental retardation live at home or in small, supervised group homes. The number of these group homes has increased markedly in the past decade, and they are an accepted presence in communities all over the United States. The residents of these facilities go out to programs, workshops, or jobs by day, attend community recreation facilities on weekends or evenings, and visit their families on holidays and at other times.

Prevention

There are only a few causes of mental retardation that can be treated medically and early enough to prevent significant disability. Among the more common ones are metabolic disorders such as phenylketonuria (PKU). If these conditions are detected soon after birth through the standard screening tests performed in the hospital nursery, they can be treated, and mental retardation will be prevented. Another condition that can cause mental retardation if not detected early in life is hydrocephalus (excess fluid causing increased pressure in the brain; see page 525). This usually is treated by draining the fluid to another part of the body to release the pressure and thereby prevent damage to the brain.

In many cases of mental retardation there is no clearly identifiable cause, and in the vast majority of cases, little, if anything, could have been done to prevent it. Unfortunately, some parents respond to this uncertainty by blaming themselves for their child's disability. Feelings of guilt about your child's retardation can lead you to make two very common mistakes: looking for magic cures and overprotecting your child. Despite claims you may hear, there are no complete cures for mental retardation, and a great deal of money or emotional energy can be wasted looking for one. It is much more important to invest your energy in coming to terms with your child's disability and helping him to develop his abilities to the maximum. Consult your pediatrician, local advocacy organizations such as the Association for Retarded Citizens, and other reputable professionals to find out what programs (such as the Special Olympics) are available in your community. Professional assistance can be extremely helpful. In the long run, however, you can be your child's most important advocate.

Overprotecting your child can result in more harm than good. Like any youngster, a child with a disability needs to be challenged in order to develop to his full potential. If you overprotect your child, you will prevent him from trying new things and you will limit his opportunities to expand his abilities. Help him make the most of the strengths he does possess. Set realistic objectives for him, and encourage him to reach them. Assist him if necessary, but let him do as much as possible on his own. You and your child will feel most rewarded when he reaches a goal by himself.

20

EARS, NOSE, AND THROAT

Colds/Upper Respiratory Infection

Your child probably will have more colds, or upper respiratory infections, than any other illness. In the first two years of life alone, most youngsters have eight to ten colds! And if your child is in day care, or if there are older school-age children in your house, he may have even more, since colds spread easily among children who are in close contact with one another. That's the bad news, but there is some good news, too: Most colds go away by themselves and do not lead to anything worse.

Colds are caused by viruses, which are extremely small infectious substances (much smaller than bacteria). A sneeze or a cough may directly transfer a virus from one person to another. The virus may also be spread indirectly, in the following manner:

1. A child or adult infected with the virus will, in coughing, sneezing, or touching his nose, transfer some of the virus particles onto his hand.

2. He then touches the hand of a healthy person.

3. This healthy person touches his newly contaminated hand to his own nose, thus introducing the infectious agent to a place where it can multiply and grow—the nose or throat. This soon gives rise to the symptoms of a cold.

4. The cycle then repeats itself, with the virus being transferred from this newly infected child or adult to the next susceptible one, and so on.

Once the virus is present and multiplying, your child will develop the familiar symptoms and signs:

- Runny nose (first, a clear discharge; later, a thicker, slightly colored one)

- Sneezing

- Slight fever (101–102 degrees Fahrenheit [38.3-38.9 degrees Celsius]), particularly in the evening

- Decreased appetite

- Red eyes

- Sore throat and, perhaps, difficulty swallowing

- Cough

- On-and-off irritability

- Slightly swollen glands

- *If there is pus on the tonsils, there may be a strep infection* (see page 547).

If your child has a typical cold without complications, the symptoms should gradually disappear after three to four days.

Treatment

An older child with a cold usually doesn't need to see a doctor unless the condition becomes more serious. If he is six months or younger, however, call the pediatrician at the first sign of illness. With a young baby, symptoms can be misleading, and colds can quickly develop into more serious ailments, such as bronchiolitis (see page 510), croup (see page 513), or pneumonia (see page 516). For a child older than six months, call the pediatrician if:

- The noisy breathing of a cold is accompanied by the nostrils' widening with each breath, or difficulty with moving breath in and out.

- The lips or nails turn blue.

- Clear mucus becomes thick and green.

- The child has a cough that just won't go away (for more than one week).

- He has pain in his ear (see *Ear Infection*, page 537).

- His temperature is over 102 degrees Fahrenheit (30.9 degrees Celsius).

- He is excessively sleepy or cranky.

Your pediatrician may want to see your child, or he may ask you to watch him closely and report back if he doesn't improve each day and is not completely recovered within one week from the start of his illness.

Unfortunately, there's no cure for the common cold. Antibiotics may be used to combat *bacterial* infections, but they have no effect on viruses, so the best you can do is to make your child comfortable. Make sure he gets extra rest and drinks extra or increased amounts of fluids. If he has a fever, give him acetaminophen. (Be sure to follow the recommended dosage for your child's age.) Never give him any other kind of cold remedy without first checking with your pediatrician. Over-the-counter treatments often dry the respiratory passages or make the nasal secretions even thicker. In addition, they tend to cause side effects such as drowsiness.

If your infant is having trouble nursing because of nasal congestion, clear his nose with a rubber suction bulb before each feeding. When doing so, remember to *squeeze the bulb part of the syringe first, gently stick the rubber tip into one nostril, then slowly release the bulb.* This slight amount of suction will draw the clogged mucus out of the nose, and should allow him once again to breathe and suck at the same time. You'll find that this technique works best when your baby is under six months of age. As he gets older, he'll fight the bulb, making it difficult to suction the mucus.

If the secretions in your baby's nose are particularly thick, your pediatrician may recommend that you liquefy them with saline nose drops, which are available without a prescription. Using a dropper that has been cleaned with soap and water and well rinsed with plain water, place two drops in each nostril fifteen to twenty minutes before feeding, and then immediately suction with the bulb. *Never use nose drops that contain any medication, since it can be absorbed in excessive amounts. Only use normal saline nose drops.*

Placing a cool-mist humidifier (vaporizer) in your child's room will also help keep nasal secretions more liquid and make him more comfortable. Set it close to him so that he gets the full benefit of the additional moisture. Be sure to clean and dry the humidifier thoroughly each day to prevent bacterial or mold contamination. *Hot water vaporizers are not recommended since they can cause serious scalds or burns.*

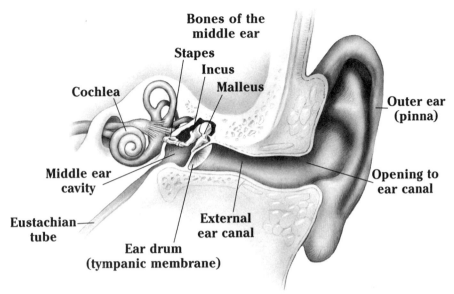

Bones of the
middle ear

Stapes

Incus

Malleus

Cochlea

Outer ear
(pinna)

Middle ear
cavity

Opening to
ear canal

Eustachian
tube

External
ear canal

Ear drum
(tympanic membrane)

Cross Section of Ear

One final note about medications: *Cough medicines or cough/cold preparations should never be considered in a child under three years of age unless prescribed by your pediatrician.* Coughing is a protective mechanism that clears mucus from the lower part of the respiratory tract, and ordinarily there's no reason to suppress it.

Prevention

If your baby is under three months old, the best prevention against colds is to keep him away from people who have them. This is especially true during the winter, when many of the viruses that cause colds are circulating in larger numbers. A virus that causes a mild illness in an older child or an adult can cause a more serious one in an infant.

If your child is in day care and has a cold, advise the teachers so that they can isolate him as much as possible from other children until his symptoms are gone. This may prevent him from spreading it to the others. Similarly, if your child would be in contact with children who have colds and you can conveniently keep him away from them, by all means do so.

Ear Infection

During your child's first few years of life, there's a significant chance that he'll get an ear infection when he has a cold. This happens because fluid often accumulates in the middle ear during colds and throat infections. If this fluid becomes infected by bacteria, it causes pain in the ear and inflammation of the eardrum. Doctors refer to this middle-ear infection as "acute otitis media."

Two thirds of all children have at least one ear infection by their second birthday. It's a particularly common problem among young children, because they are more susceptible to viral throat infections, and because their tiny eustachian tubes, which normally drain fluid from the middle ear, don't function properly during an infection.

Children under one year of age who spend time in group day-care settings get more ear infections than those cared for at home, primarily because they are exposed to more viruses. Also, infants who self-feed when lying on their backs are susceptible to ear infections since this allows formula to enter the eustachian tube, causing inflammation. Children in certain ethnic groups, notably Native Americans and Eskimos, seem to have more ear infections too. This may be due to the shape of the eustachian tube in these groups. Two things may explain the fact that, as your child enters school, his likelihood of getting a middle-ear infection will decrease: The growth of his middle-ear structures reduces the likelihood of fluid blockage; and the body's defenses against infection improve with age.

Signs and Symptoms

Ear infections are usually, but not always, painful. A child old enough to talk will tell you that his ear hurts; a younger child may pull at his ear and cry. Babies with ear infections may cry even more during feedings, because sucking and swallowing cause painful pressure changes in the middle ear. Lying down leads to changes in ear pressure, so a baby with an ear infection may have trouble sleeping. Fever is another warning signal; ear infections often are accompanied by elevated temperatures ranging from 100 to 104 degrees Fahrenheit (38 to 40 degrees Celsius).

You might see blood-tinged yellow fluid or pus draining from the infected ear. This kind of discharge means that the eardrum has developed a small hole (called a perforation). This hole usually heals by itself without complications, but you will want to describe the discharge to your pediatrician.

You may also notice that your child's hearing ability has decreased. This occurs because the fluid behind the eardrum interferes with sound transmission. But the hearing loss is almost always temporary; normal hearing will be restored once the middle ear is free of fluid. Occasionally, when ear infections recur, fluid may remain behind the eardrum for several weeks and continue to interfere with hearing. If you feel your child's hearing is not as good as it was before his ear became infected, consult your pediatrician. If you remain concerned, request a consultation with a hearing specialist.

Ear infections are most common during the cold and flu "season" of winter and early spring. When your child complains of pain in his ear during the summer, particularly after a day at the pool or the beach, he could be suffering from an infection of the *outer* ear canal, called swimmer's ear. This poses no danger to hearing, although it can be very painful and should be treated promptly. (See *Swimmer's Ear,* page 548.)

Treatment

Whenever you suspect an ear infection, call your pediatrician as soon as possible. In the meantime, follow these steps to make your child more comfortable.

- If he has a fever, cool him using the procedures described in Chapter 23, on fever.

- Give liquid acetaminophen in the dose appropriate for his age.

- Do not use eardrops unless your pediatrician authorizes them after seeing your child.

The pediatrician will look into your child's ears with a lighted instrument called an otoscope. To determine whether there is fluid in the middle-ear space behind the eardrum, the doctor may attach a piece of rubber tubing to the otoscope and blow gently into the ear to check for sensitivity and eardrum movement. This same test can be performed by an instrument that produces a printed report called a tympanogram. If a fever is present, the doctor will perform an overall examination to determine whether your youngster has any other problem in addition to an ear infection.

To treat infections of the middle ear, the doctor will prescribe an antibiotic. These are available as flavored liquids, tablets, capsules, and sometimes in chewable form. Eardrops are sometimes used to relieve pain or in certain infections that require direct application of the medication to the ear canal or eardrum area. These are prescription medications and should be used only on your pediatrician's advice. Unless your child's ear infections are associated with allergies, antihistamines and decongestants probably won't help.

An antibiotic is the primary treatment for an ear infection. Your doctor will specify the schedule for giving it to your child; it may be two, three, or four times a day. Follow the schedule precisely. As the infection begins to clear, some children experience a sense of fullness or popping in the ears; these are normal signs. There should be clear signs of improvement and disappearance of ear pain and fever within three days.

When your child starts feeling better, you may be tempted to discontinue the medication—but don't! Some of the bacteria that caused the infection may still be present. Stopping the treatment too soon may allow them to multiply again and permit the infection to return with full force. The only way to protect your child against a second infection is to give him the antibiotic for the full period recommended by your pediatrician (usually ten days).

Your pediatrician will want to see your child after the medication is gone, to check if any fluid is still present behind the eardrum. This can occur even if the infection has been controlled. This condition, known as "serous otitis," is extremely common: four to six out of every ten children still have some fluid two weeks after an ear infection is treated. In nine out of ten cases the fluid will disappear within two months without additional treatment.

On occasion an ear infection won't respond to the first antibiotic prescribed, so if your child's fever persists or he continues to complain of ear pain for more than three days, call the pediatrician. To determine if the antibiotic is working, your doctor—or a consulting ear, nose, and throat (ENT) specialist—may take a sample of the fluid from the ear. This is done by inserting a needle through the eardrum. If the analysis of this sample reveals that the infection is caused by bacteria resistant to the antibiotic your child has been taking, your pediatrician will prescribe a different one. In very rare instances, an ear infection may linger even though other drugs are used. In these cases, a child may be hospitalized so that antibiotics can be given intravenously, and the ear can be drained surgically.

Should a child with an ear infection be kept home? It won't be necessary if he's feeling well, as long as someone at day care or school can administer his medication properly. Talk with the staff nurse or your child's care-giver, and review the dosage and the times when it should be given. You also should check to be sure that storage facilities are available if the medication must be refrigerated. Medicine that doesn't require refrigeration should be kept in a locked cabinet separate from other items, and its container should be clearly identified with your child's name and the proper dosage.

If your child's eardrum is perforated, he'll be able to engage in most activities, although he may not be permitted to swim. Ordinarily, there's no reason to prevent him from flying in an airplane.

Prevention

Occasional ear infections cannot be prevented. In some children, ear infections may be related to seasonal allergies such as hay fever, which also can cause congestion and block the natural drainage of fluid from the ear to the throat. If your child seems to get ear infections more frequently when his allergies flare up, mention this to your pediatrician, who may suggest additional testing or prescribe antihistamines or decongestants.

And what about children who recover from one ear infection only to get another shortly thereafter? If your youngster has had several ear infections during the season, your pediatrician may suggest preventive antibiotics to reduce the chances of still another infection. These drugs usually are prescribed at a low dosage which is taken once or twice a day. Although ear infections may recur while this

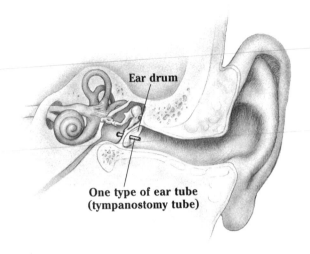

Ear drum

One type of ear tube
(tympanostomy tube)

monitoring his hearing to see if it improves with time. If the placement of ventilation tubes is proposed for your child, you should discuss his specific problem with your doctor so you fully understand the advantages and disadvantages.

If your child is given ventilation tubes, he should avoid getting water in his ears. Bathing rarely causes a problem, and swimming on the surface of the water is all right, though the doctor may want him to use custom-made earplugs. Even with earplugs, however, don't allow him to dive or swim underwater.

Repeated ear infections can be very trying for you and your child. However, rest assured that it is only a temporary problem that *will* improve as he gets older.

medicine is being taken, they usually happen much less often.

If your child continues to have ear infections despite preventive medication, he probably will be referred to an ear specialist, who may recommend that tiny ventilation tubes be inserted in the eardrum to drain the middle ear. These tubes may also be prescribed if fluid remains behind the eardrum more than three months after an ear infection, and hearing is impaired. While the tubes are in place, they usually restore hearing to normal and also prevent further infections.

The use of these tubes is controversial, because their long-term benefit is still unproven. Also, placing the tubes in the eardrum usually dictates the use of general anesthesia, requiring the child to be hospitalized for a few hours or overnight. For these reasons, the decision to insert the tubes may depend on a number of factors: the length of time ear fluid has been present, the number of recent ear infections, the degree of hearing loss, and the age of the child. For example, the operation might be justified for an eight- to twenty-four-month-old child—even if his hearing loss has been mild—since that age is very important for the development of speech and language. In an older child, the procedure might be postponed in favor of

Epiglottitis

The epiglottis is a tonguelike flap of tissue at the back of the throat. Ordinarily, it prevents inhalation of food and liquid into the windpipe when one swallows. In epiglottitis, a rare but serious condition, this structure becomes infected, usually by bacteria called *Haemophilus influenzae B*. This condition is life-

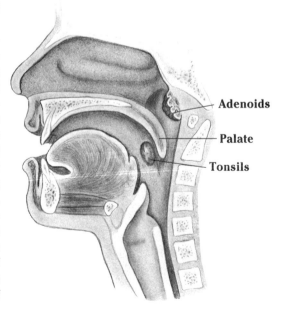

Adenoids

Palate

Tonsils

threatening, because when the epiglottis is swollen, it can block the trachea (windpipe) and interfere with normal breathing. Children between two and six years old are most susceptible to this problem.

The infection begins with a sore throat and a fever that usually is greater than 101 degrees Fahrenheit (38.3 degrees Celsius), and quickly makes your child feel very sick. His throat will become extremely sore. With each breath, he may make a harsh or raspy noise, called stridor. He may have such difficulty swallowing that he begins to drool. He probably will refuse to lie down and will be most comfortable sitting and leaning forward.

Treatment

If your child has an unusually sore throat and is drooling and/or breathing with difficulty, call your physician immediately. Because epiglottitis progresses so rapidly and has such serious consequences, do not attempt to treat it at home. After contacting your pediatrician, try to keep your child calm. Don't try to examine his throat or insist that he lie down. Also, avoid offering food or water, because that might cause vomiting, which often makes breathing even more difficult.

If you take your child to the pediatrician during the early stages of epiglottitis, the doctor may not be able to diagnose the disease. Don't hesitate to call back if the sore throat becomes much worse or drooling or stridor begins after you return home.

If your pediatrician suspects epiglottitis, you will be asked to take your child directly to the hospital emergency room. With the help of an anesthesiologist and an otolaryngologist (an ear, nose, and throat specialist), the doctor will examine your child's epiglottis. If it is severely inflamed, an anesthetic will be given and a tube will be inserted through the nose and into the trachea, bypassing the swelling and allowing your child to breathe comfortably again. In very severe cases, a tracheostomy (a breathing tube placed into the trachea through a small in-cision in the neck) may be necessary, but this is done much less often now than in the past. Your child also will be given antibiotics.

All these decisions are likely to be made very quickly, and you may feel shocked that your child needs such extreme treatment for what looks like a simple though severe sore throat. It's important to remember that epiglottitis progresses very rapidly and can become life-threatening if it goes untreated.

Prevention

A new vaccine is available to combat the bacteria that cause epiglottitis. Your child should receive the Hib conjugate vaccine at fifteen months. However, even if he has had the vaccine, consult your doctor if you know there has been an exposure to another child who has the infection. Your physician might want to take added precautions.

Hay Fever (Allergic Rhinitis/ Allergic Conjunctivitis)

If your child's nose starts to run and his eyes become itchy and red and swollen, but there are no other symptoms of a cold or an infection, he's probably having an attack of hay fever: an allergic reaction in the nose to irritants or "allergens" in the environment. There usually is no fever. The most common allergens that trigger hay fever are pollen, dust, mold, and animal dander.

Like other allergies, hay fever is often inherited, so if you or your spouse has it, your child is more likely to develop it. The symptoms may not appear immediately, however. Respiratory allergies are quite uncommon in children under age three.

It is sometimes difficult to tell the difference between a common cold and hay fever, because many of the symptoms are the same. Here are some of the signs of hay fever:

COMMON HOUSEHOLD ALLERGENS

Source	What to Do
Pets (dogs, cats, guinea pigs, and hamsters): There's no such thing as a "nonallergic" dog or cat, although some people are less sensitive to certain breeds. Contrary to popular belief, it's not the hair that causes the allergy; it's the *dander* (or skin sheddings) that become soaked in saliva or the urine of the animal.	Don't allow animals in the house. Unless your child is extremely allergic, he probably can play with pets outdoors, where he won't have such intensive exposure to the dander. When choosing your next pet, think in terms of snakes, lizards, fish, and frogs.
Mold (small pieces of plants that contain spores or seeds): Mold grows outdoors in cool, damp, dark places, such as in soil, grass, and dead leaves. Indoors, it's found in damp cellars, closets, attics, old mattresses, and pillows and blankets that haven't been aired out in a long time. It also grows in wicker baskets used as planters, on dried flowers, and on Christmas trees.	In bathrooms and other damp rooms, don't use carpeting and wallpaper. Also make sure your bathrooms have exhaust fans that work. Throughout the house, replace any carpet that's been saturated by a big water spill, or dry it completely. Avoid using vaporizers, humidifiers, and swamp coolers. You can destroy mold with several types of disinfectants, but be careful to store them in a safe place, away from curious toddlers. Sometimes a room air purifier will help remove mold spores and house dust. For some children, air conditioning helps, but for others it makes the allergy worse. Outdoors, prune and trim back large shrubs so that light comes into your house. Use nonorganic material for mulching and other landscaping tasks, and remove dead leaves and grass clippings as soon as possible.

- Sneezing, sniffling, stuffiness; itchy and runny nose (usually clear discharge)

- Tearing; itchy, red, or swollen eyes

- Coughing

- A crease on the top of the nose from frequent wiping

- Nosebleeds or sores around the outside of the nose (see *Nosebleeds,* page 545)

- Black rings (or "allergic shiners") under the eyes

- Constant red throat

- Snoring at night and breathing through the mouth because of stuffiness

- Fatigue (mostly from not sleeping well at night)

- Constant throat clearing

- Cough at night resulting from a postnasal drip

- Headache without fever

Source	What to Do
Dust: If your pediatrician tells you to get rid of the dust in your house, don't take offense. Every house has dust hiding in and on such things as upholstered furniture, mattresses, box springs, pillows, wool rugs, rug pads, stuffed animals, blankets, unfiltered furnace air, and feathers.	Make your whole house, and especially your child's bedroom, as dust-free as possible. To get started, empty his bedroom completely and clean it thoroughly. Get rid of wall-to-wall carpeting, replacing it with wooden or linoleum flooring. Cover the furnace or air-conditioner outlets with glass-fiber or cheesecloth filters, and clean wall or floor heating units weekly. Keep only one bed in the room, and cover the mattress and box spring (which should be scrubbed) with plastic dustproof casings. Use cotton or synthetic blankets, not quilts or comforters. Also rely on rubber or dacron pillows (not those filled with feathers, as they collect more dust). Clean the bedroom thoroughly at least once a week, airing it out on that day; then leave the doors and windows closed for the rest of the week. When you dust, use a damp or oiled cloth to avoid raising the dust.

| | If you use this room to sleep, it should be the most allergy-free one and should be used only for sleeping, not for playing. All toys and stuffed animals should be removed from the room. Keep your child away from attics and storage areas, too, and out of the house while extensive cleaning is being done. You might consider a room air filter, especially during high allergy seasons. |

If your child has nasal allergies, it might open the door to other problems as well. For example, he may get more sinus and ear infections (see *Sinusitis,* page 603, and *Ear Infection* page 537) or if the allergy causes eye irritation, he may be more susceptible to eye infections (see page 559). Since chronic hay fever can also interfere with sleep, your child may often be tired and cranky, which in turn can lead to behavior problems.

Treatment

Call your pediatrician when your child's allergy starts to interfere with sleeping, school, social, or other activities. To prevent or treat symptoms, the doctor probably will recommend an antihistamine, sometimes combined with a decongestant. You may have to try a few different antihistamines (or antihistamine-decongestant combinations) before you find the one that works well and has minimal side effects (see *Commonly Used Medi-*

How Allergies Develop

Each time an allergic person is exposed to an allergen, his immune system produces an antibody called IgE. The more of this antibody he makes, the more allergic he is. It may take weeks, months, or years to make a large amount of IgE, but once he has built up a reserve, his body will begin exhibiting allergic symptoms. When the allergen comes into contact with the IgE on the surface of the so-called mast cells (located in the nose, skin, eyes, intestinal tract, and bronchial tubes), these cells release chemicals—particularly one called histamine—that cause the allergic symptoms.

---

cations, page 658). The most common side effects of these medications are drowsiness, dry mouth, constipation, decreased appetite, and, occasionally, change in behavior. Sometimes an antihistamine will have a stimulating effect, causing unusual activity and/or nervousness in the child. For chronic treatment and to avoid the side effects of oral indications, your physician may recommend a prescription nose spray.

You may be tempted to use nasal-spray nose drops (which you can buy over the counter). Don't do this! Often these drops, after a few days' use, may actually cause *more* nasal congestion rather than less. Ironically, this increased congestion can be even more uncomfortable and difficult to treat than the original allergy. If your youngster's eyes are swollen, itching, and red, the physician may prescribe eyedrops in addition to antihistamines.

Perhaps the best thing you can do for your allergic child is to remove the sources of allergens from your home. Refer to the chart on page 542 for the most common culprits—and how to avoid them.

Herpes Simplex

Oral herpes is one of the most common viral diseases of childhood. This condition produces sores ("cold sores"), blisters ("fever-blisters"), and swelling of the inside of the mouth and lips. (When most people hear the word *herpes,* they associate it with genital herpes, the sexually transmitted disease; however, it is a different strain of this virus that usually causes cold sores in children.) Oral herpes is highly contagious, and is spread by direct contact, frequently by kissing. Most infants are protected by their mothers' antibodies up to about age six months, but they become susceptible after that.

When the virus is transmitted to a child for the first time, he is said to have "primary herpes." This may cause pain, swelling and reddening of the gums, and an increase in saliva, followed a day or two later by blisters inside the mouth. When the blisters break, they leave sore areas that take several days to heal. The child also may develop a mild fever and headaches, feel irritable, lose his appetite, and have swollen lymph glands for a week or so. Many children, however, have such mild symptoms that no one realizes they have the virus.

Unfortunately, once a child has had primary herpes, he becomes a carrier of the virus. This means that the virus, usually in an inactive state, remains within his system for years. However, during episodes of stress, injury to the mouth, sunburn, allergies, and fatigue, the virus can become reactivated, producing what's called "secondary herpes." This is a condition similar to but generally milder than the primary infection, and usually doesn't occur until later in childhood or adulthood.

Treatment

If your child complains of symptoms resembling those of herpes, consult your pediatrician. Primary herpes is not a serious illness, but it can make your child uncomfortable. The treatment which should be aimed at reducing this discomfort includes:

- Bed rest and sleep

- Plenty of cold fluids, including nonacidic drinks like apple or apricot juice

- Acetaminophen, if fever or excessive discomfort is present

- Mouth rinse or gargles prescribed by your pediatrician. These medications may contain a painkiller that will numb the areas affected by the mouth sores. Carefully follow the directions for use of these preparations

- Soft, bland, but nutritious diet

Never use any creams or ointments containing steroids (cortisone) if there is the slightest suspicion that the mouth sores are due to herpes. These preparations can make the viral infection spread.

Prevention

Direct contact is required to spread the herpes virus, so you should not let anyone with herpes blisters or sores kiss your child. Also, try to discourage your child from sharing eating utensils with other children. (This is more easily said than done.) If your child has primary herpes, keep him home to prevent other children from getting this infection from him.

Nosebleeds

Your child is almost certain to have at least one nosebleed—and probably many—during these early years. Some preschoolers have several a week. This is neither abnormal nor dangerous, but it can be very frightening. If blood flows down from the back of the nose into the mouth and throat, your child may swallow a great deal of it, which in turn may cause vomiting.

There are many causes of nosebleeds, most of which aren't serious. Beginning with the most common, they include:

- Colds and allergies: A cold or allergy causes swelling and irritation inside the nose and may lead to spontaneous bleeding.

- Trauma: A child can get a nosebleed from picking his nose, or putting something into it, or just blowing it too hard. It can also occur if he is hit in the nose by a ball or other object or falls and hits his nose.

- Low humidity or irritating fumes: If your house is very dry, or if you live in a dry climate, the lining of your child's nose may dry out, making it more likely to bleed. If he is frequently exposed to toxic fumes (fortunately, an unusual occurrence), they may cause nosebleeds too.

- Anatomical problems: Any abnormal structure inside the nose can lead to crusting and bleeding.

- Abnormal growths: Any abnormal tissue growing in the nose may cause bleeding. Although most of these growths (usually polyps) are benign (not cancerous), they should still be treated promptly.

- Abnormal blood clotting: Anything that interferes with blood clotting can lead to nosebleeds. Medications, even common ones like aspirin, can alter the blood-clotting mechanism just enough to cause bleeding. Blood diseases, such as hemophilia, also can provoke nosebleeds.

- Chronic illness: Any child with a long-term illness, or who may require extra oxygen or other medication that can dry out or affect the lining of the nose, is likely to have nosebleeds.

Treatment

There are many misconceptions and folk tales about how to treat nosebleeds. Here's a list of do's and don'ts:

Do

1. Remain calm. A nosebleed can be frightening, but is rarely serious.

2. Keep your child in a sitting or standing position. Tilt his head slightly forward. Have him gently blow his nose if he is old enough.

3. Pinch the lower half of your child's nose (the soft part) between your thumb and finger and hold it firmly for a full ten minutes. If your child is old enough, he can do this himself. *Don't release the nose during this time to see if it is still bleeding.*

Release the pressure after ten minutes and wait, keeping your child quiet. If the bleeding hasn't stopped, repeat step 3. If after ten more minutes of pressure the bleeding hasn't stopped, call your pediatrician or go to the nearest emergency room.

Don't

1. Don't panic. You'll just scare your child.

2. Don't have him lie down or tilt back his head.

3. Don't stuff tissues, gauze, or any other material into your child's nose to stop the bleeding.

Also call your pediatrician if:

- You think your child may have lost too much blood. (But keep in mind that the blood coming from the nose always looks like a lot.)

- The bleeding is coming only from your child's mouth, or he's coughing or vomiting blood or brown material that looks like coffee grounds.

- Your child is unusually pale, sweaty, or is not responsive. Call your pediatrician *immediately* in this case, and arrange to take your child to the emergency room.

- He has a lot of nosebleeds, along with a chronically stuffy nose. This may mean he has a small, easily broken blood vessel in the nose or on the surface of the lining of the nose, or a growth in the nasal passages.

If your pediatrician sees your child during a nosebleed, he will probably repeat the nose-holding routine described above. (If the nose is full of blood clots, it may be suctioned clean first.) The doctor may also use nose drops that constrict the blood vessels, or put cotton soaked with medication inside the child's nose. The doctor may decide to examine your child's nose with a special light to find the origin of the bleeding. If a blood vessel is found to be causing the problem, the doctor will touch that point with a chemical substance (silver nitrate) to stop the bleeding.

If the bleeding still cannot be controlled, the nose may have to be packed with gauze. Your child won't like this—it is uncomfortable—but it may be necessary. The packing is generally left in for at least twenty-four hours.

If your doctor thinks it's necessary to explore the cause of the bleeding further or to make sure your child didn't lose too much blood, a blood test will be ordered. It's extremely rare that a child will need a blood transfusion to replace lost blood.

Prevention

If your child gets a lot of nosebleeds, ask your pediatrician about using saline nose drops every day. This may be particularly helpful if you live in a very dry climate, or when the furnace is on. In addition, a humidifier or vaporizer will help maintain your home's humidity at a level high enough to prevent nasal drying. Also tell your child not to pick his nose. If he picks it at night or in his sleep, put him to bed wearing thin cotton gloves or socks over his hands and pinned to his pajama sleeve.

Sore Throat (Strep Throat, Tonsillitis)

The terms *sore throat, strep throat,* and *tonsillitis* are often used interchangeably, but they don't necessarily mean the same thing. Tonsillitis refers to tonsils that are inflamed. (See *Tonsils and Adenoids,* page 552.) When your child has a sore throat or a strep throat, the tonsils may be inflamed, or the inflammation may affect the surrounding part of the throat but *not* the tonsils.

In infants, toddlers, and preschoolers, the most frequent cause of sore throats is a viral infection. No specific treatment is required when a virus is responsible, and the child should get better over a three- to five-day period. Often, children who have sore throats due to viruses also have a cold at the same time. They may develop a mild fever, too, but they generally aren't very sick.

One particular virus (called Coxsackie), seen most often during the summer and fall, may cause the child to have a somewhat higher fever, more difficulty swallowing, and a sicker overall feeling. If your child has a Coxsackie infection, he also may have one or more blisters in his throat, which your pediatrician will look for during the examination. Infectious mononucleosis also can produce a sore throat, often with marked tonsillitis.

Strep throat is caused by a bacterium called *streptococcus.* To some extent, the symptoms of strep throat may depend on the child's age. Infants may have only a low fever and a thickened nasal discharge. Toddlers (ages one to three) may have a slight sore throat, a little fever, crankiness, decreased appetite, and swollen glands in the neck.

Older children with strep are often more ill; they may have an extremely painful throat, fever over 102 degrees Fahrenheit (38.9 degrees Celsius), swollen glands in the neck, and pus on the tonsils. It's important to be able to distinguish a strep throat from a viral sore throat, because strep infections must be treated with antibiotics.

Treatment

Any time your child has a sore throat that persists (not one that goes away after his first drink of juice in the morning), whether or not it is accompanied by fever, headache, stomachache, or extreme fatigue, you should call your pediatrician. That call should be made even more urgently if your child seems extremely ill, or if he has difficulty breathing or extreme trouble swallowing (causing him to drool). This may indicate a more serious infection (see *Epiglottitis,* page 540).

The doctor will examine your child and may perform a throat culture to determine the nature of the infection. To do this, he will touch the back of the throat and tonsils with a cotton-tipped applicator and then smear the tip onto a special culture dish that allows the strep bacteria to grow if they are present. The culture dish usually is examined twenty-four hours later for the presence of the bacteria.

Some pediatric offices now are doing quick-result strep tests which provide findings within minutes. However, when these tests are negative, their results still need to be confirmed with a twenty-four-hour culture. If the result of the culture is still negative, the infection usually is presumed to be due to a virus. In that case, antibiotics will not help and need not be prescribed.

If the test shows that your child does have strep throat, your pediatrician will prescribe an antibiotic to be taken by mouth or by injection. If your child is given the oral medication, it's very important that he take it for the full ten-day course, as prescribed, even if the symptoms get better or go away.

If a child's strep throat is not treated with antibiotics, or if he doesn't complete the treatment, the infection may worsen or spread to other parts of his body, causing more serious problems such as ear and sinus infections (see *Ear Infection,* page 537, and *Sinusitis,* page 603). If left untreated, a strep infection can also lead to rheumatic fever, a disease that affects the joints and the heart.

Prevention

Most types of throat infections are contagious, being passed primarily through the air on droplets of moisture, so it makes sense to keep your child away from people who have symptoms of this condition. However, most people are "contagious" before their first symptoms appear, so often there's really no practical way to prevent your youngster from contracting the disease.

In the past when a child had frequent sore throats, his tonsils might have been removed in an attempt to prevent further infections. But this operation, called a tonsillectomy, is much less often recommended today. (See *Tonsils and Adenoids,* page 552.) Even in difficult cases, where there is repeated strep throat, treatment with antibiotics is usually the best solution.

(See also *Swollen Glands,* page 550.)

Swimmer's Ear (External Otitis)

Swimmer's ear is an infection of the skin of the ear canal or outer ear which occurs most often after swimming or other activities that admit water into the ears. Swimmer's ear develops because moisture in the ear canal encourages the growth of certain bacteria and, at the same time, causes the skin that lines the ear canal to soften (like the white, swollen area that forms under a wet bandage). The bacteria then invade the softened skin and multiply there.

Children who play for long periods in warm water are most likely to get this infection. However, for reasons that are not clear, some children are more prone to it than others: Infants, for instance, rarely get swimmer's ear; preschool and school-age children develop it most often, usually in the summertime. At any age, injury to the canal, and conditions such as eczema (see page 631) and seborrhea (see page 630), can increase the likelihood of getting swimmer's ear.

With the mildest form of swimmer's ear, your child will complain only of itchiness or a plugged feeling in the ear, or—if he's too young to tell you what's bothering him—you might notice him sticking his finger in his ear or rubbing it with his hand. These symptoms often progress to dull pain, beginning any time from six hours to five days after being in the water. By this time the opening of his ear canal may become swollen and slightly red, and if you push on the opening or pull up on his ear, it will hurt him.

In more severe cases of swimmer's ear, the pain will be constant and intense, and your child may cry and hold his hand over his ear. The slightest motion, even chewing, will hurt a lot. The ear canal opening may actually be swollen shut, with a few drops of pus or cheesy material oozing out, and there may be a low-grade fever (rarely more than one or two degrees above normal). In the most serious infections the redness and swelling may spread beyond the ear canal to the entire outer ear.

Since swimmer's ear doesn't involve the middle ear or the hearing apparatus, any loss of hearing due to blockage of the canal is temporary. The infection rarely spreads beyond the canal into deeper tissues. If it does, however, this can be very serious and more intensive treatment is required.

Treatment

If your child has pain in his ear, or you suspect swimmer's ear, call your pediatrician. Although the condition usually isn't serious,

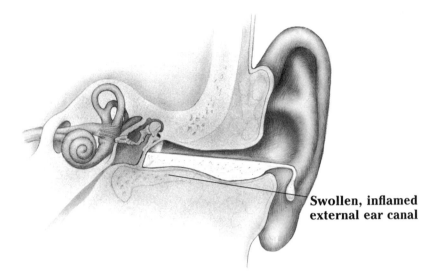

**Swollen, inflamed
external ear canal**

it still needs to be examined and treated by a doctor. Unfortunately, it's sometimes impossible for a parent to tell whether a young child suffers from swimmer's ear, a middle-ear infection, or some unrelated condition, so you should not attempt to treat it by yourself.

Until you see your pediatrician, you can help relieve your child's pain with acetaminophen, along with a heating pad (on low setting) or a hot-water bottle placed around the ear. For more severe pain in an older child you might also be able to use a codeine preparation, but you should check with your pediatrician before giving your child this or any medication other than acetaminophen.

Do *not* insert a cotton swab or anything else into the ear in an attempt to relieve itching or promote drainage; this will only cause further skin damage and provide additional sites for bacteria to grow. As a matter of fact, using cotton swabs to clean out a child's ears can, by itself, lead to infection of the ear canal. Using the swab can irritate the skin and remove the thin layer of earwax that's there to coat and protect the canal against moisture and bacteria.

At the pediatrician's office, the doctor will first examine the affected ear and then, perhaps, carefully clean out pus and debris from the canal. In mild cases this may be the only treatment your child needs, although most doctors also prescribe eardrops for five to seven days. The eardrops combat infection and thereby decrease swelling, which helps to relieve the pain. In order to be effective, however, eardrops have to be used properly. Here's how to administer them:

1. Lay your child on his side with his affected ear up.

2. Put the drops in so that they run along the side of the ear canal, permitting air to escape as the medicine flows in. You can gently move the ear to help the drops along.

3. Keep your child lying on his side for two or three minutes to make sure that the drops reach the deepest recess.

4. Put these drops in three or four times a day for the length of time prescribed. Occasionally oral antibiotics are also prescribed.

If the ear canal is too swollen for drops to enter, your pediatrician may insert a "wick"—a small piece of cotton or spongy material that soaks up the medicine and holds it in the canal. In this case, you'll need to resaturate the wick with the drops three or four times per day.

Rarely, a swimmer's ear infection is so severe that the child has to be hospitalized to receive intravenous antibiotic therapy and pain medication.

When your child is being treated for swimmer's ear, he should stay out of the water for about a week. However, he can take brief showers or baths daily and have his hair washed, as long as you sponge dry the ear canal afterward with the corner of a towel or a blow-dryer (on a very low setting, held away from the ear). Once that's done, put in more eardrops. Incidentally, swimmer's ear is not contagious, so you don't have to keep your child home from school or camp, as long as someone there can put in his drops properly.

Prevention

There's no need to try to prevent swimmer's ear unless your child has had this infection frequently or very recently. Under these circumstances, limit his stay in the water, usually to less than an hour. Then, when he comes out, remove the excess water from his ear with the corner of a towel, or have him shake his head. His ears should dry out for at least twenty minutes before he enters the water again.

As a preventive measure, many pediatricians recommend acetic acid eardrops. They are available in various preparations, some of which require a prescription. These are preferred over those that are "homemade." They usually are used in the morning, at the end of each swim, and at bedtime. Earplugs or a bathing cap sometimes help keep the ears dry and prevent this problem from occurring.

There's still another sound way to prevent swimmer's ear—by following the advice your grandmother gave you: "The only thing you should stick in your ear is your elbow." That goes for your child's ears too. Resist the temptation to clean out your child's ears with cotton swabs, your finger, or any other object. Your doctor can show you how to remove the wax from the ear with an ear bulb-syringe or an earwax softener.

Swollen Glands

Lymph glands (or lymph nodes) are an important part of the body's defense system against infection and illness. These glands normally contain groups of cells, called "lymphocytes," which act as barriers to infection. The lymphocytes produce substances called antibodies that destroy or immobilize infecting cells or poisons. When lymph glands become enlarged or swollen, it usually means that the lymphocytes have increased in number due to an infection or other illness, and that they are being called into action to produce extra antibodies. Rarely, swollen glands, particularly if long lasting and without other signs of inflammation, such as redness or tenderness, may indicate a tumor.

If your child has swollen glands, you'll be able to feel them or actually see the swelling. They also may be tender to the touch. Often, if you look near the gland, you can find the infection or injury that has caused it to swell. For example, a sore throat will often cause

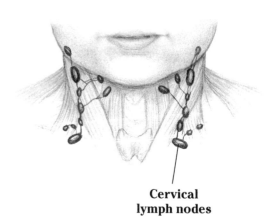

**Cervical
lymph nodes**

Common Causes of Swollen Glands

- Swollen glands in the front or sides of the neck are usually caused by an inflamed or sore throat, most often caused by a virus, but sometimes due to strep bacteria. (See *Sore Throat*, page 547.) At times, swollen glands in the back of a child's neck may mean that there is (or has been) an infection of the scalp. Occasionally a swollen gland in the neck area is mistaken for mumps (see page 600). However, this disease usually causes swelling of the parotid gland, which is located on the jaw in front of the ear and does not extend down to the neck.

- Swollen glands under the jawbone may be caused by infection in the cheek or gum or a tooth.

- Although slight swelling of the glands at the lower back of the head is often normal, it could also indicate, particularly if the glands are large and tender, that the child has a viral illness or infection.

- Swollen glands occurring only in the groin usually are a sign of an infection in the leg.

- Swollen glands in the underarm typically indicate an infection on the arm or hand on the same side as the swelling.

- Swollen glands all over the body are usually related to a general illness, such as a viral infection.

- Scratches from cats may result in swollen glands near the site of the break in the skin or even further away, depending on the location of the glands normally draining that body area.

- Swollen glands above the collarbone may be evidence of an infection or even a tumor within the chest, and should be examined by a physician as soon as possible.

---

glands in the neck to swell, or an infection on the arm will produce swollen glands under the arm. Sometimes the illness may be a generalized one, such as those caused by a virus, in which case many glands might be slightly swollen.

Treatment

In the vast majority of cases, swollen glands are not serious. Lymph node swelling usually disappears after the illness that caused it is gone. The glands gradually return to normal over a period of weeks. You should call the pediatrician if your child shows any of the following:

- Lymph glands swollen for more than three days

- Fever higher than 101 degrees Fahrenheit (38.3 degrees Celsius)

- Glands that appear to be swollen throughout the body

- Glands that enlarge rapidly, or the skin overlying them turning red or purple

As with any infection, if your child has a fever or is in pain, you can give him acetaminophen in the appropriate dosage for his weight and age until you can see the pediatrician. When you call, your doctor probably will ask you some questions to try to determine the cause of the swelling, so it will help if you do a little investigating beforehand. For instance, if the swollen glands are in the jaw or neck area, check if your child's teeth are tender or his gums are inflamed, and ask him if there is any soreness in his mouth or throat. Mention to your doctor any exposure your child has had to animals (especially cats), or wooded areas. Check as well for any recent animal scratches, tick bites, or insect bites or stings that may have become infected.

The treatment for swollen glands will depend upon the cause. If there's a specific bacterial infection in nearby skin or tissue, antibiotics will clear it, allowing the glands gradually to return to their normal size. If the gland itself has an infection, it may require not only antibiotics but also warm compresses to localize the infection, then surgical drainage. If this is done, the material obtained from the wound will be cultured to determine the exact cause of the infection. This will help the doctor choose the most appropriate antibiotic.

If your pediatrician cannot find the cause of the swelling, or if the swollen glands don't improve after antibiotic treatment, further tests will be needed. For example, infectious mononucleosis might be the problem if your child has a fever and a bad sore throat (but not strep), is very weak, and has swollen (but not red, hot, or tender) glands. Special tests can confirm this diagnosis.

If the cause of prolonged swelling of lymph nodes cannot be found in any other way, it may be necessary to perform a biopsy (remove a piece of tissue from the gland) and examine it under a microscope. In rare cases this may reveal a tumor or fungus infection, which would require special treatment.

Prevention

The only swollen glands that are preventable are those that are caused by bacterial infections in the surrounding tissue. Proper cleansing of all wounds (see *Cuts and Scrapes,* page 455) and early antibiotic treatment in cases of suspected infection are the key to avoiding involvement of the lymph nodes.

Tonsils and Adenoids

If you look into your child's throat, you will see a reddish, oval-shaped mass on each side. These are the tonsils. They produce antibodies during periods when the body is fighting infection. The adenoids cannot be seen unless you use a dentist's mirror, for they lie in the space between the back of the nose and the throat. If the adenoids or the tonsils become very large, breathing problems or difficulty swallowing may result.

While it is common for preschoolers and young children to have large adenoids, no one really knows why they enlarge. The condition may sometimes be caused by infection associated with frequent colds or allergies.

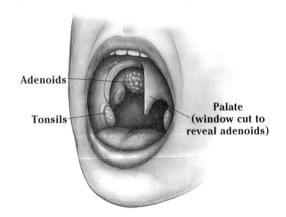

Adenoids

Tonsils

Palate
(window cut to
reveal adenoids)

Other children's adenoids are large at birth or they increase in size during the first year of life without any signs of recurring infection.

When your child's tonsils are swollen you often can tell by simply looking and listening. His voice may change slightly, as if he's talking around a large object in his throat—which he is! Then, if you look into his throat, you will see that the tonsils are larger and perhaps redder than usual.

It is not as easy to tell when your child's adenoids are enlarged. He might complain that his nose feels stuffy or that he can't smell very well, or you might notice that he seems to breathe through his mouth a lot. Most children with enlarged adenoids do not complain, however, because they are used to the problem. Except in extreme cases, swollen adenoids rarely cause any other health difficulties.

Occasional nasal obstruction caused by swollen adenoids is not something to worry about. The symptoms generally disappear once the infection or allergic reaction is over. *Persistent* swelling, however, can become a problem. You should suspect persistently swollen adenoids if:

- Your child tends to breathe through his mouth most of the time instead of his nose.

- His nose sounds blocked when he talks. (In extreme cases, the word *money* might sound like "buddy.")

- He breathes noisily by day and snores at night.

- He stops breathing for a moment or two at night while snoring or breathing noisily. (This condition, called "sleep apnea," usually doesn't cause the child to wake up.)

In extreme cases, your child may have such difficulty breathing that it interferes with the normal exchange of oxygen and carbon dioxide in his lungs. This is very rare, but important to recognize. If your child has severe breathing difficulty, seems drowsy during waking hours, and lacks energy despite what

should have been adequate amounts of sleep, consult your pediatrician.

Treatment

If your child shows the signs and symptoms of enlarged tonsils or adenoids, and doesn't seem to be getting better over a period of weeks, mention it to your pediatrician. If the doctor decides that there is *significant* tonsil or adenoid enlargement, he will recommend one of several courses of treatment:

Watching and Waiting

If you have only just noticed the symptoms, the doctor may delay further action until he is sure there's an ongoing problem. Often, enlarged tonsils or adenoids simply get smaller by themselves. However, the longer the swelling continues, the more likely it is to need treatment.

Treatment with Antibiotics

Your pediatrician may decide to give your child antibiotics in an attempt to eliminate any infection that might be causing the swelling.

Diagnosis and Treatment of Allergies

Sometimes, preventing or controlling allergy attacks will cause the enlarged adenoids to become smaller over a period of months.

Surgery to Remove Tonsils and/ or Adenoids (Tonsillectomy and Adenoidectomy)

Although these two operations (often combined and called T & A) were done almost routinely in the past and remain the most common major operations performed on children, it was not until recently that their long-term effectiveness has been adequately tested. In light of current studies, and in view of the risks that accompany any operation, today's physicians are much more cautious in recommending these procedures.

The American Academy of Pediatrics recommends that surgery be performed under the following conditions:

1. If your child has so much blockage from his tonsils and/or adenoids that it interferes with the normal exchange of carbon dioxide and oxygen in his lungs. (One sign of this may be periods of several seconds when breathing actually stops during sleep.)

2. If your child's tonsils are so enlarged that he has significant difficulty swallowing or breathing, or both. (This warrants tonsillectomy only.)

3. If the enlarged adenoids cause extreme discomfort in breathing and severe distortion of speech. (An adenoidectomy alone is recommended.)

Surgery is considered "reasonable" but not "urgent" under these conditions:

1. If your child has seven episodes of severe sore throat accompanied by strep infection or other signs of substantial illness in one year; or five such episodes in each of two years; or three in each of three years. Signs of "substantial illness" would include a fever of 101 degrees Fahrenheit (38.3 degrees Celsius) or higher, enlarged or tender lymph nodes in the neck (swollen glands), or a coating of pus on the tonsils or throat. (See *Sore Throat,* page 547, *Swollen Glands,* page 550.)

2. If there is an infection severe enough to cause a pocket of pus (an abscess) around or behind the tonsil.

3. Evidence of tonsillitis that does not clear completely over a six-month period despite antibiotic treatment.

4. Tonsils or adenoids so large that the child has difficulty swallowing or breathing or breathes through his mouth a lot, and snores loudly when asleep. (This may or may not include momentary episodes of sleep apnea.)

5. Chronically (for a minimum of six months) enlarged or tender cervical lymph nodes (the nodes below the angle of the lower jaw) despite antibiotic treatment.

6. Ear infections (see page 537) that continue to recur despite treatment with ventilation tubes.

21

EYES

Your child relies on the visual information he gathers to help him develop throughout infancy and childhood. If he has difficulty seeing properly, he may have problems in learning and relating to the world around him. For this reason it is important to detect eye deficiencies as early as possible. Many vision problems can be corrected if treated early but become much more difficult to care for later on.

Your infant should have his first eye examination by a pediatrician at birth to check for problems that may be present then. Routine vision checks should then be part of every visit to the pediatrician's office. If your family has a history of serious eye diseases or abnormalities, your pediatrician may refer your baby to an ophthalmologist (an eye specialist with a medical degree) for an early examination and follow-up visits if necessary.

If a child is born prematurely, he will be checked for a vision-threatening condition called "retinopathy of prematurity." This is especially true if the baby required oxygen over a prolonged period of time during the early days of life. While this condition cannot be prevented, in most cases—if detected early—it can be treated successfully. All-

neonatologists are aware of the threat of retinopathy and will advise parents of the necessity for ophthalmological evaluations. Parents should also be advised that all premature children are at greater risk for developing astigmatism, myopia, and strabismus and that they therefore should be screened periodically throughout childhood.

How much does a newborn baby see? Until fairly recently it was thought that the newborn infant could see very little; however, the information now available indicates that even during the early weeks of life, an infant can see light and shapes and can detect movement. Far vision remains quite blurry, with the optimal focal length being 8 to 15 inches, roughly the distance from his eyes to yours as you are nursing or feeding your baby.

Until your baby learns to use both eyes together, his eyes may "wander," or move randomly. This random movement should be decreasing by two to three months of age. Around three months of age, your baby will probably focus on faces and close objects and follow a moving object with his eyes. By four months of age, your baby should be using his vision to detect various objects close to him, which he will probably reach for and grasp. By six months of age the baby should be able to

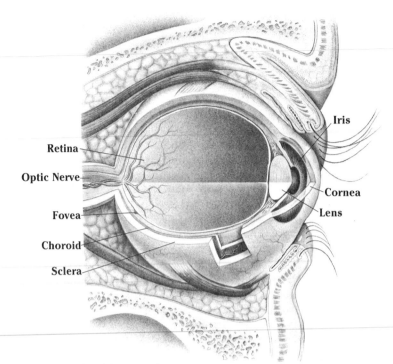

Iris

Retina

Optic Nerve

Cornea

Fovea

Lens

Choroid

Sclera

The Eye

visually identify and distinguish between objects.

Between one and two years of age, your baby's ability to see develops rapidly, so that the average two-year-old can see at approximately the 20/60 level. Between ages three and five years, the child reaches the 20/40 level, and by ages seven to nine, the child with normal vision will reach the adult visual acuity level of 20/20.

By the time a child is 14, his visual and visual-motor systems are fully developed. At this point, many eye and vision problems can no longer be reversed or corrected. This is why early detection and treatment of eye problems in children is so important and why your pediatrician will examine your baby's eyes at every routine physical examination.

If regular eye checks during pediatric visits indicate that your baby's eyes are developing normally, he should not need more formal testing until three to four years of age. By that

age, most children can follow directions and describe what they see, so testing is much more reliable. Your pediatrician may use the E-game vision screen or similar testing which enables him to estimate your child's visual acuity in reportable terms. As visual acuity should have reached the 20/40 level, any child with less than 20/40 vision should be referred to an ophthalmologist to determine the cause of the visual deficiency.

Your pediatrician's screening will also check for any evidence of eye disease and will evaluate the alignment of your child's eyes to make sure both eyes are working together.

When to Call the Pediatrician

Routine eye checks can detect hidden eye problems, but occasionally you may notice obvious signs that your child is having trouble seeing or that his eyes are not normal.

Notify the pediatrician if your child shows any of the following warning signs.

- Persistent (lasting more than twenty-four hours) redness, swelling, crusting, or discharge in his eyes or eyelids

- Excessive tearing

- Sensitivity to light

- Eyes that look crooked or crossed, or that don't move together

- Head held in an abnormal or tilted position

- Frequent squinting

- Drooping eyelids

- Pupils of unequal size

- Continuous eye-rubbing

- Eyes that "bounce" or "dance"

- Inability to see objects unless he holds them close

- Eye injury (see page 563)

- Cloudy cornea

You also should take your child to the pediatrician if he complains of any of the following:

- Seeing double

- Frequent headaches

- Dizziness

- Nausea after doing close-up eye work (reading, television)

- Inability to see clearly

- Itching, scratching, or burning eyes

- Difficulty with color vision

Depending on the symptoms your child displays, the pediatrician will probably check for vision difficulties and/or some of the other problems discussed in the remainder of this chapter.

Vision Difficulties Requiring Corrective Lenses

Nearsightedness

The inability to see distant objects clearly is the most common visual problem in young children. This inherited trait occasionally is found in newborns, especially premature infants, but it's more often detected after two years of age.

Contrary to popular belief, reading too much, reading in dim light, or poor nutrition cannot cause or affect nearsightedness. It's usually the result of an eyeball that's longer than average. Less frequently, it's due to a change in the shape of the cornea or lens.

The treatment for nearsightedness is corrective lenses—either eyeglasses or contact lenses. Keep in mind that when your child grows rapidly, so does his eye, so he may need new lenses as often as every six months. Nearsightedness usually worsens very rapidly for several years, and then stabilizes before or during adolescence.

Farsightedness

This is a condition in which the eyeball is shorter than average, making it difficult for the lens to focus on nearby objects. Most children are actually born farsighted, but as they grow, their eyeballs get longer and the farsightedness diminishes. Glasses or contact lenses are rarely needed unless the condition is excessive. If your child has eye discomfort or frequent mild headaches related to prolonged reading, he may be suffering from a severe degree of farsightedness, and should be examined by your pediatrician or pediatric ophthalmologist.

Astigmatism

Astigmatism is an uneven curvature of the surface of the cornea and/or lens. If your child has an astigmatism, his vision may be blurred. Astigmatism can be corrected with either glasses or contact lenses.

Strabismus

Strabismus is a misalignment of the eyes caused by an imbalance in the muscles controlling the eye.

A newborn baby's eyes commonly and normally wander. However, within a few weeks he learns to move his eyes together, and the wandering should disappear within a few months. If this intermittent wandering continues, or if your baby's eyes don't turn in the same direction (if one turns in, out, up, or down), the muscles controlling the eye movement on one side may be weaker than on the other. This condition, called strabismus, makes it impossible for the eyes to focus on the same point at the same time.

If your child is born with strabismus, it's important for his eyes to be realigned early in life so he can focus them together on a

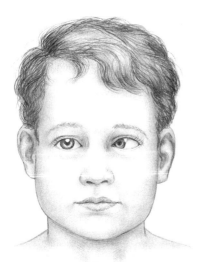

**Left eye
turning inward**

single object. Eye exercises alone cannot accomplish this, so the treatment usually involves eyeglasses, eyedrops, or surgery.

If your child needs an operation, it is frequently done between six and eighteen months of age. The surgery is usually safe and effective, although it's common for a child to need more than one procedure. Even after surgery, your youngster still may need glasses.

Some children look as though they have strabismus because of the way their faces are structured, but in fact their eyes are perfectly aligned. These children may have a flat nasal bridge and broad skin folds alongside the nose, which can distort the appearance of the eyes. This is called **pseudostrabismus** (meaning "false eyeturn") or **epicanthus.** The child's vision is not affected, and in most cases, as the child grows and the nasal bridge becomes more prominent, the child loses the pseudostrabismic appearance.

Because of the importance of early diagnosis and treatment of the true eyeturn (or true strabismus), if you have any suspicion that your baby's eyes may not be perfectly aligned and working together, it should be brought to the attention of your pediatrician, who can best determine whether your baby has an actual problem.

Strabismus may be present at birth (congenital strabismus) or it may develop later in childhood (acquired strabismus). Strabismus may develop if your child has another visual impairment, sustains an eye injury, or develops cataracts. The sudden onset of strabismus should always be reported to your pediatrician immediately. Although very rare, it may indicate the development of a tumor or other serious nervous system problem. In all cases, it is important to diagnose and treat strabismus as early in your child's life as possible. If an eyeturn is not treated early, the child may never develop the ability to use both eyes together (binocular vision); and if both eyes are not used together, it is common for one to become "lazy," or amblyopic.

Amblyopia

Amblyopia is a fairly common eye problem that develops when a child has one eye that doesn't see well or is injured, and begins to use the other eye almost exclusively. The idle eye then relaxes and becomes even weaker. In general, the problem must be detected by the age of three in order to treat and successfully restore normal vision in the affected eye by age six. If this situation persists for too long (past the age of five or six years), vision may be lost permanently in the unused eye.

Once an ophthalmologist corrects the problems in the unused eye, your child may need to wear a patch over the "good" eye for periods of time. This forces him to use—and strengthen—the eye that has become "lazy." Patching therapy will be continued for as long as necessary to bring the weaker eye up to its potential. This could take weeks, months, or even up to age nine or older. As an alternative to the patch, the ophthalmologist might prescribe eyedrops to blur vision in the good eye, thereby forcing your child to use the amblyopic eye.

Eye Infections

If the white of your child's eye and the inside of his lower lid become red, he probably has a condition called conjunctivitis. Also known as "pink eye" or "red eye," this inflammation usually signals an infection, but may be due to other causes such as an irritation, an allergic reaction, or (rarely) a more serious illness. It's often accompanied by tearing and discharge, which is the body's way of trying to heal or remedy the situation.

If your child has a red eye, he needs to see the pediatrician as soon as possible. The doctor will make the diagnosis and prescribe the necessary medication, and also will show you how to cleanse the eyelids. *Never put previously opened medication or someone else's eye medication into your child's eye. It could cause serious damage.*

In the newborn baby serious eye infections may result from exposure to bacteria during passage through the birth canal—which is why all infants are treated with antibiotic eye ointment or drops in the delivery room. Such infections must be treated early to prevent serious complications. Eye infections that occur after the newborn period may be unsightly, because of the redness of the eye and the yellow discharge that usually accompanies them, and they may make your child uncomfortable, but they are rarely serious. Several different viruses, or occasionally bacteria, may cause them, and topical antibiotics (eyedrops prescribed by your pediatrician) are the usual treatment.

Eye infections typically last up to one week and may be contagious. Except to administer drops or ointment, you should avoid direct contact with your child's eyes or drainage from them until the medication has been used for several days and there is evidence of clearing of the redness. Carefully wash your hands before and after touching the area around the infected eye. If your child is in a day-care or nursery-school program, you should keep him home until the eyes are no longer red.

Eyelid Problems

Droopy eyelid (ptosis) may appear as an enlarged or heavy upper lid; or, if it is very slight, it may be noticed only because the affected eye appears somewhat smaller than the other eye. Ptosis usually involves only one eyelid, but both may be affected. Your baby may be born with a ptosis, or it may develop later. The ptosis may be partial, causing your baby's eyes to appear slightly asymmetrical; or it may be total, causing the affected lid to completely cover the eye. If the ptotic eyelid covers the entire pupillary opening of your child's eye, or if the weight of the lid causes the cornea to assume an irregular shape (astigmatism), it will threaten normal vision development and must be corrected as early as possible. If vision is not threatened, surgical intervention, if necessary, is usually delayed until the child is four or five years of age, when the eyelid and surrounding tissue are more fully developed and a better cosmetic result can be obtained.

Most **birthmarks** and growths involving the eyelids of the newborn or young child are benign; however, because they may increase in size during the first year of life, they sometimes cause parents to become concerned. Most of these birthmarks and growths are not serious and will not affect your child's vision. Many decrease in size after the first year of life and eventually disappear entirely without treatment. However, any irregularity should be brought to the attention of your child's pediatrician so that it can be evaluated and monitored.

Some children are born with or develop **tumors** that can impair eyesight. In particular, a flat, purple-colored skin tumor, if it involves the child's upper eyelid, may put the child at risk for glaucoma. Any child having such a mark should be examined periodically by an ophthalmologist.

Small dark moles, called **nevi**, on the eyelids or on the white part of the eye itself rarely cause any problems or need to be removed. Once evaluated by your pediatrician, these marks should only cause concern if they change in size, shape, or color.

Small, firm, flesh-colored bulges on your child's eyelids or underneath the eyebrows are usually **dermoid cysts**. These are noncancerous tumors which are usually present from birth. Dermoids will not become cancerous if not removed; however, because they tend to increase in size during puberty, their removal during preschool years is preferred in most cases.

Two other eyelid problems—**chalazions** and **styes**—are common, but not serious. A chalazion is a cyst resulting from an infection of an oil gland, usually in the middle of the underside of the lid. This can lead to infection and swelling of the lid. A stye is a bacterial infection of the cells surrounding the sweat glands or hair follicles on the *edge* of the lid. Call your pediatrician regarding treatment of these conditions. He will probably tell you to apply warm compresses directly to the eyelid for twenty or thirty minutes three or four times a day until the signs of infection are gone. The doctor may want to examine your child before prescribing additional treatment, such as an antibiotic ointment or drops.

Once your child has had a stye or chalazion, he's more likely to get them again. When chalazions occur repeatedly, it's sometimes necessary to perform lid scrubs to reduce the bacterial colonization of the eyelids and open the oil gland pores.

Impetigo is a very contagious bacterial infection that may occur on the eyelid. Your pediatrician may advise you on how to remove the crust from the lid, and then prescribe an eye ointment and oral antibiotics.

Tear Production (or Lacrimal) Problems

Tears play an important role in maintaining good eyesight by keeping the eyes wet and free of particles, dust, and other substances

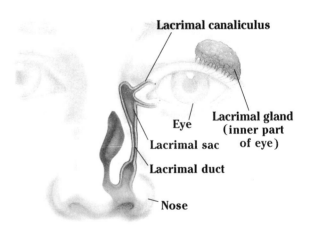

Lacrimal canaliculus

Eye

Lacrimal gland (inner part of eye)

Lacrimal sac

Lacrimal duct

Nose

that might cause injury or interfere with normal vision. The so-called lacrimal system maintains the continuous production and circulation of tears, and depends on regular blinking to propel tears across the surface of the eye, finally draining into the nose.

This lacrimal system develops gradually over the first three or four years of life. Thus, while a newborn will produce enough tears to coat the surface of the eyes, it probably will be about seven to eight months after birth before he "cries real tears."

Blocked tear ducts, which are very common among newborns and young babies, can cause the appearance of excessive tearing in one or both eyes, because the tears run down the cheek instead of draining through the duct and into the nose and throat. In newborns, blocked tear ducts usually occur when the membrane covering them at birth fails to disappear. Your pediatrician will demonstrate how to massage the tear duct. He also may recommend the use of barely warm compresses and, if there is infection, antibiotic drops or ointment. He'll also show you how to clean the eye with moist compresses to remove all secretions. Until the tear duct finally opens, the eye infection may not go away and, in fact, may move even deeper into the tear production mechanism. This condition must be watched carefully to prevent this more serious infection.

Sometimes a cyst can cause blocked or inflamed tear ducts. When this occurs and the methods described above are unsuccessful, the ophthalmologist may decide to open the blocked sac and duct surgically. Unfortunately, sometimes this procedure must be repeated more than once.

In rare cases a baby's eyes will not tear at all. When this happens, the surface of the eyes will become inflamed, and a sticky discharge will be present. If this doesn't clear by itself, the child will need eyedrops to keep the eyes wet and prevent any damage.

Cataracts

Although we usually think of cataracts as affecting elderly people, they also may be found in infants and young children. A cataract is a clouding of the lens (the transparent tissue inside the eye that helps bring light rays to focus on the retina). While rare, congenital cataracts are nonetheless a leading cause of visual loss and blindness in children.

A cataract usually shows up as a white reflection in the center of the child's pupil. If a baby is born with a cataract that blocks most of the light entering the eye, the affected lens has to be removed surgically to permit the baby's vision to develop. Most pediatric ophthalmologists recommend that this procedure be performed during the first month of life. After the clouded lens is removed, the baby must be fitted with a contact lens or with an eyeglass correction. At this time, the placement of lenses within the eye is not recommended. In addition, visual rehabilitation of the affected eye will almost always involve use of a patch until the child's eyes are fully mature (at age nine or older).

Occasionally a child will be born with a small cataract that will not initially impede visual development. These cataracts often do not require treatment; however, they need to be monitored carefully to ensure that they do not become large enough to interfere with normal vision. In addition, even if too small to pose a direct threat to visual development, cataracts may cause secondary amblyopia (loss of vision), which will need to be treated by your ophthalmologist.

In most cases the cause of cataracts in infants cannot be determined. Cataracts may be attributed to a tendency inherited from parents; they may result from trauma to the eye; or they may occur as a result of viral infections such as German measles and chicken pox or infection from other microorganisms such as toxoplasmosis. To protect the unborn child from cataracts as well as from other serious disorders, pregnant

---

Preventing Eye Injuries

Nine out of ten eye injuries are preventable, and almost half occur around the home. To minimize the risk of such accidents in your family, follow these safety guidelines:

- Keep all chemicals out of reach. That includes detergents, ammonia, spray cans, and all other cleaning fluids.

- Choose your child's toys carefully. Watch out for sharp or pointed parts, especially if your child is too young to understand their danger.

- Keep your child away from darts and pellet and BB guns.

- Teach your preschooler how to handle scissors and pencils properly. If he's too young to learn, don't allow him to use them.

- Keep your child away from power lawn mowers, which can hurl stones or other objects.

- Don't let your child near you when you're lighting fires or using tools. If you want him to watch you hammer nails, make him wear protective goggles.

- Tell your youngster not to look directly into the sun, even with sunglasses. This can cause permanent and severe eye damage.

- Never allow your child near fireworks of any kind.

---

women should take care to avoid unnecessary exposure to infectious diseases. In addition, as a precaution against toxoplasmosis, pregnant women should avoid handling cat litter or eating raw meat, both of which may contain the organism that causes this disease.

Glaucoma

Glaucoma is a serious eye disorder caused by increased pressure within the eye. It may be due either to overproduction of or inadequate drainage of the fluid within the eye. If this increased pressure persists too long, it can damage the optic nerve, resulting in loss of vision.

Although a child can be born with glaucoma, this is quite rare. More often, it develops later in life. The earlier it is detected and treated, the better the chance of preventing permanent loss of vision. If any of the following warning signs occur, you should call your pediatrician promptly.

- Excessive tearing

- Extreme sensitivity to light. (The child will turn his head into the mattress or blankets to avoid light)

- Blinking tightly

- Hazy or overly prominent-appearing eyes

Glaucoma must be treated surgically to create an alternate route for fluid to leave the eye. Any youngster who has this disease must be watched very carefully throughout his life so that the pressure is kept under control and the optic nerve and cornea are not harmed.

Eye Injuries

When dust or other small particles get in your child's eyes, the cleansing action of tears will usually wash them out. If that fails to occur, or if a serious accident affecting the eye takes place, call your pediatrician or take your child to the nearest emergency room after heeding the following emergency guidelines.

Chemicals in the Eye

Flush the eye with water for fifteen minutes, making sure you get the water into the eye itself. Then take the child to the emergency room.

Large Particle in the Eye

If the particle won't come out with tears or by flushing with water, or if your child is still complaining of pain after an hour, call your pediatrician. The doctor will remove the object or, if necessary, refer you to an ophthal-mologist. Sometimes such particles cause scratches on the cornea (corneal abrasions). These are quite painful but heal rapidly with eye ointment and patching. Corneal injuries also can be caused by blows or other injuries to the eye.

Cut Eyelid

Minor cuts usually heal quickly and easily, but a deep cut requires emergency medical attention, and probably will need stitches. (See *Cuts and Scrapes,* p. 455.) Even if the cut is minor, check to make sure it isn't on the border of the eyelid or near the tear duct. If it is, call your pediatrician right away for advice on how to handle the situation.

Black Eye

To reduce swelling, apply a cool pack or towel to the area for ten to twenty minutes. Then consult the doctor to make sure there is no internal damage.

22

FAMILY ISSUES

Adoption

If you are about to adopt or have just adopted a child, you are likely to be experiencing conflicting emotions: Along with the excitement and delight, you understandably will feel some anxiety and apprehension. It's no different with couples who conceive and bear a child themselves, except that nature gives them nine months to adjust to the situation.

Having an understanding and supportive pediatrician will be very helpful as you begin your new job as a parent. Even before you actually receive your child, the doctor can help you understand your feelings. If you are adopting a child from overseas, the pediatrician will be able to alert you to special medical issues that may arise.

Once your child is home with you, a visit to the pediatrician should be scheduled as soon as possible to make sure there are no existing medical problems. Future examinations should be scheduled as required by the child's age and medical needs, but several special counseling visits should be made during the first year to help you deal with the special concerns that may arise as you and your child start to develop a relationship.

Adoptive parents must face several issues and questions that natural parents do not encounter. They include the following:

- *How and when should I tell my child he is adopted?*

Your child should learn the truth as early as he is able to understand, which probably will be between ages two and four. It's important to adjust the information to his maturity level, so that he can make sense of it. For example, "Your parents loved you very much, but they knew they could not take care of you. So they looked for someone who also loved little children, but could not have them on their own." As he gets older and asks more specific questions, give him honest answers, but do not press information on him if he seems uncomfortable or fearful about it.

- *Are there special problems to watch for?*

Adopted children have no more or different problems than any other child of the same age and background. However, if you adopt an older child, you will need to learn as much as possible about his background, so you can provide the special support and understanding he requires.

- ***Should I tell others that my child is adopted?***

If you are asked, answer the question honestly and straightforwardly. Do not belabor the point or go into extensive detail if your child is nearby, however, as that may make him uncomfortable.

- ***What if he wants to find his "real parents"?***

Allow your child to discuss his feelings and desires, and tell him that you will help him locate them if he still wishes to do so when he is older. Don't push him into searching for them, and don't discourage him from doing so if it's important to him. As he gets older, explain any special circumstances, such as state guidelines or specific requests by the biological parents to not be identified, so he'll know how difficult it may be to trace them.

Your pediatrician may be able to help you with more detailed answers to these and other questions that arise in adoptive families.

Child Abuse and Neglect

The news is so full of reports about child mistreatment that you can't help but wonder how safe your child really is. While it's a mistake to become overprotective and make your child fearful, it is important to recognize the actual risks and familiarize yourself with the signs of abuse. More than 2.5 million cases of child abuse and neglect are reported each year. Of these, 35 percent involve physical abuse, 15 percent involve sexual abuse, and 50 percent involve neglect. Child neglect can include physical neglect (withholding food, clothing, shelter, or other physical necessities), emotional neglect (withholding love, comfort, or affection), or medical neglect (withholding needed medical care).

Most child abuse occurs within the family, often by parents or relatives who themselves were abused as children. Neglect and mistreatment of children is also more common in families living in poverty, and among parents who are teenagers or are drug or alcohol abusers. While there has been a recent increase in child abuse outside the home (by acquaintances and in day-care programs or schools), this is still relatively rare.

Signs and Symptoms

It's not always easy to recognize when a child has been abused. Children who have been mistreated are often afraid to tell anyone, because they think they will be blamed or that no one will believe them. Parents also tend to overlook symptoms, because they don't want to face the truth. This is a serious mistake. A child who has been abused needs special support and treatment as early as possible. The longer he continues to be abused or is left to deal with the situation on his own, the less likely he is to make a full recovery.

The best way to check for signs of abuse is to be alert to any unexplainable changes in your child's body or behavior. Don't conduct a formal "examination" unless you have reason for suspicion, as this may make the child fearful, but do look further if you notice any of the following:

Physical Abuse

- Any injury (bruise, burn, fracture, abdominal or head injury) that cannot be explained

Sexual Abuse

- Fearful behavior (nightmares, depression, unusual fears, attempts to run away)

- Abdominal pain, bedwetting, urinary tract infection, genital pain or bleeding, sexually transmitted disease

- Extreme sexual behavior that seems inappropriate for the child's age

Emotional Abuse

- Sudden change in self-confidence

- Headaches or stomachaches with no medical cause

- Abnormal fears, increased nightmares

- Attempts to run away

Emotional Neglect

- Failure to gain weight (especially in infants)

- Desperately affectionate behavior

- Voracious appetite and stealing of food

Long-Term Consequences

In most cases, children who are abused or neglected suffer greater emotional than physical damage. A child who is severely mistreated may become depressed or develop suicidal, withdrawn, or violent behavior. As he gets older he may use drugs or alcohol, try to run away, refuse discipline, or abuse others. As an adult he may develop marital and sexual difficulties, depression, or suicidal behavior.

Not all abuse victims have severe reactions. Usually, the younger the child, the longer the abuse continues, and the closer the child's relationship with the abuser, the more serious the emotional damage will be. A five-year-old child whose teacher slaps him occasionally in anger probably will have a milder reaction than a three-year-old whose uncle beats him every time he visits.

Getting Help

If you suspect your child has been abused, get help immediately through your pediatrician or a local child protective agency. Physicians are legally obligated to report all suspected cases of abuse or neglect to state authorities. Your pediatrician also will detect and treat any medical injuries or ailments,

recommend a therapist, and provide necessary information to those investigating the case. The doctor may also testify in court if necessary to obtain legal protection for the child or criminal prosecution of a sexual abuse suspect. Criminal prosecution is rarely sought in mild physical abuse cases but is likely in those involving sexual abuse.

Your child will benefit from the services of a qualified mental health professional if he has been abused. You and other members of the family may be advised to seek counseling so that you'll be able to provide the support and comfort your child needs. If someone in your family is responsible for the abuse, a mental health professional may be able to successfully treat that person as well.

If your child has been abused, you may be the only person who can help him. There is *no* good reason to delay reporting your suspicions of abuse. Denying the problem will only make the situation worse, allowing the abuse to continue unchecked and decreasing your child's chance for a full recovery.

Preventing Abuse

The major reasons for mistreatment of children within the family are often parental feelings of isolation, stress, and frustration. Parents need support and as much information as possible in order to raise their children responsibly. They need to be taught how to cope with their own feelings of frustration and anger without venting them on children. They also need the companionship of other adults who will listen and help during times of crisis. Support groups through local community organizations are often helpful first steps to diminish some of the isolation or frustration they may be feeling.

Personal involvement in your child's activities and supervision is the best way to prevent physical and sexual abuse outside the home. Any school or day-care program you select for a child should allow unrestricted parent visits without prearrangement. Parents should be allowed to help in the classroom on a volunteer basis and informed about selection or changes of staff members. Parents should pay careful attention to their child's reports about and reactions to his experiences at school. Always investigate if your child tells you he's been mistreated or if he is experiencing a sudden unexplained change in behavior.

While you don't want to frighten your child, you can teach him some basic rules of safety in a nonthreatening manner. Teach him to keep his distance from strangers, not to wander away from you in unfamiliar territory, to say no when someone asks him to do something against his will, and always to tell you if someone hurts him or makes him feel bad. Instead of teaching him that he's surrounded by danger, teach him that he is strong, capable, and that he can count on you to keep him safe.

Divorce

Every year over one million children in the United States are involved in a divorce. Even those youngsters who had lived with parental conflict and unhappiness for a long time may find the changes that follow divorce more difficult than anything they'd experienced before. At the very least, the child must adjust to living apart from one parent (usually the father) or, if in shared custody, to dividing his life between two homes. Because of financial changes, he may also have to move to a smaller home and a different neighborhood. A mother who stayed at home before now may have to go to work. Even if she doesn't, the stress and depression that accompany divorce may make her less attentive and loving with her child.

No one can predict specifically how divorce will affect your child. His response will depend on his own sensitivity, the quality of his separate relationships with both parents, and the parents' ability to work together to meet his emotional needs during this time. It will also depend to some extent on his age. In a very general way, you can anticipate how your child will react to divorce based on his age at the time it occurs.

Children under two often revert to more infantile behavior. They may become unusually clinging, dependent, or frustrated. They may refuse to go to sleep, and may suddenly start waking up during the night.

Children between three and five also may act more babylike, but what they may feel is that *they* are responsible for their parents' breakup. At this age, children do not fully understand that their parents' lives are separate from their own. They believe that they are the center of their family's universe and therefore blame themselves when it falls apart. In addition, children this age have an emerging sexual awareness, making identification increasingly strong. This means children will react strongly to the absence of the father. Boys often become more aggressive and defiant toward the mother. Girls may become insecure and mistrustful of males. The less contact the child has with the father, or the more tense the postdivorce relationship, the more serious these reactions are likely to be.

Your child's response to the divorce probably will be most intense during and immediately following the breakup. As he grows older, he may continue to think about the past and struggle to understand why his parents separated. For years he may have some sense of loss, which might become especially painful during holidays and on special occasions like birthdays and family reunions.

Most children of divorce wish desperately for their parents to get back together. However, it is much more difficult for them if the parents repeatedly attempt to reconcile and then part again than if the initial separation is final. When the parents act indecisively, the child is likely to become suspicious, confused, and insecure.

In rare cases, a child's behavior and self-esteem actually improve after the parents' divorce. Sometimes this is because the parents are relieved of the tension and unhappiness of a bad marriage, and now can give the child more affection and attention. Sometimes it is because the divorce ends an emotionally or physically abusive situation. Often, however, even children who have been abused by a parent still yearn for that parent's love and for the restoration of the family.

How Parents Can Help the Child

Children integrate and mirror their parents' emotions. If his parents are angry, depressed, or violent during the separation process, a child is likely to absorb these disturbing feelings and may turn them against himself. If the parents argue about him, or if he hears his name during their disputes, he may believe even more strongly that he is to blame. Secrecy and silence probably won't make him feel much better, however, and actually may intensify the unhappiness and tension he feels around him. The best approach is to be honest about your feelings but make a special effort to be loving and reassuring with your child. He will have to accept that his parents no longer love each other—and you shouldn't try to pretend otherwise—but make sure he understands and *feels* that both parents love him just as much as ever.

If your child is younger than two years, you can't get this message across very well with words. You will have to convey it through your actions. When you are with your child, try to put your own pain and worries aside and concentrate on his needs. Keep the daily routine as consistent as possible, and do not expect him to make any other major changes (such as toilet training, moving from a crib to a bed, or, if avoidable, adjusting to a new babysitter or day-care arrangement) during this transitional period. In the beginning, try to be understanding and patient if your child's behavior regresses, but if this regression continues even after the divorce is completed and your life has settled back into a regular routine, ask your pediatrician for advice.

If your child is older, he needs to feel that *both* his parents care about him and that they are willing to put their differences aside when it comes to his welfare. This means that you both must maintain an active involvement in his life. In the past, most fathers gradually withdrew from their children following divorce. Today, courts and psychologists are trying to correct this pattern, in part by making a distinction between physical and legal custody. In this way, one parent can be granted *physical custody,* so that the child can have a home base, while *legal custody* can be awarded jointly, so that both parents remain involved in decisions about the child's education, medical care, and other basic needs. The child can visit regularly with the parent who does not have physical custody. It is also possible to have both joint physical custody and joint legal custody. This arrangement has the advantage of keeping both parents fully involved with the child. However, it also may have serious drawbacks. The child, especially under ten, may feel split between his two homes, two sets of friends, and two routines. Many parents who have joint physical custody find it difficult to manage all the day-to-day decisions about scheduling, birthday parties, lessons, and schoolwork. Unless both parents are fully committed to making this arrangement work, it can lead to more conflict, confusion, and stress for the youngster. Any custody arrangement selected should give a high priority to the children's emotional and developmental needs.

Whatever your custody arrangement, you both, as parents, will continue to play key roles in your child's life. Try to support each other in these roles. As much as possible, avoid criticizing each other. Your child needs reassurance that it's still okay for him to love both of you. He needs you to help him feel that he's safe with either of you and that there's no need for secrets or guilt. If you and his other parent can't actively cooperate, at least be tolerant of each other's routines, rules, and plans, even if you have minor reservations. Under the circumstances, arguments over how much television your child watches or what foods he eats can cause him far more damage than will the TV or the snacks. If necessary, discuss your concerns when your child is not present. If a child hears his parents trying to undermine each other's authority, he may come to feel that he can't trust either of them or that he can't talk about his feelings openly. An atmosphere of hostility may make it hard for him to enjoy himself with either parent.

As your child reaches age four or five, his life will broaden to include school and neighborhood activities, and he will develop much more complex feelings about his place in the world. You and your former spouse should discuss how he behaves and what he talks about when he is with each of you. Even though you are divorced, you still share responsibility for your child, and you need to work together to resolve any emotional or behavioral problems he may develop. Be especially alert for any signs of low self-esteem, unusual moodiness or depression, or excessive apologizing or self-criticism. These may indicate that he is blaming himself for the divorce. If this is the case, and you cannot convince him that he is blameless, talk to your pediatrician. He may advise you to consult a child psychiatrist or psychologist or other mental health professional.

If you feel very depressed or disturbed after your divorce and cannot seem to regain control of your life, you cannot give your child the nurturing and support he needs. For everyone's sake, consult a professional for psychological counseling as soon as you realize you are having difficulty.

If your divorce is full of tension and anger, you may worry that the battles will never end and that your child will never recover. While it's true that some of the emotional effects of divorce may remain with your youngster permanently, he will have every chance to grow up healthy and happy if he receives the love, affection, and support he needs from his parents and other care-givers.

(See also *Single-Parent Families*, page 575; *Stepfamilies*, page 577.)

Grief Reactions

Losing a parent is one of the most traumatic events that can happen to any child, and grief is the natural response. Your child may experience grief not only if a parent dies but also if one becomes chronically or seriously ill, or if there is a divorce. (Even if he remains in touch with both parents following divorce, he may mourn the loss of the family unit as he's known it.) Children also may grieve for siblings, grandparents, a beloved care-giver, or a pet.

When a Child Loses a Parent

For a young child, the loss of a parent is an overwhelming crisis, impossible to understand. Children under five cannot grasp the permanence of death. Because of this, the first stage of grief is often a period of protest and hope that the lost parent will return. Many children will try to use fantasy to make this happen, imagining the missing parent in familiar situations or places.

Once the child begins to realize that the parent is truly gone forever, despair sets in. Infants, with their limited communication skills, generally express their distress by crying, feeding poorly, and being difficult to console. Toddlers will cry, be easily excitable and uncooperative, and may regress to infantile behavior. Older children may become withdrawn. A preschooler might have a faraway look on his face, be less creative and less enthusiastic about play during this period. The more anguished or emotionally distant the other members of the family are, the more intense a young child's despair is likely to be.

Eventually, he will emerge from this mood of despair and begin to shift his love and trust to others. This does not mean that he's forgotten the missing parent, or that the hurt has gone away. Throughout his life there will be times when he will experience conscious and unconscious feelings of loss, especially on birthdays and holidays, during special occasions such as a graduation, and when he's ill. At these times the child may voice his sadness and ask about his missing parent.

If the missing parent was the same sex as the child, these questions probably will come up frequently between ages four and seven, when he is struggling to understand his own sexual identity. In the best of outcomes, these remembrances will be brief and positive and will not create serious distress. If they are prolonged or if they noticeably disturb the child, they should be discussed with the pediatrician.

When a Child Loses a Sibling

Losing a sibling also is a devastating experience. Though it might not strike as deeply as the loss of a parent, it may be more complicated because many children, even those old enough to understand how their sibling died, may feel that in some way they are to blame. These feelings may be intensified if parents, deep in their own despair, become withdrawn or angry and unwittingly shut themselves off from the child.

The surviving sibling must watch helplessly as his parents go through the same agony of grief that he would experience if he'd lost them. He will see first the shock and emotional numbness, then denial, then anger that such a cruel thing could possibly happen. Through it all, he is likely to hear guilt in his parents' words and voices. He may interpret this guilt to mean that they were devoting time or attention to him that should have been given to his lost sibling.

His mother may feel driven to talk about her lost child, how the death occurred, and what she could have done to prevent it. The child may struggle to comfort her even as he's trying himself to comprehend what has hap-

pened. The realization that he cannot make her happy, no matter what he does, may seriously damage his feelings of security and self-esteem. If his father reacts, as many men do, by becoming restrained, short-tempered, and preoccupied with distractions outside the family, the surviving sibling may feel frightened and rejected by him.

In a household where the mother badly needs to talk and the father wants to avoid talking, the mutual support and understanding they both need is difficult to achieve, and the marriage may suffer. The surviving child will feel this stress as keenly as his grief for the sibling he's lost, and may assume that he's responsible for his parents' disputes as well as his sibling's death.

The entire family may benefit from professional counseling after a child dies. Your pediatrician can recommend a qualified family therapist, psychologist, or child psychiatrist to help you all cope with your grief and bring your family back together.

Helping Your Grieving Child

When you are grieving for your spouse or your child, it is easy to neglect your surviving child's needs. The following suggestions can help you provide the framework of love, comfort, and trust your child needs during and after the grieving process:

1. Maintain your child's familiar day-to-day routine as much as possible. Ask the people he loves and trusts—family members, familiar babysitters, or preschool teachers—to be there for him when you are unavailable.

2. Offer frequent, calm explanations, keeping in mind your child's level of understanding and possible feelings of guilt. Keep the explanations as simple as possible, but be truthful. Do not construct fairy tales that will leave him more confused or hopeful that the death can be reversed. If your child is older than three, reassure him that nothing he did or thought caused the death, and that no one is angry or thinks badly of him. To make sure he understands, it may help to ask him to repeat what you've said.

3. Get help from loved ones. It is difficult to give your grieving child all the attention and support he needs when you are grief-stricken yourself. Close friends and family members may be able to give you some relief, at the same time providing a sense of family and community for your child at a time when he may feel alone and lost. If you have lost a child, it is especially important for the family's sake that you and your spouse try to be mutually supportive during this time.

4. Be open to discussions about the loss over the coming weeks, months, and years. Even if your child appears to recover from grief faster than you do, his grieving process will go on below the surface for many years—possibly, in a quiet way, for a lifetime. He will need your continuing support and understanding as he tries to come to terms with his loss. As he grows older, he will ask more sophisticated questions about the circumstances and reasons for the death. As painful as it may be for you to recall these events, try to answer him honestly and directly. The more he understands what happened, the easier it will be for him to make his peace with it.

Should Your Preschooler Attend the Funeral?

Whether a young child attends a funeral for a loved one depends on the child's individual level of understanding, emotional maturity, and his desire to participate in this ritual. If he seems very fearful and anxious, and can't understand the purpose of the ceremony, then he probably should not attend. On the other hand, if he seems able to control his responses and wishes to be present to say goodbye one last time, attending may be consoling and actually help him deal with his grief.

If you decide to have him present, prepare him for what will happen. Also, make arrangements ahead of time for a close family member or care-giver to take the child if he needs to leave, so you can remain at the funeral. Having this extra help will also free you to meet your own emotional needs during the ceremony.

If you decide not to have your child at the funeral, you might arrange a private, less formal visit later to the gravesite. Although this, too, will be stressful, it may make it easier for him to understand what has happened.

When to Get Professional Help

You may want to consult your pediatrician for advice soon after the death has occurred. With the experience and knowledge to help you guide your child through the grieving process, the physician can help you decide how and what to tell your child, and can discuss how your child may be feeling and behaving in the months to come.

It is not possible to say how long your child "should" continue to grieve. Ordinarily, a grieving child will show signs of gradual recovery, with, at first, hours, then days, and eventually weeks when he acts pretty much as he did before the death. If he does not start to have these periods of normalcy within four to six weeks, or if you feel that his initial despair is too intense or is lasting too long, talk to your pediatrician.

Although it is normal for a child to miss a deceased parent or sibling at times, it is not normal for the preoccupation to overshadow the child's entire life for years to come. If your child seems to be thinking constantly about the death, so that his grief dominates every family occasion and interferes with his social and psychological development, he probably needs psychological counseling. Your pediatrician can refer you to a qualified mental health professional.

Your child also needs *you* to return gradually to normal functioning. After you've lost a child or your spouse, it may take many months before you are able to return to your usual daily routine, and much longer before your feelings of anguish begin to subside. If a year has passed since the death and you still don't feel that you can resume your former activities, or if your grieving is replaced by ongoing depression, it's good to seek psychological help, not only for your benefit but for your child's as well.

One- and Two-Child Families

Most newly married couples today plan to have only one or two children, compared with three or more back in the early 1960s. The reasons for this shift include a trend toward later marriage, more emphasis on careers for women, more effective methods of contraception, and the rising cost of rearing and educating children.

There are some very clear benefits to having a small family:

- Each child receives more parental attention and educational advantages, which generally raise his self-esteem.

- Children in small families, especially first and only children, tend to have higher school and personal achievement levels than do children of larger families.

- The financial costs of maintaining a household are lower.

- It is easier for both parents to combine careers with family life.

- The general stress level is lower because there often are fewer conflicts and less rivalry.

There are also some drawbacks, especially in one-child families. When all the expectations, hopes, and fears are focused on just one child, parents easily can become overprotective and indulgent without even realizing it. The child may have fewer opportunities to meet other children or to develop a sense of independence. He may be pushed to overachieve, and he may receive so much doting attention that he becomes self-centered and undisciplined.

If you have just one or two children, you may become overprotective and overattentive. This may make your child reluctant to be separated from you, hindering the development of new relationships with peers. In fact, you may have that same difficulty. Here are tips to help you keep these feelings in the proper perspective as your child matures:

- Make sure your expectations of your child are realistic for his age. Get to know other families with children the same age, and watch how these parents raise their children: when they're protective, and when they let go; how they discipline the children; how much responsibility they expect of them.

- Maintain your own adult social life as a couple (or as an individual, if you are a single parent). Taking a few hours off from each other will help both you and your child develop your separate identities. The earlier you start this pattern of separation (at least once a week, even during infancy), the easier it will be for you both to accept the increasing separation that needs to occur as he grows older.

- Let your child get to know other trusted grown-ups by having them babysit, and by including the child in group activities with other families.

- Give him plenty of opportunities to play with other children his age through play groups, nursery schools, or other children's groups.

- If you are worried about your child's health or development, get advice from your pediatrician as soon as possible. Don't let your anxieties build, and don't smother your child with unnecessary concern.

Sibling Rivalry

If you have more than one child, you almost certainly will have to deal with some amount of sibling rivalry. Competition between youngsters in a family is normal and natural. All children want parental affection and attention, and each child believes he rightly should receive all of yours. Your child does not want to share you with his brother or sister, and when he realizes he has no choice in the matter, he may become jealous, possibly even violent toward his sibling.

Sibling rivalry between younger children tends to be most troublesome when the age difference is from one and a half to three years. This is because the preschool child is still very dependent on his parents, and has not yet established many secure relationships with friends or other adults. However, even when the spread is as many as nine years or more, the older child still needs parental attention and affection. If he feels that he is being left out or rejected, he likely will blame the baby. In general, the older the child, the less jealousy he will feel toward his younger sibling. The jealousy is often most intense for preschoolers when the sibling is a newborn.

There may be days when you're convinced your children really do hate each other, but these emotional outbursts are only temporary. Despite their feelings of resentment, siblings usually have true affection for one another. You may have difficulty seeing this, however, since they may reserve their worst behavior for moments when you are present, because then they are competing directly for your attention. When you're gone, they may be fine companions. As they get older and their need for your complete and undivided attention decreases, their feelings of affection probably will overcome their jealousy of each other. Sibling rivalry that lasts into adulthood is rare.

What to Expect

You may notice the first signs of sibling rivalry even before your younger child is born. As the older one watches you preparing the nursery or buying baby equipment, he may demand gifts for himself. He may want to wear diapers again or drink from a bottle "like the baby will." If he senses that you're preoccupied with the baby, he may misbehave or act out in order to get your attention.

This unusual or regressive behavior may continue after the baby is home. Your older child may cry more frequently, become more clinging and demanding, or simply withdraw. He may imitate the baby by asking for his old baby blanket, sucking on a pacifier, or even demanding to nurse. School-age children often appear very interested and affectionate toward the baby, but are aggressive or misbehave in other ways to get attention. Among all siblings, the demand for attention is usually greatest when the parents are actively and intimately involved with the baby—for example during breast-feedings or bathtime.

As your younger child gets older and becomes more mobile, quarrels will erupt over the older child's toys and other possessions. The toddler will go straight for what he wants, without caring who owns it, while your preschooler will jealously guard his own territory. When the toddler intrudes on this space, the older child usually reacts strongly.

Sometimes, particularly when the children are several years apart, the older one is accepting and protective of the younger sibling. However, as the younger one grows and begins to develop more mature skills and talents (in schoolwork, athletics, talking, singing, or acting, for example), the older child may feel threatened or embarrassed by "being shown up." He may then become more aggressive or irritating, or start to compete with the younger sibling. The younger child, too, may experience jealousy about the privileges, talents, accomplishments, or advantages that his older sibling accumulates as he gets older.

Often, it is almost impossible to tell which child is contributing more to the rivalry.

How Should Parents React?

It's important not to overreact to jealousy between your children, especially if the older child is a preschooler. Feelings of resentment and frustration are understandable—no child wants to give up the spotlight of parental affection. It takes time for a youngster to discover that his parents don't love him any less because they have a second child to love.

If your older child starts imitating the baby, don't ridicule or punish him. You can indulge his fantasies briefly by allowing him to drink from a bottle or climb into the crib or playpen, but only once or twice at the most, and don't reward this behavior by giving him extra attention. Make it absolutely clear that he does not have to behave like a baby to gain your approval, love, or affection. Praise him when he acts "grown-up," and give him plenty of opportunities to be a "big brother (or sister)." It shouldn't take long for him to realize that he benefits more by acting maturely than by behaving like a baby.

If your older child is between three and five years old, try to minimize conflicts over space by guaranteeing some secure, protected area. Separating his private possessions from shared ones will help reduce quarreling.

It's natural for parents to compare their children, but don't do this in front of them. Each child is special, and should be treated as such. Comparisons inevitably make one child feel inferior to the other. A statement such as "Your sister is always so much neater than you," for example, will make a child resent both you and his sister, and actually may encourage him to be messy.

When your children get into an argument the best strategy usually is to stay out of it. Left alone, they probably will settle it peacefully. If you get involved you may be tempted to take sides, making one child feel triumphant and the other betrayed. Even if they bring their fight to you, try to be impartial and tell them to settle it peacefully on their own. Instead of blaming either one, explain that they're *both* responsible for creating the dispute and for ending it.

Obviously, you must intervene if the situation becomes violent, especially if the older child might harm the younger one. In this case you must first protect the baby. Make sure the older youngster understands that you will not tolerate such abusive behavior. If the age difference is large or there is any reason to suspect that violence may erupt, supervise them closely when they are together. Preventing aggressive behavior is always better than punishment, which all too often increases rather than decreases the older child's feelings of rivalry.

It is important to spend time separately with each child. Finding the right balance of attention is not always easy, but if your older child's acting out is becoming extreme, it could be a signal that he needs more of your time.

If the older sibling remains extremely aggressive, or you feel that you don't know how to handle the situation, consult your pediatrician, who can determine whether this is normal sibling rivalry or a problem that requires special attention. The pediatrician also can suggest ways to ease the tensions. If necessary, he will refer you to a qualified mental health professional.

(See also *Preparing Your Other Children for the Baby's Arrival*, in Chapter 1, page 18.)

Single-Parent Families

Single-parent families are becoming more and more common. Most children of divorce spend at least some years in single-parent households. Another increasingly large group of children live with single parents who were never married. A smaller number of children have widowed parents.

From a parent's viewpoint, there are some benefits to being single. You can raise the child according to your own beliefs, principles, and rules, with no need for conflict or compromise. Single parents often develop closer bonds with their children. When the father is the single parent, he becomes more nurturing and much more active in his child's daily life than most fathers in two-parent households. Children may also derive some benefits from being in single-parent households. For example, they may become more independent and mature because they have more responsibility within the family.

Single parenthood is not easy, though, for parents or children. It generally means less income and a lower standard of living. If you can't arrange or afford child care, getting and holding a job may be difficult. (See Chapter 14, "Part-time Care for Your Child.") Without another person to share the day in, day out job of raising the child and maintaining the household, you may find yourself isolated from other adults. When you are under stress, the child may sense and share this stress. You can easily become too tired and distracted to be emotionally supportive or consistent about rules and discipline. This can lead to distress and behavior problems for the child. Lack of a same-sex role model can sometimes add to problems.

Here are some suggestions that may help you maintain your own emotional stability while providing your child with the guidance he needs:

- Take advantage of all available resources in finding help in caring for your child. Use the guide to part-time care in Chapter 5.

- Maintain your good humor as much as possible. Try to see the positive or humorous side of everyday mishaps and conflicts.

- For your family's sake as well as your own, take care of yourself. See your doctor regularly, eat properly, and get enough rest, exercise, and sleep.

- Set a regular time when you can get out of the house and away from your child. Relax with friends. Go to a movie. Pursue hobbies. Join groups. Do things that interest *you*. Being a single parent doesn't mean that you can't have a social life of your own.

- Don't allow yourself to feel guilty because your child has only one parent. There are plenty of families in the same situation. You didn't "do it to him," and you don't need to penalize yourself or spoil him to make amends. Feeling and acting guilty won't help anyone.

- Don't look for problems where none exist. Many children grow up very well in single-parent homes, while others have a great many problems in two-parent homes. Being a single parent doesn't necessarily mean you'll have more problems or have more trouble resolving them.

- Set firm but reasonable limits for your children, and don't hesitate to enforce them. Children feel more secure and develop responsible behavior better when limits are clear and consistent. Expand these limits as the child demonstrates the ability to accept increased responsibility.

- Find some time each day to spend with your child—playing, talking, reading, helping with homework, or watching television.

- Praise your child often and with genuine affection.

- Create as large a support network for yourself as possible. Keep active lists of relatives, friends, and community services that can help with child care. Establish friendships with other families who will let you know of community opportunities (soccer, cultural events, etc.) and are willing to exchange babysitting.

- Talk to trusted relatives, friends, and professionals such as your pediatrician about your child's behavior, development, and relationships within the family.

Smaller Extended Families

Until the last few generations, most American families were two-parent ones; and nearby, perhaps even in the same house, lived grandparents, aunts, uncles, and cousins. The women were primarily responsible for caring for the children and running the household while the men worked outside the home. In many ways, this formula worked well: There were plenty of adults to look after the children. There was a built-in support system and roles were clearly defined. The children benefited the most because they had so many close social contacts and received love from so many different directions.

The extended family is not as common in American society today. Due to career obligations, opportunities, and the desire to go to new places, fewer and fewer newly married couples choose to live near their parents or close relatives.

Without regular contact with these relatives, parents and children alike need to create alternative support systems. A close friendship with another family, participation in a surrogate or foster grandparent program, or in Big Brothers or Sisters, can help replace the lost ties. So can strong and consistent religious involvement. For many families, congregational activities are a source of support and close friendships. Many other community programs such as youth and neighborhood activity centers also can fulfill these needs.

Even if your relatives are scattered, try to strengthen your child's sense of family by keeping in touch by phone and letters. Encourage your child to draw pictures for relatives, and to send his own letters when he learns to write. Exchange photographs, and make them into a photo album that grows with your child. If you have a tape recorder or video camera, make tapes of your family as "audio/video letters" to bring you closer together.

The overall intent is to balance the intimate connections of a small nuclear family with continued meaningful contacts with loved ones outside the immediate family. The values fostered and nurtured through these family relationships will be important ones for the child to model and incorporate into his way of living when he grows up. Your family's modeling of these values reinforces their importance for the growing child.

Stepfamilies

A single parent's remarriage can be a blessing for the parent and child alike—restoring the structure, stability, closeness, and security that were lost through divorce, separation, or death. A stepfamily is often financially beneficial. Moreover, the stepparent becomes an appropriate role model of the same sex as the child's absent parent.

But creating a stepfamily also requires many adjustments and can be very stressful for everyone involved. If the stepparent is presented to the child as a substitute for his absent parent, the child may feel torn by his loyalty to his real parent and may immediately reject the stepparent. There's often a great deal of jealousy between stepparents and stepchildren, as well as competition for the love and attention of the parent who has brought them together. If a child feels that his new stepparent is coming between him and his parent, he may reject the stepparent and act out in order to regain his parent's attention. The situation becomes even more complex and stressful when there are children on both sides who are suddenly expected to accept each other's parents and get along as siblings. With time, most blended families do manage to sort through these conflicts, but it requires a great amount of patience and commitment on the part of the adults, as well as the willingness to get professional help if serious problems should develop.

Suggestions for Stepfamilies

Making a smooth transition from a single-parent family to a successful stepfamily requires special sensitivity and effort from the parent and stepparent. Here are some suggestions that may help:

- Inform your former spouse of your marriage plans, and try to work together to make the transition as easy as possible for your child. Make sure everyone understands that the marriage will not change your former spouse's role in your child's life.

- Give your child time to get to know the stepparent (and stepsiblings, if any) before you begin living together. This will make the adjustment easier for everyone and will eliminate a lot of your child's anxiety about the new arrangement.

- Watch for signs of conflict, and work together to correct them as early as possible.

- Parent and stepparent should decide together what will be expected of the child, where and how limits will be set, and what forms of discipline are acceptable.

- Parent and stepparent need to share the responsibilities of parenthood. This means that *both* will give affection and attention and that *both* will have authority in the household. Deciding together how the child should be disciplined, and supporting each other's decisions and actions, will make it easier for the stepparent to assume a role of authority without fear of disapproval or resentment.

- If there is a noncustodial parent who visits the child, these visitations should be arranged and accepted so that they don't become an issue of contention within the stepfamily.

- Try to involve both biological parents and stepparent(s) in all major decisions affecting a child. If possible, arrange for all the adults to meet together to share insights and concerns; this will let the child know that the grown-ups are willing to overcome their differences for his benefit.

- Be sensitive to your child's wishes and concerns about his role within the stepfamily. Respect his level of maturity and understanding when, for example, you help him decide what to call the stepparent or introduce him to the stepparent's relatives.

As difficult as the transition may seem at first, try to remember that no family is trouble-free. Try to keep in mind that relationships between stepparents and stepchildren tend to develop gradually, over a period of one to several years, rather than over weeks or months.

An important factor in the development of the step-relationship may be support from the other biological parent. A relationship with a biological parent that precludes closeness to the stepparent may be resented by the child and may make him feel guilty whenever he is emotionally drawn to the stepparent.

Harmonious communications among all three (or four) parents can minimize this guilt, as well as reduce the confusion that a child could feel when he tries to accommodate the values and expectations of several adults. For this reason, when a child is spending time in two households, occasional meetings including all of the parents, if possible, may be very helpful. Sharing perspectives on rules, values, and scheduling communicates to the child that all his parents can talk with one another, are mutually respectful, and have his development as a central priority.

In an atmosphere of mutual respect between biological and stepparents, the child can derive the benefits of stepfamilies mentioned earlier. The child again has the opportunity of living in a household with two parents. The remarried parent often is happier and thus better able to meet the child's needs. As the child gets older, his relationship to the stepparent may give him support, skills, and perspectives. These benefits, together with the economic advantages of the stepfamily situation, may give the child a broader range of opportunities.

Twins

Having twins means much more than simply having two babies at once, and this challenge goes beyond having twice the work or pleasure. Twins quite frequently are born early and therefore tend to be smaller than the average newborn, so you may need to consult your pediatrician even more frequently than you would with a single baby. Feeding twins, whether by breast or bottle, also requires some special strategies, and the doctor can provide advice and support. (See Chapters 1 and 4.)

Twins: Fraternal vs. Identical

Identical twins come from the same egg, are always the same sex, and look very much alike. We expect them to act alike and develop in similar ways as they grow up. Because of their many similarities, they may develop extremely close emotional bonds, possibly excluding even other family members to some extent.

Fraternal twins come from two separate eggs, which are fertilized at the same time. They may or may not be the same sex, and they will not be identical in appearance, temperament, or behavior. Because of these differences, they often do not form the extremely close relationship found between identical twins. In fact, there is likely to be more rivalry.

Characteristic	Identical	Fraternal
Sex	Same	Same or different
Appearance	Identical	Many similarities, but not necessarily identical
Placenta	One	Two
Chorion bag	One or two	Two
Amniotic sac	One or two	Two
Blood types	Identical	May be identical

Raising Twins

From the very beginning it's important that you recognize your twin babies as two separate individuals. If they are identical it's easy to treat them as a "package," providing them with the same clothing, toys, and quality of attention. But as similar as they may appear physically, emotionally they are different, and in order to grow up happy and secure as individuals, they need you to support their differences. As one twin explained, "We're not twins. We're just brothers who have the same birthday!"

Both identical and fraternal twins may become either competitive or interdependent as they grow. Sometimes one twin acts as the leader and the other as the follower. Whatever the specific quality of their interaction, however, most twins develop very intense relationships early in life simply because they spend so much time with each other.

If you also have other children, your twin newborns may prompt more than the usual sibling rivalry. They will require an enormous amount of your time and energy, and will attract a great deal of extra attention from friends, relatives, and strangers on the street. You can help your other children accept, and maybe even take advantage of, this unusual situation by offering them "double rewards" for helping with the new babies and encouraging even more involvement in the daily baby-care chores. It also becomes even more essential that you spend some very special time each day alone with the other children doing their favorite activities.

As your twins get a little older, particularly if they are identical, they may choose to play only with each other, making their other siblings feel left out. To discourage the twins from forming such exclusive bonds, urge them to play individually (not as a unit) with other children. Also, you or their babysitter might play with just one twin while the other plays with a sibling or friend.

You may find that your twins do not develop in the same pattern as do other children their age. Some twins seem to "split the work," with one concentrating on motor skills while the other perfects social or communication abilities. Because they spend so much time together, many twins communicate better with each other than with other family members or friends. They learn how to "read" each other's gestures and facial expressions, and sometimes they have their own verbal language that no one else can understand. (This is particularly true of identical twins.) Because they can entertain each other, they may not be very motivated to learn about the world beyond them. This unique developmental pattern does not represent a problem, but it does make it all the more important to separate your twins occasionally and expose them individually to other playmates and learning situations.

Twins are not always happy about being apart, especially if they've established strong play habits and preferences for each other's company. For this reason, it's important to begin separating them occasionally as early as possible. If they resist strongly, try a gradual approach using very familiar children or adults to play with them individually but in the same room or play area. Being able to separate will become increasingly important as the twins approach school age. In nursery school most twins can stay together in the same room, but many elementary schools prefer twins to be in separate classes.

As much as you appreciate the individual differences between your twins, you no doubt will have certain feelings for them as a unit. There is nothing wrong with this, since they do share many similarities and are themselves bound to develop a dual identity—as individuals and as twins. Helping them understand and accept the balance between these two identities is one of the most challenging tasks facing you as the parent of twins. Your pediatrician can advise you on how to cope with the special parenting problems involved with twins. He also can suggest helpful reading material or refer you to organizations involved with helping parents who have multiple births.

Working Mothers

Some American parents still accept the notion that the "good mother" is one who gives up work to stay home with her children. In reality, working mothers are fast becoming the rule rather than the exception. In the 1990s more than half of mothers with young children are employed outside the home, and the percentage of working mothers continues to increase. Women have been moving into the work force not only for career satisfaction but also because they and their families need the income. More than one fourth of all children live in single-parent homes, with their mothers providing most of their support. About 80 percent of married working women have husbands who earn less than $30,000 a year. For the children in many of these families, the alternative to a working mother is poverty.

In some families, mothers continue to work in order to hold careers they've spent years developing. Most employers in this country are not sympathetic to working mothers who wish to take time off to be with their young children. If these women stop work even for a year or two, they may forfeit some of the advantages they've earned, and possibly lose certain career opportunities permanently.

To this day there is no scientific evidence to support the notion that children are harmed when their mothers go to work. The key influences on a child's development are the amount of stress in family life, the attitude of the family about the mother's working, and the quality of child care. A child whose family is emotionally well-adjusted and who is well-loved and cared for should thrive regardless of whether his mother has a job outside the home.

As a mother who successfully manages both an outside job and parenthood, you provide an excellent role model for your child.

He will be proud of your achievements and feel motivated to become more independent, responsible, and achievement-oriented himself. In most families with working mothers, each person plays a more active role in the household. The children tend to look after one another and help out in other ways, and the father participates in household chores and child rearing as well as breadwinning. This brings him much closer to the children and often makes him more emotionally supportive of his wife than he otherwise might be.

Problems arise if you don't want to work or if your husband resents your working. If you're working purely out of economic necessity, you may have to take a job that you won't necessarily enjoy. In that case you must be careful not to bring your frustration and unhappiness home, where it will spill over into family relationships. The message the children may receive in this situation is that work is unpleasant and damages self-esteem instead of building it.

Family relationships may suffer if both parents want to work but only one has a job, or if there is competition or resentment because one parent is earning much more than the other. Such conflicts can strain the marriage, and may make the children feel threatened and insecure. With both parents working, the need for mutual support and communication intensifies.

Even when the support is there and everyone's intentions are good, however, a two-career family has to deal with practical problems that do not arise in other families. On a daily basis you and your husband may feel so divided between family and career obligations that you have little time for a social life or each other. Both of you should cooperate on household and child-care responsibilities so that one will not end up doing most of the work and feeling resentful about it.

The decision has to take into consideration your own needs plus those of your spouse and child. If at all possible, try to delay your return to work until after the first three or four months, so that the parent-child bonding may be firmly established and maintained. Take the time to prepare yourself and your family, so that the adjustment is as easy as possible for everyone. Try to time your return to work so that stress is minimal. Your return should, if at all possible, not coincide with other major family changes, such as moving or changing schools, or personal crises such as illness or death in the family.

As a working parent you are bound to be concerned about the loss of time with your child, especially if you return to work when he is very young. You could miss some of his important milestones, like the first step or word, and you may even feel jealous of the time he spends with his care-giver in your absence. These are all normal responses, but it's important to separate your own needs from concerns about your child's welfare.

Virtually everyone agrees that the first few years of life are very important in shaping a child's future personality, but this does not mean that you are the only one able to do the shaping. In fact, day care seems to have some important benefits for young children. Those who routinely are cared for by individuals other than their parents may be slightly more independent than other youngsters. A high-quality, stimulating, and nurturing day-care program offers excellent preparation for school, both socially and in-

tellectually. From your child's point of view, the important issue is not whether he is in day care, but what quality of care he receives.

Unfortunately, despite the tremendous need for quality day care, it is expensive and often hard to find. Many parents end up spending a large share of their paychecks for part-time child care and still are dissatisfied with the quality of the care their children receive. They can, however, significantly upgrade their children's day-care programs by becoming actively involved. At the very least, this means visiting the program regularly and talking with the care-giver often and extensively. Fund raising, donating supplies, volunteering to help, and working with the staff to devise more stimulating activities are other ways to improve the quality of care without increasing the cost.

Taking an active role in your child's day care not only helps ensure his well-being, but also may reduce any guilt or misgivings you're feeling about continuing to work. Having quality child care and a good relationship with the care-giver will ease some of the worry, and being especially attentive when you are with your child will make up for some of the time you're not together. The more involved you are in all aspects of your child's life—even when you're not physically present—the closer you will feel to him and the more effective you will be as a parent.

23

FEVER

Your child's normal temperature will vary with his age, activity, and the time of day. Infants tend to have higher temperatures than older children, and everyone's temperature is highest between late afternoon and early evening, and lowest between midnight and early morning. Ordinarily, a rectal reading of 100 degrees Fahrenheit (37.8 degrees Celsius) or less, or an oral reading of 99 degrees Fahrenheit (37.2 degrees Celsius) or less is considered normal, while higher readings indicate fever.

By itself, fever is *not* an illness. In fact, usually it is a positive sign that the body is fighting infection. Fever stimulates certain defenses, such as the white blood cells, which attack and destroy invading bacteria. However, fever can make your child uncomfortable. It increases his need for fluids and makes his heart rate and breathing faster.

Fever most commonly accompanies respiratory illnesses such as croup or pneumonia, ear infections, flu, severe colds, and sore throats. It may also occur with infections of the bowel or urinary tract, and with a wide variety of viral illnesses.

In children between six months and five years, fever can trigger seizures, called "febrile convulsions." These usually happen during the first few hours of a febrile illness. The child may look "peculiar" for a few moments, then stiffen out, twitch, and roll his eyes. He will be unresponsive for a short time, and his skin may appear a little darker than usual during the episode. The entire convulsion usually will last no more than three or four minutes, and may be over in a few seconds, but it can seem like a lifetime to a frightened parent. It is reassuring to know that febrile convulsions almost always are harmless, though they should be reported promptly to your pediatrician.

A rare but serious problem which is easily confused with fever, is heat illness, or heat stroke. This is caused not by infection or internal conditions, but by surrounding heat. It can occur when a child is in a very hot place, for example a hot beach in midsummer or an overheated closed car on a summer day. Children left unattended in closed cars result in several deaths a year; never leave an infant unattended in a closed car, even for a few minutes. Heat stroke also can occur if a baby is overdressed in hot, humid weather. Under these circumstances the body temperature can rise to dangerous levels (above 105 degrees Fahrenheit [40.5 degrees Celsius]), which must be reduced quickly by cool-water

UPPER LIMITS OF NORMAL TEMPERATURES

Method	Time	3 Years and Under	Over 3 Years
Rectal temperature	2 minutes	100.4 F (38 C)	100 F (37.8 C)
Oral temperature	2 minutes	99.5 F (37.5 C)	99 F (37.2 C)

sponging, fanning, and removal to a cool place. After the child has been cooled, he should be taken immediately to a pediatrician or emergency room. Heat stroke is an emergency condition.

Whenever you think your child has a fever, take his temperature with a thermometer. Feeling the skin (or using temperature-sensitive tape) is not accurate, especially when the child is experiencing a chill. If your child is less than three years old, take his temperature rectally with a mercury rectal thermometer (see *Taking a Rectal Temperature,* page 58). If he is older, he probably can cooperate well enough for you to take his temperature orally, but make sure the thermometer remains in place for at least two minutes.

When to Call the Pediatrician

If your child is *three months or younger* and has a rectal temperature of 100.2 degrees Fahrenheit (37.9 degrees Celsius) or higher, call your pediatrician immediately. *This is an absolute necessity.* The doctor will need to examine the baby to rule out any serious infection or disease.

You also may need to notify the doctor if your child is between three and six months and has a fever of 101 degrees Fahrenheit (38.3 degrees Celsius) or greater, or is older than six months and has a temperature of 103 degrees Fahrenheit (39.4 degrees Celsius) or higher. Such a high temperature frequently indicates a significant infection, which may require treatment. However, in most cases your decision to call the pediatrician also will depend upon associated symptoms such as sore throat, earache, cough. If your child is over one year of age, is eating and sleeping well, and has playful moments, there usually is no need to call the doctor immediately. You may wait to see if the fever improves by itself or with the home treatment methods described below. If a high fever persists for more than twenty-four hours, however, it is best to call even if there are no other complaints or findings.

If your child should become delirious (acts frightened, "sees" objects that are not there, talks strangely) during his fever, call your pediatrician, particularly if this has not occurred before. These unusual activities probably will disappear when the temperature returns to normal, but the doctor may want to examine the child to make sure they are a response to the fever and not something more serious, such as an inflammation of the brain (encephalitis).

If your child has a febrile convulsion, he should be examined by your pediatrician as soon as possible, particularly if this is the first time it has occurred, or if it is more severe or prolonged than others he has had. You need to be sure that the seizure is due to fever and not to a more serious condition such as meningitis (see page 597).

Home Treatment

Fevers under 101 degrees Fahrenheit (38.3 degrees Celsius) generally do not need to be treated unless your child is uncomfortable or has a history of febrile convulsions. Even

ACETAMINOPHEN DOSAGE CHART

Dosages may be repeated every four hours, but should not be given more than five times in twenty-four hours. (*Note:* Milliliter is abbreviated as ml; 5 ml equals 1 teaspoon [tsp].)

Age	Weight	Drops 80 mg/0.8 ml	Elixir 160 mg/5 ml	Chewable Tablets 80 mg tabs
0–3 mos.	6–11 lbs. (2.7–5 kg)	0.4 ml	—	—
4–11 mos.	12–17 lbs. (5.5–7.7 kg)	0.8 ml	½ tsp	1 tab
12–23 mos.	18–23 lbs. (8.2–10.5 kg)	1.2 ml	¾ tsp	1½ tabs
2–3 yrs.	24–35 lbs. (10.9–15.9 kg)	1.6 ml	1 tsp	2 tabs
4–5 yrs.	36–47 lbs. (16.3–21.4 kg)	2.4 ml	1½ tsp	3 tabs

higher temperatures are not in themselves dangerous or significant unless your child has a history of convulsions or a chronic disease. It is more important to watch how your child is behaving. If he is eating and sleeping well, and has periods of playfulness, he probably doesn't need any treatment. If he seems to be bothered by the fever, however, you can treat it in the following ways.

Medication (Acetaminophen)

There are several medications that can reduce body temperature by blocking the mechanisms that cause a fever. These so-called antipyretic agents include acetaminophen, ibuprofen, and aspirin. All three of these drugs appear to be equally effective at reducing fever. *However, since aspirin may cause or be associated with side effects such as stomach upset, intestinal bleeding, and (most seriously) Reye syndrome (see page 490), we do not recommend using it to treat*

a simple fever. Although ibuprofen is now approved for use in infants and children, it is still relatively new and we do not know much about its side effects. Therefore, we recommend using acetaminophen.

Ideally, the dose of acetaminophen should be based on a child's weight, not his age. (See the Dosage Chart above.) However, the dosages listed on the labels of acetaminophen bottles (which are usually calculated by age) are generally safe and effective unless your child is unusually light or heavy for his age. As a general rule, do not give a baby under three months acetaminophen or any other medication without the advice of your pediatrician.

Sponging

In most cases, using oral acetaminophen is the most convenient way to treat a fever. However, in some cases you might want to combine this with tepid sponging, or just use sponging alone.

Sponging is preferred over acetaminophen if:

- Your child is known to be allergic to, or is unable to tolerate, antipyretic drugs (a rare case).

It is advisable to *combine* sponging with acetaminophen if:

- Fever is making your child uncomfortable.

- He has a temperature over 104 degrees Fahrenheit (40 degrees Celsius).

- He has a history of febrile convulsions or someone else in your immediate family has had them.

- He is vomiting and may not be able to retain the medication.

To sponge your child, place him in his regular bath (tub, bathinette, or baby bath), but put only 1 to 2 inches of tepid water (85 to 90 degrees Fahrenheit, or 29.4 to 32.2 degrees Celsius) in the basin. If you do not have a bath thermometer, test the water with the back of your hand or wrist. It should feel just slightly warm. Do not use cold water, since that will be uncomfortable and may cause shivering, which can raise his temperature. Seat your child in the water—it is more comfortable than lying down. Then, using a clean washcloth or sponge, spread a film of water over his trunk, arms, and legs. The water will evaporate and cool the body. Keep the room at about 75 degrees Fahrenheit (23.9 degrees Celsius), and continue sponging him until his temperature has reached an acceptable level (see the table of Normal Temperatures). *Never put alcohol in the water; it can be absorbed into the skin, which can cause serious problems such as coma.*

Usually, sponging will bring down the fever in thirty to forty-five minutes. However, if your child is resisting actively, stop and let him just sit and play in the water. If being in the tub makes him more upset and uncomfortable, it is best to take him out even if his fever is unchanged. Remember, fever in the moderate range (less than 102 degrees Fahrenheit [38.9 degrees Celsius]) is in itself not harmful.

Other Suggestions for Mild Fever

- Keep your child's room comfortably cool, and dress him lightly.

- Encourage him to drink extra fluid (water, diluted fruit juices, gelatin-flavored water).

- Avoid giving extremely fatty foods or others that are difficult to digest, as fever decreases the activity of the stomach, and foods are digested more slowly. There is no reason to discontinue giving your child the milk he normally drinks.

- If the room is warm or stuffy, place a fan nearby to keep the cool air moving.

- Your child does not have to stay in his room or in bed when he has fever. He can be up and about the house, but he should not run around and overexert himself.

- If the fever is a symptom of a highly contagious disease, keep your child away from other youngsters and elderly people.

Treating a Febrile Convulsion

If your child has a febrile convulsion, act immediately to prevent injury:

- Place him on the floor or bed away from any hard or sharp objects.

- Turn his head to the side so that any saliva or vomit can drain from his mouth.

- Do not put anything into his mouth; he will not swallow his tongue.

- Call for emergency medical help if the convulsion lasts more than two or three minutes or is particularly severe (difficulty breathing, choking, blueness of the skin, several in a row).

24

GENITOURINARY TRACT

Blood in the Urine (Hematuria)

If your child's urine has a red, orange, or brown color, it may contain blood. The medical term for this is *hematuria*. This can be caused by many things, including a physical injury, or inflammation or infection in the urinary tract. Hematuria also can be caused by some general medical problem, such as a defect of blood clotting, exposure to toxic materials, hereditary conditions, or abnormalities of the immune system.

Sometimes there may be such small amounts of blood in the urine that you cannot see any color change, though it may be detected by a chemical test performed by the pediatrician. In some cases, the reddish color may simply be due to something your child has eaten or swallowed. Beets, blackberries, red food coloring, phenolphthalein (a chemical sometimes used in laxatives), Pyridium (a medicine used to relieve bladder pain), and the medicine rifampin all will cause the urine to turn red or orange if your child ingests them. Any time you are not sure that one of these has caused the color change, or if the color change persists for more than twenty-four hours without explanation, call your pediatrician.

Treatment

The pediatrician will ask you about any possible injury or foods that might have caused the change in color of the urine. He will perform a physical examination, checking particularly for any increase in blood pressure, tenderness in the kidney area, or swelling (particularly of the hands or feet or around the eyes) that might indicate urinary tract problems. The doctor also will perform tests on a sample of urine.

If no urinary infection is found, the doctor may request blood tests, X-rays, or other examinations to check the functioning of your child's kidneys, bladder, and immune system. If none of these reveals the cause of the hematuria, and it continues to occur, your pediatrician may refer you to a children's kidney specialist, who will perform additional tests. (Sometimes these tests will include an examination of a tiny piece of kidney tissue under the microscope. This tissue may be obtained by surgically operating, or by performing what's called a "needle biopsy.")

Once your pediatrician knows what is caus-

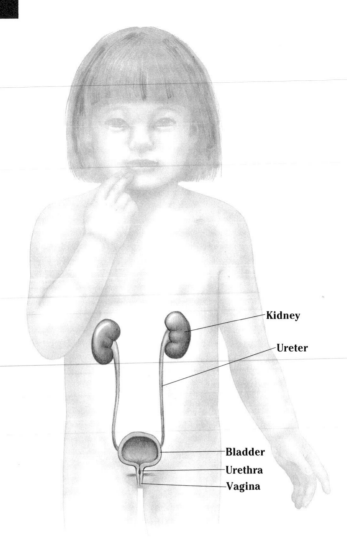

Kidney

Ureter

Bladder

Urethra

Vagina

Genitourinary System

ing the hematuria, treatment can begin. This may be as simple as rest, a change in diet, or, in some cases, special medication such as cortisone or drugs to affect the immune system. Whatever the treatment, your child will need to return to the doctor regularly for repeat urine and blood tests and blood-pressure checks. This is necessary to make sure that he isn't developing chronic kidney disease, which can lead to kidney failure. If surgery is required to correct the hematuria, your pediatrician will refer you to a urologist who can perform such procedures.

Hypospadias

Ordinarily in boys, the opening through which urine passes (the meatus) is located at the tip of the penis. In rare cases, and for reasons that are unknown, this opening appears on the underside of the penis—a condition known as "hypospadias."

Because hypospadias involves a malformation of the skin in this area, it may cause abnormal erections (called chordees) and sexual problems in adulthood. The meatus may direct the urinary stream downward, and in very rare cases there may be some blockage during urination. One of the most important reasons to correct severe hypospadias, however, is to prevent the psychological complications that can arise quite early in childhood when playmates notice the abnormal appearance of the penis.

Treatment

After detecting hypospadias in your newborn, the pediatrician probably will advise against circumcision until after consultation with a urologist. This is because circumcision makes future surgical repair more difficult.

Mild hypospadias may require no treatment, but moderate or severe forms require surgical repair. This operation may be done as early as six months or as late as eighteen months of age, but usually is recommended around the first birthday. Very often this surgery can be performed on an outpatient basis. In some severe cases more than one operation may be needed to repair the defect completely. After surgery your child will have normal urinary and sexual function, and a nearly normal-appearing penis.

Labial Adhesions

Ordinarily, the lips of skin (labia) surrounding the entrance to the vagina are separated. In rare cases they grow together to block the opening, partially or completely. This condition, called "labial adhesions," may occur in the early months of life or, less frequently, later on if there is constant irritation and inflammation in this area. In these latter cases, the problem is usually traceable to diaper irritation, contact with harsh detergents, or panties made with synthetic fabric. Usually, labial adhesions do not cause symptoms, but they can lead to difficulty with urination and increase a girl's susceptibility to urinary tract infection. If the vaginal opening is completely blocked, there is a buildup of urine or vaginal secretions behind the obstruction.

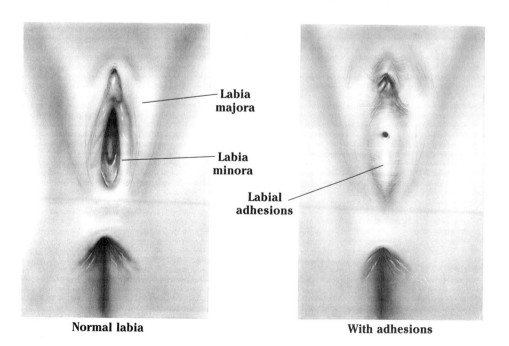

Labia
majora

Labia
minora

Labial
adhesions

Normal labia   **With adhesions**

Treatment

If the opening of your daughter's vagina appears to have closed, or looks partially blocked, notify your pediatrician. He will examine her and advise you if any treatment is necessary.

At first, the doctor will gently attempt to spread the labia. If the connecting tissue is weak, this mild pressure may expose the opening.

If the connecting tissue is too strong, the doctor may prescribe a cream that contains the female hormone estrogen for you to apply to the area as you very gently and gradually pull the labia apart over a period of time. Once the labia are separated, you will need to apply the cream for a short while (three to five days) until the skin on both sides heals completely.

In very rare cases, the adhesions (scarlike tissue that grows between the labia and holds them together) are so thick that they need to be separated with a special instrument. This must be done by the physician.

Meatal Stenosis

The meatus is the opening in the penis through which urine passes. Sometimes, particularly in circumcised boys, irritation of the tip of the penis causes scar tissue to form around the meatus, making it smaller. This narrowing, called "meatal stenosis," may develop at any time during childhood, but is most commonly found between ages three and seven. Meatal stenosis is relatively rare.

Boys who have meatal stenosis have a narrowed urinary stream. Urination may take longer, and they have difficulty completely emptying the bladder. Although rare, recurrent urinary tract infections can result from this condition.

Treatment

If you notice that your son's urinary stream is very small or narrow, or if he strains to urinate, or dribbles or sprays urine, discuss it with your pediatrician. Meatal stenosis is not a serious condition, but it should be evaluated to see if it needs to be corrected surgically. The operation is very minor, but usually will require a brief general anesthetic. There will be some minor discomfort after the procedure, but this should disappear after a very short period of time.

Prevention

Decreasing the irritation caused by certain diapers, harsh detergents, and wet, rough underclothing may help prevent the condition.

Undescended Testicles (Cryptorchidism)

During gestation, the testes develop in the abdomen of the male fetus. As he nears birth, they descend through a tube (the inguinal canal) into the scrotum. In a small number of boys, especially those who are premature,

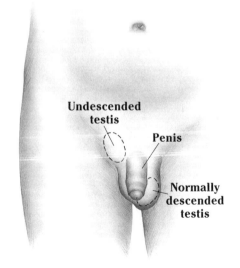

Undescended testis

Penis

Normally descended testis

one or both testicles fail to descend by the the time of birth. In many of these boys, descent will occur during the first nine months of life. In some, however, this does not happen.

The cause of undescended testicles cannot be explained in most cases. However, in some boys the following factors may play a role:

- There may not have been enough of certain hormones from the mother or the developing testicles to stimulate their normal maturation.

- The testes themselves may be abnormal in their response to these hormones.

- There may be a physical blockage that prevents descent.

- In some cases there may be a link with hormonal preparations taken by the mother during pregnancy (which is one reason why pregnant women are advised to avoid such medications).

If your child has undescended testicles, his scrotum will be small and appear underdeveloped. If only one testicle is undescended, the scrotum may look asymmetrical (full on one side, empty on the other). If the testicles are sometimes present in the scrotum and at other times (such as when he is cold or excited) are absent, and located above the scrotum, they are said to be "retractile." This condition usually is self-correcting as the child becomes more mature.

The undescended testicle may be twisted, and in the process, its blood supply may be blocked, causing pain in the inguinal (groin) or scrotal area. If this situation is not corrected, the testicle can be severely and permanently damaged. So if your son has an undescended testicle and complains of pain in the groin or scrotal area, call your pediatrician immediately.

Undescended testicles should be reevaluated at each regular checkup. If they do not descend into the scrotum by age one to two, treatment should be started.

Treatment

Undescended testicles may be treated with hormone injections and/or surgery. The lower the testes, the more likely that the hormone injections will be successful. Usually, but not always, treatment with hormones is tried first; if that is unsuccessful, the surgical approach is taken. Sometimes a hernia (see page 485) is also present and can be repaired at the same time.

If your son's undescended testicle is allowed to remain in that position for over two years, he has a higher than average risk of being unable to father children (infertility). He also has a slightly increased risk of developing testicular tumors in adult life, particularly if the testicle is left in its abnormal position. Fortunately, with early and proper treatment all of these complications can usually be avoided.

Urethral Valves

Urine leaves the bladder through a tube called the urethra, which in boys passes through the penis. During early fetal development, there are tiny "valves" at the beginning of the urethra which block the passage of urine. These normally disappear well before birth so that urine can flow freely out the end of the penis. In some boys, however, the valves remain after birth, and may cause serious problems by interfering with the flow of urine. They are called "posterior urethral valves."

Often these valves are detected by ultrasound during pregnancy, but many times they are not discovered until the newborn period, when the pediatrician finds that the baby's bladder is distended and enlarged. Other warning signals include a continual dribbling of urine and a weak stream during urination. If you notice these symptoms, notify your pediatrician at once.

Posterior urethral valves require immediate medical attention to prevent serious urinary tract infections or damage to the kidneys. If the blockage is severe, the urine can back up through the ureters (the tubes between the bladder and the kidneys), creating pressure that can damage the kidneys.

Treatment

If a child is having urinary blockage due to posterior urethral valves, the pediatrician may pass a small tube up the penis into the bladder to relieve the obstruction temporarily. Then X-rays of the bladder and kidneys will be ordered to confirm the diagnosis and to see if any damage has occurred to the upper urinary tract. A urologist will then perform surgery to remove the obstructing valves.

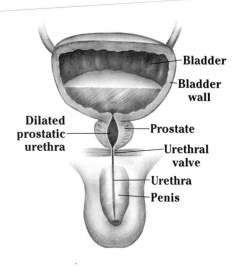

Bladder
Bladder wall
Dilated prostatic urethra
Prostate
Urethral valve
Urethra
Penis

Urinary Tract Infections

Urinary tract infections are common among young children, particularly girls. They generally are caused by bacteria that enter through the urethra, though they also can be caused by bacteria carried through the bloodstream to the kidneys from another part of the body. As the bacteria move through the urinary tract, they may cause infection in different locations. *Urinary tract infection* is a general term used for all the following specific infections.

Urethritis—infection of the urethra

Cystitis—infection of the bladder

Pyelonephritis—infection of the renal pelvis and kidney

The area most commonly infected is the bladder (cystitis). Usually, cystitis is caused by bacteria that get into the urinary tract by contamination of the urethra with stool. The urethra is very short in girls, allowing bacteria to get into the bladder easily. Thus, they tend to have urinary tract infections more frequently than boys.

Cystitis can cause lower abdominal pain, tenderness, pain during urination, frequent urination, blood in the urine, and fever. Infection of the upper urinary tract (the kidneys) will cause a more general abdominal pain and higher fever, but is less likely to cause frequent and painful urination.

Urinary tract infections must be treated with antibiotics as quickly as possible, so you should notify your pediatrician promptly if you suspect your child has developed one. A urinalysis also should be performed if your child suffers vague symptoms that cannot be explained, since these can be caused by a chronic urinary tract infection. Even if your child has no symptoms, routine urinalyses should be performed according to the Academy's recommended schedule (see page 61), and blood pressure checks should be done at each office visit.

Treatment

The pediatrician will measure your child's blood pressure and examine him for tenderness that might indicate a urinary tract infection. The doctor will want to know what your child has been eating and drinking, because certain foods can irritate the urinary tract, causing symptoms similar to those of an infection. (Drinks containing citrus juice, carbonation, and caffeine are especially likely to have this effect.) The doctor also will need to know if anyone else in the family gets urinary tract infections, since this might suggest an inherited structural abnormality that would make your child more susceptible to these problems.

Your child also will be asked to provide a urine sample for analysis. This must be collected by the "clean catch" method, so you will need to help. First, you'll use soap and water to cleanse the urethral opening (with an uncircumcised boy, hold the foreskin back). Then allow your child to start to urinate, but wait just a moment before you start to collect the sample in the container provided by the doctor. In this way, any bacteria around the outside of the urethral opening will be washed away by the first urine voided and won't contaminate the specimen. (Infants will be cleansed in the same manner but will have special urine collectors taped over the penis or vaginal opening until voiding occurs.)

The urine will be examined under the microscope for any sign of blood cells or bacteria, and special tests (cultures) will be done to identify the bacteria that are present. An antibiotic will be started immediately if an infection is suspected, although it may need to be changed after the final results of the culture are obtained (up to forty-eight hours later).

Antibiotics usually are prescribed for a two-week period. After one week your pediatrician may request another urine sample, to check the effectiveness of the treatment. If it does not seem to be working, the prescription will be changed. Otherwise, the same medication will be continued for another week.

Make sure your child takes the full course of medication prescribed, even if the discomfort goes away after just a few days. Otherwise, the bacteria may grow again, causing further infection and more serious damage to the urinary tract. After your child's treatment is complete, another urine sample will be taken to make sure that the infection is completely gone and no bacteria remain.

Most specialists now feel that after your child's first serious urinary tract infection, further tests should be done (ultrasound, X-rays, or renal scanning examinations). Your pediatrician also may conduct other tests to check kidney function. If any of these examinations indicates a structural abnormality that should be corrected, your doctor will recommend that your child see a genitourinary surgeon.

Wetting Problems or Enuresis

After toilet training is completed (usually between ages two and four), it is not uncommon for children still to occasionally wet the bed at night. This may happen as often as two to three times per week early in this period and gradually become less and less until it is completely gone at around age five.

In most cases, the best way to deal with incontinence (wetting) is to treat it as something natural and unimportant. Don't put your child back in diapers, and don't scold or punish him. This wetting usually occurs because the child's bladder is not yet large enough to hold a full night's output of urine, or because he has not yet developed the ability to awaken in response to the urge of a full bladder.

Some children continue to wet at night past the age of five. This generally is referred to as "nocturnal (nighttime) enuresis," or bedwetting. It affects one out of every ten children over the age of five. Boys make up two thirds of this group, and there often is a family history of bed-wetting (usually in the father). The reasons for bed-wetting are not fully understood, but it may be related to the fact that girls develop control over their nervous, muscular, and nighttime "full-bladder alarm systems" more rapidly than do boys. Bedwetting generally is *not* associated with other physical or emotional problems.

A much smaller number of children over age five have daytime wetting problems, and an even smaller group is unable to hold their urine both day and night. When incontinence does occur both day and night, it usually indicates a bladder or kidney problem.

If your child wets, consider the following possible causes:

- Slow development of the ability to awaken when the bladder is full

- Urinary tract infections or urethral irritation from bubble bath or detergents in bath water or, very rarely, sensitivity to certain foods

- Abnormalities in the structure of the urinary tract, such as an unusually small bladder, a partial blockage within the neck of the bladder, or muscles that don't contract properly to control urination

- Constipation, which can cause extra pressure on the bladder from the rectum

- An early sign of diabetes mellitus (see page 652), urinary tract infection (see page 592), or emotional distress caused by an upsetting event or unusual stress. This is particularly true if wetting began suddenly after six months of totally dry nights.

Signs of a Problem

When your child is starting toilet training, he is sure to have "accidents." Therefore, there is no reason to be concerned about wetting until at least six months to a year after the training is successful. Even then, it is still normal for him to have some accidents, but they should decrease, so that by age six he should have only occasional accidents during the day, with perhaps a few more at night. If your child continues to wet frequently, or if you notice any of the following signals, consult your pediatrician:

- Wet underpants, nightclothes, and bed linens, even when the child regularly uses the toilet

- Unusual straining during urination, a very small or narrow stream of urine, or dribbling after urination

- Cloudy or pink urine, or bloodstains on underpants or nightclothes

- Redness or rash in the genital area

- Hiding of underwear to conceal wetting

- Daytime as well as nighttime wetting

Treatment

Occasional nighttime wetting or daytime accidents when the child is laughing, or engaged in physical activity, or just too busy playing, is perfectly normal up to the age of five or so, and should be no cause for concern. Though annoying to you, and perhaps embarassing for your child, it should stop on its own. There probably is no need for a medical investigation. However, your pediatrician will want to know the answers to the following questions:

- Is there a family history of wetting?

- How often does your child urinate, and at what times of the day?

- When do the accidents occur?

- Do accidents occur when your child is very active or upset, or when he's under unusual stress?

- Does your child tend to have accidents after drinking caffeinated drinks, lots of water, or a lot of salty foods?

- Is there anything unusual about your child's urination or the appearance of his urine?

If your pediatrician suspects a problem, he may check a urine sample for signs of urinary tract infection (see page 592). If there is an infection, the doctor will treat it with antibiotics, and this may cure the wetting problems. Usually, however, infection is not the cause.

If there are other indications that wetting is due to more than just slow development of the full-bladder response, and the wetting persists beyond age five, your pediatrician may request additional tests, such as X-rays of the bladder or kidneys. If an abnormality is found, the doctor may recommend that you consult a pediatric urologist.

If no physical cause can be found for wetting in a child who is over five years of age, and the wetting is causing significant family disruption, the pediatrician may recommend a home treatment program. The program will vary, depending on whether your child wets during the day or night.

Home Treatment for Daytime Wetting After Toilet Training

1. Eliminate skin irritation in the genital area by avoiding the use of harsh detergents on underclothing and bubble-making products in the bath water. Also, use mild soaps for bathing, and apply petroleum jelly to protect the affected areas from further irritation from the water and urine.

2. Eliminate dietary sources of excess urine output and irritation:

- Excessive water

- Drinks that contain caffeine

3. Prevent constipation (see page 474).

4. Encourage your child to hold the urine a little longer before each urination in order to enlarge the capacity of his bladder.

Home Treatment for Nocturnal Bed-wetting Over the Age of Five

The following plan usually is helpful, but you should discuss it with your pediatrician before beginning.

1. Explain the problem to your child, emphasizing that you understand and know it's not his fault.

2. Discourage him from drinking large amounts of fluids right before bedtime.

3. Have him use the toilet immediately before bedtime.

4. Try to awaken him to use the toilet again right before *you* go to bed if he's been asleep for an hour or more. (This may be difficult if he's a very sound sleeper.)

5. Reward him for "dry nights," but don't punish him for "wet" ones. This is very important, since this is an emotional issue for both of you.

If your child is still wetting after one to three months on this plan, your pediatrician may recommend using a bed-wetting alarm device. This alarm will awaken your child automatically as soon as he begins to wet, so he can get up and complete his urination in the toilet. When used consistently and according to your pediatrician's guidelines, this conditioning method is successful for fifty to seventy-five out of every hundred children who try it.

If the bed-wetting alarm hasn't solved the problem after three or four months, your pediatrician may prescribe oral medication, but this should be a last resort. Although medication can be helpful, it can also produce side effects such as rapid heart rate, restlessness, and changes in blood pressure.

If None of the Treatments Works

A small number of children with bed-wetting simply do not respond to any treatment. Almost all will outgrow the problem by adolescence, however. Only one in a hundred adults is troubled by persistent bed-wetting. Until your child does outgrow his wetting problem, he will need a large amount of emotional support from the family, and he may benefit from counseling with his pediatrician or a child mental-health professional. He should still realize that there are things he can do to help his problem, however, and should be encouraged to continue trying to increase his bladder capacity and to avoid drinking large quantities of beverages that stimulate urination. Because bed-wetting is such a common problem, there are many mail-order treatment programs and devices being advertised. You should be wary of them, however, as there are many false claims and promises made. Your pediatrician is still your most reliable source for advice, and you should ask for it before enrolling in or paying for any treatment program.

25

HEAD, NERVOUS SYSTEM, FACE, AND NECK

Meningitis

Meningitis is an inflammation of the tissues that cover the brain and spinal cord. The inflammation sometimes affects the brain itself. Meningitis is a very serious disease that occurs rarely. When it does, however, we see it most commonly in children under five. With early diagnosis and proper treatment, a child with meningitis has an excellent chance of getting well without any complications.

The most serious kind of meningitis is caused by bacteria (several different types are involved). Children under the age of two are at greatest risk for this form of the disease. Meningitis also can be caused by viruses and other organisms such as fungi or parasites. The viral form usually is not very serious.

The bacteria that cause meningitis often can be found in the mouths and throats of healthy children. But this does not necessarily mean that these children will get the disease. That doesn't happen unless the bacteria get into the bloodstream.

We still don't understand exactly why some children get meningitis and others don't, but we do know that certain groups of children are more likely to get the illness. These are the following:

- Babies, especially those under two months of age. (Because their immune systems are not well developed, the bacteria can get into the bloodstream more easily.)

- Children with recurrent sinus infections

- Children with recent serious head injuries and skull fractures

- Children who have just had brain surgery

- Children with severe burns that may be chronically infected

- Children with certain chronic conditions such as cystic fibrosis, cancer, sickle-cell anemia, or illnesses requiring continuous respirator care or intravenous infusions

Before antibiotics (drugs that combat bacteria) were developed, 90 percent of the children with meningitis died. Of the 10 percent who survived, most were left retarded or deaf, or had convulsions. Now, the outlook is much brighter. With prompt diagnosis and treatment, 70 percent of the children who get meningitis recover without any complications.

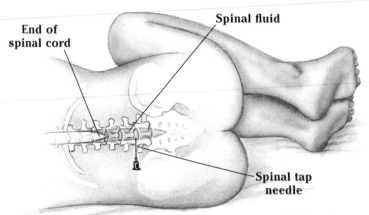

End of spinal cord

Spinal fluid

Spinal tap needle

A spinal tap is taken from the space below the spinal cord so that the needle will not touch the spinal cord.

Even most of those with complications usually have only minor ones that last just a short time. Hearing loss, however, remains an important, frequently found, long-lasting problem. Meningitis must be detected early and treated aggressively in order to be cured. This is why it's so important for you to notify your pediatrician immediately if your child displays any of the following warning signs.

If your child is less than two months old: The presence of fever, decreased appetite, listlessness, or increased crying or irritability warrants a call to your doctor. At this age, the signs of meningitis can be very subtle and difficult to detect, and thus it's better to call early and be wrong than to call too late.

If your child is two months to two years old: This is the most common age for meningitis. Look for symptoms such as fever, nausea, vomiting, decreased appetite, excessive crankiness, or excessive sleepiness. (His cranky periods might be extreme and his sleepy periods might make it impossible to arouse him.)

If your child is two to five years old: In addition to the above symptoms, a child of this age with meningitis may complain of a head

ache, pain in his back, or a stiff neck. He also may object to looking at bright lights.

Treatment

If, after an examination, your pediatrician is concerned that your child may have meningitis, he will do a blood test to check for a bacterial infection, and will also obtain some spinal fluid by performing a spinal tap. This procedure involves inserting a special needle into your child's lower back to draw out the fluid. Any signs of infection in this fluid will confirm that your child has meningitis. In that case he'll need to be admitted to the hospital for intravenous antibiotics and fluids, and for careful observation for complications. During the first days of treatment your child may not be able to eat or drink, so intravenous fluid will be used to provide the medicine and nutrition he needs. This may be necessary for up to ten days.

Prevention

Some types of bacterial meningitis can now be prevented with vaccines or antibiotics. Ask your pediatrician about the following:

Hib Conjugate Vaccine

This vaccine will decrease the chance of children becoming infected with Haemophilus influenzae bacteria. The vaccination is given by injection to children beginning at ages of two months of age. (See Immunization Alert in Chapter 10, page 283.)

Pneumovax

This vaccine is effective in preventing some infections caused by the *pneumococcus* bacteria. It is recommended for administration only to those children who are most susceptible to such infections: children with abnormal immune systems, sickle-cell disease, certain kidney problems, and other chronic conditions.

Rifampin

If your child has been exposed—either at home or during day care—to a child with meningitis caused by *Haemophilus influenzae* or the *meningococcus* bacteria, he should be placed on this antibiotic to prevent him from becoming infected. Your pediatrician will tell you how often and how long to use it. If your child shows any of the signs of meningitis, even though he is on the medication, call your pediatrician immediately.

Motion Sickness

Motion sickness occurs when the brain receives conflicting signals from the motion-sensing parts of the body: the inner ears; the eyes; and nerves in the ankles, knees, and other joints. Under usual circumstances all three areas respond to any motion. When the signals they receive and send are inconsistent—for example, if you watch rapid motion on a movie screen, your eyes sense the motion, but your inner ear and joints do not—the brain receives conflicting signals and activates a response that can make you sick. The same thing happens when a child is sitting so low in the backseat of a car that he cannot see outside. His inner ear senses the motion, but his eyes and joints do not.

The symptoms of motion sickness usually start with a vague feeling of stomach upset (queasiness), a cold sweat, fatigue, and loss of appetite. This then progresses to vomiting. A young child may not be able to describe queasiness, but will demonstrate it by becoming pale and restless, yawning, and crying. Later he will lose his interest in food (even his favorite ones), and finally he will vomit.

We do not know why this happens more often in some children than others, but it is most likely due to an increased sensitivity to the brain's response to motion. This response can be affected by previous bad car trips but usually improves as a child gets older.

Motion sickness occurs most often on a *first* boat or plane ride, or when the motion is very intense, such as that caused by rough water or turbulent air. Stress and excitement also can start this problem or make it worse.

What You Can Do

If your child starts to develop the symptoms of motion sickness, the best thing to do is stop the activity that is causing the problem. If it occurs in the car, stop as soon as safely possible and let him get out and walk around. If you are on a long car trip, you may have to make frequent short stops but it will be worth it. If it happens on a swing or merry-go-round, stop the motion promptly and get your child off the equipment.

He probably will be upset and scared, so try to help him relax. Otherwise, what should be a happy time will become a dreaded experience. Most important, do not get angry with your child, because he cannot help what is happening. Be as supportive of him as you can, or he may refuse to travel or have a temper tantrum the next time you ask him to get into the car or board a plane or boat.

Since "car sickness" is the most common form of motion sickness in children, many preventive measures have been developed. In addition to the frequent stops, you might try the following:

- Place your young child in an approved car seat, facing forward if over 18 pounds (8 kg) and able to sit well (after seven to nine months). Do not let him move around in the car. (You should not let him do this for safety reasons, anyway.)

- Let your older child (age four) sit in the front seat facing forward.

- If he has not eaten for three hours, give your child a *light* snack before the trip—which also helps on a boat or plane. This relieves hunger pangs, which seem to add to the symptoms.

- Try to focus his attention away from the queasy feeling. Listen to the radio, sing, or talk.

- Have him look at things outside the car, not at books or games.

If none of the above works, stop the car and have him lie on his back for a few minutes (still in his lap belt) with his eyes closed. A cool cloth on the forehead also tends to lessen the symptoms.

If you are going on a trip and your child has had motion sickness before, you might want to give him medication ahead of time to prevent problems. Some of these medications are available without a prescription, but you should ask your pediatrician before using them. Although they can help, they often produce side effects such as drowsiness (which means that when you get to your destination your child might be too tired to enjoy it), dry mouth and nose, or blurred vision. Less common reactions include skin rashes, blood pressure changes, nausea, and vomiting. Some children actually become agitated from these medicines rather than drowsy. The skin patch-type motion-sickness medications should never be used on young children.

Although it does not happen often, dehydration (see page 478) can occur from the vomiting and poor fluid intake that may accompany motion sickness. If you feel that your child is becoming dehydrated, take him to the nearest physician's office or to an emergency room.

If your child has symptoms of motion sickness at times when he is not involved with a movement activity—particularly if he also has a headache, difficulty hearing, seeing, walking, or talking, or if he stares off into space—tell your pediatrician about it. These may be symptoms of problems other than motion sickness.

Mumps

Mumps is a viral infection that usually causes swelling of the salivary glands, the glands that produce the digestive juices in the mouth. Thanks to the MMR (measles, mumps, and rubella) vaccine given at fifteen months and a booster at age twelve years, most of today's children will never get this disease. If your child has not been immunized, however, you

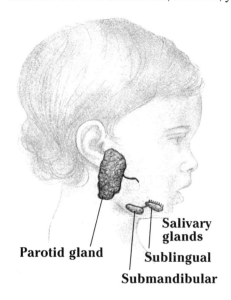

Parotid gland

Salivary glands

Sublingual

Submandibular

should know how to identify mumps and distinguish it from similar ailments.

The parotid gland, located in front of the ear at and above the angle of the jaw, is the one most often affected by mumps. However, other salivary glands in and around the face may also be involved. Though not all children with mumps appear swollen, anyone who has the virus in his system will become immune to it. Contrary to what many people think, no one can have the disease twice.

The mumps virus usually is transmitted when an infected individual coughs droplets containing the virus into the air. A nearby child inhales these particles and the virus passes through his respiratory system into his bloodstream, finally settling in his salivary glands. At this point, the virus usually causes swelling of the glands along the side of one or both cheeks. The child also may have a fever for three to five days, and will complain of pain when touching the swollen area, opening his mouth, and eating food—especially foods that stimulate the release of salivary juices. He also may experience nausea, occasional vomiting, headache, a general feeling of weakness, and loss of appetite.

In addition to the swelling of the salivary glands, there also can be swelling and pain in the joints and swelling of the testes in boys. In extremely rare cases, the virus can cause swelling of the ovaries in girls, or swelling of the brain.

Several days before the glands become noticeably swollen, the child with mumps will become infectious to others. He'll remain infectious until the swelling is gone—that is, for at least ten days after the first sign of inflammation.

It's important to note that salivary-gland swelling can be caused by infections other than mumps. This explains why some parents are convinced that their children have had the disease more than once. If your child has been immunized or has already had mumps and his cheeks become swollen, consult your pediatrician to determine the cause.

Treatment

There is no specific treatment for mumps, aside from making the child as comfortable as possible with rest, lots of fluids, and acetaminophen for fever. Although a child with the disease won't be too eager to take fluids, you should keep a glass of water or non-citrus juice nearby, and encourage him to take frequent sips. Sometimes, a warm compress over the swollen gland will give some short-term relief.

Eating solid, hard-to-digest foods may cause your child increased pain because they require extra saliva from the swollen glands. Instead, feed him soft, non-citrus foods that are easy to chew and swallow, and that place minimal demands on the inflamed glands.

If your child's condition worsens, or if he develops complications such as painful testes, severe abdominal pain, or extreme listlessness, contact your pediatrician right away. The doctor will want to examine your child to see if he needs more extensive medical treatment. However, such complications from mumps are extremely rare.

Seizures, Convulsions, and Epilepsy

Seizures are sudden temporary changes in physical movement or behavior caused by abnormal electrical impulses in the brain. Depending upon how many muscles are affected by the electrical impulses, a seizure may cause sudden stiffening of the body or complete relaxation of the muscles, which temporarily can make a person appear to be paralyzed. Sometimes these seizures are referred to as "fits" or "spells."

A convulsion (sometimes called a "grand mal seizure") is the most dramatic type of seizure, causing rapid, violent movements and sometimes loss of consciousness. Convulsions occur in about five out of every hundred people at some time during childhood. "Petit mal seizures," in contrast, are momentary episodes associated with a vacant stare or a brief (one or two seconds) lapse of attention. These occur mainly in young children, and may be so subtle that they aren't noticed until they begin affecting schoolwork.

Febrile convulsions (seizures caused by high fever) occur in three or four out of every hundred children between infancy and age five. They rarely occur after five years of age, however, and half of all children who have one febrile convulsion never have another. A febrile convulsion can cause reactions as mild as a rolling of the eyes or stiffening of the limbs, or as startling as a grand mal convulsion with twitching and jerking movements that involve the whole body. Febrile convulsions usually last less than five minutes, and ordinarily the child's behavior quickly returns to normal.

The term *epilepsy* is used to describe seizures that recur over a long period of time. Sometimes the cause of the recurring seizures is known (symptomatic epilepsy) and sometimes it is not (idiopathic epilepsy). Chemical imbalances in the blood, brain damage due to infection or injury, and lead poisoning (see page 462) are some of the conditions that can lead to epilepsy.

Some children experience sudden episodes that include breath holding, fainting, facial or body twitching, and unusual sleep disorders. They may occur just once or may recur over a limited time period. Though these may resemble epilepsy or true seizures, they are not and they require quite different treatment.

Treatment

Most seizures will stop on their own and do not require immediate medical treatment. If your child is having a convulsion, you should protect him from injuring himself by moving him to a semi-sitting position or laying him on his side with his hips higher than his head, so he will not choke if he vomits.

If the convulsion does not stop within two or three minutes, is unusually severe (difficulty breathing, choking, blueness of the skin, several in a row), call for emergency medical help. Do *not* leave the child unattended, however. After the seizure stops, call the pediatrician immediately and arrange to meet in the doctor's office or the nearest emergency room. Also call if your child is on an anticonvulsant medication, since this may mean that the dosage must be adjusted.

If your child has a fever, the pediatrician will check to see if there is an infection. If there is no fever and this was your child's first convulsion, the doctor will try to determine other possible causes by asking if there is any family history of seizures or if your child has had any recent head injury. He will examine the child and also may order blood tests, X-rays, or an electroencephalogram (EEG), which measures the electrical activity of the brain. Sometimes a spinal tap will be performed to obtain a specimen of spinal fluid that can be examined for some causes of convulsions such as meningitis (see page 597). If no explanation or cause can be found for the seizures, the doctor may consult a pediatric neurologist, a pediatrician who specializes in disorders of the nervous system.

If your child has had a febrile convulsion, the doctor may simply advise you to control the fever using acetaminophen and sponging. However, if a bacterial infection is present, an antibiotic will probably be prescribed. If a serious infection such as meningitis (infection of the lining of the brain) is responsible for the seizure, your child will have to be hospitalized for further treatment.

When seizures are caused by abnormal amounts of sugar, calcium, or magnesium in the blood, hospitalization may be required so that the cause can be found and the imbalances corrected. If epilepsy is diagnosed, your child usually will be placed on an anticonvulsant medication. When the proper dosage is maintained, the seizures can almost always be completely controlled. Your child may need to have his blood checked periodically after starting this medication to make certain there is an adequate amount present. He also may need periodic EEGs. Medication usually is continued until there have been no seizures for a year or two.

As frightening as seizures can be, it's encouraging to know that the likelihood that your child will have another one drops greatly as he gets older. (Only one in a hundred adults ever has a seizure.) Unfortunately, a great deal of misunderstanding and confusion about seizures still exist, so it is important that your child's friends and teachers understand his condition. If you need additional support or information, consult with your pediatrician or contact your local or state branch of the Epilepsy Foundation.

Sinusitis

Sinusitis is an inflammation of one or more of the sinuses (bony cavities) around the nose. It usually occurs as a complication of a viral upper respiratory infection or allergic inflammation in children over 2 years of age. These conditions cause swelling of the lining

of the nose and sinuses. This swelling blocks the openings that allow the sinuses to drain into the back of the nose, so the sinuses fill with fluid. Although nose-blowing and sniffing may be natural responses to this blockage, they can make the situation worse by pushing bacteria from the back of the nose—into the sinuses. Since the sinuses can't drain properly, the bacteria will multiply there, causing an infection.

There are several signs of sinusitis that should alert you to call your pediatrician:

- The persistence of symptoms of a cold or upper respiratory infection, including cough and nasal discharge lasting for more than ten days, without any improvement. The nasal discharge may be thick and yellow, or clear, or whitish, and the cough usually will continue during the day as well as at night. In some cases a child with sinusitis will have swelling around the eyes when he wakes up in the morning. Also, a preschooler with sinusitis sometimes may have persistent bad breath along with cold symptoms. (However, this also could mean that he has put something into his nose or has a sore throat, or that he isn't brushing his teeth!)

- Your child's cold is severe and is accompanied by high fever and thick yellow nasal discharge. His eyes might be swollen in the early morning, and he might have a severe headache that he describes (if he's old enough) as behind or above the eyes.

In very rare cases, a sinus infection may spread to either the eye or the central nervous system (the brain). If this occurs, you'll see swelling around the eye not just in the morning but all through the day, and you should call your pediatrician immediately. If your child has a very severe headache, becomes sensitive to light, or is increasingly irritable, the infection may have spread into the central nervous system. This is serious and requires immediate medical attention.

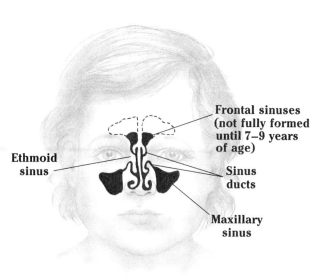

Frontal sinuses (not fully formed until 7–9 years of age)

Ethmoid sinus

Sinus ducts

Maxillary sinus

Treatment

If your pediatrician thinks your child has sinusitis, he will prescribe an antibiotic, usually for a ten- to fourteen-day period. Once your child is on the medication, his symptoms should start to go away very quickly. In most cases the nasal discharge will clear and the cough will improve over a week or two. *But even though he may seem better, he must continue to take the antibiotics for the prescribed length of time.*

On the other hand, if there's no improvement after two to four days, your pediatrician might want to conduct some further tests, after which a different medication may be prescribed or an additional one added for a longer period of time.

Wryneck (Torticollis)

Wryneck is a condition that causes a child to hold his head or neck in a twisted or otherwise abnormal position. He may lean his head toward one shoulder and, when lying on his

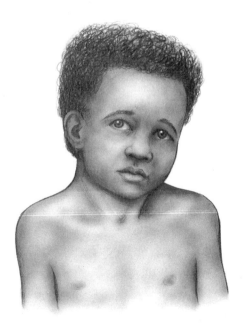

stomach, always turn the same side of his face toward the mattress. This can cause his head to flatten on one side and his face to appear uneven or out of line. If not treated, wryneck may lead to permanent facial deformity or unevenness and to restricted head movement.

There are several different causes of wryneck. These include:

Congenital Muscular Torticollis

By far the most common cause among children under age five, this condition is the result of injury to the muscle that connects the breastbone, head, and neck (sternocleidomastoid muscle). The injury may occur during birth (particularly breech and difficult first-time deliveries), but it also can occur while the baby is still in the womb. Whatever the cause, this condition usually is detected in the first six to eight weeks of life when the pediatrician notices a small lump on the side of the baby's neck in the area of the damaged muscle. Later, the muscle contracts and causes the head to tilt to one side.

Klippel-Feil Syndrome

In this condition, which is present at birth, the tilt of the neck is caused by an abnormality of the bones at the top of the spine. Children with Klippel-Feil syndrome usually have a short, broad neck, low hairline, and very restricted neck movement.

Torticollis Due to Injury or Inflammation

This is more likely to occur in older children, up to the age of nine or ten. This type of torticollis results from an inflammation of the throat caused by upper respiratory infection, sore throat, injury, or some unknown factor. The swelling, for some reason still not known, causes the tissue surrounding the upper spine to loosen, allowing the vertebral bones to move out of normal position. When this happens, the neck muscles go into spasm, causing the head to tilt to one side.

Treatment

Each type of wryneck requires a slightly different treatment. It is very important to seek such treatment early, so that the problem is corrected before it causes permanent deformity.

Your pediatrician will examine your child's neck and may order X-rays of the area in order to identify the cause of the problem. X-rays of the hip may also be ordered, as some children with congenital muscular torticollis also have been found to have dislocation of the hip. If the doctor decides that the problem is muscular torticollis due to a birth-related injury to the sternocleidomastoid muscle, you will be instructed in an exercise program to stretch the neck muscles. The doctor will show you how to gently move your child's head in the opposite direction from the tilt. You'll need to do this several times a day, very gradually extending the movement as the muscle stretches.

When your child sleeps, it is best to place him on his back or side, with his head positioned opposite to the direction of the tilt. He can be placed on his stomach if he allows you to turn his face away from the side of the muscle injury, and if he then keeps his head in this position while sleeping. When he is awake, position him so that things he wants to look at (windows, mobiles, pictures, activity) are on the side away from the injury. In that way, he'll stretch the shortened muscle while trying to see these objects. These simple strategies cure this type of wryneck in the vast majority of cases, preventing the need for later surgery.

If the problem is not corrected by exercise, your pediatrician will refer you to an orthopedic surgeon. In some cases it may be necessary to surgically remove the damaged section of muscle.

If your child's wryneck is caused by something other than congenital muscular torticollis, and the X-rays show no spinal abnormality, other treatment involving rest, a special collar, traction, application of heat to the area, medication, or rarely even surgery may be necessary.

26

HEART

Arrhythmias

The regular rhythm or beat of the heart is maintained by a small electrical circuit that runs through nerves in the walls of the heart. When the circuit is working properly, the heartbeat is quite regular, but when there's a problem in the circuit, an irregular heartbeat, or arrhythmia, can occur. Some children are born with abnormalities in this apparatus, but arrhythmias can also be caused by infections or chemical imbalances in the blood.

Your child's heart rate will *normally* vary to some degree. Fever, exercise, crying, or other vigorous activity makes any heart beat faster. (That's why a person's base heart rate is usually measured when the body is at rest.) And the younger your child, the faster his resting heart rate will be. As he gets older, his rate will naturally slow down. For example, a resting heart rate of 130 beats per minute is normal for a newborn infant, but it's too fast for a six-year-old child at rest. A resting heart rate of 50 or 60 beats per minute may be normal for an athletic teenager, but it is abnormally slow for a baby.

Even in healthy children there can be other variations in the rhythm of the heartbeat, including changes that occur just as a result of breathing. Such a normal fluctuation is called "sinus arrhythmia," and requires no special evaluation or treatment. It is *not* a sign of heart trouble.

So-called "premature heartbeats" are another form of irregular rhythm that requires no treatment at all. If these occur in your child, he might say that his heart "skipped a beat" or did a "flip-flop." Your pediatrician may check to see if the irregular beats disappear with exercise; if they do, they are not an indication of heart disease.

If your pediatrician says that your child has a true arrhythmia, it could mean that his heart beats faster than normal (tachycardia), very fast (flutter), fast and with no regularity (fibrillation), slower than normal (bradycardia), or that it has isolated early beats (premature beats). While true arrhythmias are not very common, when they occur they can be serious, causing fainting or even heart failure. Fortunately, they can be treated successfully with medication, so it's important to detect them as early as possible.

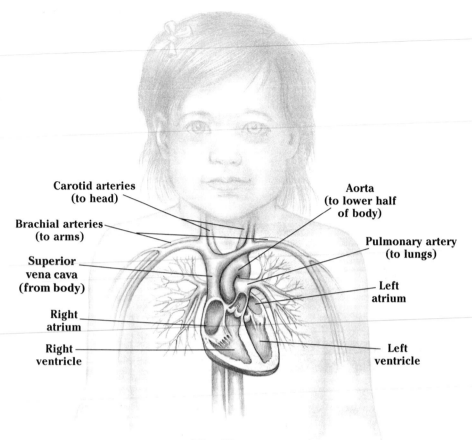

Carotid arteries
(to head)

Aorta
(to lower half
of body)

Brachial arteries
(to arms)

Pulmonary artery
(to lungs)

Superior
vena cava
(from body)

Left
atrium

Right
atrium

Right
ventricle

Left
ventricle

The Heart

Signs and Symptoms

If your child has a true arrhythmia, your pediatrician probably will discover it during a routine visit. But should you notice any of the following warning signs between pediatric visits, notify the physician immediately.

▪ Your infant suddenly becomes pale and listless; his body feels limp.

▪ Your child complains of his "heart beating fast," even when he's not exercising.

▪ He tells you he feels uncomfortable, weak, or dizzy.

▪ He blacks out or faints.

It's *unlikely* that your child will ever experience any of these symptoms, but if he does, your pediatrician will perform additional tests and perhaps consult with a pediatric cardiologist. In the process the doctors may do an electrocardiogram (ECG), so as to better distinguish a harmless sinus arrhythmia from a true arrhythmia. An ECG is really just a tape recording of the electrical impulses that make the heart beat, and it will allow the doctor to observe any irregularities more closely.

Sometimes, your child's unusual heartbeats may occur at unpredictable times, frequently not when the ECG is being taken. In that case the cardiologist may suggest that your child carry a small portable tape recorder that continuously records his heartbeat over a one- to two-day period. During this time you'll be asked to keep a log of your child's activities and symptoms. Correlating the ECG with your observations will permit a diagnosis to be made. For example, if your child feels his heart "flutter" and becomes dizzy at 2:15 P.M.—and the ECG shows his heart suddenly beating faster at the same time—the diagnosis of tachycardia will probably be established.

Occasionally, irregular heartbeats will occur only during exercise. If that's the case with your child, the cardiologist may have your youngster ride a stationary bicycle or run on a treadmill while his heartbeat is being recorded.

Heart Murmur

Technically, a heart murmur is simply a noise heard between the beats of the heart. When a doctor listens to the heart, he hears a sound something like *lub-dub, lub-dub, lub-dub*. Most often, the period between the *lub* and the *dub,* and the *dub* and the *lub* is silent. If there is any sound during this period, it is called a "murmur." Although the word is unsettling, murmurs are *extremely* common, and usually normal, occurrences.

In preschool and school-age children, heart murmurs almost always turn out to be harmless; the children require no special care, and the sound eventually disappears. These children have "normal" or so-called "functional" or "innocent" heart murmurs, caused simply by the way the blood is flowing through their hearts.

If your child has such a murmur, it probably will be discovered between the ages of one and five during a routine examination. The doctor will then listen carefully to determine if this is a "normal" heart murmur or one that might indicate a problem. Usually, just by listening to its sound and noting its lo-

cation on the chest or back, the pediatrician will be able to tell into which group it falls. If necessary, he or she will consult a pediatric cardiologist to be certain, but additional tests are usually not necessary.

On rare occasions, a pediatrician will hear a murmur that sounds abnormal enough to indicate something more than just a noisy flow of blood through the heart. If the doctor suspects this, your child will be referred to a pediatric cardiologist for special tests that will enable a precise diagnosis to be made.

Heart murmurs that can be heard during the first six months of life usually are *not* functional or innocent, and they, too, require the attention of a pediatric cardiologist. Your infant will be observed for changes in skin color (turning blue) as well as breathing or feeding difficulties. He also may undergo additional tests, such as a chest X-ray, ECG, and an echocardiogram. The echocardiogram creates a picture of the inside of the heart by using sound waves. If all of these tests prove normal, then it is safe to conclude that the baby probably has an innocent murmur, but the cardiologist and pediatrician will probably want to see him at frequent intervals to be absolutely certain.

Treatment

Innocent heart murmurs require no treatment, nor should your child be excluded from sports or other physical activities because of one. The only people who need to know about such a heart murmur are the parents and the doctor who examines him (this includes any physician who treats him in an emergency room or elsewhere). You don't need to tell school officials. They might misinterpret the information, thinking your child has a heart problem, and they could try to keep him from being physically active. For the same reason, when you complete health forms for school or camp, you should write "normal" in the heart section if your child's murmur is innocent. If there's a specific question about a heart murmur, write "normal" in the space provided.

Normal heart murmurs, incidentally, generally disappear by mid-adolescence. We don't know why they go away, any more than we know why they appear in the first place. In the meantime, don't be discouraged if the murmur is softer on one visit to the pediatrician and loud again on the next. This may simply mean that your child's heart is beating at a slightly different rate each time. The murmur will most likely eventually go away.

Hypertension/High Blood Pressure

We usually think of high blood pressure, or hypertension, as a problem that affects adults. But in fact, this condition can be present at all ages, even in infancy. About five of every hundred children have higher than normal blood pressure, though less than one in a hundred has medically significant hypertension.

The term *blood pressure* actually refers to two separate measurements: *systolic* blood pressure is the highest pressure reached in the arteries as the heart pumps blood *out* for circulation through the body; *diastolic* blood pressure is the much lower pressure that occurs in the arteries when the heart relaxes to take blood *in* between beats. If either or both of these measurements is above the range found in healthy individuals of similar age and sex, it's called hypertension.

Hypertension is more common among blacks than whites. It also seems to be more prevalent in some parts of the world; for example, it's very rare among Alaskan Eskimos, but affects as many as forty of every hundred adults in northern Japan. In many cases hypertension seems to develop with age. As a result, your child may show no signs of high blood pressure as an infant, but may develop the condition as he grows.

In most instances of high blood pressure, no known cause can be identified. However, when hypertension becomes *severe* in children, it's usually a symptom of another serious problem, such as kidney disease or abnormalities of the heart, or the nervous or endocrine (gland) system.

Fortunately, high blood pressure alone rarely causes serious problems in children, and can be controlled through dietary changes, medication, or a combination of the two. However, if hypertension is allowed to continue or become worse over many years, the prolonged extra pressure can lead to heart failure. In addition, the stress on blood vessels in the brain can cause them to burst, producing a stroke. Also, long-term hypertension causes changes in blood vessel walls that may result in damage to the kidneys, eyes, and other organs. For these reasons it's important to follow the pediatrician's advice carefully if your child is diagnosed as having high blood pressure.

Treatment

In most routine physical examinations, your child's blood pressure will be measured. This is how hypertension is usually discovered. Most often, this condition causes no noticeable discomfort, but any of the following may indicate high blood pressure:

- Headache

- Dizziness

- Shortness of breath

- Visual disturbances

- Fatigue

If your child is found to have high blood pressure, your pediatrician will order tests to see if there is an underlying medical problem causing it. These tests include studies of the urine and blood. Sometimes special X-rays also are used to examine the blood supply to the kidneys. If, as in most cases, no causative

High-Sodium (Salt) Foods
(More than 400 milligrams/serving)

Seasonings—Bouillon, salted meat tenderizers, salted spices (such as garlic salt, onion salt, seasoned salt), soy sauce, teriyaki sauce.

Snack foods—Salted pretzels, crackers, chips, and popcorn.

Commercially prepared foods—Most frozen dinners and commercially prepared entrees, also dry and canned soups.

Vegetables—Any vegetables prepared in brine, such as olives, pickles, sauerkraut, and vegetable juices such as tomato juice.

Cheeses—Processed cheese foods, some types of cheeses including American cheese, blue cheese, cottage cheese, and Parmesan.

Meat—Any smoked, cured, pickled, or processed products such as corned beef, bacon, dried meat and fish, ham, luncheon meats, sausages, and frankfurters.

Low and Moderate-Sodium (Salt) Foods
(Less than 400 milligrams/serving)

Seasonings—Spices without added salt, such as garlic powder, onion powder, and "plain" spices such as oregano, thyme, dill, cinnamon, etc. Condiments such as mayonnaise, mustard, hot pepper sauce, steak sauce, and catsup.

Vegetables—All fresh, frozen, and canned, particularly those canned with no added salt.

Fruits and fruit juices—Fruit juices, and all fresh, canned, frozen, and dried fruits.

Grain products—Pasta, bread, rice, cooked cereals, most ready-to-eat cereals, pancakes, pastries, cakes, cookies.

Dairy products—Milk, yogurt, custard, pudding, ice cream.

Meat and other protein foods—Fresh meat, fish, and eggs, unsalted nuts, dried beans and peas.

medical problem can be found, the diagnosis of "essential" hypertension will be made. (In medical terms, the word *essential* refers only to the fact that no cause could be found.)

What will the doctor tell you to do? The first step toward reducing your child's blood pressure is to limit the salt in his diet. Giving up the use of table salt and restricting salty foods can reverse mild hypertension, and will help lower more serious blood pressure elevations. You'll also have to be cautious when shopping for packaged foods; most canned and processed foods contain a great deal of salt, so check labels carefully to make sure the items have little or no salt added.

The pediatrician may also suggest that your child get more exercise. Physical activity seems to help regulate blood pressure and thus can reduce mild hypertension. Weight reduction in the obese individual also may serve to lower blood pressure; in addition, there are other health benefits from avoidance of excessive weight.

Once the pediatrician knows your child has high blood pressure, he'll want to check it at least every six months to make sure the hypertension is not becoming more severe. If it does become worse, it may be treated with medication as well as diet and exercise. There are many types of medications, which work through different parts of the body. At first the pediatrician may prescribe a diuretic, a medicine that increases urine output of salt (sodium), before trying stronger drugs. Alternatively, or if this doesn't return your child's blood pressure to normal, a drug called an "antihypertensive" will be prescribed. The doctor will initially prescribe a single drug, and then add others only if the blood pressure is difficult to control.

When your child's blood pressure is brought under control with diet or medication, you may be tempted to let him increase his salt intake or stop taking his medicine because the problem seems to be gone. However, this will only bring back the hypertension, so be sure to follow your pediatrician's instructions exactly.

Prevention

It's very important to detect hypertension early. For this reason, your child's blood pressure should be measured at least once a year.

Overweight children are more likely to develop hypertension (as well as other health problems). For this reason, watch your child's caloric intake and make sure he gets plenty of exercise.

It's also wise to keep excess salt out of your child's diet, even if he doesn't have high blood pressure. There's no clear evidence that salt causes this problem, but your child doesn't need extra salt, and once he develops a taste for it, he'll have more difficulty decreasing it if he develops blood pressure problems later in life.

27

IMMUNIZATIONS

Immunizations are available to protect your child against ten major childhood diseases: polio, measles (page 640), mumps (page 600), German measles (rubella; page 633), chicken pox (page 629), whooping cough (pertussis; page 519), diphtheria, tetanus, haemophilus infections (Meningitis, page 597, and epiglottitis, page 540), and Hepatitis B (page 66). Any of these diseases can disable or kill, so your child should be immunized against them. Immunizations also are available against influenza, rabies, and pneumococcus.

When your child is given a vaccine, he actually receives that part of the "weakened" infectious organism that is able to stimulate his body to produce antibodies against it. These antibodies then protect him against the disease, should he ever come in contact with it.

In addition, certain children may need protection against influenza (flu vaccine) or rabies (rabies vaccine). Your pediatrician will tell you if this is necessary. Except for the oral polio vaccine, all of the immunizations are injections.

The American Academy of Pediatrics recommends the schedule of immunizations appearing on page 63. Please see that page for complete details.

Side Effects

Each of the vaccines has some potential side effects. These are listed below.

Diphtheria, Tetanus, and Pertussis (given together in a single vaccine)

The side effects for the diphtheria and tetanus portions of the vaccine are similar: pain and swelling at the site of the injection and, on rare occasions, skin rash within twenty-four hours. The pertussis portion of the vaccine causes heat, redness, and tenderness at the injection site in about half the children who receive it. They also may have fever and become irritable. Inflammation of the brain also has been known to occur following vaccination, although it is so rare (1 in 110,000 immunizations) that it is not definitely known whether it is caused by the vaccine or by some other substance or infection.

These side effects and complications must be weighed against the fact that the disease itself causes far more complications than the vaccine.

Polio

Taking this vaccine will be totally painless for your child; it is taken by mouth. In very, very rare cases the virus used to make the vaccine can cause paralysis in the child who receives it. Also, because the virus will be present in the child's stool shortly after vaccination, it is possible for people handling the stool to become infected if they have not been immunized against polio. Infections following polio immunizations are extremely rare; about eight cases of paralysis occur each year in the United States.

Chicken Pox Vaccine

Adverse reactions from the chicken pox vaccine generally are mild and include redness, stiffness, soreness, and swelling where the shot was given; tiredness; fussiness; fever; and nausea. Also, a rash of several small bumps or pimples may develop at the spot where the shot was given or on other parts of the body. This can occur up to one month after immunization and can last for several days.

Measles, Mumps, and Rubella

These vaccines usually are given together in one injection. The measles part of the vaccine sometimes causes a mild rash and fever five to twelve days after it is given. Very rarely, children will have slight swelling over the jaw, as if they had mild mumps from the mumps vaccine. The rubella part of the vaccine sometimes causes joint pains and swelling or, very rarely, an inflammation of the nerves of the arms or legs.

Hib Conjugate Vaccine

Your child might be sore, red, or swollen around the site of the injection. This occurs in a very small number of cases (one out of every sixty-seven). Mild fever may develop.

Influenza

The newer vaccines have few side effects except for one or two days of soreness at the injection site; febrile reactions are infrequent.

Rabies

The new vaccines have few or no side effects in children.

Treatment for Side Effects

Before immunizing your child, your pediatrician should review with you what reactions you can expect and how to treat them. Generally, fever is managed with acetaminophen. For local reactions your pediatrician may recommend that you apply cool compresses for symptomatic relief.

If your child has any reaction that makes him uncomfortable for more than four hours, notify your pediatrician, who will want to note it in your child's records and prescribe appropriate treatment.

Children Who Should Not Receive Certain Vaccines

These vaccines do not cause serious reactions in most children. However, there are cases where they should not be given.

Diphtheria and Tetanus

If your child has had a serious reaction (rash, fever of 105 degrees Fahrenheit [40.5 degrees Celsius] or greater, fainting, or hives) to a previous dose of these vaccines, he should not receive another one.

Personal Immunization Chart

Keep a record of your child's immunization by filling in this chart. Fill in the date each time your child is immunized. If you need more of these records, contact the American Academy of Pediatrics, 141 Northwest Point Boulevard, P.O. Box 927, Elk Grove Village, Illinois 60009-0927.

	DTP	Polio	MMR	Hepatitis B	Hib	Tetanus-Diphtheria	Chicken Pox
Birth	:	:	:	:	:		:
1–2 months	:	:	:	:	:		:
2 months	:	:	:	:	:		:
4 months	:	:	:	:	:		:
6 months	:	:	:	:	:		:
6–18 months	:	:	:	:	:		:
12–15 months	:	:	:	:	:		:
15 months	:	:	:	:	:		:
15–18 months	:	:	:	:	:		:
4–6 years	:	:	:	:	:		:
11–12 years	:	:	:	:	:		:
14–16 years	:	:	:	:	:		:

Pertussis

If your child has had a seizure *before* getting the pertussis vaccine, your pediatrician may delay giving the P part of the DTP until the cause of the seizure is known, and at least six months have gone by without the occurrence of another seizure. If your child had a serious reaction to a previous dose of pertussis vaccine, no further doses of the P part will be given and Pediatric D-T will be substituted. Serious reactions include: high fever (105 degrees Fahrenheit [40.5 degrees Celsius] or greater), seizures, prolonged high-pitched and peculiar crying or screaming, collapse, or signs of brain inflammation (changes in consciousness, stiff neck, or extreme crankiness).

Chicken Pox Vaccine

Although the chicken pox vaccine is approved for use in otherwise healthy children, there are certain groups of people, such as children with a weakened immune system or pregnant women, who should not receive it. Talk to your pediatrician about whether your child falls into any of the high-risk categories and should not be vaccinated against chicken pox.

Measles, Mumps

Because this vaccine is made from egg protein, your child probably should not receive it if he is highly allergic to eggs. However, your pediatrician may want to consult with an allergist or immunologist, who can give your child special allergy tests before a decision is made concerning the use of the vaccine.

Rubella

All children who have not had this disease and who are not allergic to egg or neomycin should be given this vaccine before adolescence. It should not be given to a pregnant woman but may be given to her other children without endangering her pregnancy.

Rabies

There are no reasons not to give the rabies vaccine when it is needed.

Influenza

Flu vaccines are prepared from egg protein, so children who are allergic to eggs should not receive them.

Hib Conjugate Vaccine

There are no reasons for withholding this vaccine unless your child has a sensitivity to one or more of its ingredients. Your pediatrician will help you determine this.

28

MUSCULOSKELETAL PROBLEMS

Arthritis

Arthritis is an inflammation of the joints that produces swelling, redness, heat, and pain. Although we usually think of it as a disease of the elderly, some children also have this condition. There are four main types of childhood arthritis:

Toxic Synovitis of the Hip

This is the most common form of arthritis in children. It develops suddenly and then disappears after a short time, with no serious aftereffects. A virus is the probable cause.

Bacterial Infection

When a joint becomes infected with bacteria, a child may limp (if the hip, knee, or ankle is infected), run a fever, and feel pain upon moving the affected joint. See your pediatrician immediately if these signs or symptoms appear.

Lyme Disease

An infection transmitted by the deer tick can cause a form of arthritis (known as "Lyme arthritis" because it was first diagnosed in a

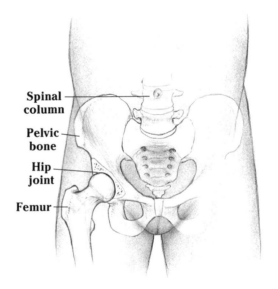

Spinal column

Pelvic bone

Hip joint

Femur

child in Old Lyme, Connecticut). The disease starts with a rash around the tick bite. Similar changes then appear on other body areas. Later, there are headaches, fever, chills, and muscular aches and pains. Although this infection can be disabling, it tends to last for only a limited time. Since its original discovery, it has been found in many other parts of the world. Antibiotics are helpful if the diagnosis is made within one month of the tick bite.

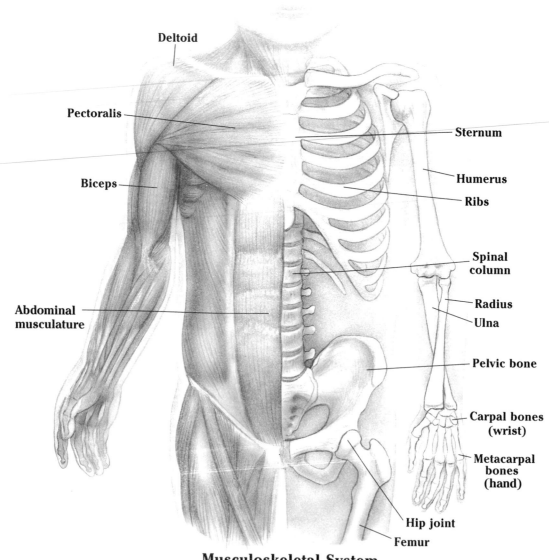

Deltoid

Pectoralis

Biceps

Abdominal
musculature

Sternum

Humerus

Ribs

Spinal
column

Radius

Ulna

Pelvic bone

Carpal bones
(wrist)

Metacarpal
bones
(hand)

Hip joint

Femur

Musculoskeletal System

How to Remove a Tick

1. Gently cleanse the area with an alcohol-soaked sponge or cotton ball.

2. Using forceps, tweezers, or fingers (protected by a tissue or cloth), grasp the tick as near to the mouth parts and as close to the skin as possible.

3. Using gentle but steady tension, pull the tick up and out. Be sure the tick is dead before disposing of it. (Alternatively, save the tick if your local health department wants it for surveillance purposes.)

4. After the tick is out, cleanse the bitten area thoroughly with alcohol or other cleansing agent.

Juvenile Rheumatoid Arthritis

Commonly referred to as JRA, this is the most common chronic (long-term) form of joint inflammation in children. Unfortunately, it also can sometimes lead to permanent damage. JRA is a puzzling disease that is often difficult for the pediatrician to diagnose and for parents to understand.

If your child has any of the symptoms described below—particularly unexplained fever, persistent joint stiffness, pain, or swelling of the joints, call your pediatrician. These all could signal the presence of arthritis.

Juvenile rheumatoid arthritis occurs most often in children between the ages of three and six or around the time of puberty. It's unusual for JRA to begin under one year of age or after age sixteen. Though this disease can be disabling, with proper treatment most children recover fully, and the condition usually disappears following puberty.

Although the exact cause of JRA is still unknown, a combination of factors probably comes into play. Researchers believe that JRA may be triggered by or perhaps related to a viral infection in children who have an abnormality in their immune (disease-resistance) system. In nonsusceptible children the viruses probably would cause only a mild illness with no lasting effect. But in some children the immune system overreacts to the viruses, particularly in the joint areas. It is the overreaction that causes the inflammation, swelling, pain, and joint damage.

The signs, symptoms, and long-term effects can vary depending upon the type of JRA that's present. A form of JRA known as systemic JRA, for instance, causes not only fever and painful joints, but also may have damaging effects on internal organs. When systemic JRA strikes the internal organs, the child can develop inflammation of the outside covering of the heart (pericarditis) or of the heart muscle (myocarditis) or the lining of the lungs (pleuritis) or of the lung tissue itself (pneumonitis). Much less commonly, inflammation occurs in the brain and its lining (meningoencephalitis).

There are two other types of JRA—pauciarticular (affecting one or two joints) and polyarticular (affecting many joints). Pauciarticular JRA can be associated with inflammation of the eye, which in turn can cause glaucoma or cataracts. Pauciarticular JRA is the most common form and it most often affects young girls. It also has the best prognosis in terms of disability and ultimate outcome.

Great strides are being made in the treatment of JRA, and often the disease can be completely controlled. Therapy is aimed at reducing inflammation. Aspirin may be used initially (this is one of the very few indications for using aspirin in children) because it's safe and inexpensive anti-inflammatory drug. It does have some undesirable side effects, such as stomach irritation. Also, because of its link to Reye syndrome (see page 490), aspirin must be discontinued if your child has chicken pox or flulike illnesses. If the aspirin doesn't work or produces unacceptable side effects, your pediatrician may decide to use one of the newer nonsteroidal anti-inflammatory drugs (sometimes referred to as "NSAIDs"). Like aspirin, these are rapid-acting drugs, but less likely to cause side effects. They are also much more expensive.

If JRA is severe and is still progressive, your pediatrician might prescribe a "slow-acting" drug containing gold. Given by injection, it's effective in six out of ten cases. (Although a pill form of this medication is available for adult use, it hasn't been approved for children.)

While there is no way to prevent JRA, it is possible to slow down progression of the disease. At times it will require a parent to do some difficult things, like forcing a child to exercise when any movement hurts. It's necessary, because if a child with JRA is inactive, his pain and deformities will increase.

JRA requires a great deal of adjustment, not only for the ill child but also for his parents and other family members. By working as a team you'll markedly decrease your child's chances of suffering permanent damage. If you need more support, your pediatrician can refer you to arthritis organizations that can assist you.

Treatment

Treatment varies depending upon the type of arthritis your child has. Treatment may include medications, exercise, physical therapy, or the use of splints. Whatever treatments are prescribed, it is essential that every step be carried out exactly as recommended. This may be difficult sometimes, particularly when your child is in pain, but it's important to carry through in order to prevent deformities and disability later on.

If infectious arthritis is diagnosed, the child may be placed on antibiotics for a time. In some cases, hospitalization may be necessary so that antibiotics can be given intravenously.

When toxic synovitis is diagnosed, only bed rest may be prescribed, or in some cases traction (gentle stretching of the joint with a system of weights and pulleys). Lyme disease, if diagnosed early (within one month of the tick bite), is treated with antibiotics. If the arthritis is severe, other medications usually will be prescribed to control the inflammation and pain until the condition gradually disappears on its own.

Bowlegs and Knock-Knees

If your toddler's legs seem to curve outward at the knees, there's probably no reason for concern. Look around, and you'll see that few young children have truly straight legs. In fact, many children between the ages of one and two appear quite bowlegged, and it's common for children from three to six to look "knock-kneed." Their legs may not look straight until the age of nine or ten.

Bowlegs and knock-knees usually are just variations of normal, and they require no treatment. Ordinarily the legs straighten out and look perfectly normal by adolescence. Bracing, corrective shoes, and exercise are not helpful and, in fact, can hinder a child's physical develoment and cause emotional difficulty.

Rarely, bowlegs or knock-knees are the result of a disease. Arthritis, injury to the growth plate around the knee (see *Fractures,* page 459), infection, tumor, and rickets all can cause changes in the curvature of the legs. Here are some signs that suggest a child's bowlegs or knock-knees may be caused by a serious problem:

- The curvature is extreme.

- Only one side is affected.

- The bowlegs get *worse* after age two.

- The knock-knees persist after age seven.

- Your child is also unusually short for his age.

If your child's condition fits any of these descriptions, you should talk to your pediatrician, who can determine the exact cause and prescribe the necessary treatment. In some cases, the pediatrician will refer you to a pediatric orthopedist for consultation and possible corrective surgery.

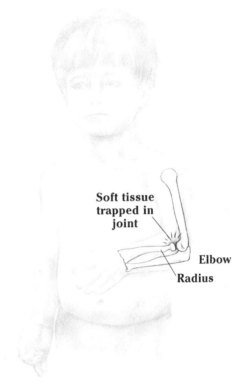

Soft tissue trapped in joint

Elbow

Radius

Elbow Injuries

Pulled elbow (also known as "nursemaid's elbow") is a common, painful injury among children under four years old. It occurs when nearby soft tissue slips into the elbow joint and is trapped there. This can happen because your child's elbow joint is loose enough to separate slightly when his arm is pulled to full length (when he's being lifted, yanked, or swung by the hand or wrist, or if he falls on his outstretched arm). The nearby tissue slides into the space created by the stretching and is trapped there when the joint returns to its normal position.

Nursemaid's elbow usually doesn't cause swelling, but your child will complain that it hurts. He probably will hold his arm close to his side, with his elbow slightly bent and his palm turned toward his body. If you try to straighten the elbow or turn his palm upward, he will resist because of the pain.

Treatment

Don't try to treat this injury yourself, because elbow pain also might be caused by a problem

such as a fracture. Instead, the injury should be examined by your pediatrician as soon as possible. To make your child more comfortable until he sees the doctor, support the arm in a sling made from a soft cloth, such as a dish towel. Don't give him food, water, or pain medication unless your physician advises you to do so.

The doctor will check the injured area for swelling and tenderness, and any limitation of motion. If an injury other than nursemaid's elbow is suspected, X-rays will be taken. If no fracture is noted, the doctor will gently manipulate the joint to release the trapped tissue. While this procedure causes some pain as it's being done, your child should feel relief almost immediately afterward. The doctor may recommend the use of a sling for two or three days while the soft tissue heals, particularly if several hours have passed before the injury is successfully treated.

Prevention

Nursemaid's elbow usually can be prevented by lifting your young child properly. Grasp him under the arms or around his body. Do not pull or lift him by holding his hands or wrists, and never swing him by the arms.

Flat Feet/Fallen Arches

At some point during your baby's first year or two, you'll probably notice that he seems to have very little arch to his feet. This flat-footedness, which may persist well into later childhood, occurs because children's bones and joints are very flexible, causing their feet to flatten when they stand. Also, young babies have a fat pad on the inner border of their feet that hides the arches (see Figure 1). You can still see the arch if you lift your baby up on his toes, but it disappears when he comes down on his heels (see Figure 2). Often the foot also turns out, increasing the weight on the inner side and making it appear even more flat.

This natural flat-footedness usually disappears by age six as the feet become less flex-

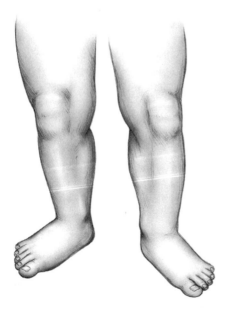

ible and the arches develop. Only about one or two out of every ten children will continue to have this kind of flat-footedness into adulthood. Even for these youngsters, however, as long as the feet remain flexible, there's no cause for concern and no need for treatment. In fact, all the special shoes, inserts, and exercises that are promoted and sold only cause more problems than the flat feet themselves, and will *not* develop an arch in your child's foot.

There are other forms of flat-footedness that may need to be treated differently. For instance, a child may have tightness of the heel cord (Achilles tendon) that limits the motion of his foot. This tightness can result in a flat foot, but it usually can be treated with special stretching exercises to lengthen the heel cord.

Very rarely, a child will have truly rigid flat feet, a condition that can definitely cause problems. Such youngsters have difficulty moving the foot up and down or side to side at the ankle. This can cause pain—though that usually does not happen until the teenage years—and, if left untreated, can lead to arthritis. This rigid type of flat foot is seldom seen in an infant or very young child, but when it does develop, it should be evaluated promptly. If your child has any foot pain, sores, or pressure spots on the inner side of the foot, or if the foot is stiff, with limited side-to-side or up-and-down ankle motion, see your pediatrician. If rigid flat-footedness is diagnosed, you'll probably be referred to a pediatric orthopedist for further treatment, which may involve surgery.

Limp

Limping in a child can be caused by something as simple as a stone in the shoe, a blister on the foot, or a pulled muscle. But a limp can also be a sign of more serious trouble, such as a broken bone or an infection, so it should be investigated early to make sure no serious problems are present.

Some children limp when they first learn how to walk. Among the causes of early limping are neurological damage (for example, cerebral palsy; see page 526). Any limp at this age needs to be investigated as soon as possible, since the longer it goes untreated, the more difficult it may be to correct.

Once walking is well established, significant sudden limping usually indicates one of several conditions:

- A "toddler" fracture

- Hip injury or inflammation (synovitis)

- Previously undiagnosed congenital hip dislocation

- Infection in the bone or joint

Toddler fracture is a mild fracture (see page 459) that can occur with minor accidents such as a slip on a newly waxed floor or a jump from a porch step or swing. Sometimes the child can explain how the injury occurred, but youngsters do so many thimgs in one day that they may have difficulty recalling exactly what happened. Sometimes an older sibling or babysitter can solve the mystery.

Hip problems that cause a limp at this age usually are due to a viral joint infection and need to be brought to the attention of your physician. When a child has an infection in the bone or joint, there usually is fever, swelling of the joint, and redness. If the infection is in the hip joint, the child will hold his leg flexed or bent at the hip and be extremely irritable and unwilling to move the hip and leg in any direction.

Sometimes a child is born with a dislocated hip which, in rare cases, goes undetected until the child starts to walk. As one leg is shorter than the other, the child will walk with an obvious limp, which will be persistent.

Treatment

If you know that your child's limp is due to a minor injury, such as a blister, cut, splinter in the foot, or mild sprain, you can apply simple first-aid treatment at home. However, most other causes need to be examined and treated by a pediatrician.

If your child has just started walking and is limping, the pediatrician should see him as soon as possible. Calls about limping in an older child may be delayed for twenty-four hours, since many of these problems disappear overnight.

X-rays of the hip or the entire leg may be necessary to make the diagnosis. This is most certainly true if there is a suspicion of a congenital dislocation of the hip. If an infection is present, antibiotics will be started immediately. (This will require hospitalization if the infection is in the joint or bone.) If a bone is broken or dislocated, it will be placed in a splint or cast, probably after consultation with a pediatric orthopedic specialist. If a congenital dislocated hip is diagnosed, referral to a pediatric orthopedist will be immediate as proper treatment, including special casting and/or bracing, should not be delayed.

Pigeon Toes (Intoeing)

If your child's feet turn inward, he is said to be pigeon-toed, or have intoeing. It's a very common problem that may involve one or both feet, and occurs for a variety of reasons.

Intoeing During Infancy

This usually is due to a turning-in of the front part of the foot (the forefoot), and is called "metatarsis adductus" (see Figure 1). It may be due to the baby's position in the uterus or other causes. Usually this condition is mild and will resolve before the child's first birthday. Sometimes it is more severe, or is accompanied by other foot deformities that result in a problem called "clubfoot." This condition requires a consultation with a pediatric orthopedist and early casting or splinting.

Intoeing in Later Childhood

If you notice that your child is toeing in during his second year, it is most likely due to inward turning of the shinbone (tibia). This condition is called "internal tibial torsion" (see Figure 2). If your child is between ages three and ten and has intoeing, it is probably due to an inward turning of the thighbone (femur), a condition called "medial femoral torsion." Both of these conditions tend to run in families.

Although intoeing should not cause worry, there are several situations that should alert you to get advice:

- When you look at the foot from the bottom while the child is resting, you see that the front portion turns inward.

- The outer side of your child's foot (opposite his big toe) is curved like a half-moon.

- The condition is severe enough to affect your child's walking or running.

If you observe any of these problems, ask the pediatrician to examine your child's feet.

Treatment

Some experts feel no treatment is necessary for intoeing in an infant under six months of age. Others feel that early treatment may be helpful. In cases where there are different opinions, it is best to follow the advice of your own pediatrician. It does appear that the majority of infants who have intoeing in early infancy will outgrow it with no treatment.

If your baby's intoeing persists after six months, or if it is rigid and difficult to straighten out, your doctor may recommend a series of casts applied over a period of three to six weeks. The pediatrician will also refer you to a pediatric orthopedist. The main goal is to correct the condition before your child starts walking.

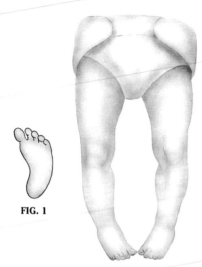

FIG. 1

FIG. 2

Intoeing in early childhood usually clears on its own, but if your child has trouble walking because of turning of the tibia, further discussion with your pediatrician and orthopedic consultant is required. The night brace, used in the past for this problem, has not been shown to be an effective treatment.

If your child's intoeing remains severe when he is nine or ten years old, he may require surgery to correct it.

Because intoeing so often corrects itself over time, it is very important *not* to use non-prescribed "treatments" such as corrective shoes, twister cables, daytime bracing, exercises, shoe inserts, and back manipulations. These do not correct the problem and are, in fact, harmful because they interfere with normal play or walking, and may even cause additional deformity. Furthermore, a child in these braces unnecessarily faces the emotional strain caused by his playmates' ridicule.

Sprains

Sprains are injuries to the ligaments that connect bones together. A sprain occurs when a ligament is stretched excessively or torn.

Sprains are very uncommon in young children, because the ligaments are usually stronger than the growing bones and cartilage to which they are attached. Therefore, the growing part of the bone might separate or tear away before the ligament is injured.

In young children, the ankle is far and away the most commonly sprained joint, followed by the knee and wrist. In a mild sprain (grade 1), the ligament is simply overstretched. More severe sprains can involve partial tearing of the ligament (grade 2) or a complete tear (grade 3). The signs and symptoms of sprains in young children can be quite similar to those for fracture: pain, swelling around the joint, and inability to walk, bear weight, or use the joint.

You should call your child's pediatrician if there is any evidence that a joint injury has occurred. Your doctor will often want to examine the child. If the pain and swelling are excessive or if there is concern about a fracture, your pediatrician may recommend a consultation with an orthopedic surgeon. The orthopedist may need to perform special X-rays to distinguish between an injury to a ligament or a bone.

When a sprain is diagnosed, the joint is usually immobilized with an elastic bandage or a splint. Crutches may be necessary in the case of a leg sprain, to prevent continued stress on the injured ligament. A cast may be necessary if the injury has been severe.

Most grade 1 sprains will heal within two weeks and without subsequent complications. In certain grade 3 injuries, especially around the knee, an operation may be necessary to repair the damage. Your child's physician should be called any time a joint injury fails to heal or swelling recurs. Ignoring these signs could result in more severe damage to the joint and long-term disability.

29

SKIN

Birthmarks and Hemangiomas

Dark-Pigmented Birthmarks (Nevi or Moles)

Nevi, or moles, are either congenital (present at birth) or acquired. They are composed of so-called nevus cells, similar to those that give dark pigment to the skin, so these spots are dark-brown or black.

Congenital Nevi

Small nevi present at birth are relatively common, occurring in one of every hundred white children. They tend to grow with the child and usually don't cause any problems. Rarely, however, these moles may develop into a type of serious skin cancer (melanoma) at some later time, usually during or after adolescence. Therefore, while you don't have to *worry* about them right away, it's a good idea to watch them carefully and have them checked by your pediatrician at regular intervals or if there is any change in appearance (color, size, or shape). He may refer you to

a pediatric dermatologist who will advise you on removal and any follow-up care.

But there's also a much more serious type of nevus—a large congenital one that varies in size from a half-dollar to as large as this book. It might be flat or raised, may have hair growing from it, and can be so large that it covers an arm or a leg. Fortunately, these are very rare (occurring in one of every 20,000 births). However, they are much more likely than the smaller ones to develop into a melanoma, so early consultation with a pediatric dermatologist is advisable.

Acquired Nevi, or Moles

Most white people develop ten to thirty pigmented nevi, or moles, throughout the course of their lives. They usually occur after the age of five, but sometimes develop earlier. These *acquired* moles are seldom a cause for worry. However, if your child develops one that's larger than a pencil eraser, is an irregular shape, or has multiple colors within its structure, your pediatrician should examine it.

One final note: probably the most common acquired dark spots on the skin are freckles. They usually appear between the ages of two and four years, are found more often on parts of the body exposed to the sun, and tend to run in families. They often become darker or larger during the summer, and are less prominent in the winter. They represent no danger and should not cause concern.

Blood Vessel Malformations on the Skin (Hemangiomas)

Your young infant has a red raised bump growing rapidly on his forehead, and a flat dark-red patch on one arm. They're quite unsightly, but are they harmful?

Hemangiomas are birthmarks that occur when a certain area of the skin develops an abnormal blood supply during early childhood. This, in turn, causes the tissue to enlarge over the course of several weeks or months and become reddish-blue. When the condition involves only the capillaries (the smallest blood vessels), the birthmark is called a "strawberry hemangioma." When the blood vessels are full-sized veins or a mixture of capillaries and veins, the hemangioma may be of a different type and have a different appearance.

Flat Angiomata (Stork Bites)

These most common blemishes on the skin usually appear on the eyelids or back of the neck. They usually disappear over the first months of life and are not serious.

Strawberry Hemangiomas

Strawberry hemangiomas, another common form of this condition, are found in at least two of every hundred babies born. Although they frequently are not noticeable at birth, they appear within the first month of life as a red raised dot. They can occur on any area of the body, but are most commonly seen on the head, neck, and trunk. Usually, a child has just a single strawberry hemangioma, but occasionally these marks will be scattered over several parts of the body.

If your infant develops a strawberry hemangioma, have your pediatrician examine it

so he can follow its course from the start. During the first six months of life strawberry hemangiomas usually grow very rapidly, which can be quite alarming. But they soon stop enlarging, and almost always disappear by the time the child is nine years old.

Quite often, the large reddish-purplish appearance of these birthmarks so upsets parents that they want to have them removed immediately. However, since the vast majority will gradually reduce in size over the second to third year of life, it's generally best to leave them alone. Studies have shown that when this type of hemangioma is left untreated, there are few complications or cosmetic problems. By contrast, those that are treated either with medication or surgery have a far greater chance of complications or unwanted changes in appearance.

At times, strawberry hemangiomas may need to be treated or removed—namely, when they occur close to vital structures, such as the eye, throat, or mouth; when they seem to be growing much faster than usual; or when they are likely to bleed profusely or become infected. Such uncommon conditions will require careful evaluation and management by your pediatrician and dermatologist.

Very rarely, these birthmarks are found in large numbers on the face and upper trunk. On such occasions, hemangiomas also may be present on organs inside the body. If this is suspected, your pediatrician may need to conduct further tests.

Port Wine Stains

Port wine stains, or flat hemangiomas, usually are present at birth and enlarge as the child grows. They are dark-red and often found on the face or limbs (usually only on one side of the body). Unlike the strawberry type, these hemangiomas don't go away, although they sometimes fade. Even so, they rarely cause any problems. On occasion, however, if they are found on the upper eyelid and/or forehead, there is a chance of a related problem in the underlying brain structures (Sturge-Weber syndrome). Or, if the birthmark is present immediately around the eye, there is a possibility that glaucoma (see page 562) may develop in that eye.

Port wine stains should be examined from time to time to evaluate their size, location, and appearance. If your child is very unhappy with this birthmark, a special covering makeup can be used. Only very rarely is surgery recommended, although laser treatment has been successful in some cases. (See also *How Your Newborn Looks,* page 112.)

Chicken Pox

Chicken pox is one of the most common childhood illnesses. This highly contagious infection causes an itchy, blisterlike rash that can cover most of the body. Children often get a mild fever along with the rash.

After your child is exposed to the virus that causes chicken pox, it can take 10 to 21 days for the rash to appear. Small blisters, which may have a red area around them, will begin to appear on the body and scalp, then spread to the face and to the arms and legs. Normally, the blisters will crust over and then heal, but tiny sores and possibly small scars may develop if your child scratches them and they become infected. There also may be minor darkening of the skin around some of the blisters, but this will gradually disappear after the rash is gone.

Treatment

From your own childhood, you may remember just how itchy chicken pox can be. You need to discourage your child from scratching, because that can cause additional infection. Acetaminophen (in the appropriate dose for your child's age and weight) may decrease the discomfort and also reduce any fever he has. Trimming his fingernails and bathing him daily with soap and water can also help prevent secondary bacterial infection. Oatmeal

baths, available without prescription from your pharmacy, will ease the itch. A prescription medicine also decreases the severity of the symptoms if started within 24 hours of the onset of the disease.

Do not give your child aspirin or any medication that contains aspirin or salicylates when he has chicken pox. These products increase the risk of Reye syndrome (see page 490), a serious illness that involves the liver and brain. If you are not sure about what medications you can safely use at this time, ask your pediatrician for advice.

Incidentally, the doctor probably won't need to see your child unless his temperature rises above 102 degrees Fahrenheit (38.9 degrees Celsius) or lasts longer than four days. But let the pediatrician know if areas of the rash become very red, warm, or tender; this may indicate a bacterial infection requiring antibiotics and a special oral anti-itch medication. And be sure to call your pediatrician *immediately* if your youngster develops any signs of Reye syndrome or encephalitis: vomiting, nervousness, confusion, convulsions, lack of responsiveness, increasing sleepiness, or poor balance.

Children may be contagious one to two days before the rash starts, and for twenty-four hours after the last new blister appears (usually five to seven days). Only individuals who have never had chicken pox are susceptible, however, so if your child has playmates who already have had the infection, and he is feeling well, he can play with them even while the rash is active. But keep him away from youngsters who have never had the disease or who aren't sure that they've had it. After he's recovered from the chicken pox, your child will be immune to it for the rest of his life.

Prevention

A vaccine to protect against chicken pox is recommended for all healthy children between 12 and 18 months of age who have never had the disease. Children under 13 who have not had chicken pox and were never vaccinated also should receive a single dose of the vaccine. Until your child has received the vaccine at one year of age, the only sure way to protect him is to avoid exposure. This is more important for newborn infants, especially premature babies, in whom the disease can be more severe. Some infants whose mothers have had chicken pox may be immune to the disease for the first few months. Susceptible children who have diseases affecting the immune system (such as cancer), or who are using certain drugs, such as cortisone, must also be careful to avoid exposure to chicken pox. If these individuals or normal adults are exposed, they may be given a special medication to provide immunity to the disease for a limited period.

Cradle Cap and Seborrheic Dermatitis

Your beautiful one-month-old baby has developed scaliness and redness on his scalp. You're concerned and think maybe you shouldn't shampoo as usual. You also notice some redness in the creases of his neck and armpits, and behind his ears. What is it and what should you do?

When this rash occurs on the scalp alone, it's known as cradle cap. But although it may start as scaling and redness of the scalp, it also can be found later in the other areas mentioned above. It can extend to the face and diaper area, too, and when it does, pediatricians call it seborrheic dermatitis (because it occurs where there are the greatest number of oil-producing sebaceous glands). Seborrheic dermatitis is a form of eczema that's very common in infants, usually beginning in the first weeks of life and slowly disappearing over a period of weeks or months. Unlike atopic or contact eczema (see page 631), it's rarely uncomfortable or itchy.

What's the exact cause of this rash? No one knows for sure. However, it certainly is influenced by the hormonal changes of pregnancy,

which stimulate the oil glands. This overproduction of oil may have some relationship to the scales and redness of the skin.

Treatment

If your baby's seborrheic dermatitis is confined to his scalp (and is, therefore, just cradle cap), you can treat it yourself. Don't be afraid to shampoo the hair; in fact, you should wash it (with a mild baby shampoo) more frequently than before. This, along with soft brushing, will help remove the scales.

As for baby oil, it's not very helpful or necessary. Many parents tend to use the unperfumed baby oil or mineral oil and do nothing else. But this allows scales to build up on the scalp, particularly over the rear soft spot, or fontanelle. If you decide to use oil, use only a little, rub it into the scales, and then shampoo and brush it out. Stronger medicated shampoos (antiseborrhea shampoos containing sulfur and 2 percent salicylic acid) may loosen the scales more quickly, but since they also can be irritating, use them only after consulting your pediatrician. The doctor also may prescribe some additional medication to treat the scales and redness.

If frequent shampooing doesn't improve the cradle cap, or if the rash spreads to your baby's face, neck, and crease areas, call your pediatrician, who will probably suggest a stronger, scale-dissolving shampoo and might also prescribe a cortisone cream or lotion. One percent hydrocortisone cream is a commonly used preparation.

Once the condition has improved, how can you prevent it from recurring? In most cases, just by frequent hair washing with a mild baby shampoo. Occasionally, a stronger medicated shampoo may be needed, but let your pediatrician make the decision.

Sometimes, yeast infections will become superimposed on the affected skin, most likely in the crease areas rather than on the scalp. If this occurs, the area will become extremely reddened and quite itchy. In this case, your pediatrician might prescribe some specific anti-yeast cream containing the medicine nystatin. If this is necessary, apply a small amount to the area three or four times a day, and rub it in well.

Rest assured that seborrheic dermatitis is not a serious infection. Nor is it an allergy to something you're using, or due to poor hygiene. It will go away without any scars and your baby will be beautiful again!

Eczema (Atopic Dermatitis and Contact Dermatitis)

Eczema is a general term used to describe a number of different skin conditions. It usually appears as reddened skin that becomes moist and oozing, occasionally resulting in small, fluid-filled bumps. When eczema becomes chronic (persists for a long time), the skin tends to thicken, dry out, and become scaly with coarse lines.

There are two main types of eczema: atopic dermatitis and contact dermatitis.

Atopic Dermatitis

Atopic dermatitis often occurs in infants and children who have allergies or a family history of allergy or eczema, although the problem is not necessarily caused by an allergy. Atopic dermatitis usually develops in three different phases. The first occurs between two and six months of age, with itching, redness, and the appearance of small bumps on the cheeks, forehead, or scalp. This rash may then spread to the arms or trunk. Although atopic dermatitis is often confused with other types of dermatitis, severe itching and the absence of previous allergy are clues that this is the problem. In half the cases the rash disappears by two or three years of age.

The second phase of this skin problem occurs most often between the ages of four and ten years, and is characterized by circular, slightly raised, itchy and scaly eruptions on the face or trunk. These are less oozy and more scaly than the first phase of atopic dermatitis, and the skin tends to appear somewhat thickened. The most frequent locations for this rash are in the bends of the elbows, behind the knees, and on the backs of the wrists and ankles. This type of eczema is very itchy, and the skin generally tends to be very dry.

The third phase, characterized by areas of itching skin and a dry, scaly appearance, begins at about age twelve and occasionally continues on into early adulthood.

Contact Dermatitis

Contact dermatitis occurs when the skin comes in contact with an irritating substance. One form of this problem results from repeated contact with irritating substances such as citrus juices, bubble baths, strong soaps, certain foods and medicines, and woolen or rough-weave fabrics. In addition, one of the most common irritants is the child's own saliva. Contact dermatitis doesn't itch as much as atopic dermatitis and usually will clear when the irritant is no longer present.

Another form of contact dermatitis develops after skin contact with substances to which the child is allergic. The most common of these are:

- Certain flavorings or additives to toothpastes and mouthwashes (These cause a rash around the mouth.)

- Glues and dyes used in the manufacture of shoes (They produce a reaction on the tops of the toes and feet.)

- Dyes used in clothing (These cause rashes in areas where the clothing rubs or where there is increased perspiration.)

- Nickel jewelry

- Plants (especially poison ivy, poison oak, and poison sumac (see page 641)

- Medications such as neomycin ointment

This rash usually appears within several hours after contact (maybe longer with poison ivy). It is somewhat itchy, and may even have small blisters.

Treatment

If your child appears to have a rash that looks like eczema, your pediatrician will need to examine it to make the correct diagnosis and prescribe the proper treatment. In some cases, he may arrange for a dermatologist to examine it.

Although there is no cure for atopic dermatitis, it generally can be controlled and often will go away after several months or years. The most effective treatment is to prevent the skin's becoming dry and itchy. To do this:

- Avoid frequent, long baths, which tend to dry the skin.

- Use skin moisturizers regularly to decrease the dryness and itchiness.

- Avoid harsh or irritating clothing (wool or coarse-weave material).

- If there is oozing or exceptional itching, use tepid (lukewarm) compresses on the area, followed by the application of prescribed medications.

Your pediatrician usually will suggest a medicated cream or ointment to control inflammation and itching. These preparations often contain a form of cortisone, and should be used only under the direction of your doctor. In addition, other lotions or bath oils might be prescribed. It's important to continue to apply the medications for as long as your pediatrician directs. Stopping too soon will cause the condition to recur.

In addition to the skin preparations, your child also may need to take an antihistamine by mouth to control the itching, and antibiotics if the skin becomes infected.

The treatment of allergic contact dermatitis is similar, although your pediatrician (or an allergist) also will want to find the cause of the rash by taking a careful history or by conducting a series of patch tests. These tests are done by placing a small patch of a common irritant (allergen) against your child's skin. If the skin reacts with redness and itching, that substance should be avoided.

Alert your pediatrician if any of the following occurs:

- Your child's rash is severe and is not responding to home treatment.

- There is any evidence of fever or infection (such as blisters, redness, yellow crusts, pain, or oozing of fluid).

- The rash spreads or another rash develops.

Fifth Disease (Erythema Infectiosum)

Rosy cheeks usually are a sign of good health, but if your child suddenly develops bright-red patches on his cheeks that are also raised and warm, he may have a viral illness known as fifth disease. Like so many other childhood illnesses, this one is spread from person to person. Recently, the specific virus causing this disease has been identified as a parvovirus. Once the virus is in your child's body, it may take from four to fourteen days for symptoms to appear.

This is a mild disease, and most children feel well even when the rash is present. However, there can be mild cold-like symptoms: sore throat, headache, pink eyes, fatigue, a mild fever, or itching. In rare cases there may be aches in the knees or wrists.

The rash usually begins on the cheeks, causing them to look as if they've been slapped. During the next few days, the arms, and then the trunk, thighs, and buttocks will develop a pink, slightly raised rash that has a lacelike pattern. Fever is usually absent or mild. After five to ten days the rash will fade, with the face clearing first, followed by the arms and then the trunk and legs. Interestingly, the rash may reappear briefly weeks or months later, particularly if your child becomes hot from bathing, exercise or sunlight, or spends time in the sun.

Treatment

While fifth disease is not serious, it may be confused with a rash that is. It also may mimic certain drug-related rashes, so it's important to inform your pediatrician about any medications your child may be taking. When you describe the symptoms over the phone, the doctor may suspect fifth disease, but he may still want to examine your child to be certain.

There is no specific treatment for fifth disease, but symptomatic relief is possible. For instance, if there's a fever over 102 degrees Fahrenheit (38.9 degrees Celsius)—which is very rare with fifth disease—or minor aches and pains, you can use acetaminophen. When cold symptoms are interfering with sleeping or eating, check with your pediatrician about using a decongestant. Itching can be relieved by using an antihistamine. Also, if your child exhibits new symptoms, feels sicker, or develops a high fever, call your pediatrician again.

Fifth disease is spread while the child is suffering the cold-like symptoms which precede the rash. By the time your child has a rash, he is no longer contagious. Nevertheless, as a rule, whenever your child has a rash or a fever he should be kept away from other children until the illness is identified by your doctor. As a precaution, you should wait until he no longer has a fever and is feeling normal before allowing him to play with other children. Your youngster also should be kept away from pregnant women (particularly in their first trimester) until the rash fades, as the virus that causes this disease may have a damaging effect on the fetus if the mother becomes infected.

German Measles (Rubella)

Although many of today's parents had rubella, or German measles, during their childhood, it is a relatively uncommon illness now, thanks to the availability of an effective vaccine against the virus that causes it. Even when it was quite prevalent, however, rubella was usually a mild disease.

Rubella is characterized by a fever (100–102 degrees Fahrenheit [37.8–38.9 degrees Celsius]), swollen glands (typically on the back of the neck and base of the skull), and a rash. The rash, which varies from pinhead size to an irregular redness, is raised and usually begins on the face. Within two to three days it spreads to the neck, chest, and the rest of the body as it fades from the face.

Once exposed to rubella, a child usually will break out with the disease in fourteen to twenty-one days. The contagious period for rubella begins several days before the rash and continues for five to seven days after it appears. Because the disease can be so mild, it goes unrecognized in about half the children who contract it.

Before the rubella vaccine was developed, this illness tended to occur in epidemics every six to nine years. Since the vaccine was introduced in 1968, there have been no significant epidemics. Even so, the disease does still occur on a smaller scale. Each year, a group of unvaccinated and susceptible teenagers, often in college-campus settings, develops the illness. Fortunately, except for causing fever, discomfort, and occasional pain in the joints, these small epidemics are of little consequence.

The situation is quite different when rubella infects a woman in the first three months of her pregnancy. In this case it can cause severe, irreversible damage to the unborn fetus. Babies born with this form of rubella (congenital rubella) may have eye disorders (cataracts, glaucoma, small eyes), heart problems, deafness, severe mental retardation, and other evidence of central nervous system damage.

What You Can Do

If your pediatrician diagnoses rubella in your child, you may be able to make him more comfortable by giving him extra fluids, bed rest (if he's fatigued), and acetaminophen if he has a fever. Keep him away from other children or adults unless you are sure that they're immunized. As a general rule, children with rubella should not be in day care or any other group setting for seven days after the rash first appears. In particular, make a special effort not to expose a child with rubella to pregnant women.

If your child is diagnosed as having the congenital form of rubella, your pediatrician can advise you on the best way to manage his complex and difficult problems. Infants born with congenital rubella are often infectious for a year *after* birth, and therefore should be kept out of any group child-care setting, where they could expose other susceptible children or adults to the infection.

When to Call the Pediatrician

If your child has a fever and a rash, and appears uncomfortable, discuss the problem with your pediatrician. If rubella is diagnosed, follow the guidelines suggested earlier for treatment and isolation.

Prevention

Prevention of German measles through immunization is the best approach. The vaccine usually is administered as part of a three-in-one shot called MMR (measles, mumps, rubella), given when the child is fifteen months old. Booster doses need to be given. (See Chapter 27, "Immunizations.")

In addition to children, other susceptible individuals should be considered for the rubella vaccine:

- Girls and women known not to be pregnant or anticipating pregnancy within three months

- Day-care personnel

- College students

- Military personnel

- Health-care personnel

There are relatively few adverse reactions to the rubella vaccine. Occasionally, children will get a rash, a slight fever, and some joint pain in the first one to three weeks after the vaccine is given. (Joint pain is much less common with the newest version of the vaccine.) *A child can be immunized even if his mother is pregnant at the time.* However, a pregnant woman should *never* be immunized herself. She also should be extremely careful to avoid contact with any child or adult who may be infected with the virus. After delivery, she immediately should be immunized.

Hair Loss (Alopecia)

Almost all newborns lose some or all of their hair. This is *not* abnormal; in fact, it is to be expected. The baby hair falls out before the mature hair comes in. Thus, hair loss occurring during the first six months is *not* a cause for concern.

Very commonly, a baby will lose his hair by rubbing his scalp against the mattress or as a result of a head-banging habit. As he starts to move more and sit up, or outgrow this head-banging behavior, this type of hair loss will correct itself.

In very rare cases, babies may be born with alopecia (baldness), which can occur by itself or in association with certain abnormalities of the nails and the teeth. Later in childhood, hair loss may be due to medications, a scalp injury, or a medical or nutritional problem.

An older child may also lose her hair if it's braided too tightly, or pulled too hard when combing or brushing. Some youngsters (under age three or four) twirl their hair as a comforting habit, and innocently may pull it out. Others (usually of an older age) may pull their hair on purpose, but deny doing it; this frequently signals emotional stress, which should be discussed with your pediatrician.

Also be aware of a condition called "alopecia areata," which is common in children and teenagers and seems to be an allergic reaction to one's own hair. In this disorder, children lose hair in a circular area, causing a bald spot. In general, when it's limited to a few patches, the outlook for complete recovery is good. But when the condition persists or worsens, steroid creams and even steroid injections and other forms of therapy at the site of the hair loss are often used. Unfortunately, if the hair loss is extensive, it may be difficult to renew its growth.

Because alopecia and other types of hair loss can be a sign of other medical or nutritional problems, hair loss should be brought to your pediatrician's attention whenever it occurs after the first six months of age. The doctor will look at your child's scalp, determine the cause, and prescribe treatment.

Head Lice

The detection of *head lice* is an all too frequent occurrence in young children who play together, share clothing or hats, or are generally in close contact. Though often embarrassing at first, head lice fortunately are not a serious medical problem. Parents should realize that almost everyone who has had children in school or child care has received a note informing them that a case of head lice had been reported in their child's classroom. This used to be confined to school-age children, but now that more children are in preschool, there has been an increase at earlier ages, as well.

Usually, you first become aware of the presence of head lice by noticing that the child has an extremely itchy scalp. Upon close inspection, you may see little white dots in the hair or on the neck at the hairline. Sometimes you may confuse this with dandruff or seborrhea. Dandruff generates larger flakes, however, while lice infestation results in more discrete dots that are usually stuck onto the shaft of the hair. Upon close examination, you may even see them move on the hair shaft. Also, the itchiness of the scalp is usually far more uncomfortable with lice than with seborrhea or dandruff.

These symptoms may indicate the presence of the head louse, *Pediculus humanus capitus,* and its eggs or nits. Try not to overreact when you first realize this. It is a very common condition, easy to treat, and does *not* reflect on your level of personal hygiene. It is merely the result of having your child in settings with other children.

If your child does have head lice, they probably were contracted through direct contact with another child at school. This contact usually comes with sharing brushes, combs, and hats or other articles of clothing.

Treatment

Once you recognize that your child has head lice, there are several treatments available. The three most widely used are:

- Lindane (brand names Kwell, Scabene), given as a four minute shampoo. *This preparation is highly toxic and should not be used with infants.*

- Natural pyrethrin based products (brand names A200, RID), applied as a ten minute shampoo.

- Permathrin (brand name NIX), applied as a ten minute rinse.

Check with your child's pediatrician to see which one he prefers.

Pyrethrin products are available without prescription; pyrethrin and permathrin products appear to have lower potential toxicity. Usually only one treatment is required for permathrin products; often a second treatment with lindane or pyrethrin products is necessary 7 to 10 days later when some of the residual eggs have hatched.

Whichever treatment you use, careful combing of the hair with a fine-tooth comb is important to remove the dead egg cases and any nits or eggs that have survived treatment. To prevent reinfection, you must also wash all bed clothes and clothing (hats are a big culprit) that have been in contact with the child for the 48 hours immediately preceding your noticing the head lice. Use the hot cycles to wash the clothes, or have them dry cleaned if you prefer.

In addition, if your child has lice, it's important to inform the child-care center or school program. If your active, engaging three-year-old has head lice, no doubt someone else in the group does, too. Because head lice are very contagious, other family members may also need to be treated and have their clothing and bedding laundered.

Hives

If your child has an itchy rash that consists of raised red bumpy areas with pale centers, he probably has hives (welts). This allergic reaction may be all over the body or just in one region, such as the face. The location may change, with the hives disappearing in one area of the body and appearing in another, often in a matter of hours.

Among the most common causes of hives are allergies to:

- Foods (berries, cheese, nuts, eggs, milk, sesame oils, shellfish)

- Drugs, either over-the-counter or prescribed. (Penicillin and aspirin are two frequent culprits.)

- Pollen from trees, grass, ferns

- Plants

- Response to infection (so-called infectious hives)

- Cold water

- Bites or stings from bees or other insects

And don't be surprised if you can't figure out the cause.

Treatment

An oral antihistamine will relieve the itching of hives. Many of them can be obtained without a prescription, but you should ask your doctor to recommend one. You may need to use this type of medication for one to three days, and give it as often as every four to six hours. Applying cool compresses to the area of itching and swelling also may help.

Still other treatments may be necessary if internal parts of the body are involved in the allergic reaction as well. If your child is wheezing or having trouble swallowing, emergency treatment should be sought. He usually will prescribe a more effective antihistamine, and may even give an injection of Adrenalin to stop the allergic response. If the allergy causing the hives also results in severe breathing difficulties, your pediatrician will help you obtain a special emergency-care kit for possible use with such reactions in the future.

Prevention

In order to prevent subsequent outbreaks of hives, your doctor will try to determine what is causing the allergic reaction. If the rash is confined to a small area of skin, it probably was caused by something your child touched (plants and soaps are frequent culprits). But if it spreads all over his body, something he ate or inhaled is most likely to blame.

Frequently, there's a pattern to the appearance of the hives that provides a clue to the allergy. For example, does it usually happen after meals? Does it seem to occur more during certain seasons, or when traveling to particular places? If you discover a specific pattern, alter the routine to see if your child improves. You will need to consider every food your child eats, even those that he has eaten without difficulty in the past. Sometimes, hives will occur if your child eats an unusually large amount of a food to which he is only mildly allergic.

Once you've discovered the cause of the problem, try keeping your child away from it as much as possible. If you know in advance that he will or may be exposed, send or bring along an antihistamine. If his allergy is to insects, keep a bee-sting kit available. (See *Insect Bites and Stings,* below.)

Impetigo

Impetigo is a contagious bacterial skin infection that often appears around the nose, mouth, and ears. Most commonly, it is caused by either the streptococcus, which also is responsible for "strep" throat and scarlet fever, or the staphylococcus, or "staph," bacteria.

If staph bacteria are to blame, the infection may cause blisters filled with clear fluid. These can break easily, leaving a raw glistening area that soon forms a scab with a honey-colored crust. By contrast, the strep bacteria usually are not associated with blisters, but they do cause crusts over larger sores and ulcers.

Treatment

Until your child can see the doctor, clean the rash well with soap and water. You may use a mild medicated soap, but don't rely on over-the-counter medications without consulting your pediatrician.

Impetigo needs to be treated with antibiotics, but your pediatrician may wish to first determine which bacteria are causing the rash in order to know what specific medication to prescribe. To identify the bacteria the doctor may break a blister or lift the crust, and take a sample of the material there. If this shows the cause is strep bacteria, some form of penicillin probably will be prescribed, but if the rash is due to a staph infection, a different antibiotic may be used. In either case, make sure your child takes the medication for the full prescribed course, or the impetigo could return.

One other important point to keep in mind: Impetigo is contagious until the rash clears, or until at least two days of antibiotics have been given and there is evidence of improvement. So your child should avoid close contact with other children during this period, and you should avoid touching the rash. If you or other family members do come in contact with it, wash the exposed site thoroughly with soap and water. Also, keep the infected child's washcloths and towels separate from those of other family members.

Prevention

The bacteria that cause impetigo thrive in breaks in the skin, so the best ways to prevent this rash are to keep your child's fingernails clipped and clean, and teach him not to scratch minor skin irritations. When he does have a scrape, cleanse it with soap and water, and apply an antibiotic cream or ointment. Also be careful not to use washcloths or towels that have been used by someone else who has an active skin infection.

When impetigo is caused by strep bacteria, a rare but serious complication called glomerulonephritis can develop. This disease causes inflammation of the kidney, passage of blood and protein in the urine, and sometimes high blood pressure.

Insect Bites and Stings

Your child's reaction to a bite or sting will depend on his sensitivity to the particular insect's venom. While most children have only mild reactions, those who are allergic to certain insect venoms can have severe symptoms that require emergency treatment.

Treatment

Although insect bites can be irritating, they usually begin to disappear by the next day and do not require treatment by a doctor. To relieve the itchiness that accompanies bites by mosquitos, flies, fleas, and bedbugs, apply calamine lotion freely onto any part of your child's body except the areas around his eyes and genitals. If your child is stung by a wasp

Insect/ Environment	Characteristics of Bite or Sting	Special Notes
Mosquitoes Water (pools, lakes, birdbaths)	Stinging sensation followed by small, red, itchy mound with tiny puncture mark at center.	Mosquitoes are attracted by bright colors, sweat, and sweet odors such as perfumes, scented soaps, and shampoos.
Flies Food, garbage, animal waste	Painful, itchy bumps. May turn into small blisters.	Bites often disappear in a day but may last longer.
Fleas Cracks in floor, rugs, pet fur	Small bump that looks like a hive. Often in groups where clothes fit tightly (waist, buttocks).	Fleas are most likely to be a problem in homes with pets.
Bedbugs Cracks of walls, floors, crevices of furniture, bedding	Itchy red bumps surrounded by a blister. Usually two or three in a row.	Bedbugs are most likely to bite at night and are less active in cold weather.
Fire ants Mounds in pastures, meadows, lawns, and parks	Immediate pain and burning. Swelling up to one-half inch. Cloudy fluid in area of bite.	Fire ants usually attack intruders. Some children have reactions such as difficulty in breathing, fever, and stomach upset.
Bees and wasps Flowers, shrubs, picnic areas, beaches	Immediate pain and rapid swelling.	A few children have severe reactions such as difficulty in breathing and swelling all over the body.
Ticks Wooded areas	May not be noticeable. Hidden in hair or on skin.	Don't remove ticks with matches, lighted cigarettes, or nail polish remover. Grasp the tick firmly with tweezers near the head. Gently remove the tick; don't leave any parts of it embedded in the skin.

or bee, soak a cloth in cold water and press it over the area of the sting to reduce pain and swelling. Call your pediatrician before using any other treatment, including creams or lotions containing antihistamines or home remedies such as baking soda, meat tenderizer, tobacco juice, ammonia, or vinegar. If the itching is severe, the doctor may prescribe cortisone ointment or oral antihistamines.

If the stinger is visible, remove it by gently scraping it off horizontally. If you try to pull it out by grasping it between two fingers, you may squeeze the venom sac and inject more of the toxin into your child's skin. Don't try to remove a honeybee stinger, because it has a barb that will stick in the skin. The stinger will dissolve after a few days, so simply wash the area well and leave it alone. Beestings and mosquito bites may be more swollen on the second or third day after the incident.

Keep your child's fingernails short and clean to minimize the risk of infection from scratching. If infection does occur anyway, the bite will become redder, larger, and more swollen. In some cases you may notice red streaks or yellowish fluid near the bite. Have your pediatrician examine any infected bite, because it may need to be treated with antibiotics.

Call for medical help immediately if your child has any of these other symptoms after being bitten or stung:

- Sudden difficulty in breathing

- Weakness, collapse, or unconsciousness

- Hives or itching all over the body

- Extreme swelling near the eye, lips, or penis that makes it difficult for the child to see, eat, or urinate.

Prevention

Some children with no other known allergies may have severe reactions to insect bites and stings as well. If you suspect that your child is allergy-prone, discuss the situation with your doctor. He may recommend a series of hyposensitization injections. In addition, he will prescribe a special kit for you to keep on hand for use if your child is stung.

It is impossible to prevent *all* insect bites, but you can minimize the number your child receives by following these guidelines:

- Avoid areas where insects nest or congregate, such as garbage cans, stagnant pools of water, uncovered foods and sweets, and orchards and gardens where flowers are in bloom.

- When you know your child will be exposed to insects, dress him in long pants and a lightweight long-sleeved shirt.

- Avoid dressing your child in clothing with bright colors or flowery prints because they seem to attract insects.

- Don't use scented soaps, perfumes, or hair sprays on your child, because they also are inviting to insects.

Insect repellents are generally available without a prescription, but they should be used sparingly on infants and young children. The most effective insecticides include DEET (diethyltoluamide). Repellents appropriate for use on children should contain no more than 10 percent DEET because the chemical, which is absorbed through the skin, can cause harm. The concentration of DEET varies significantly from product to product, so read the label of any product you purchase. Repellents are effective in preventing bites by mosquitoes, ticks, fleas, chiggers, and biting flies, but have virtually no effect on stinging insects such as bees, hornets, and wasps. Contrary to popular belief, giving antihistamines continuously throughout the insect season does not appear to prevent reactions to bites.

The table on page 638 summarizes information about common stinging or biting insects.

Measles

Thanks to measles vaccine, this disease is relatively uncommon in America today. However, people still get measles. If your child has never been immunized or had measles, he can get them if he is exposed. The measles virus is passed through the air droplets transmitted by an infected person. Anyone who breathes the droplets and is not immune to the disease can become infected.

Signs and Symptoms

For the first eight to twelve days after being exposed to the measles virus, your child probably will have no symptoms; this is called the incubation period. Then he may develop an illness that seems like a common cold, with a cough, runny nose, and pink eye (conjunctivitis; see page 559). The cough may be severe at times, and will last for about a week, and your child probably will feel miserable.

During the first one to three days of the illness, the coldlike symptoms will become worse, and he'll develop a fever that may run as high as 103 to 105 degrees Fahrenheit (39.4 to 40.5 degrees Celsius). The fever will last until two to three days after the rash first appears.

After two to four days of illness, the rash will develop. It usually begins on the face and neck, and spreads down the trunk and out to the arms and legs. It starts as very fine red bumps, which may join together to form larger splotches. If you notice tiny white spots, like grains of sand, inside his mouth next to the molars, you'll know the rash is soon to follow. The rash will last five to eight days. As it fades, the skin may peel a little.

Treatment

Although there is no specific treatment for the disease, it is important that the pediatrician examine your child to determine that measles is, in fact, the cause of the illness.

Many other conditions can start in the same way, and measles has its own complications (such as pneumonia) that the doctor will want to watch for. When you call, describe the fever and rash so that the doctor knows it may be measles. When you visit the office, the pediatrician will want to separate your child from other patients, so that the virus is not transmitted to them.

Your child is contagious from several days before the rash breaks out until the fever and rash are gone. During this period he should be kept at home (except for the visit to the doctor) and away from anyone who is not immune to the illness.

At home, make sure your child drinks plenty of fluids, and give acetaminophen in the proper dose to control fever. The conjunctivitis that accompanies measles can make it painful for the child to be in bright sunshine, so you may want to darken his room to a comfortable level for the first few days.

Sometimes bacterial infections develop on top of the measles. These most often include sore throat (see page 547), pneumonia (see page 516), and ear infection (see page 537). These must be seen by the pediatrician and usually require antibiotic treatment.

Prevention

Almost all children who receive the MMR (measles, mumps, rubella) vaccine after their first birthday are protected against measles for life. (See Chapter 27, "Immunizations.") However, up to five percent of children may not respond to the initial vaccination. For this reason, a second dose is now being recommended either at age five or upon entry to middle school, (ages 11 to 12) depending on your specific state requirements. Your pediatrician will tell you what is best for your child.

If your child has been exposed to someone who has measles, or if someone in your household has the virus, notify your pediatrician at once. The following steps can help keep your child from getting sick:

1. If he is under one year old or has a weakened immune system, he can be given immune globulin (gamma globulin) up to six days following exposure. This temporarily may protect him from becoming infected, but will not provide extended immunity.

2. If your child is otherwise healthy and over one year old, he can still be vaccinated. The vaccine may be effective if given within seventy-two hours of his exposure to an infected person, and *will* provide extended immunity. If your child has received one dose of measles vaccine, he may be given a second dose.

Poison Ivy, Poison Oak, Poison Sumac

Contact with poison ivy, poison oak, or poison sumac is a common cause of skin rash in children during the spring, summer, and fall seasons. An allergic reaction to the oil in these plants produces the rash. The rash occurs from several hours to three days after contact with the plant and begins in the form of blisters, which are accompanied by severe itching.

Contrary to popular belief, it is not the fluid in the blisters that causes the rash to spread. That occurs when small amounts of oil remain under the child's fingernails or on his clothing and are then carried to other parts of his body. The rash will not be spread to another person unless the oil that remains also comes in contact with that person's skin.

Poison ivy grows as a three-leafed green weed with a red stem at the center. It grows in vinelike form in all parts of the country except the Southwest. Poison sumac is a shrub, not a vine, and has seven to thirteen leaves arranged in pairs along a central stem. Not nearly as abundant as poison ivy, it grows primarily in the swampy areas of the Mississippi River region. Poison oak grows as a shrub, and it is primarily seen on the West coast. All three plants produce similar skin reactions. These skin reactions are forms of contact dermatitis (see *Eczema,* page 631).

Treatment

Treating reactions to poison ivy—the most frequent of these forms of contact dermatitis—is a straightforward matter.

- Prevention is the best approach. Know what the plant looks like and teach your children to avoid it.

- If there is contact, wash all clothes in soap and water. Also, wash the area of the skin that was exposed with soap and water for at least ten minutes after the plant or the oil has been touched.

- If the eruption is mild, apply a calamine lotion preparation three or four times a day to cut down on the itching. Avoid those preparations that have anesthetics or antihistamines in them, as they can often cause allergic eruptions themselves.

- Topical 1 percent hydrocortisone creams can be applied to decrease the inflammation.

- If the rash is severe, on the face, or on extensive parts of the body, the pediatrician may need to place the child on oral steroids. These will need to be given for about 10 to 14 days, with the dose tapering in a specific schedule determined by your pediatrician. This treatment should be reserved for the most severe cases. The pediatrician should be called if you notice any of the following:

  - Severe eruption not responsive to the previously described home methods.

  - Any evidence of infection, such as blisters, redness, or oozing.

  - Any new eruption or rash.

  - Severe poison ivy on the face.

  - Fever.

Ringworm

If your child has a scaly round patch on his chest or the side of his scalp, and he seems to be losing hair in the same area, the problem may be a contagious infection known as ringworm.

This disorder is caused not by worms but by a fungus. It's called "ringworm" because the infections tend to form round or oval spots that, as they grow, become smooth in the center but keep an active red scaly border.

Scalp ringworm is almost always spread from person to person. If it appears elsewhere on your child's body, he may have the type spread by infected dogs or cats.

The first signs of infection on the body are very red scaly patches. They may not look like rings until they've grown to half an inch in diameter, and they generally stop growing at about one inch. Your child may have just one patch or a cluster on one side of his body, but he probably will have no more than twenty, and they'll be only mildly itchy and uncomfortable.

Scalp ringworm starts the same way the body variety does, but as the rings grow, your child may lose some hair in the infected area. Certain types of scalp ringworm produce less obvious rings, and are easily confused with dandruff or cradle cap. However, cradle cap occurs only during infancy, and dandruff rarely appears before adolescence, so if your child's scalp is continually scaly and he's over a year old, you should suspect ringworm and notify your pediatrician.

Treatment

A single body ringworm infection can be treated with an over-the-counter cream recommended by your pediatrician. The most frequently used ones are tolnaftate or miconazole. A small amount is applied two or three times a day for at least a week, during which time some clearing should begin. If there are any patches on the scalp or more than one on the body, or if the rash is getting worse while being treated, check with your pediatrician again. He will prescribe a stronger medication and, in the case of severe scalp ringworm, probably will use an oral antifungal preparation. Your child will have to take medicine for several weeks to clear the infection.

You also may need to wash your child's scalp with a special shampoo when he has scalp ringworm. If there's any possibility that others in the family have caught the infection, they also should use this shampoo.

Prevention

You can help prevent ringworm by identifying and treating any pets with the problem. Look for scaling, itchy, hairless areas on your dogs and cats, and have them treated right away. Any family members who show symptoms also should be treated.

If your child is diagnosed with ringworm, keep him out of school or play-group settings until the condition has been controlled. Also throw away any combs, hairbrushes, or hats he has used recently.

Roseola Infantum

Your ten-month-old doesn't look or act very ill, but he suddenly develops a fever between 102 degrees Fahrenheit (38.9 degrees Celsius) and 105 degrees Fahrenheit (40.5 degrees Celsius). The fever lasts for three to five days, during which time your child has less appetite, mild diarrhea, slight cough, and runny nose, and seems mildly irritable and a little sleepier than usual. His upper eyelids appear slightly swollen or droopy. Finally, *after his temperature returns to normal,* he gets a slightly raised, spotty, pink rash on his trunk. "Oh, no!" you say. "It's measles!" But the rash spreads only to his upper arms and neck and fades after just twenty-four hours. What's the diagnosis? Most likely it's a disease called roseola—a contagious viral illness sometimes referred to as "baby measles" because it's most common in children under age two. Its incubation period is seven to fourteen days. The key to this diagnosis is that the rash appears *after* the fever is gone.

Treatment

Whenever your infant or young child has a fever of 102 degrees Fahrenheit (38.9 degrees Celsius) or higher for twenty-four hours, call your pediatrician, even if there are no other symptoms. If the doctor suspects the fever is caused by roseola, he will suggest ways to control the temperature and advise you to call again if your child becomes worse or the fever lasts for more than three or four days. For a child who has other symptoms or appears more seriously ill, the doctor may order a blood count, urinalysis, or other tests.

Since most illnesses that cause fever are contagious, it's wise to keep your youngster away from other children, at least until you've conferred with your pediatrician. Once he is diagnosed as having roseola, don't let him play with other children until the rash clears.

While your youngster has a fever, dress him in lightweight clothing and give him acetaminophen in the appropriate dose for his age and weight. (See Chapter 23, "Fever.") If his temperature goes over 104 degrees Fahrenheit (40 degrees Celsius), he may be more comfortable if you give him a sponge bath with barely cool water. Also don't worry if his appetite is decreased and encourage him to drink extra fluids. As soon as his rash is gone, he may return to all normal activities, including contact with other children.

Although this disease is rarely serious, be aware that early in the illness when fever climbs very quickly, there's a chance of convulsions (see *Seizures, Convulsions, and Epilepsy,* page 601). There may be a seizure regardless of how well you treat the fever, so it's important to know how to manage convulsions even though they're usually quite mild and occur only briefly, if at all, with roseola.

Scabies

Scabies is caused by a microscopic mite that burrows under the top layers of skin and deposits its eggs. The rash that results from scabies is actually an allergic reaction to the mite's body, eggs, and excretions. Once the mite gets into the skin, it takes two to four weeks for the rash to appear.

In an older child, this rash appears as numerous itchy, fluid-filled bumps that may be located under the skin next to a reddish burrow track. In an infant, the bumps may be more scattered and isolated. Because of scratch marks, crusting, or a secondary infection, this annoying rash is often difficult to identify.

According to legend, when Napoleon's troops had scabies, one could hear the sound of scratching at night from over a mile away! A bit of exaggeration perhaps, but it illustrates two key points to remember if you think your child has scabies: It's very itchy and very contagious. Scabies is spread only person to person, but this happens extremely easily. If one person in your family has the rash, the others almost certainly will get it too.

Scabies can be located almost anywhere on the body, including the area between the fingers. Older children and adults usually don't get the rash on their palms, soles, scalp, or face, but babies may. Adult women often develop scabies sores around their breasts, and adult males and females often get them on their genitals, armpits, arms, wrists, midriff, and lower buttocks.

Treatment

If you notice that your child (and possibly others in the family) is scratching constantly, suspect scabies and call the pediatrician, who will examine the rash and may gently scrape a skin sample from the affected area to look at under the microscope for evidence of the mite or its eggs. If scabies turns out to be the diagnosis, the doctor will prescribe one of several anti-scabies medications. Most are lotions that are applied over the entire body, then washed off after several hours. Although one treatment is usually sufficient, it may need to be repeated.

Some experts feel the whole family must be treated—even those members who don't have a rash. Any live-in help, sleep-over visitors, or frequent babysitters also should receive care.

To prevent infection caused by scratching, cut your child's fingernails, and if the itching is very severe, ask your pediatrician to prescribe an antihistamine or other anti-itch medication. If your child shows signs of bacterial infection in the scratched scabies, notify the pediatrician. He may want to prescribe an antibiotic or other form of treatment.

Following treatment, the itching could continue for two to four weeks, because this is an allergic rash. If it persists past four weeks, call your doctor, because the scabies may have returned and need retreatment.

Incidentally, there is some controversy over the possible spread of scabies from clothing or linen. Evidence indicates that this occurs very rarely. However, for peace of mind, you may want to wash your linens and bedclothes in hot water. There's no need, though, to decontaminate the baby's room or the house, since the mite usually lives only in people's skin.

Scarlet Fever

When your child has a strep throat (see page 547), there's one chance in twenty that he'll also get a rash known as scarlet fever or scarlatina. The symptoms of scarlet fever begin with a sore throat, a fever of about 101–104 degrees Fahrenheit (38.2–40 degrees Celsius), and headache. This is followed within twenty-four hours by a red and sometimes itchy rash, covering the trunk, arms, and legs. The rash is slightly raised, which makes the skin feel like fine sandpaper. Your child's face will turn red, too, with a pale area around his mouth. This redness will disappear in three to five days, leaving peeling skin in the areas where the rash was most intense (neck, underarms, groin, fingers, and toes). He may also have a white-coated, then reddened tongue and mild abdominal pain.

Treatment

Call your pediatrician whenever your child complains of a sore throat, especially when a rash or fever is also present. The doctor will examine him and check for the presence of strep bacteria. If strep throat is found, an antibiotic (usually penicillin) will be given either by injection or in pill or liquid form. If your child takes the antibiotic by mouth, it's extremely important to complete the entire ten-day course because shorter treatment sometimes results in a return of the disease.

Most children with strep infections respond very quickly to antibiotics. The fever, sore throat, and headache usually are gone within twenty-four hours. The rash, however, will remain for about three to five days.

If your child's condition does not seem to improve with treatment, notify your pediatrician. If other family members develop fever or sore throat at this time—with or without a rash—they, too, should be examined and tested for strep throat.

If not treated, scarlet fever (like strep throat) can lead to ear and sinus infections, swollen neck glands, and pus around the tonsils. The most serious complication of untreated strep throat is rheumatic fever, which results in joint pain and swelling and sometimes heart damage. Very rarely, strep throat and scarlet fever can lead to glomerulonephritis, an inflammation of the kidneys that can cause blood to appear in the urine and sometimes cause high blood pressure.

Sunburn

While those with darker coloring tend to be less sensitive to the sun, no one, regardless of complexion, is immune to sunburn and its associated disorders, and children especially need to be protected from the sun's burning rays. Like other burns, sunburn will leave the skin red, warm, and painful. In severe cases it may cause blistering, fever, chills, headache, and a general feeling of illness.

Your child doesn't actually have to be burned, however, in order to be harmed by the sun. The effects of exposure build over the years, so that even moderate exposure during childhood can contribute to wrinkling, toughening, and perhaps cancer of the skin in later life. Also, some medications can cause a skin reaction when the person taking them is exposed to sunlight.

Treatment

The signs of sunburn usually appear six to twelve hours after exposure, with the greatest discomfort during the first twenty-four hours. If your child's burn is just red, warm, and painful, you can treat it yourself. Apply cool compresses to the burned areas or bathe him in cool water. You also can give acetaminophen to help relieve the pain. (Check the package for appropriate dosage for his age and weight.)

If the sunburn causes blisters, fever, chills, headache, or a general feeling of illness, call your pediatrician. Severe sunburn must be treated like any other serious burn, and if it's very extensive, hospitalization is sometimes required. In addition, the blisters can become infected, requiring treatment with antibiotics.

Sometimes, extensive or severe sunburn also can lead to dehydration (see *Diarrhea,* page 478, for signs of dehydration) and in some cases fainting (heatstroke). Such cases need to be examined by your pediatrician or the nearest emergency facility.

Prevention

Many parents incorrectly assume that the sun is dangerous only when it's shining brightly. In fact, it's not the visible light rays but, rather, the invisible ultraviolet rays that are harmful. Your child actually may be exposed to more ultraviolet rays on foggy or hazy days, because he'll feel cooler and therefore stay outside for a longer time. Even a big hat or an umbrella is not absolute protection, because ultraviolet rays reflect off sand, water, snow, and many other surfaces.

Try to keep your child out of the sun between 10:00 A.M. and 2:00 P.M. (11:00 A.M. to 3:00 P.M. daylight saving time), when the peak ultraviolet rays occur. If that's not possible, follow these guidelines:

- Always use a sunscreen in warm weather to block the damaging ultraviolet rays. All children should use a sunscreen with a sun protection factor (SPF) of at least 15 (check the label). Those with very fair skin need the highest SPF, which is over 30. Apply the protection half an hour before going out. Many sunscreens are waterproof, but even these may need to be reapplied every three or four hours if your child spends a lot of time in the water. Consult the instructions on the bottle.

- Dress your child in lightweight cotton clothing with long sleeves and long pants.

- Use a beach umbrella or similar object to keep him in the shade as much as possible.

- Have him wear a hat with a wide brim.

(See also *Burns,* page 448.)

Warts

Warts are caused by a virus—the papilloma virus. These firm bumps (although they can also be flat) are yellow, tan, grayish, black, or brown. They usually appear on the hands, toes, around the knees, and on the face, but can occur anywhere on the body. When they're on the soles of the feet, doctors call them plantar warts. Though warts can be contagious, they rarely appear in children under the age of two.

Treatment

Your pediatrician can give you advice on the treatment of warts. Sometimes he will recommend an over-the-counter medication that contains salicylic acid. If any of the following are present, he may refer you to a dermatologist.

- Multiple, recurring warts

- A wart on the face or genital area

- Large, deep, or painful plantar warts (warts on the soles of the feet)

- Warts that are particularly bothersome to your child

Some warts will just go away themselves. Others can be removed using prescription preparations. However, surgical removal by scraping, cauterizing, or freezing is sometimes necessary with multiple warts, those that continue to recur, or deep plantar warts. Although surgery usually has a good success rate, it can be painful and may result in scarring. The earlier the warts are treated, the better the chance of permanent cure, although there is always the possibility that they will recur even after treatment that is initially successful.

If a wart comes back, simply treat it again the way you did the first time, or as directed by your pediatrician. Don't wait until it becomes large, painful, or starts to spread.

30

CHRONIC CONDITIONS AND DISEASES

Coping with Chronic (Long-Term) Health Problems

We tend to think of childhood as a carefree and healthy time of life, but some youngsters face chronic health problems during these early years. (By *chronic,* we mean conditions that last for at least three months, or require at least a month of hospitalization.) While most long-term health problems in children are relatively mild, any type of lengthy illness or disability is stressful for both them and their families.

The specific medical treatment of many chronic conditions is discussed elsewhere, under the names of those conditions. (See index.) The information that follows is aimed at helping parents deal with the emotional and practical challenges of living with any child who has a long-term illness or disability.

Getting Help

If your child is born with a serious medical problem, or develops a chronic medical condition during his first years, you may face some of the following stresses and decisions:

- The realization that your child is not perfectly healthy often leads to feelings of disappointment and guilt, and fear for his future. In trying to deal with these feelings, you may find yourself struggling with unexplained emotional swings ranging from hopefulness to despair and depression.

- You will need to select and work with a team of medical professionals who can help your child.

- You may face decisions about treatment or surgery.

- You may have to accept responsibility for giving your child certain medications, guiding him in the use of special equipment, or helping him perform special therapies.

- You will be called on to provide the time, energy, money, and emotional commitment necessary for your child to receive the best possible treatment.

- In adapting your life to meet your child's needs without neglecting other family members, you will face many difficult choices, some of which may require compromise solutions.

To avoid becoming overwhelmed, it is helpful to select one medical person as the overall coordinator of your child's medical care. This person may be your pediatrician or another health professional who is most closely involved with your child's treatment. It should be someone who knows your family well, makes you feel comfortable, and is willing to spend time answering your questions and working with other doctors and therapists involved in your child's care.

Not all of your child's special needs will be medical, of course. He may require special schooling, counseling, or other therapy. Your family may need outside financial or governmental assistance. The person who coordinates your child's medical care should also provide some guidance in obtaining this extra help, but the best way to make sure you and your child get the services and support you need is to learn about the resources and regulations that apply to special services for children with chronic illnesses or disabilities. You should also find out what you can do if the services your family receives do not meet your child's needs.

Balancing the Needs of Family and Child

For a while, the child with special needs may take all your attention, leaving little for other family members and your outside relationships. While this is normal, everyone will suffer unless you find some way to restore a sense of balance and routine to your activities. Neither your sick child nor the rest of the family will benefit if the health problem becomes the central and overwhelming issue in your family's life. Eventually your child's medical care must become a part of your daily routine rather than the focus of it.

If your child must be hospitalized, returning him to normal family and community life is vital, not only for the family but also for his health and well-being. The longer he is treated like a "patient" instead of a growing child, the more problems he may have socially and emotionally later on. While it's natural to want to protect a sick child,

overprotection may make it more difficult for him to develop the self-discipline he needs as he matures. Also, if you have other children, you can't expect them to observe rules that you allow the child who is sick or disabled to ignore.

Your child needs your encouragement far more than your protection. Rather than concentrating on what he cannot do, try to focus instead on what he *can* do. If given a chance to participate in normal activities with children his age, he probably will do things that surprise everyone.

Establishing this sense of normalcy is difficult if your child's condition is uncertain. You may find yourself withdrawing from your friends because you're so worried about your child, and you may hesitate to plan social activities if you're not sure he'll be well enough to attend. If you give in to these feelings all the time, resentment is bound to build up, so try not to let this happen. Even if there is a chance that your child's condition may worsen unexpectedly, take the risk and plan special outings, invite friends to your home, and get a babysitter from time to time so you can go out for an evening. Both you and your child will be better off in the long run if you take this approach.

Special Tips

The following are suggestions that may help you cope more effectively with your child's condition.

- Whenever possible both parents should be included in discussions and decisions about your child's treatment. Too often, mothers go alone to medical appointments and then must explain what was said to the father. This may prevent the father from getting some of his own questions answered or learning enough about the choices.

- Don't be offended if your child's doctors ask personal questions about your family life. The more they know about your family, the better they can help you manage your child's care. For example, if your child has diabetes he may need a special schedule of meals, so the pediatrician may want to suggest ways to work this diet into your family's normal meal plan. Or if your child needs a wheelchair, the doctor may ask about your home in order to suggest the best places for wheelchair ramps. If you have concerns about the doctor's suggestions, discuss them with him so you can reach an acceptable plan of action together.

- Remember that although you and your doctor want to be optimistic about your child's condition, you must be honest about it. If things are not going well, say so. Your child depends on you to speak up at these times, and to work with the doctor to adjust the treatment or find a solution that will make the situation as good as possible.

- Discuss your child's condition frankly with him and the other members of your family. If you do not tell your child the truth, he may sense that you are lying; this can lead to feelings of aloneness and rejection. Furthermore, he will imagine all the things that could be wrong—most of which may be worse than his real problem. So talk to him openly, and listen to his responses to make sure he understands. Answer his questions in clear, simple language.

- Call on friends and family members for support. You cannot expect to handle the strain created by your child's chronic condition all by yourself. Asking close friends to help you meet your own emotional needs will in turn help you to meet your child's.

- Remember that your child needs to be loved and valued as an individual. If you let the medical problems overshadow your feelings for him as a person, they may interfere with the bond of trust and affection between you. Don't let yourself become so worried that you cannot relax and enjoy your child.

Anemia

Blood contains several different types of cells. The most numerous are the red blood cells, which absorb oxygen in the lungs and distribute it throughout the body. These cells contain hemoglobin, a red pigment that carries oxygen to the tissues and carries away the waste material, carbon dioxide. When there is a decreased amount of hemoglobin available in the red blood cells, making the blood less able to carry the amount of oxygen necessary for all the cells in the body to function and grow, the condition is called anemia.

Anemia may occur for any of the following reasons:

1. Production of red blood cells slows down.

2. Too many red blood cells are destroyed.

3. There is not enough hemoglobin within the red blood cells.

Young children most commonly become anemic when they fail to get enough iron in their diet. Iron is necessary for the production of hemoglobin. This iron deficiency causes a decrease in the amount of hemoglobin in the red blood cells. A young infant may get iron-deficiency anemia if he starts drinking cow's milk too early, particularly if he is not given an iron supplement or food with iron. The deficiency occurs because cow's milk contains very little iron and the small amount present is poorly absorbed through the intestines into the body. In addition, cow's milk given to an infant under six months of age can cause irritation of the bowel and small amounts of blood loss. This results in a decrease in the number of red blood cells, which can cause anemia.

Other nutritional deficiencies, such as lack of folic acid, also can cause anemia, but this is very rare. It is probably most often seen in children fed on goat's milk, which contains very little folic acid.

Anemia at any age can be caused by excessive blood loss. In rare cases, the blood does not clot properly, and a newborn infant may bleed heavily from his circumcision or minor injury, and become anemic. Because vitamin K promotes blood clotting and is often lacking in newborns, an injection of this vitamin generally is given right after birth.

Sometimes the red cells are prone to being easily destroyed. This is called hemolytic anemia, and can result from disturbances on the surface of the red cells or other abnormalities in or outside the cells.

A severe condition which involves an abnormal structure of hemoglobin, seen most often in children of black African heritage, is called sickle-cell anemia. This disorder can be very severe and is associated with frequent "crises" and often repeated hospitalizations.

Finally, certain enzyme deficiencies also can alter the function of the red blood cells, increasing their susceptibility to destruction.

Signs and Symptoms

Anemia causes a mild paleness of the skin, usually most apparent as a decreased pinkness of the lips, the lining of the eyelids (conjunctiva), and the nail beds (pink part of the nails). Anemic children also may be irritable, mildly weak, or tire easily. Those with severe anemia may have shortness of breath, rapid heart rate, and swelling of the hands and feet. If the anemia continues, it may interfere with normal growth. A newborn with hemolytic anemia may become jaundiced (turn yellow), although many newborns are mildly jaundiced and don't become anemic.

If your child shows any of these symptoms or signs, or if you suspect he is not getting enough iron in his diet, consult your pediatrician. A simple blood count can diagnose anemia in most cases.

Some children are not anemic but still are deficient in iron. These youngsters may have decreased appetite, be irritable, fussy, and inattentive, which may result in delays in their development or poor school performance. These problems will reverse when the children are given iron. Other signs of iron deficiency that may be unrelated to anemia include a tendency to eat weird things such as ice, dirt, clay, and cornstarch. This behavior is called "pica." It is not harmful unless the material eaten is toxic (such as lead). Usually the behavior improves after the anemia is treated and as the child becomes older, although it may persist longer in children who are developmentally delayed.

Children with sickle-cell anemia may have unexplained fever or swelling of the hands and feet as infants, and they are extremely susceptible to infection. If there is a history of sickle-cell anemia in your family, make sure your child is tested for it.

Treatment

Since there are so many different types of anemia, it is very important to identify the cause before *any* treatment is begun. Do not attempt to treat your child with vitamins, iron, or other nutrients or over-the-counter medications unless it is at your physician's direction. This is important, because such treatment may mask the real reason for the problem and thus delay the diagnosis.

If the anemia is due to lack of iron, your child will be given an iron-containing medication. This comes in a drop form for infants, and liquid or tablet forms for older children. Your pediatrician will determine how long your child should take the iron by checking his blood at regular intervals. Do not stop giving the medication until the physician tells you it is no longer needed.

Following are a few tips concerning iron medication:

- It is best not to give iron with milk because milk blocks the absorption.

- Vitamin C increases iron absorption, so you might want to follow the dose of iron with a glass of orange juice.

- Since liquid iron tends to turn the teeth a grayish-black color, have your child swallow it rapidly and then rinse his mouth with water. You also may want to brush your child's teeth after every dose of iron. Though tooth-staining by iron is unattractive, it is not permanent.

- Iron medications cause the stools to become a dark black color. Don't be worried by this change.

Safety precautions: Iron medications are extremely poisonous if taken in excessive amounts. (Iron is one of the most common causes of poisoning in children under five.) *Keep this and all medication out of reach of small children.*

Prevention

Iron-deficiency anemia and other nutritional anemias can be prevented easily by making sure your child is eating a well-balanced diet and by following these precautions:

- Do not give your infant cow's milk until he is six months to one year old.

- If your child is breast-fed, give him iron-fortified foods such as cereal when solid foods are introduced. Before then, he will absorb enough iron from the breast milk. However, the introduction of iron-poor solid foods will decrease the amount of iron he absorbs from the milk.

- If your baby is formula-fed, give him formula with added iron.

- Make sure your older child has a well-balanced diet and eats foods that contain iron. Many grains and cereals are iron-fortified (check labels to be sure). Other good sources of iron include egg yolks, green and yellow vegetables, yellow fruits, red meat, potatoes, tomatoes, molasses, and raisins. Also, to increase the iron content of your entire family's diet, use the fruit pulp in juices, and cook potatoes with the skins on.

Cystic Fibrosis

Cystic fibrosis (CF) is an inherited disease that changes the secretions of certain glands in the body. The sweat glands and the glandular cells of the lungs and pancreas are most often affected, but the sinuses, liver, intestines, and reproductive organs can also be involved. Although we have made great progress in treating this disease and its symptoms, there is still no cure. Children with cystic fibrosis now live much longer than previously.

For a child to get cystic fibrosis, both parents must be carriers of the gene that causes it. In the United States, one out of every twenty white people is a carrier of the CF gene, and approximately one out of every 1600 white babies is born with the disease. The illness is much less common in the black population (one in every 17,000 live births) and even rarer among Orientals.

In the last few years, a genetic abnormality has been detected in many cystic fibrosis patients, with other gene mutations being found asmore research is done. While we do not have the capability to screen the population at large effectively for CF, that may be possible in the near future. Genetic screening and counselling is available for those with a family member with CF. Since the disease is usually fatal, this should be an important consideration for high-risk families.

Signs and Symptoms

In children with CF, the disease is not usually obvious at birth. The signs and symptoms vary, depending on the severity of the particular case and the organs that are involved. Some ot this has been related to the amount of mutation of the most common genetic abnormality. However, all children with CF excrete excessive amounts of salt in their sweat. This may cause salt crystals to appear on their skin and gives them a salty taste when you kiss them.

CF often (though not always) seriously affects the lungs, causing mucus in the airways to be thicker than normal and more difficult to cough out. A child with CF is likely to have a persistent cough, which gets worse with colds. Since the lungs' secretions remain in the airways for longer than normal, the airways are more likely to become infected, increasing the chances of pneumonia or bronchitis.

Many children with CF are deficient in the pancreatic enzymes that help to digest food. As a result, they cannot digest fats and proteins as well as they should, which results in large, bulky, foul-smelling stools. These children grow more slowly than normal and are underweight.

You should suspect cystic fibrosis and call your pediatrician if your child has frequent pneumonia (see page 516), bulky, foul-smelling stools, or fails to grow or gain normally. The doctor will order a sweat test to measure the amount of salt your child loses as he perspires. Children with cystic fibrosis excrete large quantities of salt in this manner.

Two or more tests may be required to confirm the diagnosis, since the results are not always clearly positive or negative. If your child is diagnosed as having the disease, your pediatrician will help you get the additional specialized medical help that is necessary.

Treatment

The treatment of cystic fibrosis depends upon which body system is involved with the disease (skin, lungs, digestive tract) and the severity of that involvement. In general, the goals are to:

1. Reduce secretions from the lungs

2. Replace missing or insufficient digestive enzymes

3. Reduce or replace salt loss

The Emotional Burden of Cystic Fibrosis

Because CF is a hereditary disease, many parents feel very guilty about their child's illness. But this problem is not *anyone*'s fault, so you should channel your emotional energies into your child's treatment instead. Work closely with the doctors and therapists, and do not be fooled by publicized "breakthroughs" or "guaranteed cures." If you hear of a new therapy, ask your pediatrician or CF center before spending money or trying it.

It also is important to raise your child as you would if he did not have this illness. There is no reason to limit his educational or career goals. Many CF patients grow up to lead productive adult lives. Your child needs both love and discipline, and he should be encouraged to develop and test his limits.

Balancing the physical and emotional demands created by this disease is hard on both the CF patient and his family, so it is very important that you get as much support as possible. Ask your pediatrician to put you in touch with the nearest CF center and CF support groups. The Cystic Fibrosis Foundation can also be of help. Write to: Cystic Fibrosis Foundation, 6931 Arlington Road, Bethesda, Maryland 20814.

Diabetes Mellitus

When a child has diabetes mellitus, his pancreas (a gland located in the abdomen) is not producing enough of the hormone insulin to move sugar adequately from his bloodstream into all the cells of his body, where it is needed for energy. Since the sugar cannot be used by the cells, it begins to increase in the bloodstream. This abnormal buildup, and the failure of the body's cells to receive the sugar they need for normal function, cause many severe symptoms and—if untreated—lead to life-threatening complications.

Childhood diabetes, or Type 1, most frequently appears in young children between ages four and five. This type is inherited, though special genes must be present on *both sides* of the family in order for it to develop. This means that if you have one child with diabetes, there's a chance that your other children also may acquire it. (The adult form of diabetes, or Type 2, is not due to an absolute lack of insulin but may result from or be associated with obesity. It is usually inherited from only one parent and often can be managed with diet and exercise. This form of diabetes is very rare in children.)

During the development of childhood diabetes, the pancreas cells that produce insulin (called beta cells) are destroyed. This is now known to occur rather slowly, over a period of months to years. There is evidence that this process is triggered by viral infections in children who are genetically susceptible. This is supported by the fact that childhood diabetes most often becomes symptomatic during peak times of viral infection (winter, late fall, and early spring).

If not recognized early and treated immediately, diabetes can have devastating effects, particularly in very young children. That's why it is important to notify your pediatrician *immediately* if your child displays any of the following warning signs and symptoms of the disease:

- Failure to grow and gain weight, especially in very young children

- Weight loss associated with constant hunger and eating (or sometimes with loss of appetite and decreased food intake)

- Excessive thirst

- Dehydration (See page 478.)

- Excessive and frequent urination (A previously toilet-trained child might start wetting his pants during the day or night; a baby in diapers will need his wet diaper changed constantly.)

- Vomiting, particularly if accompanied by unusual fatigue, drowsiness, or general lack of enthusiasm (This last symptom is an important one, though it appears late.)

Treatment

The pediatrician will check your child's urine and blood (preferably after a meal) for increased sugar levels and for other signs of abnormal metabolism due to diabetes (e.g., ketones in the urine). If the tests are positive and the diagnosis of diabetes mellitus is confirmed, the child usually is hospitalized for control of the disease. Injections of insulin are necessary in nearly all children.

You'll be taught how to give him the insulin injections, usually at least twice per day. (Insulin usually is administered before breakfast and dinner, and contains both short-acting and intermediate-acting forms.) The thought of administering these injections may upset you, but it's really not difficult, and when your child is older (usually age eight or older) he'll learn to give them himself. Your acceptance of these injections and your ability to give them calmly will help your child adjust to the treatment as "usual activity" and lessen his own fear and anxiety.

You'll also be taught how to test your child's blood-sugar levels (you'll need to do this several times a day) and what to do when the level gets too high or too low. Low blood sugar is treated by feeding him a sugar-containing food or drink or by injecting a substance called glucagon, which rapidly raises the blood sugar. Then an additional complex carbohydrate and protein snack is given to keep the blood-sugar level more constant. High blood sugar is treated with additional rapid acting insulin.

Your child's diet also is extremely important. He should have regular, nutritionally balanced, healthful meals, and should eat about the same amounts of food at each meal. He will also need snacks, too, at midmorning, midafternoon and bedtime to keep his blood-sugar levels stable. For snacks he should avoid pure carbohydrates (like candy), since they markedly elevate the blood sugar for a short period of time. Popular and healthy snacks for children with diabetes include:

Fruit with nuts or cheese

Granola bars (if strenuous exercise is planned)

Yogurt (plain or flavored at home with fresh fruit)

Peanut butter and crackers

Cheese and crackers

Small portions of plain ice cream

In the beginning, your pediatrician may choose to put your child on a special diet to ensure that he eats properly. The doctor may also recommend an exercise program, since physical activity with diet helps keep diabetes under control. Children with diabetes can and should participate in all activities, and they need to be encouraged to do so. They may need extra food for strenuous exercise so this is a good time to give special sweet treats. Moreover, your child's teachers must also be educated about the disease, so that the necessary routine of insulin injections, appropriate meals and snacks, planned exercise, and blood-sugar testing is maintained. You should always speak to the teachers at the beginning of the school year.

There's one other essential: emotional support for the entire family. You can get this—and learn more about the disease—from the Juvenile Diabetes Foundation (432 Park Avenue South, New York, NY 10016) and the American Diabetes Association (1660 Duke Street, P.O. Box 25757, Alexandria, Virginia 22314). The more support you have, the better you'll be able to handle this disease and the upheaval it may cause in your lives.

The more you understand about diabetes, the better the chance that your child will do well. With proper education it's now possible to control diabetes and lessen the severity of serious later complications such as eye problems, heart disease, and kidney disease.

Failure to Thrive

If you plot your child's weight and measurements, you should see a continuous upward trend, although there will be times when he gains very slowly and perhaps some weeks when he actually loses a little weight due to illness. It is not normal for him to stop growing, or to decrease in weight except for the small amount he loses during the first few days of life. If he does lose weight, it's a clear sign either that he's not getting enough to eat or that he's ill. The medical term for this condition is *failure to thrive*. Although it can occur in older children who are seriously ill or undernourished, it is most common and most dangerous during the active growth period of the first three years.

If allowed to continue for a prolonged period, this condition can become serious. Steady weight gain is especially important for infants and toddlers because it indicates that they are receiving adequate nutrition and care for normal physical, mental, and emotional development.

Usually when a child stops growing, it's due to a feeding problem that prevents him from getting as many calories as he needs. As a newborn, he may be too fussy to eat as much as he needs, or, if breast-fed, he may not be getting enough milk while nursing. Some children may require more food than their parents are able to provide. These problems must be detected and treated early in order to avoid long-term or permanent damage.

Sometimes failure to thrive signals a medical problem. The newborn may have an infection passed on from his mother during pregnancy, or he may have a hormonal difficulty, allergy, or a digestive problem that prevents nutrients from being properly absorbed into the body. Diseases such as diabetes (page 652), cystic fibrosis (page 651), or heart disease also can interfere with normal growth. If one of these is present, the child may need a special diet as well as medical treatment.

When to Get Help

Regular charting of your child's growth and comparison of his general development with others his age is the best way to make sure he is thriving. If he does not gain weight, grow in length, or otherwise develop normally, consult your pediatrician, who will measure and examine your child, ask about his diet and eating patterns, and review his medical history for signs of illness that may be contributing to his failure to thrive. The physician will try to establish exactly when the growth or weight gain stopped, and ask about any incidents or events that may have contributed to this. The pediatrician may also watch the youngster eating or nursing to see how much he consumes and how he responds to food. Sometimes a short period of in-hospital observation may be necessary.

If the doctor discovers a physical cause for the decrease in growth rate, the appropriate treatment will be recommended. If there is no physical reason, however, the pediatrician will look for emotional or social problems, particularly within the family. Such disturbances can decrease a child's appetite or alter his normal food intake and digestion. Once discovered, these difficulties can also be treated with individual or family counseling.

HIV Infection and AIDS

No one who has read a newspaper or watched a television newscast in recent years could have avoided learning something about HIV infection (which frequently leads to AIDS, or acquired immune deficiency syndrome). This new and terrifying disease usually is detected when a life-threatening infection or cancer develops in a person whose bodily defenses have been weakened. This weakness has been caused by an infection with the human immunodeficiency virus (HIV).

HIV infection was first recognized in 1981, in homosexual men who had developed either a lung infection—caused by an unusual organism known to cause disease only in people with impaired immune systems—or a cancer that had rarely occurred in young men. It quickly became apparent that these men did, in fact, have a problem with their immune system, the body system that protects against invading microorganisms or developing cancer cells.

Before long, doctors reported that groups other than gay men were becoming ill as well. Today, we know that adults can acquire HIV infection as a result of homo- or heterosexual contact with an infected person (approximately three in every four cases), intravenous drug use (approximately one in five), or transfusion of blood or blood products (approximately one in twenty).

Children, on the other hand, acquire infection primarily from their HIV-infected mothers, either *in utero* (as the virus passes across the placenta), or during delivery (when the newborn is exposed to the mother's blood and body fluids) or by ingestion of infected breast milk. Studies are still in progress, but it currently appears that HIV infection will develop in one-quarter to one-half of infants born to HIV-infected mothers.

In the past, children (and adults) receiving blood or blood-product transfusions could acquire the HIV infection if the blood donor was infected. But all blood and blood products now are screened for HIV, thus minimizing this as a possible route of transmission.

Once a person is infected with HIV, the virus will be present in his body for life. But keep in mind that HIV infection is *not* the same as AIDS. People with HIV infection may be free of symptoms for years. AIDS occurs only after the progressive erosion of the immune defense system by HIV, a process that may take many months or years. The incubation period for the development of AIDS in children who acquire HIV infection *in utero* or at birth, however, averages less than two years.

Infants with HIV infection initially may appear well, but problems gradually develop. For example, their weight and height fail to increase appropriately as they get older. They have frequent episodes of diarrhea or minor skin infections. The lymph nodes (glands) throughout the body enlarge, and there are persistent fungus infections of the mouth (thrush). The liver and spleen may enlarge.

All the above symptoms are highly suggestive of HIV infection. In the absence of a specific infection (such as the pneumonia described earlier) or cancer, this condition is called AIDS-related complex (ARC).

Eventually, if the HIV infection progresses and the body's immune system further deteriorates, the AIDS-related infections and cancers may occur. The most common of these, a pneumonia, is accompanied by fever and breathing difficulties. Even after appropriate treatment, AIDS patients will suffer repeated episodes of pneumonia if they are not placed on a preventive program.

Care of the Child with HIV Infection

In this era of AIDS, many people who are understandably fearful of this deadly disease are inappropriately cautious, and even fearful, of being with HIV-infected individuals on a regular, casual day-to-day basis. It is clear from the overwhelmingly uniform evidence that children who are HIV positive should be played with, interacted with, and loved just like all other children. HIV infections cannot be transmitted by just being held. These children need all we can give them, whether it be in a day-care center, on a one-to-one basis or in any group large or small. They are the innocent victims of circumstances well beyond their control and care-giving adults should take every opportunity to make them feel no different from any other child. Often, in fact, their circumstances have placed them in a situation or an environment which is already less than conducive to optimum growth and development. We must all do everything we can to counteract all those often present negative factors. We must contribute to their positive outlook on life.

Since even common infections can cause devastating illnesses in children with HIV infection, you must avoid exposing the child to contagious illnesses, especially chicken pox and measles. Call the doctor immediately if your child develops a fever, breathing difficulties, diarrhea, swallowing problems, skin irritation, or if he's been exposed to communicable disease. In fact, any change in the child's health status should prompt you to seek medical attention, since your child has little reserve to combat even minor illnesses.

Whenever seeking any medical attention for your youngster, be sure to inform the physician of the HIV infection so that he can appropriately assess and care for the illness (management of AIDS-related pneumonia is very different from that of the usual cases seen in healthy children) or avoid potentially injurious treatments (some live vaccines, cortisone products, and so on).

Unfortunately, there is currently no standard accepted treatment for HIV infection in children. Many physicians are intravenously administering a product called gamma globulin to boost the child's ability to ward off infection. A medication called AZT (or Retrovir) is the first licensed drug with activity against HIV. Many other drugs are being tested against HIV infection and recently a second drug, didanosine, has been licensed.

With some children, the delay in physical and mental development is the most significant finding. This means parents must seek additional help from developmental specialists (pediatricians) who can offer valuable assistance in helping to manage the problems accompanying this delay.

Most researchers now believe that because HIV is incorporated within the hereditary part of human cells, it's unlikely that a drug will soon be found to cure HIV infection. However, there's good reason to think that medications will become available to keep the infection under control, much as lifelong insulin treatment maintains the health of diabetics.

Immunizing the Child with ARC and with Symptomatic HIV Infection

Your pediatrician has up-to-date guidelines for which vaccines should and shouldn't be given. Below is a summary of the current recommendations:

Children with symptomatic HIV infection (yeast infections in the mouth, frequent minor infections, enlarged lymph nodes, enlarged liver or spleen, or overwhelming infection) as well as children with asymptomatic HIV infection should receive the following vaccines at the usual recommended age:

- DTP (diphtheria, tetanus, pertussis vaccine)

- IPV (inactivated poliovirus vaccine)

- MMR (live measles, mumps, rubella vaccine)

- HbCV (hemophilus influenza type b conjugated vaccine)

- Children with symptomatic HIV infection should, in addition, receive pneumococcal and influenza vaccines. Children with either symptomatic or asymptomatic HIV infection should *not* receive OPV (oral poliovirus vaccine). Noninfected children living in a household with HIV-infected children or adults should not receive OPV because they may excrete the virus and expose the HIV-infected family members.

HIV-infected children may experience especially severe illness due to chicken pox or measles. Following exposures to these infections, HIV-infected children should receive special immune globulin by injection.

Parents of children with HIV infection sometimes hide the diagnosis from relatives, feeling the youngster will be shunned by them. However, most families have been very supportive; indeed, they have often taken over the responsibility for care during periods when the parents need such assistance.

If You're Pregnant

If you're a woman in a high-risk group—and if you're pregnant or planning a pregnancy—you should consider having the blood test to see if you have the HIV infection. If the test results are positive, you should consider delaying pregnancy; if you are already pregnant you should discuss continuing or terminating the pregnancy with your obstetrician or pediatrician.

In the Classroom

A lot of controversy has been stirred up in recent years about permitting children infected with HIV into the classroom. Most of the anxiety is really unfounded. There is *no* risk of HIV transmission in routine classroom activities.

The virus is not spread through casual contact. It is not transmitted through the air, by touching, or via toilet seats. Almost all school-age children with HIV infection can attend a regular school.

Although transmission of HIV has not occurred in schools and day-care centers, transmission of other infectious agents such as hepatitis and herpes requires that all these settings should adopt routine precautionary procedures for handling blood, stool, and bodily secretions. The standard precaution is immediately washing exposed skin with soap and water after any contact with blood or body fluids. Soiled surfaces should be cleaned with disinfectants such as bleach (a one to ten dilution of bleach to water). Disposable towels or tissues should be used whenever possible. Schools should ensure that children wash their hands before eating; staff should wash their hands before food preparation or feeding children.

Also, it is critically important that schools incorporate education about HIV infection into their curriculum. All children should be educated about the risks of HIV transmission through sexual activity and intravenous drug use. They should be taught how to avoid exposure to blood and body fluids that might contain HIV. They should also learn that HIV is not spread through casual contact.

COMMONLY USED MEDICATIONS

Antibiotics	Reason for Use	Side Effects
Penicillin V	Strep throat; protection against rheumatic fever and bacterial endocarditis	Allergic reaction
Penicillin G, Benzathine	Strep throat; protection against rheumatic fever and bacterial endocarditis; gonorrhea	Soreness at injection site; allergic reaction
Amoxicillin	Ear, sinus, urinary tract infections; gonorrhea	Loose stools; skin rash; allergic reaction
Dicloxacillin	Infections (especially skin, impetigo) caused by staph germs	Allergic reaction
Cephalexin (Keflex®)	Alternative to amoxicillin for urinary tract infection	Allergic reaction; loose stools
Cefaclor (Ceclor®)	Alternative to amoxicillin for ear and sinus infections	Allergy; skin rash; swollen joints
Sulfisoxazole (Gantrisin®)	Urinary tract and ear infections	Allergy; skin rash
Trimethoprim / Sulfamethoxazole (Bactrim®, Septra®)	Urinary tract and ear infections	Allergy; skin rash; nausea, vomiting
Erythromycin (Ilosone®, E-mycin®, Pediamycin®)	Alternative to penicillin V; Mycoplasma pneumonia; Legionnaires' disease; impetigo; chlamydia infections	Nausea and vomiting
Rifampin (Rifadin®, Rimactane®)	Prevent meningitis due to *Haemophilus influenzae* B and meningococcus	Red/orange staining of urine
Ear Preparations		
Acetic acid solution (Vosol®)	External ear infections	None
Cortisporin® otic solution or suspension	External ear infections	None

	Reason for Use	Side Effects
Eye Preparations		
Erythromycin (Ilotycin®) ointment (0.5%)	Conjunctivitis	Puffy eyes
Gentamicin (Garamycin®) solution (0.3%)	Conjunctivitis	Puffy eyes
Sulfacetamide (Sulamyd®) solution (10%)	Conjunctivitis	Puffy eyes
Analgesics		
Aspirin	Pain; inflammation **Do Not Use For Fever Due To Any Infection**	Many—especially stomach upset; ringing in ears; allergic reactions
Acetaminophen (Tylenol®, Tempra®, Liquiprin®, Panadol®)	Pain; fever	None with suggested dose
Codeine	Pain	Dizziness; behavior changes such as hyperactivity
Agents for Common Cold		
Actifed®	Common cold; upper respiratory infections	Irritability; sleep disturbances, drowsiness
Dimetapp®	Common cold; upper respiratory infections	Irritability; sleep disturbances, drowsiness
Triaminic®	Common cold; upper respiratory infections	Irritability; sleep disturbances, drowsiness
Rondec®	Common cold; upper respiratory infections	Irritability; sleep disturbances, drowsiness
Diphenhydramine elixir (Benadryl®)	Allergic reactions; itching; motion sickness; hay fever	Drowsiness
Hydroxyzine (Atarax®)	Allergic reactions; itching; motion sickness; hay fever	Drowsiness
Robitussin®	Cough	

	Reason for Use	Side Effects
Agents for Common GI Problems		
Antacids (Tums, Rolaids, Gelusil, Maalox, many others)	Heartburn; stomach gas	Dizziness; constipation
Colace®	Stool softener	Diarrhea
Mineral oil	Stool softener	Diarrhea
Dulcolax®	Laxative	Diarrhea
Senokot®	Laxative	Diarrhea
Ipecac syrup	Empty stomach by vomiting after poison ingestion	Lethargy; diarrhea; persistent vomiting
Skin Preparations		
Bacitracin Ointment	Skin infections	None when used correctly
Silver sulfadiazine	Burns	Discoloration of skin
Pyrethrins/Piperonyl Butoxide (RID®)	Lice	None when used correctly
Hexagammabenzene (Kwell®)	Lice	May be toxic; follow directions and speak with physician

Index

Page numbers of illustrations and charts appear in italics